Yale Publications in the History of Art, 37
George L. Hersey, editor

Pre-Restoration lithograph of the west façade of Saint-Denis by A. Rouargue. From the collection of the Musée d'Art et d'Histoire de la Ville de Saint-Denis.

THE ROYAL ABBEY
OF SAINT-DENIS

from Its Beginnings to the
Death of Suger, 475–1151

SUMNER McKNIGHT CROSBY
Edited and completed by
PAMELA Z. BLUM

YALE UNIVERSITY PRESS
New Haven and London

Designed by Susan P. Fillion
and set in Centaur display and Granjon text type by
The Composing Room of Michigan, Inc.
Printed in the United States of America by
The Murray Printing Company,
Westford, Massachusetts

Library of Congress Cataloging-in-Publication Data

Crosby, Sumner McK. (Sumner McKnight), 1909–1982
    The Royal Abbey of Saint-Denis from its beginnings
to the death of Suger, 475–1151.

    (Yale publications in the history of art ; 37)
    Bibliography: p.
    Includes index.
    1. Abbaye de Saint-Denis (Saint-Denis, France)
2. Eglise abbatiale de Saint-Denis.   3. Suger, Abbot of
Saint Denis, 1081–1151—Contributions in church
architecture.   4. Saint-Denis (France)—Buildings,
structures, etc.   I. Blum, Pamela Z.   II. Title.
III. Series.
NA5551.S214C76   1987   726'.5'0944362   85-26464
ISBN 0-300-03143-2 (alk. paper)

Contents

Illustrations

**This list does not include excavations, capitals, and profiles
illustrated in the Appendixes.**

PLATES   *(following pages 502, 506, 510)*

ALBUM DRAWINGS

Asterisk indicates drawings that appear in reduced form in this volume. A complete set of album drawings is available separately in a tube.

Publisher's Note

For a publisher, the task of editing and producing a posthumous volume as complex and important for future scholarship as Sumner Crosby's life work on Saint-Denis is not approached without some trepidation. It was our good fortune to face this task with an able and tireless partner, Pamela Z. Blum, and with the kind support and cooperation of the Crosby family. We extend our thanks to the author's family and to Pamela Blum, who put aside much of her own work to become editor of this monumental volume.

Editor's Preface

In July 1982, four months before his death, Sumner Crosby delivered the manuscript for this book to the Yale University Press. The typescript totaled some seven hundred pages, plus footnotes, appendices, most of the illustrations and the nearly completed plans and elevations for the Album. But the monograph still lacked a conclusion and a bibliography; also for several chapters the annotation proved incomplete. Unfortunately the author did not live to supply those materials, nor did he ever have a chance to see and evaluate the editorial and substantive suggestions submitted by the readers of this manuscript. After his death in November 1982, the need for an editor to see the manuscript through to publication became obvious both to the Press and to the Crosby family. Aware of the imperative of making the material in these volumes available to art historians, I agreed, when asked, to act in that capacity.

The text, along with the plans and elevations and excavation drawings in this volume, represents a life's work and supersedes the earlier studies. Although part I of the text reviews some material covered in the author's first volume, *The Abbey of St.-Denis, 475–1122* (New Haven, 1942), the text also contains numerous revisions based on evidence uncovered since that earlier publication. Part II presents the long-promised study of the twelfth-century building campaigns at the abbey. With the use of photogrammetric photographs and drawings, the author's plans and elevations have attained a precision never before possible in the study of medieval monuments. Although the author published preliminary reports after each season of excavating, as well as numerous articles on the building and its sculpture, this volume, enriched by years of experience in the field, offers his final interpretations of the accumulated evidence. The evaluation of the author's findings and conclusions will continue to occupy archaeologists and architectural historians for several generations.

The author gathered his evidence in a succession of excavations between 1939 and 1977, but with an interruption during World War II and another in 1948, when permission to excavate was suspended for twenty years in favor of Jules Formigé, then the newly appointed architect in charge of the works at Saint-Denis. The text of this study often reads like a dialogue between the author and Formigé. Their disagreements arose because the Crosby study represents the work of a scholar trained in the methods of archaeology and architectural history, whereas Formigé, trained as an architect, stated in the opening paragraph of his monograph, *L'Abbaye royale de Saint-Denis* (Paris, 1960), "Le travail que je presente est celui d'un architecte." Their interpretations of the same evidence seldom coincide. Cautious in its conclusions and meticulous in the presentation of archaeological evidence, this volume provides the material crucial to an understanding of the various campaigns of construction at Saint-Denis, beginning with Sainte Geneviève's chapel and extending through the Merovingian, Carolingian, and the twelfth-century building programs sponsored, respectively, by Dagobert I and the abbots Fulrad, Hilduin, and Suger.

In agreeing to edit the manuscript, I set guidelines with the approval of the Crosby family and of the Yale University Press. All of the author's interpretations and conclusions have remained unchanged. My goals in editing the text have been to eliminate repetition, reorganize data to achieve greater concision, and revise the prose to provide more clarity and precision. Although I did not undertake a review of the author's research, as editor I have supervised the verification of all quotations and references. Faye Hirsch and Elaine Beretz, both doctoral candidates at Yale University, have performed the exacting task of verification for parts I and II, respectively. Minot Kerr assisted with chapter 4, part I. They also deserve credit for compiling the bibliography of works cited. Because the author's references did not go beyond the year 1980, I have, with no attempt at comprehensiveness, supplemented the author's annotations with references to recent literature through 1984 of particular pertinence to the text. They include citations to papers read at the conference held at Columbia University in 1981, "Abbot Suger and Saint-Denis: An International Symposium." The author's health did not permit him to assess or to incorporate any of the new material presented at the conference. Although he had intended to prepare and publish a critique of the papers, in this volume his conclusions stand unrevised and do not take into account the scholarship presented at the symposium.

My editorial additions to the text proper do little more than supply dates or provide phrases in the original language where the author has translated a passage or paraphrased it in English. In the notes, in order to distinguish editorial comments and citations from the author's references, my interpolations appear within square brackets and are consistently labeled "Ed. note."

The papers of Sumner McKnight Crosby, including sundry drafts of his manuscript for the present volume, will be put on file at The Cloisters, Fort Tryon Park, New York, New York, 10040, an adjunct of the Metropolitan Museum of Art.

The editor is indebted to many people who have given freely of their time and knowledge. Yale University Press provided me with all comments received from readers of the manuscript as the author had submitted it. The readers of that version were Jean Bony, Jane Hayward, and Philippe Verdier. The final version has profited from their expert opinions and from the bibliographical information provided by Charles McClendon after his readings of the initial and the edited versions of the chapter on the first Carolingian building campaign. Elizabeth Brown, Caroline Bruzelius, Walter Cahn, Paula Gerson, Danielle Johnson, Meredith Lillich, Gabrielle Spiegel, and Patricia Stirneman have provided continuing assistance in their areas of expertise. All deserve special mention for making the task of the editor easier.

In discharging my editing function, I was given every consideration at Saint-Denis by M. Branislav Brankovic, Architecte des Bâtiments de France, and I gratefully acknowledge the permissions he granted. Thanks to the generous cooperation of M. Bernard Manapin and his staff at the basilica and to the indispensable help of William W. Clark, I was able to clarify a number of puzzling details in the manuscript and to take the supplementary photographs, measurements, and profiles of bases needed to complete this monograph.

Under the supervision of Fred Bland and William W. Clark in New Haven and New York, Donna Carney, Stefan Halstrup, Erica Ling, and Daniel Kaplowitz completed the plans. Also guided by William Clark, Donald Sanders drew the final version of the twelfth-century choir as proposed by the author. Without doubt I owe the greatest debt of gratitude to William Clark. Keenly aware that his efforts, critical judgment, and encouragement were indispensable to the undertaking, I value his participation as much for the quality of his counsel as for the generosity of spirit animating him. I also wish to thank Judy Metro of Yale University Press for her helpful cooperation and expert guidance.

And finally I would like to express my gratitude to the author's widow, Sarah Townsend Crosby, and to Sumner McK. Crosby, Jr., whose interest has been a positive factor in achieving this book. Following the undertaking closely, they have encouraged and supported it at every turn.

Pamela Z. Blum
New Haven, Connecticut, 1984

Author's Preface

In 1932 as a first-year graduate student at Yale one of my early assignments was the selection of a topic for a research paper. My attention was immediately attracted by a title: "The so-called School of Saint-Denis in Carolingian Miniatures." Saint-Denis and Carolingian miniatures seemed of minor significance, details that would be explained when the work began. A "so-called school," however, needed exploration because of its possible significance for a new career. Initial reading soon disclosed that the school was a supposition, but not before Saint-Denis as a leading monastic institution whose history paralleled that of the French monarchy had fully engaged my attention.

By the end of that first year another Dionysian problem seemed pertinent and important—why was Abbot Suger's new twelfth-century church recognized as the first Gothic church? Scholars seemed to accept that fact but no one seemed sure why, nor, even more important, were they certain just how much of the existing building is authentic. Although I didn't realize it, my fate was then sealed. The abbey church at Saint-Denis became the title of my doctoral dissertation and has remained the focus of my research for the past fifty years.

Initially I envisioned writing a summary history of the abbey with emphasis on the remarkable sequence of men who served as abbots and patrons, with a detailed analysis of the succession of outstanding buildings erected during their abbacies. The unexpected amount of significant new material, as well as unexpected delays in permissions to explore it and the insistent demands of teaching a full schedule at Yale University delayed continuous writing until my retirement in 1978. Now, with the pressure of time, I can only hope that I will be allowed to complete the survey of those segments with which I have had personal experience. The history of post twelfth-century buildings and their decorations must become the responsibility of future generations of students. May they continue to have the challenges and surprises that made the prospect of a new season always exciting.

Henri Focillon, Professeur au College de France, and Marcel Aubert, Membre de l'Institut, introduced me to Saint-Denis and guided my studies until after the publication of my first volume in 1942. Their enthusiasm and encouragement allowed me to propose excavations within the abbey church. The unexpected discoveries of portions of the Carolingian building and of surviving masonry from Suger's unfinished twelfth-century church made it difficult to shut down the first excavations in 1939 but easier to ask for permission to begin again in 1946, after World War II. Most of the important "finds" were made during the following three summers, including the apostle bas-relief discovered early in June 1947, but they also provoked national prejudice so that my "field" research stopped in 1948, not to be renewed until the 1960s. The often widely separated fragments of early masonry made accurate plans imperative on which to locate the remnants of Abbot Hilduin's ninth-century chapel, of William the Conqueror's eleventh-century tower, and finally of the three campaigns of Abbot Suger's new Gothic building. Reconstructions of the plans of all the successive buildings are a major part of the present volume.

Seeking precision and accuracy is frustrating; they often remain elusive, especially when ground plans or elevations of medieval structures are involved. That problem has been resolved by the perfection of photogrammetry, which records within millimeters elevations and contours of stone vaults. Such studies are now available for the existing twelfth-century portions of Suger's church. The opportunity to study the exact curvatures of the ribs under both the western and eastern vaults at Saint-Denis has, in my opinion, made it possible to suggest how the twelfth-century mason controlled these fundamental features of skeletal construction. Suger's choir with its "circular string of chapels, by virtue of which the whole church would shine with the wonderful and uninterrupted light of most luminous windows"[1] can now be analyzed in a logical manner.

The three western portals, the first in the series of Early Gothic "royal portals," have been considered "deprived forever of all historical interest, and extremely ugly besides."[2] Meticulous examination of the portal sculpture from scaffolding has made it possible to detect insertions and repairs, as well as sanding, recutting, or similar surface alterations of the portal sculpture. Although we cannot undo "restorations," enough original material still *in situ,* plus heads and other fragments in museums both in this country and abroad, as well as untouched portions of the portals themselves, permit a definition of the "Saint-Denis style." Although the nineteenth century altered the aesthetic character of the sculpture, Suger's elaborate, often complex iconographic program can be recreated and expounded with more than reasonable assurance.

The accomplishment of these multiple goals could not have been realized without the help of many different talents. Over the years beginning and advanced students, sometimes new acquaintances, and numerous colleagues both here and abroad have held the ends of tape measures or climbed ladders and scaffolding to give their opinions about some out-of-reach detail. I can only hope that their recollections are as pleasant as mine.

In the preface to my 1942 volume, I expressed my gratitude to the many officials and friends who made it possible to begin these studies. The list is now a great deal longer. I appreciate the interest and special efforts made by Monsieur Henri Bonnet, Ambassadeur aux Etats-Unis, and by Monsieur Louis Joxe, Ministre des Affaires Etrangères, who made it possible to continue the excavations in 1948. Monsieur René Perchet, Directeur, Direction de l'Architecture, was always sympathetic and helpful. The late Professor Erwin Panofsky, of the Institute for Advanced Studies at Princeton, was constantly in touch with the progress of the work, as has been Jurgis Baltrušaitis in Paris. My old friend and colleague Louis Grodecki made himself available to encourage and advise my slow progress. To him and to his wife, Catherine, Sal and I owe more than passing acknowledgment for continued warm hospitality.

Jacques Devinoy in Paris, with his meticulous draughtsmanship, produced the detailed plans and sections of the excavations. His enthusiasm and friendship remain treasured acquisitions. With recourse to a plan drawn for me by Richard Gould, Fred Bland began to work with me as a graduate student in architecture and has supervised the preparation of all drawings for publication. He and his wife, Morley, endured several summers before the completion of the Métro made Saint Denis a part of Paris. Their companionship and determination made it possible to survive the longest days.

Pamela Blum substituted for my eyes when cataracts blurred my vision. She has become the expert on Saint-Denis sculpture. Without her faithful presence, the recording of alterations to the often fragile, carved decorations would remain unknown.

The skill of our son William, who deserves more than parental gratitude, produced photographic records of the church and the excavations which are more than graphic documents. Grandparental thanks are also due Timothy Crosby, who forfeited many vacation hours to make enlargements for illustrations in these volumes.

Monsieur Donzet of the Monuments Historiques in Paris has been most helpful in assuring access to the church, and Michel Fleury, in charge of all archaeological investigations in the Ile-de-France, has acceded to my requests to open new trial excavations. Most recently William W. Clark, Professor at Queen's College, CUNY, has commented helpfully on the text, and I have enjoyed stimulating dialogues with Stephen Gardner, Professor at Columbia University. In assisting me, Caroline Rollins of the Yale University Art Gallery has kept everything in order.

Sal joined me as this long assignment began in Paris. She has insisted that everything be completed. Without her patience and encouragement there would be no book.

S. McK. C.
Woodbridge, Connecticut, 1982

Short Titles and Abbreviations

Acta Sanctorum . . . Johannes Bollandus and the Bollandists, eds. *Acta Sanctorum quotquot toto orbe coluntur, vel a catholicis scriptoribus celebrantur quae ex latinis et graecis.* Paris, 1643ff, Venice, 1734ff, and Paris, 1863ff.

Acta Sanctorum Ord. Ben. . . . Mabillon, Jean and Luc d'Achéry, eds. *Acta Sanctorum Ordinis S. Benedicti in saeculorum classes distributa.* 3 vols. Venice, 1668–1772; reprinted, 1935.

Bib. de l'Ec. des Ch. . . . *Bibliothèque de l'Ecole des Chartes.* Paris, 1839/40–.

Bull. de la Soc. Nat. des Antiq. de France . . . *Bulletin de la Société Nationale des Antiquaires de France.* Paris, 1857–.

Bull. mon. . . . *Bulletin monumental.* Paris, 1834–.

Cabrol and Leclercq, *Dictionnaire* . . . Cabrol, Fernand, and Henri Leclercq. *Dictionnaire d'archéologie chrétienne et de liturgie.* 15 vols. Paris, 1907–53.

Crosby, 1942 . . . Crosby, Sumner McKnight, *The Abbey of St.-Denis, 475–1122.* Vol. 1, New Haven, 1942.

Crosby et al., *Saint-Denis* . . . Crosby, Sumner McK., Jane Hayward, Charles T. Little, and William D. Wixom, eds. *The Royal Abbey of Saint-Denis in the Time of Abbot Suger (1122–51).* New York, 1981.

D.H.G.E. . . . *Dictionnaire d'histoire et de géographie ecclésiastique.* 20 vols. Paris, 1912–.

J.S.A.H. . . . *Journal of the Society of Architectural Historians.* Louisville, KY, 1941–.

J.W.C.I. . . . *Journal of the Warburg and Courtauld Institutes.* London, 1937–.

Karl der Grosse . . . Braunfels, Wolfgang, Helmut Beumann, Bernhard Bischoff, Herman Schnitzler, and Percy Ernst Schramm, eds. *Karl der Grosse: Lebenswerk und Nachleben.* 5 vols. Düsseldorf, 1965–68.

Kohler, ed., *Vita Genovefe* . . . Kohler, Charles Alfred, ed. *Vita beatae Genovefe virginis: Etude critique sur le texte de la vie latine de Sainte Geneviève de Paris avec deux texte de cette vie.* Bibliothèque de l'Ecole des Hautes Etudes, 48. Paris, 1881.

Lecoy de la Marche, ed., *Oeuvres* . . . Lecoy de la Marche, Auguste de, ed. *Oeuvres complètes de Suger recueillies, annotées et publiées d'après les manuscrits pour la Société de l'Histoire de France.* Paris, 1867.

Mâle, *Twelfth Century* . . . Mâle, Emile. *Religious Art in France—The Twelfth Century: A Study of the Origins of Medieval Iconography.* Edited by Harry Bober. Translated by Marthiel Mathews. Bollingen Series, 90:1. Princeton, 1978.

Mém. de la Soc. Nat. des Antiq. de France . . . *Mémoires de la Société Nationale des Antiquaires de France.* Paris, 1817–.

M.G.H. . . . *Monumenta Germaniae Historica: Die deutschen Geschichtsquellen des Mittelalters, 500–1500.* The following abbreviations of series in the *M.G.H.* appear in this book:
Auct. antiq. . . . *Auctores antiquissimorum.* Edited by Carolus Halm et al. 15 vols. Berlin, 1877–87.
Diplomata imp. 1 . . . *Diplomata imperii* 1. Edited by Georg Heinrich Pertz. Hanover, 1872.
Diplomata kar. . . . *Diplomata karolinorum.* Edited by Engelbert Mühlbacher. Hanover, 1906.
Epistolae . . . *Epistolae, III–VIII. Epistolae Merowingici et Karolini aevi.* 6 vols. Edited by Ernst Dümmler and Wilhelm Gunlach et al. Berlin, 1892–1939.
Script. rer. Mer. . . . *Scriptores rerum Merovingicarum.* 7 vols. Edited by Bruno Krusch and Wilhelm Levison. Hanover, 1885–1920 and 1951.

Migne, ed., *P.L.* . . . Migne, Jacques-Paul, ed. *Patrologiae cursus completus, sive bibliotheca universalis, integra, uniformis, commoda, oecumenica, omnium SS. patrum, doctorum scriptorumque ecclesiasticorum qui ab aevo apostolico ad usque Innocentii III tempora floruerunt . . . Series Latina. [Patrologia Latina].* 221 vols. Paris, 1844–64.

Monuments Piot . . . Commission de la Fondation Eugène Piot. *Monuments et mémoires publiées par l'Académie des Inscriptions et Belles-Lettres.* Paris, 1894–.

Neues Archiv . . . *Neues Archiv der Gesellschaft für ältere deutsche Geschichtskunde.* Hanover and Leipzig, 1876–1935.

Panofsky, ed., *Suger* . . . Panofsky, Erwin, ed. and trans. *Abbot Suger on the Abbey Church of St.-Denis and its Art Treasures.* Edited by Gerda Panofsky-Soergel. 2d ed. Princeton, 1979.

Rec. des hist. de France . . . Bouquet, Martin, et al., eds. *Recueil des historiens des Gaules et de la France.* 24 vols. Paris, 1738–1904.

Suger, *De Administratione* . . . Suger. *Liber de rebus in administratione sua gestis.*

Suger, *De Consecratione* . . . Suger. *Libellus alter de consecratione ecclesiae Sancti Dionysii.*

Vie des saints . . . Baudot, Jules L., Léon Chaussin, and the Benedictines of Paris. *Vie des saints et des bienheureux selon l'ordre du calendrier, avec l'histoire des fêtes.* 13 vols. Paris, 1935–59.

THE ROYAL ABBEY
OF SAINT-DENIS

from Its Beginnings to the
Death of Suger, 475–1151

PART ONE

SAINT–DENIS, 475-1122

Saint Denis,

Legend and History

The legend of Saint Denis is one of the most colorful and complex creations in medieval sacred literature.[1] Embellished over the centuries, its interpretation has caused serious debate, often bitter controversy. "Imagine his astonishment," a recent entry in an ecclesiastical dictionary remarked about Saint Denis, "if he could have foreseen that his identity would cause rivers of ink to flow, with no other result than to complicate and confuse his history."[2] Confusion is inherent because the legend has fused the identity of three different men who lived in three different geographical locations at three different periods in history. Here in brief is a summary of the fully developed legend.

Denis, Denys, or Dionysius, the first bishop of Paris, was also known as Dionysius the Areopagite,[3] who was converted to Christianity in Athens by the Apostle Paul. Later he wrote the *Celestial Hierarchy,* a mystical treatise on the heavenly hosts and divine light. After St. Paul's death in Rome, Denis assisted Pope Clement I in organizing a mission to convert the pagans in Gaul. As the leader of a large band of bishops, he directed their work and with two devoted companions, Rusticus and Eleutherius, went to Paris. When the emperor Domitian ordered the persecution of all Christians, Denis and his companions were among the first to be arrested. After refusing to deny their faith in the presence of the prefect Fescennius, they were tortured and cast into prison. Ultimately they were led to the slopes of Montmartre, where all three were decapitated. As soon as Denis' head touched the ground, he reached down and picked it up; then, as his lips chanted psalms, he walked two miles to his chosen place of burial. Soldiers ordered to cast the bodies of his companions into the Seine were stopped on the way by Catulla, a noble lady who offered them so much wine that they fell asleep for several hours. She buried the decapitated bodies in a distant field, where hastily sown grain miraculously took root, grew apace, and completely hid the graves. After the fury of the persecution had cooled, Catulla reunited the three bodies and erected a simple monument in their memory.[4]

Chronologically the first of the three historical figures conflated into the legend was Dionysius the Areopagite, identified by Saint Luke in the Bible as one of Paul's early Athenian converts.[5] He was known as the Areopagite because he was a member of the highest court in Athens, which sat on the Areopagus, or Hill of Athena Areia (also known as Mars Hill), to the west of the Acropolis. According to Eusebius, who wrote his *Ecclesiastical History* about 320, this same person became the first bishop of Athens;[6] but no other early documents record his existence.

The second Dionysius of concern to this legend is mentioned by the highly regarded early historian Gregory of Tours, who recorded in his *Historia Francorum* that during the reign of the emperor Decius (249–251), seven men were sent into Gaul to preach and that "the blessed Dionysius, Bishop of Paris, after enduring divers torments for the name of Christ, ended this present life under the sword."[7] The oldest list of the bishops of Paris[8] and other trustworthy information about early Christian communities in Gaul[9] confirm a mid-third-century date for the establishment of Christianity in Paris;[10] but a more persistent tradition, current as early as the sixth century, identified the mission sent to France as organized by Pope Clement I, the successor of Saint Peter in Rome, at the end of the first century.[11] Saint Denis, according to this tradition, would have been over ninety years old when he was martyred; but no historical document verifies such a first-century date.

The third Dionysius associated with this legend also chose the name Dionysius the Areopagite; but he did not live until the late fifth or early sixth century. At a colloquium in Constantinople in 532, the Severians cited a group of mystical treatises, including the *Celestial Hierarchy* by a Dionysius the Areopagite, in support of their Monophysite doctrines.[12] The orthodox Catholics immediately challenged the authenticity of these writings because not one of the early Christian fathers made any reference to them.[13] Internal evidence does not allow the dating of these texts before the very late fifth or early sixth century.[14] Their author is consequently usually referred to as the Pseudo-Dionysius the Areopagite, or Pseudo-Areopagite.

These mystical writings were known in the West before the end of the sixth century.[15] All the more surprising, then, is the fact that the writings were not attributed to Dionysius of Paris until the ninth century. Hilduin, abbot of Saint-Denis, made the official identification in his *Historia Sancti Dionysii,* written between 835 and 840.[16] From then on Saint Denis, the first bishop of Paris, was recognized as a disciple of Saint Paul and as the author of the *Celestial Hierarchy*.[17]

The gradual accretion of other details to Gregory of Tours' straightforward statement can also be identified. Rusticus and Eleutherius, Denis' faithful companions, are not mentioned in the earliest texts; but they appear in the *Martyrologium Hieronymi,* an authoritative document of the late sixth or early seventh century.[18] A trench recently discovered in the crypt under the high altar of the abbey church is claimed to be the burial place of Saint Denis and his companions; this gives added significance to the fact that Rusticus and Eleutherius were not part of the legend until the end of the sixth century.[19] Such details, in spite of their possible symbolic value, could hardly fire the popular imagination as did accounts of miracles and events associated with familiar landmarks.[20] The legend of Saint Denis acquired these prerequisites in the ninth century, when the writings of Hilduin and his monks placed the martyrdom on the slopes of Montmartre and proclaimed the miracle of the *cephalophorie.*

The early texts identify the butte to the north of the Ile de la Cité as *Mons Martis* or *Mons Mercurii,* the mount of Mars or Mercury. A "happy mutation" mentioned in the *Miracula Sancti Dionysii* compiled by Hincmar at Saint-Denis between 834 and 835[21] changed *Mons Martis,* Montmarte, to *Mons Martyrum,* Montmartre.[22] By the seventh century the presence on the top of the butte of a cemetery with a church or chapel originally dedicated to Saint Denis, but known today as Saint-Pierre-de-Montmartre, is evidence of the abbey's early concern with this area.[23] Bolstered by the necessity of moving the site of their important Foire de la Saint-Denis nearer to Paris for better protection, the monks of Saint-Denis wished to extend their influence to lands around the butte, at the foot of which lay the road connecting the abbey with Paris.[24] The *felici mutatione* changed the mount of Mars to the mount of the martyrs. By the mid–ninth century the monks had incorporated the whole area into the legend of their patron saint.

In contrast to the Montmartre legend, the early texts state specifically that the martyrdom of Saint Denis took place in the village of Catulliacum, or *Cadalgo.*[25] Coins struck by Ebregisilus in the seventh century, presumably to facilitate trading and increase profits of the fair, identify the *vicus Catolacum* with the monastery of *Sci Dionysii.*[26] Archaeological evidence to be thoroughly described in subsequent chapters establishes the existence of an important Roman building in the vicinity of the abbey and of a large pagan and Christian cemetery under and adjacent to the abbey church, as well as of the foundations of a sequence of early buildings on the site. The concurrence of this written, numismatic, and archaeological evidence lends assurance to the belief that Dionysius was martyred at St.-Denis and buried under the present abbey church.

The legend of Saint Denis' retrieval of his severed head so beguiled medieval imaginations that the same miracle became associated with a number of other saints. Saint Yon at Chartres, Saint Nicaise at Rouen, Saint

Lucien at Beauvais, and Saint Piat at Tournai[27] all accomplished this difficult feat. Under such circumstances, as Saint Beuve reportedly observed, "C'est le premier pas qui compte." The origin of this miracle may be traced to the early custom of representing any beheaded martyr, except Saint Paul, as holding his head in his hands. The transition from a saint holding his head to one carrying it was an easy one.[28] The first appearance of this miracle in any medieval legend was, as might be expected, in the *Historia Sancti Dionysii* by Hilduin in the ninth century. Another detail about the saint's martyrdom— namely, the skill or ineptitude of the executioner—became the center of considerable controversy late in the Middle Ages. The canons of Notre-Dame, in Paris, claimed that one of their treasured relics was the cranium of Saint Denis; but the monks of Saint-Denis insisted that they had the entire head. The dispute appeared before the Parlement de Paris in 1410. No judgment was given, but the king had to intervene to restore order.[29]

As the reputation of Saint Denis increased and his legend acquired additional specific details, six sites in addition to the shrine became associated with his arrival in Paris and his passion. Known as the seven stations of Saint Denis, the devout undertaking the pilgrimage to the shrine would have visited each one.[30] Before the end of the eighth century the renown of the first bishop of Paris and of the abbey dedicated to him had spread beyond the confines of the Ile-de-France to southern France and even into Italy, Germany, and England.[31]

Saint Denis: Patron and Protector of the French Monarchy

Historians today are quick to recognize the importance of a favorable geographical location. There can be little doubt that the site of Saint-Denis was significant in its rise to fame. From Roman times it enjoyed the advantage of its position on the great north road close to the banks of the Seine and close as well to the heart of Paris. Roman roads remained the principal arteries for overland communication and transport throughout the Middle Ages. And the Seine from prehistoric times to the present has kept these inland communities in touch with the outer world. To these natural and classic routes of travel must be added the blessings of the fertile fields of the Ile-de-France, which with its temperate climate promised bountiful annual harvests and great forests full of game. But it was the proximity to Paris and the fact that the Ile-de-France formed the core of the royal domain that ultimately gave St.-Denis its unusual advantages.

The site of the abbey lying to the north, rather than to the south, of Paris also has its interesting implications. The establishment, or earliest development, of a small *bourgade,* or community, where the major road to the north beyond Paris crossed the small river Croult is not recorded in any document. The formation of such a *bourgade* at the bifurcation of the road leading north (today route N1) and the branch to the northwest along the Seine to Le Havre (today route N14) is at least a reasonable assumption.[32] Such a location would also have been a natural one for a Roman *castrum* guarding the northern approaches to Paris.[33] This Roman military and commercial community could have been active in the third century when Saint Denis arrived in the region to preach the Gospel. Such a community, presumably with a cemetery, could have been a logical place for an official execution. Normally, an execution such as Denis' decapitation would in Roman times have taken place outside of a city in an armed camp. The site must have been abandoned after the Franks defeated the last Roman general, Syagrius, at Soissons in 386. By the late fifth century Sainte Geneviève's description of Saint Denis' tomb as a "fearful" place would have been quite appropriate.[34]

The early Frankish kings, Clovis and his sons, who established the Merovingian dynasty, chose Lutetia (Roman Paris) for the capital of their newly created kingdom. Apparently attracted by the ideal location of the Ile de la Cité in the middle of the Seine and by the vestiges of the imperial palace and the Roman forum on the south or left bank, they established themselves in that area. Before his death in 511, Clovis founded a church on the slopes of the hill today dominated by the Panthéon to serve as his burial place. At first dedicated to the Holy Apostles, it was later known as Sainte-Geneviève.[35] His son Childebert also founded a church on the south bank to serve as his own and his family's burial place. Dedicated to Saint Vincent, protomartyr of Spain, because of relics seized on Childebert's victorious expedition to that area, the church is familiar today as Saint-Germain-des-Prés.[36] On the basis of this evidence, the first generations of the Merovingian dynasty favored the south bank of the Seine. How, then, did Saint Denis, whose shrine was six miles to the north, become the royal patron?

Although Paris was recognized as the Merovingian capital, the government was peripatetic, following the king as he moved around his domains or undertook longer excursions to maintain his authority. Since sustenance was always a problem in the early Middle Ages, the king and his court, who necessarily lived off the land, were forced to move regularly. The great forests surrounding Paris, with their streams and marshes, provided an ideal environment, abundant with game and fish. Consequently, a ring of early royal residences, often called palaces, can be identified in modern Parisian suburbs.[37] In the later decades of the sixth century, Paris and the immediate vicinity suffered a series of calamities. Gregory of Tours, who visited Paris in 587, mentions a great fire in 585 and terrible floods and epidemics, such as the one which killed the infant son of Chilpéric and Fredegonde about 580.[38] Possibly unsanitary conditions in the crumbling ruins of the Roman remains on the south bank caused such epidemics; perhaps the third and fourth generations of Clovis's descendants preferred the cleaner air of the northern forests. In fact the palace of Clotaire II (613–638), in Clichy on the right bank and that of his son Dagobert I located further north in Epinay, only a few kilometers west of St.-Denis, indicate such a preference. In this northern region the shrine of the first bishop of Paris was the most venerable. Early miracles identified with his tomb stress Saint Denis' concern for the protection of his shrine and for those who sought its refuge.

One of the first generally accepted references to the shrine at Saint-Denis is recorded by Gregory of Tours, who described the pillaging of the early church by soldiers of Siegbert in 570.[39] One of them, an officer, carried off the silk cloth sewn with precious stones that covered the saint's tomb; the officer's servant stole some two hundred pieces of gold. While crossing the Seine to return to their camp, the servant fell overboard with all of the money and could not be saved. The officer interpreted this as a sign of divine wrath and hastened to return the tomb-covering to the church. This did not, however, save him from a violent death within the year. Another of Siegbert's soldiers, equally covetous but bolder than the rest, climbed to the top of the tomb to obtain the golden dove that hung above it. His feet slipped, so that he died astraddle the tomb, *compressis testiculis,* with his lance in his side.[40]

The desire of a saint to protect his tomb from intruders, although not peculiar to the legend of Saint Denis, recurs again and again in the miracles associated with his shrine. Two legendary incidents in the life of the young Prince Dagobert, early in the seventh century, offer interesting examples.

On one occasion Prince Dagobert, with his companions, was in full pursuit of a fine stag which suddenly took refuge in the church of Saint-Denis. Although the doors stood open, neither the dogs nor the hunters could pass through them, and they departed marveling at this miraculous barrier. A little later, Dagobert was seated at a table with his tutor, Sadrigesellis, when the old man unceremoniously reached over and took a drink from the prince's bowl. Dagobert, infuriated at this act of *lèse majesté,* drew his sword and so closely cut off the portion of the beard which had touched the cup that the tutor's chin was also slashed. Dagobert's followers then set upon the old man and beat him. On hearing of this rude treatment, Dagobert's father, Clotaire II, sent for the young prince to punish him, but Dagobert, evidently remembering the hunting incident, fled to the tomb of Saint Denis. Once again the pursuers were unable to gain entrance into the church, and the prince was soon pardoned.[41]

We can only conjecture to what extent the location of the shrine and the emphasis on his role as protector influenced the identification of Saint Denis as the particular patron of French kings.[42] The selection of patron saints can be traced back to the fourth century.[43] Inherited directly from the ancient identification of special or tutelary gods, the word *patronus* had special connotations in Roman relationships between patron and client—connotations which survived as an integral part of feudal contracts.[44] The first surviving original French royal charter, written in 625 on papyrus and now preserved in the Archives Nationales in Paris, mentions *sancti domini Dioni[nsis p]eculiares p[atroni n]ost[tri],* as the special patron of Clotaire II.[45] This same formula, often abbreviated as *pec. pat. nos.,* appears in twenty-two other royal charters before the crowning of Pepin the Short in 751.[46] From Pepin's accession to the throne until the thirteenth century, almost every French royal charter relating to Saint-Denis used this identical phrase.[47] In 1120 Louis VI went even further in a proclamation naming the saint *dux et protector* (leader and protector) of France.[48]

Saint-Denis: Royal Abbey

The recognition of Saint Denis as royal patron in the seventh century was preceded in the sixth century by royal burials *ad sanctos* before his shrine.[49] Close associations between Saint-Denis and the monarchy for centuries to come date from such burials. Together with a number of early royal gifts and the granting of special royal privileges, they resulted in the recognition of Saint-Denis as the royal abbey.

The earliest written account of a royal burial at Saint-Denis mentions that of Dagobert, the infant son of Chilpéric and Fredegonde, who died about 580 during an epidemic.[50] Archaeological evidence now establishes that there was an earlier royal burial—that of Queen Arnegonde about 570— and that "during the entire sixth century nobles of high rank chose Saint-Denis as their final resting place."[51] In the context of the royal abbey, the new evidence indicates that the tradition of royal burials at Saint-Denis began not with Dagobert I in 638, but some half century earlier with Queen Arnegonde.[52] In other words, about one hundred years after the building of the first church to honor Saint Denis, his shrine attracted royalty seeking his protection as guardian of their tombs. Although no single factor or recorded reason explains their choice, the fact remains that the three outstanding Merovingian kings of the seventh century—Clotaire II (584–628), Dagobert I (628–38), and Clovis II (638–55)[53]—chose to be buried at Saint-Denis, as did Charles Martel and his son Pepin the Short, the first king of the new Carolingian dynasty.[54]

By the end of the tenth century, there were more royal tombs at Saint-Denis than in any other locality; and following the burial of Hugh Capet in 987 only three Capetian kings, Philip I, Louis VII, and Louis XI, were buried elsewhere. When Philip I chose to be buried at Saint-Benoît-sur-Loire, Suger commented that this was against the *jus naturalis,* or normal custom.[55]

Another royal custom begun in Merovingian times also gave the abbey a distinction shared with few other institutions. At an unspecified date some-time in the sixth or early seventh century, the court began to deposit copies of royal documents at Saint-Denis.[56] These carefully guarded records formed the annals for the writing of the early histories of France. *Mostier seignori,* the *Maistre abeïe,* "La ou les gestes de France sont escrites," provided the information for the *Grandes Chroniques,* also called the *Chroniques de Saint-Denis.*[57] Possibly because of these archives a school of some renown was associated with the abbey. Pepin the Short received his education there; Charles the Bald was under its protection; and almost three centuries later Louis VI studied there with the young Suger. Activities such as these enhanced the abbey's reputation, and early gifts of land and other sources of revenue, bolstered by special privileges, made Saint-Denis a powerful feudal institution.

Gregory of Tours's description of the loot taken from the church by Siegbert's soldiers in 570 and confirmation of gifts of land in 625 and 626 by Clotaire II prove that the religious community owned movable and real property before Dagobert became king. Yet Dagobert gave "so many gifts, villas, and properties in so many places that everyone marvelled."[58] His generosity so impressed his own and later generations that tradition acclaimed him as the founder of the abbey.[59]

An even more important source of revenue was the great "Foire de la Saint-Denis" founded by Dagobert in 635 or 636 for the exclusive benefit of the religious community.[60] Held in October concurrently with the celebration of the saint's feast day, the fair functioned as a marketplace for winter provisions. Not to be confused with later fairs, such as the "Foire de Saint-Mathias" in February or the "Foire du Lendit" in June, Dagobert's fair attracted foreign merchants at an early date.[61] When Theodoric III, about 680, granted complete exemption from all custom duties, the monks became especially privileged merchants.[62] Other royal concessions, including independence from the bishop of Paris, granted by Bishop Landri on 1 July 653, at the request of Clovis II,[63] and royal immunity, between 657 and 664 by Queen Bathilde, freed the monks from the most onerous feudal obligations.[64] The renewal and confirmation of these privileges preoccupied succeeding abbots at the accession of each new Carolingian or early Capetian king.

This prosperous, privileged position necessitated close relationships between the abbey and the court. For more than a century, from 867 to 968, the king himself or a powerful noble, such as Hugh the Great, assumed direction of the abbey as its lay abbot. What might appear as a great honor resulted, in fact, in a precarious position. Charles the Bald, the first king to retain the title of abbot, left the administration to the provost, the dean, and the treasurer of the abbey but put his mayor of the palace in charge of military affairs. In those troubled times during and immediately following the Norman invasions, military issues were paramount. For a while the abbey had little control over its revenues and even ran the danger of becoming a simple benefice of the counts of Paris. The traditional independence of the abbey was too strong, however, to permit this submergence; even before he was king, Hugh Capet restored the administration of the abbey to the monks and their elected abbot.[65] The distinction of having been a royal abbey in more than name alone became a permanent prerogative, which with other special functions gave the abbey its unique position.

As royal authority and dignity increased, protocol at the court that established precedence at all ceremonies became more significant. Rivalry for the primacy of the French church was intense. The archbishop of Sens claimed recognition as successor to the original primate of the fourth Lyonnais district. The archbishop of Reims based his claim in the tradition that Saint Remi had converted Clovis I to Christianity and had crowned him at Reims with holy oil from an *ampula* miraculously brought from heaven by a dove or angel.[66] The abbot of Saint-Denis vaunted Saint Denis' recognition as patron and protector of the monarchy and the abbey's right to guard and preserve the *regalia,* the symbols of authority used at coronations.

The origins of the regalia are obscure, but they may have originated in the Frankish practice of burying the king with his royal insignia. No mention of the presence of the regalia at Saint-Denis occurs until 888, when Eudes, count of Paris, removed the insignia from the abbey's treasury for his own coronation. The regalia then included a crown, the orb, the royal vestments, fibulae, an armband, and a dagger.[67] Although serious objections were unquestionably made at this appropriation, their return to Saint-Denis was very slow. The widow of Hugh Capet, crowned in 987, gave back the orb. Philip I bequeathed his crown to the abbey; later, in 1120, Louis VI signed an official act of restitution in the presence of the papal legate.[68] The act proclaimed that according to law and custom the insignia of the deceased king were to be carried to Saint Denis, leader and protector of the kingdom. In 1179, after being consecrated by his uncle Archbishop William, the newly crowned Philip Augustus received the royal insignia from the hands of another William, the abbot of Saint-Denis. After the ceremony Philip returned the emblems to the abbot, who carried them back to Saint-Denis for safekeeping in the treasury. In 1261 King Louis IX agreed that the regalia were to be kept permanently in the abbey treasury, but he also stipulated that the insignia necessary for a coronation were to be taken from the abbey to Reims for the performance of the ceremony.[69] A glance at the plates in Félibien's *Histoire de l'Abbaye Royale* shows the accumulation of these treasures at Saint-Denis before they were dispersed or melted down during the Revolution. Crowns, scepters, and elaborately ornamented vestments symbolized well the royal dignity of the abbey.[70]

The treasury also sheltered another royal emblem—the famous *oriflamme*, carried into battle by the marshal of the armies with the cry, "Monjoie Saint-Denis."[71] The first mention of the oriflamme is found in the earliest existing version of the *Chanson de Roland*, written at the end of the eleventh century. The "orie flambe" passage occurs in the account of the last great battle, which was to avenge the death of Roland and of the other great peers of France. "The best men of France are with Charlemagne: so, too, is the golden banner. The emperor goes into battle with Geoffry of Anjou carrying the *oriflamme*. It had been Saint Peter's; it had borne the name Romaine; there on the battlefield its name was changed to that of the battle-cry 'Monjoie.'"[72]

Events surrounding the threatened invasion of France in August 1124 by Henry V of Germany in league with Henry I of England gave the *vexillum*, the military standard of the Vexin, a national significance. Suger called the Vexin a fief of the abbey.[73] According to Suger, Louis VI, recognizing that Saint Denis was the "special patron, and after God, the most powerful protector of the kingdom,"[74] took the vexillum from the high altar at Saint-Denis, as though from the hand of his seigneur in the manner of a vassal acknowledging the authority of his overlord.[75] Next Louis made two strategic moves: first he blocked the English from joining the forces assembled east of the Rhine by Henry V; and then he summoned all France—"tota Francia"—to rally around him at Reims. The response to this urgent call exceeded all expectations. "Whether in our times or in those of remote Antiquity, France never acted more illustriously nor proclaimed more gloriously its unified strength," Suger proudly wrote.[76] In the face of the opposition,

Henry V withdrew, and the exultant French returned to their own lands.

The display of the vexillum, taken by Louis as *signifer,* or standard bearer, of the abbey and of its patron saint, encouraged all of France to rally behind the king; but not until the end of the twelfth century did the vexillum become identified as the famous oriflamme.[77] Before his departure on the third crusade, Philip Augustus also took the "auriflamman seu vexillum sancti Dionyou" from the altar. When he displayed the banner, "vexillum simplex, splendoris rubei," at the battle of Bouvines in 1214,[78] it was identified as "quod cum flamma habeat vulgariter aurea nomen."[79] In short, at the end of the twelfth and beginning of the thirteenth centuries the splendid red banner associated with the war cry "Monjoie Saint-Denis" and carried at the head of the French army was still identified as the vexillum of Saint-Denis and only "commonly" called the oriflamme.

Recent scholarship has concluded that it was not until long after Suger's death that the monks of the royal abbey realized their most ambitious aims. A significant gesture of King Louis IX illustrates this achievement. In 1248 he went to Saint-Denis with his eldest son to place four pieces of Byzantine gold on the altar as a symbol of the feudal head-tax paid to a sovereign lord. He departed on his crusade as a Knight of Saint-Denis, and on his return repeated the symbolic act, giving twenty-eight gold pieces to the abbey—four for each year that he was absent. His successors did not follow his example or renew this act of submission. This moment may be looked on as the climax of the monks' efforts to make their saint the true sovereign of the French monarchy.

CHAPTER ONE

Sainte Geneviève's Chapel

Only the vague outlines of the history of northern France after the collapse of Roman authority in the fourth century can be sketched with any certainty. The obscurity of these early beginnings of the Middle Ages under the leadership of Frankish, or Merovingian, kings justifies the rubric Dark Ages.[1] Such obscurity magnifies the interest and significance of the scattered facts available for reconstructing this early medieval culture. As a source adding to our meager knowledge, the first chapel built to honor Saint Denis deserves careful attention.

The legend of Saint Denis asserts that Catulla, a pious Christian woman, marked the martyrs' burial place with a monument which, the legend continues, was replaced in the fourth century by a sumptuous basilica, later destroyed during the barbarian invasions of the fifth century.[2] No authoritative texts document such a building, and the archaeological evidence is equally negative. The absence of any other fourth-century or even early fifth-century Christian churches in the region of Paris makes such a possibility even more remote.[3]

Reasonably reliable documents of the sixth century mention a basilica dedicated to Saint Denis, and only one such church in the entire area is so identified before the eighth century.[4] A more explicit text—the *Vita Genovefae,* written about 520—provides an approximate date and describes the circumstances of the building of this first church.

Born in Nanterre, Sainte Geneviève became the patron saint of Paris because she correctly predicted that the city of Paris would not suffer depredations from the dreaded Attila the Hun. She knew about the tomb, *locus ejus,* of Saint Denis in the *vicum Catolocensem* (Catolacum), which her biographer described as a "terrible and fearful" place.[5] The specific use of the phrase "locum ejus" indicates that only a tomb existed at that time. Her devotion to Saint Denis, the first Parisian martyr, inspired her to persuade priests in Paris to make a "collatio" in order to build a basilica in his honor.[6] Since Sainte Geneviève died in 512, this first building to honor the first bishop of Paris was probably built in the later years of the fifth century or early in the sixth century. A specific date, namely 495, has been proposed.[7] Although such an exact date exaggerates historical probability, I have adopted ca. 475 as a reasonable one for the building of the first church dedicated to Saint Denis.

Until recently the exact location of this first church was seriously debated.[8] Two documents mention a church dedicated to Saint Denis *in strato,*[9] which has been interpreted as referring to the church of Saint-Denis-de-l'Estrée, today called "l'église de Saint-Denis" at the western end of the rue de la République in St.-Denis, as distinct from "la basilique," or abbey church.[10] In addition to the statement in Suger's will that Saint Denis rested for three hundred years *in strato,* three small lead coffins discovered in 1577 under the sanctuary of Saint-Denis-de-l'Estrée bore inscriptions indicating that they contained vestments of the three martyrs—presumably confirmation that this was their original resting place. Yet evidence has accumulated over the years that establishes the existence of a large pre-Christian and Merovingian cemetery under and adjacent to the present abbey church. This affords a more logical site for the martyrs' burial than *in strato,* despite the reference in Suger's will.

The discovery, or uncovering, of burials around the abbey church was such a common occurrence that little if any notice was taken of those recurring incidents.[11] Viollet-le-Duc was the first to identify as Merovingian the plaster and stone sarcophagi that he found during his excavations. Although he published drawings of one of them and removed a number of stone coffins intact, the few plans and sections of his excavations provide the only extant records of where some of the sarcophagi were found.[12] Those discoveries indicate that Merovingian burials were made under the western bays as well as under the crossing of the existing abbey church.

Other early burials were discovered between 1900 and 1905 during excavations in the remains of a sixteenth-century chapel known as the Eglise des Trois Patrons, located across the rue de Strasbourg, some fifty meters to the north of the western bays of the abbey church.[13] There excavations undertaken by a Commission du Musée municipal, in the hope of finding "des choses archéologiques très curieuses," uncovered remains of a number of Merovingian burials, including three complete plaster and one stone sarcophagi. At depths varying between 2.75 m and 4.45 m below the "sol actuel,"[14] coins dating from the emperor Nero (A.D. 59–68) to the emperor Magnentius (A.D. 350–53) also came to light, as well as Roman tiles, a terracotta Christian antefix, and Merovingian weapons, fibulae, jewels, and a

Fig. 50

braid of blond hair.[15] The cemetery was a large one, for additional Merovingian sarcophagi were found in the abbey garden by Jules Formigé in
1948.[16] Also more than one hundred early burials, some of them pre-Christian, have been excavated under the transept and crossing of the abbey
church.[17] The presence of this early cemetery suggests the logical place for
the martyr's burial in the third century. The discovery of two parallel alignments of large stones that could have been foundations for a building under
the existing crossing of the abbey church confirms that this was also the
location of the first church built in honor of Saint Denis.

Pls. 2, 3A; Album no. 2

App. E.4a,b, 8, 10

These foundations are easily distinguished from any other foundation
construction at Saint-Denis. They occur under the crossing of the existing
church in an east–west alignment at exactly the same depth and are the only
large blocks decorated by unusual incised designs or by carving in low relief
and by projecting string courses. The moldings and designs identify them as
Gallo-Roman blocks, possibly of the second to third century A.D; their details
will be described more fully below. The oldest, or earliest, on this site, the
blocks served as foundations for Sainte Geneviève's chapel and established
the east–west orientations for all the successive churches on this site, as well
as creating a basic dimension that persisted in all buildings until the thirteenth century.

Viollet-le-Duc was the first to recognize these blocks as the "débris de
monuments gallo-romains," but he mistakenly interpreted them as part of
the foundations for Dagobert's church. Furthermore, for reasons not at all
clear today, on the plan of his supposed excavations of the crossing the points
marked "a," which he identified as containing this Gallo-Roman debris, do
not coincide with the location of the blocks visible today.[18] Viollet-le-Duc's
excavations in this area were limited to the space necessary for the installation
of the "caveau imperial" and consequently did not extend as far to the west as
the present excavations.

This Gallo-Roman debris was rediscovered by Jules Formigé in 1956–57,
when he undertook the removal of Viollet-le-Duc's imperial crypt. Yet
Formigé's description and interpretation of what he found must have been
written before the excavation of the area had advanced very far. Consequently, many of his conclusions are thoroughly misleading. He wrote, for
instance, "I also uncovered a wall perpendicular to the preceding ones [the
Gallo-Roman, east–west blocks] and of the same type which must have been
the western limits of this chapel."[19] No such wall exists today. Masonry
projections to the north and south, that is, perpendicular to the Gallo-Roman
blocks, occur at points roughly indicated on his plans, but they are at a much
higher level, are of quite different stones, and differ in general character. He
added, "At this point, a painted jamb of a portal with a set-back was found."
When questioned, Jean Deschamps, the foreman of Formigé's work at Saint-
Denis, could not recall such a discovery.

The consistent horizontal level of these blocks is one of their most noticeable archaeological features, suggesting that they belonged to the same structure. Unfortunately, it is no longer possible to identify exactly what they
rested upon. Their lower edges lie between 2.05 m and 2.10 m below the

1. Large stone block with pelta designs, presumably from a Gallo-roman temple reused in Merovingian foundations under nave of abbey church. Musée Lapidaire, Saint-Denis.

2. Merovingian foundations under south side of nave, showing one block with Lewis holes.

surface of the existing nave pavement, but the 1.00 m or so that has been excavated below these blocks has been almost entirely covered by a modern cement to consolidate the surfaces, so that verification of any substructure is no longer possible. The geological composition of the large blocks also differentiates them from other foundation masonry, as does their decoration.

One complete block, identical to those in the foundations, is stored at present in the Musée Lapidaire.[20] Described as a "clear beige limestone with white zones rich in microfossils," the stone probably originated in a quarry in the region of Paris that contained "lamborde [limestone] d'age lutétien supérieure."[21] The size of this block, which measures 1.25 m by 0.50 m high, and of others in the foundations suggests that the original Gallo-Roman

Fig. 1

building from which they came must have been in the vicinity of the cemetery in which Sainte Geneviève's chapel was built; certainly their transportation over any great distance would have been difficult. Some of the blocks have rectangular holes cut into their uppermost surfaces. Such holes, known as *trous de louve,* or Louis (Lewis) holes, allowed the insertion of expanding metal clamps which, when attached to ropes, facilitated the moving of the blocks. To be visible, the moldings and designs on one face of several of the blocks—their most distinctive characteristic—must have faced outward. The most dominant designs are a sequence of irregular, incised motifs typical of the frieze on the entablatures of Roman structures. These unusual, asymmetrical patterns called *pelta,* or *boucliers d'Amazones*—Amazons' shields— have been observed in paintings and mosaics as well as on architectural fragments in southern Gaul, Switzerland, the Rhineland, and England. All examples date to the third and fourth centuries A.D.[22] Above the frieze of pelta are three molded elements which may have served as a cornice for an entablature. The middle element has a sequence of two triangular motifs separated by two vertical bars, and the upper vertical band, or fillet, may be an imitation of a rope molding. Another block at the western end of the north side has four projecting moldings with crude, raised designs possibly representing foliate patterns. Comparison with a block found in the foundations at Glanum, at St.-Rémy de Provence, confirms a pre-third-century date for the Roman structure at Saint-Denis.[23] The majority of the blocks are undecorated and average about 0.40 m high by 0.50 m wide and 0.30 m thick, suggesting that they originally formed part of a solid wall, or stylobate.

The location of these blocks in reasonably straight east–west alignments which stop abruptly at both the eastern and western terminations establishes,

Fig. 2

Figs. 1, 3

Fig. 4a,b

3. Merovingian foundations under south side of nave, showing a block with a pelta design.

b

a

4. (a) Merovingian foundations under north side of nave, showing masonry block with stylized foliate designs; (b) detail of a drawing of the excavation by Viollet-le-Duc, showing masonry block in place.

in my opinion, the dimensions of Sainte Geneviève's chapel. The overall exterior east–west length measured from the eastern and western faces of the foundation blocks was 20.60 m and between the inside surfaces, 19.90 m. The interior width from the northern and southern faces of the same blocks is 9.10 m. These dimensions indicate that the first building to honor Saint Denis was not a small funerary chapel but a stone church of some importance. Although the Gallo-Roman northern and southern foundations end opposite each other, problems remain about the construction of both the eastern and western terminations of the building.

No actual masonry of the eastern terminal wall exists today.[24] The only evidence that I have been able to discover is a few photographs taken for the Archives Photographiques, Direction de l'Architecture in Paris while Formigé's excavations were in progress. Several of these photographs show the eastern portions of the eighth-century annular crypt with the foundations as

Pls. 2, 3A; Album no. 13A

App. H.7, 8

they were uncovered.[25] Although the evidence is not conclusive, changes in the foundation masonry can be identified. Two photographs (nos. 58.P.1055, 58.P.1056), supposedly taken during the same visit to the excavations, show the south side with what appears to be an agglomerate, loose mixture of black earth and uncut stones under the Gallo-Roman foundation blocks. Although the bottom of one of the photographs (fig. H.7) is out of focus, the rough fill with blocks of earth at the bottom right can be seen to change abruptly to a seemingly assembled masonry of small, irregular stones. The two photographs of the north side are difficult to understand when compared with the upper constructions visible today,[26] but a change in the lowest foundations similar to that on the south side takes place with the sudden disappearance of the fill with black earth. On both the north and south sides this change occurs as the curving masonry of the semicircular apse begins. Since no other traces of this black fill exist in this area, I have concluded that the eastern end of Sainte Geneviève's chapel was a flat wall, perpendicular to the east–west alignment of the Gallo-Roman foundations, which was removed when King Dagobert I enlarged the chapel in the seventh century. If the reconstruction of the eastern end of Sainte Geneviève's chapel must remain hypothetical, the reconstruction of the western end is more certain, and the details are interesting.

App. H.5, 8

The exact location of the western wall is marked by the juncture of the north and south alignments of Gallo-Roman blocks with foundations constructed in a completely different manner and by the remnants of a substructure running north and south. The sudden change from the east–west alignment of large Gallo-Roman blocks to foundations built of small, irregular stones in a loose sand mortar occurs on both the north and south sides exactly opposite each other. Furthermore, the westernmost, or last, Gallo-Roman blocks on each side project slightly beyond the alignment of the other blocks, and remnants of solid mortar adhere to the projecting surfaces—an indication that other masonry continued between those terminal points. At a lower level, in what must have been a trench dug into the solid subsoil, a series of misaligned, irregularly shaped stones extends across the western end of the excavation just in front of the densely packed group of Merovingian sarcophagi. This loose structure must have been intended to support the western wall between the last of the Gallo-Roman blocks. Changes occurred to this wall within a relatively few years. As shown on the plans of the burials uncovered successively by Viollet-le-Duc, Edouard Salin, and Michel Fleury, recently published in the *Dossiers de l'archéologie,* at least nine if not ten tombs have their feet (eastern ends) or heads (western ends) projecting over or onto the stones of this north–south substructure.[27] Although the projections in most instances measure only a few centimeters, the eastern and western ends of the two tombs on the southern end almost touch each other. Thus the masonry of this western wall must have been pierced or destroyed during the sixth century. As Michel Fleury demonstrated in his text, only a relative, not an absolute, chronology can be established for the dates of these tombs.[28] Since, however, the earliest Christian burial found by Salin at Saint-Denis is dated about 500, and since Queen Arnegonde was buried between 565

Fig. 5a,b

Fig. 6

Fig. 7

a

b

and 570 just to the west of tomb 11, which encroaches on the substructure masonry, such a disturbance or change must have occurred during the first half of the sixth century. France-Lanord, who examined the contents of these tombs in his private laboratory in Nancy, has proved conclusively that they were never subjected to any infiltration of water.[29] Consequently an area extending several meters to the west of Sainte Geneviève's chapel was covered sufficiently to protect it from the weather.[30] Such protection could have been provided by a wooden porch or portico, which may have extended around to cover the north side of the chapel, facing the cemetery. Although Edouard Salin does not comment on the possible infiltration of water in the tombs which he examined under the north transept, their location would have been just outside of Sainte Geneviève's chapel. Unfortunately, Salin, presumably in conjunction with Jules Formigé, did not understand the different masonries in this area. Consequently the diagrams he published in *Monuments Piot* in 1957 are completely misleading with regard to the dates of the masonry adjacent to the burials, although the dating of the burials must be correct.[31] Since this small area under the north transept is the only one to have been thoroughly examined, and since the burials uncovered date from the fourth to the seventh century or even later, the proposal that there might have been a covered portico along the north side of Sainte Geneviève's chapel must remain purely tentative, even though such a covering must have existed to the west of the chapel.

Before I discuss the interesting implications of the proportions of Sainte Geneviève's late fifth-century building and its decoration, fragments of early

5. Western corners of foundation for Sainte Geneviève's chapel, showing blocks with attached mortar: (a) northwest projection; (b) southwest projection.

masonry above the Gallo-Roman blocks must be described. Three segments of early masonry survive, more or less intact, above the Gallo-Roman foundation blocks. The coursings are characteristic of early medieval masonry called *petit appareil* because of the presence of small, unfinished stones in a coarse mortar. The stones, which average about 0.20 m long by 0.10 m high, are laid in roughly horizontal beds which have a setback nearly at the same levels in all three locations. Larger, unfinished stones, which average about 0.25 m high by 0.40 m long, in some instances as long as 1.50 m, even 1.80 m, form a middle coursing, although toward the western end they rest directly on the Gallo-Roman blocks. The best preserved and most extensive portion of this masonry is above the southeastern foundations. A smaller segment remains near the western end of the south side, and fragments of the same type can be seen above the western portions of the northern alignment of Gallo-Roman blocks. Since very few examples of such early medieval masonry have survived, there has been some doubt about the date of these wall fragments at Saint-Denis. Could they have been part of Sainte Geneviève's chapel late in the fifth century, or were they part of Dagobert's addition in the seventh century? Only recently a section of masonry has been uncovered farther to the west on the southern side. Since this fragment is located above the rubble foundations to the west of the Gallo-Roman blocks, and since it appears to be more solidly constructed, although the stones are small and unfinished, I differentiate it from the sections to the east and

6. Rubble alignment under western foundations of Sainte Geneviève's chapel with projecting Merovingian sarcophagi.

App. E.4a, 5d

App. E.4b, 8

Pl. 2; Album no. 2

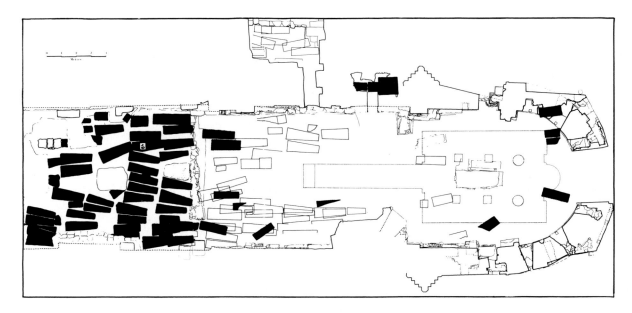

propose that the eastern portions are fifth century whereas the western one is seventh century. On the basis of these observations, my reconstruction of the plan of Sainte Geneviève's chapel measures 19.90 m by 9.10 m wide inside the Gallo-Roman blocks of the foundations and possibly 20.60 m long by 9.50 m wide inside the walls of the church itself.

Pl. 3A

Similar rectangular plans, almost exactly twice as long as they are wide—a rectangle composed approximately of two identical squares—have been noted in other small Merovingian churches. Jean Hubert even has cited this proportion as "proof that the builders of these churches were deliberately applying geometrical principles so as to safeguard the harmony of proportions."[32] Such a Vitruvian canon in a series of small Merovingian churches proposes a surprisingly sophisticated continuity between late antiquity and the early Middle Ages, which I doubt could have been conscious or deliberate. At Saint-Denis, nevertheless, the width established by the Gallo-Roman blocks and Merovingian masonry of the first church on this site was continued by extension to the seventh-century enlargement, and by normal economical reuse of existing masonry to the nave of the new, eighth-century church. By the twelfth century, as we shall see, a legend endowed the "old" building with such venerability that Abbot Suger's masons were instructed to incorporate the early masonry in their new "Gothic" construction.[33] In addition to a basic dimension, the first church also established the orientation or east–west axis for the succeeding churches, except for the chapel added to Abbot Fulrad's basilica by Abbot Hilduin in 832. In a commentary on my first volume, Jean Hubert noted that Hilduin's chapel was correctly oriented but that the axis of the existing church is not. He postulated that Hilduin's chapel had the same axis as the monastic buildings and as the tombs in the adjacent cemetery, and that the early church on this site must have had the same "normal" orientation.[34] The rediscovery of the foundations for the first

7. Plan of Merovingian sarcophagi excavated under nave and crossing by Viollet-le-Duc, Edouard Salin, and Michel Fleury (after *Dossiers de l'archéologie* 32 (1979): 22, plan 4).

church corrects such an assumption and proves that the fifth-, seventh-, twelfth-, and thirteenth-century constructions were built along the same axis.

The almost continuous foundations and some segments of masonry above them have survived to locate and identify the plan of the first church to honor Saint Denis, but details about the rest of its structure are meager and unspecific. According to the author of the *Vita Genovefae,* miracles occurred during the building of Saint Denis' chapel. The miraculous filling of a barrel with good wine for workmen who were cutting timbers in the forest can be interpreted as confirmation of the probability that the building had a wooden roof. The equally miraculous discovery of a chalk pit supplied an ingredient necessary for the mortar of the masonry walls, and the picturesque relighting of Sainte Geneviève's candle by angels after it had been extinguished by demons emphasizes the urgency of the work and Saint Denis' own interest in its progress.[35] The important factor for the development of the cult would have been the presence of Saint Denis' tomb under the church. The *Vita Genovefae* states that Sainte Geneviève encouraged the priests of Paris to build a basilica in his honor. Is the assumption that this church, or chapel, was built over Saint Denis' burial place correct? Reason buttressed by archaeological evidence would answer yes.

If Sainte Geneviève's only desire had been to honor the first bishop of Paris, she would not have had to go all the way to the cemetery in the *vicum Catolacum* to do so. Once at the cemetery, why should she have selected one particular spot, unless that spot had been associated with martyrdom? In other words, the precise location of the first church could hardly have been accidental. Jules Formigé's excited claim in 1958 that he had found the saint's burial place was marred by his explanation that the "grand fosse" in the crypt was too large for a single burial but perfectly suited for three—namely, Saint Denis and his two companions.[36] Since historians agree that Rusticus and Eleutherius were later additions to the legend, Formigé's "grand fosse" could not have been the original size of the burial place; it might have been the result of a later enlargement. The fact that this particular spot remained the focal point, that is, the location of the high altar, for all the successive churches is persuasive evidence that Sainte Geneviève chose this location for the first church because local tradition in the fifth century identified it as the burial place of Saint Denis. Later enlargements of the first church, either by Dagobert in the seventh century or by Fulrad in the eighth century, when the presence of two companions was an accepted fact, doubtless encouraged the transformation of the original single cavity into a larger, "grand fosse" capable of holding three burials. The fact that from the beginning this first church was called a basilica confirms the belief that the building contained holy relics. Sainte Geneviève's chapel, in the cemetery of Saint-Denis, can therefore be referred to as a *basilica ad corpus* and recognized as a *praecipua loca sanctorum* capable of attracting pious souls who wished to gain the favor of a powerful protector by a life of attentive service at his tomb.[39] In spite of the scarcity of documents, there is convincing evidence that such a community developed at an early date.

App. H.1

One of the first religious requirements would have been a *Passio,* or recital of the life and martyrdom of the patron saint, to be included in the liturgical readings on his feast day. That need was fulfilled at Saint-Denis by the text known as the *Passio sancti Dionysii, Rustici et Eleutherii,* or the *Gloriosae.* Emphasizing the fact that as the first *Passio* it is sparse in details and redundant in rhetoric, Levillain and Loenertz have argued that the earliest redaction must have been written in the late fifth or early sixth century.[38] The presence of Christian burials dating as early as ca. A.D. 500 strengthens the evidence for such an early community.

The size of Sainte Geneviève's basilica gave it distinction in those early years before Clovis had established his authority or selected Paris as his capital. The few details that can be associated with the church are persuasive evidence that soon after its founding a religious community developed, presumably spontaneously, to act as custodians and to provide some assurance of security in an otherwise chaotic society. As might be expected, the available evidence is inferential rather than specific, but the implications are convincing.

In 1948, as I completed the excavation of the north transept, some unopened and apparently undisturbed sarcophagi were discovered at the southeastern extremity. Circumstances did not permit their investigation, but authorities agreed that they would be examined before the consolidation and covering of the excavation began. Under pressure to complete the consolidation of this same area, workmen uncovered a Merovingian stone sarcophagus in July 1952, which they evidently investigated, for in the immediate vicinity the foreman found two bronze buckles, six beads (two of crystal, two of amber, and two in *patte de verre*), some gold threads from a textile, and other metal objects. Exclamations of surprise and indignation at the lack of proper supervision greeted the discovery, which because of a "figule digitée" must date in the second half of the sixth century. The quality of the objects indicated the burial of a lady of very high rank. Proclaimed one of the four or five most important discoveries of its type in France, it proved to be only the first of a number of similar princely burials to be uncovered under and adjacent to Sainte Geneviève's chapel.[39]

Edouard Salin has dated the earliest such burials at the beginning of the fourth century on the basis of a "follis" of Maxentius (306–312) and a bronze of Constantine I (306–337) found in the mouth of a child as an offering to Charon.[40] Michel Fleury's discovery in August 1959 of the tomb of Queen Arnegonde has marked the climax so far of these discoveries. They are still incomplete.[41]

A colorful reconstruction of Queen Arnegonde's costume shows a dark red silk tunic, reaching almost to her feet, over a violet, almost indigo blue, robe.[42] A band of purple satin embroidered with rosettes and triangles in gold thread was attached to the ends of the long sleeves of the tunic, which was held in place by a long silver and gold pin and by a large belt decorated with two lines of open triangles and gold bands. An unusually large, carved silver, two-piece buckle with gilt filigree designs and mounted colored glass in decorative compartments joined the ends of the belt. Gold earrings, two round cloisonné fibulae with garnets, small silver buckles and ornaments for the straps around her light wool stockings, two small gold pins to fasten a satin veil on her head, and a ring engraved with her name completed her adornment. Brought to Clotaire I's court in the 530s, she gave birth to Childebert in 539, and died between 565 and 570 at about forty-five years of age. A burial with such royal accoutrements proves that Saint-Denis was no longer regarded as a terrible and fearful place, nor had it been so since the beginning of the sixth century, when the first princely interments began. A religious community capable of inspiring royal confidence must have gathered around Sainte Geneviève's chapel before the end of the fifth century. Within the first century of its existence such a community was custodian of a number of noble and royal tombs.

Before the end of the second decade of the seventh century, the community included an *abbas* and *monachi* as well as *cleri vel pauperum*. These terms describe the members of an early Christian community but do not necessarily imply that it was a regular monastic order. At that time an abba generally referred to a member of the secular clergy, who was the superior of a basilica. Monachi included the lay brothers serving the basilica as well as the ordained cleri, or priests and deacons. The pauperum acted as guardians and servants. These men must have lived in a manner similar to the early groups at Saint-Hilaire-de-Poitiers, who were regulated by an unwritten code or custom brought from the Near East by Saint Martin, as described by Sulpicius Severus. This custom maintained a cenobitic, communal life, with the members under no oath. Individuals living in separate chambers, or cells, were occupied in manual labor and ate and prayed together. The fare was simple, as was the costume. All property was common, but the community could own such property in its own right.[43] The group at Saint-Denis did not become a regular monastic order until about 650, when the Rule of Saint Benedict and Saint Columban was imposed by Queen Bathilde.

Possibly the presence of royal burials inspired early gifts to the custodians and encouraged costly decorations for the church they served. The bejeweled altar covering and large sum of gold carried off by Siegbert's soldiers during the raid described by Gregory of Tours indicates that by 570 the community had received munificent but unrecorded benefactions.[44] The first recorded gift of the community at Saint-Denis is mentioned in Clotaire II's charter of 625, confirming the gift to Saint-Denis of property within the walls of Paris from a certain Dagobert, son of Baddon. This gift has been identified as an intermediate lot, possibly near the Seine, to be used for storage and implies that the community of Saint-Denis, or its agents, was already engaged in an active commerce. Such an inference is strengthened by another of Clotaire II's charters confirming a gift from John, a merchant, to Saint-Denis of several unidentified pieces of property within the diocese of Paris. John may have been motivated by a desire for salvation, but he was also a businessman who must have had some commerce with the Dionysian community— enough to justify a gift of several pieces of property. In 627 an even larger gift is recorded, namely that of Theotrude, or Theodila, who gave three villas, two in the Oise and one in the Limousin. The villa at Mero (Oise) included "cultivated and uncultivated land, woods, ponds and streams, with the farm-house."[45] Such properties must have provided an annual income, which was greatly increased by Dagobert's remarkable generosity and by the privileges acquired during his reign and that of his son Clovis II.

Before I discuss King Dagobert's patronage in the seventh century, a final detail in Sainte Geneviève's chapel—the altar and its surroundings—should be examined. Gregory of Tours mentioned the sixth-century altar on two occasions. In his *Historia Francorum* he recorded a dispute that took place before the altar between "men of high birth among the first at the court of Chilperic" (presumably Chilpéric I, 561–584).[46] Gregory used three different terms to describe the altar ensemble. First an oath was to be sworn over the tomb—*super tumulum*—of the blessed martyr Dionysius. An oath was then sworn with hands raised over the altar—*super altarum*—and, finally, during the ensuing fight, blood was spilled in front of the altar, and spears were thrown which reached the sepulchre—*ad ipsum sepulchrum*.[47] In every instance there was one tomb, one altar, and one sepulchre. Translations of the passage vary, but since Gregory of Tours was careful to use three specific terms, I believe that three different parts of the monument are identified.[48] The tomb—*tumulus*—refers to the actual tomb or burial place of the martyr, over which stood the altar and behind and to the east of which was a sepulchre, or memorial sarcophagus. The altar and sarcophagus must have been in the church above the pavement, whereas the tomb or burial place could have been in the ground underneath. Gregory's other mention of the altar in his description of Siegbert's pillaging gave additional details.

As recorded in the *Liber in Gloria Martyrum*, which is not considered to be as reliable as the *Historia*, Siegbert's soldiers found the sanctuary where the host was kept deserted by the custodians, who had probably fled for protection to Paris. As noted earlier in a different context, a sacred cloth sewn with gold and gems which covered the sepulchre (*quia sanctum tegebat sepulchrum*) was stolen. Another soldier climbed onto the sepulchre (*super sepulchrum sanctum calcare non mentuens*) in order to reach a golden dove with his lance, but his feet slipped on the sides (*elapsisque pedes, ab utraque parte, quia turritum erat tumulum*) so that he died, *compressis testiculis,* with his lance in his side.[49] The problem is the phrase *turritum erat tumulum*, since *turritum* has been variously translated as "decorated with towers" or as "a cone" or "a pyramid," or simply as "lofty, high." None of these descriptions is appropriate for a tomb under the pavement. Possibly a copyist did not distinguish between the tomb—*tumulum*—and the sepulchre—*sepulchrum*—as was done in the *Historia Francorum*. A stone sarcophagus with a "high" pitched roof was not unusual in the sixth and seventh centuries.[50] My reconstruction, therefore, for the eastern end of Sainte Geneviève's chapel would include a flat table altar placed on the pavement above the place where the patron saint was buried. Behind the altar, directly in front of the flat eastern wall of the chapel, was a stone sarcophagus with a steeply pitched cover-up roof. The first building to honor the first bishop of Paris was, consequently, a relatively large mortuary chapel built at the end of the fifth or early sixth century in a large cemetery north of Paris, where oral traditions of that time located the burial place of Saint Denis. Properly called a basilica because it was built over the remains of the martyr, it was in fact a simple rectangular building with solid foundations formed by large stone blocks, *spolia* perhaps, from a nearby Roman encampment. The masonry walls of small, irregular stones laid in horizontal beds were characteristic of early medieval construction, as was the wooden roof. Within a century this chapel had become the focal point of a religious community of some importance, especially in relation to the Merovingian court. Saint-Denis prospered during the seventh century, notably from about 620 to 655, during the reigns of Dagobert I and his son Clovis II. The chapel was enlarged and embellished and the beginnings of the abbey's immense wealth and privileged position established.

CHAPTER TWO

The Enlargement of the Basilica
under Dagobert's Patronage

I n 1846 Charles Sainte-Beuve commented on those whom history had slighted:

> I have often thought that there would be a chapter to write: About those who have a poor reputation and who do not deserve it. Montaigne forgot to do it. . . . One might begin with Augeus, to whose name has become attached that odious, almost repugnant, phrase, *the Augean stables,* and who was the richest and most royal patriarch of shepherds, according to ancient idylls. Above all one should not forget Dagobert, *le bon Dagobert,* who has left a jovial, rather ridiculous reputation, and who was possibly a great, energetic king, the *quasi-*Charlemagne of his race, dead in the flower of his age—thirty-three years old—and in the vigor of his lofty projects.[1]

Dagobert I was born into a world torn by brutal rivalries, such as those between Brunhild and Fredegonde, yet before his death in ca. 638 he had extended his authority over all of France. Immortalized as "le bon Dagobert" in a favorite nursery rhyme, he must have been an able administrator, one who reorganized royal finances and controlled internal disorders.[2] His generosity to Saint-Denis so impressed his contemporaries that he became known as the founder of the abbey. Contrary to the *Gesta Dagoberti Regis,* documents and archaeological discoveries indicate that he did not introduce monasticism at Saint-Denis nor did he build a completely new church. Yet his reputation as established by the *Gesta Dagoberti Regis*, written at Saint-Denis two centuries after his death, was so widespread and so popular that the Abbot Suger in the twelfth century as well as most historians of the abbey, even as recently as 1946, have called him "Founder of the Abbey" (*ecclesiae fundator*).[3] Enough archaeological evidence now exists to explain obscurities in the early texts, so that it is possible, in my opinion, to reconstruct at least the major outlines of what Dagobert's patronage accomplished at Saint-Denis.

The *Chronica Fredegarii* and the *Vita Eligii Episcopi Noviomagensis,* critical texts possibly written within a few years of Dagobert's death, may be considered contemporary, if not eyewitness accounts. After mentioning Dagobert's sickness at his palace in Epinay and his death and burial at Saint-Denis, Fredegarius described the rich ornaments given to the church by Dagobert and noted that he had "built around it" (*in circoito fabrecare*). The *Vita Eligii* described the decorations in greater detail and added that a new altar was "outside at the feet of the holy martyrs" (*extrinsecus ad pedes sancti martyris*).[4] The erudite, detailed explanation of these phrases by Havet and Levillain, in particular, are delightful examples of learned but nonconclusive debate, because the archaeological data available to them was limited to Viollet-le-Duc's confusing explanation of the so-called plan of his excavations.[5] Although the evidence is still fragmentary, enough masonry identifiable as post-475 (Sainte Geneviève's chapel) and pre-775 (Fulrad's construction) has come to light to provide a reasonable solution.

As noted in chapter 1, the alignment of Gallo-Roman blocks which I have identified as foundations for Sainte Geneviève's chapel stop abruptly on both the northern and southern sides at the western end of the excavation under the crossing.[6] Instead of large, cut, yellowish stones at a constant level of ca. 2.05 m below the present pavement, immediately to the west the masonry changes to a series of beds of small, irregularly shaped stones, sometimes with fragments of flint or even blocks of pure lime, extending to a depth of 2.65 m. Coarse, sandy mortar separates these stones. Similar segments of this masonry appear in nine other locations in the excavated areas under the nave and side aisles of the present church.

Evidence for the date of this masonry is circumstantial, and its attribution to the enlargement of Sainte Geneviève's chapel by Dagobert in the seventh century is deductive. Since this type of masonry is not found in the east under the Gallo-Roman blocks, it must postdate the fifth century. In other locations to the west, the same type of masonry passes under the foundations of the eighth century. The location of this masonry suggests that the major portion of this enlargement consisted of a nave (probably with side aisles) extending almost 28.00 m to the west of Sainte Geneviève's building.

The most extensive and best preserved part of the seventh-century foundations lies under the fourth bay on the north side of the nave. Extending 6.50 m from east to west and projecting 3.10 m to the south, this masonry apparently locates the northwest corner of the nave of Dagobert's building. In the fourth and sixth beds on the north side, clearly visible as an integral part of the masonry construction, rectangular cubes of lime vary in size from

Pls. 2, 3A; Album no. 2

Pl. 3B; Album no. 13B

Figs. 8, 9; App. E.7–10

Pl. 2

Fig. 8

a

b

8. (a) Merovingian, seventh-century foundations under sixth bay of nave, north side, showing lime blocks (white) as integral part of masonry; (b) detail showing carved ornament of broken stone fragments in seventh-century foundations.

0.20 m long by 0.17 m high to 0.20 m long by 0.08 m high. The presence of these lime blocks provides another indication that this construction must be Merovingian and not Gallo-Roman.[7] That conclusion is strengthened by the presence of two fragments of stone, also an integral part of the masonry, both carved in low relief with abstract, ornamental motifs characteristic of Merovingian decoration. Those original fragments were removed by Jules Formigé, who substituted the plaster casts present in the foundations today. The ornament and possible function of these fragments in the embellishment of the church will be discussed later in this chapter.

9. Seventh-century masonry, south side.

Averaging about 2.65 m, the depth of these foundations is governed by the average depth of the solid clay soil on which they rest. The masonry rises in irregularly aligned beds to a level of 1.20 m below the existing pavement. At the western end identical masonry turns to the south at an angle of almost exactly 90 degrees. Although the projection to the south is fragmentary as a result of partial dismantling during the construction of later foundations, that corner where the stones are bonded together presumably marks the northwestern limits of the nave. Later alterations obscure the western face of this wall, which contains the fragmentary lower portions of a stone sarcophagus with a north–south orientation. Under these circumstances, measurement of the thickness of the foundations becomes difficult, but the rubble mass extends ca. 0.90 m to the west, which seems to approximate the thickness at this point.

In 1947 the excavation of the north side aisle uncovered another sizeable fragment of this same rough construction. Extending 4.50 m along an east–west axis parallel to the nave foundations and to the adjacent massive *libages* of the eighth-century church,[8] the rubble construction disappears at its western end under the Carolingian foundations that project to the south and form part of the western portions of the eighth-century church. Resting on clay soil at 2.05 m below the existing pavement and rising only two or three beds to a height of about 0.50 m, the masonry is 0.70 m thick in its widest dimension.

Twenty-two years later, in 1969, after authorities had once again given me permission to excavate, we uncovered another fragment of this seventh-century masonry under the sixth bay of the north side aisle. Only 1.30 m long, it is 0.65 m wide and its upper surface lies 1.43 m below the existing pavement. Located only 0.33 m to the south of the eighth-century founda-

Fig. 10

App. C.6

10. Part of seventh-century foundations under fourth bay of north side aisle (1947 excavations). Upper, or western, end is under eighth-century foundations.

tions, this segment continues the alignment of the identical masonry found 8.50 m to the west in 1947 and must, therefore, have formed part of the north wall of the north side of Dagobert's construction.

In 1971 I opened the area under the south side aisle immediately to the east of the 1939 excavation. Beginning 1.40 m below the existing pavement and extending down to 2.20 m, rough masonry of the same type came to light. Only the northern, or inner, face could be freed, since the upper portions are covered by indiscriminate masonry extending south to join the eighth-century foundations. The western end of this fragment of the seventh-century foundations is torn away, apparently destroyed when at some later date the area was disturbed for the burial of a large stone sarcophagus. Although only 1.30 m of this foundation was uncovered, as yet it is the sole segment found under the south side aisle. Another excavation under the seventh bay of the south aisle just to the east of the iron grill failed to disclose any similar foundations. The small segment under the western side of the fifth bay, however, aligns symmetrically with the longer foundation under the north side aisle discovered in 1947, so that some evidence for the southwestern end of Dagobert's extension still exists.

App. E.2b

The junction of this seventh-century masonry with the Gallo-Roman blocks of the foundations of Sainte Geneviève's fifth-century chapel has already been identified. Until recently only the southern side of these foundations was visible, but in 1977, after a careful examination of the stone sarcophagi placed against the masonry had been completed, the foundations could be cleaned of a dense, black fill, thereby revealing the same type of petit appareil as on the south side. Since this segment, only 1.20 m in length, is in direct alignment with similar masonry farther to the west and exactly parallel to the identical masonry on the south side, that petit appareil must have been part of Dagobert's extension of Sainte Geneviève's chapel. In its western

App. E.2a

portions this extension continued exactly the width and axis of Sainte Geneviève's chapel but added both to the north and south sides what must have
been side aisles. How far these side aisles continued to the east remains
unknown, for to my knowledge no evidence of this distinctive type of foundation masonry has come to light under the crossing or side aisles of the
transept. The only possible indications for the eastern end of Dagobert's
enlargement of Sainte Geneviève's chapel are the official photographs taken
while Jules Formigé's excavations were in progress. As previously noted, the
bottom or lower portions of these photographs are not in focus and must,
therefore, be considered somewhat tenuous evidence; but several positive
conclusions can be drawn from them.

App. H.5–8

It is difficult to describe exactly what the masonry under the curving walls
of the apse was like, but it seems to consist of a rough agglomerate with
unshaped stones of various sizes. Certainly there are no carefully finished
blocks such as the Gallo-Roman vestiges to the west, and there are none of the
large libages characteristic of the eighth-century foundations. Examples of
the libages can be seen at the base of the exterior of this apse, both on the north
side under the eighth-century finished masonry and on the south side where
an opening has been excavated in the twelfth-century masonry to reveal
another such massive block. On the interior in one section on the south side to
the right of the middle section of one of Formigé's photographs, small,
irregular stones appear to have been placed in approximately horizontal beds
not unlike the petit appareil of foundations farther to the west which I have
identified as belonging to the seventh-century structure; but larger unfinished stones are present in an irregular fashion in those foundations so that
the masonry is not exactly the same. How do we explain the agglomerate
masonry at this location? When deciding in the 620s to embellish the shrine
of Saint Denis, Dagobert's first care may have been the altar and memorial
sarcophagus or shrine over the tomb at the eastern end of Sainte Geneviève's
chapel. To provide more space, the flat eastern wall of that early chapel was
replaced by a semicircular apse extending about 4.00 m to the east. For
such a relatively simple construction an agglomerate masonry in a trench dug
into the solid clay subsoil provided an adequate foundation. When Dagobert
decided that the church should also be enlarged to the west, more regular,
although still crudely built, foundations were used. In the eighth century the
eastern apse was rebuilt as an annular crypt. To do this the foundations of
Dagobert's apse were strengthened by placing massive libages around the
exterior to support the new Carolingian construction with its buttresses and
windows.

App. H.13

App. H.7

In summary, as part of Dagobert's generosity to Saint-Denis, he decided to
embellish the shrine. Balustrades, a chancel, and other decorations to be
described in the following pages were created, and the altar was moved to the
east of the earlier burial place. Such a move necessitated the destruction of the
eastern wall of Sainte Geneviève's chapel, which was rebuilt as a semicircular
apse around the newly decorated mausoleum. The move might also have
occasioned the special ceremonies recorded in the *Gesta Dagoberti* for 22 April
626.[9] This liturgical ensemble, primarily reserved for the clergy, created the

11. Section of seventh-century foundation running north–south under third bay of nave.

Fig. 11

need for additional space for parishioners and visitors. That was achieved by extending the walls of Sainte Geneviève's chapel 27.20 m to the west and by adding side aisles, 3.30 m wide, at least along the western portions. A western entrance apparently included a narrow vestibule, for there are two small segments of masonry in a north–south alignment some 3.80 m to the west of the well-defined northwestern corner of the nave. The masonry closely resembled the construction that was characteristic of the other seventh-century remnants. The reconstruction of the plan for such a western ensemble which I published in 1949[10] must, however, remain hypothetical since the whole area has now been completely explored, and there are no other similar masonries to complete this fragmentary plan. The building of a new western ensemble in the eighth century and the major foundations of the existing nave either cover or have obliterated any other fragments of the Merovingian structure.

Dagobert did more than embellish Sainte Geneviève's chapel, yet he did not build an entirely new church. As in other examples of pre-Carolingian architecture, the early rectangular chapel, or *basilica ad sanctam*, was enveloped by a larger building;[11] its structure must have been simple. Only one small section of masonry above the seventh-century rubble foundations has been uncovered, with little likelihood that more will be found. This fragment is under the southern side of the nave only a few meters to the west of the foundations of Sainte Geneviève's chapel. Covered by a plaster coating which still adheres in places to the essentially simple rubble wall construction, the surface is more continuous and uniform than the petit appareil and has setbacks that have been described above as the Gallo-Roman foundations. Because so few fragments of equally early medieval masonry have survived, good comparative examples are nonexistent. Perhaps it exceeds ordinary caution to identify this as part of Dagobert's seventh-century extension. Yet such a light construction would have been consistent with the rubblelike, relatively unstable character of the seventh-century foundations, which are quite unsuitable as supports for a solid superstructure.[12] Later descriptions of Dagobert's church transformed it into a building of regal magnificence, "constructed with a marvelous variety of marble columns."[13] It remained confused, in Suger's and all other medieval minds, with the Carolingian building which still existed in the twelfth century. Although these scattered foundations suggest that the building must have been one of the larger seventh-century churches, today prudent scholars admit that only fragmentary remains of Dagobert's extensions can be located.[14]

Scholars are also careful in their assessments of the sumptuous decorations that Dagobert reputedly lavished on Saint-Denis. According to the *Vita Eligii*,

> Eligius [Eloi][15] built a *mausoleum* for the holy martyr Dionysius in the region of Paris[16]—and above this [*super ipsum*] a marble *tugurium* marvelously worked with gold and gems,[17] also he joined the crest with a type of magnificent front [*species de fronte magnifice*]. In addition he fashioned gilded wood [*axes*] around the altar and placed on it rounded and bejeweled golden apples.[18] He diligently adorned the lectern and doors with silver metal, and he worked the cover of the throne of the altar [*tectum throni altaris*] with wood (covered with silver).[19] He also made a covering [*repam*] over the place of the old [*anterioris*] tomb,[20] and built an altar on the outside [*extrinsecus*] at the feet [*ad pedes*] of the holy martyr.[21]

Proof that the literal meaning of this passage is open to interpretation exists in the different attempts to translate it.[22] Since I cannot visualize the results of any of the previous efforts, I will add my version to the collection. I concluded initially that the passage is not descriptive in a continuous fashion, but that the different phrases are essentially notes or observations without sequential order. Four major elements are identified as distinctive parts of the new shrine. Eloi's basic decision was to move the altar to a new location beyond or to the east of the earlier one, presumably in the new apse built for this purpose. A chancel with a lectern and doors was erected around the new altar surmounted by a marble *tugurium*, or ciborium. A throne with a *tectum*, or canopy, above it stood behind the new altar, possibly with its back against the semicircular wall of the apse. Finally a *repam*, or covering, with a crested pitched roof joining a richly decorated front or pediment was placed over the pitched roof of the old sarcophagus located above the actual tomb of the patron saint. My reconstruction, consequently, would proceed from west to east, beginning with the old sarcophagus, sumptuously covered with a new pitched roof, crest, and pediment. Then came the chancel built around an altar sheltered beneath a marble ciborium. The chancel included a lectern with doors, and the posts of the enclosure were decorated with round ornaments. Finally at the eastern end, against the curving wall of the apse, a throne stood under a textile canopy.[23] This elaborate ensemble was replaced in the next century when the new church was built, but a few surviving fragments have been identified as belonging to Saint Eloi's shrine.

Perhaps the outstanding fragment is a small piece of polychromed cloisonné metalwork now in the Cabinet des Médailles of the Bibliothèque Nationale in Paris. Although positive identification is impossible, a number of scholars have accepted the convincing evidence advanced by Count Blaise de Montesquiou-Fezensac in 1940 that the fragment was originally part of the cross of Saint Eloi, supposedly placed behind the altar at Saint-Denis.[24] Such a cross is not mentioned in the *Vita Eligii,* but it figures prominently in the *Gesta Dagoberti*[25] and was evidently one of the treasures most admired by Abbot Suger.[26] Listed as No. 189 in the *Inventaire of 1631,* this .102 m × .102 m piece was reserved for the revolutionary Commission des Arts in 1793 before the rest of the cross and other major treasures were melted down in April 1794.[27]

The cross may not have been a permanent fixture of the shrine but may have been brought out for exhibition on special occasions only.[28] If so, Saint Ouen would not have included it in his description of the shrine in the *Vita Eligii.* It is known to us as a detail in the meticulously rendered, fifteenth-century painting in the National Gallery in London by the Master of Saint Gilles. The painting shows the celebration of mass at the high altar in the abbey church, in which Saint Eloi's cross rises behind the golden retable given to Saint-Denis by Charles the Bald. Although the proportions shown in the painting are distorted, the cross evidently stood about 1.98 m high, so that it would have ranked among the monumental achievements of early medieval goldsmiths.

The fragment in the Cabinet des Médailles preserves the exquisite effect of cloisonné surfaces, predominantly red, interspersed with orange, blue, and green pieces of glass in the geometrical design of the gold cloisons. When nine types of stones—presumably precious ones such as sapphires, emeralds, and mother-of-pearl—filled the empty mounts, the total effect must, indeed, have been splendid.[29]

The use of polychromy in the chancel is suggested by the description in the *Vita Eligii* and proved by fragments found during my excavations. *Axes in circuitu altaris* has been interpreted as a reference to a wooden balustrade around the altar, which Saint Eloi had covered with gold and decorated with round ornaments on the posts. Broken segments of a post with grooves cut into its sides intended to hold the panels of a chancel enclosure were found during the excavations, but they are of stone, not wood, and have traces of paint on the surfaces. These stone fragments, approximately 0.40 m long, came to light in 1947. They were found embedded under the north side of the nave in the rough masonry which I have identified as seventh-century.[30] After Jules Formigé had removed them from the foundations and replaced them with plaster casts, he put the original fragments in the Musée Lapidaire, where they can be seen today. On discovery both pieces were already broken, and the decoration on the end of one appears to have been left unfinished—a detail suggesting that the stones had been discarded and then used as part of the rubble foundations.[31]

Especially interesting is the design of the ornament carved in low relief on the exposed flat surfaces of both pieces. At first glance, this design seems to be a variant on the familiar "northern" or "barbarian" Hiberno-Saxon interlace, but closer examination reveals a sequence of discontinuous, self-contained, symmetrical motifs with both curvilinear and rectilinear elements. Although I have shown photographs to many colleagues, I have

Fig. 12

12. Detail of the *Mass of Saint Gilles* by the Master of Saint Gilles (French). London, National Gallery. The detail shows the cross of Saint Eloi rising behind the retable given by Charles the Bald for the high altar of Saint-Denis.

a
b
c
d

received little help in locating similar designs or possible prototypes.[32] Although limited, my own observations have led to Coptic illuminations, as in the Glazier Codex, ca. A.D. 400, where Harry Bober has described "a calculated mode which systematically effects discontinuity";[33] to ornaments on buckles and belts from "awarischen" graves of the sixth and seventh centuries;[34] to silver round fibulae from Gotland;[35] to tubes from a fourth-century gold necklace from Apt;[36] to a stone post from the chancel at Saint-Pierre-aux-Nonnains in Metz;[37] and to a copper-gilt, eighth-century reliquary casket from the Muotathal (Switzerland) Parish Church.[38]

The removal of the two decorated stone fragments from the foundations in which they were embedded at Saint-Denis disclosed that they fitted together to form a unit that measures 0.80 m long by approximately 0.18 m square in section.[39] More surprising is the channel running the entire length of both pieces on each of the other sides of the block. The channels measure approximately 0.04 m wide by 0.35 m deep on two sides, and 0.02 m deep on the third side. The borders of two of the channels were decorated with shallow, narrow parallel grooves with ridges in between, and the third side has a sequence of "s" curves decorating one border and a braided ribbon pattern on the other. The original stone block must, therefore, have been intended to serve as an upright, or vertical, post into which panels were inserted. Since there are three channels, this particular post must have supported three different panels at right angles to one another.[40] Fragments of other posts and of some of the panels were found during Formigé's excavations, but, to my knowledge, there is no record of where they were found or the circumstances of their discovery. Only one of the panel fragments is large enough to allow a reconstruction of the original design, which one of For-

13. Four views of a reassembled fragment of a Merovingian chancel post found under the sixth bay of the nave, as shown in figure 8b.

Fig. 13a–d

Figs. 14, 15

a   b   c   d

e   f   g   h

migé's workmen cleverly fashioned in plaster, so that the effect of one entire section—post and panel—can be seen in the Musée Lapidaire.[41] The symmetrically opposed and addossed spirals with stylized space fillers[42] that decorate the panel can be defined as a series of discontinuous, self-contained motifs in the same general terms as the more intricate "knots" on the face of the post.

Although the fragments found at Saint-Denis are in stone and the *Vita Eligii* describes the balustrade of Saint Eloi's shrine as made of wood, such discrepancies are frequent in the early Middle Ages. The fact that the Saint-Denis post was found embedded in the seventh-century foundations provides a terminal date of not later than the mid–seventh century for these carvings, a fact that may prove helpful in dating other, similar designs. Consequently St. Eloi's work on the shrine must have started before the beginning of work on the western portions of Dagobert's extension; otherwise these discarded pieces could not have been used as part of the foundations. The carving must be regarded as the work of artists at Saint-Denis, in contrast to other decorative details which may have formed part of Saint Eloi's shrine but which

14. Miscellaneous decorated stone fragments found by Formigé's workmen.

Fig. 16

15. Fragment of original stone chancel panel, found by Formigé, fitted into a piece of chancel post shown in figures 8b and 13.

16. Plaster reconstruction by a Formigé workman of a Merovingian chancel panel at Saint-Denis.

were brought to Saint-Denis from other locations. Some of a series of marble capitals apparently belong in this category of imported art.

There are three marble capitals to be seen today as part of the decoration in the crypt. Six more marble capitals exhibited in the Cluny Museum in Paris have been identified as coming from Saint-Denis. Although scholars still dispute the date of similar marble capitals found in a surprisingly large number of early medieval buildings in central and northern France, where marble does not exist, the consensus of opinion holds that they were carved in southwestern France as late as the seventh century in workshops that continued traditions inherited directly from antiquity.[43]

Capitals carved in marble are mentioned as part of the fabric of Saint-Denis in the nineteenth century, when fragments of marble shafts and capitals were found during the demolition of the north tower on the west façade.[44] Since the northern tower was built in the twelfth and early thirteenth centuries, these capitals must have been at Saint-Denis before then. Unfortunately, since there is no record of their dimensions or the style of the decoration, the question of whether Viollet-le-Duc reused those capitals from the demolition in his restoration of the crypt cannot be resolved. The lack of records has created a basic problem for the study of all capitals in the crypt at Saint-Denis as well as the so-called Saint-Denis capitals in the Cluny Museum.

When Alexandre Lenoir's Musée des Monuments Français in Paris was dissolved by Louis XVIII in 1816, the collections were dispersed in great disorder.[45] Many funerary monuments as well as other pieces of sculpture, furniture, and stained glass were sent to Saint-Denis with no information about their place of origin. The storage facilities at Saint-Denis continued to be used as a collection point throughout most of the nineteenth century, especially by Viollet-le-Duc. Confusing to the study of the marble capitals is the knowledge that Alexandre Lenoir had capitals, one of them marble, removed from the crypt of the church of Saint-Marcel in Paris when it was razed in 1806. The capitals were sent to Saint-Denis for storage. When, at the end of the century, the seven marble capitals at Saint-Denis were transferred to the Cluny Museum, no one knew whether or not the marble capital from Saint-Marcel was among them.[46] In other words, even when a piece of sculpture is known to have been at Saint-Denis during the nineteenth century, there is no proof that the object was executed or even used at Saint-Denis. "Provenance Saint-Denis" does not mean "made at Saint-Denis." Although all the marble capitals attributed to Saint-Denis are consequently suspect, I have selected three different types to demonstrate the variety of problems they present.

Among the most unusual examples are two medium size capitals (Cluny Museum, Inv. nos. 12.114A and 12.114B).[47] These original interpretations of acanthus leaves have been identified as the "raised vein" variety because the basic channels or veins of the structure of the leaves are modeled in low relief. The outline of the leaves, instead of being stylized or of a rigidly symmetrical design, is freely interpreted to such a degree that they have been called naturalistic foliate forms anticipating the botanical studies of High Gothic sculpture.[48] Similar free, leaflike patterns flow from the center of the upper zone of the capital to the corners and replace the volutes of the Corinthian composite order. Even more striking for the historian of art is the capital with almost identical leaves reused in the interior of the Baptistery of Saint-Jean at Poitiers.[49] Since capitals of this type are rare, it is tempting to suggest that they were carved in the same workshop, if not by the same artist. There is a reasonable explanation for the presence of almost identical capitals at Saint-Denis and Poitiers in the seventh century. In 628, after the death of his brother Caribert, Dagobert I led an expedition to Poitiers in order to insure allegiance to himself as the sole king.[50] In characteristically Merovingian fashion, Poitiers was looted. Part of the booty might well have been the two marble capitals, which the artistically sensitive king brought back to Paris to present to Saint Eloi to be used as part of the decoration of the shrine of Saint Denis. Such neat historical coincidences are as rare as the design of the capitals themselves.

Another of the marble capitals in the Cluny Museum might have been part of the shrine at Saint-Denis, but in this instance the evidence is circumstantial

a

b

17. Marble capitals supposedly from Saint-Denis, possibly carved in the seventh century. Now in Cluny Museum, Paris. (a) One of two identified as "raised vein" type; (b) small capital.

Fig. 17a

Fig. 17b

rather than formal or historical. The base diameter of this capital (Inv. no. 12.115) is only 0.17 m, which is small enough to be appropriate for some purely decorative rather than structural function. The carving is also of the same high quality as the other "imported" examples.

The last group I shall include in this discussion consists of three capitals that are larger than the raised-vein type and have a more conventional two-zoned Corinthian design. Two of them were reemployed as an integral part of the decoration of the twelfth-century crypt at Saint-Denis. The third example, now in the Cluny Museum (Inv. no. 12.117), although a three- rather than two-zoned capital, has the same boldly articulated, stylized Corinthian leaf-type as the two capitals in the crypt. The latter could have been part of the original twelfth-century decoration, for they adhere to Abbot Suger's predilection for incorporating antique remnants in his "modern" building.[51] Yet the possibility remains that Viollet-le-Duc had them installed there during the nineteenth-century restoration of the crypt. Questions such as these can perhaps never be answered definitively and will always be part of the mysteries of Saint-Denis.[52]

Another irresolvable problem related to Saint Eloi's shrine is the throne mentioned in the *Vita Eligii*—*sed et tectum throni altaris axibus operuit argenteis.* Could this throne have been the famous throne of Dagobert now in the Cabinet des Médailles in the Bibliothèque Nationale in Paris? Although most scholars today agree that Dagobert's throne is not Merovingian, perhaps the last word has not been said. "Le Fauteuil de Dagobert" is certainly one of the most unusual and famous pieces of furniture to have survived from antiquity and the Middle Ages. After its restoration at Saint-Denis in the twelfth century it was regularly used for the coronation of the kings of France. Originally the seat must have served as a Roman *sella curulis* for the highest magistrates. In itself a symbol of justice and authority, it was constructed as a folding chair or stool for ease of transport. "On it," Abbot Suger recorded, "as ancient tradition relates, the kings of the Franks, after having taken the reins of government, used to sit in order to receive, for the first time, the homage of their nobles."[53] No other document confirms such usage, but Lothaire I evidently sat on it in the ninth century,[54] and Napoleon I had it repaired again for his coronation and for the ceremony awarding the cross of the Legion of Honor to his officers.[55] The exact history of the throne is unclear.[56]

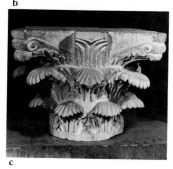

18. Merovingian marble capitals supposedly carved at Saint-Denis: (a) first capital on the right, or south, upon descending the north stairway into the crypt; (b) seventh capital, north aisle, north wall; (c) Merovingian capital now in the Cluny Museum, Paris.

Although scholars have recognized the antique origin for this type of folding seat, attempts have been made to attribute "Dagobert's fauteuil" to the workshops of Saint Eloi in the seventh century or to ninth-century Carolingian artists.[57] Even though Suger stated that he had the throne (*cathedram*) remade (*refici fecimus*), in one of the recent studies the author concluded that most probably "it is a work of the Court School (ninth century) and that it has survived substantially in the form in which it was first made."[58] Two Carolingian miniatures show similar lion-headed seats, and in both instances the upper arms or sides are missing.[59] In my opinion, such evidence, both visual and documentary, is proof that the throne had become so "worn with age and dilapidated" (*antiquatam et disruptam*) by the twelfth

Fig. 18a, b,c

Fig. 19

19. The so-called throne of Dagobert. Cabinet des Médailles, Paris, Bibliothèque Nationale.

century that Suger ordered his artisans to restore it thoroughly and to strengthen it by adding the arms and the back. The two small heads that "act as terminals to the rods that link the sides and the back together" are difficult to date, since, as minor decorations, they could have been used and reused.[60]

In summary, "Dagobert's throne" is an impressive object as well as a fascinating work of art. As such it must have been in constant use over the centuries with subsequent need for frequent repairs. Expert examination of every detail may well identify characteristics of widely divergent periods. The basic construction of the "monopod" lion legs and the criss-cross folding mechanism are, I believe, of Roman origin, brought to Gaul and left there by one of the many high authorities in the early centuries of our era.[61] Respected and preserved by succeeding generations, it may well have been used by the Frankish kings (as suggested by Suger). Possibly they transported it to different parts of their domains. For this reason the "throne" should not be considered a permanent part of any ensemble. The seat is certainly atypical of Merovingian work and, although such details as the rosettes of the central rod may have been redone by ninth-century artisans, the throne itself is not necessarily Carolingian any more than it is twelfth-century. When it was deposited at Saint-Denis is not documented, although it must have been there before the twelfth century.[62] As a symbol of royal authority its location at Saint-Denis was highly appropriate.

Over the centuries Dagobert's popularity acted as a magnet, so that many works of art and sumptuous ornaments were attributed to his generosity. Since the attributions cannot be satisfactorily documented and some of the works of art have disappeared, I shall mention them only briefly. The most elaborate description of Dagobert's church is in the *Gesta Dagoberti Regis,* written between 835 and 840 at Saint-Denis, probably by Abbot Hilduin and his disciple Hincmar, who became archbishop of Reims. By the time they were writing, whatever Dagobert had actually built at Saint-Denis had been replaced by Abbot Fulrad's eighth-century church. Thus details about the Merovingian construction and decoration were at best hearsay at the remove of one generation.[63] The initial statement that Dagobert had built the church from its foundations[64] cannot be construed to mean that he built an entirely new building, for the earlier text, the *Chronica Fredegarii,* states that he built around Sainte Geneviève's chapel (*in circoito fabrecare*) and this is confirmed by the archaeological remains. The claims in the *Gesta* that he had the interior walls and the nave arcades hung with textiles woven with gold thread and sewn with precious pearls and that the exterior of the apse was covered with pure silver[65] are not unusual in early medieval literature, but they cannot be accepted as unembroidered fact.[66] The covering of the rest of the church with lead,[67] if unlikely, remains a possibility,[68] and the silver offering box attached to the side aisle of the high altar, known as the *gazofilacium*, remained in the church at least until Suger's day.[69]

Other objects identified as Dagobert's gifts in the Inventory of 1634 or in the plates of the treasure at Saint-Denis published by Félibien in 1706 include a large, bejeweled clasp in the form of an eagle, supposedly used to fasten the king's royal robe,[70] and Dagobert's scepter, also called a "baton consulaire," topped with a golden lion ridden by a small boy. The scepter was stolen from the Louvre in 1794.[71] More enigmatic was a reliquary formerly kept in the chapel of Saint Firmin. According to the inventory only one-half was given by Dagobert, and the engraving published by Félibien shows a late Gothic, possibly fourteenth-century casket.[72] There was also a large porphyry "cuve," or tub, which legend claims Dagobert brought to Saint-Denis from Poitiers, where it had been used as a baptismal font.[73]

Another legend related to Dagobert's church was destined to influence the building of the twelfth-century church. In this instance the king is said to have summoned bishops to consecrate his new church, but the evening before,

a poor man, badly deformed and infected with leprosy, begged the guardian of the church to allow him to spend the night inside, which he was allowed to do. During the night, being awakened and praying, he clearly saw Jesus Christ, accompanied by Saint Peter and Saint Paul with the blessed martyrs Saint Denis, Saint Rusticus and Saint Eleutherius, enter the church through a window. Dressed in white robes (they) performed the sacred ceremony of dedication. Then Jesus came to the leper: "Man," he said, "when the bishops come tomorrow at dawn to dedicate this church, tell them that I have consecrated it." The healing of the man is proof of this act for Jesus, touching his face, lifted the leprous skin and threw it against the nearest stone where until today, with great admiration, it is seen glued fast. The prelates were astonished at this miracle and abstained from their dedication.[74]

The legend is not an early one for no mention of it appeared in the *Gesta Dagoberti;* but Suger knew of it when building his new church in 1144.[75] Since Suger seems to have been the first to take notice of this miraculous dedication, Levillain has concluded that it must have been invented by "a monk at Saint-Denis at the very end of the eleventh century in connection with the popular literature that developed with the First Crusade."[76]

To summarize what is known about Dagobert's church at Saint-Denis, we must admit that the archaeological remains are so fragmentary that the reconstruction of a complete or definitive plan must remain conjectural. Reasonable evidence supplemented by early written references indicates that a semicircular apse was added to the east of Sainte Geneviève's rectangular chapel and that the nave was extended about 28.00 m to the west. A side aisle, or *porticus,* 3.30 m wide was built along the north side facing the cemetery, but only one small section of masonry survives to indicate similar constructions on the south side. A fragment of masonry exists above the foundations to suggest that the construction was modest, composed of small, irregular petit appareil covered with a coat of plaster, probably polychromed. The extravagant description of the interior and exterior decorations was written after Dagobert's church had been destroyed, although fragments of a stone chancel that must have been part of Saint Eloi's new shrine still exist with unusual geometric patterns carved in low, polychromed relief. Marble capitals, expertly carved with acanthus foliate designs may have been brought to Saint-Denis to be included in the decoration of the shrine, but many unresolved problems about their original locations still remain. The small fragment of cloisonné inlay in the Cabinet des Médailles of the Bibliothèque Nationale in Paris may not actually have been part of Saint Eloi's great cross, but the intricate geometric design and colorful surface give a good example of the rich decoration that gave focus to the development of the cult of Saint-Denis in the mid-seventh century.

A summary of the religious reforms and economic growth encouraged by Dagobert I, his wife Nanthilda, their son Clovis II and his wife Bathilde will demonstrate how Saint-Denis developed into one of the richest, most powerful monastic institutions in western Europe. The introduction of a regular monastic rule at Saint-Denis has been wrongfully attributed to Dagobert I, although he tried to introduce a new custom, that of continual worship, *laus perennis.*[77] This would have necessitated a more structured life for the religious community and helped prepare it for the monastic regime imposed by Clovis II and his wife Queen Bathilde about 650.[78] They instituted the rule of Saint Benedict and Saint Columban so widely adopted throughout western Europe in the seventh century.[79] There is some question, however, as to whether the entire community at Saint-Denis submitted to this rule at that time. Evidently the clergy remained apart during this early period, and only the lay brothers became monks.[80] The basilica, nevertheless, remained the center of the community, served by both secular clergy and regular monks, until the establishment of a new régime under the Abbot Hilduin in the ninth century.

In economic terms it was not Dagobert's extravagant gifts of land and precious objects alone that made Saint-Denis so powerful in the seventh century—it was also the founding of the Foire de la Saint-Denis, the granting of independence from the bishop of Paris in 653, and the concession of royal immunity by Clovis II. These privileges gave Saint-Denis not only a stable economic existence but also placed it in such a favored position that it could not fail to prosper.

The Foire de la Saint-Denis, held in October, should not be confused with the two other fairs associated with the abbey: the Foire du Lendit, held in June,[81] and the Foire de la Saint-Mathias, held in February.[82] The Foire de la Saint-Denis is important not only because it was the earliest royal concession of this type, but also because it made possible the rapid growth of the abbey.

The original charter of the founding of the fair by Dagobert I in 635 or 636 does not exist today, although it remained in the archives of Saint-Denis until the middle of the ninth century.[83] Mention of the fair in charters of Childebert III in 709[84] and of Pepin the Short in 753 and 759,[85] and an analysis of the original document in the *Gesta Dagoberti*[86] not only confirm that Dagobert was the founder of the fair, but also indicate its character. The cult of the saint drew great crowds to the church on the ninth of October, the feast day of Saint Denis, and in this way the cult was the origin of the fair.[87] As the fair was held in October, it naturally became the great market for winter provisions, especially wine and honey, which must have been traded for the wool and furs of the northern merchants.[88] The presence of these northern merchants is attested by early charters, which refer to them as *neguciantes aut Saxonis vel quascumquelibit* (sic) *nacionis*—a proof that the fair was widely known. In the twelfth century the fair lasted for seven weeks, from 9 October to 30 November, which was thought to be the period fixed by Dagobert;[90] but none of the early documents is precise as to this, although there must have been some limits assigned for its duration.[91] At first it must have been held in the *vicum Catolacum,* but before the end of the seventh century, the danger of civil wars forced the monks to move it nearer to Paris, where there was more protection.[92] Before the end of the Merovingian period the Foire de la Saint-Denis was therefore an established annual event that attracted merchants from afar.

The abbey enjoyed the full revenue of this commerce from the beginning, although it was forced to go to court continually to protect its rights.[93] With the granting of complete exemption from custom duties by Theodoric III, between 680 and 688,[94] the monks of Saint-Denis became privileged merchants and were able to benefit more fully from the activity of the fair as well as to maintain important commercial relations with the different districts of the Frankish kingdom. It was to Dagobert, however, that Saint-Denis owed gratitude for the creation of the fair, which with later privileges was destined to make the abbey one of the most active centers of Merovingian and Carolingian Gaul.

The fair and other material gifts assured the basilica of a definite source of income, but it was the granting of independence from the bishop of Paris and the concession of immunity from royal officials that made it possible for Saint-Denis truly to benefit from this income. At the request of Clovis II, Landri, bishop of Paris, gave the basilica its charter of freedom on 1 July 653. Within the next few years, between 657 and 664, Bathilde, as regent, granted royal immunity in the name of her son Clothaire III. In order for us to understand the importance of these privileges, the charters need detailed consideration.

The original document of the episcopal privilege accorded by Landri in 653 has not survived. Once considered authentic, the manuscript in the Archives Nationales has been proven a forgery, achieved between 1060 and 1065.[95] Levillain, however, has been able to discover the contents of the original charter from information contained in confirming charters of Clovis II, 653; of Theodoric IV, 724; of Pepin the Short, 768; of Hilduin, 832;[96] and in certain other references.[97] Until the middle of the seventh century the basilica of Saint-Denis was completely under the jurisdiction of the bishop of Paris. It could own property, but the management of it depended on the bishop. The charter of Landri freed Saint-Denis and its possessions forever from this episcopal domination. The abbot and the monks of Saint-Denis were given complete control over the administration of the abbey as well as of its property. No church officer could interfere—or even enter the abbey—without their permission.[98] The bishop, however, reserved certain rights, the *jura pontifica,* which included the consecration of churches and altars, the blessing of the Holy Sacrament, and the ordination of the members of the congregation as well as of the abbot, who was freely elected by the monks.[99] Thus, although the abbey was independent, it was not exempt from some supervision by the bishop of Paris. The monks of Saint-Denis had to wait until the eighth century to receive a spiritual independence that was equal to their temporal freedom.

The grant of royal immunity was almost the last important early privilege acquired by Saint-Denis. During the succeeding centuries the monks were primarily concerned with retaining these early privileges, which naturally were altered to some extent as the abbey grew in power; but the rights of the fair, the independence from the bishop, and royal immunity remained the essential factors in maintaining this power. It is unnecessary to emphasize the tremendous importance of such immunity during the feudal régime. Once an individual or an institution received a charter of immunity from a king his property assumed the status of the royal fisc. Judicial rights over the inhabitants, collections of all public revenues, freedom from the rights of officials to hold courts, or to seize witnesses, to levy taxes, or to exercise the rights of *gite,* or procuration, not only gave the *immuniste* a highly privileged position, but made it possible for him to escape the burdens of feudal society. For the purposes of this study it is necessary only to discover when Saint-Denis was first granted a charter of immunity and how long it retained this privilege.

The existence of three charters of Dagobert I conceding immunity to Saint-Denis,[100] a confirmation of immunity by Chilpéric II of 716 that mentions another Dagobert,[101] and inferences from the *Gesta Dagoberti*[102] established a tradition that the abbey received its first immunity from Dagobert I.[103] The *Vita Bathildis,* however, states that it was Bathilde, wife of Clovis II, who conceded the immunity.[104] It is the latter statement that appears correct. All three charters of Dagobert I are forgeries executed at Saint-Denis during the eleventh century.[105] The charter of Chilpéric II states that the Dagobert mentioned was a cousin of the king—a reference to Dagobert III.[106] The implications in the *Gesta Dagoberti* are so general that they would have no real value even in a more trustworthy text. Thus the evidence pointing to Dagobert I fails completely; but the statement of the *Vita Bathildis* cannot be refuted.[107] The date of the first charter of immunity granted to Saint-Denis was, therefore, between 657 and 664.[108] The charter was owing to the generosity of Queen Bathilde, who in her desire to reform the abbey had instituted the monastic rule of Saint Benedict and Saint Columban. The privileges of independence and immunity were expressly given to soften the trials of a monastic régime and to insure that the imposed reforms would be upheld. These privileges added greatly to the power of Saint-Denis in the seventh century; but what is more important, they assured the abbey an illustrious position under the Carolingians and Capetians.

Many historians consider the end of the seventh and the early years of the eighth century as a hiatus in French history. It was the period of the *rois fainéants* (do-nothing kings), when established society seemed to disappear completely. The general conditions, however, could not have been desperate, for during the fifty years between 665 and 715 the abbey of Saint-Denis was able to consolidate its position. Although not a period of great advancement for the abbey, apparently opportunities arose that allowed the abbey to solidify the privileged position created by the generosity of Dagobert and of his immediate successors. If these years had been completely chaotic, the abbey would not have been able to emerge successfully from the turmoil attending the birth of the Carolingian dynasty.

In fact the abbey was unable to retain all of its possessions intact, and for a short time it ran the danger of losing even its independence. The monks, however, must have taken advantage of every opportunity. Although documents are scarce for this period, there is evidence that the abbey continued to receive gifts from the royal family,[109] who continued to confirm existing privileges.[110] A prosperous commerce was maintained,[111] and the resources of the abbey were exploited insofar as was possible.[112] In short, it was the interim in the development of any successful institution when every effort is made to establish the benefits of a preceding period of amazing prosperity on a permanent basis. The ability of the monks of Saint-Denis to do this ensured their survival through the troubled years between 715 and 750.

The invasion of Spain by the Arabs, completed by 713, and their continued push northward until they were turned back at Poitiers by Charles Martel in 732 seriously affected any commerce between northern and southern France. Doubtless because of this invasion Saint-Denis lost such revenues as the annual gift of oil from Marseilles given to the abbey by Dagobert. Northern France was torn by the war between Chilpéric II and Charles Martel, which resulted in loss of land and revenues not only at Saint-Denis but for all property owners—losses often irreparable. Between 716 and 719, the abbey experienced a more serious danger when Turnoaldus, bishop of Paris, was appointed abbot and subjected the monks once more to episcopal domination.[113] But this domination did not last long, for in 724 there was a new abbot, and the monks hastened to request their independence. This was granted by Theodoric IV and firmly established by the creation of a bishop of the abbey who could perform the functions claimed by the bishop of Paris.[114] Thus, although Saint-Denis suffered from the general unrest of the early eighth century, it was able to emerge with a more complete independence. Its revenues were diminished and many lands were lost forever, but losses occurred in proportion to the attrition throughout the kingdom. As soon as peace and prosperity returned under the Carolingians, the abbey was able to reap the benefits of the formative period.

The first three hundred years of the history of Saint-Denis molded the important contours of the abbey as a medieval institution. Later crises were solved on the basis of what had been established before the eighth century. Progress was made and recovery from periods of oppression was possible because of these early privileges. As new opportunities arose and new, more inclusive privileges were acquired, they were usually based on charters of the seventh century. Indeed in the history of Saint-Denis it is the Merovingian period that remains essential to an understanding of the position of the abbey at any later period.

CHAPTER THREE

Fulrad's Church

With the advent of the Carolingian dynasty the abbey of Saint-Denis immediately assumed a position that was intimately related to the monarchy. The abbey, which had enjoyed the favor of the ruling family from the beginning of the seventh century, was greatly enriched by the royal patronage of the Merovingian kings. During the second half of the eighth century this favor was transformed into a political relationship that led later kings to assume the title of lay abbot of Saint-Denis. The position of the Carolingian abbots as advisors and ambassadors of the king soon made it a royal abbey in actuality.

Since the history of the abbey from the beginning of the Carolingian period closely parallels that of the French monarchy, essentially the same documents provide the information for reconstructing the histories of the kingdom and the abbey. The name of Saint-Denis constantly appears in the *Continuatio* of Fredegarius's chronicle as well as in the *Annales Fuldenses* and the *Annales Bertiniani,* through the writings of Mithard, Flodoard, Orderic Vitalis, and finally of Raoul Glaber, Abbo of Fleury, and Fulbert of Chartres. These documents provide definite dates for establishing a chronology of events at the abbey.[1] In addition to the annals and historical literature, there are charters dealing specifically with the abbey's possessions and privileges, either granted or confirmed, in the reign of almost every king of France. A number of letters from both kings and abbots have also survived. Most of these documents exist in the original or in trustworthy copies, so there need be no question as to their authenticity.

Preparation for the Carolingian dynasty was a long process. In 639, only one year after the death of Dagobert I, Pepin I of Landen died while holding the office of mayor of the palace of Austrasia (the eastern part of the Merovingian kingdom as distinct from Neustria, the western portion). Although descendants of Dagobert "died young, worn out by precocious debauchery,"[2] the Austrasians were dominated by the Arnulfings, or Pepinids, who, as mayors of the palace, retained the power to rule.[3] Pepin II of Heristal (680–714) was succeeded by his illegitimate son, Charles Martel (714–41). "By reuniting and reinvigorating the kingdom of the Franks and by checking permanently the onrush of Islam from Spain (in 732 at Poitiers), [he] set the course of subsequent history."[4] Although he was never called king, and annexations of church lands to reward his followers earned him the church's enmity, Charles Martel gave his name, Carolus, to the Carolingian dynasty. Possibly attracted to Saint-Denis as a means of proclaiming his own legitimacy, he sent his two sons, Pepin and Carloman, to be educated at the abbey and chose the basilica as his burial place.[5]

Pepin III, the Short, and Carloman succeeded Charles Martel as mayors of the palace in 741. Pepin became sole mayor in 747. In 751 Pepin sent Fulrad, his archchaplain and abbot of Saint-Denis, with the Englishman Burchard, bishop of Wurzburg, on a mission to Rome to learn from Pope Zacharias "whether it were good or no that one man should bear the name of king while another really ruled."[6] The pope said that it was not, and in November 751, on the pope's authority, the Frankish assembly deposed Childéric III, the last of the Merovingians. The assembly then elected Pepin their new king, and he was anointed by Saint Boniface.[7] Trouble between the papacy and the Lombard king Aistulf continued, forcing the pope, Stephen II, to seek refuge in France. Sick from fatigue and the cold, he spent the winter in the abbey of Saint-Denis.[8] On 28 July 754, in the abbey church, he confirmed Pepin and his sons Charles, the future Charlemagne, and Carloman as kings of France and patricians of Rome. The ceremony evidently also included the dedication of an altar, which has caused some confusion and debate about the event and its relevance to the chronology of the building campaign.[9] Pepin's confidence in Abbot Fulrad and his interest in Saint-Denis resulted in the building of a completely new church at Saint-Denis. Since the building was begun under Pepin the Short and later texts state that Charlemagne completed it, I have chosen to identify the structure as Fulrad's church.

"A citizen of Rome, housed at the expense of the state, a mitred abbot, *'praelatus nullius'* and a prince of the church, attest that Fulrad had, in the elevation of the Carolingian dynasty and in the foundation of the Papal State, such a part that his name was associated with those of the Pope and King."[10] And yet we know very little about this enigmatic figure.[11] Born in Alsace, he entered history as the archchaplain to the mayor of the palace and as abbot of Saint-Denis.[12] After his original mission to Rome with Bishop Burchard on the matter of Pepin's accession, Fulrad often carried messages between the pope and the king. In 756, acting as the king's ambassador in Italy, Fulrad was enjoined to relay to the pope the submission of the Exarchate of Ravenna and of Emilia after the death of King Aistulf.[14] In recognition of these services the pope conferred a number of special privileges on the abbot which he retained throughout his lifetime.[15] After the death of Pepin the Short in 768, Fulrad was more attached to Carloman than to Charles[16] but continued to serve as archchaplain at the court until his death in 784. Recorded in 777, Fulrad's testament left to Saint-Denis his extensive estates in Alsace.[17] These remained an important source of revenue for the abbey and created an orientation of interest toward the Meuse–Rhine valleys that was still effective in the twelfth century. Although Fulrad's long career as abbot of Saint-Denis and royal archchaplain can be traced only in outline, he deserves recognition as a forerunner of other great dionysian abbots, such as Suger and Matthew of Vendôme. They too served as trusted advisors to their king and, carefully attending the affairs of the abbey, were both active as rebuilders of the church.

If records of Fulrad's life seem meager, documents about the building of his church are even more so. The only contemporary written source that confirms the building of a new church at Saint-Denis in the eighth century is a diploma of Charlemagne dated 25 February 775, the date of the consecration of the church (*a novo aedificavimus opere*) "which we have built with a new construction and ordered that it be decorated with properly magnificent decorations."[18] More than fifty years later the *Miracula Sancti Dionysii* informs us simply that the old church was destroyed (*diruta priori*) and that a new one was begun by Pepin and finished by Charlemagne.[19] Although the *Miracula* is historically suspect, this statement is credible because it occurs merely as an aside in the account of a miracle that occurred to one of the workmen during the construction of the church. Two other dates have been associated with the chronology of the building, namely, the consecration of an altar in 754 and the burial of Pepin the Short in 768. The consecration of an altar, presumably the high altar, at Saint-Denis by Pope Stephen II on 28 July 754 is recorded in the official calendars, but the information has been disputed, or misinterpreted. The consensus of opinion today interprets that entry simply as the consecration of an altar and not as a reference to the building of a new church. Pepin recorded his intention to be buried at Saint-Denis in one of his diplomas, dated September 768.[20] The next mention of that burial occurred about 835 in a letter from King Louis the Pious to Abbot Hilduin. The letter mentions an inscription stating that Pepin "had ordered that he be buried with great humility before the threshold of the basilica."[21] Apparently the building of the new church had progressed as far as the western bays by 768, thus permitting Pepin to specify his burial place—*ante limina*—before the threshold.[22] Abbot Suger provided the next mention of Pepin's tomb in the twelfth century, when he recorded that he began his new church by tearing down "a certain addition asserted to have been made by Charlemagne on a very honorable occasion, for his father, the Emperor Pepin, had commanded that he be buried for the sins of his father, Charles Martel, outside at the entrance with the doors, face downwards not recumbent."[23] This reference to an addition by Charlemagne will be discussed later in this chapter in relation to the archaeological remains.

The reason for the building of a new church by Fulrad and the function it was intended to fulfill deserve some attention prior to the archaeological reconstruction of the building itself. The cryptic phrase *diruta priori,* referring to the destruction of the old building, does not satisfactorily explain the construction of an entirely new church. Léon Levillain, the only scholar until recently who has seriously studied Fulrad's church, admitted that "it is impossible to specify the conditions or circumstances of the demolition of the old church."[24] No new documents have been discovered, and the extensive archaeological discoveries indicate only that a completely new structure replaced the earlier one. Other recent studies, however, provide plausible reasons for replacing the Merovingian building by a new, more impressive structure. The extended sojourn of Pope Stephen II at Saint-Denis, between 753 and 755, supplies, in my opinion, the historical background.

When Pope Stephen II left Rome for France on 14 October 753 to escape king Aistulf, he was accompanied by two Frankish envoys, Autchar (Ogier the Dane) and Bishop Chrodegang, plus a retinue of clerics and laymen. He did not return to Rome until 755. Lasting almost two years, his sojourn in France provided "ample opportunity for the Franks to become initiated to the liturgy as performed, *more romano,* according to Roman custom."[25] Three documents issued under Charlemagne record that Pepin replaced the Gallican chant by the *canticus Romanus*—a reform confirmed by Walafrid Strabon, who died in 849.[26] According to the *Libri Carolini,* the institution of this reform was intended to remove all differences between the Roman and Frankish churches.[27] At that time the terms *canticus, ordo psallendi,* and *cantilena* did not refer simply to the chant or to the melodic portions of the liturgical books but rather to a solemn recital. Thus the change to Roman usage involved the complete Roman liturgy, including processions and other ceremonial sequences. Consequently the pope and his entourage must have found the Merovingian church at Saint-Denis too small and unsuited to their ritual—limitations that could hardly have gone unnoticed by Pepin's court or by the Frankish clergy, who must also have been mindful of the prestige of the new dynasty. As a political symbol, the abbey was an obvious focal point to which the new Carolingian kings needed to point with pride.[28] How the new church fulfilled various demands will become clear in the reconstruction of the plan of Fulrad's church.

Prior to reconstructing systematically the plan of Fulrad's church, I will identify certain distinguishing features of the Carolingian construction at Saint-Denis. A small portion of the exterior masonry of the north side aisle provides the necessary information. A photograph of this eighth-century construction shows the massive foundations and the regularity of the wall that rises above them. Three tiers of large blocks, which I identify as libages, provide a solid base unmatched by any other construction at Saint-Denis. Evidently shaped directly in the quarry, the characteristic surface of these huge limestone blocks shows a sequence of concavities made by a curved tool. An average block measures 1.30 m to 1.60 m long by 0.50 m to 0.60 m high by 0.50 m to 0.80 m wide. Their weight alone obviated the use of any mortar, but we have no information about how the successive beds, or layers, were aligned along a given axis. Today many of the thin joints

Fig. 20

20. Section of eighth-century masonry under fourth bay of the north side aisle, showing libages in foundations and finished masonry of exterior wall.

between the blocks are filled with a black earth, which probably accumulated from the filling in of the trenches of the foundations.

The meticulously built wall that rises above the top level of the libages is uniformly 0.90 m thick. The exterior surface of the wall consists of carefully shaped rectangular blocks that measure 0.37 m long by 0.17 m high. The portion of the block facing toward the interior may extend as much as 0.65 m into the rubble core so that each stone is securely held in place. A distinguishing feature of this wall, the regular joints between 0.02 m and 0.03 m wide, are pointed, or filled, with a reddish mortar. Until relatively recently archaeologists believed this red mortar was used in depth in the Carolingian structure. In 1971 at my request experts from the Centre de Recherches sur les Monuments Historiques took core samples of different masonries at Saint-Denis.[29] To everyone's surprise the red cement proved to be only a few millimeters thick. Whether such a cover-joint had a practical purpose or resulted from an aesthetic preference for polychromed surfaces remains uncertain, but its presence at Saint-Denis seems to be a certain indication of Carolingian workmanship, as are the massive libages of the foundations and the regular masonry of the exterior walls.

In contrast to the fragmentary remains of Dagobert's enlargement of Sainte Geneviève's chapel, relatively extensive portions of the masonry of both the foundations and walls of Fulrad's church have been excavated at Saint-Denis. Enough clearly identifiable eighth-century construction exists to reconstruct the overall dimensions of the Carolingian plan, and many specific measurements can be determined with considerable accuracy. Yet, frustrating for the archaeologist, a number of important details remain uncertain.

Pl. 2; Album nos. 2, 14

Since no documents or texts describe the actual construction of Fulrad's church, the following chronology takes all surviving evidence into account. The Carolingian building must have been completed, or nearly so, in time for the consecration of 24 February 775, but we do not know when work began. Levillain concluded that construction must have started between 750 and 754—between Fulrad's election as abbot in 749 and the consecration of the high altar by Pope Stephen II on 28 July 754.[30] Careful study of such papal consecrations has shown that they did not always commemorate completion of a new building or of a particular part of a building, but rather the ceremony documented the moment of a papal visit and the special value associated with his consecrating an altar.[31] If my suggestion is valid, the papal presence and the introduction of the Roman liturgy motivated the building of a new church at Saint-Denis. Thus construction probably did not begin until 755, after the pope's departure from Saint-Denis for Rome. Once started, building must have been continuous, for it is reasonable to assume that work on the western portions was under way by 768, when Pepin the Short died. He could therefore choose his burial place *ante limina*.

Begun under Pepin and finished after the addition of a porch ordered by Charlemagne to honor Pepin's tomb at the western end, work apparently progressed from east to west. At the east, Dagobert's construction *in circoito*—"around" the tomb of the Saint—established the location of that tomb, to which, by the seventh century, had been added the relics of the saint's legendary companions, Rusticus and Eleutherius. Fulrad began the new church by rebuilding Dagobert's apse and by introducing a new type of crypt to protect the relics better and to enhance the opportunity for their veneration. The floor over this crypt was raised higher than the pavement of the transept and nave, thereby making the papal throne or abbot's chair in the apse visible throughout the church. The eighth-century rebuilding of the apse, however, did not alter its earlier shape or change its location.

The difference between the interior and the exterior foundations of the semicircular apse indicates, in my opinion, that the eighth-century masons built around the old apse and retained its dimensions—those based on the width of Sainte Geneviève's chapel. In the apse the interior construction of the foundations as excavated by Formigé's workmen may be seen in photographs in the Archives Photographiques in Paris.[32] The bottom, or lower, levels of these foundations are a rough, irregular rubble without either the large blocks found in the Gallo-Roman masonry to the west or the even larger libages[33] typical of the Carolingian foundations at Saint-Denis. Those libages can be seen today in the exterior foundations of the same apse on both the north and the south sides in the ambulatory of the crypt.

App. H.5–9

The photographs indicate that all of the "old" apse above the foundations was rebuilt in the eighth century. Quite visible in the photograph of the north side but much less clearly so on the south side, an alignment of large rectangular stones occurs directly above the bottom rubble foundations between the libages and the more regular masonry of what presumably was the exposed wall of the eighth-century apse.

Fig. 21; App. H.13
App. H.7, 8

Although not as well preserved as other portions of the exterior wall along the north side of Fulrad's building, this masonry has several distinguishing

21. Libage in eighth-century
apse in south side of crypt.

features. The careful preparation and solid construction of the coursing
contrast sharply with the petit appareil of Merovingian times. This was not a
renaissance of Roman techniques, for the construction is quite distinct from
the typical Roman wall. Yet this marks the revival of sound construction with
coursings of regular, precisely cut stones bound together by a crystalline
limestone aggregate of remarkable consistency.[34] In the apse the dimension
of the stones occasionally varies, but in the side aisle walls the rectangular
blocks (0.37 m wide by 0.17 m high),[35] have tolerances of only one to three
millimeters. The regular joints (between 0.02 m and 0.03 m wide) are
made more prominent by pointing with a reddish mortar characteristic of the
Carolingian masonry at Saint-Denis. Formigé and almost everyone who has
seen this masonry has assumed that all the mortar used in the walls of
Fulrad's church was colored red, but the reddish mortar in the eighth-
century apse and north aisle was limited to the exterior surface; the mortar
binding the rubble core was white. I have seen other red mortar at Saint-
Denis, notably as a layer in the base prepared for the eighth-century pavement.[36] Formigé reported that he found a tomb "enduite intérieurement de
mortier rouge," which I have not been able to locate. Also the Marquise de
Maillé noted that floors of a "ciment rose" were not rare in the eighth and
ninth centuries.[37] Mortar made with brick dust was described by Vitruvius as
"better for use," and a reddish mortar known as *khorosan* was made with
crushed terra-cotta in late Roman times.[38] Possibly the Carolingian masons at
Saint-Denis believed that the addition of fragments of red brick would
fortify the exterior surfaces against the weather. Perhaps, too, the color was

Figs. 8, 20

purely decorative—a cosmetic ornament applied to the surface to attract the eye.

Another feature of the exterior masonry of the eighth-century apse, an unusual projection between the two windows, apparently resulted from an aesthetic interest in appearance. At first glance this rectangular projection seems like a simple wall buttress added to the exterior to strengthen the wall. Examination proved that the stones are an integral part of the masonry; that the raised portions are cut from the same stones as the beds of the adjacent masonry. Furthermore such a slight projection would be an insignificant addition to a mass 1.80 m thick. Even more indicative of its decorative function is the fact that the upper portion is wider than the lower. Also, the thin bevel or impost only 0.05 m high making the transition from the upper portion (0.60 m wide) to the lower (0.40 m wide) accentuates the different widths; thus the upper portion, which projects 0.20 m from the wall surface, was deliberately made to appear heavier than the lower, which projects only 0.15 m.[39] Although it is impossible to reconstruct the missing uppermost portion of this raised decorative band, the projection must have created a play of light and shadow across the curved surface of this apse. The arrangement is reminiscent of some pre-Romanesque churches with a series of arches, often on corbels, between the projecting vertical bands. Students of early medieval architecture are familiar with this simple architectural ornament, known as Lombard bands, *plates-bandes,* or simply as decorative bands.

Fig. 22

22. Wall buttress of eighth-century apse, north side of crypt.

In my 1942 volume I proposed that the apse of Fulrad's church was polygonal on the exterior, and that there was an interior crypt with two curved passageways leading to a central recess, or confessio, where the relics of the patron saint were protected.[40] Formigé's rediscovery of the masonry of the apse has proved categorically that the exterior was semicircular, not polygonal, but his description and reconstruction of the plan of the *martyrium* are so schematic and arbitrary that the evidence for this annular crypt needs reexamination.[41] First of all the reader should remember that all vestiges of the original interior masonry of the eighth-century passages and crypt, or confessio, were removed when Viollet-le-Duc built the Imperial crypt. The only evidence of their existence survives in the early nineteenth-century plans of the crypt by Cellérier (dated 1811), by Debret (dated 1816), and by Viollet-le-Duc (dated 1846).[42] Since the interior diameter of the apse can now be measured accurately as 9.40 m, we can estimate the dimensions of the old plans.

Fig. 23

The curving passageways must have been about one-half as long as the diameter, or about 4.70 m, although all the plans show that the southern one was longer than the northern. The rectangular recess where the relics were kept must have been about 3.10 m wide from north to south and 1.70 m deep east to west.[43] Two openings are shown off the northern passageway and one narrow slit off the southern, but no entrances are indicated at the western end of either passage. Formigé stated, nevertheless, that "the entrances to these corridors turned at right angles on the north and on the south where I uncovered them."[44] If he did, subsequent work has hidden or destroyed them for I cannot find any evidence for the stairs which he described.[45] In addition the photographs in the Archives Photographiques in Paris do not show traces of such stairways. On the contrary the photograph of the north side shows that all the masonry was disrupted in the twelfth century when a base for a pier between Suger's new choir and the old transept was installed. On the south side the "bloc romain profilé d'une puissante doucine" identified by Formigé as the sill for the southern entrance is still in place, but "the two other steps placed in the corridors themselves" have disappeared, as have the corridors.[46] The masonry at this location in the crypt was reinforced in the thirteenth century, as evidenced by the large, unfinished twelfth-century bases placed haphazardly in the rubble fill which obliterated the earlier remains.

App. H.2

Other evidence presented in the following pages suggests that the entrances to the passageways may have been located at this point, but nothing remains to uphold Formigé's assertions. Fragments of the stone slabs that covered the passages can be seen embedded in the eighth-century masonry just above the splayed window openings. Prior to discussing these slabs and their implications for the size of the raised platform over the annular crypt, we should consider the problems relating to the windows opening into the confessio.

App. H.3, 4

Portions of six widely splayed rectangular windows—1.05 m wide by 0.70 m high—can be seen today opening through the eighth-century apse masonry. Yet Formigé's plan of the martyrium shows only five such openings

App. H.1

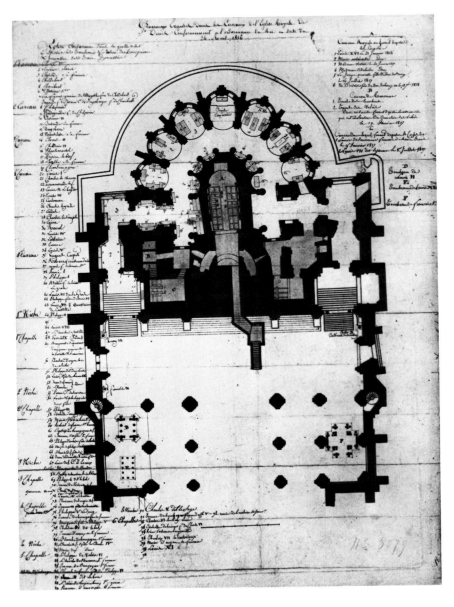

23. **Plan of crypt by Debret, dated 1816.**

still extant, and the photographs in the Archives Photographiques in Paris indicate only four. All the windows have square central posts, or "méneaux," chamfered at the corners. Formigé's plan, which apparently identified restorations by diagonal hatching, shows only the middle post on the north side as completely original (that is, filled in black).[47] Two shallow niches— 0.30 m wide by 0.35 m high—theoretically held lamps or torches to light the "couloirs," or passageways, but the Archives photographs show the interior surface of one only as blackened by smoke. Fragments of painted plaster still adhere to some of the surfaces, notably on the splayed interior of the eastern window on the south side—proof that the original masonry survives. Approximately 1.40 m from the interior the splayed portions of

App. H.3, 4, 7

the windows narrow to about 0.40 m and then splay outward. Formigé stated that plaster covered the embrasures of the windows. He noted that remains of a wooden frame to hold a window could still be seen, but I have not been able to verify this.[48]

Although details of these splayed openings onto the interior of the confessio can be questioned, the function of the apertures is apparent. Within less than a century, the exterior of the eighth-century apse was enclosed by the chapel consecrated under Abbot Hilduin in 832. In all probability the chapel itself was dimly lit, and the windows into the confessio would not have introduced much light; but they would have allowed pilgrims to glimpse the most sacred spot in the church—the presumed resting place of the patron saint. Shadows from a flickering flame inside the confessio would have intensified the dramatic effect upon viewers looking through a narrow opening from the exterior. I believe that from the eighth century on, the devout circulated around the apse and venerated the sacred relics through the splayed openings.

Fragments of stone slabs which covered the interior passageways of the annular crypt are still embedded in the eighth-century masonry just above the interior openings of the splayed windows. Since Formigé's workmen covered the interior surface of the apse masonry with a thin layer of cement, it is difficult to locate the lower level of the passageway floor. An estimate places this at about 1.65 m below our arbitrary benchmark, which is the level of the pavement in the transept and nave. With the lower side of the slabs measuring 0.80 m below the benchmark, the height of the passages would have been about 2.45 m. This would have meant that the slabs located about 1.50 m above the eighth-century pavement provided a platform that would have raised a papal throne or abbot's chair almost shoulder-high above those standing in the transept or nave. The stone fragments, 0.20 m thick, extend 3.90 m on the south side and 4.70 m on the north from the eastern periphery to the west, where they stop abruptly. This must indicate that only the surface of the apse itself was covered by such a platform—a supposition confirmed on the north side by the presence of the twelfth-century base with its lower edge 0.70 m below the benchmark, that is, at the level of the eighth-century nave pavement.

App. H.7

App. H.2

Formigé claimed that he could identify the intersection of the apse wall with the transept wall, which turned at right angles to the north and to the south, so that the apse opened directly into the transept.[49] In his plan published as the "Eglise de Dagobert Ier reconstruite par Pepin le Bref et achevée par Charlemagne," he showed the Carolingian apse with seven windows, the terminal wall of the southern transept arm with a tower, and fragments of the northern transept filled in black as though these masonries still existed.[50] If so, I have not been able to recognize them, even though I have examined all of the building above and below the transept, as well as the choir pavements, and have excavated in the crypt where these walls would have been located. In accord with his plan, the southwest corner of the transept and about 5.00 m of the south wall extending to the east have survived, identifiable by the libages typical of the eighth-century foundations beneath two beds characteristic of eighth-century masonry. The latter are interrupted, or cut, by the massive thirteenth-century foundations extending north and south that support the piers of the existing transept. These thirteenth-century foundations are a little more than 4.00 m thick. To the east on the southern side, burial chambers built at some indeterminate later date[51] extend into the exterior beyond the present south transept walls. If the Carolingian or other foundations had cut through or continued to the east through this area, some traces would exist, but they do not. Even fewer eighth-century remains exist under the north transept pavement, where William the Conqueror's eleventh-century tower replaced all but the lowest libages of the north-aisle wall, and later burials completely disrupted the remains of the eastern side of the Carolingian transept. Although I have searched diligently, I cannot find any remains of the eastern foundation wall of Fulrad's church and have been forced to conclude that those remains were completely incorporated into the thirteenth-century foundations. Such a conclusion locates the eighth-century crossing several meters to the west of the apse and necessitates a straight bay between the semicircular eastern end and the crossing.

Possible survivals of the southeast crossing structure are two large blocks,   **Fig. 24** similar to the libages of the eighth-century foundations, above the petit appareil masonry of Sainte Geneviève's chapel on the south side just to the east of the seventeenth-century *caveau des cérémonies*. Each of the blocks is over a meter wide and 0.50 m high. They do not pin-point a specific location but seem to indicate a general area for the crossing about 4.00 m west of the curving wall of the apse. The lower edges of these blocks lie about 1.15 m above the level of the eighth-century pavement—an arrangement that has an explanation in relation to the levels of the bases for the nave colonnade described in the following pages. Perhaps the most persuasive reason for the location of the blocks is that it conforms to the proportions of the rest of Fulrad's church, which are established by existing remains of the eighth-century foundations and wall structure.

From the extant foundations at the southwest corner of the transept the extension of the libages to the north establishes the alignment of the western limits of the transept arms and of the western crossing piers. Slight irreg-   **Fig. 25** ularities in the masonry above the Gallo-Roman blocks of the foundations for Sainte Geneviève's chapel may indicate the location of the western crossing piers of Fulrad's church. On the southern side just to the west of the *caveau des cérémonies* three roughly shaped stones between 0.50 m and 0.40 m wide differ from the surrounding masonry. Set at the same level as the larger libages, they occur very nearly 8.00 m to the east. Exactly opposite these stones, on the northern side three similar roughly shaped stones lie one above another. Here a curious shallow cavity some 2.20 m long seems to have been hollowed out of the Gallo-Roman blocks as though to stabilize some special load. Exactly 4.00 m to the west is the last of the bases—N8—of the north side of the nave colonnade. The significant feature of these three irregularities is their location in relation to each other. They define three corners of a rectangle approximately 9.00 m long from north to south by 8.00 m wide from east to west. If 0.50 m, or one-half the width of a Carolingian

24. South side of early, or "first," crypt, showing blocks of fifth-century foundations with *petit appareil* masonry, under two large eighth-century blocks, as restored by Formigé, ca. 1960.

25. Excavation of south transept, 1946–48, from above, showing eighth-century transept enclosed by western side of twelfth-century transept portal.

base, is added to each end of the north–south dimension, the measurement becomes 10.00 m, the width of the Carolingian nave from column center to column center. I previously assumed that the tower over the crossing of Fulrad's church—its existence documented by a text—necessitated the presence of a square crossing.[52] I now find the evidence for a rectangular crossing in those archaeological remains so compelling that the plan published in the

album of drawings has that configuration measuring 10.00 m by 8.00 m. Pl. 2; Album no. 14
The dimensions conform to the width of the bays of the nave, as established
by the column bases. In my reconstruction the Carolingian transept is equal
to two nave bays, or 8.00 m. The straight bay linking the apse and the
crossing was 4.00 m wide, the same as a nave bay. As a final observation
about the proportions of this transept, note that the arms to the north and the
south of the crossing from the center of the crossing piers to the interior of the
outer walls measure 8.00 m by 8.00 m, so that the transept consisted of
two squares flanking a rectangle—a design later repeated in the twelfth-
century western bays built by Abbot Suger. Since nothing remains of the
crossing piers, any reconstruction of their form must remain entirely hypothetical. The four supports for the tower surmounting the crossing, most
probably a wooden one, must have been masonry piers, not columns, but
whether square, rectangular, or T-shaped remains unknown.

The uneven fragments of the masonry of the southern, or terminal, wall of
the eighth-century south transept arm uncovered in 1946 contain possible
indications about the location of a Carolingian doorway into the cloister and
about the interior wall surfaces as well as information concerning the exact
location of the southwestern corner of the transept of Fulrad's church. The Fig. 25; App. G.1
exterior of the southwest corner of the transept was surrounded by, or
encased in, twelfth-century masonry, intended to provide an impressive
entrance into the new cloister. This entrance was to be a portal, its door jambs
flanked by splayed embrasures formed by two setbacks, and a trumeau
dividing the entrance. The third projection to the west is the corner buttress
of the twelfth century, not one of the setbacks. Only the trumeau and the
lower portions of the western half of the entrance exist today. The eastern
side was evidently not completed, for one bed of the typical, regular eighth-
century exterior masonry still exists at -0.50 m. On the western side at
-0.70 m, the level of the Carolingian pavement, there are two large, flat
stones. Their upper surfaces appear worn, as though they had served as the
sill of a door for many years. I believe these large stones were the top libages
of the eighth-century foundations. In the twelfth century they were decorated with a horizontal bevel to conform with the bevels of the trumeau and
continued to serve as the sill for the door from the south transept into the
cloister.

The evidence for the interior wall surface is less precise. On the eastern App. G.5
side of the twelfth-century trumeau one bed of the typical eighth-century
wall survives at -0.50 m, or about 0.20 m above the doorsill on the other
side of the trumeau. Characteristic of that period at Saint-Denis, this segment
has carefully prepared, regular stones with well-defined joints. The interior
of the same masonry, 0.90 m thick, has either been torn away or was
originally left in a rough, unfinished condition with the intention of covering
it with plaster or stucco. Since there are other examples of this procedure in
Fulrad's church, I assume that stucco finished the south transept wall, although none of the interior surfacing remains.

Having examined all remaining archaeological evidence of the eighth-
century transept, we can proceed to the more extensive evidence for the

Pl. 2; Album no. 14

structure of the nave. Surviving fragments of the exterior walls and foundations as well as bases for the nave colonnade of Fulrad's church provide positive evidence that allows a reconstruction of the entire nave plan, which measured 40.00 m overall from east to west and 20.00 m in width between the interior surfaces of the side-aisle walls. Deviations from these general dimensions will be noted.

Despite their apparent harmony, those major measurements are closely related to earlier structures on the site. The width, or north–south dimension between the centers of the bases for the nave colonnade, measures almost exactly 10.00 m, which in turn equals almost exactly 30 Carolingian feet.[53] These bases, however, were placed on the foundations of Sainte Geneviève's chapel and its extension to the west under Dagobert's patronage in the seventh century. In other words, the width of the eighth-century nave may have been determined by the width of the foundations of Sainte Geneviève's chapel. In a similar fashion the outside walls of the side aisles reflect the width of the lateral constructions of the seventh century, since the massive libages of the Carolingian foundations were placed just outside the foundations of the enlargement sponsored by Dagobert.

With respect to the proportions of Fulrad's building, a first look at the foundations of the nave suggests that the proportions may also have been dependent on earlier constructions. If the overall dimensions of the nave were, at least to some degree, predetermined, I have not been able to discover any satisfactory reason for the choice of 4.00 m as the width for the nave bays. The use of this same measurement in the straight bay to the west of the apse and in the transept of the eastern portions of Fulrad's church has already been determined. Since building progressed from east to west, this basic dimension must have been used before the nave was laid out; although I cannot explain the choice of certain dimensions, I can describe what remains of the nave construction.

The bases for the nave colonnades were, as we have seen, placed on the earlier substructures. Only the easternmost base on the north side—N8—remains over the Gallo-Roman blocks of the fifth-century foundations. Here the center of the base rests solidly on the foundation blocks, but the southern side projects beyond the limits of the foundations. To compensate for this imbalance, additional rubble in a solid mortar distinct from the fifth-century mortar was applied along the southern side of the early construction. In this way the center of the column was placed to the north of the edge of the fifth-century masonry, thereby increasing the distance across the nave between columns from 9.40 m (the distance between the interior surfaces of the fifth-century foundations) to 10.00 m, the width of the eighth-century nave. Further to the west along the north side of the nave similar reinforcement or buttressing of the early foundations occurs. In this instance the rubble and mortar reinforces work of the seventh century on the southern side of the bases. One of the best examples, N1, is still *in situ*. There the excavation could be extended down to the solid clay subsoil. Under the base an irregular mass of rubble construction from 2.00 m to 3.00 m wide projects more than 1.00 m to the south. The obvious junction between the

Fig. 26

Fig. 27

26. Foundations under easternmost eighth-century nave base, N8.

27. Western eighth-century nave base, N1, with seventh- and eighth-century foundations.

rubble masonries occurs with no bonding between the seventh- and eighth-century mortars. As in the example of the easternmost base, N8, the center of the Carolingian base is placed over the foundation, but the southern edge projects beyond the foundation limits. Presumably the reuse of the early foundations was motivated by economic reasons, but probably that early masonry was located approximately where the eighth-century masons wished to place the bases for the nave colonnade of Fulrad's church.

The outer walls of Fulrad's building were a new construction, placed just outside the seventh-century foundations. Although not enough of the early masonry has been found to determine whether the location of the old foundations influenced the newer ones and also set the east–west alignment of the walls, the influence seems probable since the walls are not exactly parallel to the bases of the nave colonnade. The eighth-century side aisles become slightly wider at the western ends than near the crossing to the east. Barely noticeable, the deviation does not exceed 0.40 m, but when these alignments were extended over longer distances, as they were in the twelfth century, other distortions occurred. In spite of such minor irregularities, the important dimensions of the Carolingian nave remain remarkably simple. The nave itself, between the centers of the columns, was twice as wide as the side aisles and one quarter the overall, interior length, with the exception of the western ensemble, which seems to have functioned as a separate entity.

Suger described this western entrance as a "narrow hall. . . squeezed in on either side by twin towers neither high nor very sturdy but threatening ruin" and called it an "addition asserted to have been made by Charlemagne."[54] He also said that it was *ab aquilone,* or "toward the north," which has provided scholars with a splendid opportunity to display their learning. Unfortunately the excavations have not completely clarified his meaning, and it does not seem likely that new evidence will be forthcoming.

First of all, no foundations or other remains indicate that this "main entrance" was on the north side of Fulrad's church. Erwin Panofsky has explained Suger's reference by demonstrating that

> the term *aquilo* had come to assume a symbolic or theological significance quite independent of its geographical or topographical one. It had come to denote the region or habitat of those who, living "in opposition to" Mount Zion, viz., to the Christian faith, can nevertheless be transformed into members thereof by conversion. And since, as evidenced by Suger himself, Mount Zion is specifically symbolized, even represented, by the sanctuary or chevet of any. . . church, we can easily see how, in the same architectural terms, the word *aquilo* could come to denote the region or habitat of those who, living in and approaching the church from a direction "opposite to" the sanctuary, can nevertheless be welcomed therein as worshippers.[55]

Although excavations have explored this whole area from the south side aisle across the nave to the exterior of the north side aisle, the remains of this western entrance are still fragmentary.[56] The extension of the Carolingian nave to the west in the twelfth century and the massive new foundations for the thirteenth-century piers traversed this area from east to west and disrupted or obliterated the eighth-century foundations. Presumably this area between the nave and side aisles would have been the location for the "twin towers" which Suger said "squeezed in" the narrow entrance hall, yet nothing remains to tell us about the size or shape of the towers. The narrow entrance hall, however, seems to have been located along the north side of the nave, where a single large stone, 1.05 m by 1.15 m, exists with two irregular, rectangular, cut holes penetrating some 0.25 m below the surface. The location and alignment of these holes suggest that they served as sockets for upright wooden posts between which a door was hung. This stone rests over large libages typical of the eighth-century foundations, set in a north–south alignment across the western end of the nave. Since these are the last, or westernmost, libages the doorway would have opened directly onto the nave. The level of the holes at 1.05 m below the present pavement indicates that there must have been a step up to the eighth-century pavement as one entered the nave.

App. B.11

Before discussing this pavement and the bases of the nave that rose above it, we must address the possibility of a polygonal apse as part of the western ensemble. Two oblique fragments of finished stones on either side of the central axis of the nave appear to be remnants of such an apse. This whole area at the entrance to Fulrad's church continued for an indeterminate length of time to be favored for burials.[57] Stone and masonry sarcophagi not only touch the existing masonry, but in several places encroach upon the foundations. Having destroyed or caused the removal of the dressed stones, the burials make it difficult to determine the original disposition. Consequently the reconstruction of the plan of any structure in this area must remain tentative. The absence of libages as foundations for this central area proves, in my opinion, that whatever was done came as an afterthought that changed the original western arrangement. The existing foundation consists of an undistinguished agglomerate mat covering roughly 3.00 m by 4.00 m under the center of the second bay from the west of the nave. The irregularly shaped foundation stones show no sign of having been fashioned by any tool, and the mortar is coarse with a large quantity of sand. Curiously, the bottom stones rest on black earth rather than on the clay subsoil below the other foundations.

The top stones in oblique alignments immediately distinguish themselves from the other masonry. Only eight such stones exist on the north side and six on the south, but they must have been deliberately arranged in this oblique fashion—an arrangement which demands attention. Although the stones vary from 1.20 m to 0.60 m in width, their upper surfaces are level, as though in anticipation of another layer or bed of similar construction. The western wall that would have completed the polygonal exterior has been torn away, but some indications of its location still exist in the fragmentary substructure. These stones, which average about 0.30 m in thickness, lie 1.30 m below the existing pavement and 0.60 m below the eighth-century pavement. Obviously it would be reckless to draw any firm conclusions from such meager evidence, but I have shown the location and position of these stones in my reconstruction of the plan of Fulrad's church.

Although the evidence for a polygonal apse in the center of the western ensemble of the Carolingian church at Saint-Denis must remain incomplete, positive evidence survives that establishes the level of the pavement of the nave to which it was joined. A fragment of the pavement of the nave of Fulrad's church was unexpectedly found intact during a small exploratory excavation in June 1969.[58] Approximately 3.00 m long by 1.65 m wide, in its largest dimensions, the irregularly shaped stones of this flooring were found under the existing pavement of the sixth bay of the north side aisle just to the west of the iron grill, or barricade, that separates the nave from the transept. The paving stones vary in size from 0.80 m to 0.30 m long and from 0.54 m to 0.20 m wide, but these dimensions prove little since each stone has its own shape that was carefully fitted into a random pattern to create a level, uniform surface. The stones, which average just under 0.10 m thick, are set in firm mortar on a carefully prepared base approximately 0.60 m thick. This base is built in a series of stratifications, or beds.

App. B.6-9

Pl. 3C; Album no. 14

Fig. 28

28. Fragment of eighth-century nave pavement under north side aisle.

The uppermost layer directly beneath the stones is a reddish mortar which must have been quite fluid when the stones were put in place since the red can be seen in the thin joints between the stones. Under the paving stones, that mortar varies from 0.06 m to 0.14 m in thickness and rests on a rubble of small, uncut stones in a coarse mortar of sand and lime, with an average thickness of about 0.15 m. Under the rubble a thin layer of white plaster 0.01 m to 0.03 m thick undulates across the fill. Below, a substratum of yellowish tan fill about 0.14 m thick rests on a bottom layer of reddish mortar, also about 0.14 m thick, placed either directly on the projections of the massive libages of the foundation or on a fill of black earth. I know of few comparable forms of groundwork for earlier or later pavements and wonder whether this example, which I was able to examine and record carefully, is owing to its proximity to an exterior wall or to some other undetected circumstance. The paving stones themselves are fine-grained limestone with a surface polished by more than four centuries of use and cleaning to the shade of light-colored, worn leather. The impression of solidity must have been enlivened by the random design of the irregular stones covering the large areas of the side aisles and the nave. Even more important than the visual effect to the archaeologist, this unusual example of mid-eighth-century taste and technique establishes a basic benchmark, or level, for the Carolingian pavement at 0.71 m below the existing pavement.[59]

Without this reference, or guideline, the problem of the bases and plinths for the colonnades between the nave and the side aisles would be even more complicated than it now is. The large, carved stone bases at Saint-Denis stand out among the surviving examples of Carolingian art in the Western world.   Figs. 29–34

Although the bases have been extolled as "fine workmanship" that is "the visible link connecting the Carolingian civilization with a past that is still obscure,"[60] the complete series has never been described and its analysis, consequently, remains thoroughly confused.

The first mention of one of these bases initiated the confusion. Described as a large stone "in the form of a die, [the object] is decorated on its four sides with ornaments of Merovingian style; this cube has had a function which remains inexplicable. It has been hollowed in the form of a receptacle, perhaps with the intention of making it into a baptismal font; all its surfaces are well preserved except for the upper one."[61] Obviously the function was misunderstood, for the cavity in the top was intended to receive the shaft of the column it supported. The decoration as a reflection of early Carolingian rather than Merovingian style will be explored shortly. This "cube" was supposedly among the debris of Lenoir's Musée des Monuments Français when Jules Quicherat and M. de Lasteyrie together with M. du Sommerand and M. Darcy selected objects for removal from the "dépôt" at Saint-Denis to the Cluny Museum in Paris in 1881. Yet Quicherat was aware that not all of the objects stored in the dépôt had come from Lenoir's museum.[62] This particular stone and another one had evidently been discovered in one of the side aisles of the basilica, where they might possibly have been placed as early as the thirteenth century. The so-called cube was returned to Saint-Denis from the Cluny Musuem with several other items in the 1950s and can now be examined in the Musée Lapidaire in the north garden of the basilica. In the descriptions which follow, it is identified as the Cluny base.

This particular base was identified as Carolingian in 1922[63] and was first associated with the Carolingian church at Saint-Denis by Jean Hubert in 1938.[64] My excavations in 1947 and 1948 uncovered four other comparable bases in their original positions under the existing nave, which confirmed their association with Fulrad's church.[65] At an unspecified moment in the 1950s workmen under the direction of Jules Formigé joined my excavations under the north side of the western nave with the excavations under the crossing by a narrow tunnel, then dug a similar tunnel along the southern side of the nave. In the process of opening these cramped passages seven large, rectangular stones or slabs were located at regular intervals, at roughly similar depths, and in alignment with the bases uncovered in my excavations. Because they occur every four meters, Formigé identified them as plinths for the original nave bases, although he confused the Merovingian and Carolingian buildings.[66] I have included those plinths with the descriptions of the Carolingian bases. One additional large and badly damaged base was also discovered under the south side of the nave, which possibly because of the limited space to examine it had escaped attention. I include it as number S3 in the sequence of the bases. Finally, in 1959, Michel Fleury uncovered one more base *in situ* under the pavement of the present crossing. That discovery completed the alignment of all of the bases for the nave colonnade of Fulrad's church but did not resolve the problem of the original location of the Cluny base.

The discordant features of the group as a whole present a number of puzzles. All the bases are different. Their dimensions and general shapes

Fig. 34

App. E.1a,b

a

b

vary both in width and height so that it is often difficult to visualize how the bases functioned as a sequence of supports with column shafts presumably of different heights. No two decorative motifs are the same. Although there are repetitions of a basic design on the same base, irregularities suggest individual freehand production. There is no set formula, no order or rhythmic repetition to create a sense of interrelatedness. I cannot detect any search for symmetry or conformity in their sequence, except of course in their strict alignment and their regular spacing. The lack of an understandable ordering may be misleading, for we must remember that this same sequence of bases remained in place as major elements of the nave construction for almost five hundred years, from about 760 to about 1260, when the transept and nave existing today were finally rebuilt. Despite the inconsistencies, if one of the missing bases should unexpectedly be discovered, anyone who had seen the others would probably perceive that it belonged to this series.

The following description of the bases and plinths identifies the location of each one according to a numbering system that begins at the western end on the north side of the eighth-century nave and continues in sequence east to the crossing, followed by the series, again in order from west to east, on the south side of the nave. Only four of the original sixteen bases can be examined where they were installed, and only three in their entirety from the clay subsoil on which the foundation rests to the top of the base *in situ*. The first, or westernmost, base on the north side of the nave, N1, is unique in the series because it has animal and bird designs carved in low, two-plane relief on its southern and eastern faces. Unfortunately, it has been so badly damaged that only fragments of the original designs survive. Two small animals facing in opposite directions on either side of a stylized tree decorate the south face. Only the faint outlines of the animals remain, and the disappearance of details, presumably once painted on the surfaces, makes comparisons difficult. In its proportions the bird outlined on the eastern face resembles the

29. Eighth-century nave base, N1: (a) south side with two animals separated by a tree; (b) east side with two birds.

Fig. 29a

symbol of Saint John of the Christ in Majesty page of the Gundohinus Gospels.[67] Certainly the figures outlined on the base in a free space, unencumbered by any geometric ornament, contrast sharply with other medieval decorations at Saint-Denis, such as those on the chancel post found in the seventh-century foundations. Possibly the presence of Pope Stephen II with his large entourage at Saint-Denis in 754 and Pepin the Short's deep involvement with Lombardy provided the historical opportunity for new artistic influences from the south.

Fig. 29b

Fig. 13

The captions for photographs of plaster casts of this base published by Formigé state that the base came from the church built by Dagobert.[68] He based his conclusion on the damage visible 0.15 m above the lower edge of the base, caused, he believed, by the installation of a later pavement. He ignored the character of the decoration, but the presence of red mortar in some of the cracks indicates that repairs were made in the eighth century.

Statistics for N1, Base and Plinth

Base	Plinth
Width (E-W): 1.00 m	Width (E-W): 1.25 m (plinth has two levels separated by a bevel. Measurement is given for the larger, lower level.)
Depth (N-S): 1.12 m	
Height: 0.65 m	Depth (N-S): (Uncertain because north face is buried in later foundations.)
Level of the lower surface below today's pavement: -0.899 m	Height: 0.28 m
Thickness of today's pavement in that area: 0.249 m	Level of upper surface: -0.899 m
Amount by which base rose above the Carolingian pavement: 0.471 m (broken and irregular upper surface)	Plinth has two levels
Amount of base lying below the Carolingian pavement: 0.179 m	
Diameter of cavity: 0.53 m (today's pavement prevents verification of this measurement.	

Because of its decoration, I refer to the second base on the north side of the nave, N2, as the "fleur de lys" base. This clearly defined cube of stone has sustained little damage, at least on its western and southern faces, which are the only ones visible. Six irregularly shaped designs, resembling fleur de lys, fill a panel on the western face, but the artist could complete only five and begin a sixth on the southern side. Outlined in low, flat relief against a plain background, these designs suggest the use of polychromy. Although no color remains, possibly the paint was applied as a paste in a technique not unlike cloisonné metalwork. Above the horizontal panels, the top of the base rises in a slanting chamfer decorated with a succession of four-petaled rosettes. Again the technique of flat relief resembles cloisonné metalwork, in this instance with crudely designed petals outlined against a bare background. The flat upper surface of the base around the circular cavity made to hold the base of the shaft of the column is also decorated with vegetal designs. Symmetrical palmette patterns enliven the four corners and intervening spaces with graceful forms devoid of any geometrical references. The photograph of

Fig. 30a

Fig. 30b

a

b

a plaster reconstruction of the complete base with the stump of a column set into the circular cavity recreates the total effect of these different designs in black and white, but we are too far removed from the early Carolingian world of the mid–eighth century to envisage how they would appear with polychromy.

30. (a) Eighth-century nave base, N2, after discovery in 1947; (b) plaster reconstruction of eighth-century nave base, N2, with restored fragment of column.

Statistics for N2, Base and Plinth[69]

Base

Width (E-W): 1.11 m	Level of top surface below today's pavement: -0.47 m
Depth (N-S): 1.06 m	
Height: 0.593 m	Amount by which base rose above Carolingian pavement: 0.34 m
Level of lower surface below today's pavement: -0.825 m	Amount by which base lay below the Carolingian pavement: 0.253 m
Thickness of pavement in area above base: 0.40 m	Diameter of cavity: 0.52 m (Not measurable today; measurement taken from plaster cast in Musée Lapidaire.)

Plinth

No dimensions taken. Plinth not excavated.

Although the tunnel under the pavement along the north side of the nave uncovered the plinths for bases N3, N4, N5, and N6, now, after the recent consolidation of the sides and floor of the tunnel, they are difficult to identify. The bases themselves were all removed, probably during either the thirteenth or nineteenth centuries. The few verifiable measurements indicate

31. Upper, or top, surface of eighth-century easternmost nave base, N8, showing the decorated chamfer.

that the plinths average 1.50 m wide from east to west, are between 0.20 m and 0.30 m thick, and that the top surfaces lie between 0.70 m and 0.80 m below the level of the existing pavement. As the excavation plan of the church indicates, the bases were carefully aligned from east to west, parallel to the axis of Fulrad's church, and spaced exactly 4.00 m apart from center to center.

The next to last base on the north side, N7, presents a problem, both because its dimensions differ from the other eighth-century bases and because it lies somewhat off axis at a considerably lower level. Its location in line with the other eighth-century bases, at a distance of 4.00 m from the neighboring plinth (N6 to the west and base N8 to the east), seems to include it in the Carolingian series, although I believe it to be a partially unfinished stone originally intended for another purpose in another location.

Discovered by Michel Fleury, the last, or easternmost, base on the north side of the nave, N8, is a large one, 1.25 m by 1.25 m. Evidently it was placed on the Carolingian pavement and rose 0.50 m above it, but how the base functioned remains uncertain. The square cavity in its upper surface (0.60 m by 0.60 m) may have supported a square pier rather than a circular column. Since it is the last support of the nave arcade preceding what would have been the crossing pier, it is indeed unfortunate that so many details remain uncertain. The damaged appearance of the upper surface containing the square cavity suggests the possibility that the base was reworked sometime between the eighth and the twelfth centuries. The only

Fig. 31

a

b

part of the carved ornament which I have seen decorates the slanting chamfer just below the upper surface. Carved in low relief, this variation on the simple palmette design appears more rounded and articulated than the flatter, two-plane reliefs of the western bases.

The sequence of eighth-century bases on the south side of the nave is more fragmentary than that on the north side, with the differences among those still extant more striking. When a small excavation was made in 1947 to confirm the presence of a base, only remnants of the first, or westernmost, base were found. The opening was filled with a solid rubble before my return the following summer, which prevented any further examination. My notes record that the vestiges measured 0.85 m by 0.95 m and that the largest of the fragments was triangular.

The two photographs of the second base, S2, located on the south side opposite the fleur de lys base of the north side, record interesting information about medieval techniques for repairs. When discovered in 1947 the sides of the base were partially covered by stone slabs hiding a thin iron band which apparently encircled the base. Since this base was abandoned in the thirteenth century when the present nave was built, and since the iron band must have been used to strengthen or repair some earlier damage to the base, the device probably dates from the twelfth century, when, as Suger wrote, he "undertook with new confidence to repair the damages in the great capitals and in the bases that supported the columns."[70] The precision with which the iron band is embedded in the stone and the care taken to hide it from view are aspects of twelfth-century techniques and aesthetics seldom well documented. Unfortunately, almost ten years passed before an official decision was reached to consolidate and preserve important features of my excavations of the mid-1940s, and I received no notice that work was about to begin. Failing to recognize the unusual features, the workmen who built a

32. Eighth-century nave base, S2, restored in the twelfth century: (a) as found in 1947; (b) after preservation in late 1950s.

Fig. 32a,b

Fig. 32b

a

b

concrete box around the base and installed a new pavement removed the remnants of the twelfth-century stone sheathing and altered the shape of the top of the base. The iron band embedded in the stone remains, but the significance of the whole ensemble can no longer be perceived.

The next base on the south side of the nave, S3, has remained unrecorded. Presumably found by Formigé's workmen when they completed the tunnel, this large stone block, 0.90 m by 0.95 m, rises to within 0.20 m of the existing nave pavement. Barely visible in the semidarkness of the tunnel, a low, essentially flat relief decorates the east, west, and northern sides of the base. Only the designs on the eastern side are distinguishable. Trilobed motifs resembling the so-called fleur de lys on base N2 have been combined and enlarged so that there is room only for four of the motifs, and only one is completely visible.

Since all of the eighth-century bases to the east of this large block on the south side of the nave have been removed, only remnants of their plinths now mark the locations. These plinths vary in size from 0.75 m by 0.90 m to 1.40 m by 1.20 m, but the levels of their upper surfaces are fairly constant at -0.85 m.

The final base to be described, the "Cluny" base, must have been one of the first eighth-century bases discovered. Although unrecorded, its discovery predated 1881, when the base was taken from Saint-Denis to Paris. By then the extensive early nineteenth-century work in the nave at Saint-Denis had been completed. Possibly Viollet-le-Duc or one of his predecessors moved the base from its original location. Yet another possibility exists. The recent excavations under the crossing have disclosed a disturbance in the early foundations under the existing southwest crossing pier which occurred as

33. Eighth-century nave base, S3: (a) from the northwest; (b) eastern side with large foliate design *in situ*.

Fig. 33a,b

a

b

c

d

early as the thirteenth century. At the time the new crossing and nave were under construction, there must have been some question about the solidity of the substructure in that location. While the thirteenth-century masons were probing the foundations, they may have removed the eighth-century base and a Gallo-Roman block below it and placed them in a side aisle of the new nave. There they remained until their removal in 1881 to the Cluny Museum in Paris. The large, unfinished twelfth-century bases crowded together at the bottom of the foundations offer evidence that in the thirteenth century there was concern with the solidity of the substructure at this particular location on the south side of the nave, and there is no Gallo-Roman block and no Carolingian base comparable to those on the north side of the nave—confirmation of the thirteenth-century strengthening of the foundations. Wherever the Cluny base was located originally, it survived as one of the best-preserved Carolingian bases at Saint-Denis.

Measuring 1.20 m square by 0.65 m in height, this large base would have risen some 0.30 m above the Carolingian pavement. The cavity, or recess, in its upper surface has a diameter of 0.53 m. Vestiges of mortar at the bottom of the cavity retain the imprint of the shaft of a column.

34. Eighth-century column base, taken from Saint-Denis to the Cluny Museum in Paris, in 1881, returned to Saint-Denis in 1960s, now in Musée Lapidaire: (a) in the Cluny Museum, faces "d" and "a"; (b) faces "a" and "b"; (c) face "c"; (d) face "d."

Fig. 34a–d

Described by Hubert as "the visible link connecting the Carolingian civilization with a past that is still obscure," the graceful designs deserve close analysis. In rectangular panels on the four sides of the base, symmetrically organized palmette designs have rhythmically curving foliate patterns organized on each side of a central axis. In two panels a vase with upright stems supporting a stylized cluster or bud provides the central element. On the other two panels, at each side of the central negative, or undecorated, space, curving foliate forms repeat rhythmical designs. This renewal, or survival, of interest in "Mediterranean" natural forms, as distinct from the "northern" abstract overall patterns, distinguishes the Carolingian revival. Wolfgang Braunfels has called attention to the resemblance of the leaves on this base to those in the Ambrosius Commentary on Luke from Corbie, dated in the third quarter of the eighth century.[71] Since the rendering of the leaves on the manuscript page was done by the application of light, flat colors, the visual effect is quite different from the curving raised relief of the carving on the base. In my opinion, a better comparison would be to the palmette ornaments below Saint Mary and Saint John on the late eighth-century reliquary casket of Bishop Altheus of Sion, Switzerland,[72] even though the symmetrical foliate decorations made with raised metal outlines created less subtle forms than those on the Saint-Denis base. Precision in symmetry governs the designs on the horizontal chamfer at the top of the base, where the axial palmettes alternate with circular voids so smoothly that it is difficult to distinguish between the positive and negative elements in the pattern.

Although the top, horizontal surface of the base has been damaged, enough of the design remains on two of the corners to identify vases with palmette motifs similar to those on the lateral panels. The resemblance of these corner decorations to those on the upper surface of the fleur de lys base, N2, suggests that they were the products of the same workshop.

The fleur de lys of base N2 still *in situ* under the existing nave pavement also has affinities with the designs on the Cluny base. The two sides visible, the western and the southern faces of base N2, as well as the chamfers and the reliefs on two of the corners of the top surface survive in almost perfect condition. The palmette designs of the upper surface compare well enough with those on the Cluny base to suggest that either the same artist carved both surfaces or the fleur de lys artist copied the work of the Cluny artist closely. I favor the second possibility because the designs on this second base lack the subtlety and fluidity of the Cluny ornament, especially in the irregular, trilobed fleur de lys aligned in rows on the lateral sides. A similar awkwardness characterizes the series of ten stylized, four-petaled rosettes that decorate the bevel, or horizontal chamfer, along the upper edge on both sides.

Fig. 30

A larger, cruder variant of the fleur de lys design is carved on the large base, S3. Here, two trilobed motifs, one inverted, are joined at their bases. The design has been enlarged so that four suffice to cover the eastern side of the base. Fragments of other low-relief ornament on the northern and western faces are indecipherable.

Fig. 33

Unfortunately, I was not present when the final base with carved decoration, N8, the easternmost one on the north side, was discovered by Michel

Fig. 31

Fleury, so I do not know the extent of the decoration. Only the top bevel is now visible from above. Equally skillfully carved, a series of adjacent palmette designs not unlike those on the horizontal chamfer of the Cluny base associate it with that group.

The available evidence points to sculptors with at least two different artistic traditions as the carvers of the bases for the nave colonnade—those trained in a region already familiar with the natural world of a Mediterranean tradition and those to whom those forms and designs were new.[73] Perhaps there were artists in the pope's retinue when he came from Italy to Saint-Denis in 752, and they may have worked alongside local artisans. The work of the local workshop reflects the influence of their new colleagues but reveals a lack of experience in the technique of low relief carving. Base N1, the only one with zoomorphic or "animal" motif, must have been carved by a local artisan who had a knowledge of other media, such as manuscript illumination.

More puzzling than the divergent styles of the carving on the bases is the apparent disregard for uniformity in height and overall size. Of the five bases still in their presumed original locations, three—N1, S3, N8—stood approximately 0.50 m above the eighth-century pavement, whereas the other two—S2, N2—attained only about one-half that height, 0.20 m to 0.25 m. Since these last two bases are located opposite each other across the nave, they raise the possibility that the base heights may have alternated, with pairs opposite each other having relatively congruent measurements. I must admit that my tentative location of the Cluny base at the eastern end of the nave would place it opposite N8, even though the two differ in size and apparently did not project above the Carolingian pavement to the same levels. Possibly the eighth-century masons were indifferent to symmetry and rhythmic alternation, yet no final solution can be proposed because there is simply not enough available evidence.

Equally enigmatic are three carved stone fragments with low-relief ornament supposedly discovered during Formigé's excavations. Unfortunately, we lack any record of where or under what circumstances they were found. Formigé published them as fragments of bases,[74] which seems most unlikely since they are only 0.08 m thick. The shallow relief carving, particularly on the largest fragment, resembles the foliate design on the upper surface of N2, the fleur de lys base, where the raised exterior outlines articulate an interior channel. The stone fragments may originally have formed part of some chancel or screen; if so, a screen carved by a local artist.

With or without carved decoration, a chancel enclosure was probably a part of the Carolingian liturgical arrangement in the eastern portions of Fulrad's building. Early in his abbacy, soon after 1122, Abbot Suger mentioned that he had "put out of the way a certain obstruction, which cut as a dark wall through the center of the church."[75] Although he does not elaborate, the obstruction could have been part of the special chancel built to accommodate the ceremonial processions that distinguished the arrival and departure of his holiness during the celebration of a papal High Mass. The presence of Pope Stephen II at Saint-Denis between 752 and 755 and the introduction of the Roman liturgy has already been mentioned as a probable motivation for building a new church at Saint-Denis. The plan must have included a *dromos* or *solea cantorum* in the eastern part of the nave. A screened enclosure extended the chancel into the nave. The western and larger of two sections—also called a *solea-schola*—was described by Thomas Mathews as formed by two parallel walls or screens that separated the central portion of the eastern nave from the rest of the church. Within the enclosure the cantors "stood in double files on either side—the boys on the inside and the men on the outside. . . ." The two double files formed the sacred or processional way through which the pope and his attendants walked on their way to the *presbyterium*, where the pope sat on his throne against the eastern wall of the semicircular apse.[76] No other documents or material evidence have come to my attention relative to this liturgical ensemble in the transept or nave of Fulrad's church. Part of the ensemble may have been replaced, possibly in the ninth century, by the elaborate, if chilly, marble and metal choir stalls, which Suger said he also replaced.[77] But I believe that in the twelfth century some of the chancel screens or barriers that formed the solea-schola for the papal processions in the mid-eighth century were still standing in the nave to "obscure the church's magnitude."

Other details about the decoration of the nave are less certain. Although hundreds of cubic meters of fill have been removed from the excavations under the nave and side-aisle pavements, the single diamond-shaped stone found in 1939 under the western end of the south side aisle remains the only hint that some of the eighth-century masonry included geometric patterns. More stones in geometric shapes should have been found had any recurrent detail such as the arches of the nave arcade or those over clerestory or side windows been so decorated. Although masonry set into geometric patterns is characteristic of Carolingian architecture, adequate evidence for this feature in Fulrad's church is lacking. On the other hand, without doubt the interior wall surfaces were painted.

When Formigé uncovered portions of the annular crypt and of the apse walls above the crypt, he confirmed Viollet-le-Duc's statement that the paintings "represented draperies very crudely drawn in grey on a white background."[78] We now identify the paintings as Carolingian. They occur on two embrasures of the splayed windows of the annular crypt and on three fragments of plaster still attached to the apse wall above the crypt. The window paintings are red marbleized surfaces with white veins surrounded by a double black border. Scattered fragments of plaster with paint have been found in the fill inside the south transept, under the side aisles, and on both sides of the nave—an indication that the interior wall surfaces were covered with painted decorations. The fragments are too small to allow a reconstruction of any part of the design. In my 1942 volume I recorded finding "such colors as blue, yellow and red ochre,"[79] and in 1970 described the fragments found under the north side aisle as follows:

> The thickness of the plaster fragments varies considerably from a thin section 0.02 m to 0.03 m thick, to chunks 0.10 m to 0.12 m thick. The thicker fragments have a continuous lavender, brick-red

color on the smooth surface. Other pieces show two or three colors apparently arranged in bands with a yellow ochre surface separated from a dark grey by a thinner band of white. On one small piece, a bright orange pigment overlayed a brick-tinted ground. Another thin fragment showed watery-green areas with white strokes and spots separated by a dark grey-brown band.[80]

The variety of colors and indications of various designs evoke possible analogies with Carolingian manuscript illumination.

In conclusion, the discovery of the eighth-century column bases and fragments of wall painting provides the first real evidence for some assessment of the beginnings of Carolingian art at Saint-Denis. Perhaps there is hardly enough painting left to justify a general statement, but it is clear that the imitation of a marble veneer, as in the crypt, or of hanging drapery on the wall of the apse is closer to the traditions of antiquity than to the abstract world of the north. These fragments of mural decoration, which antedate by a century the much more sophisticated paintings in the crypt of Saint-Germain d'Auxerre,[81] demonstrate either the direct survival or the beginnings of a deliberate revival of the world of Mediterranean Antiquity. The five stone column bases with relief decoration represent a more varied aspect of mid-eighth-century art, which is, nevertheless, related to natural, organic rather than geometric forms. The degree to which the decoration of Fulrad's early Carolingian church differed from Dagobert's Merovingian embellishments emerges in a comparison between the so-called Cluny base and the fragments from the seventh-century chancel. The rhythmically curving foliate designs on the base contrast with the overall stylized repetitive designs on the chancel screen.

The final aspects of Fulrad's church which need consideration involve the elevation and massing of volumes. Nothing remains of Fulrad's church above the level of the present pavement (presumably approximately the level of the thirteenth-century nave) located 0.71 m above the eighth-century pavement. I discussed in some detail in my 1942 volume[82] the evidence used for reconstructing the height of the Carolingian nave columns. Since no new evidence relative to the eighth-century elevation has been discovered,[83] and since, to my knowledge, there have been no criticisms of my original proposal, I shall summarize the conclusions but change the dimensions to accord with the recently established pavement and base heights.

Texts mention that marble columns with bases and capitals supported arches in the Carolingian church.[84] When I first approached the problem, I included all available fragments in the survey. With the establishment of basic dimensions for the basilica, most of those fragments have been relegated to the category of decoration as distinct from the structural ornamentation in the building. For example, no marble shafts, or fragments thereof, survive that are large enough, that is, 0.52 m in diameter, to have served as part of the nave colonnade, nor are there capitals large enough for the main arcade, unless they have been reemployed elsewhere without being recognized as Carolingian.

As I observed earlier,[85] the two southeast piers adjoining the nave in the western entrance bays or narthex built by Abbot Suger in the twelfth century provide evidence for the height of the eighth-century nave columns. Although the capitals embedded in the masonry of the piers are typically twelfth-century, they must originally have served, until the thirteenth century, as part of the junction between the old and the new, that is, between the old eighth-century nave and side aisles and the new western entrance bays. It is still my opinion that these capitals, which have no present function, reflect the height of the old, Carolingian nave colonnade. In 1940, when writing the first volume, I had not yet found positive evidence for the level of the eighth-century pavement but deduced that it was 1.10 m below the present nave pavement. Since we now know that the Carolingian pavement was only 0.71 m below the present nave, my earlier estimates for the heights of the elevation of Fulrad's church were 0.40 m too high throughout. In other words, the top of the abaci above the capitals of the nave columns stood 4.70 m, not 5.10 m, above the eighth-century pavement.

That small discrepancy would not seem of major significance, but, in this instance, the close correlation between current metric dimensions and the so-called Carolingian foot, which seemed unusually significant when I was writing my first text, can no longer be convincingly demonstrated. So many factors are involved in the construction of a sizeable building that the rigid application of abstract principles in terms of relative heights, or dimensions, appears to be less likely in the early Middle Ages that I originally imagined. General relationships among important segments or subdivisions of a structure apparently were not a preoccupation of the early medieval masons. Evidence of some indifference has already been noted in the varying sizes and heights of the bases for the nave colonnade, which must have resulted in column shafts of different lengths and even capitals of different sizes, when *spolia* or fragments from earlier or other structures were used. Since no remnants either of column shafts or capitals are known to exist, much further speculation about the nave arcade, supported on columns and capitals about 4.70 m high, seems futile. With the width of the nave bay established as 4.00 m by the remnants of the column bases still in place, and the height of columns and capitals estimated as ca. 4.70 m, the arches over each bay, presumably semicircular, must have had a radius of about 1.60 m. Thus the arcade of Fulrad's nave must have been a little more than 6.00 m high.

The central eastern bay of Suger's western ensemble must have opened directly into the junction with the old church, and that junction presumably repeated the dimensions of the old nave, with the height of the twelfth-century eastern bay in accord with the height of the Carolingian nave. Thus it seems reasonable to assume that other dimensions of the extant twelfth-century entrance bays reflect those of the eighth-century nave. The arch of this entrance bay into the nave was partially blocked up in 1841, when the supports for the new organ were built. Since the original twelfth-century arch, clearly visible from the west, is 12.70 m above the present pavement, it would have been 14.30 m above the level of the eighth-century pavement. Consequently, the old nave must have been over 14.00 m high, or a little more than twice the height of the nave arcade—a not unusual proportion for a Carolingian church.

The other measurements of the elevation of Fulrad's nave must remain arbitrary assumptions. The side aisles, to judge from the height of the nave arcade, must have been about 6.00 m high, so that a normal roof, slanting about 30 degrees, would have reached the nave walls at about 9.50 m, leaving ample room for a series of clerestory windows at least 2.00 m high to bring light directly into the nave. A miracle reported in the ninth century tells of an accident that happened while a workman was nailing boards to the roof,[86] and Suger stated that he joined a new wooden ceiling to the old one[87]—confirmation that the Carolingian nave was covered in the traditional manner by a wooden roof.

The ninth-century *Miracula* states quite simply that as "the fabric of the basilica was completed, signals [that is, bells] were hung in the tower, as was the custom."[88] Since the bells summoned the monks to their services, they "customarily" were hung over the crossing, where, readily accessible to the monk responsible for their ringing, they could be heard throughout the monastery. Another ninth-century text by Abbot Hilduin states categorically that the main altar, which was just to the east of the crossing, was "beneath the big bells."[89] As mentioned earlier in this chapter, most scholars, including myself, have assumed that such a crossing tower was built over a square crossing, but the archaeological remains indicate that the crossing was rectangular. To what extent the shape of the crossing affected the shape of the crossing tower cannot be clarified, since no images, schematic or otherwise, have survived. The model made earlier to my specifications has a square crossing tower, which must stand since no purpose is served by proposing an equally conjectural one.[90] Reconstruction of the western towers is also conjectural.

About ten years after he had ordered the demolition of the western towers of the Carolingian church, Abbot Suger described them as "twin towers neither very high nor very sturdy, but threatening ruin."[91] Suger could hardly have been enthusiastic about the proportions or appearance of the towers since he had them destroyed. Because of the obliteration of their foundations we cannot question his statement or determine either the exact location or the dimensions of those towers. Like the height and shape given the crossing tower, the form of these western towers in the model is arbitrary. Even more arbitrary are the towers proposed by Formigé for the early churches at Saint-Denis.[92] I find it quite remarkable that Formigé could specify such precise measurements, 7.795 m square, for foundations that no longer exist.

Since this chapter is concerned with Fulrad's church, the slightly later western tower, identified by Formigé as a *clocher-porche*, will be examined in the next chapter, as will the two doors he located in the nave walls. The mature and later styles of the Carolingian period, insofar as they were reflected at Saint-Denis, will also be treated in the next chapter. Fulrad's church continued Roman tradition in the basilican order of its plan.[93] Innovations such as the annular crypt and the western apse show that the masons were interested in contemporary developments, as were the artists who carved and painted its decoration.

CHAPTER FOUR

From the Death of Fulrad
to the Birth of Suger

After Fulrad's death in 784 the administration of the abbey remained in able hands. One of his disciples, Maginaire (784–97), succeeded Fulrad and continued to serve as an envoy to the pope. Maginaire's concern for the abbey's properties extended beyond Charlemagne's empire to England, where in 790 Offa, king of Mercia, confirmed possessions of Saint-Denis in London, Hastings, Pevensey, and Rocherfield.[1] The prestige of the abbot of Saint-Denis was so great that when Maginaire died in 797, the abbacy was regarded as a major prize. Charlemagne gave it as a reward to Fardulph (797–806), a Lombard who had uncovered a conspiracy against the king's life.[2] The appointment was especially favorable to the abbey, for Charlemagne's gratitude enabled Fardulph to add to the abbey's revenues and to the church's decoration, which included a new baldachino over the altar. A favorite at court, Fardulph built a palace for Charlemagne at Saint-Denis and honored the emperor's role in the revival of learning by having the seven liberal arts represented in a wall painting.[3] The next abbot, Valton (806–14) is an obscure character. He must have enjoyed cordial relations with Charlemagne, since a legend links their names. The legend relates that ten years after Charlemagne's death a monk had a vision of both Valton and Charlemagne engulfed in flames in purgatory.[4]

Hilduin (814–40), who succeeded Valton, probably belongs in the series of great abbots who headed Saint-Denis. He certainly enhanced the renown of the abbey as much as any other abbot but at the same time was one of the most enigmatic personalities in its long history. Only a few details are known about his life. Supposedly of a noble family, he played an important role in the critical years that followed the brilliant reign of Charlemagne and was closely associated with the court. By 822 Louis the Pious, Charlemagne's son, had made Hilduin his archchaplain.[5] In this position he accompanied Lothaire, one of Louis's sons, to Rome in 824. Evidently captivated by the forceful personality of that particular grandson of Charlemagne, Hilduin became involved in further intrigues against the emperor, who in 830 exiled his archchaplain to the monastery of Corbie in Saxony. This might well have been the end of his career had not one of his disciples, Hincmar, later archbishop of Reims, pleaded so successfully for Hilduin at court that in the following year he was restored to favor. He regained the royal confidence to such a degree that in 834, after another revolt of Louis's sons had failed, the emperor chose Saint-Denis as the place for the unusual ceremony of his recrowning.[6] After the death of Louis the Pious in 840, Hilduin evidently left Saint-Denis because of his disloyalty to Charles the Bald and became archchancellor for Lothaire and archbishop of Cologne as well as abbot of the monastery at Bobbio in Italy. In 844 he was sent with a delegation to Constantinople. He died on 22 November, sometime between 855 and 859.[7]

Critical studies of Hilduin's writings have suggested that he had vast ambitions both for himself and for his abbey. He was the earliest writer to identify Saint Denis with Dionysius the Pseudo-Areopagite. As royal archchaplain Hilduin must have been present in Paris at a council held in 825.[8] Surprisingly, this council staunchly supported the Byzantine as opposed to the Roman point of view in the famous iconoclastic controversy concerning the worship of images. In 827, possibly prompted by that action, the Byzantine emperor Michael the Stammerer sent rich gifts to Louis the Pious in 827, among them a Greek manuscript containing writings by the Pseudo-Areopagite. Those texts were immediately deposited at Saint-Denis in Hilduin's care. At Louis' command and with the help of his learned monks, Hilduin made a rough translation between 832 and 835.[9] This translation was kept in the abbey's archives, and the Pseudo-Areopagite's works remained obscure until on orders from Charles the Bald they were translated by John the Scot in 858.[10] Hilduin's other writings, or those that he supervised, such as the *Post Beatam ac Salutiferam* (known as the *Areopagitica,* the first manuscript to identify the Pseudo-Areopagite as Saint Denis of Paris), the *Miracula Sancti Dionysii,* and the *Gesta Dagoberti Regis*, spread throughout western Europe the renown of Saint Denis and of the royal abbey dedicated to him.[11] Numerous passages in these texts have been cited to prove that Hilduin was an archpolitician. Max Buchner, for example, claimed that Hilduin envisaged himself as vice-pope, with Saint-Denis, a second Rome, as his seat,[12] but even though such grandiose schemes may have been his boast, their realization remained remote. In fact, independence from the bishop of Paris remained one of the abbey's constant objectives, and for that reason ties between Saint-Denis and Rome were favored, as they had been under Fulrad.

Conditions in the monastery remained unsettled. By 825 the secular clergy, those who abstained from monastic vows, and the regular clergy came into open conflict. The monks faithful to their vows left the abbey, and even Benedict of Aniane and Arnoul, who had been appointed to carry out a reform in 829, were so influenced by the secular clergy that their mission failed. A Council held in 829 instituted a proper monastic regime, but during Hilduin's exile in 830, the secular element revolted, and before the reform could be considered even partially successful, a second synod was necessary in 832.[13]

Hilduin's Chapel

During these seemingly troubled years Hilduin, possibly to commemorate his return to favor after exile, built a chapel as an addition to the eastern end of Fulrad's church. Although not a major construction, this partially subter- Fig. 35 ranean chapel had several special features characteristic of Carolingian architecture. Since the detailed analysis of its history and archaeological evidence published in my 1942 volume is not readily available to many today,[14] I will provide a summary of the earlier conclusions and emphasize why I consider them to be more accurate than the reconstruction of the plan proposed by Jules Formigé, then summarized by May Vieillard-Troïekouroff in a somewhat garbled manner.[15]

While Hilduin was abbot, a charter of Louis the Pious dated 833 and an undated letter of Hilduin, plus, in 832, a record of the allocation of certain revenues for the upkeep of a chapel are the only contemporary documents pertinent to the building and dedication on 1 November 832 (?) of a new chapel. Both the letter and the charter state that this *ecclesiam* or *criptam* was *ante pedes,* against the feet of the martyrs, which means to the east of the apse of Fulrad's church.[16] Two other written references—an eleventh-century description of the precautions taken to protect the relics kept there,[17] and Suger's mention of changes to the levels of the early vaults when he was building his new chevet[18]—complete the written evidence. The documenting information hardly suffices for any reconstruction of that structure.[19]

Early attempts to reconstruct the plan of Hilduin's chapel based on interpretations of the texts, analyses of the surviving masonry in the present crypt, and allowances for the space occupied by the new altars cited in the texts has had varied results, including a proposal of a completely detached or separate construction.[20] My plan and elevation are based on a carefully Pl. 3C; Album no. 15 measured new plan of the entire crypt and on excavations in the ambulatory around the central "caveau royal." These indicate that the chapel had a central chapel flanked by parallel rooms, with the entire tripartite structure aligned about 5 degrees toward the north off the axis of Fulrad's church. Probably of one story only,[21] the structure provided for the protection and veneration of the sacred relics in a novel manner.[22]

With regard to the deviation of the axis of the side walls, the photogrammetric study of the twelfth-century vaults in the crypt has verified my earlier plan of the crypt, which was one of the first projects undertaken in my study of Saint-Denis.[23] As aligned, all four parallel walls on an axis different from the major axis of the eighth-century building and from Suger's twelfth-

century constructions belong to a single building campaign. Since Suger's masons made a determined effort to correct that deviation in order to give the twelfth-century church the same axis as the earliest churches on this site, the four parallel walls must reflect the orientation of a pre-twelfth-century structure, namely, Hilduin's chapel. In my 1942 volume I assumed that the masonry backing the blind arcades with figured capitals "had long been recognized" as dating from the ninth century.[24] Although I still believe that the walls with the twelfth-century arcading perpetuate the orientation of Hilduin's chapel, I realize that to a large extent the masonry has been repaired or replaced, and the surfaces should not be considered typical ninth-century construction.

The foundations under these four parallel walls are difficult to describe. As explained in my 1942 volume, the solid clay subsoil varies in depth and in degree of saturation.[25] This terrain borders the small river Croult, which today runs in a conduit along the southern flank of the abbey church. Possibly because at one time the area was very marshy,[26] the depth of the foundations for Hilduin's chapel varies from 0.45 m to 1.15 m with differences in construction as well. The stones resemble undressed fieldstones of different sizes and shapes. These occur particularly in the foundations on the south

35. Crypt, north ambulatory looking west, showing probable remains of Hilduin's chapel.

Fig. 36

Fig. 37

36. North ambulatory of crypt, taken from north. Exterior wall of central chamber of Hilduin's chapel.

side (crypt excavations 11 and 13 in my 1942 volume), where there is often only one bed of stones. At the western end of the north side, however (crypt excavation 3), the stones seem to have been chosen and assembled with some care. There six or seven roughly aligned horizontal beds can be distinguished. The stones at the eastern end of the northern side are more rectangular, the result of some deliberate shaping especially noticeable in the flat terminal wall that projects to the south. No similar masonry was found on the south side because of the solid rubble mat that covers the area. My reconstruction of the plan assumes a similar flat enclosing wall.

Suger described the crowds reaching to touch the relics of the Passion in Hilduin's chapel. They pressed so hard that the monks showing the relics had to flee through the windows.[27] Suger's text provides proof that there were windows in the lateral or north and south walls large enough for a man to jump through. Probably the eastern terminal walls also had window openings onto the exterior. Suger's reference to vaults of different heights in the eastern end of Fulrad's church and in the crypt joined to it implies that Hilduin's chapel was vaulted.[28]

Formigé excavated and restored the crypt extensively during the 1950s. Because his reconstruction of the plan of Hilduin's chapel differs from mine and conflicts with existing archaeological evidence, some attention must be given to his comments.[29] With respect to the chapel, his interpretations of his own excavations as well as of existing masonry and early texts present problems. He justified the removal of Viollet-le-Duc's enclosure of the eastern end of the caveau royal by characterizing Viollet-le-Duc's apse as an obvious addition or restoration which altered the original disposition and needed correction. Formigé's "corrections" were intended to return the central por-

Fig. 38

Fig. 39

37. (*above, left*) Crypt. South ambulatory showing excavation along south wall.

38. (*above*) Detail of foundations of Hilduin's ninth-century chapel, ambulatory, north wall, west end.

39. (*left*) Overall view of first excavation opened in 1938 in north ambulatory of crypt, showing ninth-century foundations.

tions of the crypt to their "original" form, which has no relation to any previous moment in the architectural history of the crypt. The caveau royal, the central chamber of the present crypt, had been the central chapel of Hilduin's addition. It was separated from the side chapels by continuous walls, much as we see them today, but the eastern end until recently was always closed off from the rest of the crypt. Now it is completely open, with an extended vault and arches improvised to join the twelfth-century construction of the hemicycle piers. On both sides the blind arcades with historiated capitals added to the walls in the twelfth century were also extended to the east by two arches supported by capitals taken from other parts of the crypt.[30]

When Formigé removed Viollet-le-Duc's apse, he also excavated the eastern end of the caveau royal, an excavation that remained open for inspection until recently. Formigé believed he had discovered the "base of its [Hilduin's chapel] semicircular apse, 4.10 m in its outer diameter. Its appearance was that of a flat horizontal mass, of which the exterior surface was covered with a smooth plaster."[31] This curving horizontal mass seemed convincing, until I tried to analyze the foundations exposed under the eastern ends of the chapel walls. Then I discovered that the entire mass was solid clay, as were the "two walls at right angles."[32] I could not discover any trace of the "smooth plaster"

Fig. 40

40. Excavation of eastern end of central chapel in crypt as left by Formigé.

or of any mortar. In my opinion, the rounded mass of clay was left by Suger's workmen in the twelfth century as they prepared the foundations for the semicircular ring of cylindrical piers of the hemicycle of Suger's crypt just to the east of the caveau royal. The clay subsoil under the entire church is not easy to remove so that only the ditch required for the new foundations was excavated in the twelfth century. Any masonry footing for the ninth-century eastern end of Hilduin's chapel would have disappeared at that time. With the recent repaving, this area at the eastern end of the caveau royal can no longer be examined.

Confusion arises from Formigé's statements that the pavement of Hilduin's chapel was 0.45 m below the twelfth- and thirteenth-century pavement,[33] that the ninth-century chapel was a little wider than the present one, and that the ninth-century walls were completely torn down, "rasés,"[34] since he labeled photographs of the interior of the caveau royal, as it is today, as the interior of Hilduin's chapel.[35] Formigé also misinterpreted Haymo's eleventh-century description of how the relics were protected.[36] The pertinent passage in that text reads, in rough translation: "Before arriving in the crypt behind the altar where (Dagobert) had the bodies of the Saints placed so deeply that one had to crawl up to the knees [usque ad genua omnino se intromittat] if anything was to be taken out, there was the small crypt [criptula], whose exterior was decorated with gold and gems [aureis gemmis],[37] which was protected by two strong locks [duabus seris diligenter], which has been built to keep the Nail and the Crown."[38] Formigé evidently ignored the distinction between the relics of the saints (reportedly put in place by Dagobert) and the relics of the Passion (supposedly given to Saint Denis by Charles the Bald) and also failed to realize that they were kept behind different altars. The saints' relics were in the annular crypt, or "confessio," behind the main altar in Fulrad's church. The relics of the Passion were in Hilduin's chapel to the east of the annular crypt.[39]

With this interpretation, the procedure for reaching the martyrs' relics as outlined in Haymo's *Descriptio* becomes understandable. The three parallel chambers in Hilduin's chapel encased the eighth-century apse so that the exterior north and south walls met the eastern wall of the eighth-century transept. This made it possible to enter the chapel directly from the church by stairs descending from the transept level in much the same way that one reaches the crypt today by means of stairs flanking the main altar to the north and south. At the west the central portion of the caveau royal is now open, permitting circulation from north to south through two wide arches, which, I believe, prior to the twelfth century were closed by doors. The two strong locks or bolts mentioned in Haymo's description would have fastened those doors. After unlocking and opening a door, one entered into the central chapel, dedicated to the Virgin, where the relics of the Passion were kept. Saint Denis' relics, in the *confessio* of the annular crypt, were to the west, visible only through the small opening into which one had to crawl in order to reach the reliquaries. "Ecce quomodo corpus sancti Dionysii munitum, nulla adimi possit arte latronum" (this was how the body of Saint Denis was protected).[40]

As an adjunct to the main building, Hilduin's chapel belongs to a series of similar structures dating from the eighth through the twelfth centuries.[41] Not unlike the eighth-century annular crypt, those additions had their origin in funerary structures designed to provide a burial place for illustrious Christians as close as possible to the tomb of a saint or martyr. A typical example of such a building, the mausoleum of the Probi, added to the west of the apse of Saint Peter's in Rome during the fourth century, is almost identical in the outline of the plan to that of Hilduin's chapel.[42] A number of small burial chambers were erected to the east of churches in Gaul from the seventh through the ninth centuries, among them Sainte-Croix of Chelles, 658; Saint-Etienne of Saint-Amand, 677; Jouarre, seventh century; Saint-Martin of Autun and the cathedral of Châlons-sur-Marne, both late in the ninth century.[43]

In the ninth century, in direct response to the growing cult of relics, a series of similar small additions were built to serve a different purpose, that of an oratory, or chapel. This concept lay behind the enlargement of Saint Ludger's crypt at Werden, about 830, and the addition to the already enlarged choir of Saint-Philbert of Grandlieu, built by the Abbot Hilbod after 847.[44] Although the addition at Saint-Philbert of Grandlieu, with its separate chapels and its circulatory passageway, has often been regarded as the earliest appearance of this type of plan, it is now evident that Hilduin's chapel at Saint-

Denis had the same characteristics and antedated Saint-Philbert by several years. Since Hilduin's chapel contained altars, it may have functioned as an oratory. But the primary purpose of that addition at Saint-Denis was to provide both protection for a number of relics and a place for their veneration that would not inconvenience or disrupt the offices of the monks in the upper, or main, church. Similar structures which added space without great expense or alteration to the church are found in a number of later churches in the Rhine Valley and in the Low Countries. Saint-Emmeram of Regensberg, Essen, Saint-Riquier, Corvey, Shaffhausen, Süsteren, Stavelot, Saint-Bartholemy of Liège, Saint-Hubert, and Malmédy all have these chapels "en hors d'oeuvre."[45]

Hilduin's chapel at Saint-Denis has significance not only as one of the earliest built, but also because its plan may have had its origin in eastern Christian architecture; the chapel belongs to a particular type of building known as the "ecclesia triplex," or triple church. The concept of symbolizing the individual yet indivisible character of the Trinity by visible means appeared in western Europe no later than the eighth century. Signifying the Trinity, a triple altar on a single base was consecrated in 782 at the monastery of Aniane. Another existed by 796 at Monte Cassino.[46] About 799 at Centula three different churches, or chapels, were interpreted in the same manner. At Lorsch there is definite mention of an ecclesia triplex before 837.[47] No identity of plan or arrangement exists between the examples just cited, but Jurgis Baltrušaitis has shown that such a definite plan existed, particularly in Asia Minor, as early as the sixth century.[48] The outstanding features of these eastern plans were the three parallel chapels, separated from each other by continuous walls. This same peculiarity occurs in Hilduin's chapel at Saint-Denis, although no text specifically refers to the chapel as a triple one. In this connection it is interesting to note that Saint Benedict of Aniane was instrumental in promoting the concept of the Trinity as a basic tenet, and that he was at Saint-Denis just before Hilduin built his chapel.[49]

It is also possible to associate this type of plan with the so-called Benedictine plan, an arrangement distinguished by a series of parallel chapels grouped in echelon formation on each side of the choir. The form was particularly popular in the eleventh century, although all of its elements appeared soon after the middle of the tenth century in the second church at Cluny.[50] At Cluny and in the later examples in Normandy, continuous walls separate the chapels, just as in Hilduin's chapel at Saint-Denis more than a century earlier.

Haymo's description of the plan written in the eleventh century allows another insight into the use of Hilduin's crypt. On certain days when the monks could supervise those who came to worship the relics, the two doors with strong locks at the western end of the 832 chapel (where it joined the eighth-century apse) could be opened, allowing the faithful to circulate from one side of the crypt to the other to venerate both the martyrs' relics through a small opening into the *confessio* to the west, and the nail and crown of thorns kept in the central chamber of Hilduin's chapel to the east. In this way the basic functions of the ambulatory around the chevets of Romanesque churches and their Gothic cathedrals were anticipated by that small crypt added in the ninth century to Fulrad's church at Saint-Denis.

The Royal Abbey and the Norman Invasions

Hilduin's successor, Louis (840–67), was Saint-Denis' first abbot of royal lineage. He was a grandson of Charlemagne and cousin of Charles the Bald. Little is known about Abbot Louis, but apparently he maintained cordial relations with both Charles the Bald and Lothaire and administered the vast domains of the abbey successfully.[51] When Louis died in 867, Charles the Bald retained the title of abbot of Saint-Denis for himself.[52] This move might be interpreted as the climax of monastic diplomacy in that the abbey became a royal abbey in fact. But, as far as we can discern, the move suggests royal expediency, since it put the supervision of the important resources of the abbey directly under the control of the king's officers. Other rich monasteries were also brought under royal control by the same device; Saint-Denis was therefore not the only royal abbey in the latter part of the ninth century. In reality this action threatened to have serious consequences. For a time it became customary for the kings to hold their plenary court at the abbey four times a year. Possibly an honor, the event also inevitably provided an occasion for dissipation on the part of the monks and placed a great financial burden on the abbey. It has even been suggested that Saint-Denis ran the risk of losing its independent status and of sinking to the level of a royal fisc.[53]

These years were also troubled ones for France; the almost annual appearance of bands of Norman raiders constituted a new and foreign menace. Saint-Denis did not escape the terrors of the Norman invasions.[54] In 841 Hilduin was forced to flee from Saint-Denis to Ferrières carrying with him the holy relics and as much of the abbey's treasures as possible. Because Charles the Bald was at Saint-Denis with his army and was forced to buy off the Danes, the devastating invasion of 845 left Saint-Denis unharmed.[55] Similarly in 857 the monks turned over a considerable sum of money to the invaders to forestall any pillaging.[56] The next year, however, Abbot Louis was captured, and the monks were forced to pay a large ransom for his release.[57] In 859 the relics were moved to Nogent-sur-Seine for protection; and the king gave the abbey land at Marnay as a retreat.[58] The location of Saint-Denis on the banks of the Seine was not very favorable at that time, since the rivers were arteries that allowed the Normans to penetrate deep into the country; yet an attack near Paris in 861 did not disturb the monastery.[59] Then, on 20 October 865 the Normans arrived before the abbey and during a siege of twenty days they pillaged the church and eventually carried off everything movable.[60] The church, curiously enough, suffered no damage at that time.[61] In 869, at the command of Charles the Bald, the abbey was fortified by an encircling wall,[62] deemed sufficient protection at that time; but in 876 the Normans reappeared, and the monks fled to Concevreux. Once again the abbey was miraculously left untouched.[63] During the great siege of Paris in 885, the monks retired to Reims with their relics and all that remained of their treasure.[64] As befitted a powerful, feudal seigneur, their abbot, Ebles of Saint-Denis (d. 893), was actively engaged in protecting Paris, where he was one of the principal commanders. Directing and taking part in the fighting, he remained in the city even though a pestilence forced the other nobles to seek safety elsewhere. When King Eudes [888–98] arrived with his troops, it was Ebles who led a party to clear the way for their entrance into the city.[65]

However dismal the events afflicting the abbey during the second half of the ninth century, doubtless the monks exaggerated their sufferings. The abbey buildings apparently escaped serious damage, and evidence suggests that the monks continued their normal existence and enjoyed a period of unusual prosperity. There exist a number of richly illuminated manuscripts, sumptuously decorated book covers, and altarpieces possibly produced at Saint-Denis between 865 and 880, yet some uncertainty remains as to whether those magnificent works of art were created in the abbey's workshops.

Scholars agree that a stylistic affinity links the decoration of the Evangeliary of Charles the Bald, known as the Codex Aureus of Saint-Emmeram (Munich, Bayerische Staatsbibliothek, Clm. 14000), the Psalter of Charles the Bald (Paris, Bib. Nat. ms. lat. 1152), the Bible of Saint Paul's-Outside-the-Walls (Rome, Abbazia di San Paolo f.l.m.), and the Sacramentary of Metz (Paris, Bib. Nat. ms. lat. 1141). On a similar basis the golden covers of the Ashburnham Gospel and of the Codex Aureus and the ivory cover of the Pericope of Henry II attributed to Luithard, as well as the large golden altar retable given by Charles the Bald to Saint-Denis and even the unusual reliquary known as the "Ecrin de Charlemagne," are attributed to the same workshop. But final proof of their manufacture at Saint-Denis is lacking, and scholars prefer to avoid specific attribution by referring to the Saint-Denis Reims style, or the Corbie Saint-Denis style, or the Palace School of Charles the Bald.[66] In spite of the considerable, often bitter discussion, the arguments of A. M. Friend, who first proposed the provenance of Saint-Denis, have yet to be contradicted in their entirety.[67] Founding his reasoning on the close relations between Charles the Bald and Saint-Denis, on specific references to the abbey in the liturgies of some of the manuscripts, and on iconographical peculiarity pointing strongly to the writings of Dionysius the Pseudo-Areopagite, Friend argued soundly and more persuasively than did other scholars in their negative rebuttals. Only a chance discovery will solve this riddle; and if I admit a certain bias in the matter, the reader should not be surprised. Wherever these sumptuous works of art were produced, certainly considerable energy and major resources were devoted to their creation. Although at times overrich in its borrowings from earlier Carolingian centers and admittedly florid in its effect, the style as an eclectic summation of Carolingian art was destined to influence eleventh- and twelfth-century art in England and Germany as well as in France.

Little remains to be said about the abbey during the last years of the direct Carolingian rulers. Charles the Bald was always numbered among the principal benefactors of Saint-Denis. In addition to the superb gold retable for the

Fig. 12

high altar, which remained in the church until the French revolutionaries melted it down, the emperor's largesse included a large, richly decorated cross located between his tomb and the Trinity Altar and seven lamps, or candelabra, that were placed in front of the same altar. All of these treasures survived the depredations of the Normans and must have lent great splendor to the choir.

After the death of Charles the Bald in 877, the abbacy of Saint-Denis was retained as a benefice by powerful nobles or by the kings themselves. Goslin (878–87), grand chancellor and cousin of the king, succeeded Charles the Bald. The valiant, warlike Ebles succeeded Goslin; and at the very end of the century Eudes, count of Paris and king of France, retained the title of abbot.

Governed in the Carolingian period by such outstanding and interesting men as Fulrad and Hilduin, and finally associated directly with the monarchy, the abbey acquired new lands; its prestige was greatly enhanced; and its church was rebuilt and richly decorated. For a time the monks were able to secure enough tranquillity to devote themselves to intellectual and artistic endeavors, but the abbey could not have profited by the confusion at the end of the century, when the last vestiges of Charlemagne's empire were disappearing and the fearful threat of the Norman raiders continued unabated. For the next two centuries the monks were preoccupied with attempts to reestablish the important position and resources of the abbey. Not until the twelfth century did Saint-Denis once again participate in national affairs and take the lead in defining new modes of artistic expression.

The Tower of William the Conqueror

The chronicle of Saint-Denis during the tenth and eleventh centuries is not brightened by startling occurrences, but punctuated by attempts to regain control over lost domains and to reestablish privileges. The many documents destroyed or lost were carefully replaced by "new copies" which often improved the wording, extended the early grants, and interpreted historical events with a freedom that was more imaginative than accurate.[68]

It is doubtful whether these "forgeries" were effective at first. The anarchy inherent in uncontrolled feudalism encouraged the independence of local seigneurs. During most of the century the abbey could scarcely manage its own affairs. Until 968 it was governed by the kings of France or by the counts of Paris. Even after Hugh Capet relinquished his title of lay abbot and allowed the monks to choose their own superior, affairs within the abbey continued unsettled.

In 994 Hugh Capet appealed to Mayeul, abbot of Cluny, to reform Saint-Denis, but this saintly abbot died en route from Cluny, and the task fell to his successor, Odilon, whose arrival was delayed until October 996. He apparently remained at Saint-Denis for some time and assumed the functions of spiritual abbot, with Robert the Pious as temporal abbot. From 1005 to 1008 Odilon appears to have been sole abbot, and he may have maintained some sort of control over the abbey until his death in 1049, even though the monk Albert had been elected abbot in 1031.

Backed by the authority of the great abbey of Cluny, Odilon's reform successfully established complete monastic rule at Saint-Denis for the first time.[69] Abolishing the division between regular and secular clergy inaugurated a true monastic rule which followed the Benedictine custom at Cluny. No evidence suggests that Cluny attempted to bring Saint-Denis into its large family of dependent priories. This would have been difficult to accomplish because of the long, jealously guarded tradition of independence at Saint-Denis.

In 1049, the monks were faced with a fantastic situation. They learned that the monks of Saint-Emmeram in Regensberg (Ratisbonne), Germany, had discovered the relics of Saint Denis in their monastery. With loud protestations against the German claim, the decision was made to open the reliquary at Saint-Denis as the most effective way to dispute the outrageous claims. Properly proclaimed, the decision included plans to expose publicly the remains of Saint Denis, which still presumably rested in the eighth-century *confessio* under the apse of Fulrad's church. The monk Haymo wrote an account of the ceremony, which took place on 9 June in the same year before a great gathering of nobles, bishops, and abbots. The chronicle describes how upon the opening of the silver casket, the bones of Saint Denis were revealed to all wrapped in a "very old" textile.[70]

Abbot Ivo (1075–94), accused of having obtained his election by bribery, received a reprimand in 1075 from Pope Gregory VII, but subsequently Ivo proved to be an able administrator. During his abbacy a large tower adjoining the church was erected with funds supposedly donated by William the Conqueror. The only mention of this tower occurs in the memoirs of Guibert, abbot of Nogent.[71] He stated that the tower was poorly built and showed signs of weakening even before its completion. The monks feared that the church might be seriously damaged if the tower were to collapse, but when it did the greater mass fell away from the church. To the horror of the spectators, the stones of the collapsing structure buried a passerby. An immediate search in the rubble uncovered the man unhurt, miraculously protected by a vault formed by falling stones. Neither Suger's writings nor any other annals of Saint-Denis refer to this event or mention the tower, and historians of the abbey have given it scant attention. Nothing was known of the plan or location until our excavations of 1946 uncovered some of the masonry under the present north transept where the north side aisle of Fulrad's nave joined the transept.[72] Easily distinguished from the eighth-century construction, that masonry replaces the Carolingian beds for approximately 10.50 m. Because the south side of the tower rests on great libages typical of Carolingian foundations at Saint-Denis, those coursings must postdate Fulrad's church. At the east end the masonry passes beneath the plinth of a base belonging to the transept, and therefore predates Suger's church. The only other known building campaigns at Saint-Denis between the eighth and twelfth centuries involved Hilduin's chapel.

A close examination of the masonry supports its identification with the tower construction. Although regularly cut, the stones lack the precision and finish of the eighth-century masonry; the surface is rougher, and the entire

Fig. 41

construction less solid. Particularly noticeable are triangular stones, placed so that the apex of the triangle projected toward the interior of the wall, presumably composed of rubble, which was either never finished or has disappeared. Remains of two large piers with angular corner setbacks and of two smaller intermediate piers of rectangular shape are easily identified. Between the smaller piers three steps lead down below the level of the Carolingian pavement.[73]

These remains of the tower permit a reconstruction of its plan with a square base of about 10.50 m on a side and with four large piers at the corners and four smaller piers between them. There must have been additional masonry piers in the interior. Although supplementary excavations were made to the north, no other remains of this type of construction were found. Evidently the royal tombs and the important foundations of the thirteenth-century transept destroyed or covered whatever was left of the tower.

Perhaps the most convincing proof that this masonry was part of the ill-fated tower occurs in the southeastern pier. Here cracks have opened. Their edges have been sheared off as if under tremendous pressure—cracks probably caused by the tower's collapse. The evidence establishes the location of William's tower at the northwest angle between the transept and the nave of Fulrad's church. The archaeological interest of this evidence lies in the late eleventh-century date of the structure, its location, and the shape of the piers. For this period there is little comparable masonry in the Ile-de-France, but the piers with their angular setbacks indicate that experiments leading to the articulated, compound pier were made in this region as elsewhere in the eleventh century. By its placement and the plan of its foundations, the tower calls to mind the large square tower of Saint-Hilaire at

41. Excavation in north transept in 1947, showing foundations of eleventh-century tower built with funds reportedly given to Saint-Denis by William the Conqueror.

Pl. 3C; Album no. 16

Poitiers, also located in the northwest angle between the transept and the wall of the north side aisle.[74]

The three steps which lead to a level below the pavement of the eighth-century church suggest that there was a crypt or oratory under the tower.[75] An excavation in 1948 to the west of the tomb of Louis XII, the area once occupied by the tower, disclosed a small vaulted chamber containing one-half of a large stone sarcophagus. The chamber appeared to be relatively recent in its construction, but possibly that portion of the sarcophagus was left there as a marker of some earlier important burial or of an especially venerated spot. The plan of Saint-Denis published by Enselin in 1708 identifies this corner as the chapel of Saint Hippolytus. After the collapse of William's tower the relics of the saint must have disappeared for Suger refers to them in vague terms.[76] Later, during the laying of the foundations for the twelfth-century nave, the relics may have been rediscovered, but not until 1236 were they officially translated to a new chapel on the north side of the new church then under construction. At a subsequent date the relics were moved as close as possible to the location of the eleventh-century tower. The possibility exists that the tower may have been intended to serve as an oratorium for Saint Hippolytus.

The bronze doors reused by Suger as the *valvas antiquas* of the north portal of the west façade may have been used in this tower. An inscription recorded by Pieresc at the beginning of the seventeenth century has been preserved in his notes in the Librairie Inguebertine in Carpentras. According to the Count Blaise de Montesquiou-Fezensac, the "lettres conjointes . . . enclavées . . . entrelacées" must date "toward the end of the second third" of the eleventh century.[77] If they do, then Airardus, who offered the doors to Saint-Denis, was an eleventh-century monk, not the Carolingian master carpenter mentioned in the ninth-century *Miracula*.[78]

Another possible element from the tower came to light during an excavation under the north side aisle which I directed in 1962. We found a stone capital of unusual dimensions and decoration lying loose in the fill just inside the twelfth-century wall that joined Suger's west bays to the old eighth-

Fig. 42

42. Capital found during excavation of north side aisle in 1962, possibly eleventh century, now at Saint-Denis in the Musée Lapidaire.

century nave. Now stored in the Musée Lapidaire, that large capital, 0.42 m in diameter at the base, 0.52 m across at the top, and 0.48 m high, is decorated with two zones of large, slightly projecting, vertically oriented forms with a center ridge. I have sought comparisons with this heavy and rather crudely carved capital in the church of the Abbaye-aux-Hommes at Caen associated with the first campaign in the 1070s.[79] Evidently with William the Conqueror's funds for building the tower came Norman masons to help in its construction.

Proposed but Unverifiable Eleventh-Century Campaigns

A number of scholars have thought that there was additional work at Saint-Denis in the eleventh century, especially in the crypt. Viollet-le-Duc and Léon Maître both believed that the blind arcades with figured capitals decorating the walls of the crypt were added in the eleventh century.[80] Maître even suggested that the rebuilding included an ambulatory around Hilduin's ninth-century chapel to provide access into the chapel from the east. Enlart bolstered the theory by citing an eleventh-century manuscript by Lambert de Saint-Omer which mentions the dedication of a church to Saint-Denis in 1088.[81] Although both Levillain and Lefèvre-Pontalis vigorously denied these theories,[82] Formigé's recent examination of the masonry in the crypt led him to propose extensive alterations and additions to Hilduin's chapel sometime in the eleventh century. Preferring it as a "second," or new, chapel,[83] Formigé included in his plan the parallel walls north and south of the "caveau royal," which I identify as part of Hilduin's ninth-century chapel. He also dated the blind arcades earlier than the figured capitals because of the large abaci, or "sommiers," above the capitals and the irregular arches above them. According to Formigé, the vault of the central chapel "en moellons à joints irréguliers, très grossièrement bâtis" is eleventh, not twelfth century.[84] To the parallel chapels, he added two rooms, one to the north and the other to the south, which he admitted were redone by Suger. Because of the thickness of their walls, he speculated that they were two towers.

Possibly inspired by Formigé's identification of "trois nouvelles chapelles accolées," Thomas Polk, a student of Jan van der Meulen, has claimed that "the evidence suggests that the crypt which Suger inherited had an ambulatory and three chapels; therefore, the irregularities of the chevet of Saint-Denis resulted from compromises caused by the imposition of a Gothic structural system in this freer, earlier, non-Gothic crypt."[85] The "evidence," it is claimed, exists in the masonry of the ambulatory and radiating chapels of the crypt, but this evidence has not been shown to me. My continued examination of the masonry has failed to corroborate either Formigé's or Polk's reconstruction of an eleventh-century crypt.

Finally Formigé wrote of a lengthening of the central chapel at the beginning of the twelfth century before Suger's election to the abbacy.[86] Formigé saw evidence for this work in an extension of the central vault and in some masonry he found under the pavement of the ambulatory to the east of the caveau royal. In both instances there is evidence to the contrary. When

Formigé removed the eastern end of the caveau royal, built by Viollet-le-Duc, the vault above also needed repairs. With pride the head mason in charge of this work showed me how he had extended the central vault to the east and joined it to the masonry over the twelfth-century piers at the hemicycle. I needed the mason's assistance to ascertain the exact juncture between the medieval and the modern vaulting, which is still difficult to see and extends overhead between the seventh capital on the north side and the eighth capital on the south side. He then challenged me to identify the abaci over the capitals which he, himself, had carved and put in place. I correctly guessed that the abacus he had carved was above the westernmost capital in the arcade along the north wall of the caveau royal.

In regard to the masonry under the pavement of the twelfth-century ambulatory, the paving stones over Formigé's excavation had been left unsealed and could be removed. (This excavation was next to the one—crypt excavation 14 in my 1942 volume—which I opened in 1939.)[87] There were four stones in a north–south alignment with the eastern faces carefully finished. In 1977, in order to discover more about this construction, I had the paving stones to the south removed and discovered that the masonry stopped abruptly. A rather large skull in the fill gave evidence that the area had not been disturbed for some time. There was no sign of the southeastern cruciform pier which is shown in the plan entitled "au début du XIIème siècle."

Very little is known about the activities of the abbey at the close of the eleventh century. The monks directed a school at the priory of Saint-Denis-de-l'Estrée, where King Philip I sent his son, Louis, for an education.[88] The monks must also have been active in the scriptorium; besides the famous *Pèlerinage de Charlemagne,* probably composed at the abbey about 1080 which spread the fame of the great Fair of the Lendit, other legends, such as the miracle describing the consecration of Dagobert's church by the hand of Christ, also appear to have been popularized at this time. The prestige of Saint-Denis as a pilgrimage place was heightened by the presence of relics of the Passion—a nail from the cross, a part of the crown of thorns—as well as the arm of Saint Simeon which had supported the Christ-child.

It is generally conceded that the regime of Abbot Adam, Suger's predecessor (1094–1122), was a pleasant but inefficient one. As befitted his position Adam attended many councils and dutifully made certain that the abbey's special privileges were renewed. Suger's reports on the state of the buildings and the domains leave little doubt about Adam's laxness. The comments of Abelard and those of Saint Bernard of Clairvaux, biased it is true, also give a dark picture of the situation. Conditions were ripe for a change, but there is little to indicate that a period of brilliance or affluence for the abbey would follow. We must turn to Suger himself if we are to understand the activities and successes at Saint-Denis in the twelfth century.

PART TWO

SAINT–DENIS, 1122-1151

INTRODUCTION

Background for a Creative Environment:
Abbot Suger and the Ile-de-France

Between 1135 and 1137 Suger, abbot of Saint-Denis, began the rebuilding of the royal abbey church—an undertaking which he said he had wished to do even while a pupil at school, should the opportunity ever arise.[1] Although his death in 1151 interrupted the completion of the new church, the innovations incorporated in the design of the western façade—with its three richly decorated "royal" portals—and in the new choir to the east—"a crown of light" with large stained glass windows and sumptuous liturgical ornaments—introduced the Gothic style to the Christian world. Two questions come to mind as to why this artistic explosion occurred in the Ile-de-France: What factors combined to produce that elusive situation—the creative environment? And to what degree did Suger himself participate in this creation, which beguiled his contemporaries and provided an inexhaustible challenge for succeeding generations? Investigation of these and other questions seems a necessary prelude to an examination of Suger's building.[2]

In his First Proclamation of the Weimar Bauhaus in 1923, Walter Gropius, the German architect, referred to "the grace of heaven" which "in rare moments of inspiration, moments beyond the control of his [an exalted craftsman's] will, may cause his work to blossom into art."[3] We should examine what political, economic, and social as well as intellectual factors encouraged the grace of heaven to smile on the Ile-de-France in the first half of the twelfth century and consider whether this rare moment was a conscious creation or a spontaneous occurrence. Among the multiple factors present were a new sense of security, new social pressures, and new philosophical challenges.

The historian interprets events to recapture the past; but the most optimistic historian cannot interpret the history of the early Capetian rulers of France in terms other than those related to confusion, anarchy, and lack of authority. The eleventh-century descendants of Hugh Capet (987–96)— Robert II the Pious (996–1031), Henri I, and Philippe I (1060–1108)— far from being rulers of France, could hardly claim dominion over their inherited rights. Robert the Pious reportedly arrived at a convocation of his royal vassals in an ox-cart whereas they came well-mounted and accompanied by armed escorts. In order to inspect his lands around Orléans, Philippe I had to be prepared to fight his way along the road leading south from Paris through Etampes, another royal county. Most of the offices that constituted the royal administration were held in hereditary succession by petty feudal nobles prepared at any time to fight the king himself.[4] Moments of royal exertion, vague intellectual stirrings, and the appearance of independent communes in both France and northern Italy capable of governing their own urban centers can be read as indications of future developments. Indeed the eleventh century closed with the almost miraculous mounting of the First Crusade in 1097 by Pope Urban II (1088–99)—the only crusade to attain its goal, the liberation of Jerusalem. Jubilation and pride must have cheered those who stayed behind, even as the victorious nobles preoccupied themselves with establishing personal kingdoms in the Near East. The crusade removed troublesome younger sons from the feudal rivalries in the west and partially opened the Mediterranean after four centuries of domination by Arab and Moslem pirates. Incentives for expanded trade appeared, and the papacy gloried in the triumph.

Events in France were, however, more typical of feudal confusion than of an incipient revival of royal prestige. In 1092 Philippe I of France chose to abandon his legal wife, Berthe, in favor of Bertrade of Monfort, countess of Anjou. Already hostile because of the king's opposition to Pope Gregory VII's reform movement, the clergy showed their indignation by repeated excommunications. Although Philippe ignored those threats, many of his vassals joined the opposition so that the king ended his reign without power. His successor, Louis VI [1108–37], son of Berthe, Philippe's first queen, is credited with reviving royal authority.[5]

On the basis of two brief references in Suger's writings, historians have concluded that the young prince Louis was educated in the monastic school of Saint-Denis-de-l'Estrée, when Suger was also a student there. They were exactly the same age, and this fortuitous common schooling has been interpreted as the beginning of a lifelong friendship, although they were probably together at school for no more than one or two years.[6] Such an attractive assumption also suggests that Suger was an intimate of the royal family, although Queen Bertrade's intense jealousy of the young prince Louis would have made this impossible until after their reconciliation in 1104. The events of his early life, including his attempted murder by Bertrade, his secret knighting at Abbéville, and his early military successes against William Rufus in the Vexin, show that Louis must have been an unusually vigorous young man with great courage and a sense of his own dignity. An avid hunter, an immense eater, and a greedy materialist, Louis had the major endowment in that moment of feudal turmoil of a love of fighting. Animated as much by a passion for personal battle as by the will to assert his royal authority, Louis VI began the consolidation of the royal domains by subduing rebellious or insolent vassals. As a result a new sense of order and personal security developed in the Ile de France, along with a respect and confidence in the king as protector and guarantor of lawful procedure. In the end, exhausted by his many excesses and so corpulent that he could not mount a horse, Louis VI le Gros named his son, Louis, as his successor and before he died arranged for his son's marriage with Eleanor, daughter of Guillaume, duke of Acquitaine. This astute political move augmented the new confidence and pride in the French crown, furthered the alignment of territories, and established the power of the king over most of France.

Louis VII (1137–80) began his reign under most auspicious conditions. The German emperor, Lothaire, had just died without a male successor. Conrad Hohenstaufen, backed by the pope and the clergy, disputed the throne with the duke of Saxony, Lothaire's son-in-law. In England and Normandy, Stephen of Blois disputed Henry I's succession with Henry's daughter, Mathilde, who was married to Geoffrey, count of Anjou. Yet the French king's moment of invincibility lasted only a short time. Quarrels over the succession to the archbishopric of Bourges and the refusal of Thibaut, count of Champagne, to recognize his feudal obligations to the king led to disputes with the pope and the clergy, including Bernard, abbot of Clairvaux (1115–53). During a vigorous campaign against Thibaut, the church of Vitri in Champagne was burned by Louis' men with 1,300 innocent people inside. Louis' chagrin was great. His remorse has been cited as a major cause leading to his organization of the Second Crusade in 1147.

Opposed at first by both clergy and vassals, Louis VII finally persuaded Pope Innocent II (1130–43) to support the crusade. He in turn ordered Bernard to join. This resulted in the abbot's famous exhortation at Vézelay in 1146. On 18 February 1147, a general assembly at Etampes accepted Louis' itinerary for the crusade and elected Abbot Suger and Count Guillaume II of Nevers co-regents of France. In contrast to the miserable failures of the crusaders, Suger maintained order and prosperity in France, so that when Louis VII returned, humiliated as well as alienated from Eleanor, he found the kingdom in good order. Also humiliated by the disgrace to his king, Suger tried to organize a new expedition. Faced by a total lack of enthusiasm as well as papal opposition, Suger finally decided to lead his own force with funds taken from his abbey's resources. Then he contracted a malarial fever during the autumn of 1150 and died on 13 January 1151. By March 1152, the king had divorced Eleanor, who within two months married Henry II Plantagenet, thereby transferring Acquitaine and all of western France to Anglo-Norman control. Louis' kingdom was once more reduced to the royal domains as under Philippe I, and France had to wait for the reign of Philippe

Auguste (1180–1223) to regain its glory. But the decade of the 1130s and the early years of the 1140s had been years of prosperity and security for the Ile de France. They were the years when Suger built the western and eastern ends of his new church.

As for the social and economic conditions, there is sound evidence that an increase in population, if not a population explosion, accompanied by expanding agricultural production, began in western Europe as early as the tenth century and became a major factor in the late eleventh and twelfth centuries. The phenomena of more food, more mouths to feed, and more people to be accommodated all helped to foster the growth of towns and an increase in trade.

Itinerant groups of individual traders braved the almost impassable roads. Bands of brigands incessantly attacked those groups, and every sort of toll or fine was levied. As the Mediterranean opened, new items became available from the East, and feudal barons began to demand unaccustomed luxuries. Seasonal fairs grew in size and became important sources of income; markets stabilized and became permanent features of the rapidly developing towns. In fact, town and market were identical, often with the same name, as in *burg,* which could refer either to a market or to the town in which it was located.[7]

Increasing numbers of artisans and merchants created urban communities, which as they prospered gradually sought independence from ponderous feudal obligations and gained a measure of self-government. This rise of the communes, or communal movement, is one of the most striking phenomena of the late eleventh and early twelfth centuries. The assumption of responsibility for city government by freely elected representatives of an urban community marked the beginning of modern European society.[8]

Astute authorities early realized the potential for direct control of new revenues in these growing economic centers. There was some hesitancy about the possibility of relaxing independent feudal control, but Louis VI granted a number of communal charters to towns in his domains, and Abbot Suger was among the first to experiment with the founding of small new towns, the villeneuves, which became important devices for repopulating devastated areas or uncultivated lands.[9] Such economic and social advances were accompanied by, if not directly related to, intellectual challenges.

There were important schools in the eleventh century, but they were isolated and represented the traditional approach to learning. Chartres, Saint-Benôit-sur-Loire, Bec in Normandy, Laon, and to a growing degree Paris attracted the best minds. The basis of their curriculum was the old system of the *trivium* and the *quadrivium.* The former explored the word by means of the disciplines of grammar, rhetoric and dialectic; the latter consisted of geometry, arithmetic, astronomy, and music.[10] Some of the cathedral schools began to specialize. John of Salisbury (c. 1115–80), for instance, went to Chartres for grammar and rhetoric and to Paris to learn logic and theology, although Laon was also renowned for its concern with theology. A brilliant mind such as his could extract from this basic foundation the ingredients for independent concepts, but his protohumanist insights were rare indeed.[11]

Peter Abelard (1079–1142) has also been identified as a medieval humanist, but one as much concerned with reason, the process of logic, as with Christian devotion. He also represented the new order in that he set himself up as an independent lecturer to whom students flocked from afar. He must have been a vain man, self-confident and self-satisfied, proud of his own abilities and achievements, scornful, abrasive, and overbearing with rivals. Yet his critics feared lest his preoccupation with logic, with the power of men's reasoning as individuals, might give his students and future generations a sense of self-importance and encourage the questioning of dogma.[12] These and other assertions threatened the authority of the Church and led to Abelard's famous condemnation by Bernard of Clairvaux.

Bernard's complex personality presents an exciting challenge to the medieval historian. Devout in the extreme, an orator capable of moving crowds or castigating kings, also much concerned with the expression of human emotion, Bernard by the analogy of divine and human love introduced a different set of values—one dealing more with the assurance of salvation than with the certainty of damnation which had preoccupied previous generations.

Although Suger's junior by ten years, Bernard was elected abbot of Clairvaux in 1115, seven years before Suger became abbot of Saint-Denis. No document establishes any relations between the two men before 1127, when Bernard wrote to Suger to congratulate him enthusiastically on the reform of the monks at Saint-Denis, and on Suger's drastic change in his own deportment.[13] By then they certainly knew each other, at least by sight, for Bernard wrote that "the only thing that disturbed me was that attire of yours and your equipage when you went about, because it appeared a bit too excessive."[14] Blasting conditions that had existed in the abbey, Bernard wrote that the community gave more easily to Caesar what was Caesar's due than to God and described the cloister as filled with soldiers and businessmen, the halls as resounding with quarrels and even worse, for women were not strictly denied access. Bernard wondered how the monks in that "synagogue of Satan," that "forge of Vulcan," could have thought godly thoughts.[15] Yet he admitted that his description of the cloister of Saint-Denis was based on hearsay, not on what he himself had seen. Characteristically, Suger made no public response, for in 1127 he had undertaken a serious reform of the monastery and of his own conduct. Twelve of Bernard's letters to Suger exist—seven, perhaps eight of them dated after 1148, when Suger was regent of France—but only two letters to Bernard from Suger are known, the second written at the very end of Suger's life.[16]

These two men, both abbots of monasteries, represent two opposite poles in temperament and in feudal society. Bernard, born of noble parents—his father, Tecelin, was a knight killed during the First Crusade—divested himself of his worldly goods to espouse ascetic self-denial in a Cistercian cloister. Suger, of humble origins, embraced the church as a way to salvation and, suspicious of extremes, approached the conduct of human affairs with prudence and moderation. Bernard's weapons were his pen and his persuasive oratory. Suger, however, took up his pen to record the events of his time and loved to tell stories to his monks late at night about his travels and the great men he had heard about or seen.[17] Although a man of action who supported his king against threat of invasion, Suger sought conversion by reason rather than by the sword and reconciliation by mediation rather than by violence. Thundering against the excesses of Cluniac art, Bernard ordered that Cistercian buildings be devoid of ornament that might distract the mind from the contemplation of the City of God.[18] Suger conceived of the church as a heavenly Jerusalem built in this world for Christian people. As a metaphor for the Holy City, the church should be adorned with bright, precious materials to the honor and glory of God and of his saints.

My understanding of Suger's church does not agree with that of Arthur Kingsley Porter, who commented that Cistercian austerity looms powerfully in the new style,[19] nor with that of Otto von Simson, who observed that "the art of Saint-Denis may reflect Bernard's ideas,"[20] but instead follows closely from Suger's own philosophy and the aesthetic rationale that guided him in building and decorating the new church. Each historian of Saint-Denis must evaluate the extent to which Abelard and Bernard influenced Suger's thought. Other philosophical currents such as Hugh of Saint-Victor's mysticism and Rupert of Deutz's complicated treatises must also be taken into account if one is to understand the intellectual milieu of the 1130s and 1140s.[21]

Any discussion of Suger as abbot and patron requires a brief overview of the artistic situation in France in the late eleventh and early twelfth centuries in order to provide perspective on Suger's innovations. Romanesque art dominated western Europe in the eleventh and first half of the twelfth centuries; in fact, it reached its climax in the 1120s and 1130s, when early Gothic concepts suddenly intruded upon the Romanesque idiom. Romanesque was nurtured in monasteries and flourished there. Conceived, at times executed, by the monks themselves, it reflected and to a large extent defined the monastic spirit. Massive mural structures covered by fireproof stone barrel vaults and illuminated by small windows provided sanctuary to those who sought protection from a savage world. The monastery was, and still is, a retreat offering security, encouraging reflection, and presenting a way to salvation. To the extent that monasteries were isolated, self-sufficient communities, Romanesque art was rural and regional.

Entrances to a retreat for those in search of redemption, the sculptured portals of churches concentrated on the end of the world, the Last Judgment, and the ever-present temptations of the flesh. Alongside biblical scenes and events from the lives of saints, capitals in church and cloister pictured a world inhabited by demons—a world of fantasy redolent with constant threats of damnation and weird, satanic creatures. But this imagery appeared in an architectural environment of rigidly defined, functional spaces. Perhaps rules and principles lay behind the ornamental or decorative forms which accented the architectural frames. Many formulae, inherited from a barbarian past or borrowed from Near Eastern artifacts, ordered and controlled abstract, vegetal designs as well as those devoted to queer combinations of animal and human forms.[22] Normal proportions, relative sizes, appropriate scale, and three-dimensional space were of no concern to these artists. Without those preoccupations artists developed abstract, ornamental relationships which ordered the fantasy of "epics of chaos," as Henri Focillon described them.[23]

Fulminating against the luxury of Cluniac churches and cloisters, Bernard of Clairvaux defined this to him unnecessary décor as "deformis formositas ac formosa deformitas" (misshapen shapeliness, shapely misshapenness)."[24]

This was a world controlled by the great mother church at Cluny, which reformed, or acquired, local monasteries along its routes of communication throughout France, northern Spain, Italy, and Britain. Cluny emphasized activities of the mind but did not impose a rigid aesthetic. On the contrary, individual monasteries were encouraged to develop their own idioms, so that Romanesque art has traditionally been studied as a series of regional styles, each with distinctive variations. A student can quickly learn to distinguish between the Romanesque of Normandy and that of Burgundy, to recognize the Roman flavor of a Provençal façade or the exuberant ornament of a Poitevin church, yet will find it difficult to isolate a Romanesque style in the Ile-de-France.[25]

In summary, Suger grew up in a rapidly changing world in which increasing royal authority encouraged a sense of security and growing trade and commerce brought activity to markets in expanding towns. A rural environment focused more and more on independently governed urban communities. Man was challenged to discover and develop his individual powers of reasoning and received increased assurance that love and understanding might lead him to salvation. Under these circumstances the fears and fantasies of the Romanesque world gave way to a new confidence, and new ways were found to express man's faith in the Christian universe.

Few men have participated more vigorously in the affairs and destinies of their generation than Suger while he was abbot of Saint-Denis from 1122 to 1151. He was, in fact, so closely associated with the events of his time that often we find it difficult to assess the extent of his participation. Certain of his ideas were sufficiently novel that years passed before they were thoroughly understood or exploited. Suger's life, from his humble origins to his renown as "father of his country," shines perhaps with less brilliance because Suger, above everything else, "excelled by being a human."[26] Today Suger lives in his writings, of which a large number have survived,[27] as well as in the stone, stained glass, and metalwork of the church at Saint-Denis, whose construction he directed. The existing portions of his new church and their decoration reveal the extraordinary force of his creative genius. After eight centuries, such rich documentation for a single person is indeed exceptional. Certainly in that monument many passages now blurred by time seem difficult to interpret, but the images they evoke remain astonishingly vivid and precise.

Much has been written about Suger. Few historians of France fail to mention him. In 1780 the Académie Française announced a competition for the best eulogy in his memory. Twelve volumes were printed in response.[28] Although few of them contained any critical analysis, some were imaginative, some amusing. During the nineteenth century serious studies began to appear,[29] and Suger continues to fascinate medieval scholars.[30]

The history of his early years shows that he was destined by fortune, by personal charm, and by special talents to play an active role in his times. Born in 1081 either in Argenteuil or in Saint-Denis itself of obscure parents (about his father, only the name Helindanus is known), Suger entered the abbey as

an oblate in 1091 when he was ten.[31] The custom of giving or vowing a child
to a monastery was a device available to humble people burdened with too
many children or desirous of providing a son with access to an education and
a career. By Suger's own account, he was a student at Saint-Denis for more
than ten years.[32] That must have been the time when, frequenting the
archives and the library, he read widely and studied the charters and other
documents relating to the abbey's possessions and privileges. The knowledge
proved invaluable in later years. By the time Suger was twenty-five, his
unusual talents were recognized, and he began his public life as a representa-
tive of Adam, abbot of Saint-Denis, at the Council of Poitiers in 1106.[33] A
year later he was present at the consecration of La Charité-sur-Loire by Pope
Paschal II. There he took advantage of the meeting to plead successfully the
cause of the abbey in its recurrent struggle for independence from the bishop
of Paris.[34] Later that spring he accompanied Abbot Adam to the stormy
meeting between the pope and the German emperor, Henry V, at Châlons-
sur-Marne.[35] From this time on he repeatedly attended councils or undertook special missions either for his abbey or for his king.[36]

As early as 1107 Suger was also given an opportunity to display his
abilities as an administrator. Appointed deputy for the abbey's priory of
Berneval in Normandy, he was able within two years to reorganize this
small, abandoned domain so that it was capable of contributing annually to
the abbey's revenues.[37] That success prompted Abbot Adam to give Suger
the more difficult assignment in 1109 of deputy to Toury-en-Beauce. This
prized territory on the road from Paris to Orléans had been menaced for
many years by the lords of Puiset, who seized merchants for ransom, destroyed crops and plundered or killed the inhabitants. The local authorities
were cowed by the fierce attitude of Hugues de Puiset; but Suger determined
to rid the country of this typically brazen feudal lord. To settle this issue
Suger led soldiers, and this was not the only time he took an active part in the
conduct of warfare.[38] He also proved astute in striking at the core of feudal
unrest by encouraging the young king to assert his royal authority at the
beginning of his reign.

During the winter of 1122, while returning from a royal mission to Pope
Calixtus II at Bitonto in southern Italy, Suger learned of Abbot Adam's death
and of his own election to the abbacy of Saint-Denis.[39] Quoting Ps. 112:7,
Suger wrote that he had been "elevated from his dung heap to sit among
princes."[40] As abbot of Saint-Denis Suger often sat among princes, and
oscillating between two poles, the temporal and the monastic, his life became
divided between the activities of court and cloister.

Immediately after his election as abbot on 12 March 1122, Suger had to face a
difficult situation involving Peter Abelard. After his humiliating mutilation
in Paris in 1119, Abelard, seeking refuge at Saint-Denis, entered the monastery as a monk under Abbot Adam. The life of a monk hardly suited
Abelard. In his autobiography, the *Historia Calamitatum,* he referred to
Adam as a man "as much the more corrupt of habits and renowned for
infamy as he was the others' superior by his prelacy."[41] While enjoying the
hospitality of the abbey, Abelard soon gave offense by questioning the identi-

fication of Saint Denis with the first-century Dionysius who had heard Saint
Paul preaching on the Areopagus in Athens and been converted [Acts 17:34].
Abelard, citing a passage he discovered in the writings of the Venerable Bede,
announced that Saint Denis, the first bishop of Paris, was not the same
Dionysius converted by Saint Paul, but rather Dionysius, bishop of Corinth, a
much less illustrious person.[42] As Panofsky has observed, this amounted to
lèse-majeste. Furious, Abbot Adam had Abelard arrested and thrown into
prison, from which he escaped to take refuge in Provins under the protection
of Thibaut, count of Champagne. Adam refused to release Abelard from his
vows and threatened excommunication, but the abbot died shortly thereafter,
leaving his successor, Suger, to settle the affair. Reportedly unsympathetic at
first, Suger soon agreed on the advice of the king's councillor, Etienne de
Garlande, to allow Abelard to retire to a place of his own choosing, but with
the promise that he would remain a monk of Saint-Denis. From then on
Suger apparently ignored the unhappy scholar and took no part in his later
persecutions. Panofsky labeled Suger's actions as "characteristically, of a
strictly official and entirely impersonal nature," and even questioned
whether Suger ever read any of Abelard's writings.[43] Yet since Suger was
always alert to what was happening around him, I can hardly believe that he
was ignorant of Abelard's major arguments. The sculpture of the three
western portals of Suger's new church is evidence of a preoccupation with the
Trinity and other questions raised by Abelard's searching mind.

Although preoccupied with the reorganization of the abbey's properties
and with certain essential repairs to the church and claustral buildings,
Suger, in the first years of his abbacy, made a number of extended trips. In the
two years following his election, he traveled twice to Italy and once to
Mainz.[44] The splendor of his retinue on the road, more appropriate for a
count than an abbot, had drawn the ire of Bernard of Clairvaux. Yet Suger's
tactful attention to the comfort and well-being of the monks at Saint-Denis
enabled him to accomplish the reform of the monastery in 1127 without undue
unrest. He displayed similar tact when faced by opposition to his building
campaign, which necessarily involved the destruction of the old church,
every stone of which was venerated as a sacred relic of the miraculous
consecration by Christ and Saint Denis.

The first twenty-three chapters of Suger's De Administratione record his
improvements to the abbey's domains, whose revenues he often tripled or
quadrupled.[45] Improved management of rundown properties, persistent recovery of ignored or lost rights, and development of unused lands by the
founding of villeneuves produced an annual income of more than 800
silver pounds as well as wine, grain, and wood for the abbey's needs. Three
fairs added another 500 pounds to the revenue, although profits of the
individual fairs cannot be estimated.[46] In calendrical order the first fair, on 24
February, celebrated the consecration of the "old" church. The least important of the three fairs, probably because it was held in midwinter, it probably
lasted no more than a week. No document records its inception, which may
have been in the late ninth century but was probably later.

The Foire du Lendit, or indictum, became the most famous Saint-Denis fair, as we have already noted.[47] Suger regarded it as such, for the charter of 1124, granted by Louis VI after he returned victorious from Reims, included complete control of the Lendit revenues by the abbey. Opening on the second Wednesday after the feast of Saint John in June, the fair lasted from ten to sixteen days. Although scholars dispute the date and cause of its origin, no document mentions the Foire du Lendit before the eleventh century. The name itself relates the fair to the announcement of the beginning of a religious event, or feast. Such an event occurred on 9 June 1053, when the reliquaries of Saint-Denis and his companions were opened to refute the claims of the monks of Saint-Emmeran, Regensberg, that they held the real relics. Also involved were the relics of the Passion, described before the end of the eleventh century as being a gift to Saint-Denis by Charles the Bald. The Lendit prospered in the early twelfth century to such an extent that Suger, who had no part in its foundation or early expansion, took pains to see that the abbey received all of its revenues.

Instituted by Dagobert and therefore the oldest, the third fair, the Foire de la Saint-Denis, celebrated the feast of Saint Denis on 9 October.[48] The fair lasted seven weeks until the feast of Saint Andrew and consequently was the longest of all of the fairs and presumably equally profitable. Suger's failure to mention this fair in any of his writings has minimized its importance in the literature, but his omission is characteristic. He seemed to take for granted many customs of long standing that involved no new action and passed over them in his writings. Yet confirmation of the charter of 5 December 1118 in 1122, almost immediately after his election as abbot, shows Suger was not negligent.[49] As early as the seventh century the danger of civil wars had forced the monks to move the site of the fair to the gates of Paris near Saint-Martin-des-Champs. In this way the fairs of Saint-Denis extended outside of the abbey, probably long before the founding of the Lendit.

In addition to the revenue from the abbey's domains and from the three fairs, Suger devised special privileges and occasions to raise funds for his new church. In 1125, on 15 March he offered freedom from the onerous tax of *mortuum manum* to the inhabitants of Saint-Denis in return for the payment of two hundred pounds.[50] This sum, destined for the *renovandum et decorandum* of the entrance to the monastery, seems precise but remains difficult to interpret.

The manner in which Suger obtained precious gems to embellish the golden altar frontal seems characteristic of his ingenuity. He recalled how, when "following our example," kings, princes, and many outstanding men "took the rings off the fingers of their hands and ordered, out of love for the Holy Martyrs, that the gold, stones, and precious pearls of the rings be put" into the front panel of the new altar dedicated to Saint Denis and his companions. In similar fashion "archbishops and bishops deposited there the very rings of their investiture as though in a place of safety."[51] He also quoted from the Roman Breviary—"Lapides preciosi omnes muri tui" (All thy walls are precious stones)—to obtain gifts of gems when the first stone of the foundations for the new crypt was laid in the presence of the king on 14 July 1140.[52]

As a thoughtful administrator, anxious to protect and care for his new church and for the comfort of the monks, he made a number of special endowments. One of them endowed the appointment of an "official master craftsman" to repair the stained glass windows;[53] this established precedents that lasted until the French Revolution, although we cannot tell how long Suger's funds survived.[54] Other projects, such as an annual revenue of more than two hundred pounds for the completion of the new church, seem to have collapsed with his death. Evidence of his meticulous attention to details occurs again and again in his description of difficulties encountered while the church was being built. One problem was resolved by the discovery of a quarry near Pontoise,[55] another by a successful search in the forest of Rambouillet for trees large enough to provide roof beams for the juncture between the old and new portions.[56]

Suger wrote the life of Louis le Gros to raise "a monument more durable than bronze,"[57] and to tell the story of his administration "lest, after our demise, the church be diminished in its revenue."[58] This practicality is characteristic of everything he did, but his concept of history was a record of past events on which judgments were made. For this reason the archives of his abbey were particularly significant, and he is credited with putting them in such good order that the library of Saint-Denis had no rival in France. These were the records that provided the basis for the great histories of France and made Saint-Denis the "maistre abeïe." Suger wrote as a storyteller, intent on captivating his audience. Chronological sequence was not significant, nor was the exact wording of the frequent quotations, set down as he remembered them from earlier readings. Alliterations and plays on words abound in his writings—a literary device then very much in fashion.[59] His student exercises in grammar would have served him in writing the verses he had inscribed on the new doors:

Nobile claret opus, sed opus quod nobile claret
Clarificet mentes, ut eant per lumina vera.[60]

Often his choice of words and quite arbitrary grammatical constructions obscure the meaning of descriptive passages, which become understandable only when confronted with extant visual evidence. The well-known reference to "geometrical and arithmetical instruments"[61] used in laying out the plan of the new choir so that the central nave of the old church would have the same dimensions as the central part of the new choir and the dimensions of the new side aisles would coincide with dimensions of the old side aisles motivated the beginning of my excavations in 1938. That passage defies interpretation without precise knowledge of the dimensions involved. In fact, literal translations often distort the intended meaning to the same degree that Suger's selections of details or events to be recorded cannot be considered all-inclusive. In other words, Suger's prose may at times be purposefully symbolic and make more than one reference, just as the images that decorated his church often have multiple iconographic allusions. Our standards for clarity and precision in prose or for the "sense of beauty tempered by reticence"[62] in the ornament of a church need not lead to the conclusion that Suger lacked taste. Such standards or definitions only create barriers between us and Suger's twelfth-century world.

Also difficult, and perhaps misleading, is any attempt to pinpoint his intellectual status.[63] Panofsky identified Suger as a protohumanist.[64] Other medievalists omit him entirely from the list of great moral and intellectual leaders of the time or label him as "one of those great men, who directed art into new paths."[65] His devotion to the classics and his concern with human values qualify him as a humanist. The didactical ordering of the interrelated themes carved on the western portals associate him, in my mind, with the scholastic process; but the fact that he did not construct any theological treatises or enter into any of the major debates on nominalism or realism, on heresies or mystical love may justify his exclusion from the company of such theologians as Anselm, Abelard, and Bernard. As with many outstanding personalities, Suger's interests were widespread, and although he may not have displayed the universal talents of the great Renaissance geniuses, he was inextricably involved in the significant currents of his time. The following chapters will focus on his participation in the building of his new church and the degree of its originality.

Suger's contemporaries often commented on his prodigious memory, which served him well in his administration of the abbey.[66] Doubtless he was relying on a well-stocked visual memory when he summoned bronze casters and chose sculptors to decorate the new portals.[67] During his wide travels he took note of works of quality that met his standards. Four times he made the long trip to Italy, twice to attend Lateran synods and twice to confer with Pope Calixtus II; and twice he went south into Apulia, visiting Monte Cassino, Benevento, Salerno, Bari, and Gargano as a pilgrim.[68] Having been sent to Montpellier in 1118 to meet Pope Gelasius II, and having accompanied young Louis VII when he went to Bordeaux to meet Eleanor before their wedding in Poitiers in 1137,[69] Suger also knew southern and southwestern France. Early in his career he lived on the Norman coast of the channel as prior of the small monastery at Berneval, not far from Fécamp, where he admired the strong administration of Henry Beauclerc, later Henry I of England.[70] In 1131 he accompanied Pope Innocent II to a conference in Rouen, possibly going with him as far as Liège in Belgium.[71] He must have seen the imperial cathedrals of the Rhineland when he attended the Reichstag in Mainz in 1125,[72] and he knew Burgundy well from traversing it on his trips to Italy; documents record his presence at La Charité-sur-Loire in 1107, Cluny in 1130, Châteauneuf-sur-Loire in 1135, Auxerre and Sens in 1138.[73] Although we cannot trace the exact routes he followed or choose between alternate possibilities, his travels took him into regions that contained most of the important Romanesque churches in France, Italy, and the Rhineland.

As this study of the building campaigns will suggest, artists from almost all of the regions visited by Suger participated in Suger's campaigns of construction. They included bronze founders, jewelers, and enamel workers from the valleys of the Rhine and the Meuse, masons and stonecarvers from Normandy, Burgundy, and southwestern France, mosaicists from Italy, and "many masters" of stained glass from "different regions."[74] Suger also speaks of an increase in "very good textiles,"[75] some of which may have been woven or embroidered in the abbey, and certainly scribes and illuminators were employed in the great library. Instead of working as independent or separate masters of their different crafts there is conclusive evidence that the artists worked closely together. They employed similar decorative motifs and imitated each others' techniques to create harmonious ensembles. Such an international workshop was the ideal environment for the emergence of a new style, and Suger to a remarkable degree was the ideal patron to foster and encourage its development.[76]

Suger's own humble origins and his early introduction into the royal court and the papal curia quite naturally led to an admiration for pomp and circumstance. Bernard's criticism of an abbot who traveled with an armed escort of sixty horsemen has always been considered to be a reference to Suger.[77] Yet under certain circumstances he knew how to use ceremony strategically. For example, when he organized a week-long hunt in the forest of Rambouillet, he invited the local seigneurs to join him in order to impress them with the abbey's feudal rights in that area.[78] In 1137 when Pope Innocent II celebrated Easter at Saint-Denis, a magnificent procession rode from Saint-Denis-de-l'Estrée to the abbey on richly caparisoned horses between trees decorated with precious textiles. Suger's unabashed delight in the colorful costumes, the pope's great mitre encircled with a golden band, the crowds of people, and the splendid feast held after the mass in the decorated cloister is reflected in his detailed description of the occasion.[79] Such celebrations, in his opinion, were offerings to God and man, and he organized with equal pleasure the consecration of his new church—first the west works on 9 June 1140 and then the east end on 11 June 1144. At the latter event King Louis VII, Eleanor of Aquitaine, as well as the Queen Mother, nobles of the court, and a great assembly of archbishops, bishops, and abbots accompanied the relics of the patron saints to their new location in the new choir.

That choir, with its crown of stained glass windows, colored floor mosaics, and richly decorated altars, best exemplifies Suger's aesthetics. The verses Suger had inscribed on bronze doors of the western entrance encapsulate his all-pervasive theme of light—light that penetrated the shadows of the church and by its glittering reflections captivated the eye and illuminated the mind:

> The dull mind rises to truth through that which is material
> And, in seeing this light, is resurrected from its former submersion.[80]

In another passage he described the rapture engendered by his contemplation of precious stones in the altar ornaments:

> Thus, when—out of my delight in the beauty of the house of God—the loveliness of the many-colored gems has called me away from external cares, and worthy meditation has induced me to reflect, transferring that which is material to that which is immaterial, on the diversity of the sacred virtues: then it seems to me that I see myself dwelling, as it

were, in some strange region of the universe which neither exists
entirely in the slime of the earth nor entirely in the purity of Heaven;
and that, by the grace of God, I can be transported from this inferior to
that higher world in an anagogical manner.[81]

That anagogical principle by which terrestrial, or material, beauty enables
the spirit to rise above itself and join the absolute was based on the *Mystical
Theology* written by Dionysius the Pseudo-Areopagite. As noted in part I,
Dionysius the Pseudo-Areopagite was identified in the ninth century as the
same Dionysius converted by Paul in Athens (Acts 17:34) and was also
believed by the monks at Saint-Denis to be the first bishop of Paris, their
patron saint. For Suger, then, the *Mystical Theology* preserved the words of
Saint Denis, and in them Suger found the justification for the rebuilding and
sumptuous decoration of the choir. The most convinced sceptic can hardly
doubt Suger's good faith or fail to remark on the perfect accord between
doctrine and action.

In the same chapter Suger developed his basic concepts:

To me, I confess, one thing has always seemed preeminently fitting:
that every costlier or costliest thing should serve, first and foremost, for
the administration of the Holy Eucharist. *If* golden pouring vessels,
golden vials, golden little mortars used to serve, by the word of God or
the command of the Prophet, to collect the *blood of goats or calves or the
red heifer: how much more* must golden vessels, precious stones, and
whatever is most valued among all created things, be laid out, with
continual reverence and full devotion, for the reception of the *blood of
Christ!* Surely neither we nor our possessions suffice for this service. . . .
The detractors also object that a saintly mind, a pure heart, a faithful
intention ought to suffice for this sacred function; and we, too,
explicitly and especially affirm that it is these that principally matter.
[But] we profess that we must do homage also through the outward
ornaments of sacred vessels, and to nothing in the world in an equal
degree as to the service of the Holy Sacrifice, with all inner purity and
with all outward splendor.[82]

The attainment of all outward splendor, spectacles offered to God and man,
light to lead the dull mind from the material to the immaterial motivated
Suger, for he believed that he was translating the words of Saint Denis into
stone, glass, precious metals, and jewels. The severe simplicity of Cistercian
architecture, devoid of ornament, could never have excited the western mind
as did the majestic Gothic cathedrals illuminated by shimmering colored
light reflected by precious liturgical vessels, brightly decorated altars, and
intricately embroidered vestments.

Suger not only recorded the details of his administration, but also had his
name inscribed or his image represented again and again in the new church.
He wished to ensure that posterity would remember his name and his
achievement.[83] He took care to provide for a celebration of his anniversary as
sumptuous as those for Dagobert, Charles the Bald, and Louis VI, the abbey's
great benefactors.[84] Such aggrandizement lies in the tradition of the *chansons
de gestes* of the twelfth century, but when contrasted with Abelard's ar-

Fig. 43a,b

a

b

43. (a) Figure, restored in nineteenth century, of Abbot Suger at feet of Christ in lintel zone of tympanum of the central portal of the west façade; (b) *Sugerius Aba,* figure at the feet of the Virgin in the Annunciation panel of the window of the Infancy of Christ, Chapel of the Virgin.

rogance and disdain, Suger's candor seems almost childlike. How pathetic and human was his fear that his achievements would be forgotten!

As a final consideration, the question remains of how much Suger actually participated in the construction of the new building. Enthusiastic scholars have cited Suger's references to the use of "geometrical and arithmetical instruments" in the planning of the choir and his description of the rib vaults that threatened to collapse during a severe storm[85] to suggest that he acted as his own architect for the entire building. So popular was this belief in the nineteenth century that Suger appears in the company of the most renowned men in the history of western architecture carved on the frieze surrounding the base of the Albert Memorial in London (completed 1875).[86] He stands between William of Sens, architect of Canterbury, and Anthemius of Tralles, architect of Hagia Sophia. Yet in a study of the building of Saint-Denis the master mason or masons exhibited a technical knowledge acquired only by years of experience. Suger's active career did not include the necessary technical experience; no document even implies that he acquired such technical training. But an extraordinarily active client, he was in many ways the ideal patron.

Knowledgeable about the building centers in western Europe, Suger selected from their workshops when he chose and summoned artists skilled in every technique. His able administration of the abbey's finances made those summonses attractive and guaranteed funds that put no limitations on their work. The result was an international gathering of artists and craftsmen capable of creating new combinations, new forms for which prototypes did not exist. As abbot, he could direct the progress of the work, and his participation in the daily problems of the *chantier* showed that his enthusiasm and preoccupation with the project were greater than those of the ordinary patron. For example, when a number of large beams were needed, he told how he lay awake in bed pondering the problem and the next morning departed as early as possible for the abbey's forest near Rambouillet. When he summoned the local keepers of the forest to tell them of his requirements, they "smiled, or rather would have laughed at us if they had dared," certain that no such beams had been left standing after the Castellan of Chevreuse had built his palisades and bulwarks.

> We, however—scorning whatever they might say—began, with the courage of our faith [and with a knowledge of the forest gained during a week of hunting] . . . to search through the woods; and toward the first hour we found one timber adequate to the measure. Why say more? By the ninth hour or sooner we had, through the thickets, the depths of the forest and the dense thorny tangles, marked down twelve timbers (for so many were necessary) to the astonishment of all, especially those on the spot.[87]

Evidently Suger was equally involved in the discovery of a quarry near Pontoise with stone of unusual quality for the columns of his new addition.[88] He could gloat over the acquisition of a horde of jewels for which he "gave four hundred pounds . . . though they were worth much more"[89] and repeatedly spoke of his delight and pride in carrying forward the building of the church.

Suger is usually portrayed as a man of action, a doer rather than a thinker. Panofsky says simply that "Suger had no ambitions as a thinker"[90]—an assessment that may be justified if only his writings are taken into account. In the next chapters interesting implications will emerge, however, as we examine some of the references in his writings to the new building and evaluate them in terms of the building itself. He recorded enough details of the iconography of the portals and windows to prove that he was fully conversant with the themes presented.[91]

CHAPTER FIVE

The Western Bays: The Beginning
of Suger's First Campaign

Textual Sources for Dating

Aliteral interpretation of the reasons Suger gave for building a new church at Saint-Denis is not commensurate with the actual results. Unquestionably after three hundred and fifty years of constant use the old building needed repair and was also much too small. His simple statement that from the time he had been a student in the abbey's school he had wanted to restore and repaint the old walls is straightforward and natural, but why should he have ordered those repairs at great expense if he already had plans to replace the old building with a new one?[1] On feast days or special occasions, especially when relics such as the nail and the crown of thorns were displayed to the public, it is not surprising that the old building was overcrowded. Suger graphically described how women were forced to "run toward the altar upon the heads of men as upon a pavement with much anguish and noisy confusion"[2] or "squeezed in by the mass of strong men as in a winepress, exhibited bloodless faces as in imagined death," and "cried out horribly as though in labor" or "miserably trodden underfoot" were "lifted up by the pious assistance of men above the heads of the crowd," and "marched forward as though upon a pavement" or "gasping with their last breath, panted in the cloisters of the brethren to the despair of everyone."[3] Even the monks "who were showing the tokens of the Passion of Our Lord to the visitors had to yield to their anger and rioting and many a time, having no place to turn, escaped with the relics through the windows."[4] Allowances should be made for Suger's tendency toward rhetorical exaggerations, but his account raises the question of why construction began in the west rather than at the eastern end, where the overcrowding was greatest.

Although Suger mentioned a number of details about the western bays, such as the triple portals with bronze doors, the strong towers, the crenellations, and the upper chapels, he overlooked many significant innovations. We find no reference, for example, to the statue columns that flanked the portals or to the rose window in the façade; both were to become integral parts of the Gothic vocabulary of forms. The development of new stylistic formulae may appear as bold reactions to earlier concepts, but the measure of importance of any innovation lies in the manner in which it is adopted by succeeding generations. Only the historian can judge the true significance of change or invention, but the judgments of historians as often as not reflect their individual biases or favorite theories.

According to Otto von Simson, "Suger undertook the rebuilding of his church in order to implement his master plan in the sphere of politics."[5] Behind von Simson's skillful summaries of the implications which he found in the *Descriptio,* in the *Pèlerinage de Charlemagne,* in the *Pseudo-Turpin Chronicle,* and in the *False Charter of Charlemagne* for the glorification of Saint-Denis lies the assumption that Suger was directly involved in their composition or promulgation.[6] Recent scholarship in this area shows how tenuous such an assertion must remain.[7] In my opinion the sequence of events in the building of Suger's church reflects much less complicated, practical preoccupations; Suger wished to glorify Saint Denis and his companions with his new building and naturally wanted it to surpass any previous building.

Why, then, did he begin with the western portions? In an almost uncanny manner Suger seemed to have known intuitively that his plan for the church would not be completed. Hoping that "Divine Mercy . . . might join a good end to a good beginning by a safe middle,"[8] he began the inscription of the new choir by stating:

> Once the new rear part is joined to the part in front,
> The church shines with its middle part brightened.[9]

Explaining why he stopped work on the western towers, he wrote, "if, in our own time or under our successors, work on the nave of the church would only be done betweenwhiles, whenever work on the towers would afford the opportunity, the nave would not be completed according to plan without much delay or, in case of any unlucky development, never."[10] This, of course, was exactly what happened; the stumbling block was the old church, which Suger and his contemporaries believed had been built by Dagobert and on which "by the testimony of the ancient writers, the Highest Priest, our Lord Jesus Christ, had laid His hand."[11] Today we know that the "old" church standing in Suger's day was not Dagobert's enlargement of the first chapel but rather the Carolingian church begun by Abbot Fulrad under Pepin the Short and consecrated in the presence of Charlemagne and his court on 24 February 775. Possibly the legend of the consecration by Christ had its origins in the miraculous appearance of Christ to Saint Denis in prison the night before his martyrdom, as recorded in the *Miracula Sancti Dionysii,* compiled between 834 and 836; but no written account of the consecration of Dagobert's church appeared before the eleventh century.[12] Given popular imagination, by the twelfth century every stone of the extant "old" building was venerated as a sacred relic. Any damage or destruction involving that sacred building would have been regarded as a sacrilege.

Consequently, after his election as abbot, Suger first acted to repair the old walls and to have them painted with "gold and precious colors."[13] Evidence of such repairs was discovered during our excavations in the nave in 1948.[14] But, Suger continued, "even while this was being completed at great expense, I found myself, under the inspiration of the Divine Will . . . encouraged . . . to enlarge and amplify the noble church consecrated by the Hand Divine." He recorded that he did so with the "counsel of wise men and the prayers of many monks."[15] Yet their decision to begin at the western end seemed motivated by practical reasons. Such a move entailed only the destruction of "a certain addition asserted to have been made by Charlemagne"[16] which to the popular mind would not, therefore, have been part of Dagobert's sacred church. The repair and redecoration of the old building and the destruction of a later addition to that building apparently would have mollified critics by calming any fears that the venerated building would disappear. Perhaps Suger hoped that the magnificence of the new façade and the entrance bays would so dwarf the old nave that he would gain support for completing the church. Apparently this is exactly what occurred; before the enthusiasm engendered by the consecration ceremonies for the new entrance had waned, Suger proceeded to lay the foundations for the new eastern end which, he hoped, would lead to the completion of the new building even at the expense of the old nave.

The question remains as to when Suger's first campaign of construction began. Because so many monuments and objects lack documentation, historians of art in seeking accurate dates depend on subjective or stylistic criteria which are always open to new interpretations. Precise dates for the two consecrations at Saint-Denis contribute in no small measure to the abbey's historical renown, but evidence for the actual start of work is less certain.

Suger recorded that he himself undertook the rebuilding of the old church. Thus work could not have begun before 12 March 1122, when he became abbot. In his testament, or will, written on 17 June 1137, just before he left for Bordeaux and Poitiers to attend the marriage of Louis VII and Eleanor of Aquitaine, he instructed the *cellarius* of the abbey to make certain that funds continued to be available for the completion of projects then underway. These included "novi et magni aedificii ecclesiae augmentione" (the new and magnificent addition to the building of the church).[17] In other words, work on the new church had started before June 1137; but no document records when the workshops were organized or planning for the new building began.

On the assumption that Suger undertook the rebuilding of the church to "implement his master plan in the sphere of politics," von Simson stated that the abbot "seems to have conceived the plan to rebuild the church immediately after the events of 1124,"[18] when Louis VI went to Saint-Denis to receive the *vexillum,* the military standard of the Vexin, on his way to Reims to oppose the emperor Henry's invasion.[19] There is no evidence supporting the tenuous assumption that plans for the building were conceived as early as 1124.

In a charter of 15 March 1125, however, Suger referred to the building of a new entrance to the monastery. This charter freed inhabitants of Saint-Denis from the feudal custom of *mortmain* in return for the payment of two hundred pounds, a sum to be used "ad introitum monasterii Beati Dionysii renovandum et decorandum."[20] This Panofsky has construed as a reference to the church proper, or the western portals.[21] Taking an opposite view, Ernst Gall concluded that "monasterium" referred to the abbey and "ecclesia" would apply to the church.[22] Although Suger may have used the terms interchangeably,[23] plans of the abbey before 1779 locate the principal gate into the monastery at the southwest corner of the enclosing walls. That gate was known as the "porte de Suger," a tradition which strongly suggests that he built the southwestern entrance to the monastery, one distinct from the entrance to the church. Also the legend on Martinet's engraving of the "Principale Porte du Cloître St. Denis" says that the fortified towers were built by Suger, and the engraving shows crenellations which, to judge from their simplicity, could very well date from the twelfth century.[24] Because this entrance gate also included adjacent structures, the expenditure of a sum as large as two hundred pounds seems reasonable.[25] In addition, during the early years of his abbacy Suger was fully occupied with duties at the court and, by 1127, with the reform of the monastery. Given those preoccupations, I seriously question whether his plans for a new building and the workshops could have materialized before 1130.

Fig. 44

Suger implied that work at the beginning proceeded slowly: "While at first, expending little, we lacked much, afterwards, expending much, we lacked nothing at all and even confessed in our abundance."[26] His testament of 1137 also mentions that in addition to work on the new church, he undertook the construction of a large "domus hospitum," as well as renovations and repairs to the dormitories and the refectory and the enlargement of the treasury.[27] Characteristically, Suger began by asserting the comfort and well-being of the monks, and to reassure them further he restored the old church. Such an extensive building program necessitated the organization of a sizeable workshop, which may well have assembled in the early 1130s; but progress was slow and work on the new west portals and entrance bays could have been delayed until about 1135.[28] This work, we know, began by the "tearing down" of the entrance to the old church. Our new plans and excavations allow us to suggest how the plan for the new western bays was laid out.

Plan

The examination and analysis of every part of the present church at Saint-Denis must begin with an evaluation of the restorations and alterations

44. Engraving by Martinet of the main entrance to the abbey, presumably constructed during the abbacy of Suger.

which in most instances have changed the original twelfth- or thirteenth-century disposition. That holds true especially for the study of the western bays.

The most drastic changes to these bays began after Napoleon's visit to Saint-Denis in August 1811. Displeased with the slowness of the work of restoration, he transferred its direction from Jacques Cellérier to Pierre Fontaine.[29] He also gave orders that had disastrous consequences: foremost among them, the general raising of the level of the pavement of the transepts, nave, and western bays to bring the heights of those pavements nearer to that of the choir.[30] One half century later, between 1860 and 1870, Viollet-le-Duc restored the pavements of the transepts and nave to their original, thirteenth-century level, but did nothing about the pavement of the western bays, which remains to this day at the early nineteenth-century height. Since the original twelfth-century pier bases lie hidden beneath that pavement, a reconstruction of the plan of the twelfth-century bases at the original pavement level is a necessary prelude to any consideration of the plan and elevation of the western bays. Excavation of some of the bases and photogrammetric studies of the vaults now allow a reasonably accurate reconstruction of the original plan and elevation.

Because lightning had struck the spire of the north tower in 1837, one of Viollet-le-Duc's first duties at Saint-Denis was to verify the solidity of the

Figs. 45a,b, 47

Figs. 46a, 47; Album no. 17

a

foundations of the west façade and north tower. In 1847 he opened an
excavation in front of the buttress to the north of the central portal and
another just to the north of the interior eastern face of the pier between the
center and north portals (pier no. 2 in the diagram). Extending 4.20 m below
the present pavement, the interior excavation exposed a small portion of the
original pier base, which showed a completely different plan and profile from
the nineteenth-century bases visible above the pavement today. Viollet-le-
Duc left this excavation open beneath a heavy stone slab to provide the access
which allows continued observation of the condition of the foundations.[31]
Yet until I had the slab lifted in 1939, the twelfth-century bases seem to have
been ignored. The excavation was enlarged in 1959 under the direction of
Jules Formigé and under my direction again in 1962, 1967, and 1971. Unfortunately, these enlargements were limited by the instability of the fill under the
nineteenth-century pavement as well as by finances and time.

My further excavations made it possible to record portions of piers nos. 9,
10, 11, and 12 as well as the northwest face and half of the southwest face of
pier no. 6, most of the interior of pier no. 2, and also the arrangement of the
masonry as it continues across the interior of the central portal. In addition,
the excavations provided information about one-half of the northeastern side
of the base of pier no. 3, about the interior of the north portal, and about a
small portion of the base of pier no. 1.

Figs. 47, 50; App. A.1

Fig. 45a,d; App. L.1, 2

b

c

d

45. Bases of the west bay piers: (a) bases installed by Cellérier early in the nineteenth century; (b) original twelfth-century pier bases of west bays excavated under existing nineteenth-century pavement— northwest face of pier no. 6; (c) detail of northwest face of pier no. 6; (d) excavated twelfth-century bases on eastern face of pier no. 2

5. 47

5. 46a

Unfortunately none of those rather scattered excavations has provided the complete plan of any pier or of an entire bay, but important supplementary information permits a satisfactory reconstruction of the entire plan of the twelfth-century bases. The photogrammetric rendering of the contours of the four twelfth-century vaults of the ground floor of the western bays shows very accurately the dimensions, angles, and sequence of most of the abaci above the capitals of the clustered piers. The plan of the abaci placed over the excavated portions of the bases of piers nos. 2 and 6 indicated that the plan of the abaci repeats the plan of the bases, except for the bevels, or horizontal chamfers, which decorate the bases. In other words, by adding 0.20 m to the plan of the abaci an accurate plan of most of the twelfth-century bases can be drawn. The excavation of piers nos. 9, 10,[32] 11, and 12 and photographs of the remaining abaci make it possible to reconstruct with reasonable accuracy the plan of the northeastern and southeastern bays.[33] With that plan available, we learn a great deal about twelfth-century architectural procedures.

"In carrying out such plans my first thought," wrote Suger, "was for the concordance and harmony of the ancient and the new work."[34] This desire to achieve a "congruent coherence" between the old, eighth-century building and his new one reflected his respect for the popular belief in the legend of Christ's consecration of the old church. Suger's master mason interpreted those "first thoughts" both literally and figuratively.[35] The new entrance would include a monumental western structure joined to the old nave by five bays. Those five bays were to be treated as a continuation of the old nave by repeating very closely the alignment and the dimensions of the eighth-century colonnade. To the west of the junction bays, the entrance bays were to be a two-storied fore-church built in the most contemporary manner, faced

Pl. 2; Album no. 17

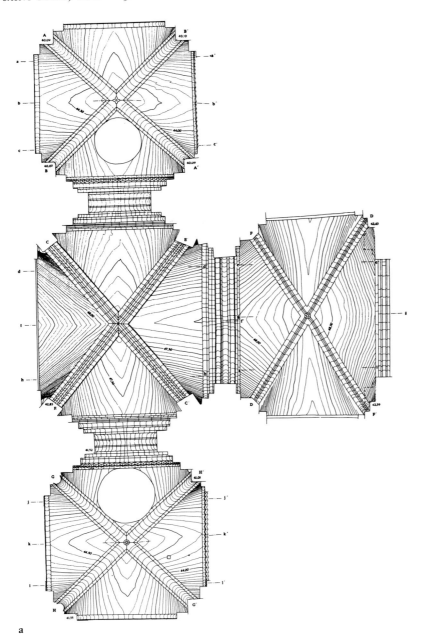

a

46. (a) Photogrammetric analysis of the twelfth-century vaults of the ground floor, western bays; (b) (*opposite*) photogrammetric analysis of the twelfth-century vaults of the upper story: northwest chapel (*left*); northeast chapel (*right*).

by a decorative western façade surmounted by "turrium altarum et honestarum" (high and noble towers).[36] The contrast between the two portions would be striking, although both structures were to be based on dimensions taken from the old church.

When the master mason prepared for the new structures by tearing down the western portions of the old church, the nave and side aisles of the old building would have been fully exposed, at least temporarily, at the west. At that time ropes continuing the alignment, or axes, of the Carolingian nave colonnades could easily have been extended over the new site. Such ropes

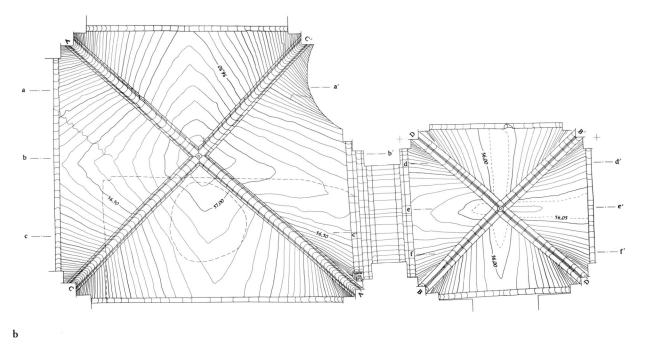

b

would also have continued, or established, the old nave dimensions in the new building. By a knotted string or a board cut to the appropriate lengths, the spans of the old bays, such as the distance between the inner faces of the bases (3.00 m), the width of a base (ca. 1.00 m), or the approximate distance between the centers of the nave columns (4.00 m), could also have easily been recorded. Those devices would have been portable anywhere on the site.

Precision was not always a prerequisite. When, for instance, irregularities in the foundations of the old western entrance made it difficult to place a base in a new junction bay exactly 3.00 m from the last, or westernmost, base of the old nave, the distance became 3.20 m; the next base measured only 2.90 m farther to the west—both apparently acceptable discrepancies. As noted in our description of the eighth-century bases, the sizes of those massive stone blocks differed from one another for no apparent functional or aesthetic reason. Such minor irregularities were normally compensated for by adjustments in the masonry—an instinctive adjustment for an experienced mason. Since all but one of the socles,[37] or bottom slabs, for the bases of the junction columns were uncovered during our excavations,[38] their exact locations have been recorded along with the continuing slight difference in the measurements.

When, however, the plan of the western bays was in preparation, different procedures were followed with more precise results. It is not my intention to present the procedures followed by the twelfth-century masons. Such a proposal would be presumptuous, but I have discovered a reasonable number of concerns, or intentions, which the master mason at Saint-Denis incorporated into his design for the western bays as he prepared his plan. These

Fig. 48
Pl. 2; Album no. 17

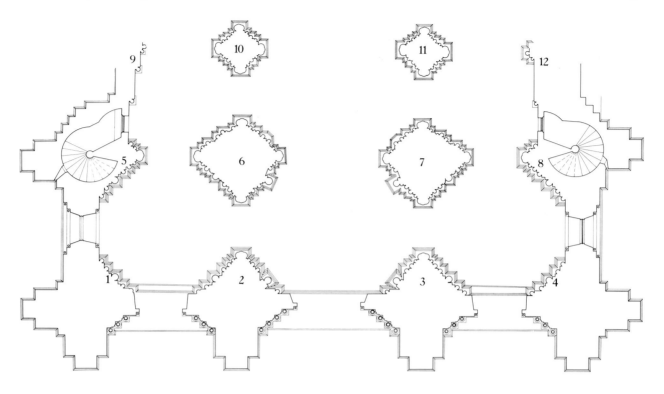

47. Reconstruction of the plan of
the original, twelfth-century pier
bases.

different preoccupations are discussed without any suggestion of priority or
sequence, although some details are related to others. I have tried to avoid the
temptation to label certain characteristics as stylistic criteria, because style is
essentially a subjective concept open to individual interpretations.

Although the discussion of the foundations will be presented as part of the
structure of the west bays in the next chapter, the major dimensions of the
plan for these bays were determined before the laying of those foundations
began. Excavations in front of the west façade and on the exterior of both the
northern and southern sides of the westernmost bay have uncovered enough
of the twelfth-century foundations to prove that the finished masonry of the
buttresses extends to within a few centimeters of the limits of the foundations.[39] Unquestionably the master mason had determined the overall dimensions of the plan before the start of construction. The evidence is limited
to the westernmost entrance bay, immediately inside the portals—a part of
the plan of primary interest to the master mason. The western fore-church, as
already stated, included a nave of two bays flanked by north and south aisles,
but in the second, or eastern, bay the master mason had to reduce the
dimensions of the western bay to make a transition to those of the junction
bays. This resulted in irregular, often awkward, compromises.

Our study must, therefore, concentrate first on the plan of the western bays
of the fore-church. When the master mason initially conceived the design for
them, he planned that they should be vaulted with heavy diagonal arches—a
fact proven by the prominent diagonal projections that began at the lowest
level of the bases, approximately in the centers of every face of each pier.

Fig. 50

48. Original plinth of a twelfth-century column from the junction between the western entrance bays and the twelfth-century extension of the eighth-century nave. Excavated in 1939, south side of nave.

Fig. 46a

Those diagonal arches will be explored in some detail in the next chapter, but their presence on the photogrammetric study of the vaults led me to an interesting insight. When the diagonal lines of the arches are extended, they intersect with those of the adjoining vaults near the centers of the piers. Those intersections form the corners of a rectangle and of two lateral squares. The rectangle in the center measures 8 m by 10 m and the squares to the north and to the south each measure 8 m on a side. The dimensions have particular significance since they are also the dimensions of the eighth-century crossing and of the transept arms of the old church. Even though the angles of the rectangle and squares lie hidden within the masonry of the piers of the west bay and cannot be seen, the master mason and his masons, and Abbot Suger as well, knew about this "congruent coherence" between the old and the new building.[40] Now that we know the meaning of Suger's phrase we can admire the subtle sensitivities of these twelfth-century masons.

The master mason must also have been aware of the importance of the diagonal arches under the rib vaults, for he experimented with their visual treatment in conjunction with the supporting piers and even adopted the diagonal rather than the parallel or perpendicular emplacement of the great piers themselves. For a number of years I have emphasized the importance of the diagonal faces of the piers, which resulted in octagonal rather than cubical volumes, as a major feature of the first campaign of building at Saint-Denis.[41] In many ways that preoccupation with diagonality was to prove among the most generative contributions to the development of the Gothic formula.[42] At present comments must be limited to those features apparent in the plan alone.

Only in the two central bays of the west work do the bases under the diagonal arches repeat the diagonal emphasis of the arches. Possibly designing to accent the centrality of these bays and their ultimate function as volumes leading into the nave of the new church, the master mason seems to have been somewhat uncertain about how to place the diagonal bases of the central entrance bay. The two bases opposite each other on piers nos. 6 and 7, for instance, are not perpendicular to the diagonal of the arches, as they are on piers nos. 2 and 3. The reason for this oblique placement is not immediately

Fig. 47

Figs. 46a, 47

obvious, although it must have been deliberate, for approximately the same angle occurs on both sides of the bay.

Such a detail also emphasizes another significant feature of the master mason's planning of the entrance bays which I discovered by accident. As I tried to ascertain everything I could about the western bays, I placed a tracing of the plan in reverse over the plan of the bases. I saw immediately that the plans on each side of the central east–west axis were identical. The north side was the mirror image of the bases on the southern side. The southeast face of pier no. 1 was, for example, the same as the northeast face of pier no. 4, only in reverse; the same is true of the southwest face of pier no. 6 and the northwest face of pier no. 7, where the oblique projecting bases under the diagonal arches are located. The visual coherence enhanced by such a balance of seemingly complex sequences will be elaborated upon later in this chapter. The sequence of projections and setbacks must have been designed by the master mason, who had them stabilized in the form of templates, presumably made of wood. Since the multiple fascicules of the massive clustered piers were intended to surmount each projection, the master mason must have envisaged the total ensemble when he fashioned his first templates.

As stated earlier, I do not intend to propose the sequence of steps or procedures that ordered the laying out of the plan, but there are certain observable principles needing identification. Although the bases for the columns of the junction bays seem to have been spaced according to the distance between the inner surfaces of the eighth-century bases, that is, 3.00 m, the spaces between the piers of the west bays were evidently controlled by measurements taken from the approximate centers of the piers, on the basis of 4.00 m rather than 3.00 m units.[43] The plan of the west bays repeats, it will be recalled, the dimensions of the eighth-century transept, namely, in the 8.00 m x 10.00 m rectangle flanked by two 8.00 m squares.

The 10.00 m dimensions resulted from the direct transference of the width of the eighth-century nave onto the new site, and the 8.00 m dimension was twice the distance between the centers of the columns of the old nave. The 4.00 m length seems to have been the measure that related the interior to the exterior plans of the west bay. A first glance at the plan shows the contrast between the diagonal definition of the interior volumes and the rectilinear shape of the exterior buttresses. This contrast between dynamic and static design underlines the ability of the master mason to recognize appropriate designs. The massive verticality of the buttresses provides important accents in the western façade and emphasizes their strength and stability as supports for the towers. Less apparent, the exterior limits, the northern, southern, or western faces of the buttresses, measure almost exactly 4.00 m from the corners of the squares used to lay out the interior plan. Furthermore, the small angular projections between the northern and southern corner buttresses continue the diagonal lines of the interior arches, as do the small projections of the other buttresses.[44] Those details establish relationships between the interior and exterior plans, although certain differences between the design of the western façade and the inner dimensions of the western portals indicate the flexibility on the part of the masons as their

Pl. 2; Album no. 17

work progressed. Slight differences between the northeastern and southeastern buttresses must also have been caused by the difficulties experienced
in building the eastern bay to join the junction bays extending the old nave.

The eastern bay was an integral part of the west fore-church, continuing
its mass with an upper story, but in plan that bay appears as a compromise,
with its reduced dimensions making the transition to those of the old eighth-
century nave. Unfortunately neither the northern nor the southern side has
been completely excavated, so that important questions, such as the reasons
for many discrepancies between their two exteriors, cannot be satisfactorily
explained. Presumably some earlier building hindered construction on the
north side, and the southern side required some widening to accommodate
the new bays. There are, it must be admitted, a number of inconsistencies for
which no logical answer seems adequate, but a few features need attention.

As noted, the original plans of piers nos. 10 and 11 were altered, both in
the thirteenth and in the nineteenth centuries.[45] A small excavation in 1967[46]
uncovered the eastern side of pier no. 11 and enough of the northern and
southern sides to prove that it had been built as a cruciform square pier, of
which only the core on the west side remains visible today. Soundings in the
masonry of pier no. 10 and in pier no. 11 as well prove that they originally
had the same plan.[47] Not only were the plans square, but their axes were
parallel, not diagonal to the central axis; yet the three setbacks on each side
resulted in clustered column shafts to conform with the center piers. These
two piers also follow the measuring system of the junction rather than that of
the west bay. The plan of the base was 3.00 m square, and the bases were
located 3.00 m from the westernmost bases of the junction.[48] The same
3.00 m rather than a 4.00 m unit was also used in locating the center of
piers nos. 6 and 7 to the west, with the measurement from the centers of piers
nos. 10 and 11 to the centers of nos. 6 and 7 approximately 6.00 m. The   Fig. 49a
northern wall of the junction bays, for instance, is joined directly to the
eighth-century nave wall and is only 0.80 m wide, in contrast to the
0.90 m width of the older wall. That wall of the junction bay is a simple,
continuous construction without projections or decoration, except for the
incised masons' marks on almost every stone. They confirm a twelfth-century date. At the western end, where the wall of the junction meets that of the
fore-church, the foundations became irregular, but not enough of the area
has been explored to provide a reasonable explanation. On the south the
junction wall is quite different. For no apparent reason, this wall does not
continue directly in alignment with the old south side aisle wall, but overlaps   Fig. 49b
only 0.40 m of the eighth-century masonry. The wall is a massive construction, 1.16 m thick, with its interior surface carefully finished by two
bevels, or horizontal chamfers, running its entire length. Masons' marks, not
unlike those on the northern wall, provide evidence of a twelfth-century date.
This southern wall has bevels continuous with those on base no. 12 and
identical to those on all the other bases. This detail may indicate that the wall
was built as the western bays were being completed. The northern side,
therefore, may well have been built earlier, possibly as the work began to
provide a material link between the old and the new.

a

b

49. Excavation of the side aisles, showing the eighth-century nave wall in foreground, joined to the new entrance bays by the twelfth-century junction wall: (a) north side aisle; (b) south side aisle.

This discrepancy between the construction of the north and south sides of the nave is an unusual feature of the plans of Saint-Denis in the twelfth century. The major problem involving Suger's last campaign and his desire to join the two ends with a "bright middle" will be treated at the end of this volume, but curiously, a similar disparity in dimensions and actual structure existed when the building first began.

After this review of details in the plan of the western bays and the bay joining them with the old church, one further conclusion deserves mention before we touch on problems concerning the structure. When the master mason, undoubtedly in consultation with Abbot Suger, planned the western entrance bays as a fore-church with a central nave flanked by side aisles and with upper chapels, neither he nor the abbot foresaw the middle part of the new church as a wider structure that would include a nave with double side aisles. The significant aspect of the first campaign is that the western bays were built with single aisles adjusted to join the old Carolingian nave. The master mason who planned the new façade and entrance bays was succeeded by another master mason, or masons, who planned the subsequent campaigns for the completion of Suger's church. In fact, certain details about the structure seem to indicate that a new master mason was in charge before the western bays had been completed.[49]

Structure

FOUNDATIONS

The preceding analysis of the plan of the western bays mentioned in many instances how the plan, as such, anticipated important details of the structure. This section will examine the structure with particular attention to the innovations and details peculiar to the first campaign at Saint-Denis.

Suger, according to Viollet-le-Duc, did not pay enough attention to the foundations of his building, which he said were built "in haste and with parsimony."[50] Yet, after almost eight and a half centuries, the west façade and entrance bays still stand, despite the new threat from the rumbling subway only a few meters away under the parvis. The foundations, apparently, have not failed.

Excavations have exposed five different areas of the western foundations, all of which afford useful evidence of the construction (see appendix A). At first glance the rubble footing of the lower portions appears inadequate, but the more carefully constructed upper levels evidently have consolidated the entire mass. The areas to the west, to the east, and to the north of the present church were used as a cemetery which dated back to Roman times; burials continued under the Merovingians in the fifth, sixth, and seventh centuries. Viollet-le-Duc's drawings of his excavations opened in 1847 to investigate the solidity of the foundations for the western towers show early sarcophagi on the northern and southern sides as well as in front of the western portals.[51] The drawing of the sarcophagi to the west proves difficult to interpret. The eastern halves of two sarcophagi shown (labeled f and g) must have extended into the foundations or perhaps have been broken off because of them. The elevation section A–B shows one of them (f) cut off but suspended in the fill outside of the foundation. Possibly out of respect for the early burials, the twelfth-century workmen left those portions of the sarcophagi in place. Viollet-le-Duc's elevation drawing of the buttress and foundations from the west does not include the sarcophagi, and when I first requested the excavation no evidence of them remained.

That same elevation shows a sketch of what might be a piece of sculpture, an inverted foliate capital, incorporated into the second and third courses of

Fig. 50

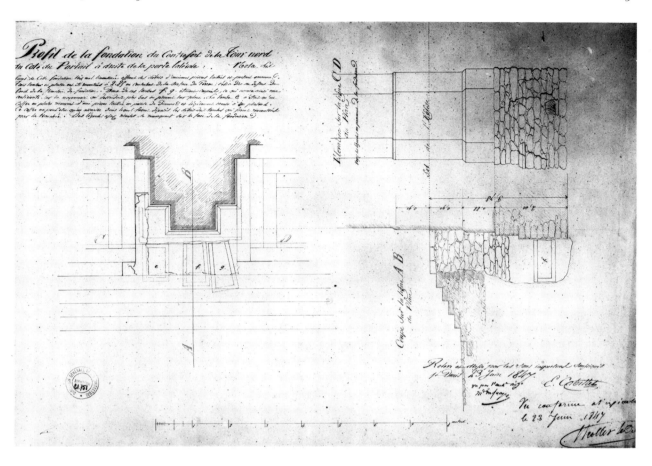

Fig. 51

the rubble masonry. When I first opened this excavation in 1939, that piece of sculpture, a capital, was embedded in the foundations.[52] In 1959 Formigé placed it in the Musée Lapidaire, where it remains to this day. The capital is thought to have come from Fulrad's eighth-century building. Other fragments of capitals were used in the twelfth-century foundations. Two pieces of a capital found at the base of the north tower were also removed to the Musée Lapidaire by Formigé.[53]

The twelfth-century masons showed a concern for solidity and precision in these foundations. In the excavation which I opened in 1939 under the colonnade of the south side in one of the junction bays linking the western bays and the old nave we uncovered a relieving arch as an integral part of the foundations.[54] The masons must have found the subsoil still soft or humid where an old well had been filled in, for the foundations there descend to a greater depth than elsewhere. Over this particular spot a rudimentary reinforcing arch was built into the rubble masonry of the foundations.

ENTRANCE AND PAVEMENT LEVELS

The accuracy of the exterior perimeter of the foundations in relation to the superstructure which they support offers additional evidence of the care

50. Plan and elevation of Viollet-le-Duc's excavations in front of the buttress to the right of the left (north) portal of the west façade.

taken in constructing the foundations. Possibly to limit the amount of labor required to dig the trenches for the foundations, as well as to limit the amount of material required for the masonry, the periphery of the exterior of the rubble foundation extends only a few centimeters beyond the finished masonry of the buttresses. This minimal projection may be seen in the plans and sections of Viollet-le-Duc's drawings, which we verified when the excavations were enlarged. As already noted, such accuracy must have been the result of careful planning before work on the foundations began.

Because only one small area of the interior of the foundations has been explored, observations for that area must remain preliminary. When Viollet-le-Duc excavated the interior of the base of pier no. 2, he examined the foundations as well. Although detailed in the upper portions, the section in the drawing is sketchy for the lower foundations. Still empty when I visited it in 1938, the hole has for some reason been filled in. Therefore the photograph and measured drawings, which we made at that time, remain the only available evidence. The foundations begin some 0.60 m to the north of the base but do not follow the perimeter of the masonry as they do on the exterior. Although properly labeled rubble masonry, the construction appears to have been much more carefully assembled on the interior than on the exterior, with larger, more regular stones aligned on an angle to follow what appears to be a grid connecting the piers. This arrangement leaves the interior of the bay with only loose fill. The presence of this loose, unstable fill was confirmed by Edouard Salin in 1956, when he excavated an early burial brought to his attention by Jules Formigé.[55] Although the interior foundation is deeper than the foundation in front of the exterior buttress, the difference is only 0.30 m. This has no significance because the level of the solid clay subsoil under the entire church undulates with depths varying every few meters. The rubble foundations seem to have been built as a level substructure, since both the interior and the exterior lie 1.80 m below the existing pavement. This level has generally been identified as the level of the original pavement, or parvis, but the enlargement of the excavations in front of the façade in 1967 and 1971 produced new evidence.[56] Since the discoveries on the exterior differ from those on the interior, let us begin with the masonry found in front of the central and northern portals.

Solid stone walls or benches 2.25 m thick rise 1.00 m above the rubble foundations and effectively block each of the doorways at that lower level. Both the exterior and the interior surfaces are sheathed in large blocks averaging 0.65 m wide by 0.70 m high. These were carefully finished with the close, diagonal striations typical of twelfth-century tooling and with masons' marks. The same broad horizontal bevels found throughout the masonry of the western bays also articulate the uppermost coursing. The interior of the wall is rubble construction topped by an additional layer of rubble rising another 0.40 m. Beginning under the western-, or outermost, columns of the portal embrasures, the walls or benches stretch laterally, that is, north and south, across the portals. As the workmen excavating eastward reached the jambs of the doorways, they pierced holes through the fill into the interior, thereby disclosing finished stones 0.15 m high by

51. Lower portions of a capital reused in the twelfth-century foundations of the northwest corner of the west bays, originally uncovered by Viollet-le-Duc.

50

A.2

App. A.3, 4

App. A.5

0.40 m wide sealed in the top of the rubble. Although only some 0.30 m of those stones were uncovered under the central portal, over 0.80 m of a similar stone at the same level was found under the north portal. That masonry seemed to be the sills for the doorways. These sills measure 0.52 m below the existing pavement—dimensions congruent with the measurements for the original bronze doors installed by Suger and still in place in the seventeenth century.

In his description of Saint-Denis published in 1625, Jacques Doublet recorded that the bronze doors of the central portal were 15 *pieds* high, and those of the north portal 14 *pieds* high.[57] At that time the *pied de Paris,* or the *pied du Roi,* was the approximate equivalent of 0.325 to 0.328 meters in our metric system.[58] This gives a dimension for the twelfth-century bronze doors between 4.88 and 4.92 m high. The height of the existing central portal as given in the photogrammetric elevation of the west façade is 4.38 m high. The additional 0.52 m to meet the sill under discussion produces 4.90 meters—a figure compatible with measurements given by Doublet.

A twelfth-century sill at this level, however, raises a number of other problems, but before examining them, we need to consider the perplexing situation presented by the masonry in front of the western portals. No exterior surface, either on the buttresses or on the benches across the portals, retains any trace of masonry which could have provided access to the elevated sills of the doorways. Most of these surfaces were marred by the nineteenth-century cement and rock fill built for the existing approach to the portals. Certainly earlier masonry steps against these stones of the building would have left some mark, especially if the steps had been in place for any length of time.

Information about different levels around the exterior of the abbey church remains vague,[59] despite earlier conjectures. Viollet-le-Duc stated that "le sol du parvis était 60 centimètres plus bas"; but he failed to say from what level he took that measurement.[60] The short article on parvis in his *Dictionnaire* says that he found traces of the paving of the parvis at Saint-Denis "du temps du Suger," and that this paving was "en contre-bas du sol exterieur," that is, below ground level, yet he gave no measurement.[61] In the plans and elevations of his excavations of May and June 1847 in front of the façade and at the bases of the north and south towers there is no identification of exterior levels.[62] Formigé's location of the twelfth-century parvis at 1.68 m below the present pavement of the western bays remains undocumented.[63] Until more positive evidence becomes available I can state only that the pavement between the embrasures of the central and northern portals was approximately at the same level as the twelfth-century sills and that there is no evidence of steps rising to them from the west.

Evidence for the level of the interior pavement of the western bays has been found, although confirmation in the form of additional paved surfaces *in situ* would be welcome. Sealed tightly against the finished surfaces of the setbacks of the southwestern face of pier no. 6 are fragments of a solid masonry construction between 0.08 m and 0.09 m thick. The smooth upper surface appears to have been part of a pavement. That pavement must

App. A.6a

have continued around the base to the north, as evidenced by the marked discoloration of the surfaces of the base at that same level. Similarly, somewhat fainter traces of the level can be seen on the surfaces of pier no. 2 directly to the west, where they were recorded by Viollet-le-Duc, but he did not suggest any date for the pavement.[64] As noted earlier, Viollet-le-Duc's drawing of this same section of the excavation of the interior of pier no. 2 indicates that the earliest ("primitif") paving was on top of the rubble foundations. I have not been able to discover any evidence for that pavement around the bases of piers nos. 2, 3, or 6. In my opinion the discovery of a fragment of the pavement of Fulrad's Carolingian church under the north side aisle[65] established a level that conforms more closely with the level of the paving fragments against pier no. 6 than would a lower pavement resting on the twelfth-century rubble foundations. My proposed reconstruction, therefore, places the pavement of the twelfth-century entrance bays 1.40 m below the existing pavement in those bays, 0.80 m below the present nave pavement, and just 0.09 m lower than the eighth-century nave (-0.71 m), to which the western bays gave access. Since the sill of the central portal was approximately 0.52 m below the present level, and our best evidence places the interior pavement 1.40 m below the same level, some ramp or series of steps must have made it possible to descend from the entrance doorway to the interior pavement.

Fragmentary remains of what may have been the supporting masonry for a series of steps on the east side of the central portal were discovered during a brief trial excavation in 1973. The area was so cramped and the fill so unstable that to avoid damage to the remains that had been uncovered work stopped shortly after it had started.[66] Three levels of loose, aggregate masonry topped by plaster surfaces were found against the southeastern face of pier no. 2. These levels rise about 0.15 m as they recede to the west toward the portal. Although a similar small fragment of masonry was found clinging to the surface of the second bevel of pier no. 3 on the southern side of the portal, not enough masonry has been uncovered to allow even a preliminary reconstruction of the stairway which must have been in this immediate area.

No such masonry has, as yet, been discovered in the fill inside the north portal, although my enlargement of this initial exploratory *sondage* by Formigé was restricted by interesting, unidentifiable changes in the lower fill. There are also a number of other details that differ from the central portal. Two beds of dressed twelfth-century limestone with bevels at their top edges stretch across the inside of the portal, but the faces of these beds project eastward, as though they were benches. Their heights, 0.50 m and 0.37 m, respectively, are the same as the lower two beds across the central portal, but they are much too high to have functioned as steps. A third bed with a carved molding of a flattened scotia and lower torus exists in the south corner, which has been mutilated to such an extent that no positive conclusions can be drawn. In the fill just to the west of the level of the bottom bed is a layer of conglomerate 0.10 m thick. Since this layer lies 1.40 m below the present pavement level, the conglomerate must have functioned as a base for the twelfth-century pavement. Thus the lowest bed or bench would have

Fig. 47

App. A.9

App. A.10

App. A.11

been covered by the pavement. Only with additional evidence can a reasonable hypothesis be suggested for the construction and function of this portal. Presumably the south portal would have repeated the disposition of masonry and levels found in the north doorway.

Although our information about the original levels of the entrances to the western bays is fragmentary and incomplete, new evidence has allowed a number of significant conclusions. Future discoveries, we hope, will corroborate our proposals in regard to the foundations, the monumental pier bases, and the various levels within the bays.

Rubble masonry topped by dressed stone blocks became increasingly common for Gothic foundations under the pavement, but they seem to be among the many innovations that appear at Saint-Denis. Yet the presence of the carefully executed bevels that ultimately disappeared beneath the pavement, or were completely hidden by steps, is perplexing. They could represent evidence of the mason's concern for "strong material foundations" properly executed or they could have compensated for miscalculations in estimating the level of a pavement to be "congruent" with the old church. No satisfactory answers are yet available. Equally perplexing are the different heights of the bevels between facing pier bases, such as those of piers nos. 2 and 6. Possibly such a variation accented the fact that piers nos. 6 and 7 stood independently of the rest of the construction, but such a suggestion must remain hypothetical until the other bases have been uncovered.

In summary, approach from the west was at the level of the doorway sills, at least between the portal embrasures and the buttresses where the masonry has been excavated. The presence of a *parvis* extending farther to the west would not have been exceptional, but no evidence exists for it or establishes its level relative to the portals. The height of the doorway sills 0.52 m below the present pavement has confirmation in the dimensions given for Suger's original bronze doors as well as in the archaeological evidence of the excavations. Since that level was considerably higher than the interior pavement, which conformed closely to the pavement height of the eighth-century, or old church, the arrangement required four or five steps on the interior of the central doorway to allow descent into the narthex bays. Given the unknowns, the arrangements inside the north and south portals remain uncertain.

PIER BASES

The original twelfth-century bases visible only in the excavations under the present pavement have already been mentioned in relation to the reconstruction of the plan of the western bays and to the construction of the foundations.[67] These bases, or substructures for the piers, consist of two distinct parts: the massive, angled socles that rest on the foundations and the smaller moldings supporting each of the attached colonnettes.

At Saint-Denis the bases of the western bays must have been impressive. Built in three beds of large blocks of stone, they rose 1.20 m above the rubble foundations, or 0.85 m above the pavement. The surfaces recede in a series of three bevels, or horizontal chamfers, which soften the angularity of the

projections and setbacks but, in their stark simplicity, heighten the monumental effect.

These three horizontal bevels evidently formed a continuous band around
the inner walls of the western bays. The excavations have uncovered them
from pier no. 1, south across the north portal, around pier no. 2, across the
central portal and on pier no. 3 as well as on piers nos. 9 and 12. Presumably
they continued along the north and south walls and around piers nos. 5 and 8
but stretched eastward only on the southern wall of the junction bays leading
to the old nave. Similar bevels also surrounded the bottom portions of piers
nos. 6 and 11. If my location of the twelfth-century pavement level is correct,
only the two upper bevels would have been visible, but their presence as a
continuous horizontal band would have created a powerful base for the
masonry above. Mention has already been made of the slight difference in the
heights of the vertical courses and bevels of piers nos. 2 and 6, which
provoked the speculation that such a subtle differentiation may have been
intended to emphasize the isolation of the two great piers under the towers
from the rest of the masonry.[68]

The presence of this continuous accent just below eye level does not
conform to the normal definition of a socle for a column or pier but rather to
the ground or basement course, *soubassement,* which appeared at Fountains
Abbey about 1135 and in the eastern end of Speyer in the late eleventh and
early twelfth centuries. In its function on the exterior such a construction
increased the thickness of the masonry at the base of the walls, provided a
more satisfactory visual transition from the horizontal ground to the vertical
walls, and furnished a runoff for rain. The soubassement course on the
interior at Saint-Denis lacked those functional purposes, yet asserted the
solidity of the foundations for the lofty towers which were planned but not
built in the first campaign.

Above the top bevel of the soubassements is a plinth, 0.14 m high, supporting the molded bases of the attached colonnettes of the piers. Of more
than one hundred and fifty such bases, so far only eight have been uncovered
in the excavations. Six of them are on the northwest face of pier no. 6, another   Fig. 45b,d; App. A.6b, 7, 10
flanks the north jamb of the central portal, and one flanks the north jamb of
the north portal. Embedded in the nineteenth-century mortar under the
present paving, all have suffered damage. In order to make this discussion of
the base profile of the western bays more comprehensive, I am including the
best preserved ones of the upper chapels, which were carved within a year or   Fig. 52a,b; App. L.5–11
two of those at ground level. The early Saint-Denis bases have particular
importance in any study of twelfth-century profiles because they are firmly
dated in the last years of the 1130s.

A full count of the column or colonnette bases carved for the interior of the
western bays totaled more than two hundred. Seventy of these surrounded
the two great piers nos. 6 and 7. The six original bases on the northwest face   Fig. 45b,c; App. L.1, 2
of pier no. 6 share the same main features, two tori separated by a scotia—
quite normal mid-twelfth-century elements. Although now severely eroded,
the tori, faceted rather than rounded in section, distinguish that particular
profile. Since those original bases have all these features in common, I assume

that they continued around the entire pier and in all likelihood occurred on pier no. 7. Thus they probably appeared on one-third of all the bases. Although two bases in the upper chapels have similar faceted top tori (now badly eroded), the closest parallels for the bases of pier no. 6 exist in the lower portions of the western towers at Notre-Dame de Chartres, under construction in the late 1130s and 1140s.[69]

App. L. 6, 7

Fig. 52a

Another recurrent base profile of the Saint-Denis western bays consists of a quarter-round upper torus, a half circle scotia flanked by two filets, and a flattened lower torus of a slightly greater height than the upper torus. Characteristically, the two tori are nearly in vertical alignment, with the upper one set back slightly. One of the best preserved bases with that profile survives in the upper southwest chapel, on the south wall as support for the west colonnette of the right, or western, window. Almost identical profiles can be seen throughout the upper chapels, and since it existed in the interior on the north side of the north, or left, portal (under the present pavement), that form probably predominated on the bases along lateral walls and engaged piers at the ground level.

App. A.10

Among the various base profiles, two are particularly interesting. On the west wall, in the right, or north, window of the upper south chapel the left colonnette has a somewhat eroded base with a continuous scallop on the lower torus which evolves into fully developed foliate spurs. Four spurs in the form of lizards ornament the base of the center colonnette of the northwest window between the center upper and lower chapels. More unusual is the large base for a column at the junction between the western bays and the old nave which was found intact in 1939 at the western end of the south side of the nave. Unfortunately, in 1940 as World War II began this excavation was filled in, and the base is no longer visible. Photographs show it clearly, and I have a full-scale profile of it. Rising 0.40 m (15 3/4 in.) above a plinth, the socle has a slightly concave horizontal chamfer. The molded base consists of a quarter-circle top torus with a semicircular scotia flanked by two filets, not unlike the bases already described, although on a larger scale. Below the scotia are two tori; the lower, larger one overhangs the socle, which produces an interesting profile.

Fig. 52b

Fig. 53; App. L.14

PIERS

The surfaces of the piers with the multiple attached colonnettes closely resemble the clustered pier. As to the authenticity of their surfaces, until 1958 they were covered by a thick coating of heavy whitewash, or *badigeon,* applied in the early nineteenth century when the interior of the church was being transformed. Because this badigeon was drying and flaking off, Jules Formigé ordered a complete cleaning of all the surfaces, which brought to

a

b

c

52. Bases of upper chapels: (a) south upper chapel, south wall, base of colonnette on right side of westernmost window; (b) base of center colonnette, with spurs in the form of lizards, westernmost window between central and north upper chapels; (c) chamfered base of pier, central upper chapel, west wall, to right of entrance from south chapel.

53. Last, or westernmost, twelfth-century base for a column on the south side of the nave in the junction between the entrance bays and the eighth-century nave, excavated in 1939.

light innumerable twelfth-century masons' marks incised on most of the stones.[70] The presence of these marks, placed there by each mason as a record of his work against ultimate payment, provides proof that the original surfaces survive unmodified by Debret's nineteenth-century chisels.

Fig. 54a–d

The large piers nos. 6 and 7 and the heavy masonry enclosing every bay overcompensate as solid supports for the towers planned to rise above them. If placed parallel to the axis of the nave, piers of this size, as well as the engaged piers of the adjacent bays, would have filled the bays and been visually awkward. Awareness of that potential problem may have prompted the master mason to arrange the piers diagonally to the main axis, thereby creating octagonal, related volumes and establishing a fundamental Gothic principle. Since the decisions relative to the size and articulation of the piers were made when the projections and setbacks of the pier plans were laid out, the number and relative sizes of the engaged columns and colonnettes were also part of the original planning.

Because the attached columns and colonnettes are not contiguous, but instead are separated by flat surfaces of varying dimensions, strictly speaking, these are not true clustered piers.[71] The colonnettes were carved from the angle of the block of stone, which resulted in rigid vertical lines on each side of the rounded surface. Under the diagonal ribs and transverse arches, the larger columns needed more space. Therefore the edges of the stone block were cut back, accenting the projection of the columns from their background plane. The unusual triplets of colonnettes forming the large columns under the transverse arches which appear much later in such English Gothic churches as Wells and Exeter[72] have no Romanesque precedents to my knowledge. Each column or colonnette corresponds to similar moldings in the vaulting arches. That continuity in molded forms serves to carry the eye from the bases to the capitals and into the vaults, then leads across to the counterparts on the opposite pier. Continuity with variety remained a principle basic to the Saint-Denis aesthetic, a principle demonstrated also by the important series of carved capitals decorating the piers.

Figs. 55a, 67b

Figs. 55d, 56

CAPITALS

App. K.
1–21

Among the many series of early- to mid-twelfth-century capitals, those of the ground level of the western bays at Saint-Denis are remarkable for the state of their preservation. Covered, as were the shafts of the great piers, by a heavy coating of badigeon early in the nineteenth century, they escaped the disastrous recutting of the later restorers. In addition, their location inside the building sheltered them from the eroding effects of the weather and industrial pollution. Since their cleaning in 1951, they appear almost as sharp and effective as when they were carved in the late 1130s. They also exist in sufficient numbers—more than 150 (the same obviously as the colonnettes which have just been discussed)—to provide a significant corpus worthy of much more attention than they have ever received.[73]

Students of antiquity observe that normally a capital should be proportioned to the diameter of the column or shaft supporting it. The medieval mason ignored that classical principle, for he realized that the multiplicity of shaft diameters in a clustered pier would have resulted in a disagreeably incoherent sequence of capitals of varying sizes. Consequently, at Saint-Denis, although the diameter of each capital conforms to the diameter of its column or colonnette, the heights are uniform in each grouped sequence. In the massive masonry construction of the Saint-Denis western bays, the pier capitals have no structural function; but they have the important visual one of providing strong horizontal accents between the vertical columns and shafts and curved arches of the vaults. The number, condition, and firm dating of these capitals make them interesting elements in the study of the change from Romanesque to Early Gothic ornament.

Fig. 55a
Only the dominant type and a few unusual examples among the western capitals will be analyzed here. I have chosen the capital under the diagonal rib on the southwestern face of pier no. 6 as a characteristic Saint-Denis type. Fundamental to the design of this foliate capital is the stylized acanthus leaf, which has origins traceable back to Roman and to early medieval examples. In the late eleventh and early twelfth centuries, the simple striations of this multilobed leaf developed into a decorative pattern quite independent of a natural form or of any earlier examples. At Saint-Denis the confidence and technical skill shown by the sculptors prove that they were not experimenting with new forms but rather elaborating and perfecting familiar concepts. Capitals almost identical to this type at Saint-Denis exist in and around Paris in both large and small churches.[74]

Although the acanthus leaf is usually associated with Corinthianesque derivatives, the example under discussion demonstrates how independent the artists were of earlier prototypes. Tall, full leaves frame a smaller symmetrical pattern on the axis of the capital. Emerging from behind and rising above these foreground patterns the tops of similar forms project and curl over as supports for the corners of the abacus. Visible in the top center, the bare, bell-like core around which the designs were carved achieves the transition from the cylindrical column to the rectangular abacus. This relatively simple arrangement, easily read from below, accents perfectly the shape of the capital. The deep incisions dividing the foliate forms create shadows and

a

b

c

d

54. (a–d) Twelfth-century masons' marks from the western bays.

a

55. Twelfth-century capitals: (a) on the southwest face of pier no. 6, in the westernmost bays; (b) on the southeast face of pier no. 1, pair on left; (c) on the southeast face of pier no. 2, capital below the diagonal rib on left; capital supporting wall rib on right; (d) on southwest face of pier no. 5, capital beneath transverse rib; (e) on northeast face of pier no. 4, capitals on right.

b

c

d

e

56. Northwestern face of pier no. 7 in the western bays.

lights that enliven the entire surface. Particularly effective, the rhythmical flow of the curving planes develops as they rise from the simple design at the bottom to the more complicated details at the top. A perfectionist whose control of his tools allowed him complete freedom, the sculptor achieved a fascinating balance between the smallest details and the overall design. This control, enlivened by a vivid imagination, also allowed him to create a seemingly endless series of variations on the same theme, as illustrated in the sequence of eight capitals across the southwest face of pier no. 6. In fact, among all the capitals in this series I have found only two with identical designs[75]—further proof of the determination of Suger's masons to avoid monotonous repetition.

    Fig. 55b

    Among the variations within the stylized acanthus leaf group in the western bays, three deserve particular notice. First are those capitals where the spaces within the leaves apparently were drilled, creating sharp, staccato accents.[76] Another group has triangular leaves positioned alternately up and down, which resulted in a compact overall pattern.[77] Quite unusual, indeed unique in the series, the large capital on the northeast side of pier no. 7 has leaves that project more fully; then suddenly on the east side, the design changes to an abstract "water-leaf" design. Another type, a combination of acanthus and "water-leaves," occurs, but in the second instance the design is a continuous one with the small acanthus patterns as the bottom zone and larger plain water-leaves as the upper zone.[78] Quite distinct from the acanthus leaf series, several designs are based on a vine or scroll motif. There are at least five variants of this type.[79] And finally there is a five-zoned or -tiered capital under the diagonal rib on the northeast face of pier no. 2 with small, flat, turned over designs resembling a fleur-de-lys.

Fig. 55c; App. K.10a

Fig. 58b
Fig. 55d

Fig. 55e

App. K.21b

    To counter the constant variation in capital design, the astragals and abaci are continuous and link each series of capitals above and below with uninter-

rupted horizontal moldings. The southwest face of pier no. 6 illustrates the Fig. 55a
effect of these bands, which continue across the undecorated masonry surfaces to bind together the whole ensemble. Yet the sequence of capitals
cannot properly be described as continuous, or frieze, capitals since they
occur at many different levels and, as on pier no. 6 southeast and pier no. 7
northwest, are often separated by undecorated or blank masonry. The simple Figs. 56, 58a,b
astragals are not semicircular tori, but have slightly angled profiles which
may have been intended to create a subtle harmony with the faceted tori of
the bases below. The abaci with much more complicated moldings create a
solid base for the springing of the multirolled arches of the vaults.

ARCHES

These arches, both the transverse running north–south and east–west, and
the diagonal ribs, complete the bays and tie their various parts into integral
units. As shown in our discussions of the different parts of the pier structure
from the soubassements to the abaci, the number and general character of the
moldings of the vaulting arches were enumerated and provided for when the
basic plan was first laid out. In the plan the essential basis for the entire
structure was established in the fundamental thicknesses of the masonry of
the walls and piers. The arches under the vaults are directly related to these
masonry divisions, which appear to have been set at 2.20 m. If the wall ribs Figs. 46a, 57a,c
are included, the transverse arches between piers nos. 6–2 and nos. 6–5, and
those between piers nos. 7–3 and nos. 7–8, all measure 2.20 m. Obviously we
do not know how the twelfth-century masons calculated these measurements, but the close approximation of wall masonry and the overall thicknesses of the arches cannot be ignored, nor can the relation to the use of a
1.00 m stick in laying out the plan. Such massive construction corresponds,
as mentioned again and again, with the function of these western bays as
foundations for the high, heavy towers above. The differences among the
profiles of these arches not only reflect the Saint-Denis masons' predilections Fig. 57a–d
for variety in visual effects but also are significant to the total effect of the
different bays.

The diagonal ribs most frequently reproduced in textbooks are the northwest and southwest bays. There a single large torus (0.36 m in diameter)
flanked by two smaller tori (0.13 m in diameter) projects 0.32 m from a Fig. 57a,c
rectangular base. The overall dimensions of the rib are 0.62 m in width and
0.39 m in projection. Such a heavy arch, spanning a distance of only
7.20 m, would not have been required in the construction of the vault (the
thickness of its webbings will be discussed in the following pages), nor would
the rib have contributed greatly to the solidity of the masonry, surrounded as
it is by walls and arches 2.20 m thick.

To the same degree the arches between the piers do not correspond to the
structure of the vaults but rather to the entire western mass stabilizing the
lower level for the heavy vaults to be built above them. Careful examination
of the courses of the masonry in the arch between piers no. 3 and, for instance,
no. 7 (that is, the arch on the north side of the southwest bay), discloses that
there are five different orders, beginning with the large lowest order, which

a

c

57. The quadripartite twelfth-century vaults of the western entrance bays. West is at bottom edge, north at viewer's right. The viewer is standing below the vault, facing west and looking up: (a) northwest bay; (b) central west bay; (c) southwest bay; (d) central east bay; (e) (*overleaf*) upper northwest chapel; (f) (*overleaf*) upper northeast chapel.

148

b

d

e

f

has a trefoil section repeating the profile of the east and west attached columns of the respective supporting piers. There are then two distinct orders on the north side, each with a roll and a concave chamfer and three similar orders on the south side with the southernmost decorated by a sawtooth molding. The other arches surrounding the northwest and southwest vaults resemble this one, but in the central bays the diagonal ribs differ from those in the lateral bays, and from each other.

The ribs of the west center bay are almost exactly the same width as those of the south and north bays, that is, 0.60 m, but the profile contrasts markedly. Two tori, 0.15 m in diameter, flank a central ovoid or slightly pointed torus, which projects 0.30 m beyond them. The design gives the ribs a lighter, more articulated appearance than those of the lateral bays. The central ribs of the eastern bay also differ in that their widths are narrower, 0.40 m, and the profile consists of two equal tori 0.15 m in diameter separated by a small, angular filet which does not project beyond the tori. Before I discuss the possible psychological effect of these different rib profiles and the different heights of the vaults, a detailed study of the actual structure of the vaults themselves is in order.

Fig. 57b

Fig. 57d

VAULTS

Seven of the twelve original twelfth-century vaults over the western bays exist today essentially in their original form.[80] The photogrammetric rendering of the contours and profiles of six of these vaults allow accurate analysis of their construction. When regarding them as an ensemble, one's first reaction is to the extraordinary diversity of structural forms which are combined to create a coherent whole. I shall begin by an enumeration of the variety among the structural details and then attempt to define the results of their combinations.

Fig. 46a,b; Album nos. 4, 5

The construction of a ribbed vault began with the erection of wooden scaffolding on which the stone arches were raised. The flexibility, or maneuverability, of this wooden framework was fundamental to the concept of Gothic skeletal construction and is clearly demonstrated by the changing centers of the arcs of the diagonal ribs, or ogives, as they are identified in the photogrammetric diagrams, of the Saint-Denis western bays. The two ribs of the central bay west—C-C' and E-E'—have diameters of 8.50 m with radii of 4.25 m swung from a center raised 0.30 m above the baseline of the arc. This same radius, 4.25 m, was used for the northwest and southwest diagonal ribs (A-A', B-B', G-G', and H-H'). In this instance the centers are 0.20 m above the baseline and lie 0.50 m on each side of its median point, which results in a slightly broken, or pointed, arch—an incipient *arc en tiers-point*. The ribs of the central eastern vault (D-D' and F-F') appear quite irregular but a center exists from which the same radius, 4.25 m, traces all but the eastern portions of the arches, which are arbitrarily extended down and outward beyond a baseline to fulfill the structural demands.

Fig. 46a; Album no. 4

Other ribs display even greater flexibility. The northwest upper chapel, for instance, has an irregular plan to accommodate the large circular staircase in the northeast corner. The diagonal rib A-A' has a diameter of 9.74 m where-

Fig. 46b; Album no. 5

a

58. (a) Southeastern face of pier no. 6; (b) northeastern face of pier no. 7 in the western entrance bays.

as the intersecting diagonal rib, C-C′, measures 8.66 m, yet the curves of both arches are traced by radii of 4.80 m. In the first instance, A-A′, the center is very close to the center of the baseline; but in the second, C-C′, the centers lie 0.50 m on either side of the median point. The last twelfth-century vault available for analysis covers the upper northeast bay, which has a square plan. Here the diagonal ribs, B-B′ and D-D′, have the same profile, traced almost exactly according to the classic arc-en-tiers-point,[81] except that the baseline is not divided into three equal segments to locate the centers for the radii, which measure 4.00 m each. This measurement of 4.00 m is interesting in relation to the building of the western bays, for it also appeared as a basic module in the laying out of the plan of the exterior buttresses.

Although we are aware of the importance of the wooden scaffoldings under the vaults and of the skill with which they were handled, we cannot reconstruct exactly how they were built in the twelfth century, nor do we know how thick or heavy the forms were on which the masons placed the stone *voussoirs* as they erected the arch. The way the masons calculated the

b

support of these forms which resulted in the finished profile of the arch also remains in question. Even though there are no answers to such questions, it is permissible to observe that the use of radii measuring 4.25 m or 4.00 m in five of the six vaults in question can hardly be a coincidence when the same measurement apparently was used in laying out the plan of the same bays.

A major aspect in the construction of rib vaults is the structural and aesthetic advantage of attaining level crowns for the vault compartments, or severies. At Saint-Denis the relatively level vault crowns were achieved by springing the armature of arches from different levels. Indeed the variety of levels, marked by the different heights of the capitals in the great clustered piers, is one of the distinguishing features commented on by most scholars when they mention the western vaults at Saint-Denis. The central eastern bay provides one of the most striking examples. There the capitals marking the springing of the transverse, wall, and diagonal ribs are located at four different heights. The result, as seen in the eastern faces of piers nos. 6 and 7, resembles the arrangement of the tubes of a mighty organ. More familiar to

Fig. 58a,b

students is the springing of the large diagonal ribs of the northwestern and southwestern bays at a level approximately 1.20 m lower than the adjacent arches.

Fig. 57a,c

FENESTRATION

The clustered shafts of the great piers, the multiple moldings of the massive arches, the carved capitals that mark the springing of the arches would have little effect, if they were obscured by poor lighting; and the master mason strove to solve this problem by still further variations in the vaults. In order to profit from a large window opening directly into the central western bay through the west façade, the master mason raised the crown of the western transverse arch 2.00 m above the keystone of the intersecting diagonal ribs and constructed this western web as a rampant vault rising to the top of the window. Rampant vaults were not an innovation, but this particular one at Saint-Denis is, to the best of my knowledge, the first Early Gothic example and confirms the assurance with which the Saint-Denis masons solved their challenges. Possibly less successful, another solution for enlarging windows and introducing light diagonally into the interior occurs in the northwestern and southwestern bays, where the exterior openings rise 0.30 m above the crowns of the transverse and wall ribs with somewhat awkward results. Unless the viewer is within a few feet of the wall below, the tops of the windows appear to be blocked. Yet additional light is admitted thanks to the sharp downward angle of the sill of the window embrasures.[82] Conscious exploitation of such diagonal, or slanting, beams of light also becomes evident in the treatment of the openings from the upper chapels into the central western bay. Resembling windows, these openings have five steps which descend from the upper chapel pavement level to the bottom of the north and south bay openings. The arrangement allows the light from the upper chapel windows to penetrate to the floor of the central bay.[83] Such deliberate structural adjustments demonstrate the masons' preoccupation with every detail of the architectural design.

Fig. 67a

Fig. 67c

MASONRY AND DESIGN PROBLEMS

In an earlier article, I referred to the problem of the thickness of the vaults over the southwestern bay.[84] Now I wish for more conclusive evidence to determine the thicknesses for all of the western vaults. Holes cut through the vaults of the southwestern and northwestern bays in the eighteenth century to facilitate the hanging of the bells in the towers show that these vaults are now 0.90 m thick; that certainly seems excessive. A sondage made in the southwestern corner of the southern upper chapel, presumably under the direction of Jules Formigé in 1959, indicated that the dressed masonry of the south wall and southwestern corner extended two beds, 0.70 m, below the present floor level.[85] This masonry rests on rough rubble, but there is no sure evidence for an earlier pavement or floor level. My observation that the original thickness of the vault at its crown "seems" to have been 0.20 m thick may be an overstatement since another sondage, evidently made at the same time in the northeastern corner, just inside the window opening into

Fig. 57a,c

Fig. 59

59. Trial excavation in the southwestern corner of the southwestern upper chapel by Jules Formigé, subsequently filled in.

the lower bay uncovered rubble masonry directly below the present floor level. The existing floor of this upper chapel is very uneven, and mortar appears to have been laid over it at different times. Yet the hole cut through the western vault, which exposes a perfect section of the vault masonry, does not show traces of different mortars at different levels. Until new evidence becomes available, the problem of the original thicknesses of the twelfth-century western vaults must remain among the many unsolved problems in the study of Suger's church.

Even more enigmatic details exist in the structure of the eastern bays, which, it will be remembered, were built as a transition from the larger entrance bays to the narrower dimensions of the old nave. In the central eastern bay, for instance, the opening to the nave was partially filled in 1841 when the organ loft was added. The outer, higher arch presumably was intended to conform to the height of the old nave. Given that congruence, the question arises as to why the crown of the central vault rises 1.43 m higher than the crown of the vault to the west, as though the transition from west to east was ultimately to have been a progression to higher elevations. The masons who built the vault had to extend their technical skills since the springing of the eastern ends of the diagonal ribs is 1.20 m lower than that of the western ends of the same arches. Also the eastern profiles of the arches had to be distorted or twisted to an angle in order that they might rest on the double capitals provided for them. Such dexterity is proof of the masons' skills, but there may have been quite different causes for such irregularities. Their search for coherent design related to functional requirements is also evident in the northern and southern wall ribs for which the corresponding attached colonnettes are raised above the capitals under the diagonal ribs by 2.40 m in the west and 3.60 m in the east. It is interesting to note that the same shafts for the wall ribs which pass uninterruptedly by the string course below the window opening into the upper chapel might be cited as a pro-

a

b

60. (a) Junction of north wall of the thirteenth-century nave with the western bays, showing eastern half of the northeast buttress, as excavated by Jules Formigé; (b) detail of northeast buttress of the western bays.

Fig. 67d

totype for similar uninterrupted shafts that rise from the pier bases to the springing of the vaults in the thirteenth-century nave at Saint-Denis,[86] though such a filiation is admittedly tenuous. The design of the north and south elevations of the central eastern bay, a tall arch topped by a smaller arched opening over two smaller arches on a central column compares well with the elevation of the crossing bays and with that originally in the choir of Saint-Germain-des-Prés in Paris as well as those elevations in the cathedral of Sens.[87] I have proposed a similar design as a possible solution for a reconstruction of the elevation of Suger's choir. In spite of seemingly awkward solutions to some of the structural problems, the master mason who built the eastern central bay was alert to current aesthetic trends and may have been instrumental in proposing new solutions.

In the lateral bays, where the reduction of width of the side aisles had to be achieved, a number of problems resulted in awkward solutions. On the north side, where work evidently started first, decisions about such details as the width of the circular staircase inside of pier no. 5 that would lead to the upper chapels must have been overlooked. After the first seven beds of the masonry to the east of the buttress were in place, the mason must have realized that the exterior was not thick enough to allow for the outer circumference of the stairway; as an accommodation, two setbacks were extended 0.30 m by 0.50 m on corbels to increase the thickness of the wall at this particular point.[88] At least that is the only explanation I can offer to account for the two badly weathered capitals forming part of the masonry. (These were noted by Viollet-le-Duc in 1846 in his drawing of the north elevation of the base of the north tower.) Because this entire area was one of Formigé's last centers of interest, the exterior of the twelfth-century masonry as well as the northwestern corner of the thirteenth-century nave have been completely exposed down to the level of the rubble foundations. The finished masonry including a typical twelfth-century bevel and, just above the bevel, a prominent multiple molding not unlike a string course may now be clearly seen. There is no

Fig. 60a,b

Fig. 61; App. K.12

61. North side of the interior of the northeastern bay of the western entrance bays.

way of determining whether all this masonry was intended to be above or below ground in the twelfth century,[89] or whether the capitals were added to minimize the results of a miscalculation made in the early stages of construction.

Other puzzling details need attention. Under the northwest corner of the vault of the same northeastern bay is a curious large capital decorated with two apelike creatures. The capital sits on three small colonnettes resting on a triangular corbel decorated by a crouching figure. The ensemble was obviously inserted into the surrounding masonry, possibly while construction was in progress, for there are two distinct masons' marks incised on two stones adjacent to the capital.[90] Speculation about the function of such a fantasy is obviously futile, but the diagonal position of the capital recalls the fact that only three other capitals in the eastern bays are placed diagonally, and none is so positioned in the southeast bay, which suggests that the new aesthetic principle of diagonality was still in its infancy.

The massive masonry around the exterior of the southern circular staircase in pier no. 8 may indicate that problems relative to the stairway were better understood by the time work was started there, and that construction of the

a   b

fore-church had in fact begun on the north side. The south stair also descends farther than the north staircase and consequently may better preserve the original disposition.

The sounding made by Formigé's workmen above pier no. 11 in the northeast corner of the southeast bay revealed a fragment of the original twelfth-century transverse arch and vaulting surface. Although they discovered only the springing of the slightly stilted transverse arch and less than a meter of the vault itself, enough survives to prove that the twelfth-century vault was above or slightly higher than the existing thirteenth-century vault and that the diagonal rib must have sprung from the same level as the transverse arches. In an earlier chapter attention was called to the capitals encased in the lower masonry of both piers nos. 11 and 12. Their foliate decoration is the same as that on the other twelfth-century capitals of the same piers, but the lower level led me to propose that this might have been the height of the eighth-century nave arcade. Since there are two such capitals, and since the height they reflect seems satisfactory as the height of the Carolingian side aisle, I believe that the proposal is valid, but I must admit that given the evidence it is difficult to reconstruct all of the details of the structure of the piers in the twelfth century.

62. (a) East side of southeastern chapel of western bays, showing twelfth-century capitals at different levels and exploratory holes in masonry of piers and vaults; (b) detail of exploratory hole in the east side of the vault of the southeast chapel of the western bays, showing original lower portions of twelfth-century arch and vault still in place.

Fig. 62a,b

UPPER CHAPELS

The upper chambers of the western bays at Saint-Denis were planned as part of the original ensemble to serve as chapels, with altars and relics. As an integral part of the western structure, they provided a solid platform on which the twin towers were placed. Suger mentioned them in three different passages which identify their dedications but only hint at their liturgical or symbolic functions. The first reference, in his *Ordinatio* of 1140–41, identifies Hugh, the archbishop of Rouen, and other bishops as performing the dedication of the "new church" (nova ecclesia) on 9 June 1140, including an upper (superius) oratory of Saint Romanus and two lower (inferius) oratories, on one side that of Saint Hippolytus, on the other that of Saint Bartholemew. Suger also stated that lights for the three chapels were to be endowed by the rent from a property adjacent to the cemetery which he had purchased from William de Cornillon.[91]

In his *De Consecratione,* Suger elaborated on the dedications. The upper chapel, "most beautiful and worthy to be the dwelling place of angels," was dedicated "in honor of the Holy Mother of God, the eternal Virgin Mary, of Saint Michael the Archangel, of All the Angels, of St. Romanus (who rests in that very place), and of many other saints whose names are inscribed there." The lower, *inferius,* chapel "on the right [they dedicated] in honor of Saint Bartholomew and many other saints; the lower chapel on the left, however, where St. Hippolytus is said to rest, in honor of him and Sts. Lawrence, Sixtus, Felicissimus, Agapitus and many others."[92] Earlier in the same chapter, Suger stated that "we chanted in celebration of this ceremony a polyphonic praise." Finally, in his *De Administratione,* Suger described the chapel of Saint Romanus in these terms: "How secluded this place is, how hallowed, how convenient for those celebrating the divine rites has come to be known to those who serve God there as though they were already dwelling, in a degree, in Heaven while they sacrifice."[93] In this instance, however, he said that the lateral or side chapels were "in the lower nave of the church" (in inferiori testudine ecclesiae)[94] and that on one side the chapel was dedicated to Saint Hippolytus and his companions and on the other to Saint Nicholas. Although there are some discrepancies among these descriptions, there is little doubt that they all refer to the three upper chapels.

Although Suger and his contemporaries regarded the upper chapels as worthy of the angels, there is some doubt about how long the chapels continued in active service. Even a most enthusiastic young priest might have found the climb up the circular stairs arduous—the equivalent in our terms of at least four floors—and there is evidence that by the thirteenth century the chapels had fallen into disuse. In 1236, according to the so-called *Chronicon S. Dionysii ad Cyclos Paschales,* the relics of Saint Hippolytus were transferred to the newly finished chapel in the west corner of the north transept.[95] By inference Saint Hippolytus's resting place was already considered so unworthy that a new chapel was thought necessary. Frankl pointed out that the central upper chapel seemed designed for security and might have served as a treasure room ensuring the safety of relics.[96] By the eighteenth century, at the

63. North opening between upper central and northwestern chapel, showing monolithic colonnettes and bases with chamfered corners.

latest, this central chapel must have been almost abandoned, for when the organ was installed in 1841 the large pedal bellows that provided the air pressure for the pipes were placed there. The bellows remain there today, along with remnants of the mechanism that ran the clock formerly installed in the western rose window. The side chapels seem to have suffered more grievously, for evidence indicates that wooden floors and partitions were built into them, and even fires were lighted there which blackened parts of the upper arches. As recently as World War II the south tower was used as an observation post by German soldiers billeted there, and at the same time remote portions of the crypt were used by the French Resistance to store arms and supplies.

In their monograph of 1925, Vitry and Brière stated that the capitals of the upper chapel "comptent parmi les élémens décoratifs les plus intacts de l'église; il paraissent avoir echappé à toute restauration."[97] Unfortunately this is no longer true. With a few notable exceptions, the capitals of the windows and openings between the chapels have been badly damaged or replaced by modern cement blanks. The webbing of the vaults and the profiles of the diagonal ribs of the center and south chapels indicate that they were rebuilt at some unknown date; but other details of the structure appear untouched.

Although today the proportions of the upper side chapels seem more lofty

App. K.22–24

and elegant than those of the bays below them, this would not have been the case when the ground floor pavement was at its original twelfth-century level. Yet there are marked differences between the upper and the lower bays. Immediately noticeable is the relative simplicity of the masonry of the north and south chapels. No rounded colonnettes or attached columns mold the surfaces of the piers as they rise to the springing of the vaults accented by simple continuous string courses. Even the bases lack any moldings, except for a horizontal chamfer, or bevel.[98] The arches under the vaults have simple tori, but the plain surfaces of the masonry accent the essentially mural construction.

Fig. 57e,f

Two new details—one structural and the other decorative—first appear in the upper chapel. The tall, slender colonnettes flanking the windows in the north and south chapels were built as part of the adjoining masonry in a sequence of beds, yet equally tall and slender colonnettes of the windows opening from the central chapel to the side chapels are monolithic. Such monolithic detached shafts were widely used in Early Gothic buildings.[99] Although they occur in Anglo-Saxon work and more frequently in Norman churches of the late eleventh century,[100] I know of no examples in the Ile-de-France predating these upper shafts at Saint-Denis. Described in France as colonnettes en délit, such shafts have both a structural and a visual function. They were cut in the quarry horizontally, or parallel to the limestone beds, but were put in place with these beds running vertically. When set vertically, the colonnettes acted as rigid struts in the horizontal beds of the masonry. Also, since they were detached, standing free from the adjacent masonry, they provided vertical, linear accents wherever they were used. Another detail, purely visual, evidently introduced into the Ile-de-France at Saint-Denis, is the chamfered edges of the projections of the engaged piers of the center chapel.[101] The simple cutting of the edges of the rectangular blocks of stone creates planes that are diagonal to the other surfaces, thereby softening the transitions between them.

Fig. 63

Figs. 52c, 63

The presence of these details in the central upper chapel prompted me, in an earlier paper, to question whether two different master masons were responsible for the west work and the choir, or whether one unusually sensitive and capable young man might have been able to create what at first glance seem to be quite different architectural entities.[102] Later in this volume, our examination of the crypt and choir will note that similar chamfers occur in the crypt, on the bases of the columns of the ambulatory of the choir, and even on the embrasures of the south transept portal. Monolithic shafts are also present in the radiating chapels of the choir. Discussion of the question of one or two master masons, however, will be more meaningful after the study of the second campaign to the east.[103]

THE TOWERS

Before we consider the west façade and the western portals, the last important part of the western ensemble, the "high and noble" towers, needs attention. Suger assured us that from the very beginning he intended that his new church would have "twin towers"[104] over the main western entrance.

64. South side of southwest tower.

He also told us that, before the end of 1148 or early in 1149 (when he was still writing his *De Administratione*), work was under way "upon the front towers," one of which was "already completed."[105] In other words, before his death in 1151, one of the western towers was finished and work on the other one had at least started. Since he called them "twin towers," he presumably intended that their design would be similar. For that reason our reconstruction of the twelfth-century façade has identical, if mirror image, towers. The actual design of the north tower, as shown in drawings and engravings before its destruction, was not the same as the south tower. The *attachements* prepared for Debret in 1838 show details apparently executed later than those of the south tower, so that the north tower must have been built for the most part after Suger's death and consequently does not belong in this study.[106] The south tower, finished before Suger's death, deserves a careful examination.

Figs. 64, 68

Fig. 72
Figs. 82, 83

65. Detail of lower arches of southwest tower.

A distinction of the tower is that it is not flush with the plane of the western façade but is set back on the mass of the western bays. Because of rebuilding and restoration of the upper portions of the façade in the four-teenth and again in the nineteenth centuries[107] the exact amount of the original setback proves difficult to estimate. The photogrammetric elevation of the west façade indicates that the southern face of the tower is set back 0.50 m from the exterior of the west bays. Such a distance seems reason-able since the twelfth-century crenellations were probably flush with the masonry of the façade. Thus 0.50 m would provide just enough space for a *tour de rond*, or passageway, behind the crenellations. In any case, since the crenellations would have created a strong visual break between the façade and the tower, we can be certain that the towers were not designed as a continuous entity as, for instance, at Jumièges, La Trinité in Caen, or Chartres.

From the top of the present crenellations to the top of the upper balustrade, the south tower measures 21.20 m. There are two levels with open arcades. The lower one has two openings, 1.40 m wide by 6.70 m high, topped by pointed arches, *en tier points*. Two attached colonnettes with badly eroded capitals flank the openings, and the arches have two rolls. The openings appear to be pierced through the masonry, which creates a proper sense of solidity at the base of the tower. The continuous abaci at the springing of the arches provide the necessary horizontal accent binding the arches together.

The upper, or top, level has three arched openings separated by cylindrical piers. The openings have slightly different widths, measuring 1.30 m, 1.50 m, 1.40 m, respectively, from north to south, but have a uniform height of 7.10 m. The arches also vary slightly: the north one is pointed but the other two are semicircular. The moldings of the arches almost replicate those of the level below, but the capitals are cruciform to support the rolls, or tori, of the receding arches. Such cruciform capitals are unusual and provide another detail suggesting the presence of Norman or Anglo-Norman masons in Suger's workshops. The capitals in place today are either recent or were replaced during the nineteenth-century restorations, but their cruciform

Fig. 65

App. K.33a

66. Timberwork for holding bells inside southwest tower.

shape must be original, as indicated by the presence of a number of seemingly original abaci. The top balustrade also dates from the nineteenth century, and there is some question about the presence of such a balustrade in the twelfth century, when a simple corbel table at the top would have been more customary. The present pitched roof above the balustrade is another nineteenth-century feature of purely arbitrary proportions and pitch. Since Suger spoke of this tower as "already completed" there is good reason to doubt that he planned a spire.

Although Debret's restorers seem to have worked on most of the details, the design of the tower, except for the crowning pitched roof and balustrade, can be regarded as twelfth-century. The presence of original masons' marks on the inside of the small circular staircase that mounts from the platforms to the top offers further confirmation for the date. Square or slightly rectangular towers were most common in northern regions, as at Speyer, Corvey, Tournai, and Caen. The Saint-Denis tower is more open and lighter in design than those mentioned, although the progression from two to three openings was familiar, as seen especially in the eastern towers of the Tournai transept. Suger spoke of the towers as "high and lofty," and since he intended to have them "richly" decorated, their function in the program of the first campaign may have been primarily visual. Perhaps the hanging of bells in such towers was taken for granted, but we have no specific evidence for any bells there before the fourteenth century. The sturdy wooden scaffolding inside the south tower today, which serves to isolate and contain the vibrations of the bells from the masonry, must date from that time or later, since the great *bourdon* still hanging in the south tower was not installed until 1772. With the towers originally an important part of the western façade complex, the discussion of their program or function must await the analysis of the façade itself.

Fig. 66

a

b

c

d

67. Four of the eight photographs used for photogrammetrics of central bays of west work: (a,b) ground story, south side, moving west to east; (c,d) triforium level, south side, moving west to east.

68. The west façade of the abbey church of Saint-Denis.

CHAPTER SIX

The West Façade
and the Western Portals

The Restorations

Fig. 68

For every aspect of Suger's church at Saint-Denis analysis must begin with the restorations and alterations that have changed the original disposition. Although particularly true of the plan of the western bays, knowledge of the restorations to the west façade and western portals is even more urgent. Just before the middle of the nineteenth century, when extensive restorations by François Debret had been terminated by his dismissal as architect in charge of Saint-Denis,[1] the façade was described as follows: "mutilated façade, deprived forever of historical interest, and extremely ugly besides."[2] Since then most scholars have been so suspicious of the façade as a whole and of its details, including the portals, that they hesitated to accord to twelfth-century masons and artists the credit due them.[3] Although, as the following survey will prove, the additions and changes to the façade have indeed been extensive, no historian of medieval architecture or sculpture can afford to ignore Saint-Denis as the earliest in the series of Gothic façades.

In its exposed position, the western façade can hardly have escaped damage during the fifteenth and sixteenth centuries,[4] but the first recorded deliberate modification took place in 1771, when the portals were considered too small for the elaborate canopies and decorations used in the processions for special occasions. The most serious aesthetic damage resulted from the removal of the statue columns in the embrasures of all three portals, as well as the trumeau figure of Saint Denis in the central portal.[5] Although damage

167

69. Drawing of the destruction
of the northwest tower.

must have been done during the Revolution, there is no record of what
happened to the portals or to the façade. In 1806, during the first years of the
restoration ordered by Napoleon, the raising of the level of the pavement
altered the proportions of the portals. For the west façade the most disastrous
period occurred under François Debret after a bolt of lightning damaged the
thirteenth-century spire of the north tower in 1837. This accident gave Debret the opportunity to apply for new funds to restore, or redo, the entire
façade, including all the sculpture of the portals. This work, which completely altered the fabric of the façade, must be reviewed in some detail.

Fig. 69

By rebuilding the north spire with stone much heavier than the original,
Debret made a grave error that threatened the stability of the entire façade.
The miscalculation led to his dismissal. During the rebuilding of the north
spire, Debret had covered the façade with scaffolding which gave his workmen unlimited access to the entire elevation. Almost every stone was transformed in some way. The intricate restoration of the portal sculpture will be
described shortly, and only the major additions and transformations to the
façade above the portals will be summarized here. In a typically meticulous

70. Debret's proposal for the restoration of the west façade, approved 15 February 1838.

Fig. 70

nineteenth-century manner Debret prepared *attachements,* or detailed drawings, with coded color washes. Some included references indicating his proposed restorations for the entire façade. The precision of the drawings which survive today in the archives of the Monuments Historiques[6] can be deceiving, since comparisons with recent photographs show that many details were never executed.[7] A simple enumeration of what was done, however, demonstrates the extent of the disfigurement. The roll moldings and arches of the

a

b

71. Sculpture reworked or added by Debret to west façade: (a) detail of kings under blind arcade, added; (b) detail of band of abstract ornament, added; (c) one of four figures of Apostles, added; (d) signs of the Evangelists in spandrels of rose window, added; (e) decorated moldings framing rose window, partially restored.

lancets above the portals were recarved, if not replaced, and bizarre geometrical designs with commemorative inscriptions of lamentable epigraphy were incised into the originally unornamented surfaces of those blind arcades. Four small statues on pedestals carved in relief were added in the spandrels between the three arches over the north and south portals. Large horizontal bands of abstract ornament were introduced into the masonry under the upper windows on the north and south sides of the façade. Projecting string courses at the level of the original string course under the rose window were continued across the buttresses that flank the façade. A blind lancet arch was added at the upper level to each of the four buttresses. At the same level blind arcades containing the figures of eight kings in all (each ca. 1.00 m high) were cut into the originally blank masonry of the façade below the north and south towers. Four medallions with relief figures of the animals representing the four Evangelists were also added to the spandrels of the rose window; framing the rose window, the roll moldings containing a frieze of decorative busts were recarved; and the crenellations crowning the top of the façade were rebuilt. Few, if any, details of the carved decoration such as capitals or string courses remained untouched. In order to save the entire structure, the north tower had to be dismantled by Debret's successor, Viollet-le-Duc.[8]

App. K.
32a–f,
33a–c

The Design of the Façade in the Twelfth Century

This rapid summary of the major alterations is a prelude to the explanation of a reconstruction of the façade as I believe Suger's master mason designed it.

c

d

e

The rather static, somewhat mechanical reconstruction, based on the photogrammetric elevation prepared by the Institut Géographique National de France in 1968, provided the basis for the more lively pencil drawing by Gregory Robeson. The first deviation from the photogrammetric elevation involved the entrance and the level of the sills of the doors. The original twelfth-century elevation was achieved by superimposing the elevation of the excavation in front of the central and north portals onto those portals. In describing the discovery of the original sills 0.52 m below the existing

Fig. 73

Fig. 72

72. Reconstruction of west façade as envisaged by Abbot Suger. Drawn by Gregory Robeson.

pavement and of solid masonry benches 0.40 m below the sills that extend across both portals, I explained the lack of evidence for steps rising to the sills from the west. As a possible architectural solution to the problem, the reconstruction drawings indicate three broad, low steps between the embrasures of the portals; but we must bear in mind that such steps remain hypothetical. They have no archaeological basis. On the other hand, the masonry benches across each portal below the sills are archaeological facts for which a satisfactory architectural explanation remains elusive.

73. Reconstruction of twelfth-century design of west façade, based on photogrammetric analysis.

In Robeson's pencil drawing only general indications refer to the restoration of the three portals. The northern tympanum has been left blank, since we have no information about the lost mosaic which Suger stated he had ordered for that location.[9] Only the second archivolt over the north portal and the inner archivolt over the south portal were decorated.[10] The statue columns on the embrasures of all three portals are vaguely indicated, and the trumeau of the central portal with its statue of Saint Denis is restored to its original position. All of these details will be examined more fully in the section on the iconography or symbolism of the façade.

In the reconstruction Debret's additions and embellishments have been eliminated from the façade, and the masonry is shown unadorned as it appears in the early engravings. The tracery of the rose window has been redrawn to conform more closely to the design of the twelfth-century rose window in the north transept of Saint-Etienne in Beauvais,[11] but without any surrounding radial figures. Finally, the crenellations are shown flush with the façade masonry with simple rectangular openings, as they are on the west façade of Notre Dame in Etampes.[12] Although the north tower was not finished before Suger's death and early engravings show that its design was not the same as that of the south tower,[13] in the reconstruction the north tower appears as a reverse, or mirror image, of the south tower on the assumption that Suger's master mason intended to build twin towers.[14] All surface decoration has been removed from the lower tiers of the façade below, and the roofs over the towers are arbitrarily drawn as simple caps without balustrades or any other ornament.

The following analysis of the structure and design of the façade will be based on this reconstruction of what I believe Suger's master mason envisaged as the major entrance to the royal abbey. "The façade of Saint-Denis is not a screen attached to the western portions of the church. It was intended to serve as a monumental entrance into the royal abbey and it was conceived as an integral part of the two western bays to which it provides immediate access. The façade, therefore, must be studied in the context of the entire western ensemble, and not merely in terms of its own composition."[15] Carleton Granbery's admirable strip-away study shows the relationship of the interior and the exterior so clearly that further comment is scarcely needed. The different levels of the prominent string courses on the façade reflect the fact that the vaults of the lateral (north and south) bays are lower than those of the central bay and that consequently the upper chapels have different volumes, as demonstrated in the tall windows to either side of the central rose. The correlation is not an exact one, however, as explained earlier in the study of the lighting of the west bays, because of the extension, or enlarging, of the lower windows above the level of the springing of the vaults. This search for as much direct light as possible necessitated a rampant vault in the central bays and the somewhat awkward blocking of the lateral windows by the lateral vaulting arches.

Another unusual structural feature was the building of the three portals with stone different from that used for the mural construction of the façade.[16] The portal masonry is aligned in regular beds measuring almost exactly 0.295 m high, whereas the beds of the masonry above the portals or in the

Fig. 74

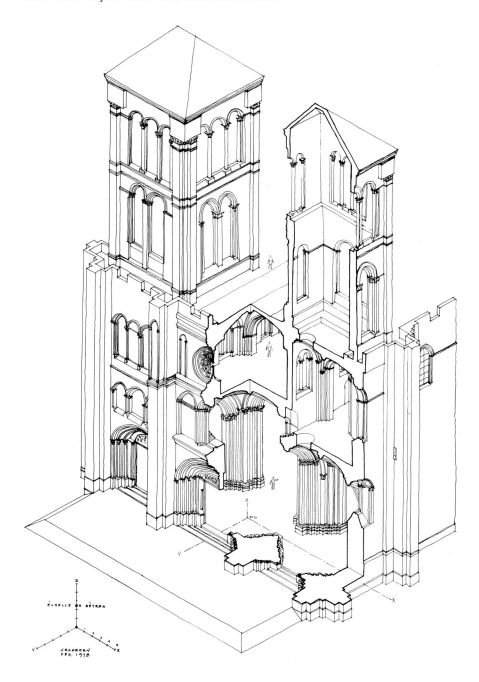

74. Isometric reconstruction and analysis of design of construction of western bays. Drawn by Carleton Granbery.

adjacent buttresses vary in height from 0.12 to 0.48 m. The regularity of the portal masonry provided a key for the detection of alterations. The quality of the limestone in the portals is superior to that of the blocks used for the fabric of the structure. The finer-grained stone facilitated the carving of many details in the sculpture.[17]

Before we consider the complicated program of the sculpture and its relation to the meaning or symbolism of the entire façade, some references to its overall design seem appropriate. The study of the arrangement and relationships between the major features of the decoration of the west façade reveals some unexpectedly interesting implications about twelfth-century procedures. Although the final or definitive sequence of such procedures remains uncertain, proof that geometrical proportions rather than mathematical measurements established these relationships deserves to be demonstrated.

The location of major elements of the design as well as the discrepancies in measurements between the portals was established when the plan of the western bays was first conceived. The positions and spacing of the prominent vertical buttresses were determined when the decision to align the major supports of the new construction with the old nave was made. Consequently, the two central buttresses measured on axis are 10.10 m apart, the same as the width of the old Carolingian nave. The exterior, or corner, buttresses are not precisely symmetrical in their lateral dimensions, evidently because they were aligned with old exterior walls of the Carolingian side aisles which were not exactly the same width. As a result, between the inner surfaces of the buttresses, the south portal measures 6.10 m in width, whereas the north portal, again between the inner surfaces of the buttresses, measures 5.80 m in width. Such minor discrepancies can be verified on the photogrammetric elevation and would remain unnoticed if they had not resulted in other deviations in the façade design.

So many different features respond to different combinations and to different propositions that it is frustrating not to be able to discover how the master mason designed the western façade or what constituted his primary preoccupations as he did so. Yet it appears that he had a controlling design or master plan from which he inadvertently deviated slightly in the beginning but to which he adhered with remarkable consistency in finishing the building.

The diagrams superimposed on the proposed reconstruction of the western façade were drawn before all the details of the reconstruction, such as the tops of the towers, had been fully deliberated. The photogrammetric elevation allows precise measurements across the façade and discloses minor differences as well as major divisions. The various series of arches and openings are contained by or enclosed in a square 25.30 m which extends from the bench across the portals to the lower edge of the openings in the crenellations and across the portals between the inner faces of the lateral vertical buttresses. This square is not rigidly divided into equal parts because the major vertical axis of the central portal is not in exact alignment with the axis of the upper rose window, and the northern side is slightly narrower than the southern. Superimposed triangles seem to locate important parts of the design. A large equilateral triangle with its base on the bench below the portals has its apex exactly in the center of the rose window. If this triangle is inverted, its baseline touches the tops of the arches over the windows opening into the upper north and south chapels, and its apex lies in the middle of the central portal, but with the slight deviations to the south because the schema reflects the slight difference in the width of the north and south sides. Gerald Allen as a student in my graduate seminar in 1971 devised and drew these

Fig. 75a,b

Fig. 75a

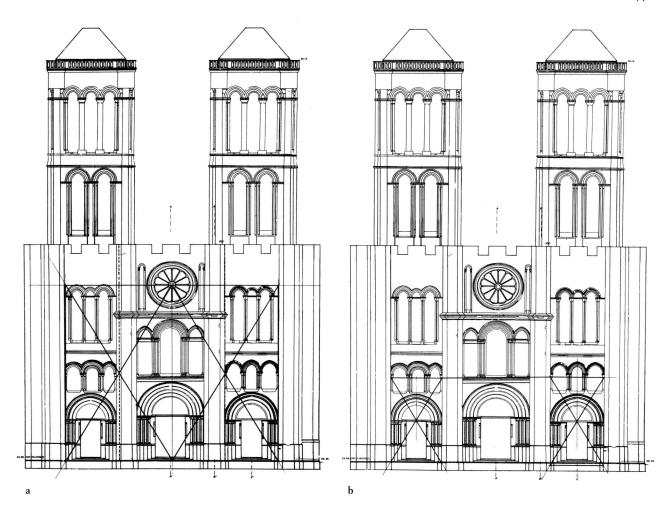

a   b

diagrams. He concluded, "There are several amazingly precise shapes on the façade, but, in the case of the square, they do not multiply into anything larger or, in both cases, break down into anything smaller."[18] He found a number of other shapes that could be diagrammed, but the progression or connections among them remained elusive.

I believe there are quite practical reasons for the slight deviations but have not discovered any system that might produce the overall design. The location of such major elements as the vertical buttresses was determined when the decision was made to align the major supports of the new construction with the old nave. Thus, as noted above, the two central buttresses measured on axis are 10.10 m apart, which is exactly the width of the old Carolingian nave. The lateral, or north and south corner, buttresses were not aligned directly with the old side-aisle walls but were in some way influenced by the difference in the width of the old aisles because the same difference, 0.30 m, exists between the width of the north and south sides of the façade.

Proof that the twelfth-century master mason relied on geometrical figures rather than mathematical measurements for his proportions exists in this

75. (a) Reconstruction of twelfth-century design of west façade with superimposed triangles; (b) reconstruction of twelfth-century design of west façade with analytical triangles superimposed on lateral bays.

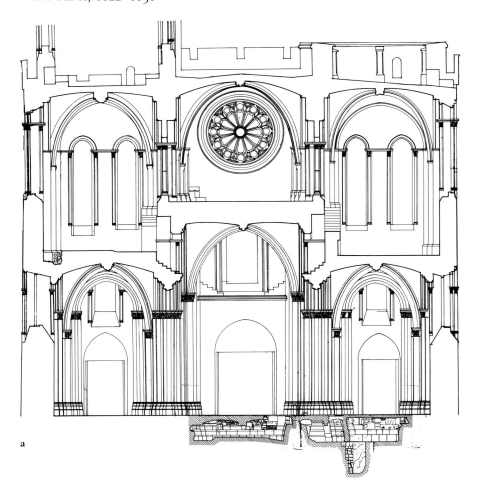

a

76. (a) A section looking west through the three western bays, including the excavated bases of the twelfth century; (b) (*opposite*) a reconstructed section through the three western bays which shows the reverse of the west façade.

slight mathematical difference of which the mason was evidently not aware until construction had progressed above the portals.[19] With the south portal measuring 6.10 m between the inner faces of the flanking buttresses, the equilateral triangles with such a base will be higher than similar triangles drawn with sides equal to 5.80 m, the width of the north portal between the buttresses. A diagram clearly demonstrates the slight tilt or deviation from the horizontal that resulted from these different heights and shows how the string course above the central portal reflects the same deviation; yet all horizontals above that level are correct. Although there is no evidence to prove how measurements were determined, that is, from which base to which height, it is certain that plane geometry produced the proportions of different parts and their relations to other parts. Certain adjustments such as horizontals controlled by plumb lines could be verified, but other maladjustments such as the slight shift in the vertical axis resulted in awkward displacements, including the different dimensions of the blind lancets located at the level of the rose window and the restricted space for the right, or south, lancet in contrast to that for the north one.

Fig. 75b

b

Similar displacements must account for the rather curious differences between the interior and the exterior of the west façade. The three portals, for instance, which appear to be symmetrically placed between the exterior buttresses are noticeably off-center between the piers of the interior. The central portal is 0.40 m closer to the northern pier than it is to the southern one, and by the same amount, the crown of its arch lies to the north of the crown of the central vault. Each side portal is squeezed, as it were, toward the exterior. Such irregularities would have disturbed neither the medieval workman, who made whatever adjustments were necessary as the structure advanced, nor the contemporary observer, but they are evidence of some of the problems that arose in the process of building a relatively complex design.

Fig. 76a,b

The Portals

The image of three arches in which the center one is larger than the side ones is reminiscent of the Roman triumphal arch, with which Suger was certainly familiar.[20] Historians of Roman civilization have described the triumphant emperor passing with his legions through the arch in an act of purification and cleansing, on his way to be received as a divine power in his heavenly city. This expression of an emperor's divine relation to the deity was emphasized by Ottonian emperors in the tenth and eleventh centuries in their revival of imperial architecture.[21] Such an interpretation would seem perfectly appropriate for the Saint-Denis portals as the entrance to the royal abbey, particu-

Fig. 77

77. Three western portals.

larly since Suger admittedly admired the antiquities of Rome. Yet architec-
turally the triumphal arch was a separate entity, unassociated with a
monumental ensemble, and Suger himself referred to the portals in quite
different terms.

In his description of the consecration ceremonies of the western portals,
Suger mentioned "the one glorious procession of these three men [the
bishops of Meaux, Rouen, and Senlis]," who left the church through a single
door. The three bishops, acting as one, proceeded to perform the holy consecration of the three doors in a single act, and "thirdly, they reentered
through a single door of the cemetery."[22] The reiteration of the numbers
three and one referring to the three portals, as well as the procession itself,
was to "imply Trinitarian symbolism."[23] That is further confirmed by the
presence of a dove and the bust of God the Father holding a disk with the
apocalyptic Lamb—the symbolic representation of the Trinity—on the keystones of the two outer archivolts of the central portal.[24] The number three is
repeated again and again in the design of the façade: three vertical elevations
of three divisions between the buttresses; three arches over each of the three
portals (in each instance, a single window flanked by two blind arcades);
three arches (two windows separated by a blind arch) as the top division of

Fig. 78

78. Restored figures of dove and bust of the Deity holding the Agnus Dei as symbols of the Trinity on the archivolts of the central portal, west façade.

the north and south elevations; and three open arcades as the top story of the south tower, presumably intended also for the north tower. If we can be certain about any of the details of Suger's church, it is that he intended the three portals as well as the entire façade to embody a reference to the Trinity.

Answers to other questions about the Trinity are more difficult, but the possibilities expose how complex such references may be, especially in the context of other themes that combine to constitute the whole. The problem of representing the Trinity in visual form always has been a challenge. As Adelheid Heimann succinctly stated, "The artistic imagination, always on dangerous ground when it attempted to represent the Trinity, showed a definite reluctance to give shape to the threefold God of the Creation, and though the scriptural interpretation sustained the dogma throughout the Middle Ages, there are only rare and isolated examples in pictorial art to compare with the impressive sequence of texts."[25] The representation on the archivolts at Saint-Denis is, to the best of my knowledge, the first to incorporate the Trinity into a complex scheme of judgment and salvation in monumental sculpture.[26] I shall only summarize the possible interpretations that refer directly to Saint-Denis.

"In the beginning was the Word, and the Word was with God, and the Word was God." The opening chapter of the Gospel according to Saint John describes the beginning of the Christian universe—the beginning of Christian history. As the Triune God, the Trinity was the creator of the world, and as the beginning was the Alpha, whereas the Last Judgment, as the end of the world, was the Omega. Thus the Trinity and the Last Judgment on the axis of the central portal at Saint-Denis established the time frame—the entire span of Christian history—for the themes of the portals. The association of the Trinity with the beginning of the world was probably familiar to Suger, who could have seen a fresco in Saint-Paul-Outside-the-Walls in Rome which showed the Trinity at the beginning of the Creation cycle. This representation is unusual for it is one of very few early examples which substituted the Lamb for the body of Christ.[27] In another context the Trinity was interpreted as the supreme hope and desire of man—for on earth the faithful see the image of the Trinity "as through a glass darkly" [King James; the Douay Version reads "in a dark manner"] but after the Last Judgment they will see the Trinity perfectly, "face to face" (1 Corinthians 13:12). The representation of the Trinity, seen face to face, becomes the assurance of Salvation.

In the archivolts of the central portal the Trinity is placed not only on the central axis of the portal and of the church, but also in the middle of twenty-four elders, or patriarchs, of the apocalyptic vision of the Second Coming of Christ. The twenty-four elders became a standard reference to the apocalyptic vision of John of Patmos, as preliminary to but distinct from the Last Judgment itself. These twenty-four kings, seated on thrones and holding "harps and golden vials" (Apocalypse 5:8), were a popular theme in art during the early Middle Ages[28] but did not appear in monumental sculpture until the twelfth century.[29] The most familiar example occurs in the tympanum at Moissac, which Emile Mâle considered to be a direct copy of the famous page in the Beatus of Saint-Sever.[30] But, although the miniature shows God holding a disk with the Paschal Lamb in one hand and a scepter with a dove in the other, the symbols of the Trinity were not included in the sculpture at Moissac. At Saint-Denis the elders are shown with the Trinity, which has been separated from Christ, but there are no signs of the Evangelists as at Moissac. Perhaps such omissions or changes are not of great significance, but the fact emerges that we find no prototypes for the complicated juxtaposition of themes at Saint-Denis. The Trinity with God holding the apocalyptic Lamb may be unusual, but the Lamb is appropriate in conjunction with the twenty-four elders, who, since they appeared in heaven, symbolized the Celestial Jerusalem, as they adored the Lamb, representing Christ, the means of Salvation (Apocalypse 5:8). In the twelfth century the Trinity was considered to have been present at the Last Judgment in the person of Christ so that a close link was forged between the Trinity in the archivolts and the Christ in the central tympanum.[31]

"The massive figure of Christ, one of the more controversial and generally disparaged sculptures at Saint-Denis, dominates the entire portal."[32] Although the restorations were extensive and included the filling in and obliteration of the important iconographical detail of the wound below his right breast caused by Longinus's spear and the addition of an appalling nineteenth-century head, we concluded that the figure of Christ "retains its original pose and, in general, its twelfth-century form and stylized drapery arrangement."[33]

Fig. 79

Fig. 80

79. Central portal, west façade.

80. The tympanum of the central portal, west façade (all heads are nineteenth-century restorations).

A simple description of the unusual image of Christ reveals that more than one reference was intended. He is at once seated on his throne and suspended on the cross. The upper torso, placed directly in front of the cross, has the right side bared, which would have shown his wound. With arms outstretched he holds a scroll in each hand. Above him the lower two of the four angels support the arms of the cross; a third carries the crown of thorns, and the fourth carries two objects in veiled hands.[34] The lower torso of the seated figure of Christ appears enframed by a mandorla-like throne. His outspread knees are covered by a tunic and mantle, and his feet rest on a footstool, or socle. He is flanked by a row of seated figures, six Apostles on his left, six on his right, plus immediately to his right the figure of the Virgin, who clasps the ends of a veil in her raised hands. At the far left and right of that row stand two angels. The one on the left with a trumpet stands above a figure holding an upright lamp; the other carries a flaming sword directed toward a barred gate with a figure kneeling before it. In the lowest zone at the feet of Christ small naked bodies of the resurrected dead emerge from their tombs. In that row the figure of Suger immediately to the right of Christ kneels in his tomb with his hands clasped in prayer. In spite of the seeming complexity of these images, all can be identified and together with the other figures of the portal present a series of interwoven themes relating to the Last Judgment and to the Salvation of mankind. The dominant theme is the Last Judgment, but the upper and lower portions of Christ's figure also reveal his two natures—the

Fig. 81

184

Son of God enthroned in a mandorla and the Son of man at the moment of his Crucifixion. As the Son of God he appears as the apocalyptic God announcing the end of the world and as the ultimate judge of the blessed and the damned.[35]

The trumpeting angel, the resurrection of the dead, and, in the first archivolt, the scenes of heaven and hell all make direct references to the Last Judgment. These scenes are supplemented by the Apostles, seated *in collegio,* representing the church at the Last Judgment, and *in disputatione*—as the teachers of men.[36] Even more unusual, since their appearance at Saint-Denis seems to be the first one in monumental sculpture, are the representations of the Wise and the Foolish Virgins carved on the jambs of the doorway and at the far left and right in the lintel zone of the tympanum. The Wise Virgins on the left jamb, with upright lamps, were able to go with the bridegroom into the marriage, but the Foolish Virgins, who had not brought oil for their lamps, found the door shut against them (Matthew 25:1–13). This parable refers both to the saved and the damned at the time of Judgment and to the apocalyptic Second Coming of Christ, which may occur at any time. The Wise and the Foolish Virgins carry the message "Watch ye therefore, because you know not the day nor the hour [when the Son of Man cometh]" (Matthew 25:13).

The twenty-four elders in the outer archivolts, seated on thrones, hold musical instruments and vials. They make another direct reference to the

81. The figure of Christ on the tympanum of the central portal, west façade.

Fig. 79

vision of the end of the world, when the apocalyptic Christ will release the forces to destroy all evil forever. To complete this reference to the Second Coming, the bust of Christ, as the keystone to the inner archivolt, appears as the "sign of the Son of man in heaven . . . coming in the clouds of heaven with much power and majesty" (Matthew 24:30). From his left and right two angels approach carrying small naked figures representing souls. They are the angels who "with a trumpet and a great voice . . . shall gather together his elect from the four winds, from the farthest part of the heavens to the utmost bounds of them" (Matthew 24:31). The central figures of the second archivolt, between the Son of man and the Trinity above, are two censing angels. These angels emerging from clouds typify the care with which the entire iconographic program of the portals was conceived and woven into a coherent entity. The clouds associate the angels with the sign of the Son of man below "coming in the clouds," but the censers carried by the angels signify an act of worship—the adoration of the Lamb—directly above them. The Lamb is also adored by the twenty-four elders in the outer archivolts, so that each individual theme amplifies and complements the context of the whole. In a similar manner the figure of Christ on the cross   Fig. 81
magnifies the symbolism of the portal.

Christ, the Son of man and also of God, endured his final agony in order to save mankind. Christ is shown with his arms outstretched in front of the cross to display the stigmata. Hovering angels support the cross and carry other signs of the Passion—the crown of thorns and the nails.[37] The Virgin Mary, directly to his right in the row of Apostles, raises her veil to her cheek in a gesture of mourning for her crucified Son.[38] This gesture can also be interpreted as that of a suppliant pleading for mercy—a direct reference to the Virgin as an intercessor for the salvation of souls at the Last Judgment. Such a conflation of Christ the Savior and Christ the Judge did not make its first appearance at Saint-Denis, as I shall demonstrate shortly; but the possibility that the Apostle immediately to Christ's left represents John the Evangelist[39] increases the probability of a reference to intercession at the Last Judgment, inasmuch as Saint John, when paired with Mary on Christ's right, represents the western concept of the Deisis. There does not seem to be any precedent for this type of Deisis before Saint-Denis. From its early appearance in Byzantine art, where the Virgin is paired with John the Baptist, not John the Disciple, the Deisis symbolized intercession for mankind.[40] At Saint-Denis this triumverate, in the center of the tympanum, assures the faithful that they may be numbered among the blessed, who will see the Trinity "face to face."

The conflation of Christ on the cross and Christ at the Last Judgment made its appearance in western art before Saint-Denis. Medieval scholars have cited the Romanesque tympanum of Beaulieu in the Corrèze, which Emile Mâle proposed as the example that inspired Suger, and used this as evidence that Suger called artists from southwestern France to join his workshop.[41] Yet the date of the tympanum at Beaulieu is uncertain, and scholars today who favor a date contemporary with, or even later than, the western portals at Saint-Denis disallow a direct relationship between the two programs.[42] There are other examples, however—notably that of the mural decoration of Saint George at Oberzell on the island of Reichenau in Lake Constance, with a probable date in the eleventh century[43]—which might have established the idea, if not precise prototypes, for this type of Christ. Relations between Saint-Denis and communities north and east of Paris to the Rhine and farther east began as early as the eighth century and continued under Suger.

One additional, rather puzzling historical aspect of the unusual portrayal of the crucified Christ as Christ of the Last Judgment should be mentioned. Although such a figure became familiar on the great Gothic portals of the thirteenth century, it was virtually ignored during the half century following Saint-Denis. Christ, as shown in the center of the tympana of Early Gothic Royal portals of the second half of the twelfth century, reverted to the typically Romanesque figure of the apocalyptic Christ surrounded by the four symbols of the Evangelists. Only at Notre-Dame at Corbeil and then on the south portal of the west façade at the cathedral of Laon was the Saint-Denis version carved again before its thirteenth-century appearance on the central portal of the south transept at Chartres in the 1220s.

THE BRONZE DOORS

Other features of the Saint-Denis western portals, such as Suger's great bronze doors, also failed to influence later programs. Today the double doors of the central portal "have the pretension of being a reconstruction of Suger's work. . . . It goes without saying that this reconstruction, done in 1842–43, with no documentation, has no value; it is an assemblage of motifs borrowed from stone sculpture or from stained glass windows and the style, as well as the technique, are deplorable."[44] Restored in 1663,[45] but partially ruined by 1771, the original bronze valves were melted down in 1794, although they were still considered "très belles et très riches"[46] when they were carried off. Unquestionably they would number among the most important products of Suger's workshop.

Suger himself admired the doors and considered them a proper entrance to his new church, for he wrote: "Bronze casters having been summoned and sculptors chosen,[47] we set up the main doors on which are represented the Passion of the Saviour and His Resurrection, or rather Ascension, with great cost and much expenditure for their gilding as was fitting for the noble porch. Also [we set up] others, new ones on the right side and the old ones on the left."[48]

Other descriptions of the doors, by historians and one by an artist, were made before they disappeared. The earliest one, written at the beginning of the sixteenth century, is the longest. Doublet wrote:

> One enters into the place in front called the Parvis and from there into the church by three large portals, which occupy all the lower part of the façade, each of which is double [deux battans]: these are covered with bronze with figures, all of which were formerly gilded with fine gold. The middle door measures 15 pieds high and 12 and a half wide; the

other, on the right hand on entering, measures 13 pieds high and 8 and
a half wide; the third, on the left, measures 14 pieds high and 8 pieds
wide.[49]

Earlier in his voluminous text, where he summarized Suger's writings,
Doublet added a few interesting details about the doors:

> He [Suger] said . . . that he brought several expert founders and
> sculptors to decorate and enrich the doors of the principal entrance to
> the church, on which one sees the Passion, Resurrection, Ascension and
> other scenes *with the figure of above-mentioned Abbot prostrated on the*
> *ground* all in bronze: and that he went to great expense both for the
> metal and for the gold that was used; also for the doors of the
> right portal on entering, which he enriched with *metal, gold and enamel,*
> leaving for the third portal on the left side the old doors, which were
> from the first building of the church.[50]

After recording the inscriptions in gilt bronze letters on the central doors, he
added: "On the old doors of the old church built by the King Dagobert this
was written in very old letters, interlaced one with other and difficult to read:

> *Hoc opus Airardus coelesti munere fretus*
> *Offert ecce tibi, Dionysi, pectore miti.*

And lower down, under two figures, one of a bishop and the other of a monk,
are written these words in the same very old letters: *Airardus Monachus:*
Sanctus Dionysius. Which Airard presents to Saint Denys two doors. Here
two large doors are over the wood covered with bronze."[51] A seventeenth-
century inventory adds a detail about the medallions of the center doors: On
the right door Suger had himself represented in a wrinkled monk's habit
(*froc plissé*), with a monastic tonsure, abbot's crozier in hand; he was lying flat
on the ground at the feet of Christ seated with the pilgrims at the table of
Emmaus.[52] Only one drawing of the doors is known, done about 1600 by
Vincenzo Scamozzi. Unfortunately, the single page he devoted to Saint-   **Fig. 82**
Denis includes a plan of the entire church, a sketch of the façade, a section
through the choir, a detail of the interior of the Valois chapel, as well as a
rough sketch of the main doors—*Porta mag. di. Bronza.*[53] The drawing is
skillfully done but so small and sketchy that no details are included. Yet it
establishes that each of the doors had four medallions, or round frames,
enclosing four scenes.

Suger recorded the verses concerning the consecration of 1140 which he
had inscribed or attached in copper gilt letters (in an unspecified place), and
also the verses which he specifically says were on the door. The consecration
verses read:

> For the splendor of the church that
>   has fostered and exalted him,
> Suger has labored for the splendor
>   of the church.

Giving thee a share of what is thine,
  O Martyr Denis,
He prays to thee to pray that he
  may obtain a share of Paradise.
The year was the One Thousand,
  One Hundred, and Fortieth
Year of the Word when [this structure]
  was consecrated.[54]

The verses on the door were:

Whoever thou art, if thou seekest to
  extol the glory of these doors,
Marvel not at the gold and the expense
  but at the craftsmanship of the work.
Bright is the noble work; but, being
  nobly bright, the work
Should brighten the minds, so that
  they may travel, through the true lights,
To the True Light where Christ is the true door.
In what manner it be inherent in
  this world the golden door defines:
The dull mind rises to truth through
  that which is material
And, in seeing this light, is resurrected
  from its former submersion.[55]

The information in the original references to the main doors can be summarized as follows: the two valves were large, measuring (as Doublet recorded and as our excavations confirmed) 15 pieds high by 12 1/2 pieds wide, the equivalent in metric measurements of 5.25 m high by 3.40 m wide. The bronze reliefs must have been cast in eight separate pieces, then attached to a wooden core—a procedure that differentiates them from the Byzantine type, which were flat panels incised with scenes or figures, often inlaid with different colored metal. Suger must have seen doors of this type in Italy at Monte Cassino, Salerno, and elsewhere. Bronze panels cast in low relief existed at San Zeno in Verona. As at San Zeno, normally the panels were square or rectangular, so that the roundels at Saint-Denis were unusual. Apparently Suger's artists had a predilection for circular frames, which have survived in the stained glass windows, in the floor mosaics, and in the works of the month carved on the jambs of the south portal. These last are particularly interesting in relation to the bronze doors, for the roundels of foliate patterns seem to imitate metalwork. Today, of course, the heavy accumulation of black grime on the surfaces of all the portals augments that resemblance,[56] but the frames surrounding the scenes of the months may be a deliberate attempt to emulate in stone the forms on the adjacent doors.

Paula Gerson, who studied an enlargement of the Scamozzi drawing of the doors, claimed that the circular frames around the scenes on the doors

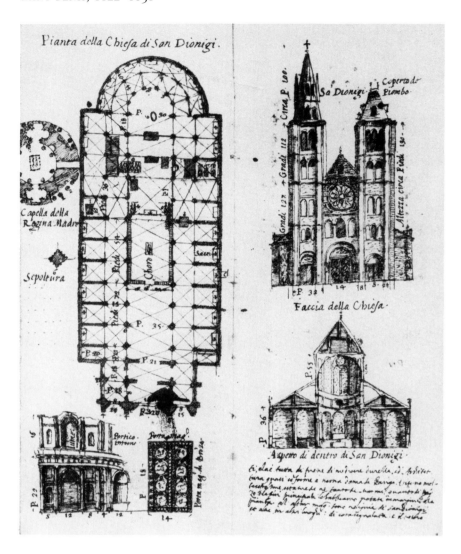

were flat bands which could have held the copper-gilt letters of Suger's verses, and she has attempted to associate one line of the verse with each scene. She has suggested that there were four scenes of the Passion on the left door and that the scenes and verses on the right door were:

> Crucifixion: "To the True Light where Christ is the
> true door"
> Resurrection: "In what manner it be inherent in
> this world the golden door defines"
> Supper at Emmaus: "The dull mind rises to truth
> through that which is material"
> Ascension: "And, in seeing this light, is
> resurrected from its former submersion."[57]

82. Drawings of Saint-Denis by Vincenzo Scamozzi, about 1600.

It is indeed unfortunate that Scamozzi's drawing is so small that all details are completely blurred, and attractive suggestions such as this must remain hypothetical.

Although it is impossible to tell where or how the verses were placed on the doors, other twelfth-century inscriptions at Saint-Denis, such as those in the stained glass medallions of the radiating chapels in the choir, are placed in horizontal lines within the medallions in irregular fashion, and the inscriptions identifying each of the Apostles on the bas-relief discovered in 1947 are also irregularly placed.[58] Most of the lettering on the bas-relief was carved in raised relief, not incised—another instance where the sculptor shows the influence of metalwork. At Saint-Denis the ubiquity of haphazard arrangements of inscriptions would seem to preclude the proposal of an orderly sequence in the frames of the medallions.

Although the first reference in the verses to the doors seems aimed, as Panofsky said, "at the more sophisticated of his [Suger's] critics,"[59] Suger's inscription focused attention on their golden appearance. Later (in line 7) the golden door defines the manner in which light is made apparent in this world, so that the mind, which has been brightened by the doors (the noble work), "may travel through the true lights, to the True Light where Christ is the true door." In other words, the bright doors, which are material and which therefore should really be admired for their craftsmanship, may resurrect the dull mind to the truth and to Christ, who is the door to Salvation. The doors become more than a conventional entranceway, both because of their material brightness, which leads the mind to the immaterial light, and because of the scenes which remind the observer that Christ rose through his Sacrifice and Resurrection to his Ascension and ultimate association with God.

The theme of the doors as the entrance to the celestial kingdom, or *porta coeli,* is emphasized by the symbolic meaning of the Wise and Foolish Virgins, located on the jambs which framed the bronze doors. The figures under canopies lead the eye and thoughts toward the tympanum. There on the lintel, *in superliminare,* below Suger's figure at Christ's feet, the inscription asked that he, Suger, be "mercifully numbered among Thy own sheep."[60] This reference to Christ as the Good Shepherd alludes again to the concept of Christ as the door to Salvation.

Finally, the verses on the golden doors "amount to a condensed statement of the whole theory of 'anagogical' illumination," as expounded by Dionysius the Pseudo-Areopagite.[61] The figure of Saint Denis on the trumeau that divided the doorway brings into focus the theme of the entire portal as the way to Salvation. Suger and his contemporaries believed Saint Denis had written the *Ecclesiastical Hierarchy.* The concept embodied in his works of rising from the material to the immaterial, from Christ's Passion to his Ascension, is repeated in the arrangement of the scenes of the different parts of the portal. Suger found inspiration in that idea for the verses on the doors. Also before his martyrdom Saint Denis had confessed his belief in the Trinity (represented in the apex of the portal); the saint's image on the lowest level of the portal represented man, the material being. The parable of the Wise and the Foolish Virgins on each side of the doors leads up to the tympanum, where the crucified Christ, also the judge, will select those who will enter the Celestial Kingdom to see the Trinity "face to face."

THE STATUE COLUMNS

Saint Denis represented on the trumeau in the center of the portal as a statue column also provided a visual link with the statue columns in the embrasures flanking the portal. Originally decorating all three portals, statue columns epitomize the problems that face any scholar interested in Saint-Denis. No written document has established that they were in place in the twelfth century, and only scattered fragments survive today. Let us first survey the evidence for their presence on Suger's portals. Although the full-length statues attached to and backed by columns appear to have been one of the most important innovations of Suger's workshops, and their imagery seems to summarize Suger's basic beliefs, he never mentioned the figures in his writings. Also there is no medieval document that even recognized their existence. The first indications of their presence on the sides of the portals that I have found appear in the eighteenth-century drawing by Martellange and in Vincenzo Scamozzi's sketch of 1600, where a little wishful thinking helps to interpret the darkened embrasures as indications of some type of decoration. A few years later, in 1706, Félibien provided the first written documentation for the statue columns: "On the sides of each portal are large statues of kings, of queens and of other principal benefactors of this church."[62] In 1718 or 1719, because he thought that the statues represented the earliest kings and queens of France, Bernard de Montfaucon commissioned the artist Antoine Benoist to make separate, detailed drawings of each statue column. Some of these drawings have survived in the Bibliothèque Nationale in Paris.[63] They remain the best available evidence for all of the figures, including three originally in the cloister at Saint-Denis.

Figs. 82, 83

Figs. 84a–d, 85b–d

One-half century after Benoist made that first visual record of the statue columns, all of them were dismounted from the portals and disappeared. That deliberate mutilation of the twelfth-century portals occurred in 1771 and included the removal of the trumeau figure of the central portal, which represented Saint Denis as bishop. The elimination of the trumeau enlarged the doorway and facilitated the passage of funerary cortèges. The monks also decided to replace the statue columns of the embrasures with more classical, undecorated columns.[64] Some remnants of the original statue columns must have been left around the abbey, for the minister Quinette reported that some twenty-four heads, "debris from medieval sculpture, coming from the destruction of the portal," were still to be recovered from the abbey.[65] In 1774 one of the statue columns from the cloister was sold to the Marquis de Migieu for his château at Savigny-lès-Beaune.[66] A curious watercolor by A. Lenoir, dated 1793, bears the legend, "La montagne à St.-Denis—vue de la montagne établis avec les statues des rois en 1793 sur la place qui précède celle de l'église de l'abbaye." The entrance to the "montagne" is framed by three statues

Fig. 85a

Fig. 86

83. Drawing of the west façade by Martellange, 1741.

wearing crowns. The two upright figures function as jambs, and a third carried on their heads acts as a sort of lintel. The sketchy delineation of the figures allows no conclusions as to whether they were from tombs or statues from the portals. Although I have searched the squares, or "places," in front of the church as well as the abbey gardens to the south and east of the church, no vestige of the "montagne" remains nor is it remembered at Saint-Denis today.[67]

Figs. 87, 88, 89

We find no mention of the statue columns during the revolutionary or postrevolutionary periods, except that of the organist Gautier, who recorded the removal of the figures in 1771. When serious archaeologists began to study Saint-Denis in the 1840s, the statue columns were mentioned, but the Montfaucon plates made from the Benoist drawings were regarded with some skepticism. In his "Notes" the Baron de Guilhermy, for instance, wrote, "Legrand d'Aussy declares, after his experience, that the drawings of Montfaucon's work have not the slightest resemblance to the originals, changed poses, accessories and emblems suppressed, draperies modified, different heads."[68]

As the decades passed, however, historians realized that, although the nineteenth-century restorations had indeed been excessive and disfiguring, most of the original iconography of the portals had been preserved.[69] Relatively recently scholars have identified fragments of the statue columns: the two heads in the Walters Art Gallery in Baltimore,[70] the head in the Fogg Art Museum in Cambridge, Massachusetts,[71] another head in a private collection in Paris,[72] and an almost complete small statue column from the cloister now in the Metropolitan Museum of Art in New York City.[73] Those sculptures have shown the details of the Montfaucon plates to be much more accurate than had been believed. In fact, comparisons with the Benoist drawings[74] as reproduced by Montfaucon led to the identification of the heads and of the figure from the cloister. Scholars have also assumed that the Montfaucon plates show the statue columns in their original order on the portals, but proof for such an assumption is still lacking.[75]

Fig. 90a
–d

Uncertainties about the dating of the statue columns raised the question of whether they were carved before or after the royal portals at Chartres cathedral. Although at first Wilhelm Vöge believed that the statue columns of the west façade of Chartres preceded those at Saint-Denis, he later corrected himself. With that reversal he recognized the Saint-Denis statues as the initiators of this new sculptural concept in northern France.[76] In 1941 Marcel Aubert established the date of 1145–50 for the western portals at Chartres,[77] and shortly thereafter, in an unpublished thesis for the Ecole de Louvre, one of his students proposed that the Saint-Denis statue columns should be dated after the death of Suger in the 1150s.[78] The argument rested on stylistic

a

b

84. Drawings of the trumeau figure and statue columns of the central portal by Antoine Benoist for Bernard de Montfaucon. Paris, Bibl. Nat. ms. fr. 15634: (a) trumeau figure of Saint Denis, fol. 33; (b) statue column of a queen, right embrasure, fol. 56; (c) Old Testament figure, left embrasure, fol. 59; (d) Old Testament figure, right embrasure, fol. 49.

conclusions based on the drawings and on Suger's failure to mention the figures. Subsequent critical opinion voiced by Louis Grodecki in his impressive survey "La Première Sculpture Gothique"[79] has definitively reversed this sequence and accepted the statue columns represented by the Benoist drawings, the scattered fragments in American museums, and the head in a Parisian private collection as part of the decoration of the portals of Saint-Denis at their dedication on 9 June 1140.

That date, although widely accepted by scholars, still posed problems.[80] The Saint-Denis statue columns become historically the first major ensemble of this favorite Gothic portal decoration, but the figures themselves were not tentative, hesitating attempts to achieve a new formula. Although our evidence is sadly incomplete, the remaining heads and the one small cloister statue, plus the drawings, constitute an impressive group of technical and aesthetic achievements. The surviving evidence gives striking proof of the originality of Suger's workshops, but the study of the statue columns is both a challenge and a frustration. The columnar statues flanked each of the portals, with three statue columns on each side of the lateral portals and four to a side in the central portal. These plus the central trumeau figure gave a total of twenty-one statue columns for the western portals. As for the additional three statue columns attributed by Montfaucon to the cloister,[81] their placement and iconographic significance in the cloister program remains an unknown. Two of the three represented crowned kings, one holding a scepter, the other a book; the third male figure, scroll in hand, wore a melon-shaped cap with an ornamental band. Of the portal statue columns only the central trumeau figure of Saint Denis wore the miter and vestments of a bishop, which differentiated him from all of the other nonroyal portal figures. Of the twenty other statues in the embrasures, four were women, one crowned,[82] and sixteen were men—eight crowned and eight wearing caps. Five of the nonroyal headdresses had ornamental bands, and the sixth a jeweled brooch. All of the men were bearded, and six had long hair reaching to or flowing over their shoulders. Only three statues had bare feet; two of these were male, one female. The drawings give no evidence of any canopies or decoration over the statues, but fourteen of the figures stood on some sort of a console or support, nine with animal, foliate, or human forms indicated. None of the drawings is complete with respect to the console, so that to estimate the total height of the statue columns is difficult.

Possibly the most tantalizing, perhaps unanswerable, questions about the portal statue columns concern their original sizes as well as the proportions within the figures. Evidently uniformity was not a primary consideration for mid-twelfth-century artists, as proven by the magnificent statue columns of the "portail royal" of the west façade at Chartres cathedral. There both the size and the relative proportions vary from figure to figure. For estimating size and proportions the Benoist drawings prove useless, since he drew them all to the same scale, and in a typically eighteenth-century manner the proportions appear more or less normal. A comparison of a photograph of the Metropolitan Museum's statue of a king with the Benoist drawing of the same king shows the degree to which the eighteenth-century aesthetic modi-

84a

. 87,
89

5a,b

c

d

a

b

c

d

fied the twelfth-century forms. Not only is the head of the statue proportionally much smaller than in the drawing, but the elongated and attenuated
twelfth-century figure has been changed to a robust, solid figure–type in the
drawing. A further comparison between this drawing and the engravings
showing the figures associated with the Walters Gallery heads and with the
Parisian head of a queen gives no indication that the Metropolitan statue
from the cloister is only 1.17 m high, whereas with the other heads measuring
0.35 m to 0.36 m in height, the statues of the western portals must have
been over 2.30 m tall. Although all of the drawings of the portal figures are
of the same height, the columns now in place on the embrasures of the north
and south portals average 2.27 m from the column base to capital, and the
larger columns flanking the central portal average 2.75 m high. One might

Figs. 87,
88, 90d

85. (a) Statue column from the cloister at Saint-Denis. Metropolitan Museum of Art,
New York; (b) drawing of statue column from cloister now in the Metropolitan
Museum of Art by Antoine Benoist for Montfaucon. Paris, Bibl. Nat. ms. fr. 15634, fol.
46; (c,d) drawings of statue columns from the cloister by Antoine Benoist for
Montfaucon. Paris, Bibl. Nat. ms. fr. 15634, fols. 45 and 42.

86. Watercolor by A. Lenoir
entitled "La montagne à St.
Denis," dated 1793, Paris, Louvre.
A. Lenoir, Aquarelles et Dessins,
vol. 4 "St. Denis," sheet 17.

conjecture that the additional 0.48 m of the central portal columns was filled by the supporting console figures drawn beneath all eight of the central portal figures, but the drawings also show six of the figures from the lateral portals with consoles or console figures beneath their feet. Thus the presence or absence of consoles under the statue columns does not provide any clue to the total height of the statue or to the proportions of the figure itself. Comparisons with other figures carved or drawn by Suger's artists proved equally irrelevant in the search for the original proportions of the statue columns. No norm or canon of proportions for figures prevailed.[83] Also, in spite of the fact that today the columns of the north and south portals measure 2.27 m in comparison to the 2.75 m for the columns of the central portal, the four existing heads all have approximately the same dimensions—0.35 m to 0.36 m high by 0.22 m to 0.20 m wide. The two heads that came from statues of the central portal ("Clothaire III" in Baltimore and the "Queen of Sheba" in Paris) are slightly smaller (0.35 m high) than those assigned to the north portal ("Childebert" in Baltimore and the Fogg Museum head, which measure 0.36 m high). A "normal" proportion of 1:7 would result in a statue 2.35 m high; that height could have been accommodated on the central portal but would have resulted in a statue 2.52 m high—one much too large for the north portal. Obviously the problem of relative proportions for the statue columns cannot be solved unless new evidence becomes available.

Of the twenty-one portal figures only three, perhaps five, can be given reasonable identifications. In addition to the trumeau figure of Saint Denis, Gerson identified the middle statue on the left, or north, embrasure of the right portal as Moses.[84] In the drawing the figure holds a tablet which might be interpreted as one of the tables of the law, Moses' identifying attribute.

Fig. 87c

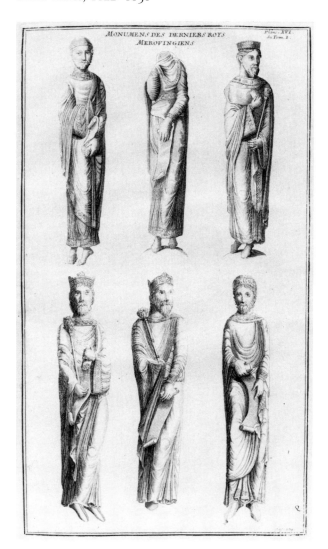

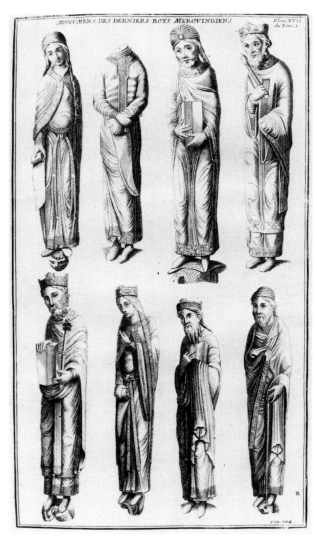

Léon Pressouyre, in his article publishing his discovery of the head of a queen from one of the Saint-Denis statue columns, chose not to carry his identification beyond its royal character.[85] Yet I agree with Gerson that, in all likelihood, the queen was intended to represent the Queen of Sheba.[86] If Gerson's comparisons are accepted, then it would be reasonable to follow her proposal that the kings standing on each side of the queen in Montfaucon's plate 17 should be identified as King Solomon and King David. Until some future discovery adds to our knowledge about the statue columns, further attempts at identification remain purely speculative.

Suggestions about possible interpretations for the groups as a whole have provided a more fruitful approach. Félibien's assumption that the statues represented "kings and queens and other benefactors"[87] was a reasonable guess, but only a guess. In the early eighteenth century, thinking that the figures were kings and queens of the First Dynasty in France,[88] Montfaucon

87–89. Engravings of the lost statue columns of the western portals from drawings by Antoine Benoist: (87) (*above, left*) left portal; (88) (*above*) central portal; (89) (*opposite*) right portal.

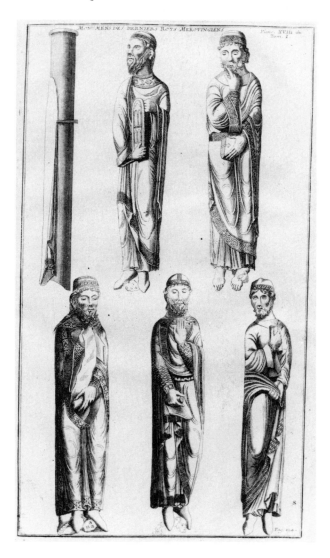

had the drawings made for his first volume, but his identifications were never taken seriously. By the middle of the eighteenth century, however, scholarly consideration began to interpret the figures in biblical terms. As early as 1756, Abbé Lebeuf recognized that many of the statues were not royal rulers but Old Testament patriarchs who might, among other possibilities, represent the concordance between the Old and New Testaments or the concepts of *regnum et sacerdotium,* of secular and ecclesiastical authority.[89] Since then a variety of symbolic themes have been proposed: the royal ancestry of Christ, as in the Tree of Jesse; Christ's genealogy according to the Gospel of Matthew (Matthew 1:5–6);[90] the Old Testament as the foundation for the New Testament;[91] the different books of the Holy Scriptures;[92] royalty as both the ancestors of Christ and representatives of secular order.[93]

Since Suger made no reference to the statue columns, it may be presumptuous to suggest what symbolic meanings he might have assigned to

90. Original heads from the lost statue columns of the western portals: (a) Inv. no. 27.22 and (b) Inv. no. 27.21, from the Walters Art Gallery, Baltimore, Maryland; (c) acq. no. 1920.30, The Fogg Museum of Art, Harvard University, Cambridge, Mass.; (d) head of a queen in the collection of Jean Osouf, Paris, France.

them. Yet there is abundant evidence that the images in his programs carried multiple meanings. For example, the Christ of the central tympanum represented both the Crucified Savior and the Judge at the end of the world; the Virgin seated to his right with her hands raised carried the idea of the mourning mother and of man's supplicant for mercy at the Last Judgment.

Each of the three western portals had its own iconographical theme which supplemented the entire vision. In the same manner, the statue columns in each doorway referred to symbolic themes of the portal as well as having meaning when read horizontally as an ensemble. As a sequence, the statue columns formed a horizontal band of vertical accents across the façade. The visual continuity of that sequence bound the portals together. As kings and queens and patriarchs of the Old Testament, the statue columns may have evoked Suger's belief in a balance of power, but as Gerson has shown, besides regnum et sacerdotium, they also expressed the teachings of the Pseudo-Areopagite, who saw the ecclesiastical and mundane hierarchies as a reflection of the celestial hierarchies.[94] The ecclesiastical hierarchy, or Church, could lead mankind to Salvation. The crenellations at the top of the façade assert that Saint-Denis was the protector of the monarchy and the kingdom as well as of the mortal remains of the royal dynasties.[95] The statue columns at the bottom or lowest level of the façade seemed to affirm Suger's loyalty and support for his king and his Church.[96]

Lateral Portals

Before examining the question of how the north and south portals supplemented the iconographical program of the central one and contributed to the overall meaning of Suger's triple portal program with its trinitarian connotations, we must first determine how much the extensive alterations and restorations of the eighteenth and the nineteenth centuries have aborted the original iconographic intentions. Especially in the north portal, the alterations and restorations have so obscured the original details that attempts to resolve the many enigmas could be hazardous. First, as noted above, the raising of the level of the pavement of the western bays and of the nave in the early nineteenth century has changed the proportions of all three of the western portals. The original sill of the north portal uncovered during my enlargement of the excavation in front of the western facade lies 0.52 m below the present pavement at the same depth as the sill for the central portal. The measurements for the north portal lack the correspondences that are present in the central portal between the bronze doors and the measurement from sill to tympanum. Doublet's height of 14 pieds for the left doors would equal 4.55 m to 4.59 m, but the measurement from the sill to the present tympanum in the north portal equals 4.40 m, some 0.15 m to 0.20 m less than the doors. The discrepancy could be attributable to the fact that the mosaic tympanum installed by Suger was still in place in the early seventeenth century.

91. North portal of the west façade.

Of the original decoration of the north portal, only the heavily restored relief carvings on both jambs of the doorway and the figures in the outer archivolt survive. Because an entirely new tympanum was installed in 1771 when the statue columns were removed, possibly all of the sculpture of the north portal was more severely restored and recut in the eighteenth and again in the nineteenth centuries than elsewhere.[97] Although most of the surfaces have been recut and many details replaced, enough remains to indicate what was originally intended.

There is no question that the Signs of the Zodiac always decorated the jambs of the doorway. Published in 1788, the earliest description of the zodiac at Saint-Denis noted that three of the signs were missing—namely, Leo,

Fig. 91

Fig. 92a,b

a

b

Cancer, and Virgo—and that the Gemini, now at the top of the right jamb, should have been placed at the top of the left jamb above Taurus.[98] Although attempts have been made to suggest how the complete series of twelve signs might have been arranged, all proposals are purely conjectural.[99] There is no literary or material evidence to contradict Galaisière's early statement that the irregularities were due to the "capriciousness of the architect."[100] Whether or not all of the signs were originally present does not alter the fact that these astrological signs were part of the twelfth-century iconographic program.

Although the cosmological significance of the Signs of the Zodiac is assured, the meaning of the relief figures on the outer archivolt about the doorway is less certain. Today both of the archivolts of the north portal have figurate carving, but the inner archivolt was undecorated until 1839.[101] Tests show that the stone of the outer archivolt is the same as the stone of the central portal and that the voussoirs measure 0.295 m—the basic dimension of all the twelfth-century stones in the portals.[102] The figures in the center of the archivolt occupy seven voussoirs. The keystone contains a bust of Christ with outstretched arms framed by a mandorla supported by two angels. His right

92. The jambs of the north portal with the carvings of the Signs of the Zodiac: (a) left, or north, jamb; (b) right, or south, jamb.

Fig. 91

hand is a replacement, and also the upper portion of the tablet he holds, as is the band inserted in the lower portion of the tablet to repair the eroded joint between the two voussoir stones. Yet the repairs are backed by the original tablet. Christ's open left hand touches the finial terminating what appears to be a flowering scepter. Although lightly recut, the fleuron is original, and restored portions of the attribute and hand are backed by remnants of the original forms; therefore the restorations perpetuate the twelfth-century arrangement. The lower edge of the mandorla merges with the undulating, cloudlike waves from which the central figure emerges. The circular shape of the mandorla is unusual, but the light recutting did not change the original form.

Below and flanking this central group, and obviously related to it, are two unusually elongated figures with crossed legs—each figure covering five and a half voussoirs. Scholars still speculate about the identity of those figures.[103] Both of them reach upward to receive the objects with veiled hands. The figure to Christ's right has bare feet but the figure to his left wears shoes. Although most of the drapery has been severely recut, there are comparable drapery stylizations in the central portal.

In the lowest tier of the archivolt two groups of three figures complete the decoration. On both the left and right sides two figures, apparently conversing, stand in front of and below a third figure. Of this third figure only the head, shoulders, and one hand pointing upward are visible. That gesture establishes a relationship between the lower groups and the upper figures. Although both groups have been generally recut, and, in the case of the left hand of the left front figure on the right side, details of the fingers obliterated, the original iconography has survived. Otto von Borries concluded that the groups filled a compositional or formal function and had no discernible bearing on the program.[104] Such space-fillers would have been unique in twelfth-century sculpture, but until some clue comes to light no guess is better than another. Such a clue possibly existed in the lost mosaic which Suger ordered for the tympanum, so once again the student is faced with lack of information.

Several years ago in a short article I described the chance discovery of the lower portion of the tympanum, carved for this north portal in 1771.[105] At that time I commented on the similarity of the iconography between the present nineteenth-century tympanum and the one carved in 1771, with the suggestion that such a continuity in subject matter might be an indication that the eighteenth-century example also followed a tradition established by the original twelfth-century mosaic. On this tenuous basis I then suggested that the scene depicted in the mosaic might have been the martyrdom of Saint Denis and his companions. Another hypothesis, equally tenuous, proposed that the mosaic depicted an enthroned Virgin and Child. This proposal subsumed Suger's special veneration of the Virgin and the possibility that he might have seen such mosaics on one of his trips to Italy.[106]

Suger acknowledged that his choice of a mosaic was "contrary to modern [that is, contemporary] custom."[107] Panofsky surmised that this choice "can best be accounted for by Suger's predilection for everything that shines and glitters."[108] Possibly the choice was motivated by Suger's admiration for the achievements of antiquity as well as for those of his Carolingian predecessors. But aesthetic preferences do not inform us about the iconography. The subject of the destroyed mosaic may never be discovered, but the symbolic implications of the portal as a whole may exist in the surviving fragments of its decoration, namely, the doorjambs and the outer archivolt.

The Signs of the Zodiac on the doorjambs were certainly not intended as an isolated theme. As in so many other instances, their implications are understood fully when combined with other images, in this case when considered as pendants to the Works of the Months carved on the jambs of the south portal. The Works of the Months represent the terrestrial cycles of human activity, and the Signs of the Zodiac specify the cosmic progression of the heavenly spheres. The two lateral portals, therefore, provide another dimension to the Alpha and Omega of the central portal; but instead of being read within the framework of each portal, they reach across the façade to unite the triple entrance into a single ensemble. The Signs of the Zodiac, however, unlike the Wise and the Foolish Virgins on the jambs of the central portal, apparently have no relation to the upper tympanum and the outer archivolt, which may have presented a coherent concept.[109]

The theme of Christ with outstretched arms bestowing attributes or distinguishing between such fundamental concepts as the Old and the New Law, the Church and the Synagogue, appeared at Saint-Denis in the medallion of the anagogical window in Suger's choir. In the head of the window Christ with the seven gifts of the Holy Spirit crowns the Church, *Ecclesia*, and unveils *Synagoga*.[110] On the outer archivolt of the north portal Christ holds in his right hand what could have been the tablet of the Law but is possibly a book; in a gesture of acclaim his open left hand indicates the flowering scepter. The two figures who reach up to receive or to display these attributes are not differentiated by any detail in their costumes, except the bare feet of the figure on Christ's right. These two figures have been identified as Peter and Paul or as Moses and Aaron,[111] but no one has carried the implications of the whole scene to what seems to me the logical conclusion— one that is thoroughly compatible with Suger's convictions.

The two attributes, a tablet or book and a scepter, are recognized insignia of ecclesiastical and secular authority. The distinction between Church and State, as well as their equal responsibilities in maintaining order in the Christian world, was of immediate significance at the time of the investiture struggle, in which Suger may well have participated.[112] An unusual factor in this early representation of regnum et sacerdotium is the lack of distinction between the two figures who hold the attributes, but the bare feet of the figure with the tablet symbolizing sacerdotium and the shod feet of regnum with the scepter are appropriate, as is the fact that Christ holds the tablet but gestures toward the scepter. A further possibility encompassing the groups at the lowest level of the archivolt identifies them as people of varying status being shown the divine origin of the two realms of Christian authority. In such a context my earlier suggestion that the subject of the tympanum mosaic might have been the martyrdom of Saint Denis and his companions becomes quite unsuitable, and some other representation more in harmony with the concept of regnum/sacerdotium seems indicated.

The Virgin and Child in Majesty, the throne of wisdom, or *sedes sapientiae,* proposed by Von Borries,[113] would provide coherence, for a *sedes sapientiae* appears between the bishop and the king in the St. Anne portal at Notre-Dame in Paris and later on the Gnadenpforte at Bamberg, where the confrontation of the two powers (in the latter instance, St. Peter and Henry II) takes place "under the tutelage of the incarnate Logos."[114] Another symbol, often seen in mosaics, could have been a Fountain of Life, which in Suger's terms would be interpreted as a fountain of reason. In the opening lines of his *De Consecratione*, which repeat Neoplatonic doctrines as stated by the Pseudo-Areopagite, we read that those who crave to participate in the supreme and eternal reason may "drink wholesomely from the fountain of the reason of eternal wisdom."[115] Such interesting possibilities remain pure conjecture, since no documentary evidence of any type exists at present to support one or another proposal.

To complete this examination of the north portal, let us consider briefly the possible relation of the statue columns and the old bronze doors to an interpretation emphasizing regnum et sacerdotium. The Montfaucon plates showing the Saint-Denis statue columns remain our clue for their original order. Plate 16 shows the six figures he attributed to the north portal. Four of the statues are kings with crowns and scepters, another (shown as headless) must have been a queen or royal personage, to judge by the rich orphreys decorating the costume, and the one remaining figure with a nonroyal head-dress standing at the extreme right presumably represented a patriarch or prophet.[116] In this instance the law of the Old Testament and secular law may be said to be equally represented—a suitable reference to equality of authority. The "old" doors, supposedly with a figure of the donor, Airardus, in the costume of a monk,[117] and a figure of a bishop, were reused from an earlier building so that their original meaning or reference contributes little to the twelfth-century imagery. Although the condition of this portal precludes any definitive assertions, I believe that enough remains of the figures in the outer archivolt to suggest that Suger's fundamental belief in a balance of power between Church and State, between sacerdotium et regnum, was a dominant theme, one which could also be recognized in the statue columns.

The imagery of the sculpture on the right, or south, portal is more easily described but the symbolic reference may be less evident. In the south portal the tympanum was a relief sculpture, not a mosaic, and the inner instead of the outer archivolt had figures carved on the voussoirs. On the jambs of the south doorway, complementing the Signs of the Zodiac of the north portal, all twelve Works of the Months are represented in an order reading up the right jamb and down the left. The early engravings of Le Gentil de la Galaisière prove that all of the signs were in place before the Revolution, and the drawing of the façade by Cellérier shows that both the tympanum and the inner archivolt were carved before Debret began his restorations.[118]

The twelve scenes symbolizing the annual work cycle differ from the Signs of the Zodiac in many ways, although as groups they complete and intensify each other's significance. The abstract, mystical cosmology of the

Figs. 87, 88, 89

Fig. 93

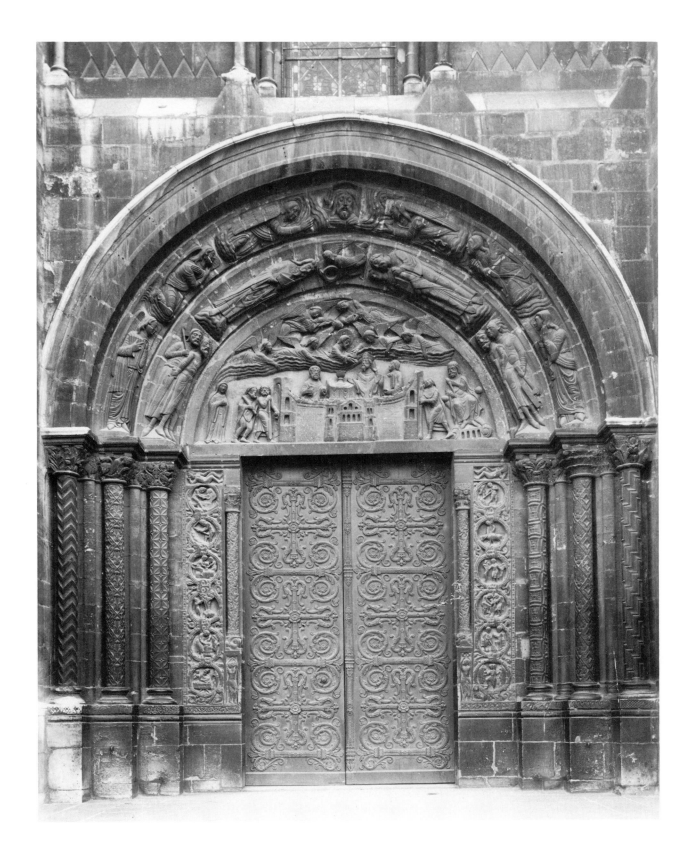

93. South portal of the west façade.

zodiac contrasts with the terrestrial activity of mankind, and together they define the dimensions of our cognate being. Personifications of man's seasonal activities may not reach as far back into antiquity as do the Signs of the Zodiac, although the works appeared in Roman times as gods and goddesses and by the middle of the fourth century were depicted as the activities normal to every month.[119] In addition to the contrast between abstract and naturalistic imagery, the Works of the Months are shown in round medallions created by vegetal rinceaux issuing from lionlike masks in contrast to the rectangular frames of the zodiac. I shall comment here only on a few unusual ones.

The first medallion, January, Janus with two heads, one young and one old, seems to bring a youthful figure out of a gate or tower on the left and to push an old figure into the gate on the right. This imagery is quite unusual; in fact, this appears to be the earliest known example and is unique in the twelfth and thirteenth centuries.[120] September is represented by two men seated on a cask which they are filling, an unusual motif in French art that usually stands for October. November, with a man butchering a pig over a barrel and another pig hanging in a tree, is also an atypical scene. The naturalistic representation of the men, young and old, of their postures, and of the details distinguishes this series at Saint-Denis from its immediate predecessors at Saint-Lazare, Autun, and at La Madeleine at Vézelay.[121] Another unusual feature of the Saint-Denis series is the seemingly reversed order of the months, which, from right to left, reads up the right jamb and down the left. Mirroring this arrangement, the Signs of the Zodiac on the north portal read in the normal order, that is, from the left jamb to the right. The symbolic implication of that deliberate ordering which leads the eye and mind from the outside inward toward the central portal offers further proof of the subtlety and careful thought behind the organization of the entire portal program.[122]

In addition to the scenes in the cycles, a number of figures carved on the jambs seem primarily decorative, although some may have been intended to add to the symbolic references of the program as a whole. In all three portals the small, richly carved colonnettes placed at the inner corners of the jambs include heraldic birds and eagles and also tiny nude figures in combat with each other or with monsters as they climb through intertwined vines.[123] No symbolic intent has been attributed to this decoration or to the four very low relief figures under all of these colonnettes, who stand with their arms raised above their heads as a gesture of support. Although these figures may have been inspired by antique Atlas-types, no iconographic meaning has been attributed to them or to the two small reclining men in the narrow frames under the Signs of the Zodiac.[124] Two more small, reclining figures, in this instance nude, are placed at the top of the jambs of the south portal. In an earlier study I proposed that originally there were four such figures which symbolized the four seasons, the four rivers of paradise, or the four cardinal points of the compass—imagery which would have completed the universal environment represented by the Signs of the Zodiac and the Works of the Months.[125] Our examination of these small nudes identified them as original, although all of the surfaces have been recut.[126] Yet in the absence of a place

Fig. 95

Fig. 94

Figs. 92, 94, 95

for two more such figures, I must admit that I have no persuasive explanation as to their original meaning.

No such confusion about intended meaning exists for the figures and scenes carved in the tympanum and on the inner archivolt of the south portal, although most scholars, myself included, were until recently reluctant to consider them as part of the original sculpture of the portals.[127] Yet Vöge in 1894, Emile Mâle in 1922, and Von Borries in 1942–43 all recognized that the surfaces had been restored, and Mâle concluded that the "general composition" was original.[128]

The scene in the tympanum is the miraculous last Communion, according to legend offered by Christ in the company of a host of angels to Saint Denis and his companions while they were in prison the night before their execution. Emerging from wavy clouds, Christ and the angels occupy the upper part of the tympanum. In the lower portion, the prefect Fescennius, who condemned Saint Denis, is seated on his throne at the far right; the prison with the three saints and an altar is shown in the center. On the far left Larcia, who had condemned Saint Denis but was later converted to Christianity by his faith, stands behind the executioners at the prison gate. Although this

94. The left, or north, jamb of the south portal with scenes symbolizing the Works of the Months, July through December (top to bottom).

95. The right, or south, jamb of the south portal with scenes symbolizing the Works of the Months, January through June (bottom to top).

Fig. 96

96. Tympanum and archivolts of the south portal.

composition is most unusual for the twelfth century, a number of manuscripts prove that the scene and the details were known as early as the middle of the eleventh century.[129] In the apex of the inner archivolt a hovering angel carries a martyr's crown; below on the left, Saint Denis holds his bishop's miter, and on the right his two companions, Rusticus and Eleutherius, appear at the same level. Two pairs of executioners with their swords and axes occupy the lowest tier of the inner archivolt. Emile Mâle asserted that Suger was "the first to have consecrated a portal to the glory of a saint; there was nothing similar before him."[130] Such a statement overlooks the north transept portal at Autun dedicated to Saint Lazarus, which had the Raising of Lazarus carved on the tympanum. Scholars accept a date of shortly after 1130 for the Autun portal[131]—evidence that Suger was not inventing a new concept but rather adapting a new custom to his own purposes.

The martyrdom of Saint Denis, the subject introduced into the iconographic program of the western façade by the south portal, raises the question of why emphasis was given to the mystical communion of Saint Denis rather than to the actual scene of martyrdom or even to the miraculous *cephalophorie,* when he picked up his head and walked away. Although the choice of this particular scene has been explained as emphasizing the intimate relationship between Christ and Saint Denis and the saint's special function as a bishop to lead the initiated Christians to perfect knowledge,[132] the scene of the Communion can be understood on its own terms. The Sacrament allows the faithful to participate in the mysteries of Christ and through him to attain salvation, which as we have seen is a major theme of the central portal and of all the portals as the gates to the Heavenly City. At a time when heresies involving the Trinity and transubstantiation were current, this quite unusual miracle may have been chosen to impress the faithful and heighten the prestige of Suger's patron saint, thereby establishing the preeminence of Saint Denis and his special prerogative to lead the people to salvation. The Golden Legend states that the heads of the three saints were cut off as they confessed the Trinity, a connection which underscores in yet another way the interdependence of the portals.

Another possible reference to leadership may have resided in the six statue columns on the embrasures of the south portal. When Benoist did his drawings, one of the statue columns (identified as belonging to the south portal in Montfaucon's plate 18) had already disappeared. The remaining five, as noted earlier, seem to form a harmonious group: they have similar decorated caps and tunics distinguished by goffered sleeves. All but one of the figures held a scroll, the exception being the statue of Moses, who held a tablet of the law. Katzenellenbogen observed that, beginning in Carolingian times, the virtues of Old Testament kings and early Jewish leaders were invoked in the coronation rites of French kings, who were regarded as their spiritual successors.[133] He also noted that "the names of Abraham, Isaac, Jacob, Joseph, Moses and Joshua, together with those of David and Solomon were showered time and again on Carolingian rulers by their court poets." Without wishing to assert that the statue columns of the south portal should be identified as these specific Old Testament leaders, I cannot refrain from commenting on the suitability of their inclusion among the statues at Saint-Denis.

A possibility exists that the new bronze doors executed on Suger's orders for this south portal might have enlarged on this theme of leadership; but, as we mentioned in our first discussion of the doors, almost nothing is known about them. After describing Airardus on the north door, Félibien, in his description of Saint-Denis as it appeared early in the eighteenth century, stated briefly, "One still sees on the center of the door of the other side-aisle [that is, the south portal] a monk [réligieux] in the costume of a 'chanoine,' such as was worn by the monks of Saint-Denis at the end of Charlemagne's reign when they left (or changed from) the monastic costume."[134] Félibien believed that the Airardus depicted on the north door was the monk who fell from the scaffolding while Fulrad's Carolingian church was under construction. He considered that image to be one of the oldest, showing a Saint-Denis monk dressed in eighth-century manner, whereas recent scholarship suggests a date for the doors no earlier than the eleventh century.[135] The description gives no information about the other figures, so that we remain ignorant about the iconography of these bronze doors and their contribution, if any, to the sculptural program of the portal.

But in summary we need not question the contribution of the south portal as a whole to the iconographical program of the ensemble. Closely allied to the zodiac of the north portal, the Works of the Months emphasize the terrestrial environment of mankind, and the miraculous Communion in the tympanum demonstrates the earthly rite that leads to Christ and Salvation.

Emphasis is given to the patron saint, Denis and his companions, as martyrs, which amplifies the references of the central portal in terms of the saint's ability to lead the way to the Light.

Finally, we will examine Suger's objectives for the building and decoration of this first campaign as I understand the evidence. Suger's first campaign, which he referred to as the *nova ecclesia,* or new church, was not a piecemeal construction. From the moment the foundations were laid, the master mason knew about the entire project; and although details may have been refined or changed during the three or four years that the workshops were active on these western portions, there is no evidence of major changes. The presence of identical masons' marks on stones in the foundations and at the top of the south tower is additional proof of the continuity of the work, which may correctly be considered as a unit. As a unit these western bays, with upper chapels, formed a separate mass, an impressive block, almost independent of the rest of the church to the east. Such a western structure had special connotations, which developed in the eighth and ninth centuries but began their liturgical obsolescence late in the tenth century, only to reappear as a deliberate revival under the German emperors in the eleventh and twelfth centuries.[136] Suger and his master masons and clerical advisors used traditional formulae to introduce new concepts, so that the western bays at Saint-Denis are at once a revival of Carolingian forms, and its decoration a forerunner of Gothic encyclopedias. Even though these western bays were thought of as an entity with their own special functions, they were, from the beginning, considered part of a larger whole.

One of Suger's major concerns was to insure that his new building would be harmonious with the old one, and at the same time modern. To achieve that concordance, earlier proportions and measurements were subtly incorporated into the new plans. We noted how the eastern bays of the new entrance acted as a juncture with the old, eighth-century nave and how the western central bays were rectangles flanked by squares, all repeating the dimensions of the eighth-century transept arms and crossing. Yet the structure with massive *soubassements* for the great, clustered piers supported ribbed vaults of varying shapes, reflecting the area vaulted. The result is a sequence of different volumes which express both the functions of these bays as solid supports for the towers above and as a preparation for the new building about to be entered. Suger also hints, although we could wish for more graphic descriptions, at the function of these bays in relation to the liturgy when he mentions the dedication ceremonies and the chanting of "a polyphonic praise,"[137] presumably in conjunction with monks who were chanting in the eastern portions of the old church. More specifically, in describing the dedications of the upper chapels, he called them "worthy to be the dwelling place of angels" and wrote how those who celebrated the divine rites in the chapels were "already dwelling, in a degree, in Heaven."[138]

The traditional connotations of such twin-towered western masses emphasize these references. E. Baldwin Smith convincingly demonstrated the long history of towered structures in relation to such concepts as the heavenly fortress, the city of God, and particularly as the *porta coeli,* the gates to heaven.[139] Under Charlemagne strong political associations developed, later revived by the Ottonian emperors and the imperial successors of the Holy Roman Empire, which promoted the identification of these western masses as the church of the emperor—a *Kaiserkirche.* More recently Carol Heitz has stressed the liturgical origins of the medieval "western churches" and the increasing accent on the worship of the *Salvator mundi,* the Savior of mankind, in these western portions.[140] Unfortunately none of these recent studies has given any consideration to Suger's twelfth-century program for the Saint-Denis western bays. Confirmation of most of these ideas becomes increasingly evident in an examination of the details of his building and his references to it.

The symbolism of the whole ensemble is clarified and amplified by the elaborate iconography of the western portals. The Romanesque portal, even the three western doors of La Madeleine at Vézelay, were directly associated with the symbolism of the architecture to which they provided access. At Saint-Denis the association of themes of the portals is extended to include the entire western mass. The Trinity depicted on the apex of the archivolts of the central portal is understood in the three portals, dedicated in an elaborate ceremony in which three participants acted as one. This emphasis of units of three was carried up across the façade in the repetition of three arcades to the top of the towers and existed even in the interior in the *ecclesia triplex,* the triple church of the upper chapels. The reiterated emphasis on the assurance of Salvation in the crucified Christ, as judge of the blessed and the damned, is echoed in the traditional consecration of this western mass to the cult of the Savior.[141] Even more explicit is the inspiration Suger found for his verses on the bronze doors in the writings of Dionysius the Pseudo-Areopagite. The mystic's ideas reemerge in Suger's description of the upper chapels as the abode of angels, with Saint Michael the Archangel as the protector of the Gates to Heaven. A final principle, possibly in Suger's mind the most important one, was manifested in the new series of statue columns. These references to *Regnum* and *Sacerdotium,* to royal and priestly authority, supplemented by the Signs of the Zodiac and the Works of the Months and also the crenellations and the rose window all combined to proclaim the royal stature of the abbey and the respect due Saint Denis as the patron saint and protector of the French monarchy.

Although such massive western structures were doomed to disappear as the Gothic cathedral developed, Suger's elaboration of the western portals and of the west façade emerged as distinguishing features of the great cathedrals of the thirteenth century.

CHAPTER SEVEN

The Crypt and Choir (1140-1144)

Textual Sources

Whether the concern is architecture, sculpture or stained glass, the major stylistic problem, posed by the workshops at Saint-Denis, is the same: namely the origin of Gothic art. In architecture the problem has already been often raised; and we can even consider that it has been resolved."[1] Indeed, for more than a century scholars have used the choir of Abbot Suger's new church as the point of departure for their definitions of Gothic architecture. Yet no detailed analyses of the plan and of the structure of either the crypt or the choir have been attempted. Such an analysis is the goal of this section.

Documentary sources anchor this second campaign of Suger's building program in history. They also illuminate his aesthetic predilections; but many questions remain unanswered. Although these texts are among the most familiar of Suger's writings, they require a review here for what they tell us about the dates of the construction, its progress, its liturgical function, and its symbolism.

The decision to build a new chevet to the east of the old Carolingian nave and transept had been reached before work on the new western bays had been finished. Such a decision is not surprising. Suger admits that he was invigorated by the success of the new front part[2] and that the abbey's finances were flourishing—"while at first, expending little, we lacked much, afterwards, expending much, we lacked nothing at all."[3] Also the workshops were organized and still on the site. Any delay might result in the dispersal of the workmen. In order to ensure a continuity of work, Suger ordered that the holy water used for the consecration ceremonies of 9 June 1140 be saved so that it could be mixed with the mortar for the new foundations.[4] Apparently preparations for these foundations began immediately after the ceremonies of 9 June 1140, since by 14 July the "excavations [had been] made ready for the foundations."[5] The decision to enlarge the eastern end rather than to work on the nave was also consistent with Suger's original decision to "respect the very stones [of the old church], sacred as they are, as though they were relics."[6] A new choir to the east would relieve the "congestion around the Holy of Holies [*Sanctum Sanctorum*—or high altar]";[7] it would also involve the destruction of only a small portion of the old building. The passage involving the destruction of the old apse has always been difficult for translators and has provoked "some honest High School work on its analysis" by Panofsky.[8] His paraphrase is clear, but I have taken the liberty of changing it a little to conform to the masonry now visible in the crypt: "It was decided to remove the apse which formed the upper part of the sanctuary wherein were kept the relics of our Patron Saints. This apse [the eighth-century one], lower than the present [or twelfth-century one] was removed all the way down to the top surface of the crypt [Hilduin's ninth-century *ecclesia triplex*] to which it was attached"; so that "this crypt might offer its top as a pavement to those approaching by either of the two stairs, and might present the chasses of the Saints, adorned with gold and precious gems, to the visitors' glances in a more elevated place."[9] Enlarging the choir but removing as little as possible of the old church was Suger's basic objective. The results far exceeded such modest intentions.

Suger's elaborate ceremony on 14 July 1140 marked the official beginning of work on the new chevet. He described the procession,[10] which included bishops and abbots as well as King Louis, as "beautiful by its ornaments and notable by its personages." All "descended with humble devotion to the excavations made ready for the foundations." Suger also said, "that which we proposed to carry out had been designed *loculento ordine* [with brilliant or luminous order]"[11]—that is, the plan of the chevet. This plan, to be examined in detail shortly, is surprisingly sophisticated and precise. Preparation for the entire chevet from the crypt "to the summit of the vaults above" the choir must have required careful consideration over a period of several months. In other words, the decision to proceed with the new chevet must have been taken no later than the winter or early spring of 1140.

The description of what we would call the ceremony for the laying of the cornerstone includes other interesting details. King Louis, Suger, and other abbots and monks laid foundation stones with their own hands. Although this would seem to imply dressed stones or ashlar, excavations have revealed that the foundations under the crypt consist of a rubble mat. This, of course, does not preclude the placing of stones in mortar made from the holy water. Unfortunately the excavations did not uncover any of the gems which Suger said "certain persons also deposited as they chanted, 'All thy walls are precious stones.'"[12] They also chanted Psalm 86 [King James, 87]: "The foundations thereof are in the holy mountains: the Lord loveth the gates of Sion . . . ; glorious things are said of thee, O city of God." This reference equated the chevet with the holy city of Mount Sion.

Work on the new chevet progressed rapidly—"for three years we pressed completion of the work at great expense, with a numerous crowd of workmen, summer and winter, lest God have just cause to complain of us."[13] Later, when he wrote his *De Administratione,* the "three years" became "three years and three months," during which "the Hand Divine . . . allowed that the whole magnificent building [be completed] . . . from the crypt below to the summit of the vaults above, elaborated with the variety of so many arches and columns, including even the consummation of the roof."[14]

Since, according to Suger's calendar, work began on 14 July 1140, the building would have been completed in mid-October 1143—a remarkably short time, indeed. Yet if all of his references are to be interpreted literally, work advanced even more rapidly. One of Suger's best known and most controversial accounts relates the story of the great storm that occurred on 19 January when Geoffroy, bishop of Chartres, stood in front of the high altar at Saint-Denis celebrating a mass on the anniversary of the death of Dagobert.

> The Bishop, alarmed by the strong vibrations of these [arches] and the roofing, frequently extended his blessing hand in the direction of that part and urgently held out toward it, while making the sign of the cross, the arm of the aged St. Simeon; so that he escaped disaster, manifestly not through his own strength of mind but by the grace of God and the merit of the Saints. Thus [the tempest], while it brought calamitous ruin in many places to buildings thought to be firm, was unable to damage these isolated and newly made arches, tottering in mid-air.[15]

The portions of this passage involving the construction of the vaults will be reconsidered in the analysis of the elevation of the choir, but the pertinent implications here concern the progress of the work, which I believe needs reexamination. Following Léon Levillain's comments,[16] many scholars have assumed that the choir was finished in three years and three months, that is, by October 1143, and that work on the vaults must have been under way earlier that same year or in January 1143, before the great storm.[17] In other words, almost all of the construction had been finished very early in 1143, only two and a half years after the laying of the foundations. Even my own enthusiasm for Suger's abilities questions the possibility of his erecting such a complex structure, especially one so novel, in such a short time.

A terminal date for the completion of the chevet is provided by the consecration celebrated on 11 June 1144. Although the structure must have been completed by then, probably such decorations as the great cross would have been added later. In actuality the date of the consecration was arbitrary; Suger says that "we fixed, upon deliberation and with the gracious consent of his Royal Majesty Louis the Most Serene King of the Franks (for he ardently wished to see the Holy Martyrs, his protectors), the date of the ceremony for the second Sunday in June, that is to say the third day before the Ides, the day of the Apostle Barnabas."[18] Doubtless the work progressed rapidly, but, agreeing with Panofsky's interpretation of the phrase "three years and three months" as a symbolic reference to the Trinity,[19] I would place the miracle of the storm on 19 January 1144, not 1143.[20] This would allow another year for construction, and provide a timetable still consistent with the 11 June consecration. Such details are not of great importance, but they demonstrate how accurately we can reconstruct many of Suger's actions.

Although Suger says that the choice of 11 June 1144 as a date for the dedication of the new choir suited the convenience of King Louis VII, there had to be other considerations. Doubtless the lovely June weather in the Ile-de-France was a factor in planning a magnificent ceremony to which many notables were invited and which would certainly attract large crowds. Inclement weather usually discourages attendance. To be a successful event of more than passing interest, the ceremonies had to include members of the royal family and court, dignitaries of the church, and many other notables whose presence would enhance the prestige of the royal abbey. Then, in turn, the brilliance of the new architecture with its stained glass would astound them all.

"We sent invitations by many messengers, also by couriers and envoys, through almost all the districts of Gaul and urgently requested the archbishops and bishops, in the name of the Saints and as a debt to their apostolate, to be present at so great a solemnity."[21] A copy of this invitation would be a most interesting document, especially in regard to the phrasing of the "debt to their apostolate." Probably the phrase was a formula without serious implications; but modern historians might infer that acceptance of such an invitation acknowledged some obligation to the patron saint or, to some degree, his superiority. In his list of those to whom invitations were sent, Suger gives the whole affair political overtones by mentioning only archbishops and bishops, not fellow abbots and other clergy. Not until later in his account of the ceremonies does he mention the participation of archdeacons, abbots, and other honorable persons.[22] The list of prelates mentioned by Suger as having visited Saint-Denis while the new church was under construction includes those present at the consecration ceremonies of the western bays on 9 June 1140, at the verification of the relics of the altar of Charles the Bald on 9 October 1141, and at the consecration of the crypt and choir on 11 June 1144.[23]

At the ceremony on 11 June 1144 not only most of the above list were present, but also "Our Lord King Louis himself and his spouse Queen Eleanor, as well as his mother, and the peers of the realm [who] arrived two days before [*perendie*].[24] Of the diverse counts and nobles from many regions and dominions, of the ordinary troops of knights and soldiers there is no count."[25]

Such a gathering demanded a great deal of planning and forethought, but Suger said without pretension that he was "not so much [intent upon] external matters (for these we had already ordained to be provided in affluence without argument)."[26] Yet he admitted that "in June almost all victuals were scarce," and that he was worried about finding enough mutton, since there was "a plague among the sheep born that year." The problem was solved by the unexpected appearance of a Cistercian monk with a very great flock of rams sent by his brethren, which "I bring to your Paternal Grace . . . so that you may keep what you like and send us back what you do not like."[27] This passage gives evidence that Suger had quite human failings, since he admitted to irritation at the monk's interruption, which detained him on his way to mass. "A little irritated," Suger at first had answered "without too much civility" before hearing the mission of the monk.[28]

Suger's love for lavish ceremonies could not be better demonstrated than by his attention to every detail: the preparation of the sacramental implements, the "arrangements by which the eager and so sacred procession of so many persons might smoothly wend its way throughout the church, within and without,"[29] even to the protection of the procession by the king and his retinue. The ceremonies evidently began with the arrival of the royal family on Friday, 9 June. On Saturday the various relics to be consecrated in the new altars were taken "out of their chapels and, according to custom, placed . . . most honourably in draped tents at the exit of the [monks'] choir."[30] That Saturday night, the night office, Matins, was expanded into an all-night service (*pervigilium*).[31] Evidently Suger fervently hoped that the legendary, miraculous consecration of the "old" church would be repeated, for he "devoutly implored [that] our Lord Jesus Christ . . . might deign mercifully to visit the holy place and to participate in the holy ceremonies, not only potentially but also in person."[32] Early Sunday morning, 11 June, the prelates "arranged themselves in episcopal manner [that is, in hierarchical order] . . . in the upper choir between the tombs of the Martyrs and the altar of the Saviour,"[33] that is, the western, or central, part of the new choir. Then,

> so great a chorus of such great pontiffs, decorous in white vestments, splendidly arrayed in pontifical miters and precious orphreys embellished by circular ornaments, held the crosiers in their hands [and] walked round and round the vessel . . . so piously that the King and the attending nobility believed themselves to behold a chorus celestial rather than terrestrial, a ceremony divine rather than human. The populace milled around outside with the drive of its intolerable magnitude; and when the aforesaid chorus sprinkled the holy water onto the exterior, competently aspersing the walls of the church with the aspergillum, the King himself and his officials kept back the tumultuous impact and protected those returning to the doors with canes and sticks.[34]

Following the consecration of the new structure,

> we proceeded to the translation of the sacred Relics and approached the ancient and venerable tombs of our Patron Saints; for thus far they had not been moved from their place [in the eighth-century *confessio*]. After prostrations, the pontiffs as well as our Lord the King, and all of us so far as we could in view of the narrowness of the room, inspected . . . the venerable shrines. . . . Forthwith muscles are moved, arms are

thrust out, so many and so important hands are laid on that not even the seventh hand was able to reach the sacred shrines themselves. Therefore, our Lord the King himself, injecting himself into their midst, received the silver chasse of our special Patron from the hands of the bishops—I believe, from the hand of the Archbishop of Reims and Sens, the Bishop of Chartres and others—and led the way out as devoutly as nobly. A marvel to behold! never could anyone see such a procession, apart from that which had been seen on the occasion of the old consecration by the Heavenly Host.[35]

When the relics of the patron saints reached the ivory door in Hilduin's chapel,[36] they were joined by the relics which had been taken out of the draped tents in front of the monks' choir and were carried on the shoulders of bishops, counts, and barons. This procession then advanced

through the cloisters with candlesticks, crosses, and other festive ornaments and with many odes and hymns. . . .
   When [the procession] had returned to the church and had ascended by the stairs to the upper altar, destined for the rest of the Saints . . . the rites were performed at the new main altar which was to be consecrated in front of their new tomb; the consecration of this [new main altar] we entrusted to the Lord Archbishop of Reims, Samson. The rites were also splendidly and solemnly performed at the other twenty altars that were to be consecrated.[37]
   . . . After the consecration of the altars all these [dignitaries] performed a solemn celebration of Masses, both in the upper choir and in the crypt, so festively, so solemnly, so different and yet so concordantly, so close [to one another] and so joyfully that their song, delightful by its consonance and unified harmony, was deemed a symphony angelic rather than human.[38]

Detailed descriptions such as these enliven our imagination and almost allow us to be present as the simultaneous celebration of ten masses and sounds of another ten voices in the crypt filled the new choir.
   Were such ceremonies repeated? Were they part of the program of the new choir? Such questions must be borne in mind in our examination of the plan and structure of this second campaign.
   This review of the textual sources for the study of the chevet would be incomplete if it did not include a few references made by Suger to the symbolic meaning of the structure and also the original inscriptions record-ing the initial dedications of four of the radiating chapels of the choir. The latter were uncovered in the late 1950s when Formigé ordered all surfaces cleaned. The dedication inscriptions incised on the corbel under the fifth rib of the vault of the chapel between the two windows read as follows (I have used Panofsky's rather than Formigé's identification of the chapels):[39]

Fig. 97

Chapel of the Innocents (no. 3): In nomine sanctissime Trinitatis consecratum est hoc altare a venerabili Patre S.[40] Noviom[ens]i

97. Chapel of the Holy Innocents. Detail showing an inscription commemorating the consecration of the altar to the Saints Innocents in 1144.

Episcopo in honore sanctorum Innocentium anno Incarn[ati] V[erb]i MCXLIV.

Chapel of Saint-Cucuphas (no. 6): In nomine S[ancti]ss[im]e Trinitatis consecratu[m] est hoc altare a v[enerabil]i P[atr]ie A.[41] Atrebatensi Ep[iscop]o in honore s[ancti] Cucuphatis an[n]o D[e]i MCXLIV.

Chapel of Saint-Eugene (no. 7): In nomine sanctissime Trinitatis consecratum est hoc altare a venerabili Patre A.[42] Constantiarum episcopo in honore sancti Eugenii anno Dei MCXLIV.

Chapel of Saint-Hilary (no. 8): In nomine sanctissime Trinitatis consecratum est hoc altare a venerabili Patre R.[43] Ebroicensi episcopo in honore sancti Hilari anno Dei MCXLIV.

In a complicated metaphor based on Psalms 47:3 and 45:6 Suger referred to his new choir as "*Mount Zion, . . . the city of the Great King,* in the *midst* of which *God will not be moved;* but [in the choir of Saint-Denis], will not disdain, *moved* by the entreaties of sinners, to be placated and propitiated by the sweet-smelling burnt offerings of the penitent." This "midst," that is, the choir, was "raised aloft by twelve columns representing the number of the Twelve Apostles, and, secondarily by as many columns in the side-aisles signifying the number of the [minor] Prophets."[44] In such a structure, according to the Apostle Paul, "you are no more strangers and foreigners; but you are fellow citizens with the saints, and the domestics of God. Built upon the foundation of the apostles and prophets, Jesus Christ himself being the chief cornerstone: In whom all the building, being framed together, groweth into an holy temple in the Lord. In whom you also are built together into an habitation of God in the Spirit."[45] Suger cleverly took these words of Saint Paul, who he believed had been the teacher of Saint Denis, and transformed them into the basic concepts of the Pseudo-Areopagite concerning the spiritual, or immaterial, and the material spheres: "the more loftily and fitly we strive to build in a material way," the more we, ourselves, spiritually, are "builded together for an habitation of God."[46] This symbolism of the Pseudo-Dionysius is complemented by Suger's emphasis on "the elegant and praiseworthy extension in [the form of] a circular string of chapels, by virtue of which the whole [church] would shine with the wonderful and uninterrupted light of most luminous windows [a crown of light], pervading the interior beauty;"[47] there the celebration of simultaneous masses "was deemed a symphony angelic [a celestial choir] rather than human." In Suger's mind, the chevet harmonized with "the upper chapel [of the western bays] most beautiful and worthy to be the dwelling place of angels." Pseudo-Dionysian metaphysics established the hierarchy of the angelic kingdom, and Suger's second campaign built a terrestrial abode for its counterpart, the ecclesiastical hierarchy on earth.

Alterations and Restorations

Tourists who visit the crypt today are impressed by its solemnity, its intimate associations with kings and queens whose mortal remains still rest there, and by the impressive masonry casually identified by the guardian-guide in general terms. The student finds the crypt fascinating because of its long history, but the serious archaeologist soon realizes that all is confusion. Extensive alterations and so-called restorations, some as recent as the 1970s, have transformed most of the surfaces and falsified important details. The crypt, not unlike the west façade, has suffered grievous indignities, which amount to tragic misrepresentations of what should be an exciting and instructive experience looking back into the long history of the royal abbey. The remains of the earliest buildings have already been examined. This section will concentrate on changes to Suger's twelfth-century crypt. Plans for the crypt were formulated early in 1140 while work on the western bays was still in progress. The ceremony for the laying of the first foundation stones was celebrated on 14 July 1140.

The first changes to Suger's crypt occurred less than a century after its completion. Begun soon after 1230,[48] the rebuilding of the upper portions of the choir entailed the reinforcement of the cylindrical piers of the choir hemicycle and of the two straight bays of the western portions of the choir.

Because four western piers were inadequately supported in the crypt, four solid, circular piers were added there as the work began. These crypt piers are easily identified in the north and south ambulatories today by their thirteenth-century crocket capitals, by their polygonal, not square, bases, and by their projections up to and presumably through the barrel vaults of the ambulatories. The last must have occasioned some work on the vaults, but no important changes occurred elsewhere in the crypt.

Pl. 2; Album no. 2

The minor alterations in the two lateral western chambers at the north and south of the stairs leading to the crypt seem to date from the rebuilding of the transept in the thirteenth century. In the northern chamber, where the royal remains were placed after their rediscovery in 1817,[49] a thirteenth-century crocket capital can be seen in the northwestern corner. Since everything below the capital is covered by the storage area, I have found no explanation for the capital or its function. Similarly in the southern chamber in the northeastern corner of the transept chapel of Saint John the Baptist, where Du Guesclin's tomb is located, the base of the thirteenth-century pier projects below the level of the nave, presumably to insure the solidity of the pier's foundations.

Between the mid-thirteenth century and 1683, when Marie-Thérèse, the wife of Louis XIV, died, no record mentions work in the crypt. Yet before 1683 excavations were made to build subterranean burial chambers, or *caveaux,* under the eastern bays of the transept. Some of that work unquestionably altered the western portions of Suger's crypt; but, possibly to avoid pillaging, those caveaux apparently were kept secret. At the present writing one such chamber with two "rooms" and numerous niches lies under the chapel of Saint John the Baptist in the south transept.[50] With the possible exception of a plan dated 24 February 1811, presumably drawn for Cellérier as a project, none of the earliest known plans of the crypt shows those chambers. Cellérier's plan indicates another such "vault," or chamber, with three tiers of coffins under the north transept, but no traces of it have survived. Abbé Bossuet must have referred to the chambers in his funeral oration of 21 August 1670 for Henriette Anne Stuart, wife of Philippe de France, duke of Orléans:

Fig. 98b

> Elle va descendre à ces sombres lieux, à ces demeures souterraines, pour y dormir dans la poussière avec les grands de la terre, comme parle Job, avec ces rois et ces princes anéantis, parmi lesquels à peine peut-on la placer, tant les rangs y sont pressés, tant la mort est prompte à remplir ces places.[51]

In 1683 no room could be found for the dead queen, Marie-Thérèse. Royal engineers sent to Saint-Denis constructed a corridor that linked the small chamber built in 1514 by Louis XII for Anne de Bretagne to the central part of the crypt to the east (namely, the eighth-century *confessio*) and to the central part of Hilduin's ninth-century crypt.[52] The latter, the larger space, became the "caveau royal."[53] Presumably in 1683 the caveau was sealed off from the rest of Suger's crypt, thereby altering the twelfth-century arrangement which had first modified Hilduin's crypt, especially at the eastern end

a

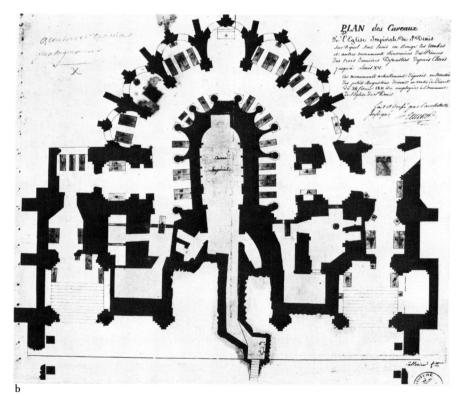

b

98. Early plans of the crypt: (a) before 1793; (b) by Cellérier, ca. 1811; (c) by Debret, 1816; (d) by Viollet-le-Duc, 1846.

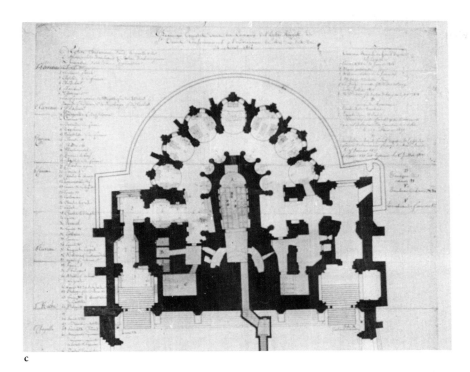

c

d

of the central portion. After the 1683 closure, the only access to the caveau led from the transept crossing southwest of the high altar between the tombs of Louis III and Philippe III le Hardi, down a series of steps, and through the small chamber built by Louis XII. That chamber was known from then on as the "caveau des cérémonies." There the most recently deceased king was placed until the arrival of his successor's coffin forced his removal to the caveau royal. After 1683 the crypt as a whole was left deserted. Its destiny seemed that of a graveyard. No religious services had been performed there since the sixteenth century.[54] Then the Revolution engulfed France, and in October 1793 the mobs from Paris arrived at Saint-Denis. To celebrate 10 August 1792, the anniversary of the downfall of the throne, Barrère had demanded before the national convention that the "mausolées fastueux" at Saint-Denis be destroyed: "La main puissante de la république doit effacer impitoyablement ces épitaphes superbes et démolir ces mausolées qui rappelleraient des rois l'effrayant souvenir."[55] The principal target was, of course, the caveau royal.

In 1793, Hubert Robert made one of his famous paintings of destruction and ruin, which he entitled *La violation des caveaux de Saint-Denis*.[56] Had Hubert Robert been a Piranesi, rather than a romanticist, this sketch could have provided one of the few records of the depredations at Saint-Denis. Unfortunately, the sketch is purely imaginary, with a background recognizable as the choir and transept rising above a gaping hole supposedly torn in the vault of the caveau royal. The masonry shown as large, dressed blocks of stone could not have come from that part of the crypt. In fact, no precise records of the damage caused by the mobs exist, but Chateaubriand's memorable lines leave a vivid image.

Fig. 99

> Saint-Denis est désert, l'oiseau l'a pris pour passage, l'herbe croît sur ses autels brisés; et, au lieu du cantique de la mort, qui retentissoit sous ses dômes, on n'entend plus que les gouttes de pluie qui tombent par son toit découvert, la chute de quelque pierre qui se détache de ses murs en ruines, ou le son de son horloge, qui va roulant dans les tombeaux vides et les souterrains dévastés.[57]

Damages were aggravated by the total neglect of the entire structure until 1806, when Napoleon decreed the restoration of Saint-Denis.

As elsewhere throughout the building, the alterations and restorations that followed proved to be as disastrous and depleting as the willful destruction by the mobs and the transport of the royal monuments and stained glass to Paris by Alexandre Lenoir.[58] The first work, under Jacques-Guillaume Legrand, 1806–07, is described as the "deblayement," or basic removal of debris, from the interior and from the exterior ditches.[59] The work of his successor, Jacques Cellérier, had more serious consequences.[60] Although the official order for the return of royal tombs to Saint-Denis is dated 16 December 1816, evidently Cellérier, before his dismissal in 1811, made plans for alterations in the crypt where the tombs were to be placed.[61] These plans included such major changes as the creation of new, monumental staircases under the chapels of Notre-Dame-la-Blanche and Saint John the Baptist at the north-

Fig. 98b

99. *La violation des caveaux de Saint-Denis,* **painting by Hubert Robert, 1793. Original now in Musée de Carnavalet, Paris.**

ern and southern extremities of the transept, the leveling of all the floors in the crypt, and the creation of plaster niches around the exterior of the caveau royal for the display of tombs. This project entailed quite indiscriminate cutting through or into the earlier masonry, with obviously dangerous consequences to the stability of the structure. Evidently Napoleon gave these plans to Pierre Fontaine, Cellérier's successor;[62] but since Fontaine was dismissed in 1813, most of the work must have been accomplished under François Debret. The best and most detailed description of this work is by Viollet-le-Duc, who undertook to remedy the damage:

Fig. 98c

> On fit dans les caveaux du tour de choeur [that is, in the crypt],
> abandonnés depuis longtemps de tristes ouvrages; pour consolider les
> murs du caveau central (qu'il était facile du rest de réparer dans leur
> forme ancienne, puisque ces murs ne portent pas de charge) on eut
> l'idée de bâtir des niches en cul-de-four appareillées à la moderne, entre
> les grosses colonnes qui jusqu'alors avaient été isolées. . . . Outre que
> l'appareil de ces niches contraste désagréablement avec l'architecture des
> cryptes, cette construction fit disparaître une arcature Romane qui se
> voyait sur le parement extérieur du mur nord du caveau central.
>   Pour établir une communication entre tous ces caveaux qui
> d'autrefois étaient indépendants les uns des autres, on perçu à même
> des massifs sans autre précaution que de mettre quelques platebandes
> en fer aux arêtes des linteaux. On voulait donner un même niveau au

100. Detail of the capital of a pier of the hemicycle of the crypt, showing evidence of the recutting of the sculpture.

sol de tous ces caveaux, et pour obtenir ce résultat on creusa jusqu'à plus de deux mètres dans un massif très dur sur beaucoup de points . . . les attachements font mention de tous ces ouvrages si compromettans pour la solidité de l'edifice. On changea la disposition du caveau central, en bâtissant un cul-de-four là où se trouvaient autrefois un mur plat et une arcature . . . et enfin on recoupa quatre et cinq centimètres au diametre des colonnes des bas-côtés du choeur [the round piers of the hemicycle in the crypt] pour y appliquer un stuc noir enlevé plus tard.[63]

The evidence still visible on the inside (that is, the side facing the central chamber) of the round piers in the ambulatory indicates that the cutting back of the original twelfth-century surfaces was only one or two centimeters, not four or five.[64] The effect was the same, however, for the vigor of the original designs of the capitals was completely lost. Today all of the abstract vegetal decoration on the capitals of piers and on those in and outside the radiating chapels appears crisp and static, even though the seemingly infinite variations in the designs are attributable to the artists of the twelfth century. Such transformations from lively modeled surfaces to sharp but lifeless ones typify work under Debret's direction, as already noted in the western portals and upper portions of the façade. Another detail mentioned by Viollet-le-Duc as typical of Debret's work was the "platebandes de fer," or flat, iron bars, placed under the lintels of the niches in the crypt. They are exactly like the one that still supports the lintel of the central portal of the west façade.

His information about the leveling of the floors of all the rooms in the crypt indicated that in many places the change involved the disruption of more than 2.00 m in a very solid masonry. Dated 1846, a plan of the crypt by Viollet-le-Duc included as part of his first lengthy report to the administration has metric measurements inscribed in many rooms, especially on the

Fig. 100

App. K.34–92

Fig. 98d

south side. These numbers may indicate the different depths that were dug out; if so in some instances there must be errors.[65] The problem is not a major one, although it demonstrates again how many details in the structure of Suger's building defy positive solutions.[66]

After the disruption to the crypt for the purpose of installing the royal tombs, which was completed in 1818,[67] little was done that affected the architecture of the crypt until 1847, when Viollet-le-Duc undertook the task of restoring it, insofar as possible, to its original state. Although on his arrival at Saint-Denis in 1846, Viollet-le-Duc faced the immediate problem of the need to demolish the north tower of the west façade, he also began at once to consolidate the masonry of the crypt. This entailed the removal of the niches around the central chamber and the restoration of the surviving masonry. Although the work can be described as consolidation, two of Viollet-le-Duc's sketches indicate that it might more properly be called a reconstruction. Dated 14 June and 31 July 1848, these drawings show what he found when the plaster niches which surrounded the exterior of the caveau royal had been removed. In the details drawn, the voussoirs of the original arches of the arcade added by Suger to Hilduin's ninth-century crypt were more or less intact; but the shafts of the small columns had been removed, as had most of the abaci and bases and also the capitals with carved scenes. Since the historiated capitals are significant in the history of twelfth-century sculpture in the Ile-de-France, it is interesting to note that of the six emplacements for capitals shown in the two drawings, only one retained any indication of the sculpture, which I cannot identify as part of any of the capitals known today.

Fig. 101a,b

When Suger built his new ambulatory around the central portion of Hilduin's crypt, he must have rebuilt the eastern end of the central chapel. Presumably he wished to preserve as much as possible of the old crypt, which had protected the sacred relics of the Passion, and possibly wanted to close it off. There is no evidence of exactly where the relics of the Passion were kept in his new chapel;[68] and no positive evidence has survived indicating exactly how Suger closed the eastern end of the central chamber. The reconstruction of the plan suggested by Lefèvre-Pontalis, which has a flat wall decorated with arcades, conforms to the other twelfth-century work and to the fragments of the masonry still in place.[69] Viollet-le-Duc rebuilt the exterior of the eastern end with two angular flat walls and a buttress which remained in place until Formigé's transformations of the 1950s.

Viollet-le-Duc's major reconstructions affecting the twelfth-century crypt focused on the caveau royal, although he apparently modified or removed a number of other details which are shown in Cellérier's and Debret's plans of 1811 and 1816. These details include walls at the western ends of the north and south ambulatories and a room outside the northwestern chapel, presumably an addition by Debret. Begun in 1859, the other major work done by Viollet-le-Duc in the crypt, namely, the building of an imperial crypt for the Bonaparte dynasty ordered by Napoleon III, did not affect the masonry of Suger's crypt. By 1875, Viollet-le-Duc had completed the restoration there and, except for a few minor changes, the crypt remained untouched until Formigé's major alterations in 1958–59.

Fig. 98b,c

Fig. 102

a

b

101. Drawings of the crypt by Viollet-le-Duc: (a) detail of exterior wall, south side of the central chamber in 1848; (b) detail of exterior of central chamber, south side, window opening and arch to west.

Jules Formigé, chief architect at Saint-Denis from 1945 until his death in 1961, did his most important work in the crypt. Because I have no access to whatever records he kept my observations are based entirely upon what I have observed in the crypt today contrasted with its condition when I began my studies in 1935. I have also drawn upon a few conversations with the foremen in charge of the work during the 1960s and 1970s. Formigé concluded his chapter on the crypt with a statement of his purpose: "In the restoration of this crypt, I made every effort to remove all the additions that disfigured it and I only redid parts of the pavement that were missing. The crypt, therefore, can be seen in its ancient condition, which allows one to admire this magnificent ensemble to which nothing can be compared, either in France or elsewhere."[70]

The architecture of the crypt itself bears witness to his arbitrary interpretation of its "ancient condition." In some instances Formigé's extensive changes might be interpreted as restorations, although I have no evidence of any documentary or other record to substantiate his work. After removing the floors of all the radiating chapels, for instance, he installed new pavements at the same level as that of the ambulatory. He enlarged the windows of the radiating chapels by lowering their sills to the presumed twelfth-century level. His most drastic decision involved the opening of the east end of the central portion of the crypt, the caveau royal, as though it had once been an integral part of the twelfth-century ensemble.

102. A view from the east of the interior of the crypt in 1978, as restored by Formigé.

Two photographs in Formigé's book identified as "before" and "after" *dégagement*, or "disengagement," show a typical "restoration."[71] The eastern end of the caveau royal has not been disengaged or freed, it has been completely removed, accompanied by skillful adjustments in the adjacent masonry.[72] The arcades of the north and south walls have been extended to the east, possibly in imitation of Lefèvre-Pontalis's reconstruction of this central portion in Suger's time.[73] With twelfth-century capitals arbitrarily taken from other parts of the crypt, the modern arcades are clever reproductions of those to the west. For example, until the late 1950s, the capital showing Saint Benedict seated with Totila, king of the Goths, kneeling in front of him was the first capital on the south wall as one entered the crypt on the south side. Another two capitals, now on the south wall of the central chamber (the tenth and eleventh from the west), in pre-Formigé times faced each other in the caveau royal at the level of the transverse arch just to the west of the semicircular apse.[74]

Quite deceptive is Formigé's extension of the barrel vault to the east. It is difficult to ascertain whether the existing vault over the old caveau royal is the original ninth-century vault of Hilduin's crypt or whether it was redone in the twelfth century. No documents tell us, but the unfinished irregular surfaces of the rectangular stones in the reasonably parallel beds are different from those surviving in other twelfth-century vaults in the crypt and elsewhere at Saint-Denis. Formigé's mason, Campo, was so accomplished technically that he duplicated the older portions of the vault perfectly; only careful inspection reveals the differences between the old and new surfaces. With considerable pride Campo verified my identification of the actual joint. After admitting that it had been difficult to design the arches at the eastern end that would make a smooth transition to the twelfth-century masonry of the hemicycle piers, he asked if I could identify the new abaci which he himself had carved in imitation of earlier ones.[75] Even though before his time the central portion had always been closed off from the rest of the crypt, he expressed no concern about the archaeological validity of his changes and additions.

Other changes in the crypt included the opening of the large arches at the western end of the caveau royal to facilitate the circulation of tourists.[76] The entrance stairs from the northern transept were also rebuilt. When the doorway was reopened, evidence of earlier masonry was uncovered. This led to the unexpected discovery of part of the base of the twelfth-century pier between the elevated choir and lower crossing of Suger's new church. Unfortunately the fragments were dismounted and reinstalled so carelessly that doubt exists about the original shape of the pier and about its exact location. The same doubts surround details of the plan or structure of the crypt today when one evaluates them in terms of its original function or significance. If care is exercised, however, and references to trustworthy sources are constantly checked, the crypt can provide vital information about the preparations for the building of Suger's new "crown of light," the ambulatory and radiating chapels above.

Crypt and Choir Plans

Fortunately Suger's ambulatory and the radiating chapels enclosing the choir have survived virtually intact so that we can study in detail the degree to which the master mason succeeded in meeting the abbot's specific requirements. Much more complicated than the western bays, which were designed to provide an impressive approach and entrance into the new building, the plan of the new eastern end represents a brilliantly subtle response to a sophisticated program. To examine these subtleties, the plans of the crypt and choir must be accurately recorded, and the two structures cannot be considered as separate entities. The upper portion, or choir, was designed to satisfy the abbot's intentions, and the crypt functioned as a solid foundation for that choir. The exact locations of the masonry supports demand particular attention, since the relationships among the columns, piers, and buttresses not only inform the articulation of the interior spaces, but also bear responsibility for any irregularities or distortions in the structure of the vaults.

To achieve an accurate plan is difficult when the structure, a partially subterranean one such as the crypt, has masonry built in periods as much as four centuries apart and involves isolated chambers often on different alignments.[77] Although the alterations and restorations just reviewed may have changed some of the pavement levels in the crypt, the relatively simple masonry which rests directly on the foundations must represent the original twelfth-century disposition. Formigé's rebuilding in the eastern portions of the caveau royal created an exception to this—a problem to be analyzed shortly.

As I began my studies in the abbey church, the plan of the crypt was one of my first preoccupations. We measured and remeasured for it again and again, and I published the results in my first volume.[78] In 1970, when the photogrammetric recording of the contours of the vaults became available, our efforts were rewarded. Only a few changes were needed to make the location of almost every detail of my plan conform to the accurate record provided by photogrammetry. A major difficulty remained, however, since the photogrammetric renderings included only the interior construction and lacked any reference to the irregular exterior buttresses between the radiating chapels. The form and alignments of these buttresses are important for an understanding of the structure of the entire chevet. Yet having rechecked the exterior details with a transit within the last few years, we are confident that the accompanying plan is accurate.

The same holds true for the choir plan, which presented much less of a problem than the crypt. When we checked the exact location of the ambulatory columns, an interesting deviation became apparent in the photogrammetric elevations. Those slender supports for the complicated arches and radiating ribs of the ambulatory vaults are not exactly perpendicular. The abaci above the capitals project slightly outward over the bases so that a plumb line suspended from the top of an abacus falls beyond the outer edge of the base. I have checked this curious deviation from a ladder, and although

Figs. 106, 110c; Pl. 2; Album nos. 9, 19

Fig. 118a; Pl. 1; Album nos. 1, 10

Fig. 103

the overhang varies only from 0.045 m to 0.091 m, it is present in every column. Because this overhang is always on the outer side, that is, the side facing the radiating chapels, deviation from verticality must have been caused by some unexpected pressure from the inside, possibly occasioned when the hemicycle cylindrical piers were replaced in the thirteenth century. The fact that the deviation is not consistent but varies from column to column strengthens such a hypothesis. Consequently in the plan of the choir the bases of these ambulatory columns still in their original locations do not conform precisely to the photogrammetric location of the abaci. The bases lie very slightly toward the inside, but the deviation is so slight that it can hardly be drawn even with a very fine line.

We can begin analyzing the accurate plans of the crypt and the choir once we have reviewed the recently summarized texts revealing Suger's *desiderata* for the new chevet. Suger's original and most obvious purpose was to enlarge the church, especially the eastern end, where "the brethren who were showing the tokens of the Passion of our Lord to the visitors had to yield to the anger and rioting and many a time, having no place to turn, escaped with the relics through the windows."[79] Although this passage must refer to Hilduin's ninth-century crypt, where the relics of the Passion were kept before Suger's rebuilding, the eighth-century apse with the high altar was also quite small. He also wrote elsewhere of similar occasions when "no one, because of their very congestion, could [do] anything but stand like a marble statue, stay benumbed or, as a last resort, scream."[80]

More important than the need to enlarge the eastern end was Suger's decision to move the relics of the patron saints from their protected seclusion in the confessio under the high altar. He wished to "present the chasses of the Saints, adorned with gold and precious gems, to the visitors' glances in a more elevated place."[81] Such a bold idea reflected Suger's confidence in royal authority and the ability of the king to provide security in the realm. Fortunately the portion of Hilduin's partially subterranean crypt just to the east of the high altar that rose above ground provided an excellent platform, raised more than 3.50 m above the pavement of the nave. The new choir was built over the ninth-century vaults.

In addition to a raised platform Suger desired a "circular string of chapels" with large stained glass windows so that "the whole church would shine with . . . wonderful and uninterrupted light."[82] These chapels should be "so close" to each other that the celebration of simultaneous masses at their altars would create a symphony deemed "angelic rather than human."[83] Finally, the ensemble was to be achieved "loculento ordine," (with luminous order) by means of "geometrical and arithmetical instruments" so that the central portion of the new choir and its inner ambulatory would have the same dimensions as the old nave and side aisles. Quoted in its entirety, the passage in question contains additional significant details:

> Moreover, it was cunningly provided that—through the upper columns and central arches which were placed upon the lower ones built in the crypt—the central nave of the old nave should be equalized, by means

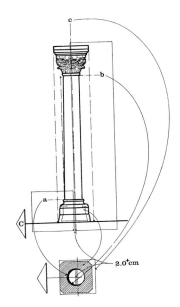

103. Photogrammetric diagram showing vertical alignment of ambulatory column.

of geometrical and arithmetical instruments, with the central nave of
the new addition; and, likewise, that the dimensions of the old side-
aisles should be adapted to [Panofsky used "equalized with"] the
dimensions of the new side-aisles, except for that elegant and
praiseworthy extension, in [the form of] a circular string of chapels, by
virtue of which the whole [church] would shine with the wonderful
and uninterrupted light of most luminous windows, pervading the
interior beauty.[84]

Since the old nave was 10.00 m wide from column axis to column
axis[85] and since the distance between the centers of the first two columns of
the curve of the hemicycle in Suger's new choir also measures almost exactly
10.00 m, it seems reasonable to accept his statement that the new nave
was "equalized" with the old. The old side aisles, however, were over
5.00 m wide,[86] whereas the new ambulatory (side aisle) is only about
3.50 m wide. In order to explore different possibilities that may explain
such a discrepancy, we must first turn to certain details of the crypt and choir
plans.

The superimposition of the photogrammetric "plan des voutes" of the
choir over the vaults of the crypt proves how "cunning" (*sagaciter*) Suger's
masons were. The columns and arches of the choir really are "placed upon"
the columns and arches of the crypt, with the exception of a uniform overhang or projection of the ambulatory bases beyond the masonry piers between the radiating chapels in the crypt—a phenomenon to be investigated
later in this chapter. Precision and uniformity with variety continued to be
dominant characteristics at Saint-Denis.

Another fundamental principle was the strict observance of bilateral symmetry. The structural components in the choir are much simpler and sparer
than the massive piers of the western bays, but the thin columns and curved
segments of masonry have been carefully aligned on each side of a median
axis so that they have the same shapes and occupy identical mirror positions
on the north as on the south. The spaces, or voids, which dominate the
interior repeat each other in extent and configuration on each side of an
invisible divider. Yet the progression of changing shapes is neither repetitive
nor static, due to subtle changes in the location of points of organization.

In the crypt a dominant feature immediately observable in the photogrammetric plans is the presence of the semicircular arcs of the arches between the
columns of the hemicycle and between the columns of the ambulatory and
between the chapel piers. At first glance the segments of semicircles formed
by the hemicycle and ambulatory arcs appear concentric, binding the entire
plan into regular compartments, as in the plan published by Ernst Gall and
Otto von Simson.[87] A comparison of this arbitrary, schematic rendering of   **Fig. 104**
the Saint-Denis plan with the ground plan based on actual measurements
and photogrammetric renderings underlines the dynamic quality of the
existing structure in contrast to the schematic interpretation. The vitality
results from the slightly eccentric arrangement of the three central radiating
chapels. From their centers, which lie on an arc, lines can be drawn that

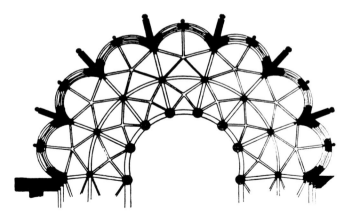

104. Plan of the ambulatory and radiating chapels of choir, 1140–44.

converge on a point almost 2.00 m to the east of the major focal midpoint of the median axis.[88] I shall return to the significance of the focal point shortly but should first comment on the three central, or eastern, radiating chapels. Since the centers of those chapel vaults are farther from the semicircular arc formed by the ambulatory columns and by the arc of the chapel piers in the crypt, the chapels themselves are larger than the four to the west. This is quite

noticeable in the crypt, where the eastern, or axial, chapel is obviously larger than the others, but in the choir above the greater size can be perceived only in the extended length of the central, or fifth, rib of the vault.[89] Another factor of interest in the master mason's plan is its organization not only on the basis of the masonry supports, but also around spatial units such as the centers of vaults—or points in space above the head of the observer. As at Saint-Denis, such subtle refinements are often sensed intuitively rather than perceived directly by means of material, or objective, boundaries. Thus the significance of many designs cannot be judged solely on the two-dimensional plan of the structure; the critic must also take into account the existence of that structure in space.

The focal point in the middle of the median axis, an invisible spot, can illustrate this idea through its numerous interesting implications for the mason's spatial effects. We discovered this focal point as we were rechecking measurements in the choir. A temporary, small altar had been placed in the choir for the daily performances of the liturgy. The celebrant, when facing east in front of the altar, stood directly under the convergence, or keystone, of the ribs of the vault over the hemicycle.[90] When he looked to the east and rotated his head from one side to the other, the columns of the hemicycle and of the ambulatory would line up with the masonry between the radiating chapels, so that he could see only the windows—in actuality a "crown of

Fig. 105

105. (Left and right) "Crown of light." Ambulatory and radiating chapels as seen from the altar located under keystone, or convergence, of the ribs of the vault above the hemicycle.

light." At this place, where Suger must have stood many times, one is immersed in light and is "resurrected' from one's "former submersion."[91]

When located on the plan of the crypt or of the choir, that spot under the hemicycle keystone proves to be the central, or median, point of the entire chevet. Not only is it one-half the distance between the old confessio under the high altar to the west and the eastern extremity of the central radiating chapel (the exterior face of the central buttress), but it also marks one-half the distance between the northern and southern boundaries of the chevet at their widest, or westernmost, dimension. With that dimension equaling 30.00 m, and one-half of it 15.00 m (at the median or central point of the east–west axis), the latter is also the distance in the old eighth-century church from the center of a nave column across the nave to the inside wall of the opposite side aisle. Was it the combined dimension of nave and aisle in the old church that was "equalized" in Suger's choir? Panofsky recognized the linguistic distinction made in the *De Consecratione* between the nave and the side aisle. He emphasized the use of the word "quantitas" (dimension) for the side aisle, without stressing the verb "adaptaretur," as opposed to "aequaretur," which referred to the nave.[92] Another possible interpretation of "adaptaretur" takes into account the approximate width of the ambulatory, which when measured between the inner faces of the hemicycle and ambulatory column bases equals 2.50 m.[93] Thus if both the north and the south ambulatories are included, the measurement could be construed as 5.00 m—the approximate width of the old side aisles. Should this be called "adapting" rather than "equalizing"?

The focal point in the choir is easy to locate because of the keystone of the hemicycle vault. It is less apparent in the crypt. I attach significance to the median, or middle, point between the old confessio under the high altar and the exterior of the easternmost buttress, which lies within the old caveau royal, or central chapel, of Hilduin's ninth-century crypt. That point is located between the rectangular pilasters just to the east of the sixth colonnette from the west along the north and south interior walls of the central chapel. Until recently this spot would have been just east of the transverse arch that marked the beginning of the semicircular apse that closed the central chapel. As demonstrated earlier, evidence is lacking about the original eastern end of Hilduin's chapel as well as about changes to it that must have occurred in the twelfth century. Since the median point was the center for the arcs that located the hemicycle and radiating chapel piers, it must have been visible or open to the east when the plan of the crypt was laid out. In other words, the eastern end of Hilduin's ninth-century crypt must have been removed when Suger's new crypt was begun. The approximate western limit of that removal can be seen in the crypt today at the joining of Formigé's new eastern extension to the older western vault over the central chapel. A north–south line drawn at this point intersects the western limits of the radiating chapels and marks the eastern limits of the parallel walls constructed on the same axis as the central chapel. They were the northern and southern exterior walls of Hilduin's crypt.

Pl. 2

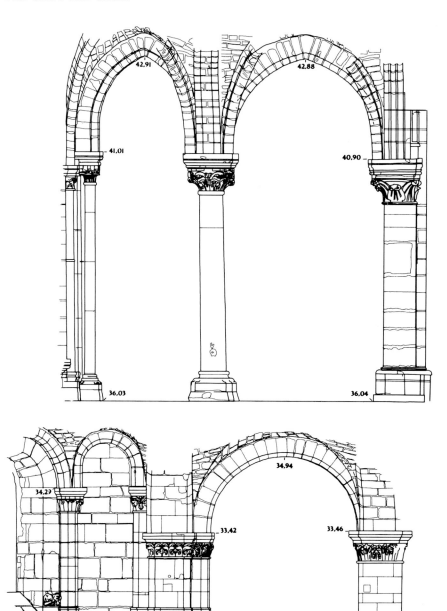

106. Photogrammetric elevation
of crypt and choir axial chapels
(chapel no. 7).

Confirmation of the significance of these arcs in the location of the hemicycle and ambulatory columns exists in the "étonnants ports-à-faux" (astonish-
ing overhangs), as Formigé called them[94] of the ambulatory column bases
beyond the chapel masonry in the crypt. The superposition of the photogrammetric plans of the crypt and choir vaults demonstrates this overhang   Fig. 106
and shows that the overhang is caused by the fact that the ambulatory in the
crypt is slightly wider than the ambulatory in the choir. Earlier I speculated

about the possibility that the choir ambulatory width was "adapted" to equal one-half the width of the old side aisle, 2.50 m. Consequently the overhang which Formigé claimed was a "century in advance of its successors" may have resulted from an arbitrary "adaptation" and does not represent a "daring" structural innovation.

During the initial discussions about the building of the choir, agreement must have been reached quickly that the axis of the new choir should continue the alignment of the old nave and new western bays. Such a concordance was essential. There had been no problem in the first campaign at the western end because the western portions of the old church were torn down, thereby allowing a direct sighting into the old nave. At the eastern end, the apse and eastern walls of the old transept were certainly still standing at the time of the consecration on 9 June 1140 and possibly, but not certainly, when the foundation ceremony of 14 July took place. In the crypt the process of alignment with the old nave axis was, therefore, more difficult. Access to the old nave must have existed through the entrance stairs on each side of the confessio, and probably a window or aperture adjacent to the high altar allowed the relics in the confessio to be seen from above. Ropes could have been stretched, or sightings made, through such openings, but alignment with the old axis would have been especially difficult because the walls of Hilduin's crypt were on an axis about 5° to the north of the old axis.[95] As a result the new axis, as seen in the center radiating chapel of the crypt, deviated slightly, about 1° 30′, to the north. Possibly not until the hemicycle piers were put in place did this deviation become apparent.[96] At least the location of the hemicycle piers seems to shift to the south in relation to the radiating chapel masonry in the crypt. As a result, the transverse arches from the hemicycle to the radiating chapel piers are awkwardly out of line with the axes of the masonry between the chapels. The deviation becomes increasingly evident as one progresses to the west, particularly on the south side. Since the choir columns were placed over the crypt piers, the misalignment was repeated between the hemicycle and ambulatory columns of the choir.[97]

Another even more radical series of irregularities occurs in the placement of the exterior buttresses between the radiating chapels, which project from the chapel masonry at angles seemingly independent of the interior structure. These wall buttresses, which rise from the foundations of the crypt to the summits of the choir chapels, must be recognized as integral to the structure of the chevet. They are not applied units nor are they later additions. No two buttresses repeat the same angle or projection in succession. Their positions seemed haphazard, until I realized that the plans of those on the north side mirror those on the south.[98] The bilateral symmetry in the planning of the crypt and choir has already been emphasized, as it was in the plan of the western bays. In that first campaign the mirror images belong to the category of design devices that resulted in visual coherence between the different faces of the massive piers. The mirrored arrangement of the buttresses on the exterior of the chevet presumably served a functional purpose, counteracting and stabilizing the lateral thrusts of the interior vaults. When I first observed these oblique buttresses I wrote: "Since these buttresses continued upward

Pl. 2

between the radiating chapels of the choir, they must have been designed as supports either for the vaults of the chapels or possibly for the high vaults of the hemicycle of the choir."[99] In recent years scholars have noted other oblique wall buttresses in the construction of mid-twelfth-century chevets, such as those at Saint-Martin-des-Champs.

The question arises as to whether it is coincidental that the distances of 2.70 m between the centers of the hemicycle piers is also the measurement from those same midpoints across the ambulatory in the crypt, as well as the constant of the radii of the arcs of the ribs of the vaults over the ambulatory and radiating chapels of the choir. What conclusion, if any, should be drawn from the fact that angles of both 30° and 27° recur between the centers of the ambulatory and hemicycle columns and vault centers? Apparently a decagon–pentagon combination will locate the centers of the three eastern chapels in the crypt, but does such a geometrical instrument function for the rest of the plan?[100] Melodic harmonies based on mathematical intervals in such a fundamental musical instrument as the monochord may have inspired the master mason as he located points on the median axis.[101] Cosmological mysticism, or the symbolic order of the universe, may have dominated the mind that conceived the "circular string of chapels" as epicycles on eccentric arcs radiating from equidistant centers.[102] Possibly the *loculento ordine,* the luminous order, was related to the series of rotating squares derived from the *ad quadratum* system of proportional relationships involving "true" measure.[103] Possibly the master mason had these and similar analogies in mind as he devised the initial plan for the crypt, which controlled the plan of the choir. Certainly his reduction of masonry supports to allow light to pervade the interior spaces would not have been possible without expert technical knowledge of the potentials of the ribbed vault, to which we must now turn our attention.

CHAPTER EIGHT

Crypt Structure

Figs. 106, 110c

Almost every historian of Western architecture has extolled the choir of Saint-Denis while ignoring the structure of Suger's crypt.[1] But now photogrammetric renderings of the contours of the vaults and elevations of the crypt have provided opportunities for gaining new insights into its structure.

The crypt, as we have already noted, was built to provide a raised platform for the exhibition of the sacred relics and to preserve the venerable remains of the old buildings which had protected the relics of Saint Denis and his companions, as well as those of the Passion of Our Lord. As a structure the crypt functioned as foundations for the choir above. Its carefully dressed masonry recalls, in a much more sophisticated manner, the dressed faces of the foundations of the western bays. But the crypt, of course, is a complete structure, not just a few beds of finished masonry.

Although only scattered and very limited areas of the rubble foundations under the crypt have been examined, enough has been seen to give us some idea of their construction and form. The discussion of Hilduin's ninth-century chapel noted that the area to the east of the early church bordered on the small river Croult. Consequently the almost marshy ground has a water table not far above the solid clay subsoil which underlies the whole area. Proof of the competence of Suger's masons as engineers emerges in the photogrammetric elevations of the crypt and choir, where the levels of the

243

107. Detail of twelfth-century foundations under radiating chapels.

Fig. 107 pavements and superstructure are so uniform that no settling or movement took place over the centuries. The foundations that I have been able to examine consist of a very solid cement rubble extending only a little more than 1.10 m below the pavement.[2] Since the crypt pavement is 2.00 m below the present nave pavement and the average depth of the clay subsoil on which the eighth- and twelfth-century foundations rest is 2.60 m below that

108. Crypt ambulatory, south aisle, facing east.

109. Crypt, radiating chapel no. 7.

pavement, the crypt foundations must have been laid into a trench dug at least 0.50 m into the solid clay. In view of the difficulty in removing this heavy clay, the twelfth-century workmen probably did only what was essential. I have seen a small portion of the exterior limit of the foundation on the north side,[3] a section of the interior face under the radiating chapels,[4] and a section of the curved interior masonry under the hemicycle piers.[5] Except on the exterior, the foundations do not extend beyond the limits of the masonry they were built to support. From these limited excavations I concluded that the twelfth-century foundations formed segments of arcs under the radiating chapels and hemicycle piers. They consist of a solid agglomerate sunk as a mat into the heavy clay, which made them stronger than the metaphoric "walls of precious stones" extolled by Abbot Suger.[6]

Although the plan of the crypt established the contours and proportions of the elegant choir above, all of the crypt masonry is heavy and solid. The hemicycle piers are squat, massive cylindrical constructions of large, curved stones, presumably with a rubble core. Compressed bases provide the footing, and a wide, decorated, continuous capital with a large abacus crowns each pier.[7] The walls between the radiating chapels are equally massive. Facing the hemicycle piers on the outer side of the ambulatory, compound piers curving slightly to conform to the curvature of the arches over the chapel openings also project to support the heavy transverse arches of the vaults. The bases, shafts, continuous carved capitals, and abaci moldings repeat the vertical dimensions of the hemicycle piers. The compound piers are not free-standing but are continued to the exterior by the walls separating the chapels. Defining the interiors of the circular radiating chapels, these curving walls increase in thickness as they extend to the exterior.[8] They terminate in

Fig. 108

Fig. 109

a

b

asymmetrical wall-buttresses between each chapel.[9] Such masonry certainly lives up to Suger's description of "strong material foundations."[10]

Above these ample supports, the arches and vaults proved equally solid. The major arches vary in width, but they form a solid framework for the groin vaults of the ambulatory.[11] The curving lateral arches form powerful concentric bands of masonry—particularly visible in the photogrammetric plan of the crypt vaults. In their effect the arches resemble segments of a rim reinforcing the periphery of a wheel. Four wall arches consolidate the lower portions of the vault compartments in each of the radiating chapels.

Such transverse and lateral arches distinguish the Romanesque groin vaults of northern Europe from those in the south, which derive more closely from Roman antecedents.[12] The arches were built first, creating a freestanding armature not unlike the construction of a rib vault but without any diagonal arches and ribs. The groin vaults at Saint-Denis are distinguished for the small-cut stones and the precision and flexibility of the design.

The curving ambulatory around the old caveau royal terminates in straight bays that lead to the western stairs to the upper church. Combined with the "circular ring of chapels," the design created a variety of shapes to be vaulted. Straight barrel vaults with penetrations cover the western ends of the north and south ambulatories. Triangular compartments with tripartite groin vaults make the transition in front of the western radiating chapels to the irregular, quadripartite vaults of the curving eastern sections of the ambulatory. Finally, the radiating chapels, each with two windows, were successfully covered with five-part groin vaults. None of these forms was an innovation at Saint-Denis; antecedents at least fifty years earlier exist in England.[13] But the precision of the stereotomy and the uniformity of the

110. Crypt vaults: (a) north aisle with combined masonries of different periods; (b) north ambulatory, vault adjacent to radiating chapel no. 2; (c) photogrammetric analysis of the twelfth-century crypt vaults.

Figs. 106, 110b,c

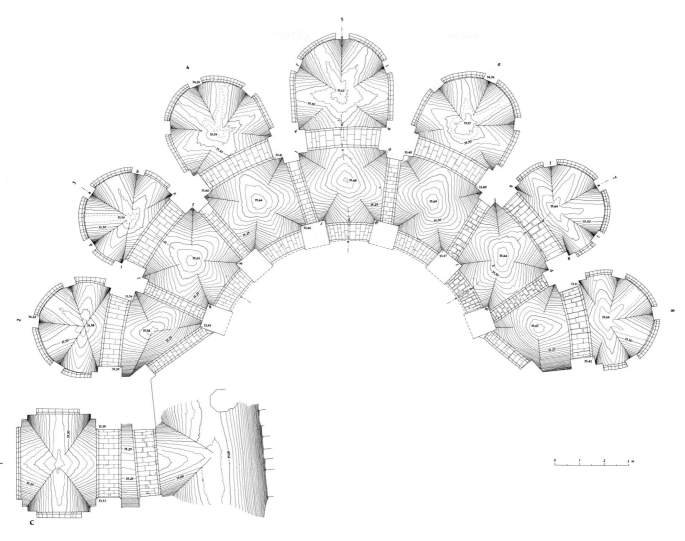

dimensions are characteristic of the skill and advanced knowledge of Suger's masons.

The crypt vaults at Saint-Denis offer an unusual opportunity to observe how such vaults were constructed in the mid-twelfth century. In most instances the intrados, or underside, of the Romanesque groin vault has been covered with stucco or with some type of plaster. It is difficult to accept at face value the often very beautiful, detailed representation of masonry construction in nineteenth- or early twentieth-century publications. The photogrammetric, detailed representation of the vaults of the axial chapels at Saint-Denis is accurate and more trustworthy for careful analysis than photographs or direct observation. But even this representation remains two-dimensional and does not indicate such details as the oblique cutting of the ends of many stones where they form part of the groin itself. The resulting sharp, clean edge must have been cut as the stone was placed on the wooden centering, possibly with some smoothing or finishing after the wooden forms were removed. The curved surfaces of the stones also create the clear, uniform volumes of the vault compartments, which demonstrates an extraordinary technical mastery. The same virtuosity distinguishes the curving vaults of the circular stairways in the western bays. The crowns of the vaults, however, must have been difficult to build. The photogrammetric contours, identified as 35.50 m (above sea level), show large, relatively flat or undefined areas.

Presumably the same or similar wooden forms under the arches and vaults were moved from bay to bay as the building progressed. The photogrammetric records confirm this in that the three elevations of bays 3, 5, and 7 and the diameters and heights of the transverse arches over the ambulatory are uniform. All three diameters are 2.70 m, and the heights of the crowns vary only a few millimeters—4.23 m, 4.29 m, 4.24 m. The radius of the semicircular arch in each instance measures 1.50 m, indicating that the center of the arch was raised 0.10 m above the baseline, a reasonable height for the base, or bottom, beams of the wooden form. The profiles given for the curves of the diagonal arches, in this instance the groins, and intersections of the vault compartments, are less consistent. They are not drawn according to the system of the *voûte en anse de panier* (three-centered arch), nor do they conform to a segment, or section of an oval, or ovoid outline.[14] In my opinion, these profiles resulted from the intersection of the wooden centerings and were not drawn or constructed as independent arches. Yet a number of the profiles have the same dimensions, such as a diameter of 4.40 m with a crown of 2.20 m in the ambulatory vault or 3.90 m by 1.30 m in the radiating chapels—an indication that the same wooden centerings and arch forms were moved and reemployed as the construction advanced. The presence of broken or slightly pointed profiles, particularly in the ambulatory vaults, should not be interpreted in relation to the development of Early Gothic vault construction but rather as the normal result of conventional Romanesque building techniques. (They should not be identified as *arcs d'ogives,* as they are in the photogrammetric sheet of crypt profiles, for they are not separately built arches.)

Fig. 102

Another detail deserves mention in the structure of the crypt. In this instance it can be seen only on the exterior. The undulating periphery of the contiguous chapels, separated only by the buttresses, is accented by a series of arches above the arches of the windows. The result is what appears to be two overlapping segments, or sleeves, of cylindrical masonry. The effect is decorative, since the curving masonry is broken into two planes, and the shadows of the upper arches create rhythmical accents that unite the ensemble and carry the eye from chapel to chapel. This decorative principle may have had its origins in the decorative bands, so familiar to students of early Romanesque architecture, which became an integral feature of German Romanesque in the eleventh and twelfth centuries.[15] I mention them in this section on the crypt structure, for these upper arches add to the thickness of the chapel masonry and load the upper portions where the vaults exist. At the crypt level the arches are round with only a small chamfer to soften the angle

Fig. 111

111. Exterior view of crypt chapel no. 8, the westernmost radiating chapel on the south side.

of the window arch, in contrast to the treatment of the windows and overlapping arches of the choir above.

To complete this analysis of the exterior of the crypt, mention should be made of the western extremities. On the north side the first chapel is rectangular. Today there is a door opening onto the exterior which provides access into the crypt. Originally there must have been a window to light the altar of this chapel. A second arch above the opening continues the same double arch construction of the radiating chapels. On the south side an awkward angle of the adjoining masonry interrupts and distorts the western springing of the upper arch. This is evidence of some error in the measurement on the southern side when the straight, or ninth, chapel was under construction. The masonry, which projects 1.00 m to the south before it is replaced by the construction of the sacristy built in the fifteenth century, must be part of the original twelfth-century building. The continuation at an oblique angle of the base molding confirms this, as does the string course molding just below the choir windows.[16]

This description of the details of the crypt structure completes my preliminary consideration of the structure of the eastern end. Next a similar examination of the details of the structure of the ambulatory and radiating chapels of the choir above will provide the basis for a comparative study of the existing portions of Suger's chevet, followed by a reconstruction of the upper portions of the twelfth-century choir demolished in the thirteenth-century campaign of rebuilding.

In summary, the crypt consists of a sequence of individual vaults separated by heavy transverse arches which break the continuity of the curving ambulatory. The separation of the spatial volumes becomes even more explicit in the radiating chapels, which are isolated from each other by massive walls. This heavy masonry covered by groin vaults over individual additive units of space conforms to the normal definition of Romanesque architecture and hardly prepares us for the structure of the choir above.

CHAPTER NINE

Choir Structure

Fig. 112

Fig. 108

Only a small portion of the structure of Suger's choir stands today, but the nine bays of the ambulatory and the seven radiating chapels have established his master masons among the most creative builders of all time. It was not that they invented new technical or structural forms[1] or introduced original solutions to accommodate a living liturgy, but they exploited possibilities inherent in a relatively novel concept of stone masonry to allow light to pervade interior space. "Luminous order," order ordered by light, was Suger's objective. The way his masons achieved that objective is the prime concern here.

The coherent, explicit plan essential to that order must have been devised in some detail before the summer months of 1140, when the first foundations for this second campaign were prepared. But although the ambulatory and radiating chapels of the crypt provide the substructure for those same elements in the choir above, none of the structural components of the crypt anticipates the diaphanous radiance of the choir ensemble. Structural details such as column bases, capitals with abaci, or segmental stone vaults are common to both crypt and choir (see appendix J), but the proportions of individual details, the assurance of a stone armature held in stable tension by skillful counterbalance (in contrast to defined, separate volumes enclosed by static forces), must be experienced in order to be comprehended.

112. Interior of choir ambulatory
and radiating chapels.

Unfortunately we know nothing about the master mason who had the imagination to propose this "crown of light" and the daring to realize it. Because so many significant details in the plan of the crypt are also incorporated into the plan of the choir—the asymmetrical alignments of the buttresses between the chapels, for instance—we must assume that he was among the experienced masons who devised the new plan. Other less technical details such as a few masons' marks, a reasonable continuity in molding profiles, and the expanded use of monolithic colonnettes indicate that he and his companions were part of the team who built the western bays. Is it possible or useful to be more precise? No sequence of specific details, no major structural or aesthetic system betray training or experience in one particular geographical locality or region. Unquestionably in consultation with Abbot Suger, those masters responsible for building the new eastern end of Saint-Denis enjoyed the challenge of new ideas and dared to incorporate them into stone masonry, and there is much to be learned from the remains of the structure of Suger's new choir.

Presumably the extrados, the upper and outer surface, of the vaulting of the crypt was exposed as a platform for the masons as they began to build the choir, its ambulatory, and its radiating chapels. We know very little about the type of foundation which that platform provided because we lack information about the composition of the vault construction over the crypt. Although I have examined all surfaces carefully, no opening or perforation through the vaults has come to my attention. Since those surfaces have been altered, repaved, and recovered innumerable times, precise information about the original material composing the vaults probably has not survived. I know of no measurements that record the thicknesses of the vaulting surfaces, although exterior dimensions indicate that in most areas the rubble construction which must cover the carefully executed curved surfaces of the various groined vaults in the ambulatory crypt and the adjacent radiating chapels exceeds 0.50 m. Because the direct sightings necessary for photogrammetry were not available, the photogrammetric elevations of bays 3, 5, and 7 of the crypt and choir are not continuous. In bay number 5, the axial bay, the height of the intrados of the lateral wall arch is recorded as 35.25 m (above sea level), and the level of the pavement of the choir chapel above is given as 36.02 m, a difference of 0.77 m. This is a substantial figure which seems generous as an average thickness for the crypt vaults. Other recorded heights in the choir ambulatory prove that there has been almost no movement in the masonry construction. For example, the heights of the abaci above the capitals of the ambulatory columns as recorded in the photogrammetric elevations are 41.02 m, 41.01 m, and 41.01 m (above sea level). The figures testify to a remarkable stability over a distance of more than 15.00 m. One of the many mason's secrets still hidden from us is the way they checked such heights. Given today's measurements, there can be no question about the adequacy of the crypt structure as a support for the choir above.

Today we admire Suger's masons for their audacity in building the choir ambulatory and radiating chapels with minimal masonry supports. The abbot mentioned only the masons' ability to locate the "upper columns and central arches . . . upon the lower ones built in the crypt."[2] The implications are that the lower structure was hidden from view by the crypt vaults. Consequently the upper columns had to be located by the geometrical and arithmetical instruments, which were also used to equalize the old and the new naves. Apparently Suger's masons were able to diagram with considerable accuracy the location of different parts of the lower structure, and without being able to see it they could transfer the location of the crypt hemicycle piers and chapel masonry to the platform above the crypt vaults. The arc of the semicircle establishing the location of the hemicycle columns traced the location of the centers of those piers in the crypt and of the columns in the choir, but the perimeter of the semicircle on which the radiating chapel masonry was located marked the inner limits of the masonry walls between the crypt chapels. Thus, as the aligned but noncontinuous photogrammetric elevations indicate, when the centers of the columns of the upper, or choir, ambulatory were located on this same perimeter approximately one-half of the upper, or choir, column base projected beyond the limit of the crypt masonry in an overhang, which Formigé described as "étonnant."[3] Consequently I interpret the location of the choir, or upper, ambulatory columns as evidence of twelfth-century geometrical and arithmetical planning rather than as a precocious use of the structural imbalance characteristic of certain thirteenth-century Gothic structures.

Even though the cylindrical piers of the choir hemicycle were replaced in the thirteenth century, the exact locations of all the structural elements of Suger's choir survive today. Since the later hemicycle columns continue to hold up the inner periphery of the twelfth-century ambulatory vaults, they necessarily occupy the locations of the earlier supports—a fact confirmed by the incorporation of the lowest bed of the twelfth-century plinths in the bases of the thirteenth century. These remnants of Suger's construction have been

Fig. 106

Pls. 1, 2; Album nos. 1, 2

Fig. 106

Fig. 113

Fig. 114

113. An abacus of one of the hemicycle piers, showing the remnants of the ribs of the twelfth-century arcade on the right side, joined to the ribs of the thirteenth-century arcade on the left side.

114. (*far left*) A base of one of the thirteenth-century hemicycle piers, showing the incorporation of a portion of an original twelfth-century plinth.

115. (*above*) The base of an ambulatory column as restored in the nineteenth century.

cut and reshaped so that they no longer provide information about the dimensions or configuration of the original hemicycle supports. Of course the ambulatory column bases also remain in their original locations, but they have been "restored." Unfortunately, there are no drawings or untouched examples to indicate the original shapes. The chamfered corners of the plinths, for example, might be original, but they appear unusually sym-

Fig. 115

116. A detail of the bases of the columns, colonnettes, and masonry between the radiating chapels in the choir.

metrical and complete. Although the plinths for the piers in the central upper chapel of the western bays were cut so that they continued the chamfer of the edges of the compound piers, only the upper corners of the plinth were cut away. There are no chamfers at all on the attached, unfinished pier bases excavated on the south side of Suger's proposed nave. Thus, although there are hints of chamfered plinths before the choir ambulatory columns, later bases along the nave have none, nor has the original twelfth-century base found by Formigé on the northeast side of the crossing. The bases of the ambulatory piers between the chapels do not repeat the profile of today's bases of the ambulatory columns or of the colonnettes between the radiating chapels. The reason for such variation in the design seems unclear, but perhaps the differences reflect the masons' preferences for variety.

Figs. 52c, 63

Fig. 120a; App. L.15

Fig. 116

The continuous plinth in all the chapels has a relatively short vertical rise, then a wide but slightly slanted bevel. Above the bevel the final section, also relatively short, rises vertically again. The plinth supports the colonnette bases and a continuous molding which in each chapel repeats the profile of the colonnette bases and links them across the mural masonry. Their spurs recut, the molded profiles of those bases show a somewhat flattened lower torus, a pronounced, shallow middle scotia, topped by a smaller torus, with the tori aligned on an almost vertical plane.[4]

To emphasize my earlier observations, there is no positive evidence to establish how extensive the thirteenth-century repairs were or whether the modern restorers adhered to or deviated from the earlier designs.[5] For this reason little serious attention has been given to the influence of Saint-Denis on mid-twelfth-century visual effects in architecture. Much more attention has been focused on the structure of the choir above the supporting bases, with the accent on the vaults rather than on the columnar supports for the vaults.

The major columnar supports in the choir were, of course, the hemicycle and ambulatory columns, but the colonnettes of the radiating chapel masonry should also be included. With the possible exception of the hemicycle supports, which were replaced in the thirteenth century and about whose structure we have no evidence, all of these vertical elements are monolithic shafts.[6] At least some of the ambulatory columns still consist of single pieces of stone, cut directly from the quarry—and presumably all of the ambulatory columns were originally similar single pieces of stone.[7] As mentioned earlier, Suger's account of the pulling of stone for the column shaft from the quarry at Pontoise probably is a reference to the columns of the junction between the old, Carolingian nave and the new western entrance, but we can be assured that shafts of similar dimensions were available for the building of the choir. As with the smaller colonnettes *en délit,* such vertical shafts functioned as rigid props in terms of the structure. They must account for the remarkable stability of the choir as indicated in the almost unchanging heights of the abaci above the ambulatory columns. Even though the colonnettes of the peripheral masonry of the radiating chapels are set into the masonry (with the exception of those under the transverse arches to the ambulatory columns or under the median, "fifth" rib of the vault), they effectively mask the masonry as mural structure and add to the linear definition of the "radiant" choir.

Figs. 105, 116

Various horizontal accents contrast with the vertical supports. The capitals over the ambulatory columns provide strong light and dark contrasts under the vaults, as do the smaller colonnette capitals of the radiating chapels. The structure of the capitals of the ambulatory demonstrates quite explicitly the way this architectural detail functions, and few examples exist that perform the function with more daring. The ambulatory capital had to provide the transition from the circular shape of the column to the rectangular surface of an abacus almost exactly twice the size of the column shaft. Concentrated on the square surface of the abacus are the diagonal thrusts of eight different arches. Consummate courage, confidence, and skill combined to conceive the possibility of gathering this bundle of opposing forces above such a slender support. Indeed, the column shaft appears to function more as a tether holding the straining arcs to the pavement rather than as a support assuring their stability above the heads of the observers. Although these ambulatory capitals are freestanding, self-contained, isolated units, the following discussion of the vaults will emphasize that the radiating chapels of the choir include not only the outer periphery of curving masonry and the large stained glass windows but also the spaces extending to the ambulatory columns, which are covered by the same five-ribbed vaults. Consequently, the capitals over the colonnettes of the outer periphery should be considered with those of the ambulatory columns.

App. K.96–105

Fig. 117

Dominating the capitals and colonnettes in the radiating chapels, the slightly larger intermediary, freestanding colonnettes between the chapels receive the transverse arches springing from the ambulatory columns. By their increased dimensions all of the components of those freestanding colonnettes—their bases, shafts, capitals, and particularly the abaci and en-

117. The ambulatory column and vaults in the center of the picture demonstrate the tetherlike appearance of these supports.

tablatures above the capitals—maintain a reasonable relationship proportionally with the much larger ambulatory columns and capitals, although the size differences between them remain apparent. More varied than elsewhere, the decoration of the capitals within the chapels includes human masks, griffons, and sirens (see Appendix N).[8] All of the elements are linked to each other by the unusual continuous abaci, which provide a strong horizontal accent directly beneath the curving surfaces of the vaults.

The vaults themselves seem to defy any simple description. The radiating chapels and ambulatory present "a complexity of overlapping forms which, however, in no way diminishes the clarity and simplicity of the whole."[9] Although Frankl may have wished to include all aspects of the chapels in his very perceptive analysis, I find his words "clarity and simplicity" especially pertinent to the structure of the vaults. The armature of stone arches, five over each chapel and four over the ambulatory bays, reaches from the vault centers over varying linear dimensions to unite constantly changing spatial volumes into a coherent entity. Now the photogrammetric analyses of these vaults can demonstrate how the master masons achieved a simple and logical control of these irregular areas. Although, for example, the horizontal distances in bays 3, 5, and 7 vary from 3.44 m (bay 7, ribs g–h) to 5.00 m (bay 5, ribs d–e), the apex or height of the crowns of the vaults above the abaci of the supporting columns is always exactly the same—2.50 m. Further analysis shows the radii of the arcs of the different ribs as consistently identical— 2.70 m. In other words the arches of the rib vaults were built on similar or identical wooden forms or centerings, which as construction progressed could be moved from bay to bay. Only the outer, or peripheral, segments of

Fig. 112

Fig. 118a,b

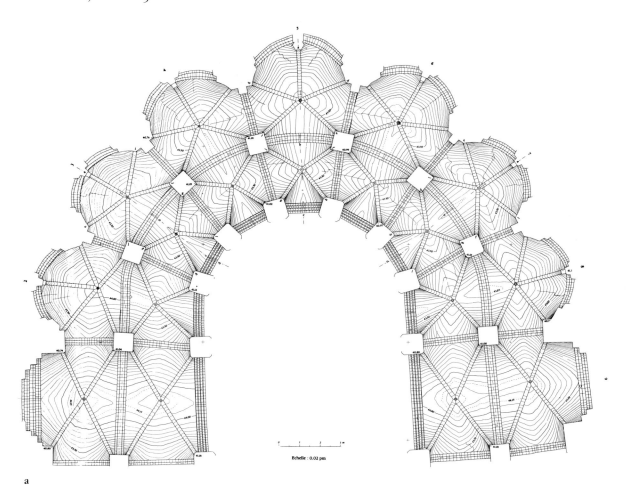

a

these wooden forms were set in place, because the centers for the radii of the
arches were constantly changing. The centers for the arcs g–h in bay 7, as
quoted above, lie 1.00 m on each side of the median, or center, of the
baseline, whereas the centers for the arcs d–e in bay 5 are only 0.25 m on
each side of the middle of the baseline. The result, in structural terms, was
absolute uniformity with almost complete flexibility. The rigid control of the
stone armature under the vaults produced related, coherent spaces and
united them into a comprehensible whole.

Such comprehensibility would not have been an important factor in the
clarity of the whole without adequate lighting—one of Suger's major preoccupations. The quality of this light in its original density is difficult to assess.
Fragments of the twelfth-century stained glass still survive in some of the
eastern windows, but they are almost lost amid the nineteenth-century restorations.[10] The trained eye can detect the original pieces and respond to the
vibrant pale blues in the center area of the Tree of Jesse window and in a few
medallions in the chapel of Saint Peregrinus to the north. Suger described
only scenes in the windows of the three easternmost chapels, which led to the

118. (a) Photogrammetric diagram of the vaults of the ambulatory and radiating chapels;
(b) a five-arched vault of an
axial chapel of the choir.

b

assumption, no longer held, that the four other radiating chapels were originally decorated by the griffon design still to be seen in the northern chapels.[11] After a painstaking and expert examination, Louis Grodecki concluded, however, that "il est certes impossible, aujourd'hui, faute de renseignements historiques valables, de décider de l'emplacement primitif, et la forme générale elle-même, des vitraux à griffons."[12] Thus it is impossible today not only to decide about the location and general form of the windows "à griffons," but also to reconstruct Suger's windows in their entirety. Yet enough remains to tell us a good deal about their complicated iconography[13] and to enable us to appreciate their high quality. Imagine the prismatic effects of multicolored light enhanced by the oblique angles of the windows and the concentration of illumination on the altars in the center of each chapel, with flickering candles supplementing the light from the windows during the celebration of the masses. The extraordinary brilliance within this crown of light still stimulates the imagination and quickens emotions.

Yet flights of imagination are inhibited and the images clouded because the central portion of Suger's choir was entirely rebuilt in the thirteenth century. That rebuilding less than one hundred years after the completion of the choir poses a number of questions. We lack documentation concerning the cause for the rebuilding, as well as information about the original twelfth-century elevation. We do not know whether it had three or four stories; and the method of buttressing the vaults is another unknown.

Before taking up these problems let us review evidence for the completion of Suger's choir. Suger said explicitly that he "pressed the completion of the work at great expense, with a numerous crowd of workmen, summer and winter."[14] He also stated that the "Hand Divine . . . allowed that whole magnificent building [to be completed] . . . from the crypt below to the summit of the vaults above . . . including even the consummation of the roof."[15] None of his writings is more unambiguous; he left no room for doubt about the completion of the choir.

Although historians of Saint-Denis have assumed that some structural weakness in Suger's building necessitated its rebuilding,[16] excavations both inside and out prove that the twelfth-century foundations of the chevet are still solid. Continuous under the chapels of the crypt, the rubble mat extends below the dressed masonry of the exterior buttresses. That footing contrasts with the loosely built foundations of the western bays seen by Viollet-le-Duc. Yet the presence of four massive cylindrical piers built in the western portions of the north and south ambulatories of the crypt in the thirteenth century indicates that some strengthening of the foundations was considered necessary prior to the construction of the new thirteenth-century choir. In my opinion the rebuilding of the central portions of the choir resulted primarily from a continuing desire for concordance and harmony, not from a structural flaw. The upper portions of Suger's choir at the end of the new *rayonnant* nave and transepts would have looked as incongruous as the Carolingian nave must have appeared between Suger's new western entrance and his choir to the east.

Despite the absence of any masonry vestiges to suggest what the twelfth-century elevation of the choir included, speculation has persisted about whether tribune galleries existed above the ambulatory vaults, whether the high vaults over the choir were sexpartite, and most recently whether there were early flying buttresses.

Possibly because of an erroneous identification of the western upper chapels as tribune galleries, Viollet-le-Duc stated categorically that a vaulted gallery existed over the side aisles of Suger's church in the same manner as at Noyon and Notre-Dame of Paris.[17] This same assumption was repeated by Georg Dehio and von Bezold,[18] who nurtured the concept of a "school of Saint-Denis," exemplified by the group of four-storied churches built in the second half of the twelfth century in the Ile-de-France. The majority of scholars interested in Gothic architecture have concurred, so that Michel Anfray in 1939 could write that "all archaeologists agree that there were vast tribunes over the side aisles" of Suger's church,[19] and Paul Frankl included tribunes in the sketch of Suger's choir published in the first edition of Erwin Panofsky's *Abbot Suger*.[20] The slender, seemingly fragile supports of the ambulatory, presumably equally slender in the original hemicycle, have always led me to question the plausibility of a vaulted tribune gallery over the ambulatory.[21] In the second edition of Panofsky's *Abbot Suger,* the sketch of the choir elevation drawn under my direction does not include such tribunes.[22] My initial doubts about the possibility of supporting the masonry of tribune galleries on the slender shafts of the choir ambulatory columns have not been dispelled by expert opinions to the contrary. Because not even a single remnant or small fragment of twelfth-century masonry remains above the vaults of the ambulatory and radiating chapels, and because Saint-Denis geographically did not belong to the group of northern churches built with tribunes, I continue to question the presence of galleries in the choir of Suger's church.

More positive reasons argue against the possibility of sexpartite vaults over the choir, in spite of the repeated assertions of a number of authorities.[23] Jean Bony has argued against such a possibility,[24] and the archaeological facts confirm that a sequence of single columns was the intended support for Suger's proposed nave with double side aisles. In addition, there is no indication of the normal alternation of supports usually present under sexpartite vaults.[25]

Until recently the problem of how the upper portions of Suger's choir were buttressed had received little attention. Into this vacuum came Fitchen and Conant's radical solution based on a new interpretation of Suger's description of the great storm that shook the unfinished vaults of the new choir.[26] They argued that the arches over the choir that "swayed hither and thither" were early flying buttresses—an interpretation less convincing than Panofsky's philological analysis.[27] Given the evidence, most scholars agree that flying buttresses were not built in the Ile-de-France until some thirty years after Suger's choir.[28]

An attempt to determine heights of important levels within the elevation of the structure must precede any proposal concerning the design and elevation of the upper portions of Suger's choir. Even though rebuilt in the thirteenth century, the existing hemicycle piers with their capitals and abaci continue to support the twelfth-century ambulatory vaults and must, therefore, perpetuate the heights, within a few centimeters, of the original hemicycle columns—that is, 5.00 m above the choir pavement. Since the hemicycle arches today also open below the vaults of the twelfth-century ambulatory, their heights of plus or minus 7.00 m must also approximate those of Suger's hemicycle. The twelfth-century arcade probably had a string course about 1.00 m higher—or circa 8.00 m above the level of the choir pavement—which marked the extrados of the ambulatory vaults. On the assumption that Suger's desire for "concord and harmony" would have resulted in a reasonably continuous level of the high vaults from one end of his building to the other, and on the assumption also that the central chapel above the western bays of his first campaign was intended to have opened into a "new" nave, an estimated total height for the crowns of the "high" vaults of about 20.00 m above Suger's choir pavement seems reasonable. Consequently there must have been approximately 12.00 m between a string course above the hemicycle arcade and the choir vaults—space enough for either two or three upper stories in the elevation of Suger's choir.

As noted above, earlier historians of Romanesque and Gothic architecture almost took it for granted that Suger's choir was originally built with tribune galleries over the ambulatory vaults and that he intended to build similar galleries over the side aisles of his new nave. This would have placed Suger's building in the so-called northern group of four-storied structures along traditional lines. Today, although no new evidence has come to light, scholars are inclined to place Suger's building more in the sphere of Parisian practices than elsewhere, and I believe that certain features at Saint-Denis in the twelfth century support that association.

Although the exact dates and progress of the enlargement of the eastern end of Saint-Martin-des-Champs in Paris cannot be determined, current scholarship agrees that the irregular, awkward ambulatory and radiating chapels are contemporary with, if not earlier than, Suger's new chevet at Saint-Denis.[29] Relationships between the two monastic communities are assumed rather than explicit, but the concept of an ambulatory with communicating radiating chapels certainly associates the two structures as architectural ensembles more closely than is possible with other pre-mid-twelfth-century undertakings.[30] The relative assurance of Suger's achievement at Saint-Denis contrasts with the tentative relationships between different levels and structural forms at Saint-Martin-des-Champs, but some connections between the programs of the two buildings must have existed. Similar ideas that may have informed the beginning of new buildings do not necessarily imply similar structural techniques, but it is interesting that similar, if not identical, irregular alignments characterize the exterior buttresses between the chapels in the chevets both at Saint-Denis and at Saint-Martin-des-Champs. At Saint-Denis, as already observed, the wall buttresses between the radiating chapels of the crypt and choir project obliquely outward. That is,   Pls. 1, 2; Album nos. 1, 2
they are not constructed as symmetrical projections between the curving perimeters of the chapels. At Saint-Martin-des-Champs we find similar oblique wall buttresses, but they are almost entirely covered by the slanting roof over the ambulatory and radiating chapels. Close observation from the ground and photographs from above disclose this irregularity clearly, but one must gain access to the spaces above the radiating chapels to be able to see how obliquely the massive wall buttresses are aligned.[31]

To my knowledge no adequate explanation for this particular phenomenon, infrequent or restricted as it may be, has yet been proposed. Measurements are difficult to determine, as is the exact recording of slight changes in axes or alignments. I still believe in my earlier assumption that these early Gothic masons were concerned with what they assumed were thrusts or pressures exerted by, or within, the high vaults over the semicircular choirs; but since the few other examples that have been recorded do not seem to follow similar patterns or angles, no specific theory or explanation has as yet proved satisfactory. Perhaps accurate observations of additional examples will eventually allow the formulation of a reasonable theory.

Another important Parisian workshop was active in the eleventh and twelfth centuries at Saint-Germain-des-Prés. The new choir there consisted of two straight bays preceding an ambulatory with five radiating chapels.

Although presumably completed for the dedication by Pope Alexander III on 21 April 1163, "it is impossible to assign a precise date for the new construction."[32] Doubtless in many ways the earlier choir at Saint-Denis provided an exemplar for the builders of Saint-Germain-des-Prés. Because of that, information about a number of features now destroyed at Saint-Denis may be rediscovered in the details of the Parisian abbey. Rather than present a comprehensive demonstration of the architectural similarities, I shall emphasize two details of particular interest to this discussion, both of which William W. Clark treated in his perceptive article.[33] A later addition, the flying buttresses at Saint-Germain-des-Prés were built late in the twelfth century "under the influence of the shop working on the nearby nave of Notre-Dame, Paris."[34] Clark's diagram of these buttresses at the end of his article shows graphically how the buttresses were built off-center in relation to the masonry of the radiating chapels.[35] Analyzing an earlier study by Louis Barbier,[36] Clark pointed out how "the builder changed the geometric regularity in the hemicycle vaults to achieve visual unity in the choir space." With that in mind, Clark concluded that the "stability of the chevet of Saint-Germain-des-Prés did not depend on the use of flying buttresses."[37] His diagram demonstrated how the axes of the masonry between the radiating chapels are aligned to concentrate on the geometric center of the choir, whereas the axes of the added flying buttresses converge on the keystone of the hemicycle. A certain amount of diagrammatic manipulation supported his reasoning, but I am not yet convinced that enough evidence exists for a definite explanation of this interesting irregularity.

Clark's reconstruction of the interior of the Saint-Germain-des-Prés choir is also pertinent to any hypothesis about the original elevation of Suger's choir. With minor changes such as the curvature of the arches, I believe that the three-story elevation with a simple arcade opening into the space over the ambulatory vaults and an ample clerestory as a third or top story under the high vaults at Saint-Germain-des-Prés may well have reproduced Suger's choir more accurately than any other building in the Ile-de-France or elsewhere.[38] (A three-story elevation was not unusual in the twelfth century.) Although the ambulatory and radiating chapels of Suger's choir demonstrate how Suger's masons achieved unusual and unexpected results with conventional forms, we have no way of knowing with what degree of originality or refinement of detail they handled the choir elevation. Those of us fascinated by the beginning of Gothic art feel that lack acutely.

Fig. 119

In conclusion, this study of the structure of the remaining portions of Suger's original choir has pointed to the uncertainties about the authenticity of many details, such as column bases and other carved elements. Yet the once almost mysterious structure of the rib vaults over the ambulatory and the radiating chapels has been clarified by the photogrammetric analyses of the contours and elevations of the remaining twelfth-century portions. The use and presumable reuse of the same wooden centerings or forms on which the rib arches were built assured a uniformity which the eye senses even when it does not recognize the extent of the identity of the curvatures. Different linear dimensions were combined into harmonious volumes by the repetition

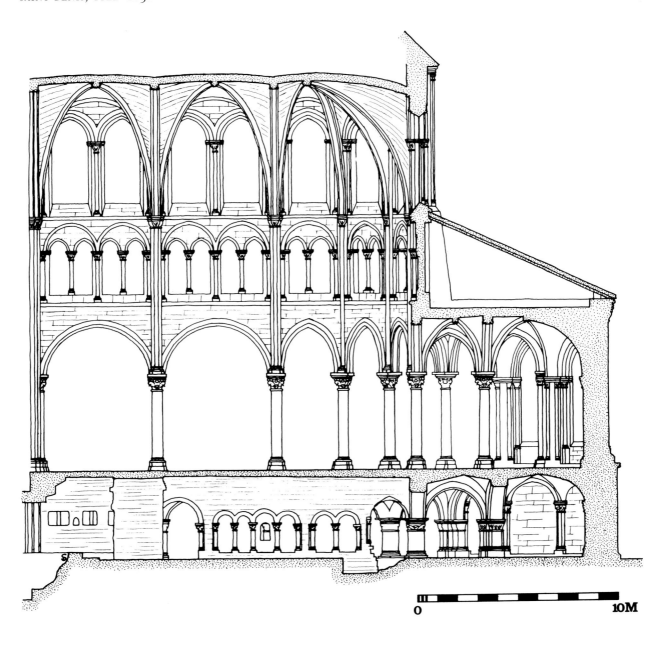

of identical curved segments. The result is a sequence of constantly shifting, interrelated controlled spaces enclosing the central dominant volume of the choir. Unfortunately the rebuilding of the central portions of the choir in the thirteenth century deprives us of a complete understanding of Suger's construction. After a discussion of the various hypotheses about the structure of the choir, its elevation and supports, the possibility of tribune galleries over the ambulatory at Saint-Denis was dismissed. The affinities between the

119. Sketch of a proposed elevation of Suger's twelfth-century choir. Drawn by Donald Sanders.

eccentric buttresses at Saint-Denis, at Saint-Martin-des-Champs, and at Saint-Germain-des-Prés supported the proposal of a three-story elevation for Suger's choir not unlike the original one at Saint-Germain-des-Prés.[39] A final chapter on the evidence for the twelfth-century transept and nave will complete this survey of Suger's church.

CHAPTER TEN

Suger's Unfinished Transept and Nave

Suger wrote repeatedly of his desire to finish his church with a bright new middle that would join the new eastern and western ends, but he also voiced his apprehension that this work would never be finished. Now positive archaeological evidence establishes that he began both the transept and the nave but that nothing was completed as he had planned. Since only summaries of the recent excavations have been published and since Formigé's analysis of this evidence is as inaccurate and misleading as Viollet-le-Duc's plan of his excavations under the transepts and nave,[1] I shall analyze that text and the archaeological discoveries in some detail.

The division of Suger's *De Administratione* into chapters does not perpetuate all of the rubrics of the early manuscripts, nor do the printed texts invariably provide a word-for-word transcription of the manuscript. This has particular importance for an interpretation of chapters 28 and 29, where Suger described his "eagerness" to complete work on the church.[2] In the printed version Suger concluded chapter 28 with the statement: "Eager to press on my success . . . we devoted ourselves to the completion of the work and strove to raise and to enlarge the transept wings of the church so as to correspond to the form of the earlier and later work that had to be joined."[3] Chapter 29 begins "Quo facto," translated as "This done" or "Cela fait," which has usually been interpreted to mean that the work on the transepts had been finished by 1148, when the writing of the *De Administratione* was complete.[4] The manuscript, however, reads: "Quo de continuatione utriusque operis facto" (This—the continuation of other works—being done).[5] The "utriusque operis," or other works, may refer to the western towers mentioned in the following phrase of the same sentence rather than to the "transepts" in the previous sentence; or, more likely, the phrase alluded to the completion of the second campaign—the new crypt and choir. In any case "utriusque" need not mean the transepts, upon which, according to the archaeological evidence, work was initiated but never completed.

Begun in 1946 under my direction and carried forward under the crossing by Formigé and Fleury, the excavation of the transept wings brought to light meager evidence about the twelfth-century masonry in those areas. In fact, only three fragments of twelfth-century work were found. They include the southwest embrasure and the trumeau of the south transept portal designed to open into the cloister; the western, interior portion of the north transept portal; and the western portion of the twelfth-century pier on the north side of the choir hemicycle, found between the raised choir pavement and the lower level of the pavement of the Carolingian eighth-century nave.

Although this masonry reveals many of Suger's intentions, many of its details are puzzling. Just to the south, or right, of the northern staircase into the crypt, the remains of that northwestern pier between the choir and the present transept originally included 0.34 m of the western engaged column with its molded base and the two northern setbacks of the socle. In 1959, when Formigé reinstalled the pier, for some unknown reason the middle, or northwestern, projection was omitted so that only a portion of the fragment can be seen today. Formigé's reconstruction of the plan of this pier[6] does not conform to the masonry discovered; thus the archaeologist faces a series of questions: first, what was the precise location and orientation of this pier? next, have any other fragments been altered or omitted? third, how does one reconstruct this unusual pier, which was designed to achieve the transition between the two different levels of the choir and transept pavements? fourth, was the fragment in fact a crossing pier, as Formigé stated, or instead the junction pier between the choir and an eastern aisle of the transept, designed to provide space for the stairways giving access to the choir from the west? and finally, did the eastern face of this pier at the choir level include enough of a column to be counted as one of the twelve columns of the choir? According to Suger, these represented the twelve Apostles.[7]

On the basis of the photograph in the Archives Photographiques in Paris taken during the discovery of the fragments of the pier, I have attempted a reconstruction to meet those questions, but I must admit that I propose it tentatively as a hypothetical part of the plan. Some of the details, however, such as the moldings of the base of the engaged column and of the socle below survive as valid twelfth-century details. As such they provide interesting comparisons with similar details of masonry excavated in other parts of the transept and with other portions of Suger's construction.

The diameter of the western engaged column of this pier is 0.52 m, a measurement which conforms exactly to the diameter of other twelfth-century freestanding or attached column shafts, for example, the monolithic

Fig. 120a

Fig. 120b,c

Fig. 119
Pl. 1; Album no. 20

a

b

ambulatory columns of the choir and the columns of the juncture between the western entrance bays and the old Carolingian nave. The molded base of this attached column has two tori separated by a scotia and spurs at the angle of the socle. The socle, which includes a sloping cavetto and a tall, slightly inclined bevel, differs from the profile of the base discovered at the southwestern end of the junction to the Carolingian nave. The base itself, however, with the two tori in almost vertical alignment and spurs at the angles, is similar if not identical to the twelfth-century bases of the subsidiary colonnettes between the radiating chapels of the choir—a congruence which associates the pier with Suger's second campaign.

If, as seems logical, the pier was built as part of the choir, we must find how it compares with the other vestiges of the twelfth-century transept uncovered by my excavations of 1946 and 1947. I have found no affinities between the pier in question and fragments excavated under the north transept, but the masonry found under the south transept yielded good comparisons. Begun early in the summer of 1946 at a time when France was still recovering from the tragedies of the Occupation, the latter excavation started with the removal of the pavement on the northeast side of the thirteenth-century pier (the ninth from the west), at the northeastern corner of the monument to François I. Almost immediately we uncovered the socle of an engaged pier. Its dimensions and profile are identical with the two socles farther to the west, found under the existing south side aisle exterior wall in 1939. The socle with a sloping cavetto and plinth over a tall sloping bevel, or horizontal chamfer, is the same as the socle of the pier discovered by Formigé in 1959 on the northwestern side of the choir. Given that comparison, the relationship between the choir construction and the work on the twelfth-century south transept seems obvious—a relationship to be explored more fully after we review the results of all the excavations.

As the excavation of the south transept progressed to the east more early masonry came to light. Directly under the marble paving slabs, as though left in place to support the nineteenth-century pavement, a large, irregularly shaped construction was uncovered. Formigé identified this masonry as part of the exterior of the façade of the south transept but he called it a "buttress

c

120. Twelfth-century pier base between transept and choir, north side: (a) base as originally found; note the two setbacks; (b) the same base as reinstalled by Formigé, photographed from the north; (c) the same base as reinstalled by Formigé, photographed from the south.

Figs. 25, 122a

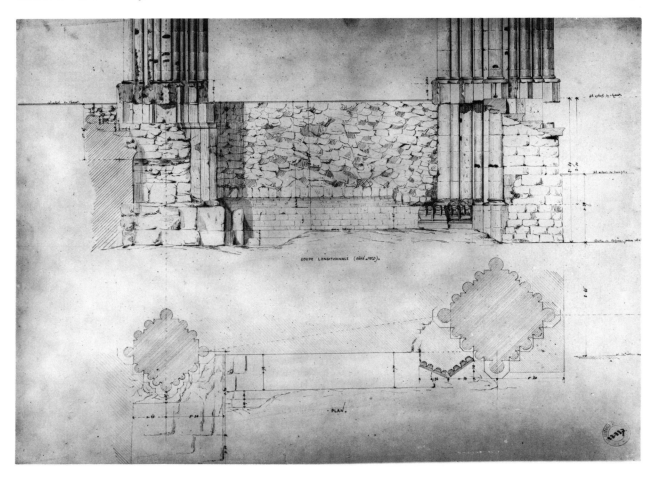

COUPE LONGITUDINALE (côté sud).

· PLAN.

with three set backs with a little farther on a slightly projecting band."[8] The western projection of this construction should be called a buttress, but the three setbacks to the east with carefully executed chamfers on their angles form much too large a mass to be interpreted as part of a buttress. The projections, or setbacks, have differing dimensions, which diminish as they proceed to the east, and I interpret them as two setbacks and the jamb of the western embrasure of a transept portal which would have opened into the cloisters. The enclosing masonry is carefully finished with the typical twelfth-century diagonal striations on the outer faces, but on the interior instead of a rough, irregular rubble core we found a large rectangular block. As the excavation neared completion the removal of the fill against the interior, or northern, side of this masonry revealed large blocks, or libages, typical of the eighth-century Carolingian foundations. This discovery identified the stone enclosed by the twelfth-century masonry and the wall extending to the east as the southwestern corner of the Carolingian, or old, transept.

Suger's workmen had, indeed, preserved the old, venerated stones and had strengthened and buttressed them.[9] The excavation proved that a third twelfth-century campaign had started to construct a new south transept

121. Elevation and plan of Viol-let-le-Duc's excavation.

Pl. 2

b

a

which was attached or placed against and around the southwest corner of the "old" eighth-century transept. Consequently the twelfth-century transept had approximately the same dimensions as the Carolingian structure. The twelfth-century masonry continues westward without interruption so that the socle for the twelfth-century engaged pier uncovered as we began the excavation aligns with the transept portal. Thus the transept would not have projected to the south beyond the walls of the nave—an interesting feature of Suger's new church.

Unfortunately the eastern part of this nonprojecting transept, if completed, was destroyed or covered over in the thirteenth century when the foundations for the existing transept were built. Contradicting Viollet-le-Duc's elevation drawing of excavations, which seems to show twelfth-century masonry placed against the eastern arm of the "old" transept foundations, and also despite Formigé's random, disconnected remarks about windows and bases of columns in this area,[10] my *sondages* and careful examination of all available substructures have not revealed any vestiges of the eastern sides of either the eighth- or twelfth-century transept.

The survival of fragments of what must have been part of a trumeau for the south portal provides evidence for the width of the portal, as it was planned by Suger's masons. Since a trumeau divides a portal, the vestige establishes that the eastern embrasure would have begun 1.80 m to the east of the trumeau—a measurement mirroring that of the extant western portion of the portal. I have used this dimension in my reconstruction of the south transept plan.

The form of the trumeau deserves attention. Resting directly on a large block, or libage, of the Carolingian foundations, four blocks of limestone finished with twelfth-century striations, two to a side, flank a fragment of a broken marble column shaft. Carved with a slanting bevel, the lower two blocks extend to surround the shaft, as though to enclose it and hold it firmly

122. South transept excavation: (a) two setbacks of twelfth-century portal; (b) lower portions of a twelfth-century trumeau from the south transept portal.

Fig. 121

Fig. 122b

Album no. 20

in place. Their resemblance to metal clasps, or bezels, used to hold a stone or jewel in place seems inescapable. Possibly the marble shaft of this fragment survived from the old building. Perhaps considered by Suger to be precious, the shaft was mounted just as his goldsmiths mounted antique cameos in the new altar decorations. The corners, or angles, of the two upper stones of the trumeau are chamfered in the same manner as the setbacks in the embrasure to the west. Those chamfers are also reminiscent of the piers of the chapel above the central bays of the western complex. Although a minor detail, the chamfers offer additional proof that the construction of the south transept is coherent with the other portions of Suger's new church. In contrast with the more normal symmetrical setbacks of the western portals, the plan of this south embrasure shows that the two setbacks have different dimensions. As yet I have not found any comparable examples.

Fig. 52c

Another detail of the masonry of this southern ensemble deserves mention. Even a cursory glance at the photograph of the trumeau shows the marked contrast of the masonry on each side. To the right, or east, the blocks of stone in the second, or upper, bed of masonry are very regular. Although their width is slightly greater than the beautifully preserved regular blocks of the eighth-century, north side-aisle masonry, their height is the same. The presence of red mortar in the joints confirms that this wall was part of the Carolingian church. On the left, or western, side of the trumeau the masonry differs. Three large blocks extend from the embrasure to the trumeau. They have a typical twelfth-century bevel or horizontal chamfer. In interpreting these different masonries, I concluded that the workmen began construction on the western side of the transept by enclosing the southwestern corner of the Carolingian transept in the new masonry and placed the trumeau in the middle of what they intended to be the new south portal. Work evidently stopped there, which left the northeastern corner of the old transept intact.

Fig. 25

App. C.5

Comparable evidence of unfinished work exists under the north transept. Later in the summer of 1946 we began to remove the pavement of the north transept. Immediately under the pavement at the western end, just inside or to the east of the iron grill that separates the transept from the nave, we uncovered well-preserved, finely executed masonry. Under the middle of this transept aisle several meters of the exterior wall of the north side aisle of the Carolingian church have survived. Directly to the north and in alignment between the thirteenth-century piers, we found twelfth-century masonry, and above the twelfth-century foundations trapezoidal socles rested on carefully finished beds. Although the quality of the stone, the diagonal striations of the surface, and the slanting bevel of the socles closely resemble those of other twelfth-century masonry at Saint-Denis, the shape of the socles is completely different from the socles for the engaged piers of the south side of the nave. The difference between the twelfth-century masonries on the north and south sides of the nave is both striking and puzzling.

Fig. 123

App. D.4

Since the foundations under the northern masonry, but not those on the southern side, could be excavated, the construction on the north needs attention prior to any speculation about the finished masonry of the socles. Upon descending into the excavations today, one's sense of the proximity of the

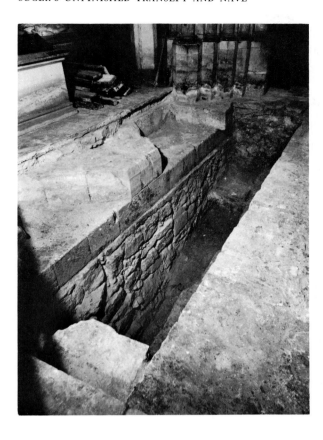

123. Remains of a twelfth-century pier base from the north transept excavation.

earlier and later foundations is heightened by the lack of light and the unexpected depth of the excavation. Both the eighth- and the twelfth-century foundations were placed directly on the solid clay subsoil. Since Suger's new transept enclosed the old one and did not project to the north, the trench for the twelfth-century foundations was dug immediately outside the eighth-century side aisles. In places the distance between the eighth- and the twelfth-century foundations is so slight that there hardly seems room for Suger's workmen to have set the stones in place. Yet envelopes of new masonry enclosing an earlier church were not uncommon in the Middle Ages. Given that procedure, the new construction could begin without interrupting the services in the old building. The masons could build the foundations and construct the new walls up to the springing of the arches for the vaults before destroying the old structure. If necessary there could be a pause if sufficient funds were unavailable to complete the new building. Apparently this is exactly what happened at Saint-Denis; but the interval between the laying of the new foundations and the completion of a new nave lasted almost a century.

Although more than 25.00 m of this interior, or southern, surface of the twelfth-century north aisle wall was excavated, less than 2.00 m of the exterior, or northern, face of this wall could be investigated.[11] The two small sections uncovered, however, established the width of the wall and indicated that solid wall buttresses project to the north and, spaced at the same regular intervals of the interior bays, strengthen the wall.[12]

App. F.14

The foundations under this exterior north aisle wall are typical of twelfth-century construction at Saint-Denis. Irregular, unfinished stones of varying sizes were laid in roughly horizontal beds. No debris or fragments from earlier buildings have been found as part of this masonry. Carefully leveled at the top, a bed of thin, uniform stones forms a reasonably regular surface which provides a good footing for the finished mural masonry. In general the rough, irregular stones of these foundations resemble those of the foundations under the western bays of the first campaign, but the masonry of the nave appears to be more carefully constructed. Proof of the solidity of the foundations under the north aisle lies in the fact that they still serve as the east–west links between the piers of the existing thirteenth-century north side aisles and transept piers.

Fig. 50; App. F.12

The dressed masonry placed directly on the prepared upper surface of these northern foundations is best preserved in the eastern part of the excavation immediately to the south of the monument to Louis XII. There three beds of masonry were finished with almost machinelike precision. Presumably intended as the lowest portions of the engaged piers of the exterior wall of the north aisle, the trapezoidal socles sit directly on this first, or bottom, bed. The socles measure 0.70 m across the southern, or smaller, side, the face of which is flush with the bottom bed of the foundations. The diagonal sides measure 1.10 m, and the socle extends 0.90 m back (to the north), from the southern face of the lowest bed to a finished surface, the presumed plane of the side-aisle wall.[13] In the excavated eastern bay a second horizontal bed extends between the trapezoidal socles. Measured from the wall plane, that bench is 0.50 m wide, or almost exactly one-half the width of the first, or lowest, bed.

Fig. 123; App. F.11, 13

The easternmost socle, the most striking feature of that bay, extends 1.70 m to the south from the presumed interior face of the north wall. This socle is built of two layers of masonry, and the upper layer has the same bevel as the other two socles. Only the western side, the southwestern angle, and 1.50 m of the southern face of the socle exist today. Since the adjacent masonry to the east uncovered by the excavation consists of an agglomerate mass with no distinguishing characteristics, the eastern side of the socle was either destroyed or left unfinished. A sequence of rectangular cavities, empty when they were uncovered, has led me to conclude that as burials continued in the church this whole area was filled in and altered at some later but indeterminate date.[14]

To return to the large socle, in the overall plan of the excavations the socle is directly opposite or symmetrical to the embrasure of the south transept portal. I interpret the size and location of the socle as positive evidence of the beginning of the western part of the twelfth-century north transept. Another unusual aspect of this large socle is the extension of its southern extremity beyond the twelfth-century foundations to a point where it rests on a substructure which I have identified as part of the eleventh-century tower. Because the immediately adjacent eleventh-century masonry lies only

1.00 m to the south and rises to the same height or level as the top, or upper, surface of the twelfth-century socle, we have definite proof that the construction of the twelfth-century north transept was never finished.[15]

When I first summarized these excavations in 1947, I stated with considerable assurance that "construction [of the transept] began on the north side proceeding from east to west . . . [and that] the profiles of the bases on the south side were indications of a later date perhaps about 1170."[16] Thirty years later, with new archaeological details available, such as the northwestern pier of the choir crossing, I am much less confident. Formerly considered the normal progression, the concept of a metamorphosis of forms from relatively simple to relatively complex details has been proven erroneous. Thus the remains of monumental socles and simple, angular benches of the northern transept do not necessarily belong to a campaign that predates the south portal, where we find seemingly more sophisticated chamfered angles of compound socles with curved profiles. In fact, as noted, the forms of the south portal and adjacent socle share details also found in both the western and eastern portions of Suger's new building, whereas it is difficult to discover details to compare with the shape of the northern trapezoidal socles.[17] Even the monumental socles of the massive piers of the western bays have many more setbacks and projections.

Work on the northern side of the nave appears to have progressed less far than that on the south side. The socles of the northern side have been found only in the two eastern bays, whereas the compound socles of the southern side continue westward to the second bay from the west. Unquestionably two different groups of masons directed by two different master masons were responsible for the two different campaigns intended to join the eastern and western ends of Suger's church; yet it is difficult, if not impossible at present, to give one campaign priority over the other.

In conclusion, although we are unable to assign precise dates or to explain why the two campaigns which began the work on the transepts and nave of Suger's church were different, we know that the twelfth-century work was begun on both the north and the south sides. Carried forward from east to west, this work would have joined the choir to the western entrance bays. Even though nothing was ever finished, we can assert that both master masons adopted the same program for the transepts and the nave and can propose reasonable reconstructions for their plans. Although the bases for the engaged piers from which the vaults of the side aisles were to spring have different conformations on the north and south sides, they are spaced exactly the same distance apart—4.00 m on the east–west axis; also the bays of the new nave were to have been exactly the same width as the bays of the Carolingian church. In other words both master masons respected Suger's dictum that the new building should preserve the old one. There is no evidence, however, that "Suger limited [his work in the nave] to burying the Carolingian columns in his pillars and to fortifying the arches so that they could support the heightened wall."[18] One of the bases of the eighth-century nave colonnade is still bound by an iron band, presumably added by Suger's masons when they first restored the old church. Presumably there were

Pl. 2; Album no. 20

others also in need of repairs, but they were not part of a project to prepare the old nave to be vaulted.

Additional proof that the same overall plan was adopted by the master masons who directed the work on the north and on the south sides may be found in the fact that both lateral walls are symmetrically aligned on each side of the central axis of the old church. Furthermore, the new socles on each side not only lie 4.00 m apart, spaced as were the bases of the old nave, but also follow a direct north–south alignment with each other and with the existing eighth-century bases. The plan for the new nave, therefore, must have anticipated the replacement of the eighth-century nave columns with the new twelfth-century bases and shafts. The lateral, north and south walls were begun outside the walls of the old church so that the new structure would literally have been an "enlargement" of the old. This enlargement increased the distance from the nave colonnade to the lateral walls from 5.00 m to 8.00 m. Doubtless by design, not coincidence, the division into two side aisles would have resulted in aisle bays measuring 4.00 m by 4.00 m. Such an aisle colonnade would have continued the alignment of the ambulatory columns of the western bays of the new choir. Although neither the new nave columns nor those of the double side aisle were ever put in place, I have reconstructed the plan of Suger's intended nave on this basis.

Although the twelfth-century nave and aisle colonnades were never built, the presence of twelfth-century bases used as fill and as part of the thirteenth-century foundations under the crossing proves that preparations for their construction were under way before all work stopped in the twelfth century. Three such bases were recently uncovered on the south side of the excavation under the present crossing. Another one was found earlier by Formigé, who mistook it for part of the southwestern junction pier between the new choir and the old transept.[19] Only one side of these bases can be seen at present, so we do not know whether they were finished or not. From what is visible they appear to be of slightly different dimensions and have slightly different profiles. On the assumption that the plinths are square and that top surfaces, as indicated by the upper tori molding, are circular, I suggest that these bases were intended for the nave or aisle colonnades and were still lying around in the chantier when the thirteenth-century foundations were begun. As large blocks of solid limestone they could function perfectly well as part of the new foundations. Other twelfth-century fragments, such as an engaged foliate capital and part of a drum of an engaged column, were found embedded in the thirteenth-century foundations on the south side of the nave, and an almost perfectly preserved engaged capital with affronted griffons was discovered in the foundations of pier 13 of the north transept.[20]

App. F.2, 3

Such details, though fragmentary and very limited, combine with the dimensions of the outer side-aisle socles to suggest a possible elevation for Suger's nave. Of primary concern in such a reconstruction, of course, is Suger's insistence on harmony and concordance. In my reconstruction of Suger's choir, I explored why I favored a three-story elevation with an open arcade between the hemicycle arcade and the clerestory windows. Because of Suger's search for concordance I also adopted the design of the second, or eastern, central bay of the western ensemble as a possible design in the choir. For the same reason I would propose the twin arched opening under a single arch as the design for the middle story of the nave.[21] Doubtless the crown of the nave vaults would have been the same as that of the choir vaults, but since the nave pavement was 3.34 m lower than the choir pavement, the main arcade would have been 10.88 m high, resulting in a proportion of almost 1 to 1 between the arcade and the two upper stories. Because of Suger's predilection for columnar supports and also because twelfth-century bases designed for such cylindrical shafts have survived in the thirteenth-century foundations under the crossing, I conclude that the nave and aisle supports must have been cylindrical. Finally, in the reconstruction of the plan of Suger's church I have shown the crossing piers as symmetrical to the socle of the northwest pier of the choir hemicycle.

Figs. 67d, 119

Conclusion[1]

When Abbot Suger began his new abbey church at Saint-Denis in the mid-1130s, he was fulfilling a boyhood dream. Some forty years had passed since he had entered the gates of the monastery as an *oblatus,* only ten years old, and his ideas, expressed in the different parts of the new building, continued to develop as the construction advanced. Although he died in 1151, as the nave and transept were just beginning to rise above the ground, his vision of this new house of God was so apparent that we can comment on the entire structure. The building proceeded in three successive campaigns. Each major part of the church was intended to signify different fundamental beliefs about the Christian universe and its successful existence. Order in the temporal realm dominates the first campaign, the western façade and the entrance bays, dedicated on 9 June 1140. The celestial hierarchy, the realm of light, and the verities of sacred literature were given material existence in the second campaign, the new eastern choir, dedicated on 11 June 1144. Although destined to remain unfinished during Suger's lifetime, the nave, or central body of the church, was to join the two ends and invoke the authority of the papacy by a direct reference to Saint Peter's basilica in Rome. Before we examine the details that justify the recognition of such an elaborate program, a brief summary of the early buildings dedicated to Saint Denis—patron and protector of the French monarchy—will strengthen the proposal that symbolic intent was present in Suger's new building.

Toward the end of the fifth century, when northern France was all but deserted, Sainte Geneviève (who became the patron saint of Paris because she had insisted that Attila the Hun would not reach the city) was disturbed that the tomb of Denis, the city's first bishop, was in such a fearful place. She persuaded the priests of Paris to solicit enough funds to build a chapel over the burial place of the bishop in the cemetery of the village of Catulliacum, now St.-Denis, about four Roman miles directly north of the city. The chapel immediately became one of the *praecipua loca sanctorum* of Gaul, and throughout the sixth century nobles of high rank at the Merovingian court chose to be buried in or near the simple rectangular building, whose dimensions—approximately thirty-five by seventy meters—made it one of the more important masonry structures in the area. About 570 Queen Arnegonde, wife of Clotaire (the grandson of Clovis) and mother of Chilpéric, was buried just outside the western entrance, the first in a long series of royal burials at Saint-Denis. After Dagobert I and his son, Clovis II (ca. 645), the monastery was fully established and royally endowed to such an extent that when the Carolingian dynasty replaced the Merovingian, Pepin the Short, the father of Charlemagne, was anointed in the abbey church by Pope Stephen II. Even earlier, Charles Martel, Pepin's father, had sent his sons to be educated at Saint-Denis, apparently in the hope that association with so many former kings and queens would give them an aura of royalty. He also chose Saint-Denis as his own burial place. Although Charlemagne was buried at Aix-la-Chapelle in his own palace chapel, after the death of Hugh Capet in 987 only three French kings—Philip I, Louis VII, and Louis XI— were not buried at Saint-Denis. The abbey church had indeed become the *nécropole dynastique,* where the regalia and the royal standard, the oriflamme, were protected. Saint Denis, the patron saint, was recognized not only as the first bishop of Paris and as the patron and protector of the French monarchy, but also as the Areopagite, author of mystical treatises destined to become an integral segment of medieval philosophy. Nurtured in such an environment, Suger, when he became abbot of Saint-Denis in 1122, not surprisingly envisaged the building of a great new church. What is surprising is that he succeeded in introducing so many new ideas and in perfecting so many technical advances and that his masons introduced a new style, the Gothic, which dominated western Europe for the next three centuries.

Let us turn to an examination of the details of the three successive campaigns of building. Normally the construction of medieval churches began at the eastern end, so that services could be conducted undisturbed as soon as possible in the new environment. Why, then, did Abbot Suger begin at the western end? Although Suger does not record the fact, there was evidently considerable opposition to any proposal to replace the old building with a new one. A legend had developed that the old church had been built by Dagobert I and that the building had been miraculously consecrated by Christ himself, accompanied by Saint Denis, his companions, and a host of shining angels. Yet the legend ignored the fact that Dagobert's embellishments at Saint-Denis were completely replaced by Fulrad's new church, dedicated in 775 in the presence of Charlemagne and his court. The account of the miraculous consecration does not appear in writing until the late eleventh century, but apparently popular opinion accepted it so enthusiastically that every stone of the church standing in Suger's day was venerated as though it were a relic, and passions were so fervid at that time that they could not be ignored. Suger, who had spent hours as a student in the abbey's archives, recalled that the western end of the old church was said to be an addition built by Charlemagne, so that it did not actually belong to Dagobert's venerable shrine and could, consequently, be torn down with impunity. Such clever reasoning, however, hardly justified the need for such a monumental new entrance, elaborately decorated with sculpture and surmounted by high and noble towers. Obviously Suger knew that such towers would dominate the plains north of Paris and that they would constantly call attention to the abbey.

Scholars have commented on these twin towers and noted similar towers above the façade of William the Conqueror's great abbey church of Saint-Etienne at Caen, in Normandy. Originally outside the town walls, that church provided an impressive entrance to the ducal capital. Suger may well have seen it during his early years, when he served as prior of the small church of Berneval, near Fécamp in Normandy. But before Suger began his own new church, he had made many other trips for his abbot and his king. Three times he went to Rome, even to Bitonto at the southern tip of Italy. He traveled to Bordeaux in southwestern France to be present at the wedding of Louis VII and Eleanor of Aquitaine. In 1124 he was present at the Reichstag in Mainz to represent the claims of Saint-Denis. He must have visited most of the important monasteries and growing communities of the early twelfth century in western Europe, with the exception of England, and he evidently traveled with attentive eyes and a retentive memory. When he summoned artists from many lands to build and decorate his new church, he remembered the most active and interesting workshops he had visited. Masons, sculptors, and artists expert in other techniques came to Saint-Denis with different backgrounds and training. Suger must have encouraged them to assist him in formulating the details of the new programs. The west façade and the western bays illustrate how successfully these different ideas could be incorporated into a single program.

The façade at Saint-Denis, for example, is not just an exterior embellishment. The twin Norman towers are not flush with the plane of the façade but are set back on the mass of the entrance bays so that they become an integral part of the whole western structure. These western bays have two stories with upper chapels which function independently of the rest of the building. Such a western mass, or *westwerke,* was introduced into ecclesiastical architecture in Carolingian times and further developed in the Ottonian imperial basilicas of the tenth and eleventh centuries in the Rhine Valley. The westwerke were symbols of secular, royal authority distinct from the authority of the Church, which was presided over by the clergy at the eastern end of the building. Suger does not tell us that he had this in mind, but the forms certainly suggest such an intention, and his contemporaries would not have misunderstood the references.

An unusual feature at Saint-Denis is the presence of crenellations crowning the top of the façade. The ones we see today are restorations, rebuilt in the fourteenth and nineteenth centuries. Proof that they were part of the original design is Suger's mention of *superiora frontis propugneula* "both for the beauty of the church and, should circumstances require it, for practical purposes." Similar crenellations over gateways can be traced back to early antiquity and are present in early images of the Temple of Solomon. At Saint-Denis they remind us that the patron saint was protector of the monarchy and that the church guarded the regalia and the oriflamme.

Directly below the crenellations is a rose window, the first, to my knowledge, to appear as an integral part of the design of a western façade. Erwin Panofsky described the rose as "superimposing a magnificent *Non* upon the *Sic* of the big window beneath it" and added that "the very concept of an isolated circular unit conflicted with the ideals of Gothic taste in general." Others, however, such as Jurgis Baltrušaitis, have noted the frequency with which circular patterns (like the wheel-scheme as a cosmic metaphor) came to be used in the High and late Middle Ages as a formal means of organizing ideas.[2] At Saint-Denis the rose opened into the central upper chapel, where it could also be seen from the eastern choir. Such a circular, solar disk was added to the wall of the western apse at Worms, another of the Rhenish imperial basilicas. There it framed the emperor when he sat in his throne at the western end of the nave. Unfortunately Suger does not record any purpose or meaning for the rose window at Saint-Denis. In fact, he does not even mention it. If such an "isolated circular unit conflicted with the ideals of Gothic taste in general," the presence of rose windows in almost all Gothic façades is a peculiar phenomenon in the history of taste.

Any discussion of the west façade at Saint-Denis must include some comment about the triple portals which gave access to the interior. One of the many new features of the portals at Saint-Denis is that there are three arched openings immediately adjacent to each other. The image of three arches with the central one larger than the side ones recalls the famous Roman triumphal arches of Constantine or the one at Orange, in the Rhone Valley, both of which Suger must have seen. As noted earlier, Roman writers have described the triumphant emperor with his legions as he passed through the arch as an act of purification and cleansing on his way to be received as a divinity in his heavenly city. This concept of the emperor's filial relation to the deity was reiterated by the Ottonian emperors of the tenth and eleventh centuries, and the idea of purification as one entered the Church of God would be appropriate for western portals. Suger, however, refers to them in quite different terms. His account of the dedication on 9 June 1140 describes "one glorious procession of . . . three men" who left the church through a single door. The three bishops, acting as one, proceeded to perform the dedication of the three doors in a single act and reentered the church through a single door. The reiteration of the numbers one and three certainly implies a trinitarian symbolism, an implication confirmed by the carved imagery of the central portal. There, at the top of the two outer archivolts on the central axis of the portal and of the whole church is a dove attended by angels with, immediately below, the bust of God the Father holding a disk which contains the Paschal Lamb—the symbolic representation of the Trinity. The Trinity was a vital theological question in the second quarter of the twelfth century, so the orthodox statement at Saint-Denis is in clear support of papal authority. The Trinity also represented the beginning of the Christian universe and of Christian time. Such multiple references complicate the possible interpretation of the exact meaning of the iconography at Saint-Denis, but they also demonstrate the interrelation of the major themes of the Old and New Testaments.

The dominant theme at Saint-Denis is the Last Judgment depicted in the tympanum, the archivolts, the decorated jambs, and the original bronze doors of the central portal. In contrast to the almost literal representation of St. John's magnificent apocalyptic vision on the tympanum at Moissac, carved only some fifteen years before Saint-Denis, the Last Judgment on Suger's portal is depicted by various references. Christ the Judge, dominating everything, reveals his two natures as Son of God and Son of man. As judge, Christ summons the dead to appear from the grave, shown in the lintel beneath his feet. He is also shown at the moment of the crucifixion with outstretched arms and his right side bared and pierced by the spear of Longinus. These specific images are supplemented by the trumpeting angel awakening the dead, by scenes of heaven and hell awaiting the blessed and the damned, and by less traditional ones, such as the Apostles seated *in collegio,* representing the Last Judgment. The Apostles converse with each other *in disputatione*—a scholastic reference to their role as teachers of the people. Even more unusual are the Wise and Foolish Virgins holding both upright and overturned lamps on the jambs of the portal. In the lower extremities of the tympanum one maiden prepares to enter heaven while the other, on Christ's left, kneels before a barred door. This parable from Matthew (25:1–12) refers both to the blessed and the damned at the time of judgment and to the apocalyptic Second Coming of Christ. Reference to the Second Coming is completed in the archivolts surrounding the tympanum by the images of the twenty-four elders of the apocalypse, seated on thrones and holding vials and musical instruments. The elders, or patriarchs, with the symbol of the Trinity in their midst, symbolize the celestial Jerusalem. On the outer archivolt the elders are shown framed by an intertwining garland or vine, a favorite motif for the ancestors of Christ in representations of the Tree of Jesse, seen in the stained glass window added a few years later when Suger's new choir was finished at the other end of the church. The possible association of the patriarchs with the ancestors of Christ leads us to one of the most original and influential innovations in the sculpture of the western portals—the statue columns that originally decorated the embrasures of all three portals.

No statue columns exist today on the western portals, but a few fragments in scattered museums and a series of eighteenth-century drawings prove that such statues did exist. Although Suger made no mention of them, scholars today accept the idea that these important figures were part of the original program for the western portals and agree that they must have been the earliest ensemble in the long series of statue columns that became an integral feature in Gothic portal design. The statue columns were removed from Saint-Denis in 1771, probably because of their damaged condition, and only heads of four statues are known to exist today: three in this country (two in the Walters Art Gallery in Baltimore, one in the Fogg Art Museum in Cambridge, Massachusetts), and one in a private collection in Paris. The drawings of twenty-four statue columns done in 1718 or 1719 by Antoine Benoist for Bernard de Montfaucon's *Les Monumens de la monarchie françoise,* published in 1729, are now in the Cabinet des Manuscrits in the Bibliothèque Nationale in Paris. Although there has been some question about the accuracy of the details in the drawings, a comparison of the existing heads and of a surviving statue from the Saint-Denis cloisters, now in the Metropolitan Museum of Art in New York, proves the drawings to be quite faithful. In the Montfaucon plates the figures are shown in the order they presumably appeared in the portals. One figure may be identified with certainty: the figure of Saint Denis, wearing a miter, on the trumeau of the central portal. The figure holding tablets is probably Moses, and the woman with long braids may have represented the Queen of Sheba. The earliest descriptions called the statues "kings and queens and other benefactors." Montfaucon named them after the kings and queens of the first dynasty, the Merovingians. In 1751 Abbé Lebeuf said that they were Old Testament figures showing the royal ancestry of Christ and the concordance between the Old and New Testaments, and also that they referred to *regnum et sacerdotium* (secular and spiritual authority), identifications still agreed with today. The presence of royalty prominently displayed on the entrance portals was certainly appropriate to the royal abbey, and the emphasis on regnum et sacerdotium was a basic premise of Suger's philosophy.

The carved jambs of the lateral portals as they exist today show the Works of the Months on the south portal and the Signs of the Zodiac on the north. The latter scenes, in rectangular frames which alternate with purely decorative panels, have been rearranged or altered so that three of the signs—Leo, Cancer, and Virgo—are missing, but enough remains of the other signs to make identification positive. On the south portal, all of the Works of the Months in circular garlands are shown in order so that when considered with the Signs of the Zodiac on the north portal they add another dimension to the Alpha and Omega of the central portal: namely, the concept of the cosmic and the terrestrial worlds.

Suger wrote that he had a mosaic affixed to the tympanum of the north portal, but there is no description to tell us whether it was a decorative design or some scene. The unusual mosaic was removed in 1771, at the same time as the statue columns. A carved tympanum showing Saint Denis and his two companions being taken from prison to be decapitated replaced the mosaic, but, since it was considered to be ugly, it too was replaced, in 1837, by the sculpture in place today, which shows an equally unattractive variant of the same scene. Only the outer of the two archivolts on the north side was carved in the twelfth century. Although heavily restored, there are enough fragments remaining to suggest that the bust of Christ with outstretched arms in the center reached to give, or receive, a scepter on his left and a book or tablet on his right. Christ's right hand is veiled and the figure below it has bare feet, while his left hand is uncovered and the figure below it wears shoes. Quite possibly this archivolt was intended to refer to regnum et sacerdotium, symbolized by the scepter and shod feet and the book and bare feet. One of Suger's major preoccupations was thus given further emphasis.

If important details are lacking for a complete understanding of the significance of the north portal, the details of the south portal are much clearer. Suspect in terms of their authenticity, the tympanum and, in this case, the inner archivolt have now been proven to be of the same stone as the central portal and, although the details have all been cleaned or recut, the scenes and figures as a whole are considered original, as claimed by Wilhelm Vöge in 1894 and again by Emile Mâle in 1922. The tympanum depicts the miraculous last Communion offered by Christ and a host of angels to Saint Denis and his companions while the three were in prison awaiting execution. Christ and angels in wavy clouds occupy the upper part of the tympanum. In the lower portion, the prefect Fescennius, who condemned Saint Denis, is seated at the right on his throne, while the prison with the saints and an altar occupies the center. The blessed Larcia, who was converted to Christianity by Saint Denis, waits outside as two executioners enter the prison from the left. The elongated figures on the inner archivolt are easily recognizable as an angel holding a martyr's crown at the center, Saint Denis holding his bishop's miter on the left, and his two companions, Rusticus and Eleutherius, on the right. At the bottom of the archivolt are two pairs of executioners with their swords and axes. The choice of this particular episode in the passion of the patron saint has been explained as emphasizing the intimate relationship between Christ and Saint Denis and the saint's special function as a martyred bishop to lead the initiated to salvation. *The Golden Legend* recounts that the three saints' heads were cut off as they confessed the Trinity, a detail supplying another possible meaning for the triple portals.

One additional major part of the symbolism of the western portals remains to be examined, the bronze doors which Suger says he installed in each of the three portals. Melted down in 1794 during the French Revolution, the bronze reliefs have completely disappeared, and little is known about the side doorways—Suger says that the north ones were old—so I shall simply mention in passing the text which Suger had inscribed on the central doors. Scenes of Christ's Passion, Resurrection, and Ascension were depicted in low relief on the eight medallions of the two panels, which, since they were originally gilded, shone brightly, at least during Suger's lifetime. Panofsky saw the verses as a condensed version of the whole theory of "anagogical illumination" expounded by Dionysius the Pseudo-Areopagite, which complete the symbolism of the first campaign and express a fundamental concept underlying the building of the entire new church.

In this summary of the multiple interpretations of so many details in the construction and decoration of the western façade and entrance bays, I have tried to be impartial. The reader is invited to select his or her own major theme for emphasis as the underlying symbol Suger wished to convey. My own vision extends from the "high and noble" towers above the mass of the western bays down past the crenellations, the rose window, and the triple arcades to the three portals, bound into a single unit by the horizontal band of statue columns and by the statue of Saint Denis in the center. With kings, queens, patriarchs of the Old Testament, and saints, the theme of the balance of authority between regnum et sacerdotium remains dominant. The emphasis is on the Christian Church in this world and on the human personalities who embodied Christian truth to Abbot Suger and his advisors. In conclusion I shall summarize the dominant symbols I perceive in the new east end and the nave that was intended to join the two ends.

The difference between the symbolism of the western bays and that of the eastern choir is the difference between literal exposition and intuitive response. At the western end, the actual forms of the architecture—crenellations, circular window, arched doorways with images carved in stone—all invite specific, often multiple interpretations. By contrast, in the eastern portion, where the monks' liturgy took place, the environment created by an emotional reaction to colored light and to bright, shining surfaces evokes abstract, metaphysical responses. The difference is that between the material world of our cognitive experience and the immaterial universe of celestial hierarchies. Abbot Suger reflects this difference in his description of the laying of the foundations for the crypt. For the procession to perform the dedication of the eastern end, the prelates arranged themselves in ecclesiastical order reflecting the hierarchies of celestial order and walked round and round the choir "so piously that the king and attending nobility believed themselves to behold a chorus celestial rather than human." After the simultaneous consecration of twenty altars, all these dignitaries performed a solemn celebration of masses, both in the upper choir and in the crypt, "so festively, so solemnly, so different[ly] and yet so concordantly, so close [to one another] and so joyfully that their song, delightful by its consonance and unified harmony, was deemed a symphony angelic rather than human." We have no evidence that such a simultaneous celebration of masses was a regular occurrence, but the "circular string of chapels," the nine contiguous, radiating chapels around the ambulatory are a perfect solution for such a program. Suger's master mason proved his genius by his construction of this "crown of light," these adjacent chapels open to one another, illuminated by large stained glass windows so that the "whole [church] would shine with the wonderful and uninterrupted light of most luminous windows, pervading the interior beauty."

The striking contrast at Saint-Denis between the crypt and the choir above it demonstrates vividly the difference between Romanesque and Gothic construction. Both levels have the same plan. Indeed, the crypt functions as foundation for the choir; but the structure contrasts the solidity of mural construction, groin vaulting, enclosed volumes, and reflected light with the diaphanous construction of minimal support, articulated skeletal rib vaults, and the maximal introduction of refracted colored light. Once again historians of architecture know of no prototype for Suger's choir. Suger tells us that his masons "cunningly provided that . . . the central nave of the old church should be equalized, by means of geometrical and arithmetical instruments, with the central nave of the new addition; and, likewise, that the dimensions of the old side aisles should be equalized with the new side aisles, except for that elegant and praiseworthy extension in [the form of] a circular string of chapels." This seems a very simple, straightforward statement. Unfortunately, this passage cannot be interpreted literally. The new choir is not exactly the width of the old nave, nor are the new side aisles (the ambulatory around the choir) the same dimensions as the old side aisles. The masons' *instrumentis* may have been some application of Hugo of St. Victor's "practical geometry." The recent photogrammetric plans and elevations of the crypt and choir prove how accurate their construction is. The levels of the abaci of the capitals over the ambulatory columns on the north side vary, for instance, only ten centimeters from those on the south side, and the segmental arcs of the rib vaults all have the same radii. These discoveries demonstrate an unexpected mastery of the construction of the wooden scaffolding on which the stone armature was built and show how carefully conceived was the entire fabric of this "circular string of chapels."

For Suger and his contemporaries this architectural beauty was enhanced by the costly vessels and other decorations made for the new choir. A basic tenet of Suger's philosophy was that "every costlier or costliest thing should serve, first and foremost, for the administration of the Holy Eucharist." His own peasant background may have accounted for his admiration of glittering things as well as a lack of restraint that may have resulted in rather garish combinations. The few liturgical vessels that survived the melting pots of the Revolution bear witness to this taste, as well as to Suger's respect for Roman antiquities such as cameos or porphyry and crystal vases, which his artisans embellished with new mountings. Only his written descriptions and a Flemish painting survive to give us some idea of his golden altars and of the great golden crucifix, more than six meters high, with its enamel plaques and complicated iconography. Suger's well-known passage from his *De Administratione* shows how perfectly these lavish ornaments could be explained in terms of the basic Neoplatonic philosophy of Dionysius the Pseudo-Areopagite, whom Suger believed to be his patron saint, the blessed Saint Denis:

Thus, when . . . the loveliness of the many-colored gems has called me away from external cares, and worthy meditation has induced me to reflect, transferring that which is material to that which is immaterial, on the diversity of sacred virtues: then it seems to me that I see myself dwelling, as it were, in some strange region of the universe which neither exists entirely in the slime of the earth nor entirely in the purity of Heaven; and that, by the grace of God, I can be transported from this inferior to that higher world in an anagogical manner.[3]

Clearly Suger intended the same for his new choir. With its luminous windows and gem-encrusted ornaments, it seemed to be neither of the slime of this earth nor entirely of the purity of heaven—a material celestial Jerusalem and earthly abode of God.

Suger certainly planned to complete his new church and probably hoped that the new transept and nave would signify the successful joining of the terrestrial to the celestial realms.

> Eager to press on my success, since I wished nothing more under heaven that to seek the honor of my mother church which with maternal affection had suckled me as a child, had held me upright as a stumbling youth, had mightily strengthened me as a mature man, and had solemnly *set me among the princes* of the church and the realm, we devoted ourselves to the completion of the work and strove to raise and to enlarge the transept wings of the church [so as to correspond] to the form of the earlier and later work that had to be joined [by them].[4]

His apprehension that this would not be accomplished, however, proved justified. Our excavations in the transepts and nave show that work was started on both the north and south sides, as a sort of envelope around the old eighth-century building, but neither side progressed very far, so that the old nave remained standing until it was replaced in the thirteenth century. Enough remains to prove that the new nave was to be two meters wider on both sides than the old one but that the old bay width—four meters from center to center—would be maintained, as would the width of the central nave, even though work on the interior of the new nave was never begun. The proportions of the side aisles as well as the presence of the ambulatory and the radiating chapels in the choir are adequate proof that double side aisles on each side of the nave were planned by Suger's master mason. The fact that work stopped, probably shortly after Suger's death in January 1151, meant that there was no consecration and therefore no inscription or dedication that might provide a clue about Suger's intentions, although the verses he recorded in his *De Administratione* as the inscription for the new choir refer to the nave:

> Once the new rear part is joined to the part in front,
> The church shines with its middle part brightened,
> For bright is that which is brightly coupled with the bright,
> And bright is the noble edifice which is pervaded by the new light;
> Which stands enlarged in our time,
> I, who was Suger, being the leader while it was being accomplished.[5]

The recent discovery of bases—carved for the new nave but used only to shore up the foundations of the thirteenth-century crossing—proves that columns, not piers, would have been the supports. Now, a colonnaded nave with double side aisles was a distinguishing feature of Old Saint Peter's in Rome. Although we cannot prove that Suger had such a reference in mind, it is true that the great third church at Cluny had double aisles, as did Saint-Sernin at Toulouse, and that in both instances allegiance to Rome was a major element in their existence. It may not be too much of an exaggeration to suggest that Suger's new nave was to have been an explicit reference to the papacy as a juncture between the terrestrial regnum of the western bays and the celestial sacerdotium of the choir.

By the middle of the seventh century, therefore, Saint-Denis was one of the important monasteries of northern France. It was also closely allied to the ruling dynasty and an active center for the arts. Destined to remain a royal abbey over the centuries, its church was, successively, one of the earliest, if not the first of the great Carolingian basilicas; the first Gothic structure; and, after the completion of the new transepts and nave in the thirteenth century, one of the first examples of the *rayonnant,* or refined Gothic style. Indeed, Suger's twelfth-century building was one of the last important monastic churches, for the focus of medieval culture was to shift to the growing urban centers and to the secular cathedral. Saint-Denis bears witness to the vitality of the monastic environment as a creative milieu in the new style of the twelfth century.

APPENDIXES

EXCAVATIONS, CAPITALS, AND PROFILES

The different masonries uncovered by the excavations in the abbey church at Saint-Denis have been described in chronological sequence in the preceding text. The following appendixes describe each excavation according to its locality within the church:

A   West Façade and Western Bays
B   Western Bays of Nave
C   North Aisle
D   South Aisle—Western End
E   Eastern Bays of Nave
F   North Transept
G   South Transept
H   Crypt

Ed. note: The elevations drawn from the excavations were done over many decades and at many different scales. When the scale is known, it has been included.

The following appendixes provide supplementary measurements, a survey of capitals, and selected base profiles:

J   Chevet structure
K   Capitals
        West Bays, Ground Floor and Upper
    Chapels
        West Façade
        Crypt
        Choir
L   Profiles

APPENDIX A

West Façade and Western Bays

Excavation of the west façade and of the western bays of Abbot Suger's church at Saint-Denis was begun before 1850 and was still actively carried forward in 1975, more than one hundred years later. Only a relatively small area has been investigated and many important questions remain unanswered. In 1847, when Viollet-le-Duc was appointed to succeed Debret as architect in charge of Saint-Denis, one of the most urgent problems was the stability of the western portions. He investigated them by uncovering the foundations in front of, or to the west of, pier no. 2 between the central and northern portals of the west façade (A.1) as well as the foundations inside the same pier (A.2). These excavations were left open under heavy paving slabs, which has allowed continued observation. There is, however, no record of that arrangement until 1938, when I was given permission to lift the slabs, take photographs, and make measured drawings of the foundations that remained as Viollet-le-Duc had left them. Be-

tween 1957 and 1959 Formigé enlarged the interior excavation, exposing the impressive bases of the northwest side of pier no. 6 and a small portion of the interior of the north portal.[1] In 1967 I began excavations that I hoped would result in an understanding of the many uncertainties about the twelfth-century construction. Difficulties prohibited extensive investigation, so many questions remain for future investigation. A summary of our discoveries and of unsolved problems follows.

Undoubtedly the most important discoveries achieved by enlarging the exterior of Viollet-le-Duc's excavation to the west of pier no. 2 were fragments of the sills for the central and north portals. Excavation under the pavement in front of the western portals, without the benefit of modern equipment, was a laborious, slow, and consequently expensive project. Large blocks of miscellaneous debris sealed in a solid mortar had to be broken by mallet and chisel by a single workman taking care not to damage the twelfth-century masonry which we wished to reveal. To our consternation, work had progressed only a small distance beyond the outer, or westernmost, embrasure of the central portal when a massive twelfth-century construction seemed to block the doorway (A.3). The diagonal striations of the surface, the presence of masons' marks and of a slanting horizontal bevel, as well as the penetration of the stones under the embrasure of the portal (A.4), identified the masonry as contemporary with that of the portal above. These two beds of large blocks, averaging 0.65 m wide by 0.57 m high, extended to the south across the portal and later were found in the same north–south alignment across the north portal as well. No evidence of steps or other approach to this level (1.00 m above the rough, rubble foundations) has been discovered, so that I have been forced to conclude that the wall, or bench, as I shall refer to it, was considered to be part of the foundations for the western entrance. When this area was finally excavated and an opening pierced to the interior, the bench proved to be 2.10 m wide. This was a satisfactorily solid horizontal link between the piers that rose to support the upper structure, including the "high and noble towers."

The opening pierced to the interior was through a light fill above the rubble on top of the bench (A.5). The uppermost stone, sealed on the rubble, measured 0.15 m high by 0.40 m wide. Although under the central portal only about 0.30 m of a comparable stone extending to the south was uncovered, a similar stone with a flat upper surface at exactly the same level (0.52 m below the present pavement) in the excavation extended some 0.80 m to the north from the southern jamb of the north portal. Such a level for the original sills of both north and central portals produces dimensions for the doorways that coincide exactly with the dimensions given for the original bronze doors by Doublet at the beginning of the seventeenth century—doors described with such pride by Suger in the twelfth century. Consequently, I identify these stones as the sills for the two portals. I can only explain the finished bench across the portals as part of the foundations which would have been hidden under some sort of a pavement in front of the portals.

Although Formigé enlarged Viollet-le-Duc's excavations at the bases of piers nos. 2 and 6, he did not extend them far enough to reveal some very interesting but perplexing evidence about the entrance bays. Excavation under the pavement of the interior of the western bays has so far proved to be quite different from the arrangement in front of the portals. On the interior the nineteenth-century pavement is supported by a series of shallow, concave vaults. The fill is relatively light, noncompacted earth which yields easily to a pickax and shovel. In some areas, this fill appears to be in a series of layers or striations which should be investigated with more care and method than we could manage, hampered as we were by very restricted space in which to work. In fact, until the nineteenth-century pavement is removed and all of the bays restored to their original levels, no satisfactory solution can be proposed for the many enigmas that remain concerning the original disposition of Suger's first campaign in the building of his new church. Consequently, I can make only preliminary and tentative proposals.

Among the most interesting discoveries are the following three details. The impressive base, or *soubassement,* for the northwestern side of pier no. 6, first uncovered by Viollet-le-Duc, was further exposed by Formigé, but the southwest face remained hidden in the fill (A.6a). As can be seen in the photograph (A.6b), our investigation of the southwest face did not include the lower 0.35 m of the fill because there was a relatively solid, level mat or form that differed from the loose material above it. As we continued to free the southwest face of the base of pier no. 6, fragments of mortar were found adhering to the angular projections of the base. Against the second such projection, and set back, we found a section measuring roughly 0.12 m long by 0.07 m wide and between 0.08 m and 0.09 m thick, with a smooth upper surface, which I have concluded must have been part of the floor covering of these entrance bays. The level of this presumed pavement is 1.40 m below the existing western pavement, or 0.80 m below the present nave pavement, and only 0.08 m below the level of the Carolingian pavement to which it was joined in the twelfth century. Obviously, more extensive evidence for such a pavement must be found before positive conclusions can be reached. The same holds true in regard to the interior dispositions of both the central and northern portals.

One small paving stone was removed by For-migé's workmen at the northern end of the central portal opening where it joined the interior of the southeast side of pier no. 2. Enough of the fill below was also removed to allow a man to descend almost 1.80 m. The base of the attached colonnette and of three horizontal bevels of the soubassement extending to the south were discovered (A.7), but no attempt was made to continue or complete the excavation. When I first explored this *sondage,* I decided to extend the opening to the south across the central portal, which was easily done. Because of the limited space, our tunnel was barely 0.50 m wide—just enough to allow a shovel to be manipulated. The bevels of the soubassement continued across the inside of the portal and onto the base of pier no. 3 (A.8). They conformed to the findings on bases no. 2 and no. 6. The sill of the doorway, however, was discovered only 0.50 m below the present pavement, and a fragment of the twelfth-century pavement came to light, still attached to the base of pier no. 6 (1.40 m below the same pavement). I then realized that steps, or possibly a ramp, must have existed to provide access from the entrance doorway down to the interior pavement. The only available area to investigate at that time was the still unexcavated southeast face of pier no. 2. The fill at this point seemed to be very loose and unstable so only a small area was removed, beginning at the eastern face of pier no. 2, which had been uncovered by Viollet-le-Duc. As we advanced to the west, fragments of mortar began to appear in the fill, some of them still attached to the finished stone of the base (A.9). These fragments extended to the south in the fill, which we consequently left untouched. They also appeared at higher and higher levels until we reached the diagonal projection of the base under the rib of the central vault. At this point, the mortar fragments in the fill and those still clinging to the base were only 0.30 m below the level of the sill of the central portal. I concluded that they must be remnants of a form, or support, for a series of steps leading from the interior pavement to the central portal doorsill. I cannot insist that these mortar fragments are positive evidence

for such steps; but until more extensive excavations have cleared this area, no other conclusions seem to be available for the western entrance into Suger's new church.

Our excavation of the interior of the north portal provided more puzzling evidence about these western doorways. Formigé's workmen removed a paving stone at the southern extremity of the north portal, but their investigations were very limited. We extended this opening to the north, across the interior, to the base of pier no. 1, but our discoveries only served to complicate the whole problem. In fact, although many of the same elements discovered inside the central portal are present inside the north portal, their position and sequence seem to deny a logical solution. Similar horizontal bevels stretch across the portal opening, but only the two lowest levels remain. A third, upper level exists at both extremities. The bottom bed of masonry, 0.50 m high, is continuous across the portal but the second bed, 0.35 m high, is set back toward the exterior, to the west, 0.30 m as though to form a step (A.10). Such a step, consequently, would have been 0.35 m high, an impossibility under normal conditions. Above the third, or top, bevel on the southern side of the portal there is a fourth bed of solid masonry with a molded surface consisting of two shallow tori separated by an equally shallow scotia. This molding stops abruptly without any indication that it continued, so that the masonry of this southern side of the portal appears fragmentary (A.11). Careful investigation of the bottom of the fill inside, or to the east of, this north portal disclosed that there were stratifications of different colored materials. The space was so limited that we decided not to try to enlarge the excavation, but rather to wait until a proper approach from the east might disclose how these enigmatic indications should be interpreted.

None of the excavations done in the western bays under my direction were major undertakings, although, in every instance, they provided important confirmations. In three different instances, excavations begun in the nave or under the side aisles were extended to the west in tunnels. Such extensions under the south and later under the north aisles uncovered the original twelfth-century bases for piers no. 9 on the north and no. 12 on the south (A.12).

Although the limited space allowed only partial excavation, enough was disclosed of each base to record its location and major dimensions which conformed with other twelfth-century details in the western bays. As can be seen on the plan (pl. 2; album no. 2), the bases differed in size and form, which seems to agree with our earlier observation that for some as yet unexplained reason the north and south sides of the junction between the new entrance bays and the old nave, as well as the project for a new nave, were built to conform to different programs.

In July 1967 small excavations were made at the junction of the western bays and the nave.[2] One of them uncovered a solid mortar mat, 0.08 m to 0.14 m thick, which may have been part of the support for the early pavement of the junction bays. Another, larger hole under the confessional placed against the eastern face of pier no. 11 completed the plan of that pier as it existed before the thirteenth-century nave was built. This excavation had to be literally chipped out from a heavy rubble fill which evidently had been part of the nineteenth-century consolidation of the area in preparation for the organ console built at the western end of the nave in 1841. The base for the eastern portions of pier no. 11, removed when the nave was built in the thirteenth century, was found intact with one drum of the attached column of the eastern projection (A.13). The drum measured 0.52 m in diameter, a recurring dimension in Suger's building.

A.1. Exterior of pier no. 2 as opened by Viollet-le-Duc in the mid-nineteenth century, showing finished masonry of buttress above rubble foundations.

A.2. Interior, or northeastern, face of pier no. 2 as left by Viollet-le-Duc, reopened by the author in 1938. This shows depth of twelfth-century foundations.

A.3. Exterior of north portal as uncovered by author in 1967, showing finished twelfth-century foundation masonry and original doorway lintel in place.

A.4. Exterior of central portal as uncovered in 1967, showing twelfth-century portal embrasures and doorway lintel above massive finished foundations.

A.5. Detail of excavation of exterior of central portal, showing rubble masonry above twelfth-century foundations under doorway lintel.

a

A.6. Interior excavation of pier no. 6: (a) southwest face showing fragments of pavement sealed against pier setbacks; (b) detail of northwest face.

b

A.7. Excavation of interior of central portal, north side, showing beveled masonry, damaged base, and colonnette of portal embrasure.

A.8. Excavation of interior of central portal, south side.

A.9. Excavation of interior of central portal, north side, showing plaster fragments in the fill as possible forms for descending entrance stairs.

A.10. Excavation of interior of north portal, north side, showing descending benches and damaged twelfth-century bases and colonnettes.

A.11. Excavation of interior of north portal, south side, showing fragments of finished twelfth-century masonry and moldings that are difficult to interpret.

A.12. Excavation of south aisle extended under eastern portions of west bays in 1939, showing twelfth-century base for pier no. 12.

A.13. Excavation of pier no. 11 in 1965, showing remnants of original twelfth-century eastern portions of base removed in thirteenth century when new nave was built.

A.14. Excavation of foundations under north side of northwest tower, left open by Viollet-le-Duc.

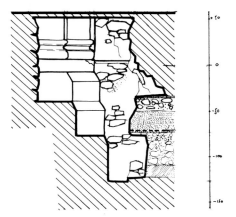

A.15. Elevation of interior excavation, west façade, north portal, looking north.

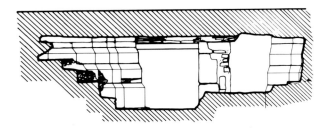

A.16. Elevation of excavation of piers no. 2 (left) and no. 6 (right), looking north.

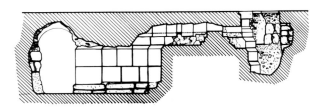

A.17. Elevation of excavation of pier no. 2 and west façade, looking north.

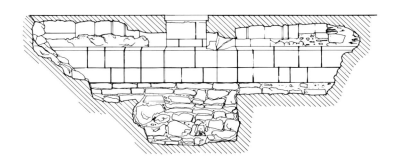

A.18. Elevation of exterior excavation, west façade, left side of central portal.

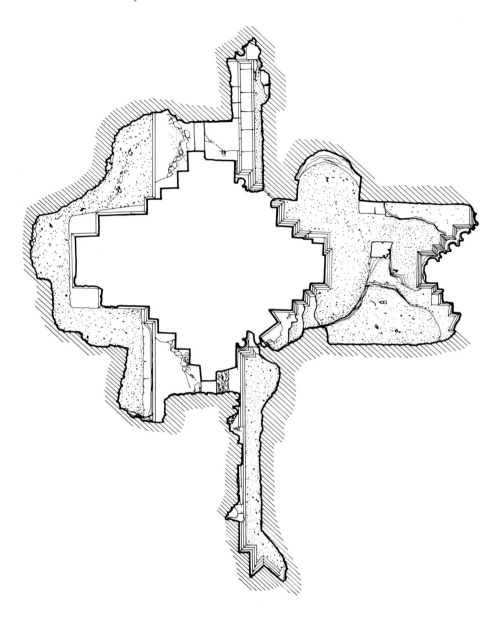

A.19. Plan of excavations at west façade, exterior (left), interior (right), with piers nos. 2 and 6.

APPENDIX B

Western Bays of Nave

Two different excavations explored the western bays of the nave and had unexpected results. The first one, in 1939, opened a trench along the first two bays of the south side of the nave (B.1). The exact location of three columns of the twelfth-century junction with Fulrad's church was clearly marked by the socles of the bases of the two eastern columns and by the presence of the complete base for the western column (B. 2). This western base was buried in the nineteenth-century cement of the foundations for the organ loft so that it was in almost perfect condition. Unfortunately, the pressure of the impending German invasion made it necessary to seal the base under the pavement again. Thus the only available evidence are my photographs and a full-scale tracing of the profile. The tall plinth with a concave bevel, the slightly projecting large torus under an almost classic succession of a smaller torus, deep scotia, and upper torus provide a perfect example of the work done by Suger's workmen in the late 1130s (app. L.14).

Two sections of masonry projecting to the north in line with similar projections under the south side aisle proved to be part of the western ensemble of the eighth-century church (pl. 2; album no. 2), which was more fully exposed almost ten years later when the north side of the nave was excavated.

By August 1947 enough of the pavement in front of the second and third bays of the north side of the nave was removed to allow a preliminary investigation (B.3). The western end revealed socles for bases of two columns of the twelfth-century junction exactly opposite those found in 1939 on the south side of the nave (pl. 2; album no. 2). Under the eastern end, which was extended by tunneling under the pavement, we were surprised and delighted to discover two large stone bases of the Carolingian nave *in situ*. As described in detail in chapter 3 above, the first or western base was badly damaged, but the second base (B.4), with a circular cavity in the top side to receive the shaft of a column, was virtually intact. The low relief carvings and the problem of the different sizes of the bases are discussed in the text.

In the spring of 1948 another season of digging at Saint-Denis began. The trench in the west bays along the north side of the nave was enlarged to the south until most of the second, third, and fourth bays were uncovered. The most unusual feature brought to light was evidence, as I have concluded, for a polygonal western apse added to, or finished, by Charlemagne in honor of his father, Pepin the Short (B.5–9). Because only the first bed of stones remains, the angular alignment that suggests the polygonal form cannot be considered conclusive evidence. Numerous later burials have disturbed the area to the west, for which no clear solution seems available. The completion of the north side excavation revealed two additional interesting features: a portion of the northwest corner of the seventh-century church and a stone with holes apparently to stabilize the vertical jambs of an entrance doorway next to the western apse (B.9,10). The discovery of the two Carolingian stone bases on the north side of the nave provided not only the alignment of the eighth-century nave columns but also the distance between the nave columns, which agreed exactly with the spaces between the bases of the twelfth-century junction. With that information available, it was possible to identify the location of the Carolingian bases on the south side of the nave. That summer we made two small excavations to explore two such locations. Only fragments of the western base could be found, but the base for the second column was uncovered with unexpected results. A circular cavity in the upper, or top, surface provided for a column shaft 0.52 m in diameter, as in the second base on the north side of the nave, but the base itself was tightly bound by an iron band, which originally had been hidden from view by a stone outer facing. Although Formigé, followed by Vieillard-Troïekouroff, stated that the base was "recollée au mortier rouge,"[1] the notes I made when I discovered the base in 1948 make no mention of a red mortar. Consequently, I believe that the repairs were made by Suger's workmen, as mentioned in his *De Consecratione*.[2] Unfortunately, when this base was prepared for conservation under the pavement, the workmen did not understand the significance of this damaged remnant, so that little remains today.

B.1. South side of the 1939 excavation of the western bays of the nave looking southwest.

B.2. Original base for a column of the twelfth-century nave junction as found in 1939.

B.4. An eighth-century nave column base, decorated with stylized foliate designs (the "fleur de lys" base, N2) in the process of being uncovered in 1947.

B.3. The opening of the north side of the excavation of the western bays of the nave in 1947.

B.5. Looking down on the nave excavation in 1948.

B.6. The eighth-century western apse seen from the northeast.

B.7. The nave excavation being prepared for a reinforced
concrete covering. The eighth-century western apse can be
seen in the center of the photograph.

B.8. North side of eighth-century western apse showing the shallow foundations.

B.9. Eighth-century foundation libages under north side of nave.

B.10. The northwest corner of the foundation for the seventh-century nave.

B.11. Eighth-century foundation blocks with holes possibly to hold the jamb posts of the door.

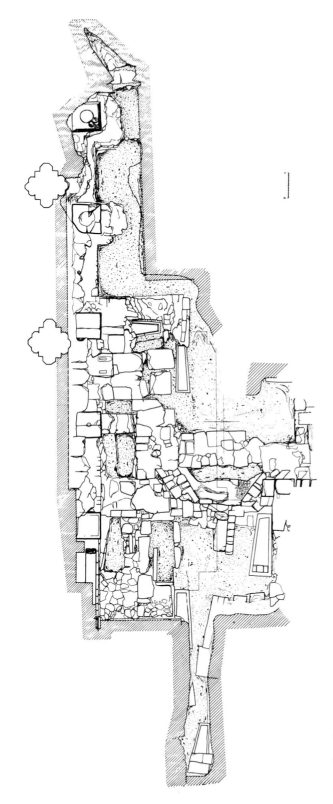

B.12. Plan of excavations of Carolingian western polygonal apse and of the north side of the nave.

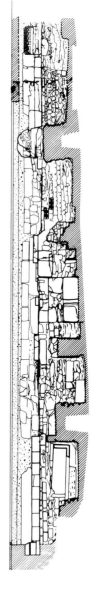

B.13. Elevation of excavations of western section, north side, of nave, showing Merovingian and Carolingian masonry and footing for twelfth-century bases of the junction bays.

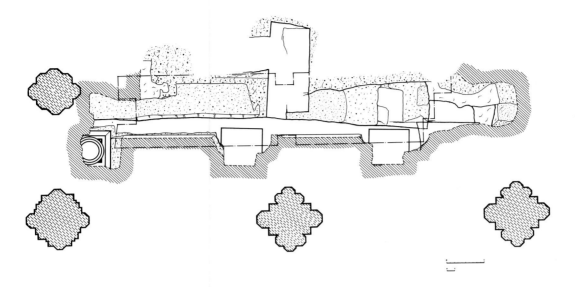

B.14. Plan of excavation of south side of Carolingian nave.

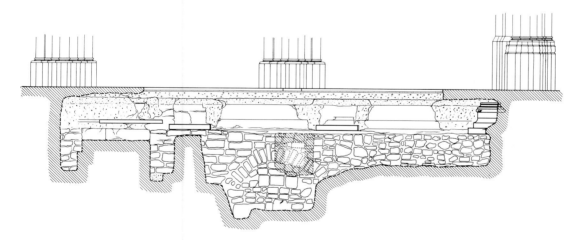

B.15. Elevation of excavation of south side of nave, looking south, showing twelfth-century base of western junction bay to right and footing for twelfth-century bases of junction bays.

APPENDIX C

North Aisle

Trial holes were opened in the north side aisle during the summer of 1947 in the hope that a corner of the Carolingian west façade might be found to match that found in 1939 under the south side aisle pavement. Two such masonry projections were uncovered in direct alignment with those to the south but they were not the same type of masonry (C.1). Under the north aisle the Carolingian remains, projecting to the south, include only the great *libages* of the foundations. They are very fragmentary, having been thoroughly disrupted when the trenches for the east–west foundations for the twelfth-century junction and later for the thirteenth-century nave traversed this area.

Once the existing pavement had been removed the continuity between the walls of the Carolingian church and those of the twelfth-century junction was clearly established, and the precise point of juncture could easily be seen (C.2). Not only is there a break in the masonry construction but there is also a twelfth-century wall buttress on the exterior to reinforce this

particular point. Another obvious but puzzling feature is the fact that on the north the twelfth-century junction wall extending to the west (C.3) is quite different from the one under the south side aisle. The north wall measures 0.75 m wide in contrast to 1.15 m on the south, and the north wall has a flat, unbroken inner surface without the two parallel horizontal bevels so prominent on the southern wall. This difference continues to be an unresolved problem. Two additional excavations have explored the western end of the north aisle, as will be explained below. Other, more positive evidence about the early buildings was discovered under the north aisle pavement.

The excavation was extended to the east into the third bay of the present side aisle. Directly in line with the eighth-century wall under the north transept, another almost perfectly preserved section of the north side of Fulrad's church was uncovered (C.4). Three carefully aligned beds of regularly finished stones 0.36 m long by 0.17 [?] m high, with the relatively prominent joints covered with a reddish mortar, distinguish this early Carolingian masonry. Equally distinctive and well preserved are the three levels of the massive libages of the foundations (C.5). Only the exterior, or north side, of this wall could be completely excavated because fragments of another, different masonry wall were found only 0.50 m to the south of the libages of the foundations. Because of the narrowness of the space between the two constructions only the upper portions of this southern wall could be investigated.

In sharp contrast to the Carolingian construction, which was solid, the interior wall crumbled as we attempted to free it from the surrounding fill. A little more than four meters long, 4.30 m to be precise, this essentially rubble masonry parallels the east–west alignment of Fulrad's building, or it would be more proper to say that the eighth-century wall is on the same axis as this rubble masonry, which must be the older of the two constructions (C.6). At its western end the rubble wall disappears under a Carolingian libage which projects to the south as part of the eighth-century western ensemble, so that the wall must have been in place before Fulrad's church was finished. I have associated this type of masonry with the enlargement of Sainte Geneviève's early funerary chapel, undertaken by King Dagobert about 630. More substantial rubble masonry will be described in the next section on the nave excavations. Until better evidence is available I shall continue to identify all of that rubble construction as Merovingian.

On the outside, or to the north, of the eighth-century wall, twelfth-century foundations and the first bed of twelfth-century finished masonry continue the east–west alignment of the beginning of Suger's nave (C.7). This western portion, however, is less advanced than in the transept, for there are no plinths above the first bed of finished masonry— evidence that work stopped on this north side of the nave somewhere between the third bay of the present nave and the beginning of the transept. The implications of this evidence in regard to Suger's church are discussed in chapter 10 above.

In the west end of this north aisle excavation, as mentioned earlier in this section, we uncovered masonry for which there is, as yet, no adequate explanation. The junction wall between the old Carolingian nave and the new, twelfth-century entrance bays continues until it reaches the northeast base—base no. 9—of the entrance bays. For some as yet unexplained reason, 2.80 m to the east of this base the junction wall encounters a solid mass of rubble, which rises to within 0.73 m of the present nave pavement. The level of the rubble, it will be recalled, is ca. 0.02 m below the level of the Carolingian pavement (C.9) found in 1969 at the eastern end of the north side aisle, but there is no evidence to account for the rubble mass in this particular location. The vertical face of the junction wall stops abruptly at the base against which it is placed without any attempt at continuity. The base, at least that portion of the base which could be freed from the surrounding rubble, seems to conform to the masonry of the entrance bays. Buried in the cement under the nineteenth-century paving, the top of the base measures 0.60 m across the southern face, which projects 0.30 m from the north wall. Two horizontal bevels add 0.20 m so that the bottom of the base measures 0.80 m from east to west and projects 0.50 m from the north. Unfortunately, this area could not be properly cleared so that I do not have a real understanding of the forms or sequence of masonries disclosed by the excavations.

In 1968 an attempt was made to resolve some of these problems. The pavement in front of, or to the south of, the entrance to the baptistry, or westernmost chapel, on the north side of the nave was removed. In this instance no problems were solved and we were left with another enigma. A wall with slightly damaged surfaces, including a horizontal bevel, joins the east–west junction wall at right angles from the north. Only a little more than 1.00 m of this wall could be uncovered before it was buried in the solid cement foundations of the baptistry. The western side of this wall is also covered so that no evidence exists about its possible function or destination.

C.1. General view of north aisle excavation in 1948 looking
west.

C.2. Detail of junction of the eighth-century wall (right) and of the twelfth-century wall.

C.3. Continuous twelfth-century junction wall from west.

C.4. Interior, or south side, of eighth-century nave wall.

C.5. Exterior, or north side, of eighth-century nave wall, showing three levels of foundation libages and three beds of finished masonry.

C.8. Excavation of east end of north side aisle in 1971, showing fragment of seventh-century foundations between empty plaster sarcophagus and eighth-century foundations.

C.6. Remnants of seventh-century foundation wall (right) inside of eighth-century north aisle wall and foundations, looking east.

C.7. Excavation in 1967 of west end of north aisle, showing twelfth-century junction wall and unexplained projection at right angle to north.

C.9. Vestiges of the eighth-century floor pavement as found in 1971 under the eastern end of the north side aisle with an unidentified small marble base.

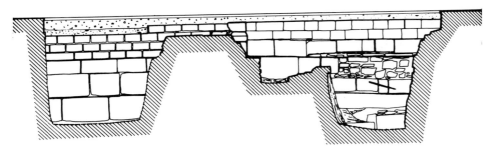

C.10. Elevation, north aisle, junction of eighth- and twelfth-century masonry, looking south.

C.11. Elevation, north aisle, looking west, showing section of eighth-, twelfth-, and sixth-century masonry.

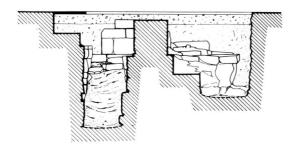

C.12. Elevation, north aisle, looking east, eighth- and twelfth-century masonry.

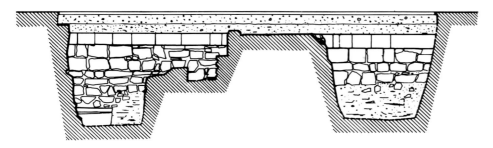

C.13. Elevation, north aisle, looking north, twelfth-century wall.

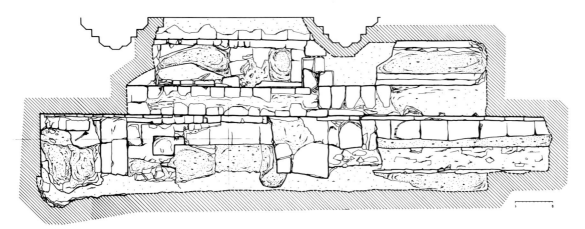

C.14. Plan of 1954, north aisle, west to east.

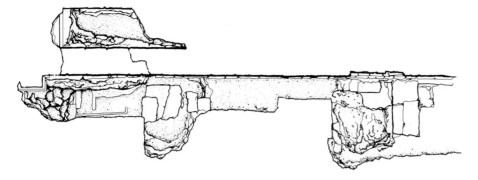

C.15. Plan of 1962, north aisle, west end, west to east.

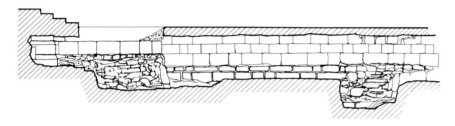

C.16. Elevation, north aisle, west end, west to east, looking
north.

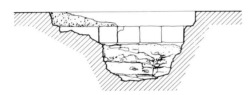

C.17. Elevation, north aisle, west end, east–west wall looking
south, 1968.

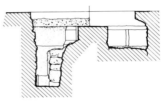

C.18. Elevation, north aisle, west end, south side of twelfth-
century junction wall, looking west.

APPENDIX D

South Aisle—Western End

Primarily because the area seemed quite free and relatively unused, excavation of the south aisle began in June 1939. Because this was my first major excavation, I lacked not only experience but also comparative material on which to base an opinion about any findings. There had been no important excavations in the church since those of Viollet-le-Duc in the mid-nineteenth century. The workmen hired by the Monuments Historiques in Paris were just as naïve and curious as I. Mallard, the architect in charge of Saint-Denis, agreed to the removal of a few slabs of the marble pavement in the middle of the aisle as a trial sondage.[1] I had chosen this particular spot because it was on the line between the twelfth-century masonry of the west bays and the ambulatory columns of the choir to the east. To everyone's surprise and my delight, a well-preserved fragment of a carefully finished wall running east–west was disclosed (D.1). Mallard then agreed to the extension of the exacavation to the east and west.

After the marble slabs of the flooring had been taken up as carefully as possible in the hope of reusing them, a layer of solid cement about 0.08 m thick had to be removed. The marble paving had been laid down while the cement was still fluid, with the result that the joints between each piece of marble were securely sealed and had to be sawed open by hand—a slow, time-consuming process. After soaking the area in water overnight, we were able to prize loose each slab. The cement underneath was then broken up and the fill exposed. Any solid construction or fragment of masonry was easily distinguishable from the loose earth fill, which was removed by a shovel and piled on the edge of the pavement. In most instances, the fill had been thoroughly disturbed in preparing for later burials—a recurrent event through the entire church. Because of these burials, little trustworthy information could be discovered in the fill, except for unusual circumstances.[2] Although the fill was carefully inspected as it was loosened and again after it had been lifted out, nothing of interest was found.

The wall that was uncovered by the excavation appeared to be relatively intact, although its upper surface was rough and had portions broken away or demolished. One break contained a portion of a tracery or window decoration which must have predated the 1230s, when the wall was torn down, but no other similar pieces were found. Our interest was centered on the inner, or northern, side of the wall, which proved to be composed of three beds of carefully finished stones, just over 1.00 m in all. The distinguishing factor was the presence of two horizontal bevels, 0.10 m high, which continued the entire length of the wall (app. L.16). As our work progressed and I became better acquainted with the physical characteristics of the first, or beginning, phase of Suger's building, I realized that these horizontal bevels were a dominant feature of the bottom, or ground level, structure. They varied in their dimensions. In this instance, the south-aisle wall, the upper bed is 0.35 m high and the lower one 0.40 m high, with both bevels 0.10 m high (D.10). The western end of the excavation had to be continued in a tunnel under the pavement in order not to obstruct circulation in the church. Under the stairs leading from the nave up to the pavement of the western bays, the wall terminated in the base of pier no. 12, which also had the two bevels. The total length of this twelfth-century junction wall was just over 9.50 m long. Its eastern end joined foundations of quite a different character.

At a point almost exactly opposite pier no. 2 of the nave, the foundations under the pavement of the south side aisle make a right-angle turn to the north (D.9). Without other comparable masonry on which to base an opinion, I suggested, in my first volume, that these foundations must have been those of the southwestern corner of Abbot Fulrad's eighth-century church (D.2).[3] Subsequent excavations have confirmed this opinion. The distinctive surface treatment of the foundation blocks, which resulted in a series of concavities (D.3), did not appear in the well-preserved Carolingian remains under the pavement of the north aisle or north transept. Among the last excavations that I directed in 1977–78 was an extension of the eastern end of this south side aisle exploration. The results were disappointing in that we did not find any seventh-century foundations similar to those under the north side aisle.

One of the more unexpected discoveries, in 1939, was the presence of two bases of the unfinished twelfth-century nave (D.4). These two distinctive portions of Suger's building exist under the south side-aisle wall of the present church. One of these bases may still be inspected under the removable paving stone next to the second thirteenth-century pier base. Two additional, identical bases were found under the south transept pavement (D.12). This confirms the fact that, before the thirteenth century, construction was started on a nave that would have joined the western and eastern ends of Suger's new church. The different design of the bases on the southern side compared with those found on the northern side remains one of the unsolved mysteries at Saint-Denis.

D.1. (*opposite*) **View along twelfth-century wall under south aisle pavement joining eighth-century to new, twelfth-century entrance bays.**

D.2. Southwest corner of eighth-century foundations of
Fulrad's church.

D.3. Eighth-century foundations at southwest corner of
Fulrad's church.

D.4. Twelfth-century pier base outside, to south, of twelfth-century junction wall under south side aisle pavement.

D.5. Eastern end of junction wall under south side aisle.

D.6. Western end of junction wall, as it meets foundations of twelfth-century western bays.

D.7. Undocumented plaster constructions under south side aisle.

D.8. Interior surface of eighth-century south side aisle wall uncovered in 1971.

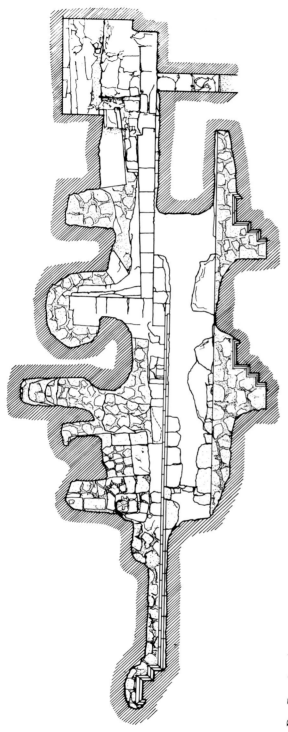

D.9. Drawing showing plan of south aisle excavation (west to east).

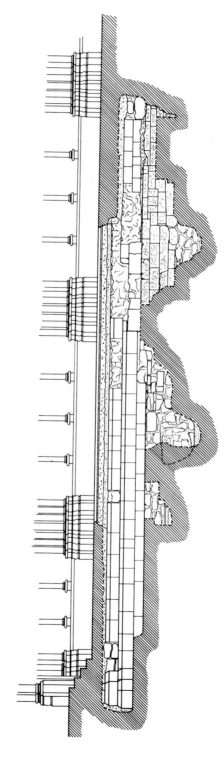

D.10. Elevation drawing of south aisle excavation shown in fig. D.9 (east to west).

329

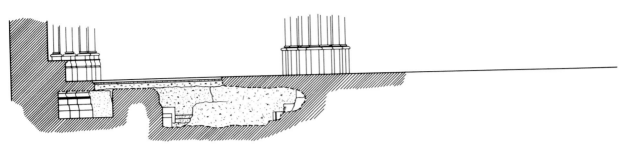

D.11. Elevation drawing of south aisle excavation showing twelfth-century plinth for Suger's nave (north to south).

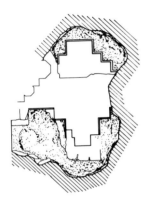

D.12. Drawing showing plan of south transept excavation, east of seventh south aisle wall pier from west. Drawing oriented with north at top of page.

APPENDIX E

Eastern Bays of Nave

After the summer excavations in 1948 my permissions were terminated, and I soon learned that I was persona non grata to Formigé. Since I have never seen his notes or records of the work he directed at Saint-Denis, especially in the late 1950s, I have no knowledge of the chronology of his excavations. This account of the excavations at Saint-Denis after 1948 is based, therefore, on my own post facto observations and conversations with such workmen as Jean Deschamps. The description continues in a west to east sequence but does not include restorations or changes made after 1977, when I last visited Saint-Denis.

Dug presumably by Formigé's workmen, in the hope of finding more decorated bases from the nave of Fulrad's church, two tunnels under the pavement of the north and south sides of the nave connected the excavations of the western bays of the nave with those under the crossing (E.1a,b). The excavations uncovered only one such base on the southern side of the nave. This large, badly damaged fragment could only be partially excavated because of its proximity to the thirteenth-century foundations for the present nave. The socles for the other eighth-century nave bases were found in place so that an accurate, if somewhat perplexing, reconstruction of the plan of the Carolingian nave can be proposed (pl. 2; album no. 2). The easternmost Carolingian base on the north side of the nave was found by Fleury, as he completed the excavation of the crossing. It can be partially seen today under the removable paving slabs to the southeast of the northwest crossing pier (fig. 31). The original foundations have been incorporated into the modern covering for the crossing.

In terms of the early buildings at Saint-Denis the most interesting discoveries under the crossing were the foundations of the two earliest churches—Sainte Geneviève's fifth-century chapel and King Dagobert's addition—as well as vestiges of the eighth-century annular crypt built for Fulrad's church. Resting directly on the solid clay subsoil, the foundations for Sainte Geneviève's early chapel are easily distinguished from any other foundation at Saint-Denis (E.2a,b, E.4a,b). Large light beige, sandstone blocks, a number of them with unusual incised designs, are aligned from east to west on the southern and northern sides under the crossing. Originally part of a Gallo-Roman temple, including the entablature, they were reemployed to support the light masonry walls of a simple rectangular chapel over the spot where Saint-Denis was believed to have been buried. Their east–west alignment and basic dimensions remained constant during the successive rebuildings of the church in later centuries. Added to by Dagobert in the seventh century, the chapel was completely rebuilt just after the middle of the eighth century by Abbot Fulrad, who began his new church by adding an annular crypt to the eastern end of the early chapel. The crypt was discovered by Viollet-le-Duc when he built the imperial crypt under the crossing, but unfortunately we have no complete records of exactly what remained in the nineteenth century. As explained in the text, the remains to be

seen in the crypt today are almost entirely the result of Formigé's reconstruction, with only portions of the eighth-century windows, including fragments of the mural decoration, incorporated into an often undocumented, arbitrary restoration. The desire to make the crypt an attractive, historically accurate adjunct to the guided tours of the royal monuments continued to preoccupy the attention of the official architect, Donzet, in charge of Saint-Denis. The other focal point of attention in the areas under the east bays of the nave and the crossing is the large Merovingian burial ground (E.3), which was first investigated by Viollet-le-Duc and is now under the supervision of Michel Fleury, Directeur des Antiquités historiques de Paris et Ile-de-France. The examination of these early burials has yielded an extensive collection of early medieval jewelry. If all of the early objects found by different excavators of Saint-Denis could be brought together, a truly significant, if not unique, exhibition of early medieval jewelry would result.

a

E.1. Tunnels under nave connecting western and eastern nave
excavations: (a) north side, looking west; (b) south side,
looking east.

b

a

E.2. Eastern ends of seventh-century foundations as they join foundations of fifth-century chapel: (a) north side (top half); (b) south side (bottom half).

b

E.3. North–south alignment of Merovingian sarcophagi across western end of Sainte Geneviève's chapel.

a

E.4. East–west alignment of remnants of Merovingian
foundations for Saint Geneviève's chapel: (a) north side; (b)
south side.

b

E.5. Plan. Nave bays 2, 3, and 4.

E.6. Plan. Eastern bay of nave and crossing, west to east.

337

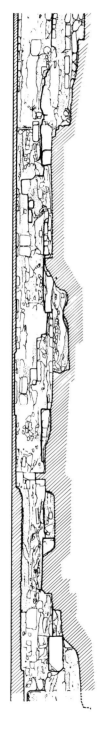

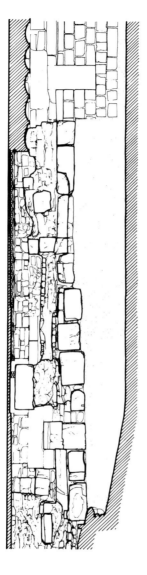

E.7. Elevation. North side, west to east. Nave bays 2, 3, and 4.

E.8. Elevation. North side, west to east. Eastern bay of nave and crossing.

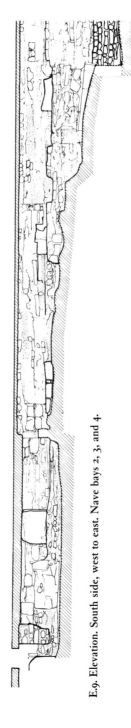

E.9. Elevation. South side, west to east. Nave bays 2, 3, and 4.

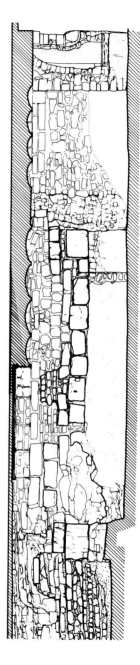

E.10. Elevation. South side, west to east. Eastern bay of nave and crossing.

APPENDIX F

North Transept

Trial excavations in the north transept in the open area south of the tomb of Louis XII and Anne de Bretagne and at the western end next to the iron grill were opened during the summer of 1947 (F.1). They uncovered a well-preserved Carolingian wall, plinths for attached twelfth-century bases, and fragments of an unfamiliar masonry that seemed to replace the eighth-century construction.

The Carolingian wall was completely excavated. It remains the best example of eighth-century masonry at Saint-Denis (F.4–6). Three superimposed sequences of massive libages provide a solid foundation, above which three beds of carefully finished, regularly cut stones 0.38 m by 0.18 m high exhibit an unexpectedly high quality of mid-eighth-century masonry. A distinguishing feature is the reddish mortar covering the relatively wide joints between the stones, which creates a polychromed appearance. Almost 10.00 m of this north exterior wall of Fulrad's building extends east–west before it disappears into or is cut by a different construction, a little

more than 6.00 m to the west of the transept. This masonry is distinct from any other at Saint-Denis.

In what was the corner between the north arm of the transept and the wall of the north side aisle of the eighth-century building there is a large pier, 2.10 m by 1.90 m (F.7, 8). Not only is such a pier unusual in this location but there are chips and cracks in the masonry which give the appearance of a damaged surface. When the excavation reached the solid clay subsoil, 2.60 m below the existing pavement, I also discovered that the pier rested on large libages identical to those of the Carolingian foundations. I realized then that the pier belonged to a structure that had replaced part of Fulrad's church. In addition to being a pier quite unlike any structural form in the Carolingian building, the stone is noticeably different. Described in geological terms as a beige-yellowish limestone of medium fine grain, without apparent microfossils, these stones can be distinguished, even by an untrained eye, from the whiter, fine-grained stones of Fulrad's church. As explained in chapter 3, the damaged pier and the adjacent masonry to the west, which also rests on Carolingian foundations, must have been built as the southern part of William the Conqueror's tower about 1080.

Less than a meter to the north of the alignment of the eighth- and eleventh-century masonry, this north transept excavation uncovered the foundations and three beds of finished masonry of the nave begun to connect the western entrance bays to the eastern chevet of Suger's church (F.11). In contrast to the south transept, where burials hindered the investigation of the twelfth-century foundations, the limited space between the early and later buildings on the north side evidently discouraged interment at any time so that we encountered only cramped quarters as we removed a relatively light fill down to the solid clay subsoil.

At first glance these twelfth-century foundations appeared to be as carelessly built as those under the west façade and entrance bays, but closer inspection showed that the seemingly rubble construction was more compact and solidly built than expected (F.12, 13). No signs of any movement could be detected. Although the irregular stones were of varying sizes—0.45 m by 0.30 m down to 0.20 m by 0.10 m—they were aligned vertically with the upper masonry, as were the foundations of the west façade. Although we had no opportunity to determine the width or thickness of these foundations, the wall they supported was 1.80 m thick with buttresses every 4.00 m that projected another 0.90 m to the north, so that the structure was intended to have been massive enough to support the new nave vaults. The top of the foundations is a series of long, flat stones ranging from 0.50 m to 1.00 m long and averaging a little more than 0.10 m thick, arranged to provide a flat, level surface for the finished masonry of the superstructure.

The first bed of these finished blocks is in striking contrast to the rubble foundations on which it rests. The stones, precisely 0.35 m high and from 0.40 m to 0.50 m wide with regular, continuous surfaces, show no evidence of exposure or use. My notes and photographs do not record any signs, such as masons' marks on the stones, and, because the nave was never built, there is no trace of any pavement.

The bottom edge of the stones lies 0.97 m below the surface of the existing pavement, so the top of this first bed would have been about 0.07 m above the eighth-century pavement. In these two western bays of the north transept, portions of five plinths for bases of the attached piers of the north aisle rise above the regular blocks of the first bed of finished twelfth-century masonry.

These large, trapezoidal plinths project 0.90 m from the twelfth-century side-aisle wall (F.11). They measure 2.20 m along that wall and 0.70 m across the southern face, which is 0.40 m above the first bed of finished masonry. The upper, or top, 0.12 m is a horizontal bevel, or chamfer, typical of the masonry of the western bays. Built of finished stones of varying dimensions, they have a rubble core. The easternmost plinth, which must have been intended as a juncture with the nonprojecting transept of Suger's church, is larger than those along the wall, but only the western side was discovered by the excavation. The eastern portion, as explained in the text, apparently was never finished. In this eastern bay, there are also two receding benches between the angular plinths; the first, or lower, one is 0.20 m high by 0.40 m wide and the second one is 0.15 m high by 0.30 m wide (F.13). The presence of these horizontal levels against the wall recalls the fact that the new cathedral of Sens was possibly started before Suger began his western bays and that the new eastern ambulatory, with similar receding levels or benches against the outside wall, may date from the later 1140s. It is difficult, nevertheless, to propose a specific date for the building of this northern side of Suger's nave, which contrasts so markedly with the southern side.

In the mid-1950s the extensive north transept excavation was covered with a reinforced concrete slab; the south transept excavation was covered with removable iron grills that provided access to iron ladders descending into the areas left open for future inspection and checking. Although much of my work has been severely criticized or completely misinterpreted by Formigé and by Edouard Bernard Salin, the chief architect, M. Donzet of the Monuments Historiques allowed me to make several small excavations. One of these extended, in 1969, the north transept discoveries to the west. Just outside the iron grill that closes off the transept, a few paving stones were removed with unexpectedly rewarding results. Under the western end, at a depth of 1.43 m under the existing pavement, a segment 1.30 m long of a roughly built wall, 0.65 m wide, was found just inside, or to the south, of the familiar large libages of the Carolingian foundations. Since this masonry closely resembled and was in direct alignment with foundations uncovered in 1947 under the north aisle 8.50 m to the west, I have identified it as part of Dagobert's seventh-century enlargement of Sainte Geneviève's fifth-century chapel.[1]

The eastern end of this same excavation disclosed even more unexpected results. Only 0.71 m under the existing paving, portions of the pavement of Fulrad's eighth-century church were found intact.

F.1. Overall view of north transept excavation from the triforium passageway. The monument to Louis XII and Anne de Bretagne is in the lower right corner.

F.2. Detail of west end of north transept excavation as it was being opened in 1946, showing carved capital as it was found embedded in thirteenth-century foundations.

F.3. Detail of carved capital found in thirteenth-century foundations as illustrated in fig. F.2.

F.4. Western end of north transept excavation showing
eighth-century exterior wall, with three levels of foundation
libages topped by three beds of finished masonry.

F.6. Detail of interior of eighth-century wall shown in figs.
F.4 and 5.

F.5. Detail of eighth-century exterior wall shown in fig. F.4.

F.7. Eastern end of north transept excavation, showing
unidentified tombs in eastern, or bottom, portions of
photograph and eleventh- and twelfth-century masonry to the
south, or left, of the monument to Louis XII.

F.8. Southeastern pier of eleventh-century tower, showing eleventh-century masonry under twelfth-century crossing pier in upper left portion of photograph.

F.9. Eleventh-century tower, south side, showing intermediate smaller pier and sequence of steps.

F.10. Southwest corner of eleventh-century tower.

F.11. Northeast end of the north transept excavation, showing eleventh-century masonry on right side of photograph and twelfth-century foundations under twelfth-century pier bases on left side.

F.12. Twelfth-century foundations under northeast end of north transept excavation.

F.13. Twelfth-century pier base partially covered by thirteenth-century pier on northern side of north transept excavation.

346

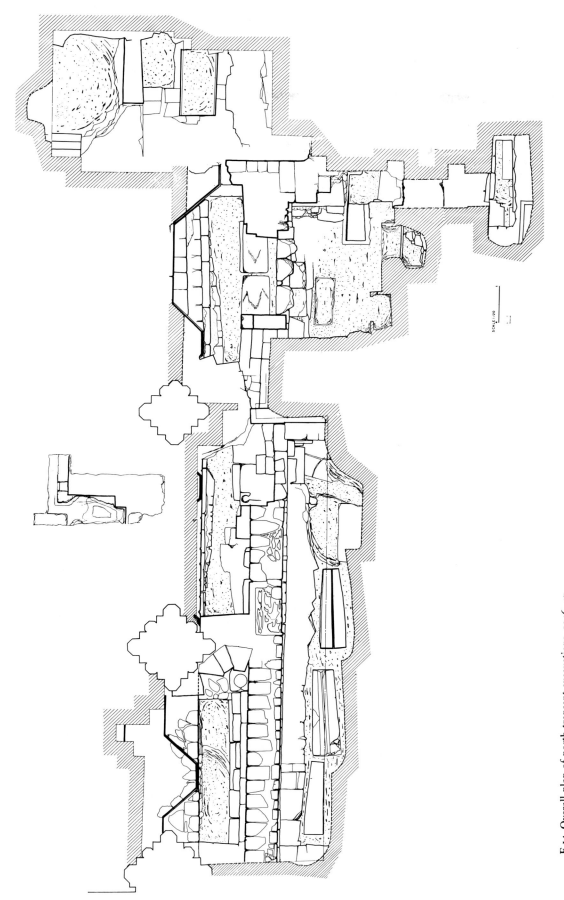

F.14. Overall plan of north transept excavations, 1946–47, west to east.

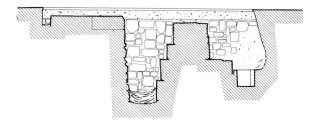

F.15. Elevation of western end of north transept excavation looking east.

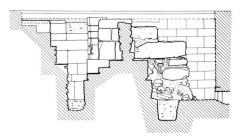

F.16. Elevation of eastern end of north transept excavation looking east.

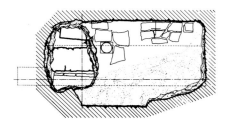

F.17. Plan of excavation in north aisle excavation of 1968, west to east, showing Carolingian pavement and unidentified base.

APPENDIX G

South Transept

During World War II all work at Saint-Denis obviously was suspended. The guardian at Saint-Denis appointed by the Monuments Historiques, M. Quatre-sous, having been badly wounded in the first war, remained *in situ,* and I was able to reestablish relations soon after arriving in Paris in September 1944. Permissions to excavate were granted during the spring of 1946, and we began work that June. Because of our discoveries under the south side aisle in 1939, I decided to begin in the south transept, where ultimately one of our most extensive and interesting excavations was opened (G.1). Not only eighth- and twelfth-century constructions were found, but also a number of undisturbed sarcophagi, one of which had an almost perfectly preserved carved bas-relief of the twelfth century as a cover (G.16c).

Work began auspiciously at the base of the transept pier just to the north of the monument of Francis I and Claude de France. As soon as the marble paving and its cement support had been removed (in the same manner as previously described), a well-preserved twelfth-century pier base, identical to the two found under the south side aisle and in direct alignment with them, came to light (G.2). This was proof that work on a new nave had been begun before the thirteenth century. Following the principle that early masonry, once uncovered, should be exposed as fully as possible, we removed the paving to the east of this initial opening. A twelfth-century wall continued the east–west alignment of the pier base. The inside, or north side, of this wall was covered by a loose earth fill, which we removed in order to explore the twelfth-century foundations, which projected out from the wall in a sort of bench. Much to our surprise and some consternation, we soon discovered that we were in the presence of a burial in the loose fill without any coffin or other protection. Several small, partially glazed clay vases with fragments of charcoal inside were found near the head and crossed feet. Although colleagues in Paris, including friends from the Monuments Historiques, were consulted, no instructions or suggestions about procedure were forthcoming. No one came to inspect the burial, so that after several weeks the bones were carefully put aside in order to proceed with the excavation. Subsequently, we found in the fill many similar vases containing charcoal, with holes pierced in their sides (G.14). Their shapes and glazes suggested to some pottery experts a probable date in the fourteenth or fifteenth centuries, or possibly even later. I had no experience or training in the proper treatment of burials and was disappointed not to be able to find someone who would be responsible as the excavation continued. Soon another burial was uncovered. This time it was a stone sarcophagus with a cross in low relief on the cover. Since no assistance or advice could be found, we decided to postpone further digging in this area and made no attempt to examine the foundations.

The twelfth-century wall, uncovered with the compound base as we opened this excavation, extended to the east, so we continued to remove the marble pavement of the transept. Only two meters from the base, the masonry became a conglomerate mass, but some of the finished surfaces continued to the south. As the area directly to the east of the monument to Francis I was uncovered, the outlines of a large construction began to appear. Soon it was evident that we were uncovering the embrasure, the left jamb, and two setbacks of an important portal as well as an adjacent wall buttress (G.3). The presence of a continuous horizontal bevel and the diagonal striations on the outer surfaces of the masonry identified the ensemble as twelfth-century construction. We realized we had found the south transept portal that opened from the church into the cloister. We did not realize at first that only the western embrasure of the portal existed.

As we uncovered and cleaned the masonry of this western embrasure, we found that the inner core differed from the outer, twelfth-century construction. In fact, it soon became apparent that the southwestern corner and the two setbacks of the portal had been built around, or added on to, the corner of another building (G.4). When the masonry, as it continued to the east, was followed across the transept arm, it stopped abruptly. It was cut through or

intercepted by a totally different foundation, which continued to the north and to the south under the massive piers of the eastern side of the existing transept (G.1, 5). At last I understood the sequence of the different masonries in this area. The east–west wall running across the transept must have been the termination of the south transept arm of Fulrad's eighth-century church. Confirmation that the east–west transept wall was an eighth-century construction was made when the interior, or northern, side of the wall was completely cleared. This disclosed, as foundations, a sequence of the massive libages typical of Carolingian building at Saint-Denis (G.6). In the late 1140s, when Suger's masons began to join the new eastern choir to the new entrance bays to the west, they built around the southwestern corner of Fulrad's transept. They left this standing in accordance with Suger's intention to "retain as much as we could of the old walls."[1] To enhance the new southern entrance to the cloisters, a trumeau was added against the Carolingian masonry (G.1, 7). Only the bottom of this trumeau remains *in situ,* but it is typical of Suger's interest in metalwork and in antiquity. A fragment of a marble column is enclosed in limestone in much the same manner as a piece of jewelry. As I studied the Carolingian masonry, preserved as part of Suger's south transept, I realized that only the western portions had been altered in the twelfth century. To the east of the trumeau, two beds of an eighth-century wall still existed (G.6), but to the west of the trumeau, this wall had been removed and two larger stones with a continuous horizontal bevel served as the sill for a new doorway (G.7). The well-worn surface of this sill proved that it had been heavily used. Unfortunately, as already mentioned, the eastern side of the early transept was either destroyed or included in the massive foundations for the thirteenth-century transept so that the reconstruction of the plan of Fulrad's Carolingian church remains incomplete, and there is no evidence of the precise nature of the twelfth-century work in this area.

Because of the unusual interest of this south transept excavation in terms of both the eighth- and twelfth-century buildings at Saint-Denis, every effort was made to make certain that all the remains of early building were uncovered. The excavation was extended to the west, although the solid substructure for the royal tombs limited our work to the continuation of the open space of the south side aisle (G.9, 10). Nothing was consequently recorded in the two southwestern bays of the transept. Under the aisle pavement to the west of the transept pier, where this excavation had been started, enough eighth-century masonry was found to ascertain that the southern wall of Fulrad's church had been continuous from the west to the transept. Enough space existed at the base of nave pier no. 6, where the transept joins the south aisle, to remove the marble pavement in the hope that the base of a twelfth-century pier might be discovered. Both the interior, or northern, side and the exterior buttress of such a pier was found, although the limited area that could be explored allowed only the upper portions of the base to be uncovered. This completed our search for structural remains under the south transept; however, one small opening was made thirty years later, just inside the iron grill, in an attempt to find additional Merovingian, seventh-century foundations. This trial hole was unsuccessful so that our reconstruction of Dagobert's enlargement of Sainte Geneviève's chapel remains incomplete.

This summary of our excavations in the south transept during the summer months of 1946 and 1947 would be incomplete without further mention of the quite unexpected discovery of a number of undisturbed burials. As I mentioned earlier, I have no experience in the proper handling or treatment of such burials, so that, whenever it was possible, we left them undisturbed. An example of how difficult it was to persuade a qualified person to come to Saint-Denis to remove an untouched burial occurred when the remains of a bishop, with his vestments intact, were found in the fill to the south of the portal which has just been described (G.15). The bishop was in a large but very plain plaster sarcophagus. Unfortunately, while the loose fill was being removed (so that the twelfth-century portal could be more properly examined) a crack appeared in the sarcophagus, which made it possible to see the interior. This also made it advisable to move the bishop to avoid damage to his remains. All the experts were

on vacation or involved in tasks some distance from Paris. Finally, an experienced archaeologist was found who would be in Paris over the weekend. Although his specialty was prehistoric caves, especially the skeletons of the large bears who had inhabited them, he agreed to see what he and two assistants could do. His only free day was Sunday, so that we found ourselves examining the bishop's remains in the excavation just over twenty meters away from the high altar where High Mass was being celebrated. That afternoon, after a metal sheet had been skillfully inserted under the bishop, everything was successfully removed to a secluded room in the crypt. The bishop's vestments had borders decorated with silver thread, which were almost perfectly preserved, as were his knitted gloves, still clasped around a wooden crozier. His well-preserved leather boots suggested the late thirteenth or early fourteenth century as a date for the burial. Officials agreed that everything should be done to preserve the vestments, but the last time I visited that room in the crypt only dust could be seen. *Sic transit gloria.* The next year my permissions were not renewed, and Jules Formigé assumed control of the excavations.

Other vestiges of burials were found in the fill, including the ends of two Merovingian plaster sarcophagi. One had incised decorations which included a Greek cross inscribed in a circular band, two smaller similar Greek crosses, and two series of three concentric circles with raised centers (G.11). The other fragment of undecorated plaster had the name Adalwinus crudely incised into the inner surface (G.12). When I last saw these fragments they were stored haphazardly in the Musée Lapidaire, over which I had no control. Just inside, or to the north of the south portal—1.20 m to be exact—a heavy stone sarcophagus was discovered resting on the solid clay at the bottom of the fill. The stone appeared to be granite with a crude Maltese cross carved in very low relief on the exterior head, or western end (G.13). The interior had not been disturbed. The deceased was wrapped in coarse, dark material with two cloth strips in the form of a cross on the outside of the face and shoulders. Diagonally across the torso was a rope which may, it was suggested, have secured the body to a wooden board when it was brought to Saint-Denis from another locality to be placed in the stone sarcophagus for final burial. Although these contents were thoroughly examined after I was excluded from the chantier, I never saw any report or heard any conclusions about the date of the burial, which was also true of other apparently untouched sarcophagi, whose presence and location I indicated to the workmen when I left.

The most surprising, completely unexpected discovery occurred early in June 1947.[2] A workman clearing the fill at the northern edge of the excavation uncovered a modest plaster sarcophagus sealed with a stone cover (G.16a). In spite of the location of the cover (only 0.25 m below the existing pavement), the burial appeared undisturbed. Further clearing revealed a most unusual feature—carving on both ends of the lid. When we had removed the fill around the sarcophagus, we could see that the undersurfaces also had decoration (G.16b). I then telephoned Marcel Aubert, Membre de l'Institut and Conservateur-en-Chef at the Louvre, and asked him

to be present the following day for the removal of the sarcophagus lid. When that moment came, none of us was prepared for the splendor of the carving which embellished the entire undersurface (G.16c).[3]

The twelve Apostles are shown under richly decorated arcades, with saints Peter, carrying large keys, and Paul in the center. Each Apostle is identified by his name, in raised relief letters, as though they were embossed in metal—a technique with which the artist was certainly familiar. Over eighty different patterns present a compendium of twelfth-century ornament. The unfinished condition of many details, especially on the right end, proves that the carving was never completed. Because so many details can be compared to the sculpture on the western portals and on the capitals of the crypt, I have suggested a date of the mid-1140s, but the authors of the Metropolitan Museum Catalogue concluded that the Apostle's relief was destined for the tomb of Abbot Suger, which tends to support a date of about 1150.[4]

G.1. Overall view from above of south transept excavation in 1947, west to east.

G.2. Twelfth-century pier base installed for Suger's new nave.

G.3. Western embrasure of unfinished twelfth-century south transept portal, showing two splayed setbacks between the door jamb (right) and the projection of a wall buttress (left).

G.4. Top surface of western embrasure of unfinished twelfth-century transept portal, showing eighth-century masonry in foreground surrounded by twelfth-century portal masonry.

G.5. Interior, or northern, side of twelfth-century transept terminal, taken from the northwest to show eighth-century libages as bottom beds of foundations.

G.6. Right, or east, side of twelfth-century south transept
doorway, showing part of twelfth-century trumeau with
chamfer and eighth-century wall masonry above eighth-
century libages.

355

G.7. Left, or west, side of south transept doorway, showing
eighth-century foundation libages under twelfth-century sill
and embrasure with chamfers.

G.8. Interior, or north, side of south transept excavation looking west, showing disrupted eighth- and twelfth-century foundations with cloth-covered twelfth-century plaster sarcophagus on right, formerly covered by the Apostle bas-relief.

G.9. Eighth-century foundations under south side aisle to west of south transept.

G.11. Decorated fragment of plaster sarcophagus possibly of the sixth or seventh century, found under eastern end of the northern side of the south transept excavation in 1947.

G.10. Interior, or north, side of eighth-century wall under eastern end of south side aisle.

G.13. Undated stone sarcophagus with two Maltese crosses.

G.12. Plaster end of a Merovingian sarcophagus possibly of the sixth or seventh century, with inscribed name Adalwinus, found in 1947 under eastern end, north side of the south transept excavation.

G.14. Partially broken terra-cotta pots found with charcoal inside accompanying burials, probably of the fourteenth or fifteenth century, under the pavement of the south transept.

G.15. Plaster and rubble unopened sarcophagus of a fourteenth- or fifteenth-century bishop found under the south side of the south transept.

a

b

G.16. Plaster sarcophagus with stone top found under
northern limits of excavation of south transept: (a) as found
on 4 June 1947; (b) details of carved decoration of stone cover
as seen before removal; (c) underside of stone cover after
removal from plaster sarcophagus, showing the twelve
Apostles under arcades.

c

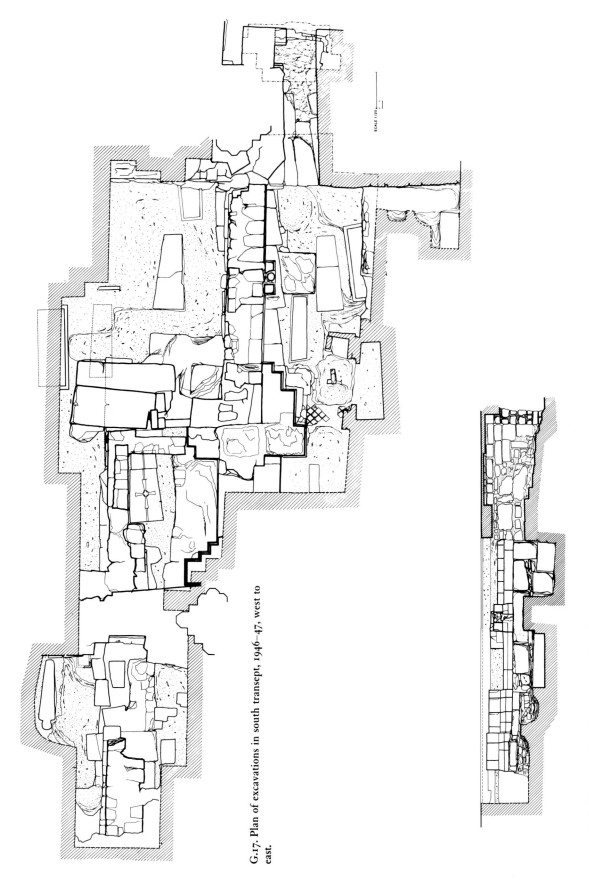

SCALE 1/20

G.17. Plan of excavations in south transept, 1946–47, west to east.

G.18. Elevation of south transept terminal, showing exterior eighth- and twelfth-century masonry.

APPENDIX H

Crypt

The excavations in the crypt ambulatory and central chamber, most of which were done in 1938 and 1939, have been described and analyzed with plans and elevations in my first volume. Since no new discoveries affecting those areas have come to light, I refer students to the pertinent pages, especially in chapter 8, with illustrations 47–65 and 74–85. On the other hand, the extensive work under the direction of Jules Formigé in the 1950s has never been properly analyzed. When I arrived in 1961 with the intention of completing my studies of the abbey church, I found that none of Formigé's explorations, beyond the material in his book, would be available to me. None of his plans or references to excavations had been deposited in the archives of the Monuments Historiques, so with the approval of the French authorities and with the assistance of students in the École des Beaux-Arts plans and elevations of the extensive work under the pavement of the crossing and eastern bays of the nave were prepared. Although I was not present as the excavations progressed nor was I able either to discuss the results with any one responsible or to study the results before they were prepared to be exhibited, I was allowed to record what is still available and to draw my own conclusions. As explained in the early chapters of this book, I believe that these particular excavations uncovered remains of the earliest buildings on this site, of Sainte Geneviève's fifth-century chapel, of Dagobert's seventh-century enlargement, and of Fulrad's completely new eighth-century church.

H.1. Interior of the eighth-century apse as restored by Formigé in the late 1950s with the "grande fosse," or supposed original burial place of Saint Denis and his companions, Rusticus and Eleutherius, in the foreground.

H.2. North side of eighth-century annular crypt as restored by Formigé. Formigé's reinstallation of the twelfth-century base from Suger's church can be seen on the extreme right.

H.3. South side of eighth-century annular crypt as restored by Formigé.

H.4. Detail of south side of eighth-century annular crypt, showing fragments of supposedly original wall painting.

H.5. Formigé's restoration of the eighth-century crypt in progress. Note that this is the north side but that no twelfth-century base can be seen. © Arch. Photo. Paris/s.p.a.d.e.m., **MH58.P.1059**/v.a.g.a., New York, **1986.**

H.6. Formigé's restoration of the south side of the eighth-century crypt. © Arch. Photo. Paris/s.p.a.d.e.m., **MH58.P.1056**/v.a.g.a., New York, **1986.**

H.7. Formigé's restoration of the south side of the eighth-century apse in progress. Note the change in the structure of the bottom foundations. © Arch. Photo. Paris/s.p.a.d.e.m., MH58.P.1055/v.a.g.a., New York, 1986.

H.8. Formigé's restoration of the north side of the eighth-century apse. Note the rough foundations. © Arch. Photo. Paris/s.p.a.d.e.m., MH58.P.1060/v.a.g.a., New York, 1986.

H.9. View through the eastern end of the eighth-century apse toward the ninth-century chapel. Note the foundations on both sides of the temporary passageway. © Arch. Photo. Paris/s.p.a.d.e.m., **MH58.P.1054**/v.a.g.a., New York, 1986.

H.10. Photo taken during Formigé's removal of Viollet-le-Duc's imperial crypt, looking to the northwest at the foundations of a thirteenth-century crossing pier. © Arch. Photo. Paris/s.p.a.d.e.m., **MH58.P.1058**/v.a.g.a., New York, 1986.

H.11. Detail of the north side of the eighth-century apse misinterpreted by Formigé as the remains of a stairway. Note the fragment of possibly original wall painting. © Arch. Photo. Paris/s.p.a.d.e.m., MH58.V.1656/v.a.g.a., New York, 1986.

H.12. Exterior of eighth-century apse, north side, showing eighth-century wall buttress.

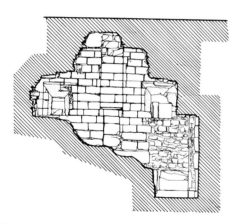

H.13. Measured drawing of elevation of the north side of the exterior of the eighth-century apse, showing windows opening on each side of the wall buttress.

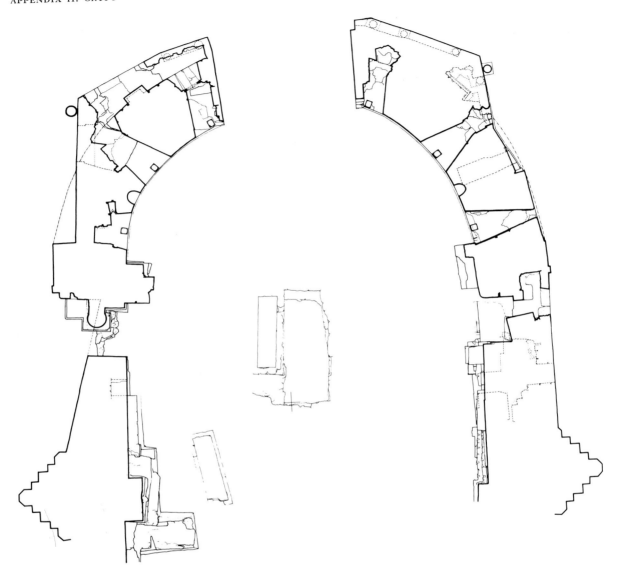

H.14. Plan of eighth-century apse.

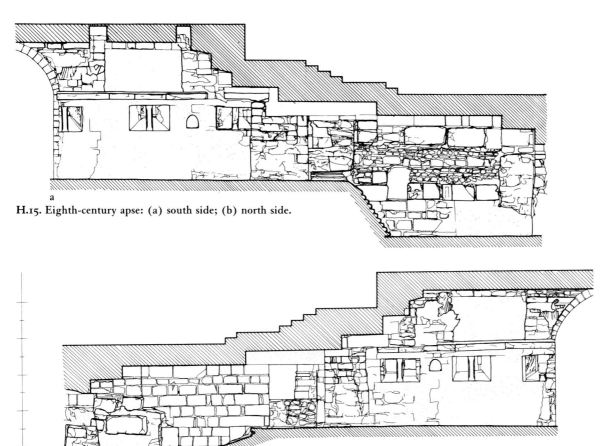

H.15. Eighth-century apse: (a) south side; (b) north side.

APPENDIX J

Chevet Structure

In contrast to the compact solidity of the enclosed spaces in the crypt, the choir presents a "complexity of overlapping forms which, however, in no way diminishes the clarity and simplicity of the whole."[1] As an aid to the analysis of the structural techniques and the proportions of these "Early Gothic" volumes, the statistics comparing the dimensions of the crypt and choir prove relevant.

Statistics, in my experience, are usually suspect, since dimensions, or other numerical data, used se-

lectively can fortify a particular thesis. Yet listings are necessary as a matter of record and, when treated as such, can be telling. The following comparative table of the details of the structure of the crypt and the upper ambulatory and radiating chapels of Saint-Denis emphasizes how different the two structures are, to the degree that it is difficult to realize that they were designed by the same master mason and built by the same workmen.

Comparative Table of Crypt and Choir Structural Details

	Crypt		Ambulatory	
Foundations	Rubble mat approximately 1.10 m thick		Masonry platform over vault approximately 0.50 m thick	
Cylindrical supports:	*Height*	*Width*	*Height*	*Width*
Base	0.31	0.94–1.06	0.65	0.96
Shaft to astragal	1.10	0.82	3.50	0.46 (top)–0.51 (bottom)
Capital	0.46	0.86–1.08	0.52	0.52–0.94
Abacus	0.18	1.00–1.06	0.28	0.94–1.10
Overall	2.05		4.95	

(The capitals of both the crypt and the choir include the astragal as well as the echinus between the carved portion of the capital and the abacus above.)

CHOIR VAULTS

	Ambulatory			Chapel		
	No. 3	*No. 5*	*No. 7*	*No. 3*	*No. 5*	*No. 7*
Diagonal ribs: Base	3.60–4.20	3.70–3.90	3.50–4.20	4.70–4.80	5.00–5.00	4.80–4.90
Keystone height above base		2.50			2.70	
Crown of vault		2.80			3.00	
Radius of diagonal arc		2.70			2.70	

Transverse Arches

	Ambulatory			Chapels		
	No. 3	*No. 5*	*No. 7*	*No. 3*	*No. 5*	*No. 7*
Base	2.56	2.58	2.66	1.60	2.28	1.64
Keystone height above base	1.92	1.90	1.98	1.78	1.88	1.90
Crown of vault	2.42	2.40	2.48	2.24	2.34	2.30
Radius to key	2.42	2.40	2.48		1.50	
Radius to vault		2.70			(above stilt, irregular)	

Lateral Arches

	Hemicycle	*Ambulatory*	*Chapels in crypt*
Base diameter	1.85 (1.90)	3.52	1.93 (2.34 axial)
Keystone height	1.90 (2.20 axial)	1.80	
Radius			

CRYPT VAULTS

Diagonal of Groins

	Ambulatory	*Chapel*
Base diameter	4.40–4.80	3.90 (4.40 axial)
Crown height above diameter of base	2.20	1.30

Transverse Arches

Base diameter	2.70
Keystone height	1.60
Crown of vault	1.90
Radius	1.35

Lateral Arches

	Hemicycle	*Ambulatory*	*Chapel windows*
Base diameter	2.00 (0.08)	3.20 (0.10)	1.70
Crown height	1.20 (0.14)	1.50 (0.20)	0.60
Radius			

Window Dimensions

	Width	*Height*
Crypt Chapels	1.86 (0.02)	2.30
Choir Chapels	1.30–1.50 (2.20 axial)	4.30

APPENDIX K

Capitals

The carved capitals that decorate the twelfth-century portions of Suger's church were almost entirely ignored by scholars of medieval art[1] in the belief that every detail of this type at Saint-Denis must have been completely recut in the nineteenth century. I include photographs of most of the seemingly limitless number of capitals that decorate the piers and columns or colonnettes flanking the exteriors and interiors of all openings such as doors and windows.

In the late 1950s, when Jules Formigé was in the process of "restoring" Saint-Denis, his workmen removed a thick covering of *badigeon,* or heavy whitewash, which had been applied early in the nineteenth century to all surfaces of the western bays, including the capitals of the piers.[2] To everyone's surprise, the capitals emerged in almost pristine condition and had escaped recutting or scraping, to present an unusually extensive series of capitals carved in the late 1130s. In order to begin this survey with original examples, I have placed these ground-level capitals of the western bays at the beginning of the series

(K.1–21), and followed them by a selection of those in the upper chapels of the fore-church (K.22–24). Until recently those chapels served as storage areas for old liturgical furniture or pieces of scenery for seasonal decorations used during Christmas or Easter. The architecture and its decoration were equally ignored. Many of the capitals have had to be completely replaced, usually by modern blank forms, but a sufficient number of original fragments remain to prove that the same effort and care were devoted to the building of these upper chapels as to other portions of the twelfth-century church.

After those two preliminary series, the capitals follow a more geographical order from west to east, beginning with three portals (K.25–33). Although they were cleaned by Debret's workmen in the 1830s, the capitals retain the original designs and, to a large extent, the sense of the carving. Our careful examination of the figurate sculpture of the portals proved that although many details were replaced or recarved in the eighteenth and nineteenth centuries, the original twelfth-century iconography was almost always followed.[3] This was also true of the capitals.

Above the portals, the west façade is divided by the prominent wall buttresses into three vertical sections, and three horizontal levels reflect the inner disposition of the vaults. These levels are marked by triple arches with colonnettes and capitals, which vary in the degree of their restoration. Of more than three dozen such capitals, I have chosen some twenty to represent the series, which includes quite a number of fanciful grotesques (K.32–33). The capitals flanking the windows on the north and south exteriors were seriously weathered, but a few demonstrate that they had the same type of ornament.

As for the crypt, which served as the foundation for the luminous choir at the eastern end of the church, the appendix of capitals includes only six examples of the large circular bands of foliate ornament surmounting the hemicycle piers in the crypt (K.34–38). As I first walked around these piers, I noticed that each band included a small, unrestored section of the carving. Presumably preserved by workmen under the direction of Viollet-le-Duc in the 1840s, this small section shows the condition of the original carving before it was restored. A student can observe the difference between the original worn, eroded surfaces and the recut, precisely carved decorations after restoration. The band capitals of the radiating chapels have all been thoroughly recut, which even the most unpracticed eye can perceive. Since I believe that these chapel decorations were treated in the same manner as the hemicycle piers, I have included photographs of almost the entire series as examples of twelfth-century design (K.39–95). They show the same search for constant variation that was apparent in the western capitals, although they must be regarded as nineteenth-century carving.

The capitals of the choir above the crypt, especially those above the ambulatory columns, are usually admired as outstanding examples of mid-twelfth-century carving. Because every detail of the carving is sharp and clear, I suspect some recutting, although this series certainly must be regarded among the most interesting examples of early Gothic decoration (K.96–105). The designs of the smaller capitals of each radiating chapel are much more varied, and they include grotesques and animal forms; I therefore represent them in spite of many obvious examples of later recarving (K.106–14). Finally, almost all the exterior capitals flanking the chapel windows were completely recarved in the 1830s, and many of them must have been replaced. I include a selection of their photographs to show variations on this type of ornament, many of which presumably repeat the original design (K.115–21).

In summary, this appendix offers more than a selection of the different series of capitals that ornament the twelfth-century portions of the abbey church at Saint-Denis. Intended primarily for students or specialists, the seemingly repetitious series of photographs demonstrates the almost inexhaustible inventiveness of these masons, who must have come from many different regions to create a coherent ensemble recognizably distinct from Romanesque prototypes but not as yet modeled after the forms of nature. Only a reasonably complete series can provide material for comparative studies. As such, I hope this appendix will prove to be more than a simple record of the achievements of Suger's craftsmen.

West Bays (K.1–24)

Hailed by Formigé after the western bays had been cleaned of the nineteenth-century heavy whitewash covering as "intact as though they had just been carved,"[4] these western capitals, carved soon after Suger had begun the building of his new church in the late 1130s, constitute an outstanding series of well-preserved Early Gothic decoration. After seven centuries of exposure, it is, indeed, remarkable that so many details remain intact and their surfaces apparently untouched.

Since these capitals are seen in the series of five or more surrounding each bay, I have arranged the photographs starting in the northwest corner of the northwest bay to follow from left to right so that all capitals are shown as though the observer were standing in the center of successive bays from north to south, the westernmost bays followed by those to the east before the beginning of the thirteenth-century nave. The schematic diagram (fig. 47) shows the numbering of piers of the western bays.

West Façade (K.25–33)

The capitals of the west façade are shown in two series: those on the embrasures of the three portals, where originally there were statue columns, and those flanking the windows and blind arcades of the upper portions of the façade. Although the two series must have been carved within a few years of each other, they are quite distinct. The capitals of the portals are larger and, since they could be seen at relatively close range, the details are more carefully executed. Treated as a continuing series of adjacent entities, their decoration, that is, the design of the capital itself, is continued onto the capitals of the adjoining smaller columnar surfaces, which were carved from the same blocks of stone. Of the fourteen capitals, six include animal or human heads and bodies reminiscent of the Romanesque world of forms. The capitals of the upper arches have been more severely weathered and often completely restored or replaced. Of the almost one hundred examples, fewer than twenty of the latter are illustrated. A section is included, at the end, to show a few of the remaining examples from the window openings of the northern and southern exterior sides of the west bays.

Crypt (K.34–95)

The large crypt under Suger's luminous choir has been so thoroughly restored and rebuilt that only the romantic enthusiast, thrilled by memories of the past, will be tempted to stay after the regular guided tour returns to the upper church, that is, unless the visitor is interested in the study of capitals. The large, circular capitals of the piers of the hemicycle around the eastern end of the old *caveau royal* have already

been discussed in this appendix, and the series of historiated capitals decorating the blind arcades around the central portions of the crypt are being studied by Pamela Z. Blum in a monograph in preparation.[5] There are also the purely decorative capitals of the radiating chapels around the ambulatory. Normally ignored by the medievalist as nineteenth-century decorations, this extensive series deserves, in my opinion, more than a passing glance. Certainly all of these capitals were thoroughly scraped, even recut, during the restorations of the first half of the nineteenth century, but, as proved by the hemicycle capitals, the original designs were carefully followed, so that the seemingly infinite variations of stylized vegetal ornament should be studied as examples of twelfth-century low-relief decoration. In this section, I illustrate the complete series, beginning on the north side in clockwise order, since only such a sequence can demonstrate the extent and degree of twelfth-century inventiveness.

Choir (K.96–114)

Twelve or more carefully carved capitals decorate each one of the radiating chapels that surrounds the ambulatory of the choir at Saint-Denis. Most of the capitals were cleaned, some quite thoroughly, in the first half of the nineteenth century, and most of them are half hidden in the shadows, so that little attention has been given to their often quite unusual decoration. Admittedly I have not examined these surfaces and do not, therefore, differentiate between the completely new, the partially recut, and the possibly old examples in this extensive series. Floodlights made possible the photographs which are presented in a selected series beginning at the western end on the northern side of the ambulatory. The series, or groups, of capitals are arranged from left to right, so that fig. K.96 is the right side of the first chapel on the north side of the ambulatory.

a

K.1a–d. Southeast face pier no. 1

b

c

d

a

K.2a–c. Northeast face pier no. 2

b

c

a

K.3a–c. Southwest face pier no. 5

b

c

a

K.4a–d. Northwest face pier no. 6

b

d

c

a

K.5a–c. Southeast face pier no. 2

b

c

a

K.6a–c. Northeast face pier no. 3
(See figure 55a for southwest face pier no. 6)

b

c

K.7. Northwest face pier no. 7

a

K.8a–c. Southwest face pier no. 7

b

c

a

K.9a–b. Southeast face pier no. 3

b

a   b

K.10a–b. Northwest face pier no. 8

K.11. Northeast face pier no. 4

K.12. Southeast corner pier no. 5

K.13a. Detail, north wall

K.13b. Detail, capital, north wall

K.14. Northwest face pier no. 10

a

K.15a–b. Northeast face pier no. 6
(See figures 58 a and b for southeast face pier no. 6
and northeast face pier no. 7)

b

K.16. Southwest face pier no. 10

K.17. Northwest face pier no. 11

K.18. Southeast face pier no. 7

K.19. Northeast face pier no. 8

K.20a. Southwest face pier no. 11 with *sondage* in vault

K.20b. South wall and *sondage* in pier no. 11, near lower capital

K.21. North wall and northwest face pier no. 12

K.22a. Central chapel, east, variations on water leaf design

K.22b. Southwest chapel, south side

K.22c. Northwest chapel, south side

K.22d. Northwest chapel, south side

K.23a. Center west chapel, south side

K.23b. Center west chapel, west side

K.23c. Northeast chapel, north side

K.24a. Southwest chapel, west side

K.24b. Northwest chapel, north side

K.24c. Center west chapel, south side

K.24d. Center east chapel, north side

K.24e. Center east chapel, south side

K.24f. Center east chapel, south side

a

K.25a–b. Central portal, details of abaci, left embrasure

b

c

K.25c–e. Central portal, details of abaci, right embrasure

d

e

K.26a. North portal, left embrasure, ensemble

K.26b. North portal, left embrasure, detail

K.27a. North portal, right embrasure, ensemble

K.27b. North portal, right embrasure, detail

K.27c. North portal, right embrasure, detail

K.28a. Central portal, left embrasure, ensemble

K.28b. Central portal, left embrasure, detail

K.28c. Central portal, left embrasure, detail

K.29a. Central portal, right embrasure, ensemble

K.29b. Central portal, right embrasure, detail

K.30a. South portal, left embrasure, ensemble

K.30b. South portal, left embrasure, detail

K.30c. South portal, left embrasure, detail

K.30d. South portal, left embrasure, detail

K.31a. South portal, right embrasure, ensemble

K.31b. South portal, right embrasure, detail

K.31c. South portal, right embrasure, detail

K.32a. Upper arcade, south side, south window

K.32b. Lower arcade, south side

K.32c. South side, middle arch

K.32d. South side, middle

K.32e. South side, second level

K32f. South side, middle window, second level

K.33a. South tower, south face, upper arcade

K.33b. South tower, east face, upper arcade

K.33c. South tower, north face, upper arcade

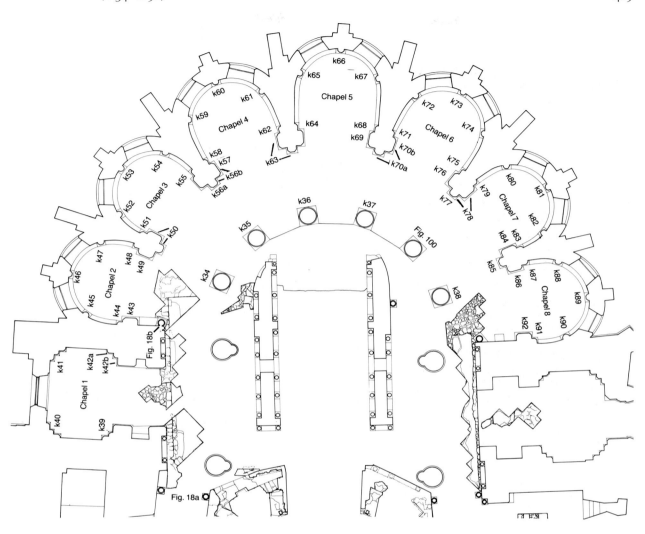

Diagram of the crypt showing the location of capitals K.34–92
in the ambulatory and radiating chapels.

K.34. Pier no. 1

K.35. Pier no. 2

K.36. Pier no. 3

K.37. Pier no. 4
   (See fig. 100 for pier no. 5)

K.38. Pier no. 6

Crypt chapel no. 1, north side (K.39–K.42)   K.39.   K.40.

K.41.   K.42a.

K.42b.

Crypt chapel no. 2 (K.43–K.49) K.43.

K.44.

K.45.

K.46.

K.47.

K.48.

K.49.

Crypt chapel no. 3 (K.50–K.56)　　　　　K.50.

K.51.

K.52.

K.53.

K.54.

K.55.

K.56a.

K.56b.

Crypt chapel no. 4 (K.57–K.63)

K.57.

K.58.

K.59.

K.60.

415

K.61.

K.62.

K.63.

Crypt chapel no. 5 (K.64–K.69) K.64.

K.65.

K.66.

K.67.

K.68.

K.69.

Crypt chapel no. 6 (K.70–K.77)   K.70a.   K.70b.

K.71.   K.72.

K.73.   K.74.

K.75.

K.76.

K.77.

K.79.

Crypt chapel no. 7 (K.78–K.85)   K.78.

K.80.

K.81.

K.82.

K.83.

K.84.

K.85.

Crypt chapel no. 8 (K.86–K.92) (see also fig. 109)   K.86.

K.87.

K.88.

K.89.

K.90.

K.91.

K.92.

K.93–95. Crypt chapels, Albert Alexandre Lenoir drawings,
Paris, *Bibliothéque des Arts Decoratifs,* Collection Maciet,
Donation André Lenoir, vol 48/11

93

94

95

(*Opposite*) Diagram of the chevet showing the location of the exterior capitals K.115a–121c and placement of interior capitals.

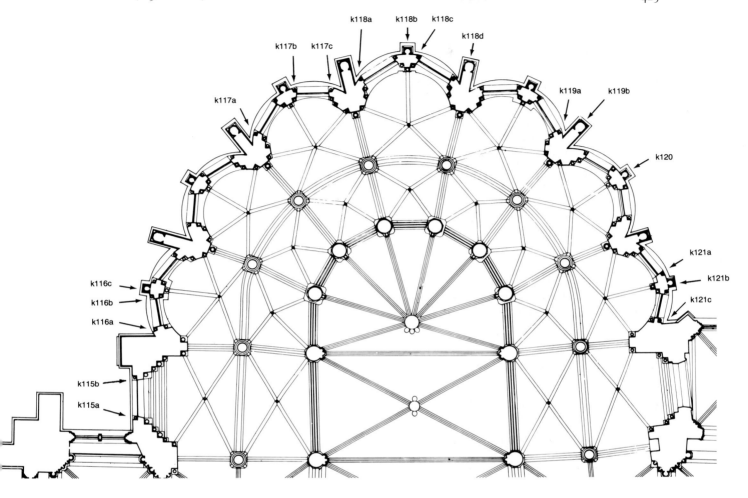

K.96. Capital no. 1

K.97. Capital no. 2

K.98. Capital no. 3

K.99. Capital no. 4

K.100. Capital no. 5

K.101. Capital no. 6

K.102. Capital no. 7

K.103. Capital no. 8

K.104. Capital no. 9

K.105. Capital no. 10

a

K.106a–c. Chapel no. 1

b

c

K.107a–c. Chapel no. 2

a

b

c

a

K.108a–c. Chapel no. 3

b

c

a

K.109a–b. Chapel no. 4

b

a

K.110a–b. Chapel no. 5

b

K.111a–b. Chapel no. 6

a

b

a

K.112a–c. Chapel no. 7

b

c

K.113a–e. Chapel no. 8

a

b

K.114a–c. Chapel no. 9

c

a

b

K.115a–b. Rectangular chapel, NW

a

b

K.116a–c. Radiating chapel no. 1

c

a

K.117a–c. Radiating chapel no. 3

b

c

a

b

K.118a–d. Radiating chapel no. 4 (axial chapel)

c

d

K.119a–b. Radiating chapel no. 5

K.120. Radiating chapel no. 6

a

b

K.121a–c. Radiating chapel no. 7

c

Profiles

Profiles of column bases have been considered reliable evidence for the dating of architectural ensembles. In the abbey church at Saint-Denis, rebuildings and restorations have made such architectural details questionable, but excavations and other investigations have made quite a number of original profiles available. In this appendix, I present a number of such details. Since the different parts of Suger's building are accurately dated and since the profiles vary widely, I show them only with mention of their specific location and approximate date.

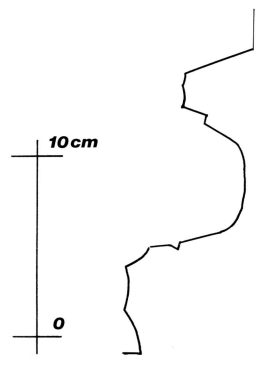

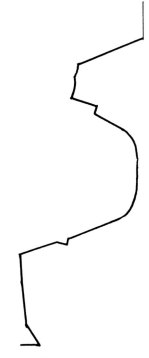

L.1. Western bays, excavated original twelfth-century base. (Pierre Rousseau)

L.2. Western bays, excavated original twelfth-century base. (Pierre Rousseau)

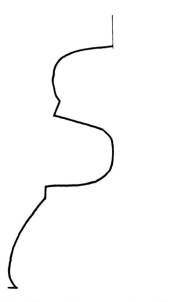

L.3. Western bays, center bay, tribune, west window. (Pierre Rousseau)

L.4. Western bays, center bay, tribune, west window. (Pierre Rousseau)

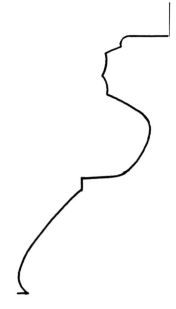

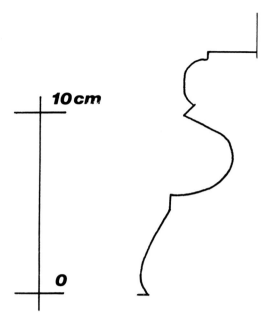

L.5. Western bays, upper story, northwest chapel, west window. (Pierre Rousseau)

L.6. Western bays, upper story, northeast chapel. (Pierre Rousseau)

L.7. Western bays, upper story, northeast chapel. (Pierre Rousseau)

L.9. Western bays, upper story, central chapel, window opening into southwest bay of south chapel, central colonnette.

L.10. Western bays, upper story, south chapel, west wall, right window, left colonnette.

L.8. Western bays, upper story, central chapel, window opening into northwest bay of north chapel, central colonnette.

L.11. Western bays, upper story, south chapel, west wall, left window, left colonnette.

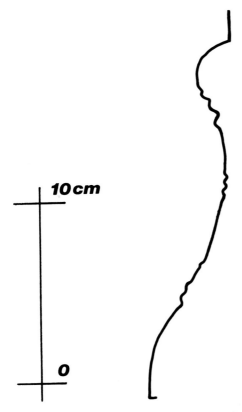

10 cm

0

L.12. Western façade, central portal, right embrasure, intercolonnette between third and fourth setback.

L.13. West façade, molding of plinth, central portal, right buttress.

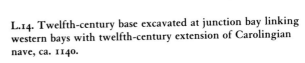

L.14. Twelfth-century base excavated at junction bay linking western bays with twelfth-century extension of Carolingian nave, ca. 1140.

446

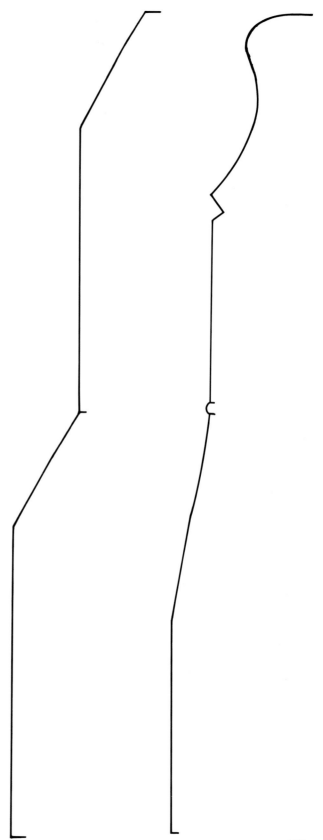

L.15. Twelfth-century base excavated by Formigé at northeast crossing, ca. 1144.

L.16. Profile of plinth, interior of northern exterior wall of first campaign linking the twelfth-century western bay with the Carolingian nave, ca. 1140.

L.17. Profile of socle and plinth of twelfth-century nave, southern exterior wall, second bay from west, second campaign, after 1144.

447

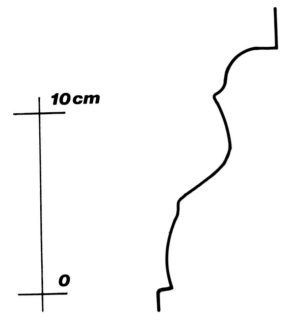

L.18. Crypt, south ambulatory, north arcade, second colonnette from west.

L.19. Crypt, south ambulatory, south arcade, second colonnette from west.

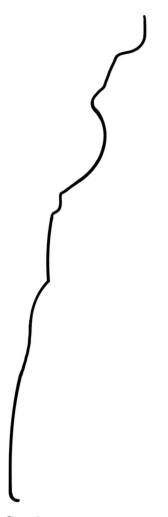

L.20. Crypt, *caveau central,* south arcade, second colonnette from west.

L.21. Crypt, base and plinth of first twelfth-century pier of ambulatory on north side.

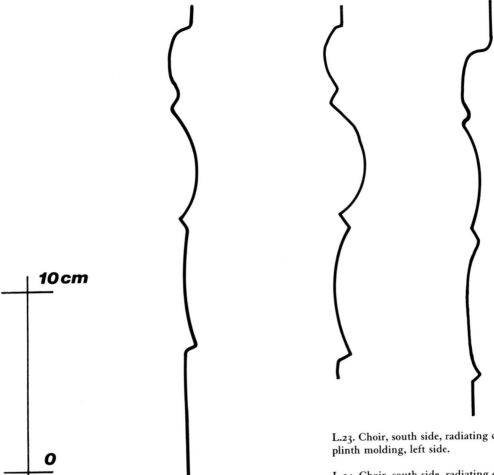

10 cm

0

L.22. Choir, south side, radiating chapel no. 5, continuous plinth molding, right side.

L.23. Choir, south side, radiating chapel no. 5, continuous plinth molding, left side.

L.24. Choir, south side, radiating chapel no. 6, continuous plinth molding.

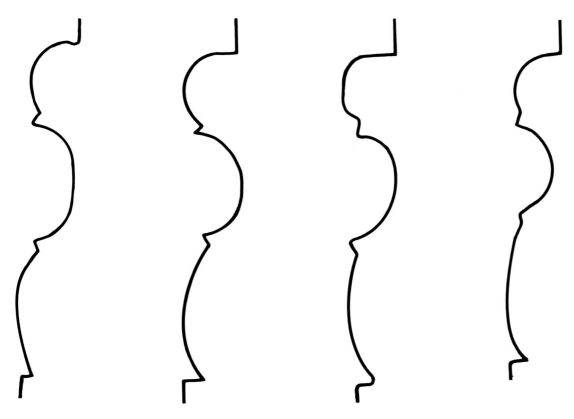

L.25. Choir, south side, radiating chapel no. 5, base of first colonnette, left side.

L.26. Choir, south side, radiating chapel no. 5, base of second colonnette from left.

L.27. Choir, south side, radiating chapel no. 6, base of first colonnette, left side.

L.28. Choir, south side, radiating chapel no. 7, base of first colonnette, right side.

L.29. Twelfth-century base excavated at junction of nave and western bays.

L.30. Western bays, section of continuous molding above plinth.

Notes

AUTHOR'S PREFACE

1. [**Ed. note:** Suger, *Libellus alter de Consecratione Ecclesiae Sancti Dionysii,* in Erwin Panofsky, ed. and trans., *Abbot Suger on the Abbey Church of St.-Denis and its Art Treasures,* 2d ed., ed. G. Panofsky-Soergel (Princeton, 1979), pp. 100–01.]

2. [**Ed. note:** "Façade défiguré, dépourvue à tout jamais d'intérêt historique et fort laide d'ailleurs." Adolphe Napoléon Didron, "Achèvement des restaurations de Saint-Denis," *Annales archéologiques* 5 (1846): 109.]

INTRODUCTION TO PART I

1. In order to differentiate between the saint, the abbey dedicated to him, and the suburb north of Paris in which the abbey is located, I shall refer to the saint as Saint Denis (without a hyphen), to the abbey as Saint-Denis (with a hyphen), and to the suburb as St.-Denis.

2. "Et quel aurait été son étonnement, s'il avait pu prévoir que sa personne ferait couler des flots d'encre, sans autre résultat que de compliquer et d'obscurcir son historie." "Saint Denis, premier evêque de Paris," *Vies des saints et des bienheureux selon l'ordre du calendrier avec l'historique des fêtes,* ed. Benedictines of Paris (Paris, 1952) 10:270 (hereafter cited as *Vies des saints*).

3. The Garnier-Flammarion 1967 paperback edition of *La Légende dorée* introduces a number of the saintly legends with comments on the meanings of the different names. The one on Saint Denis begins, "Denys veut dire qui fuit avec force. Il peut venir de *dyo,* deux, et de *nisus,* élévation, élevé en deux choses, savoir quant au corps et quant à l'âme. Ou bien il vient de Dyana, Vénus, déesse de la beauté; et *syos,* Dieu, beau devant Dieu. Selon d'autres il viendrait de *Dyonisia,* qui est, d'après Isidore, une pierre précieuse de couleur noire servant contre l'ivresse" Jacques de Voragine, *La Légende dorée,* 2d ed. and trans. J.-B. M. Roze (Paris, 1967) 2:272.

4. *La Légende dorée,* or "Golden Legend," mentioned in the previous note is the medieval compilation of the lives of all the saints, arranged according to calendrical order of their feast days. Written before 1264 by Jacobus de Voragine, or Varazze, later archbishop of Genoa, it has been published in a number of editions.

In addition to the translation by J.-B. M. Roze, originally published in Paris in 1900 and reprinted in 1967 with an introduction by Hervé Savon, there is another French translation by Téodor Wyzewa, *La Légende dorée,* 3 vols. (Paris, 1929) (for Saint Denis, see 3:674–82), and an English version, *The Golden Legend,* tr. Granger Ryan and Helmut Ripperger (New York, 1969).

The bibliography on the legend of Saint Denis is much too extensive to quote here. Among the more elaborate documents are: Abbé Eugène Bernard, *Les Origines de l'église de Paris. Etablissement du christianisme dans les Gaules. Saint Denys de Paris* (Paris, 1908); Abbé Valentin Dufour, "Les VII stations de Saint Denis," *Bulletin du Bouquiniste* 29 (1872): 211–19, 243–46 (hereafter cited as Dufour, *Bull. du Bouquiniste* 29); E.-M. Gaucher (pseud.), *Saint Denis, martyr, sa sainte vie, ses reliques, avec invocations; historique et courte description de la basilique; tombe célèbre; les funérailles royales (Louis XVI et Marie-Antoinette),* 1: *Saints patrons du diocèse de Paris* (Saint-Just-en-Chaussée, Oise, 1900); Léon Maître, "Le Culte de Saint Denis et de ses compagnons," *Revue de l'art chrétien* 51 (1908): 361–70; René Héron de Villefosse, *Histoire de Paris* (Paris, 1948), 6–8; Henri Moretus-Plantin, "Les Passions de Saint Denys," in *Mélanges offerts au R. P. Ferdinand Cavallera* (Toulouse, 1948), 215–30. See also Emile Nourry (Pierre Saintyves, pseud.), *En Marge de la Légende dorée* (Paris, 1931); Robert Boussuat, "Traditions populaires relatives au martyre et à la sépulture de saint Denis," *Le Moyen âge* 62 (1956):479–509; Gabrielle M. Spiegel, "The Cult of Saint Denis and Capetian Kingship," *Journal of Medieval History* 1 (1975):43–69, and Spiegel, *The Chronicle Tradition of Saint-Denis* (Brookline, Mass., 1978). For earlier sources for the legend of Saint Denis, see Hilduinus, *Areopagitica sive sancti Dionysii vita* and *Passio sanctissimi Dionysii,* in *Patrologia Latina, Cursus completus, Series secunda* 106, ed. J. P. Migne (Paris, 1851), cols. 14–50 (hereafter cited as Migne, ed., *P.L.*); and Jean Mabillon and Luc Achéry, eds., *Miracula* or *Vita S. Dionysii episc. Paris.,* in *Acta Sanctorum Ordinis S. Benedicti in saeculorum classes distributa* 3, pt. 2 (Venice, 1734), 311–29.

5. "But certain men adhering to him, did believe: among whom was also Dionysius, the Areopagite." (Acts 17 : 34). [**Ed. note:** All biblical quotations have been taken from the Douay edition of the Vulgate.]

6. "Moreover he mentions that Dionysius the Areopagite was converted by the Apostle Paul to the faith, according to the narrative in the Acts, and was the first to be appointed to the bishopric of the diocese of Athens," Eusebius, *The Ecclesiastical History* 4.23, trans. Kirsopp Lake (London, 1926), 1:379.

7. [**Ed. note:** Latin text, "De his vero beatus Dionisius Parisiorum episcopus, diversis pro Christi nomine adfectus poenis, praesentem vitam gladio imminente finivit."] *Gregorii episcopi Turonensis libri historiarum X,* 1, 30, ed. Bruno Krusch (hereafter cited as Gregory of Tours, *Historiae Francorum,* Krusch, ed.), *Monumenta Germaniae Historica* (hereafter cited as *M.G.H.*), *Scriptores rerum Merovingicarum* (hereafter cited as *Script. rer. Mer.*) (Hanover, 1951) 1, pt. 1:23; English translation, Gregory of Tours, *The History of the Franks* 1, xxviii, 2 vols., ed. and trans. O. M. Dalton (Oxford, 1927), 2:20. [**Ed. note:** For the Latin text, see also Grégoire de Tours, *Histoire des Francs, livres I–VI, texte du manuscrit de Corbie, Bibliothèque Nationale, ms. lat. 17655* Collection de textes pour servir à l'étude et à l'enseignement de l'histoire, ed. Henri Omont (Paris, 1886) 2:19–20 (hereafter cited as Grégoire, *Histoire des Francs,* Omont, ed.); and the

recent English translation, Gregory of Tours, *The History of the Franks,* trans. L. Thorpe (Harmondsworth, 1974), 87.] See also Godefroid Kurth, *Etudes franques,* 2 vols. (Paris, 1919), 2:117–206; and Elie Griffe, *La Gaule chrétienne à l'époque romaine* (Paris, 1947), 1:74–75, 90–91, 110.

8. The earliest list of the bishops of Paris to have survived is in a ninth-century sacramentary in the Bibliothèque Nationale, Paris (B.N. lat Ms. 2291, fol 6v); Louis Duchesne, *Les Fastes episcopaux de l'ancienne Gaule* (Paris, 1900), 2:460–61. See also Felix-G. de Pachtère, *Paris à l'époque gallo-romaine* (Paris, 1912), 122–23, 129; and Griffe, *Gaule chrétienne,* 1:64–66.

9. The first authentic record of Christians in Gaul is the letter sent from Lyons and Vienne to the churches of Asia and Phrygia, describing the Roman persecution in 177; Eusebius, *The Ecclesiastical History* 5.1, trans. Lake, 1:407–37. For a thorough discussion of these early Christian communities, see Griffe, *Gaule chrétienne,* 1:3–116.

10. Although most scholars today accept a mid-third-century date for the first Christian community in Paris, a recent comment questions the possibility: "il est certain que la date de 250 est beaucoup trop ancienne et on ne peut donc prendre à la lettre l'ensemble du recit [i.e., la mission de Saint Denis racontée par Grégoire de Tours]. . . . On peut en tous cas le [Saint Denis] considérer comme le premier missionaire, du moins comme l'organisateur de l'Église de Paris." Roger Aubert, "Denys (Saint), premier évêque de Paris," *Dictionnaire d'histoire et de géographie ecclésiastique,* 20 vols. (Paris, 1912–), 14:264 (hereafter cited as *D.H.G.E.*).

11. Some of the texts related to the early history of Saint-Denis, such as the *Gloriosae,* the *Vita Genovefae,* and two poems by Fortunatus, mention this Clementine tradition, evidence that the tradition was current as early as the sixth century. [Fortunatus], *Passio sanctorum martyrum Dionysii, Rustici et Eleutherii* [*Gloriosae*], ed. Krusch, *M.G.H., Auctorum Antiquissimorum* (Berlin, 1885) 4, pt. 2:101–05 (hereafter cited as Krusch, ed., *Gloriosae*); *Vita Genovefae virginis Parisiensis,* ed. Krusch and Ernst Dümmler, *M.G.H., Script. rer. Mer.* (Hanover, 1896) 3:204–38 (hereafter cited as Krusch, ed., *Vita Genovefae*); *Vita beate Genovefe virginis* 6, 15, ed. Charles Kohler, *Etude critique sur le texte de la vie latine de Sainte-Geneviève de Paris avec deux textes de cette vie,* Bibliothèque de l'Ecole des Hautes Etudes 48 (Paris, 1881) (hereafter cited as Kohler, ed., *Vita Genovefe*); Fortunatus, *De Basilica domni Dionysi, Carminum Epistolarum Expositionum, lib. 1,* 11; and [Fortunatus], *Carminum Spuriorum Appendix* 6, *M.G.H., Auct. Antiq.,* 4, pt. 1:13–14, 383–84. Such early confusion about the identity of Saint Denis seems reasonable since the *D.H.G.E.* lists sixteen martyrs or early bishops of that name, including Saint Denys, pope (258–68); Denys the Great, bishop of Alexandria (died 264); Denys of Corinth, first bishop of Athens; Saint Denys, bishop of Milan (355–62); Saint Denys, sixth bishop of Vienne (mid–fourth century). *D.H.G.E.,* 14:247–48, 248–53, 261–62, 263, 311. [**Ed. note:** See also *Passio sanctorum martyrum Dionysii Episcopi, Rustici, & Eleutherii qui passi sunt VII. [sic] Idus Octobris,* in Michel Félibien, *Histoire de*

l'abbaye royale de Saint-Denys en France (Paris, 1706), pièces justicatives: clxiii–clxv (published after a MS then in the chantry of Notre-Dame de Paris). For a discussion of the texts of the *Gloriosae* (earliest c. 475), see Moretus-Plantin, "Les Passions de Saint Denys," 215–30.] See also Elie Griffe, "Les Origines chrétiennes de la Gaule et les légendes Clémentines," *Bulletin de littérature ecclésiastique* 56 (1955): 3–22.

12. See *Vies des saints*, 10:263–67. The author of this excellent summary, with bibliography, noted that the choice of the name Dionysius the Areopagite by the mystical author of the late fifth or early sixth century was probably deliberate because of his concern with the "Unknown God." See also René Roques, "Denys le Pseudo-Aréopagite 1, L'État de la question," *D.H.G.E.*, 14:265–75. In addition to the *Celestial Hierarchy*, the writings of the Pseudo-Areopagite include *On Divine Names*, *Mystical Theology*, the *Ecclesiastical Hierarchy*, and eight letters. There are also supposedly apocryphal works on geometry, orthography, grammar, etc. See n. 15 below. [**Ed. note:** See inter alia, Maurice de Gandillac, ed. and trans., *Oeuvres complétes du Pseudo-Denys, l'aréopagite* (Paris, 1943).]

13. There is no mention anywhere of the Pseudo-Areopagite's writings during the first five centuries; but their authority went unchallenged at a later Lateran synod in 649. *Vies des saints*, 10:264.

14. The author's familiarity with the decisions of the Council of Chalcedon in 451 and the unmistakable influence of the Neoplatonists, especially of Proclus, who died in 487, preclude a date before the late fifth century. Most scholars now accept a date of about 510. See Roques, *D.H.G.E.*, 14:266–75.

A recent opinion stated that the author of these writings "not only concealed his identity very effectually from posterity, but also ensured for his writings, for more than a thousand years, a respect and an authority which they would certainly not otherwise have acquired, and in consequence, through a misapprehension without parallel in either sacred or profane literature, much of his teaching has become embedded in the theological tradition of the West." David Knowles, *The Evolution of Medieval Thought* (New York, 1962), 56.

15. The writings of the Pseudo-Areopagite are mentioned by Gregory the Great in 593; by Pope Martin I at the Lateran synod in 649; by Pope Agathon in 680; by Bede in his *Expositio in Marcum* between 710 and 720: Roques et al., *D.H.G.E.*, 14:265–310. A gift of "libros" from Pope Paul I to Pepin the Short between 758 and 763 included "Dionisii Ariopagitis geometricam, orthografiam, grammaticam, omnes Greco eloquio scriptas," *Codex Carolinus*, ed. Wilhelm Gundlach and E. Dümmler, *M.G.H., Epistolarum* 3, *Merowingici et Karolini aevi* (Berlin, 1892), 1:529; see also Léon Levillain, "Etudes sur l'abbaye de Saint-Denis à l'époque mérovingienne 1, Les Sources narratives," *Bibliothèque de l'Ecole des Chartes* 82 (1921): 29–30 (hereafter cited as *Bib. de l'Ec. des Ch.*).

16. King Louis the Pious requested Abbot Hilduin to write the *Historia sancti Dionysii*, also referred to as the *Post beatam ac salutiferam*, after its opening words, or more popularly as the

Areopagitica, Migne, ed., *P.L.*, 106:9–50; *Epistola ad Hilduinum, Epistolae variorum inde a morte Caroli Magni usque ad divisionem imperii* 20 (ann. c. 835), ed. E. Dümmler, *M.G.H., Epistolarum* 5, *Karolini aevi* (Berlin, 1899), 3:327–35.

17. Although Hilduin's *Historia sancti Dionysii* was the first official proclamation that Saint Denis, bishop of Paris, was the Pseudo-Areopagite, the identification had been made several years earlier when Greek ambassadors first came to the French court in 824 to persuade Louis the Pious to influence Pope Eugenius II in favor of a compromise with respect to the famous iconoclastic controversy. The first meeting was in Rouen in the fall of 824, and the identification was further recognized at a council in Paris in the early spring of 825. On their return to Constantinople, the ambassadors (among whom was Thodore, the grand Econome), announced "la découverte sensationnelle que Denys, l'illustre Aréopagite converti par S. Paul, était mort et reposait auprès des lointains Barbares d'Occident." See Raymond J. Loenertz, "La Légende de S. Denys l'Aréopagite. Sa genèse et son premier temoin," *Analecta Bollandiana* 69 (1951): 234.

In 1120, when Abelard was a monk at Saint-Denis (after his castration), he had the temerity to question this identification. He announced to the monks, on the authority of the venerable Bede, that the original Greek Dionysius was Denis of Corinth in the second century, rather than the first bishop of Athens, disciple of Paul, in the first century. This so infuriated Abbot Adam of Saint-Denis that Abelard had to take refuge with Count Thibaut of Champagne. Félibien, *Histoire*, 147–48.

18. Duchesne dated the *Martyrologium S. Hieronymi* between 592 and 600. He suggested that it was written at Auxerre: Louis Duchesne, "A propos du *Martyrologe Hiéronymien*," *Analecta Bollandiana* 17 (1898): 441–446. Bruno Krusch dated it between 627 and 628 and identified its origin at Luxeuil: Krusch, "Zum Martyrologium Hieronymianum," *Neues Archiv der Gesellschaft für altere deutsche Geschichtskunde* 20 (1895): 437–40; Krusch, "Zur Afralegende und zum Martyrologium Hieronymianum," ibid., 24 (1899): 289–337; Krusch, "Nochmals das Martyrologium Hieronymianum," ibid., 26 (1901): 349–89. See also Levillain, *Bib. de l'Ec. des Ch.* 82 (1921): 15–16.

No mention of the two companions occurs in the writings of Gregory of Tours, Fortunatus, or Fredegarius, in the *Vita Genovefae*, or in the five earliest royal charters. They appear in a charter of Clovis II and its confirmation by Theodoric IV, in 724, and by Pepin the Short, in 768; but they did not become an integral part of the legend until after 774. Julien Pierre Eugène Havet, *Questions mérovingiennes, Oeuvres de Julien Havet* (Paris, 1896), 1:221–25; Pachtère, *Paris à l'époque gallo-romaine*, 177, app. 3; Henri Leclercq, "Abbaye de Saint-Denis," in Fernand Cabrol and H. Leclercq, *Dictionnaire d'archéologie chrétienne et de liturgie*, 15 vols. (Paris, 1913–53) 4, 1: cols. 590–91; Levillain, *Bib. de l'Ec. des Ch.* 82 (1921): 14–19, 22.

To my knowledge there was no early commentary on possible interpretations of the name Eleutherius as being associated with the Greek concept of freedom or of Rusticus as being simple or

19. See Jules Formigé, "Communication sur les travaux récents de la basilique de Saint-Denis. Séance de 3 avril 1957," Institut de France, *Académie des Beaux-Arts* (Paris, 1957): 82 [**Ed. note:** Also Jules Formigé, "Comptes rendus des dernières découvertes dans la basilique de Saint-Denis," *Bulletin de la Société Nationale des Antiquaires de France* (1957):75–76]; and Jules Formigé, *L'Abbaye royale de Saint-Denis* (Paris, 1960), 2.

20. Léon Levillain has emphasized that the presence of the two companions is significant proof that the original text of the *Gloriosae* must have been written late in the fifth or early in the sixth century, when a preoccupation with the demonstration of the verity of the Trinity was important in the struggle against Arian heretics. The three saints were still regarded as symbolic of the Trinity in the ninth century, as indicated by the formula *a Patre Filioque* in the confession of the saints in unison according to the *Post beatam et gloriosam*—a formula introduced into the Nicean Creed in the eighth century in connection with reforms of the liturgy. See Levillain, *Bib. de l'Ec. des Ch.* 82 (1921): 15, 18–19.

21. Hincmar, later archbishop of Reims, wrote the *Inventio* and the first two books of the *Miracula* while he was a monk at Saint-Denis. The text has been judged purely imaginative and allegorical with no historical value. See Levillain, *Bib. de l'Ec. des Ch.* 82 (1921): 58–71. [**Ed. note:** *Miracula sancti Dionysii*, in *Acta Sanctorum Ordinis Benedicti*, ed. Jean Mabillon, *saeculum* 3, pt. 2 (Paris, 1772), 343–64.]

22. "Qui olim (ut perhibent) Mons-Martis, nunc felici mutatione Mons-Martyrum dicitur." (Mabillon, ed., *Miracula* or *Vita s. Dionysii* 2, 38, *Acta Sanct. Ord. Ben.*, saec. 3, pt. 2, p. 325); "Quorum memoranda et gloriosissima passio e regione urbis Parisiorum in colle qui antea mons Mercurii . . . nunc vero mons Martyrum vocatur": Hilduinus, *Passio sanctissimi Dionysii* 36, Migne, ed., *P.L.,* 106:50. It should be noted that Fredegarius, in the seventh century, referred to it as "in monte Mercore," *Chronicarum quae dicuntur Fredegarii Scholastici libri IV cum Continuationibus* 4, 55 (ann. 627), ed. Krusch, *M.G.H., Script. rer. Mer.* (Hanover, 1888), 2:148 (hereafter cited as Krusch, ed., *Chronica Fredegarii*); and that as late as the end of the ninth century the historian Abbon, in his account of the siege of Paris by the Norman invaders, consistently referred to it as Mons Martis. Abbon, *Le Siège de Paris par les Normands,* verses 196, 326, 334, ed. H. Waquet (Paris, 1942), 2:80, 90.

23. The church of Saint-Pierre is a twelfth-century building, heavily restored at the end of the nineteenth century. Documents of the ninth and tenth centuries mention earlier churches, and the presence of seventh-century marble capitals as well as early plaster sarcophagi proves that the church and the cemetery date from Merovingian times. See Francois Deshoulières, "L'Eglise Saint-Pierre de Montmartre," *Bulletin monumental* 77 (1913): 5–30 (hereafter cited as *Bull. mon.*); Michel Roblin, *Le Terroir de Paris aux époques gallo-romaine et franque* (Paris, 1951), 208–10 (hereafter cited as Roblin, *Terroir*); and more recently Denise Fossard, "Montmartre, l'église Saint-Pierre, anciennement

Saint-Denis," in May Vieillard-Troïekouroff, Denise Fossard, et al., "Les Anciennes églises suburbaines de Paris (IVème–Xème siècles)," *Paris et Ile-de-France, mémoires publiés par la Fédération des Sociétés Historiques et Archéologiques de Paris et de l'Ile-de-France* 11 (1960): 217–25 (hereafter cited as Vieillard-Troïekouroff et al., "Les Anciennes églises suburbaines").

24. Fossard, in Vieillard-Troïekouroff et al., "Les Anciennes églises suburbaines," 221–25.

25. "Quanta veneratione et amore dilexit Catulacensem vicum, in quo sanctus Dionisius et passus est et sepultus." Krusch, ed., *Vita Genovefae,* 17:221. "In loco qui dicitur Cadolago," "Testament de l'Abbé Fulrad" (ann. 777), in Félibien, *Histoire,* pièces justicatives LVI, p. xxxviii. For the possibility that Catulliacum was originally a Roman villa, see Roblin, *Terroir,* 64.

Another perplexing, if subordinate, question which continues to plague scholars in regard to Montmartre is the discrepancy in the distances, presumably between Paris or Montmartre, and St.-Denis, as recorded in the early texts. The factors in the problem are that the *Passio sancti Dionysii* by Hilduin states that Saint Denis walked two Roman miles (*per duo*) from the place of execution to the place of burial [**Ed. note:** Migne, ed., *P.L.,* 106:47]. The *Vita Genovefae* says that he was executed "in quarto [milario] ab eadem urbem" or four Roman miles from the city (Paris). [**Ed. note:** Krusch, ed., *Vita Genovefae,* 17:221.] The *Gloriosae* identifies the place of execution simply as "in sexto ab urbe memorato lapide" [**Ed. note:** Krusch, ed., *Gloriosae,* 104]; and finally, the old high altar in the abbey church had, as one of its four supports, an adaptation of an original Roman *borne milliare* (milestone) with the inscription "M.P. VIIII," or nine Roman miles. The ensuing arithmetic becomes amusingly complicated and ultimately inconclusive. Count Blaise de Montesquiou-Fezensac ingeniously proposed that the inscription on the altar support, namely, nine Roman miles, must have been taken from an original *borne* in the vicinity of St.-Denis and that, regarded more or less as a sacred relic, it was used as part of the altar. The "in sexto lapide" of the oldest of the texts—the *Gloriosae*—should be interpreted as six Gallic *lieues* [leagues] rather than as Roman miles, and six Gallic *lieues* were the equivalent of nine Roman miles, that is, the same as the *borne*. When the place of execution was situated on Montmartre, an adjustment had to be made, which is recorded in the "in quarto ab urbem" of the *Vita Genovefae,* the earliest extant version of which was done in the late eighth century. This *in quarto,* or four, plus the "in duo," or two miles of the *cephalophorie* equals the "in sexto" of the *Gloriosae:* Blaise de Montesquiou-Fezensac, "'In sexto lapide,' l'ancien autel de Saint-Denis et son inscription," *Cahiers archéologiques* 7 (1954): 51–60. A further observation notes that the "M.P. VIIII" on the Roman *borne* would be the equivalent of 13 kilometers 300 meters, so that Roman measurements from Paris may have originated in the Roman forum on the Mont-Sainte-Geneviève. Paul-Marie Duval, *Paris antique des origines au troisième siècle* (Paris, 1961), 242.

26. Anatole de Barthélémy, review of Charles Kohler, *Vita beatae genovefe virginis: Etude critique sur le texte de la Vie latine de*

Sainte Geneviève, in *Bulletin du comité d'histoire et d'archéologie du diocèse de Paris* 1 (Paris, 1883), 98; Julien Havet, "Questions mérovingiennes V, Les Origines de Saint-Denis," *Bib. de l'Ec. des Ch.* 51 (1890): 22–29; Cabrol et Leclercq, *Dictionnaire,* 4, 1:592, n. 14; Adrien Blanchet and A. Dieudonné, *Manuel de numismatique Française* (Paris, 1912), 1:208, 274. "Le droit de tenir un marché, d'y avoir une monnaie spéciale, et d'en percevoir les revenues sont liés ensemble dans la plupart des cas," Paul Huvelin, *Essai historique sur le droit des marchés et des foires* (Paris, 1897), 163–64.

27. A special study of the miracle lists 134 saints who achieved this miracle, Nourry, *En Marge de la Légende dorée,* 240–41. See also William M. Hinkle, *The Portal of the Saints of Reims Cathedral: A Study in Medieval Iconography* (New York, 1965), 14–16.

28. Levillain has suggested that the early text of the *Gloriosae* changed what had been an appearance, that is, trembling lips ("lingua palpitans") that confessed God, into an actual event. Levillain, *Bib. de l'Ec. des Ch.* 82 (1921): 49. For other possible interpretations, see Hervé Savon, "Introduction," ed. Roze, *La Légende dorée,* 1:10–11.

29. For a full account of this dispute, see H.-François Delaborde, "Le Procès du chef de Saint Denis en 1410," *Mémoires de la Société de l'Histoire de Paris et de l'Ile-de-France* 11 (Paris, 1884) [1885]: 297–409. A mid-thirteenth-century variant concerning Saint Denis' loss of his cranium appears in the Chronicle of Phillip of Mouskes. In this account Saint Denis curiously enough is credited with the conversion and baptism of Clovis's wife, Clothilde. This act so enraged Clovis that he sawed off the saint's cranium. Unconcerned, Saint Denis replaced his cranium and continued the conversion, to the king's amazement: *Chronique rimée de Philippe de Mouskes,* 2 vols., ed. Baron de Reiffenberg, Collection des chroniques belges (Brussels, 1836–38), 1:18. See Hinkle, *Portal of the Saints,* 41.

30. The six stations in Paris were Notre-Dame-des-Champs (today on the sites of houses at 13 and 15 rue Pierre-Nicole), where the saint supposedly first met with his converts; Saint-Etienne des Grès (on the site of the Ecole du Droit, rue Cujas), supposedly his first cathedral; Saint-Serge et Saint-Bacchus (on the site of the Sorbonne, rue Saint-Jacques), where the Trinity was first invoked; Saint-Denis-du-Pas (behind Notre-Dame on the Ile-de-la-Cité), where his tortures began; Saint-Denis de la Chartre (on the site of the Palais de Justice), where he was imprisoned; and the Martyrium on the slopes of Montmartre, where Hilduin says he was martyred. The seventh day of the Octave, 9–16 of October, was celebrated in the basilica at St.-Denis. See Dufour, *Bull. du Bouquiniste* 29: passim; Vieillard-Troïekouroff et al., "Les Anciennes églises suburbaines," 74–78, 79–84 (for Saint-Benoît le Bétourné, formerly Saint-Serge et Saint-Bacchus), 85–89 (for Saint-Etienne des Grès, formerly Saint-Etienne), 211–17 (for the Martyrium on Montmartre). See also the *Vies des Saints,* 10:270–88. The authors noted that the feast of Saint Denis is a double rite, first class with an octave. *Vies des Saints,* 10:285.

[**Ed. note:** In addition, see Fernand Cabrol, "Octave," in *The Catholic Encyclopedia* 11 (New York, 1911): 204, where octaves for saints are documented in the eighth century and Easter and Christmas octaves by the fourth.]

31. In the sixth century a chapel was dedicated to Saint Denis in Bordeaux. In 775 Charlemagne confirmed the abbey's possessions in Italy: Charter of 14 March 775, ed. Engelbert Mühlbacher, *M.G.H., Diplomatum Karolinorum* 1 (Hanover, 1906), 135 (hereafter cited as *Diplomata Kar.*). Abbot Fulrad left many important domains to the abbey in northeastern France and the Rhineland: Michael Tangl, "Das Testament Fulrads von Saint-Denis," *Neues Archiv* 32 (1907): 167–217. In 790, Offa, king of Mercia, confirmed Saint-Denis' possessions in England: "Charte d'Offa Roy des Merciens" (ann. 790), in Félibien, *Histoire,* pièces justicatives, LXII: xlii–xliii; and William Henry Stevenson, "The Old English Charters to St. Denis," *English Historical Review* 6 (1891): 736–42.

32. Since the very early history of Paris and its environs must remain obscure, historians will continue to favor one theory, rather than another, in regard to the first Christian communities. The most objective study of the whole problem, in my opinion, is the detailed work of Michel Roblin, based on careful research into the origins of the different names of geographical localities. He concluded that there was no reason not to accept that the separation of the oldest roads, leading north from Paris, after having crossed the small river Croult necessarily led to the establishment of a "bourgade commerciale," similar to all the others in the *civitas* at river crossings. *Catulliacus* he identified as "un simple villa romaine," near which the martyrdom of Saint Denis took place. Since there are indications that there were Christian burials in the neighboring cemetery during the third and fourth centuries, it would be unreasonable to believe that a Christian community did not exist there before Sainte Geneviève in the fifth century. Roblin, *Terroir,* 206–08. For a more traditional summary, see Jacques Dubois, "L'Emplacement des premiers sanctuaires de Paris," *Journal des Savants* 153 (1968): 40–41. See also the brief assertive summary in Alain Erlande-Brandenburg, *Le Roi est mort, Etude sur les funérailles, les sépultures et les tombeaux des rois de France jusqu'à la fin du XIIIème siècle* (Geneva, 1975), 68.

33. Vauban, the renowned seventeenth-century military engineer, chose this same site for his great "couronne du Nord," designed to provide exactly the same protection for Paris.

34. [**Ed. note:** "Nam terribilem esse et metuendum locus ejus nemini ambigendum est." Kohler, ed., *Vita Genovefe,* 6, 15:20.]

35. Vieillard-Troïekouroff et al., "Les Anciennes églises suburbaines," 165–88. See also Eugen Ewig, "Résidence et capitale pendant le haut Moyen Age," *Revue historique* 230 (1963): 25–72.

36. Vieillard-Troïekouroff et al., "Les Anciennes églises suburbaines," 89–114.

37. The following sites around Paris are identified by Roblin, *Terroir:* to the west, Reuil (p. 257); to the south, Palaiseau (p. 291) and Bouneuil (p. 310); to the east, Chelles (p. 222) and Nogent (p. 219); to the north, Conflans (pp. 199–200), Cormeilles (p. 200), Bezons (pp. 202–04), Chatou (p. 203), Saint-Denis (pp. 206–08), Epinay (pp. 207–08), Clichy (pp. 210–12),

Nigeon (p. 214), and Luzarches (pp. 249–50). Note that almost two-thirds were north of the city.

38. Vieillard-Troïekouroff et al., "Les Anciennes églises suburbaines," 48–50, 52.

39. Gregorius episcopus Turonensis, *Liber in Gloria martyrum* 71, *Gregorii episcopi Turonensis libri octo Miraculorum,* ed. Krusch, *M.G.H., Script. rer. Mer.* (Hanover, 1885), 1:535–36.

40. For a more detailed description of the tomb, see below pp. 26, 36.

41. *Gesta Dagoberti I. Regis Francorum* 2, 4, 7–11, ed. Krusch, *M.G.H., Script. rer. Mer.* 2, 401–04.

42. Three other national saints—Saint Rémi, Saint Martin, and Sainte Geneviève—did not enjoy the special prestige of Saint Denis. Saint Rémi, the "Apostle of the Franks," was the saint of the coronation of kings; but his shrine at Reims was under the control of the counts of Champagne, who, though vassals of the king of France, often contested his authority. Saint Martin, sometimes called the patron saint of France, was venerated at Tours, which was equally distant from the center of Merovingian and Carolingian authority. Sainte Geneviève, the patron saint of Paris, although extremely popular, as a woman could hardly have been accepted as a patron of the Salian Franks. See Sumner McKnight Crosby, *The Abbey of St.-Denis, 475–1122* (New Haven, 1942), 48 (hereafter cited as Crosby, 1942). See also Hinkle, *Portal of the Saints,* especially 23–43.

43. In 386 Ambrogio, bishop of Milan, recognized saints Gervais and Protais as the *patroni* of his church. See Cabrol and Leclercq, *Dictionnaire,* 13, 2:2514–15.

44. Numa Denis Fustel de Coulanges, *Les Origines du système féodal, le bénéfice et le patronat pendant l'époque mérovingienne. Histoire des institutions politiques de l'ancienne France* 5 (Paris, 1890), 205–52.

45. Original papyrus, Paris, Archives Nationales, K1, no. 7, in Philippe Lauer and Charles Samaran, *Les Diplômes originaux des Mérovingiennes, Fac-similés phototypiques avec notices et transcriptions* (Paris, 1908), 4 and pl. 1; Cabrol and Leclercq, *Dictionnaire,* 4, 1:624–25.

46. Seven out of twelve Merovingian kings after Clotaire II used the formula, which appears in twenty-two out of thirty charters I have examined.

47. One exception was Philip I (1060–1108), who called Saint-Rémi his patron. The formula disappeared from royal charters when the chancellery was reorganized after the battle of Fretteville in 1194, when Philip Augustus lost his official records. From then on the title of the abbey in royal charters became *beati Dionysii in Francia,* or *Saint Denys en France.*

48. "Tanquam duci & protectori suo": "Charte du Roy Louis VI" (ann. 1120), in Félibien, *Histoire,* pièces justicatives CXXIII: xciii.

49. For the origin and meaning of *ad sanctos,* see Bernhard Kötting, *Der frühchristliche Reliquienkult und die Bestattung im Kirchengebäude* (Cologne, 1965), 24–28.

50. "Quem cum maximo merore deducentes a villa Brinnaco Parisius, ad basilicam sancti Dionisi sepelire mandaver-

unt," Gregory of Tours, *Historiae Francorum,* Krusch, ed., 240; Dalton, ed., *Gregory of Tours* 2:206.

51. Edouard Salin, "Les Tombes gallo-romaines et mérovingiennes de la basilique de Saint-Denis (fouilles de janvier-février, 1957)," *Mémoires de l'Institut Nationale de France, Académie des Inscriptions et Belles-Lettres* 44 (1960): 192.

52. "Dagobert, mort à Saint-Denis en 629, y fut enterré, et Saint-Denis devint, aux depens de Saint-Germain-des-Prés, le lieu de sépulture des Mérovingiens." Vieillard-Troïekouroff et al., "Les Anciennes églises suburbaines," 91, n. 4.

53. After Clovis II the location of the Merovingian royal tombs varied or is not recorded. Clotaire III was buried at Chelles and Theodoric III at Saint-Vaast. The location of the tombs of the other "rois fainéants" is uncertain.

54. The Carolingian royal burials at Saint-Denis include Charles Martel (mayor of the palace), Pepin the Short, his son Carloman, Charles the Bald, and two of the sons of Louis II, but not Charlemagne or Louis the Pious.

55. Suger wrote that Philip had been heard to say that he chose not to be buried at Saint-Denis because he had not been attentive to the abbey and that, among the tombs of so many noble kings, his would attract little notice. See Suger, *Vita Ludovici Grossi Regis* 12, ed. Lecoy de la Marche, *Oeuvres complètes de Suger* (Paris, 1867), pp. 46–47 (hereafter cited as Lecoy de la Marche, ed., *Oeuvres*); *Vie de Louis le Gros* 13, ed. and trans. Henry Waquet (Paris, 1929), pp. 84–85 (hereafter cited as Waquet, ed., *Vie de Louis*). Erlande-Brandenburg has attempted to explain some of the "multiple reasons" for Philip I's choice of Saint-Benoît-sur-Loire, *Le Roi est mort,* 75–76.

56. "Saint-Denis, qui était à l'époque mérovingienne le dépôt où se conservaient les actes royaux," Arthur Giry, *Manuel de diplomatique* (Paris, 1884), 2:483.

57. See Joseph Bédier, "L'Abbaye de Saint-Denis et les chansons de geste," in *Les Légendes épiques,* 3d ed. (Paris, 1929), 4:122–75. [**Ed. note:** See also Spiegel, *The Chronicle Tradition,* passim.]

58. "Tante opes ab eodem et villas et possessiones multas per plurema loca ibique sunt colate, ut miraretur a plurimis," Krusch, ed., *Chronica Fredegarii* 4, 79:161. The identification of Dagobert's gifts of land to Saint-Denis is impossible today, especially because his renown inspired numerous later forgeries. The list of such possessions compiled by Jacques Doublet, *Histoire de l'Abbaye de S. Denys en France* (Paris, 1625), 173, is legendary. See Crosby, 1942, 58, n. 26.

59. The tradition was still so firmly entrenched in 1926 that the thirteenth centenary of the founding of the abbey was celebrated at Saint-Denis. Only the serious protest of Paul Lesourd in the *Figaro* of 5 October 1926 prevented the installation in the abbey church of a commemorative plaque to Dagobert as founder. See Levillain, "Etudes sur l'abbaye de Saint-Denis à l'époque mérovingienne IV, Les Documents d'histoire économique (suite)," *Bib. de l'Ec. des Ch.* 91 (1930): 9, n. 2.

60. For a thorough study of the founding of this fair and of its importance, see Levillain, ibid., 7–65.

61. As early as the eighth century, Anglo-Saxon and Flemish

merchants attended the fair: "De illa festivitate sancti Dionisii in idipso pago Parisiaco de omnes necuciantes, tam Saxsones quam Frisiones vel alias naciones promiscuas, de quascumque pagos vel provincias ad festivitate sancti Dionisii martyris, tam in ipso marcado quam et in ipsa civitate Parisius." Charter of Pepin the Short, 8 July 753, ed. Mühlbacher, *M.G.H., Diplomata Kar.* 1, 6, p. 9. In the twelfth century the fair lasted for seven weeks from 9 October to 30 November. A reminiscence of the fair may still be visited in the famous "flea market" at the Porte de Clignan-court on the plain of Saint-Denis. The Fair of Saint-Mathias may date from the end of the ninth century, but it is probably later. The famous Foire du Lendit was, according to medieval tradi-tion, founded by Charles the Bald, but Levillain doubted this. See Levillain, "Essai sur les origines du Lendit," *Revue historique* 155 (1927): 241–76.

When Dagobert founded the fair, he also, presumably, estab-lished a *monetarius,* or coin maker, with the right to mark his coins with his name. This explains the coins made by Ebregisilus at *Catolaco* (see above, n. 26). Originally the revenue belonged to the royal fisc; but when all rights to the fair were given to the abbey by Theodoric III, Ebregisilus marked the coins *Sci Di-onysii.* The presence of a monogram on these last coins corrobo-rates the late seventh-century date, for the monogram belonged to Chardiricus and Chaino, abbots of Saint-Denis from 672 to 706. See Huvelin, *Essai historique,* 164; and Levillain, *Bib. de l'Ec. des Ch.* 91 (1930): 59.

62. This charter gave exemption from all duties, such as "pontaticus, portaticus, pulviraticus, rodacus, salulaticus, cispetaticus," and any other "redibicio," and covered not only boats on any French river and carts on any road, but also all beasts and even men carrying goods of the abbey or merchants acting for the monks. It applied to any place where taxes were levied, such as "civitates, castella, vici, portus, pontes publici," and "reliqui marcadi," or any market. See Levillain, ibid., 264–76.

63. Levillain has made a thorough study of this *privilegium,* "Etudes sur l'abbaye de Saint-Denis à l'époque mérovingienne III, *Privilegium* et *Immunitates* ou Saint-Denis dans l'église et dans l'état," *Bib. de l'Ec. des Ch.* 87 (1926): 21–53. Until the middle of the seventh century the basilica of Saint-Denis was completely under the jurisdiction of the bishop of Paris. It could own prop-erty, but its management depended on the bishop. The charter of Landri freed Saint-Denis and its possessions forever from this episcopal domination. The abbot and monks of Saint-Denis were given complete control over the administration of the ab-bey as well as of its property. No church officer could interfere with or even enter the abbey without their permission. The bishop, however, did reserve certain rights, the *jura pontificalia,* which included the consecration of churches and altars; the blessing of the Holy Sacrament; and the ordination of members of the congregation as well as of the abbot, who was freely elected by the monks. Thus, although the abbey was independent, it was not exempt from a certain supervision by the bishop of Paris. The monks of Saint-Denis had to wait until the eighth century to

receive a spiritual independence that was equal to their temporal freedom.

64. Once an individual, or an institution, received a charter of immunity from the king, his property assumed the status of the royal fisc. Judicial rights over the inhabitants, collections of all public revenues, freedom from the rights of officials to hold courts or to seize witnesses, to levy taxes or to exercise the rights of the *gîte,* or procuration, not only gave the *immuniste* a highly privileged position, but made it possible for him to escape the majority of the burdens of feudal society. The attribution to Queen Bathilde of the according of immunity to Saint-Denis and the relevant documents are exhaustively examined by Levillain, *Bib. de l'Ec. des Ch.* 87 (1926): 53–97.

65. Félibien, *Histoire,* 92–111.

66. For an account of the rivalry in regard to the coronations, see Hinkle, *Portal of the Saints,* 26–30.

67. Percy Ernst Schramm and Florentine Mütherich, *Denk-male der deutschen Könige und Kaiser. Ein Beitrag zur Herr-schergeschichte von Karl dem Grossen bis Friedrich II, 768–1250* (Munich, 1962), 33–40.

68. Text of the original charter of Louis VI reprinted in Félibien, *Histoire,* pièces justicatives CXXIII: xcii–xciii.

69. See ibid., pièces justicatives CLXXVII:cxxv, and Hinkle, *Portal of the saints,* 36.

70. Félibien, *Histoire,* 536, 538, 540, 542, 544, pls. I–V.

71. The derivation of "Monjoie" from the Latin "meum gaudium" or "Mons Gaudii" has various interpretations. Fol-lowing the popular theory held by DuCange and Joseph Bédier, "Mons Gaudii," a holy hill, was sometimes located in Rome, sometimes in Jerusalem, or better still in Paris, where the refer-ence was obviously to Montmartre. See "Mons Gaudii," in Charles DuFresne DuCange, *Glossarium mediae et infimae Latinitatis* (Graz, 1954), 4:510–11; and Bédier, *Les Légendes épiques,* 2:237–52. More recently Laura Loomis has pointed out that the "Monjoie" of the *Chanson de Roland* referred to Char-lemagne's renowned sword, "joyeuse": "It held in its pommel the tip of the Passion Lance," which opened Paradise to misera-ble mortals. Laura Hibbard Loomis, "The Oriflamme of France and the War-Cry 'Monjoie' in the Twelfth Century," in *Studies in Art and Literature for Belle da Costa Greene,* ed. Dorothy Miner (Princeton, 1954), 76.

72. [**Ed. note:** For this paraphrase, see Loomis, "The Ori-flamme of France," p. 67; for the complete version:

Then they mounted up, they clamor for battle,
They shout "Monjoie" and Charles is with them.
Geoffrey of Anjou carries the oriflamme:
It once belonged to Saint Peter and its name was "Romaine,"
But it had taken the new name Monjoie there.

(Gerard J. Brault, ed. and trans., *The Song of Roland. An Analyt-ical Edition* (University Park, Pa., 1978), 2:189, verse 225, lines 3091–95.)]

73. See Robert Barroux, "L'Abbé Suger et la vassalité du Vexin en 1124. La Levée de l'oriflamme, la Chronique du

pseudo-Turpin et la fausse donation de Charlemagne à Saint-Denis de 813," *Le Moyen age* 64 (1958): 7–8. Two passages in Suger's writings and an original charter signed by Louis VI in 1124 describe the county of the Vexin, a buffer zone between Normandy and the Ile-de-France, as a fief of the abbey. Suger, *Vita Ludovici Grossi* 27, Lecoy de la Marche, ed., *Oeuvres*, 116 [**Ed. note:** See also below, n. 75]; Waquet, ed., *Vie de Louis* 28, p. 221; Suger, *De Administratione* 4, Lecoy de la Marche, ed., *Oeuvres*, 161–62 [**Ed. note:** Vilcassini siquidem, quod est inter Isaram et Ettam, nobilem comitatum, quem perhibent immunitates ecclesiae proprium beati Dionysii feodum]; and for the Charter of Louis VI dated after 3 August 1124, Félibien, *Histoire*, pièces justicatives I, CXXIV: xciii; and Achille Luchaire, *Louis VI le Gros. Annales de sa vie et de sa règne* (Paris, 1890), 160, no. 348.

74. [**Ed. note:** "Et quoniam beatum Dionysium specialem patronum et singularem post Deum regni protectorem.] Suger, *Vita Ludovici Grossi* 27, Lecoy de la Marche, ed., *Oeuvres*, 115; Waquet, ed., *Vie de Louis* 28, p. 220.

75. [**Ed. note:** "Rex autem vexillum ab altari suscipiens quod de comitatu Vilcassini, quo ad ecclesiam feodatus est, spectat, votive tanquam a domino suo suscipiens, pauca manu contra hostes, ut sibi provideat, evolat; ut eum tota Francia sequatur potenter invitat." Suger, *Vita Ludovici Grossi* 27, Lecoy de la Marche, ed., *Oeuvres*, 116; Waquet, ed., *Vie de Louis* 28, p. 220.]

76. [**Ed. note:** "Quo facto nostrorum modernitate, nec mutorum temporum antiquitate, nihil clarius Franci fecit, aut potentiae suae gloriam, viribus membrorum suorum adunatis, gloriosius propalavit, quam cum uno eodemque termino de imperatore romano et rege anglico, licet abens, triumphavit."] Suger, *Vita Ludovici Grossi* 27, Lecoy de la Marche, ed., *Oeuvres*, 121; Waquet, ed., *Vie de Louis* 28, p. 230.

77. See Loomis, "The Oriflamme of France," 73.

78. Ibid., 72.

79. Ibid. In the south transept of Chartres a window in the clerestory depicts Jean Clément du Mez, marshall of France in 1225, receiving the banner from the hands of Saint Denis. The banner is red, not golden. For a good color reproduction, see Louis Grodecki, *Chartres*, trans. Katharine Dalavenay (New York, 1963), 69.

CHAPTER 1. SAINTE GENEVIÈVE'S CHAPEL

1. Clovis I was the first Frankish chieftain to establish his control over such other early barbarian nations as the Burgundians (in 500) and the Visigoths (in 507). Clovis's grandfather Merovée defeated Attila the Hun in 451; consequently the first dynasty of the French (Frankish) nation is known as Merovingian. See Ernest Lavisse, *Histoire de France* (Paris, 1903), 2:94–95; Charles William Prévité-Orton, *The Shorter Cambridge Medieval History* (Cambridge, 1952), 1:150–51.

2. "Antedicta tamen materfamilias [Catala], horum non immemor secretorum, cum primum persecutionis vidit tepuisse fervorem, locum sanctorum ossa martyrum servantem, qua

oportuit sollicitudine requisivit; atque inventum eminentis mausolei constructione signavit. Unde postmodum Christiani basilicam supra martyrum corpora magno sumptu cultuque eximio construxerunt." *Passio Sancti Dionysii* [*Gloriosae*], 11, ed. François Arbellot, in Arbellot, *Etude sur les origines chrétiennes de la Gaule. Première partie: Saint Denys de Paris* (Paris, 1880), 107–08. Vincent Davin, *Les Actes de Saint Denys de Paris, Etude historique et critique* (Paris, 1897), 10. The presence of such a Constantinian church at St.-Denis was taken for granted by Jules Formigé, who even published a plan of it, Formigé, *Abbaye royale*, 4–5, fig. 3.

3. Vieillard-Troïekouroff et al., "Les Anciennes églises suburbaines," 226–29.

4. See Gregory of Tours, *Historiae Francorum* 5, 32, and 34, ed. Krusch, *M.G.H., Script. rer. Mer.* 1, pt. 1:237, 240–41; idem, ed. Dalton, *Gregory of Tours* 2:203, 206; idem, *Liber in Gloria martyrum* 71, ed. Krusch, ibid., pt. 2:535–56; and Fortunatus, *De basilica domni Dionysi, Carminum Epistularum Expositionum*, lib. 1, 11 and [Fortunatus], *Carminum Spuriorum Appendix* VI, *M.G.H., Auct. Antiq.* 4, pt. 1:13–14, 383–84. [**Ed. note:** See also below, n. 8.]

5. See introduction, n. 34, for Latin text, Kohler, ed., *Vita Genovefe*, 6, 15:20. [**Ed. note:** See also the variant, "nam terribilem esse et metuendum locum ipsum, nulli habetur ambicum." Krusch, ed., *Vita Genovefae*, 222.]

6. "Nam fervens devotio erat ipsi beatissime Genovefe ut in honorem sancti Dionysii episcopi et martyris basilicam construeret." Kohler, ed., *Vita Genovefe*, 6, 15:18–19; [**Ed. note:** See also the variant, "Devotio erat Genovefae, ut in honore sancti Dionisi episcopi et martiris basilicam construeret sed virtus deerat"] Krusch, ed., *Vita Genovefae*, 222. See also Griffe, *Gaule chrétienne*, 3:106; Roblin, *Terroir*, 208.

7. Levillain, "Les Plus anciennes églises abbatiales de Saint-Denis," *Mémoires de la Société de l'Histoire de Paris et de l'Ile-de-France* 36 (1909): 148–50 (hereafter cited as *Mém. de la Soc. de l'Hist. de Paris* 36). His arguments were based on the reasoning that there was only one church dedicated to Saint-Denis before the dedication of the Carolingian church in 775, and that Suger in his *Testamentum* repeated a tradition that the saint's relics rested for three hundred years "in strato." See below, n. 9.

8. As recently as 1978 Gabrielle Spiegel wrote, "Two sites for Geneviève's church are possible," Spiegel, *The Chronicle Tradition*, 15. In my two earlier books I accepted the possibility that the first church might have been on a location other than the present one: Crosby, 1942, 67–70; and *L'Abbaye royale de Saint-Denis* (Paris, 1953), 11–12.

9. "Hujus ancilla corruptore admisso dominam timens, ad Ecclesiam beati Dionysii quae Strata dicitur confugit." *Miracula* or *Vita s. Dionysii* 1, 24, ed. Mabillon, *Acta Sanctorum Ord. Ben.* saec. 3, pt. 2, p. 318. "In strata vero ubi dominus noster post Dominum ter beatus Dionysius tanto trecentorum annorum tempore quievit." Suger, *Testamentum* (1137), in Lecoy de la Marche, ed., *Oeuvres*, 339.

10. The major arguments, which I summarized in my 1942

volume, 67–70, are in Havet, *Bib. de l'Ec. des Ch.* 51 (1890): 7–32; and Levillain, "Etudes sur l'abbaye de Saint-Denis à l'époque mérovingienne, II, Les Origines de Saint-Denis," *Bib. de l'Ec. des Ch.* 86 (1925): 84–95. The "église" at the western end of the rue de la République is one of the few churches entirely designed and built by Viollet-le-Duc between 1864 and 1867.

11. In 1812, for instance, a stone sarcophagus was unearthed in front of the west façade on an axis with the central portal. Proclaimed as the tomb of Pepin the Short, it was finally described as "une sépulture vulgaire de moine ou de laïc, comme on en découvre chaque fois qu'on fouille au pied des murs de l'église. Cette année même on en a trouvé un assez grand nombre." Ferdinand le Baron de Guilhermy, *Monographie de l'église royale de Saint-Denis* (Paris, 1848), 219 (hereafter cited as Guilhermy, *Monographie*).

12. The extant drawings are in Paris, Archives des Monuments Historiques. Viollet-le-Duc mentioned others which he said were "déposé dans les précieuses archives que nous possedons à Saint-Denis." These precious documents have disappeared. Possibly they were in the pile of papers which I found on the floor in a corner of the "Orangerie" under a hole in the roof. Although an official attempt was made to move them to Paris, the dripping water had reduced the paper to powder. Eugène Viollet-le-Duc, "L'Eglise impériale de Saint-Denis," *Revue archéologique,* nouv. sér. 3 (1861): 350; see also Crosby, 1942, 12, n. 28. One of the best preserved of the stone sarcophagi has been stored under the north staircase leading up to the choir. Others were stacked unceremoniously outside to the east of the chevet.

13. *L'Eglise des Trois-Patrons à Saint-Denys en France. Fouilles et découverts* (Saint-Denis, 1906), 16 plates.

14. Since the level of the ground in 1906 is impossible to determine, comparisons with the depths under the abbey church are uncertain.

15. *L'Eglise des Trois-Patrons,* 28–29, pls. XIII, XV.

16. Jules Formigé's excavation in the abbey garden between the iron grill along the rue de Strasbourg and the north side of the nave was opened in 1948, not 1938, as stated in his *Abbaye royale,* 15, fig. 14, and p. 48.

17. Edouard Salin, "Sépultures gallo-romaines et mérovingiennes dans la basilique de Saint-Denis," *Fondation Eugène Piot. Monuments et mémoires publiés par l'Académie des Inscriptions et Belles-Lettres* 49 (1957): 93–128; Edouard Salin, "Les Tombes gallo-romaines et mérovingiennes de la basilique de Saint-Denis (fouilles de jan.-fév. 1957)," *Mémoires de l'Institut Nationale de France. Académie des Inscriptiones et Belles-Lettres* 44 (1960): 169–262, and plates. A plan showing the location of these burials has been published by Michel Fleury, who has most generously allowed me to include them in my own plan: see Michel Fleury, "Les Fouilles de la basilique depuis Viollet-le-Duc," *Dossiers de l'archéologie* 32, *Decouverts à Saint-Denis* (Jan.-Feb. 1979): 20, 21, 22, plans 2, 3, 4 (hereafter cited as Fleury, "Les Fouilles," *Dossiers de l'archéologie* 32).

18. Viollet-le-Duc, *Dictionnaire raisonné de l'architecture française du Xème au XVIème siècle* (Paris, 1868), 9:227–28, fig. 9.

19. Formigé, *Abbaye royale,* 5. [**Ed. note:** "J'ai également découvert un mur perpendiculaire aux précédents et de même nature qui aurait limité à l'ouest cette chapelle."]

20. This block may have been removed from the foundations by Viollet-le-Duc's workmen, since a similar one is described in a communication by Jules Quicherat in 1881, who reported that it was found in one of the side aisles of "la basilique" and was among the items removed to the Cluny Museum in Paris. See Quicherat's report in Augustine Prost, "Séance du 11 Mai," *Bulletin de la Société Nationale des Antiquaires de France* 42, 5 sér., 2 (1881): 177.

21. See the author's files: "Etudes pétrographiques 1971–1973," no. 1, by A. Blanc and C. Jaton, *Centre de Recherches sur les Monuments Historiques.* Formigé described the stone as "pierre jaune de Saint-Leu," *Abbaye royale,* 5. [**Ed. note:** When sorted and catalogued, the Crosby files will be housed at The Cloisters of the Metropolitan Museum of New York, Fort Tryon Park, New York.]

22. See Adrien Blanchet, *Etude sur la décoration des édifices de la Gaule romaine* (Paris, 1913), 37, 97, 114, 115, 125, 127. I have noted other examples from Sens and Strasbourg illustrated in René Louis, "XIXème Circonscription-Sens," *Gallia* 8 (1950): 177, fig. 13, 179; and J.-J. Hatt, "Circonscription d'Alsace," *Gallia* 28 (1970): 317, 319, fig. 3, as well as a shield held by Modesty in combat with Lust in a miniature in a *Psychomachia* of Prudentius of the ninth century from St. Gall, Reichenau or Constance, John Beckwith, *Early Medieval Art* (London, 1964), 91, fig. 72.

23. Henri Rolland, "Les Fouilles de Glanum (Saint-Rémy-de-Provence) de 1945 à 1947," *Gallia* 6 (1948): 163, fig. 22.

24. Three sections or elevations of excavations made by Viollet-le-Duc, supposedly while he was constructing the "caveau impériale" in 1859–60, exist in the Archives Photographiques, nos. 206160, 206162, 206164. For reproductions of the first two of these drawings, see Formigé, *Abbaye royale,* 164–65, figs. 144–45. Although I have puzzled over these beautifully executed drawings for more than forty years, I am still confused and must admit that I do not understand them. The overall key to which the letters must refer does not, to the best of my knowledge, exist. Two of the elevations with plans of the piers—nos. 206160, 206162—must be of the east–west excavations under the western bay of the choir, where the thirteenth-century piers are not in alignment. Earlier in his book Formigé seemed to refer to these elevations, although he used different reference numbers—nos. 23336-23337—ibid., 41, n. 1. [**Ed. note:** Formigé was citing the inventory numbers which the Monuments Historiques had assigned to the drawings.] He identified what he called "égouts," or drainage tunnels, for the marshy soil around the fifth-century building. The large decorated fragment shown in photograph 206160 (ibid.: fig. 145) resembles the Gallo-Roman block at the western end of the alignment on the north side, but nothing similar exists where Viollet-le-Duc indicated (fig. 4b). Possibly the legends, numbers, and letters have been reversed, so that the elevations should be interpreted differently, but the only similar underpinning for twelfth-century piers that

I have seen is under the two piers to the north and south of the crossing—not under the crossing piers.

25. I discovered these photographs in the photographic service of the Monuments Historiques, 3 rue de Valois, in Paris, by chance. If there are others, I am not aware of them. [**Ed. note:** The photographic service is now located at 4, rue de Turenne, Paris 75004.]

26. The upper portions, for instance, do not show the twelfth-century base or other details.

27. Fleury, "Les Fouilles," *Dossiers de l'archéologie* 32:22, plan 4.

28. Fleury and Albert France-Lanord, "La Tombe d'Arégonde," *Dossiers de l'archéologie* 32:27–28.

29. A. France-Lanord, "La Fouille en laboratoire, Méthodes et resultats," *Dossiers de l'archéologie* 32:66.

30. The custom of covering Early Christian cemeteries has been studied by Richard Krautheimer, "Mensa-Coemeterium-Martyrium," in *Studies in Early Christian, Medieval and Renaissance Art* (New York, 1969), 35–58.

31. Salin, *Monuments Piot* 49 (1957): 95, 96, figs. 1, 2.

32. Although Jean Hubert cited no references and could not have known about the plan of Sainte Geneviève's chapel at Saint-Denis, he wrote, "Small monastery churches of the seventh century found at Saint-Denis, Jouarre, Nivelles and Echternach show the simplest ground plan that can be adopted for a sacred edifice: a plain rectangle, but a rectangle which in fact is exactly equal to two squares. Here is proof that the builders of these churches were deliberately applying geometric principles so as to safeguard the harmony of the proportions." Jean Hubert et al., *Europe of the Invasions,* trans. S. Gilbert and J. Emmons (New York, 1969), 31.

33. [**Ed. note:** Suger, *De Administratione* 29, Panofsky, ed., *Suger,* 50–53: "reservata tamen quantacumque portione de parietibus antiquis . . . ut et antiquae consecrationis reverentia et moderno operi juxta tenorem coeptum congrua cohaerentia servaretur."]

34. Jean Hubert, "Séance du 10 juillet," *Bulletin de la Société Nationale des Antiquaires de France* (1945–47): 177.

35. Krusch, ed., *Vita Genovefae,* 18–21:222–24.

36. Formigé, "Séance du 3 avril 1957: Communications sur les travaux récents de la basilique de Saint-Denis." Institut de France, *Académie des Beaux-Arts, Années 1956–57* (Paris, 1957): 82; *Abbaye royale,* 2, fig. 2.

37. Levillain, *Bib. de l'Ec. des Ch.* 86 (1925): 44–49; Crosby, 1942, 53–54.

38. [**Ed. note:** See Levillain, *Bib. de l'Ec. des Ch.* 82 (1921): 6–17.

39. A letter, Louis Grodecki to author, dated 12 September 1952 described this discovery, which had eluded Edouard Salin as well as Jules Formigé. It was this find that prompted Salin's renewed attention to Saint-Denis and led to his subsequent investigation.

40. Salin, *Monuments Piot* 49 (1957): 102.

41. Michel Fleury and Albert France-Lanord first published the discovery, "Les Bijoux mérovingiens d'Arnegonde," *Art de France* 1 (1961): 5–18. For the most recent studies, see Fleury and

France-Lanord, "La Tombe d'Arégonde," *Dossiers de l'archéologie* 32:27–42; Fleury, "Le Monogramme de l'anneau d'Arégonde," ibid.: 43–45; Florence André and Gilbert Mangin, "Les Bijoux d'Arégonde," ibid.: 50–65; France-Lanord, "La Fouille en laboratoire," ibid.: 66–99. Maria R. Alföldi showed that *Arnegundis* is the genitive of *Arnegunde,* "Zum Ring der Königin Arnegunde," *Germania* 41 (1963): 55–58. See also David McKenzie Wilson, "A Ring of Queen Arnegunde," *Germania* 42 (1964): 265–68.

42. A color reproduction of this costume is in Peter Lasko, "Prelude to Empire," in *The Dawn of European Civilization—The Dark Ages,* ed. David Talbot Rice (London, 1965), 201; and in Fleury and France-Lanord, "La Tombe d'Arégonde," *Dossiers de l'archéologie* 32:38–39.

43. Levillain, *Bib. de l'Ec. des Ch.* 86 (1925): 52–62, 66–69; Crosby, 1942, 54–55.

44. See above, introduction, p. 8.

45. Levillain, *Bib. de l'Ec. des Ch.* 91 (1930): 5–7; Crosby, 1942, 56–57.

46. Grégoire, *Histoire des Francs,* Omont, ed., 177; Gregory of Tours, *Historiae Francorum* 5, 32, Krusch, ed., 237. [**Ed. note:** Latin text, "Erant enim maiores natu et primi apud Chilpericum regem."]

47. The incident occurred in 579 (according to Havet, *Bib. de l'Ec. des Ch.* 51 [1890]: 14), when a Parisian woman was accused of adultery. Her father upheld her innocence, to which he would swear over the tomb of Saint Denis. Having sworn with his hands raised above the altar, he was accused of perjury, and fighting between the two parties began.

48. See ibid., 30; Levillain, *Mém. de la Soc. de l'Hist. de Paris* 36 (1909): 152–53; Dalton, ed., *Gregory of Tours* 5, 32, vol. 2:203.

49. [**Ed. note:** See Gregory of Tours, *Liber in Gloria martyrum* 71, Krusch, ed., *M.G.H., Script. rer. Mer.* 1, pt. 2 (Hanover, 1885), p. 536;] and Levillain, *Mém. de la Soc. de l'Hist. de Paris* 36 (1909): 153.

50. See, for example, the tombs of the crypt of Jouarre, Hubert et al., *Invasions,* 65–66, figs. 77–78.

CHAPTER 2. DAGOBERT'S ENLARGEMENT OF THE BASILICA

1. Quoted by Henri Leclercq in Cabrol and Leclercq, *Dictionnaire,* 4, 5, from Charles Augustin Sainte-Beuve, "Histoire de la royauté, par M. J.-V. Le Clere," *Portraits contemporains* (Paris, 1846) 2:400. [**Ed. note:** "J'ai souvent pensé (nous dit Sainte-Beuve), qu'il aurait un chapitre à écrire: *De ceux qui ont une mauvaise réputation et qui ne la méritent pas.* Montaigne a oublié de la faire. Que de noms en appel contre le hasard y trouveraient place! . . . Il faudrait commencer par Augias, au nom duquel cette locution d'*étables d'Augias* a rattaché une idée odieuse et presque infecte, et qui était le plus riche et le plus royal patriarche des pasteurs, tel que nous l'a réprésenté l'antique idylle. On n'y oublierait pas surtout Dagobert, *le bon Dagobert,* qui a laissé une

réputation débonnaire et assez ridicule, et qui fut peut-être un grand roi, énergique, le *quasi*-Charlemagne de sa race, mort à la fleur de l'âge (à trente-trois ans) et dans la vigueur de ses hauts projets."]

> 2. C'est le roi Dagobert
>   Qui met sa culotte à l'envers. . . .
>   Le grand Saint Eloi
>   Lui dit: Ô mon Roi—
>   Vot' Majesté
>   Est bien mal culotté:
>   Et bien! lui dit le roi,
>   Je vais la remettre à l'endroit.

Chanson de France pour les petits français, arranged by J. B. Weckerlin (Paris, 1980), 22–23.
See also Lavisse, *Histoire de France,* vol. 2, pt. 1, pp. 158–61; and Robert Barroux, *Dagobert, roi des Francs* (Paris, 1938). This small biography is, as the author says, "ni d'érudition ni de fantaisie" (ibid., p. 9).

3. Suger, *De Administratione,* 33, Lecoy de la Marche, ed., *Oeuvres,* 203; Panofsky, ed., *Suger,* 2, 70–71; Doublet, *Histoire,* 173; Félibien, *Histoire,* 10–15; Levillain, *Bib. de l'Ec. des Ch.* 91 (1930): 9, n. 2; Krusch, ed., *Chronica Fredegarii* 4, 79, M.G.H., *Script. rer. Mer.* 2, p. 161; Krusch, ed., *Vita Eligii Episcopi Noviomagensis* 1, 32, M.G.H., *Script. rer. Mer.* 4 (Hanover, 1902), pp. 688–89. See also above, introduction, n. 59.

4. Krusch, ed., *Chronica Fredegarii,* M.G.H., *Script. rer. Mer.* 2, p. 161; Krusch, ed., *Vita Eligii,* M.G.H., *Script. rer. Mer.* 4, p. 689. The *Chronica Fredegarii* is considered more trustworthy than the *Vita Eligii.* See Crosby, 1942, 192. [**Ed. note:** See also below, n. 14.]

5. [**Ed. note:** Viollet-le-Duc, *Dictionnaire,* 9:227–29, fig. 9. See also below, p. 36 and n. 21.]

6. This location is less than 1.50 m to the west of the thirteenth-century crossing piers of the existing church.

7. See Crosby, "Excavations in the Abbey Church of St.-Denis 1948. The Façade of Fulrad's Church," *Proceedings of the American Philosophical Society* 93 (1949): 350, n. 1. [**Ed. note:** See also the most recent proposal of a date around 550 for the western extension by Carol Heitz, "Saint-Denis," in Patrick Périn and Laure-Charlotte Feffer, eds., *La Neustrie. Les Pays nord de la Loire de Dagobert à Charles le Chauve (VIIème–IXème siècles)* (Paris, 1985), 164–65.]

8. The *Petit Larousse illustré* (Paris, 1916), 556, defines *libage* as "moellon, grossièrement equarri, qu'on emploie dans les fondations ou dans l'intérieur d'une muraille."

9. "Decimo Kal. maias transtulit," Krusch, ed., *Gesta Dagoberti* 17, M.G.H., *Script. rer. Mer.* 2, p. 406. This "translation" caused a great deal of discussion because it also involved the possibility that Saint Denis was originally buried in another location. See Havet, *Oeuvres,* 194–206.

10. [**Ed. note:** See Crosby, *Proceedings of the American Philosophical Society* 93 (1949): 351, fig. 4. Location of doorway does not appear on this plan.]

11. Hans Erich Kubach, "Die vorromanische und ro-

manische Baukunst in Mitteleuropa," *Zeitschrift für Kunstgeschichte* 18 (1955): 157–98. Note especially St. Severin, Cologne, p. 163. See also Friedrich Oswald, Leo Schaefer, Hans Rudolf Sennhauser, *Vorromanische Kirchenbauten, Katalog der Denkmäler bis zum Ausgang der Ottonen* (Munich, 1968) 2, p. 155 for St. Severin, Cologne; p. 180 for St. Nazarius, Lorsch; p. 233 for St. Peter and Paul, Neustadt; and p. 255 for St. Severin, Passau. See also Karl Heinrich Krüger, *Königsgrabkirchen der Franken, Angelsachsen und Langobarden bis zur mitte des 8. Jahrhunderts* (Munich, 1971), 177–89.

12. As I have noted several times, Formigé's description of the early remains at Saint-Denis, including Dagobert's construction, must be ignored. The plan, for instance, identified as "Eglise de Dagobert Ier reconstruite par Pépin le Bref et achevée par Charlemagne" does not include any Merovingian masonry. Formigé, *Abbaye royale,* 51, fig. 40.

13. [**Ed. note:** "Quam cum mirifica marmorearum columnarum varietate componens."] Suger, *De Consecratione* 2, Lecoy de la Marche, ed., *Oeuvres,* 215–16; Panfosky, ed., *Suger,* 86–87. Suger believed that the church standing in his time had been built by Dagobert. He based his description of the church on passages in the *Gesta Dagoberti* (Krusch, ed., *Gesta Dagoberti* 20, M.G.H., *Script. rer. Mer.* 2, p. 407); and on Aimon's *Gesta Francorum* (Aimon, *De Gestis Regum Francorum* 4, 33, in Martin Bouquet, ed., *Receuil des historiens des Gaules et de la France* [Paris, 1741] 3:134). See especially Levillain, whose conclusion that our knowledge is "vague et peu sur" can now be modified, Levillain, *Mém. de la Soc. de l'Hist. de Paris* 36 (1909): 150.

14. See Vieillard-Troïekouroff, "L'Architecture en France du temps de Charlemagne," in Helmut Beumann, Bernhard Bischoff, Hermann Schnitzler, Percy Ernst Schramm, eds., *Karl der Grosse, Lebenswerk und Nachleben* (Düsseldorf, 1966) 3:336–43 (hereafter cited as Vieillard-Troïekouroff, *Karl der Grosse* 3); and Hans Sedlmayr, "Die politische Bedeutung des Virgildomes," *Mitteilungen der Gesellschaft für Salzburger Landeskunde* 115 (1975): 146. Both of these articles will be discussed more fully in the following chapter on Fulrad's eighth-century church.

15. The *Vita Eligii* is attributed to Saint Ouen, a contemporary of Saint Eloi (588–659). The latter is known as the Apostle of the Belgians and Frisians. According to legend, Eloi was born near Limoges, where he was apprenticed as a youth to the master of the mint. He became a coiner to Clotaire II, Dagobert's father, and then treasurer for Dagobert. Renowned as an artisan in precious metals and jewels, he decorated the tomb of Saint Germain, the bishop of Paris. As proof of his honesty, he made two elaborate chairs for Clotaire II when he was supplied with materials intended for only one. Eloi became bishop of Noyon. He is still popular as the patron saint of goldsmiths. See Krusch, ed., *Vita Eligii,* M.G.H., *Script. rer. Mer.* 4, pp. 634–35, and passim.

16. A *mausoleum* referred specifically to the tomb or coffin of a martyr but has been interpreted as the entire liturgical ensemble. [**Ed. note:** The description in the *Vita Eligii* 1, ibid., pp. 688–89, is as follows: "Praeterea Eligius fabricavit et mausoleum

sancti martiris Dionisii Parisius civitate et tugurium super ipsium marmorem miro opere de auro et gemmis. Cristam quoque et species de fronte magnifice conposuit necnon et axes in circuitu throni altaris auto operuit et posuit in eis poma aurea, retundiles atque gemmatas. Operuit quoque et lecturium et ostia diligenter de metallo argenti; sed et tectum throni altaris axibus operuit argentis. Fecit quoque et repam in loco anterioris tumuli et altare extrinsecus ad pedes sancti martiris fabricavit."]

17. *Tugurium* is defined as an instrument used during the celebration of the mass to allow a celebrant to partake of the holy wine. Levillain has translated *tugerium* (sic) as the "ciboire de l'autel." Levillain, *Mém. de la Soc. de l'Hist. de Paris* 36 (1909): 156, 218, n. 2. Blaise de Montesquiou-Fezensac, *Le Trésor de Saint-Denis* (Paris, 1973) 1:4, published a translation of the passage by Jean Hubert which avoided a literal rendering: "par dessus, un *tugurium* de marbre d'un merveilleux travail, d'or et de pierres précieuses, ainsi que la crête et le fronton."

18. *Axes in circuitu altaris auro* for Levillain became, "Dans le choeur, il aurait aussi couvert de feuilles d'or la balustrade qui entourait l'autel," Levillain, *Mém. de la Soc. de l'Hist. de Paris* 36 (1909): 156. Hubert's translation in Montesquiou-Fezensac, *Trésor* 1:4, reads, "et il couvrit d'or la balustrade du bois placée autour du trone de l'autel."

19. *Tectum throni altaris*. Levillain, *Mém. de la Soc. de l'Hist. de Paris* 36 (1909): 157, treated this as "le dais du siège du célébrant"; and Hubert, in Montesquiou-Fezensac, *Trésor* 1:4, rendered it as "le toit abritant le trône de l'autel."

20. *Repam* in Levillain's text was "une sorte de ciboire," Levillain, *Mém. de la Soc. de l'Hist. de Paris* 36 (1909): 156. Hubert did not translate the word. *Anterioris* has both a spatial and a temporal context. Both Levillain and Hubert chose the temporal, "ancien." Levillain, ibid., Hubert, in Montesquiou-Fezensac, *Trésor* 1:4.

21. *Extrinsecus ad pedes* for Levillain meant, "extérieurement aux pieds du martyr, c'est à dire à l'est," Levillain, *Mém. de la Soc. de l'Hist. de Paris* 36 (1909): 156. Hubert, in Montesquiou-Fezensac, *Trésor* 1:4, preferred "au dehors, aux pieds du saint martyr."

22. Chronologically the list begins with Félibien, *Histoire*, 10–11; Maître, "Le Culte de saint Denis et de ses compagnons (suite)," *Rev. de l'art chrétien* 52 (1909): 83–84; Levillain, *Mém. de la Soc. de l'Hist. de Paris* 36 (1909): 156–158, 217–22; Levillain, *Bib. de l'Ec. des Ch.* 86 (1925): 25–27; Formigé, *Abbaye royale*, 52–57; Hubert, in Montesquiou-Fezensac, *Trésor* 1:4.

23. The author of the *Vita Eligii* was careful to choose different words, *repam, tugurium,* and *tectum,* to describe the covering over the old tomb, the new altar, and the throne. I have tried to recognize these distinctions.

24. Montesquiou-Fezensac, "Une Epave de trésor de Saint-Denis," *Mélanges en l'honneur de M. Fr. Martroye* (Paris, 1940), 289–301.

25. Krusch, ed., *Gesta Dagoberti* 20, *M.G.H., Script. rer. Mer.* 2, p. 407.

26. Suger, *De Administratione* 33, Lecoy de la Marche, ed., *Oeuvres,* 198; Panofsky, ed., *Suger,* 62–63.

27. Montesquiou-Fezensac, *Trésor* 1:53.

28. For a description of the cross from the 1634 Inventory, see ibid., 213–15.

29. For a reproduction in color, see Hubert et al., *Invasions,* 242, fig. 266.

30. Crosby, *Proceedings of the American Philosophical Society* 93, no. 5 (1949): 350, fig. 3. The same fragments are incorrectly identified as having been found by Jules Formigé, Hubert et al., *Invasions,* 55, fig. 67. Formigé may have referred to one of these fragments as "un piedroit de porte peint avec feuillure," belonging to the first chapel, Formigé, *Abbaye royale,* 5.

31. [**Ed. note:** The traces of paint surviving on the fragment suggest that the carver had completed the sculpture and had highlighted the design with color as a final touch. The reason for the unfinished end remains unclear; possibly that portion was to have been set into a posthole, and therefore would not have been visible.]

32. Hubert stated categorically that "this counter-curve motif occurs in exactly the same form in gold filigree-work of the 6th and 7th centuries." Hubert et al., *Invasions,* 352, no. 67. I have been unable to locate such "exact" prototypes.

33. Harry Bober, "On the Illumination of the Glazier Codex. A Contribution to Early Coptic Art and Its Relation to Hiberno-Saxon Interlace," in Helmut Lehmann-Haupt, ed., *Homage to a Bookman* (Berlin, 1967), 42.

34. Gyula László, *Steppenvölker und Germanen* (Vienna, 1970), 53–56, figs. 20–24. These are interesting examples of additive, discontinuous designs.

35. Bernhard Salin, *Die altgermanische Thierornamentik* (Stockholm, 1935), 89, fig. 212.

36. André Dumoulin, "Recherches dans la région d'Apt," *Gallia* 16 (1958): 219, fig. 25.

37. Carol Heitz, "Communication sur le chancel de Saint-Pierre-aux-Nonnains à Metz," *Bull. de la Soc. Nat. des Antiq. de France* (1975): 103. The two lower designs are described as "deux entrelacs de serpents, l'un abstrait, l'autre très vivant." For early medieval chancels, see also Fernand Benoit, "La Basilique Saint-Pierre et Saint-Paul à Arles, Etude sur les cancels paléochrétiens," *Provence historique* 7 (1957): 8–21.

38. Barry A. Kaplan, "*Bursae Eleganter Gemmatae.* The History of an Abandoned Liturgical Instrument" (M. A. thesis, Yale University, 1972), 35, figs. 58–61; and Linus Birchler, *Die Kunstdenkmäler des Kantons Schwyz—Gersau, Kussnach und Schwyz,* in *Die Kunstdenkmäler der Schweiz* (Basel, 1930) 2:254–57. Here the design is described as "two four-lobed interlace knots in double-traced repoussé."

39. The lateral measurements of the fragments removed by Formigé's workmen vary from 0.17 m to 0.19 m.

40. A similar post at Metz with three channels "ne pouvait se trouver que quelque part au centre et cantonner, soit l'escalier de montée centrale, soit une petite estrade avancée dans la nef," Heitz, *Bull. de la Soc. Nat. des Antiq. de France* (1975): 99–100.

41. [**Ed. note:** See also Formigé, *Abbaye royale,* 54–55, figs. 43, 44.]

42. The design has also been described as resembling "an

enlargement of the curves and counter-curves which were a favorite motif with the barbarian goldsmiths." Hubert et al., *Invasions*, 55. See also ibid.., 54, 55, figs. 66, 67, and the description on 352, nos. 66 and 67. The "large extant fragment" which Hubert says was the basis for the plaster reconstruction of the whole slab at Saint-Denis measures only 0.15 m by 0.12 m and includes only one of the design motifs.

43. The most detailed analysis of these capitals is by Denise Fossard, "Les Chapiteaux de marbre du VIIème siècle en Gaule—Style et évolution," *Cahiers archéologiques* 2 (1947): 69–85. Unfortunately, she did not note the different dimensions of the so-called Saint-Denis examples included in her discussion. [**Ed. note:** See also Vieillard-Troïekouroff, "Les Chapiteaux de marbre du Haut Moyen-Age à Saint-Denis," *Gesta* 15 (1976): 105–11; J.-P.C., "Chapiteau," in P. Périn and L.-C. Feffer, eds., *La Neustrie*, 193–94, no. 52; and for the dimensions, below n. 47.] Jean Hubert in his *L'Art pré-roman* (Paris, 1938), 96–97, suggested a date of 749–54 because of the resemblance of the Saint-Denis capitals to those in the "Torhalle" at Lorsch. In a later text he did not illustrate the marble capitals in the Cluny Museum, but he dated those in the Baptistery of Saint-Jean in Poitiers as "about seventh century." Hubert et al., *Invasions*, 351, nos. 49–50. François Eygun, "Le Baptistère Saint-Jean de Poitiers," *Gallia* 22 (1964): 166, argued for a sixth-century date. Léon Levillain judiciously referred to the capitals in question as "mérovingiens," *Mém. de la Soc. de l'Hist. de Paris* 36 (1909): 151. See also Jean Cabanot, "Chapiteaux de marbre antérieurs à l'époque romane dans le département des Landes," *Cahiers archéologiques* 22 (1972): 1–18, "toute tentative de datation apparaissant encore bien prématurée" (ibid., 1); and Mary Larrieu, "Chapiteaux en marbre antérieurs à l'époque romane dans le Gers," *Cahiers archéologiques* 14 (1964): 109–57.

44. In his notes Ferdinand de Guilhermy wrote, "On trouve employé dans le clocher des fûts et des chapiteaux de marbre blancs," Paris, Bibliothèque Nationale, *Ms. Nouvelles acquisitions françaises*, 6121, fol. 94. See also Albert Lenoir, *Architecture monastique* (Paris, 1852), 1:228–29. We have no information about the exact location or about Viollet-le-Duc's disposition of the capitals.

45. Louis Grodecki, *Les Vitraux de Saint-Denis* (Paris, 1976), 1:46. [**Ed. note:** On the collection and dispersion of the artifacts, see inter alia Louis Courajod, *Alexandre Lenoir. Son Journal et le Musée des Monuments Français*, 3 vols. (Paris, 1878–87).]

46. Vieillard-Troïekouroff, "Les Anciennes églises suburbaines," 127, n. 3.

47. The inventory numbers and dimensions of the capitals in the Cluny Museum are as follows:

12.114A (H. 0.42 m, D. 0.30 m) [**Ed. note:** Exhibition no. 605.]

12.114B (H. 0.42 m, D. 0.30 m) [**Ed. note:** Exhibition no. 606.]

12.115 (H. 0.26 m, D. 0.17 m) [**Ed. note:** Exhibition no. 609.]

12.116 (H. 0.27 m, D. 0.21 m) [**Ed. note:** Exhibition no. 610.]

12.117 (H. 0.35 m, D. 0.23 m) [**Ed. note:** Exhibition no. 607.]

12.118 (H. 0.29 m, D. 0.22 m) [**Ed. note:** Exhibition no. 608.]

The marble capitals in the crypt at Saint-Denis measure:

NN 7 (H. 0.30 m, D. 0.27 m at the base) [**Ed. note:** Location, north aisle, north side, seventh from west.]
NS 1 (H. 0.37 m, D. 0.28 m at the base) [**Ed. note:** Location, north aisle, south side, westernmost position.]
SS 8 (H. 0.39 m, D. 0.26 m at the base) [**Ed. note:** Location, south aisle, south side, eighth from west.]

Jules Formigé accounted for the different sizes of the capitals by suggesting that they came from different claustral buildings built by Dagobert at Saint-Denis. Formigé, *Abbaye royale*, 8.

48. Denise Jalabert, *La Flore sculptée des monuments du Moyen âge en France* (Paris, 1965), 26 and pls. 3a, 3b.

49. The upper zone of the Poitiers capital is different, with rosettes in place of volutes and a band with bead and reel ornament between them. For illustrations, see Hubert et al., *Invasions*, 43, fig. 50; Eygun, *Gallia* 22 (1964): 164, no. 7 on diagram. The Poitiers capital measures 0.39 m in height.

50. Eygun, *Gallia* 22 (1964): 137–72.

51. [**Ed. note:** See inter alia Suger, *De Administratione*, Panofsky, ed., *Suger*, 46–47, 67–73.]

52. The Corinthian marble capitals may also be compared to those at the palace chapel in Aachen. See Felix Kreusch, "Im Louvre wiedergefundene Kapitelle und Bronzebasen aus der Pfalzkirche Karls des Grossen zu Aachen," *Cahiers archéologiques* 18 (1968): 73, fig. 1. The measurements are 0.477 m high by 0.290 m wide at the base, dimensions somewhat larger than those at Saint-Denis. There is a similar capital from La Mendicidad de Seville described as a "normal" visigothic Corinthian design of the second half of the seventh century. See Blas Taracena Aguirre, Pedro Batlle Huguet, and Helmut Schlunk, *Ars Hispaniae* (Madrid, 1947) 2:246, fig. 252.

[**Ed. note:** Vieillard-Troïekouroff cited the third capital in the crypt at Saint-Denis among the Merovingian survivals. See *Gesta* 15 (1976): 106, no. 2. Identified as SS 8 in note 47 above, that capital, except for the inclusion of an astragal, is a duplicate of the capital labeled NS 1, in note 47, and illustrated by the author in fig. 18b. Troïekouroff described the latter as "très restauré, s'il n'est pas moderne," ibid., 107. Certainly if original, it has been heavily recut, which raises the question of which was the model and which the copy and the further question of when the copy was made—whether in the twelfth century or in the nineteenth. Carbon dating would be useful in settling the matter.]

53. Suger, *De Administratione* 34, Lecoy de la Marche, ed., *Oeuvres*, 204; Panofsky, ed., *Suger*, 72–73. [**Ed. note:** "In qua, ut perhibere solet antiquitas, reges Francorum, suscepto regni imperio, ad suscipienda optimatum suorum hominia primum sedere consueverant, tum pro tanti excellentia officii, tum etiam pro operis ipsius precio, antiquatam et disruptam refici fecimus."]

54. Lothaire's portrait in his Psalter, written soon after 842—now in the British Library (Add. Ms. 37768)—shows the king

seated on a throne with lion heads and legs very similar to Dagobert's throne. See Hubert, Jean Porcher, and W. F. Volbach, *The Carolingian Empire* (New York, 1970), 285, fig. 296.

55. A copy of the throne is kept at Saint-Denis, to the left, or north, of the high altar. For some time it has been used by the celebrant at High Mass.

56. Charles Lenormant, "Notice sur le fauteuil de Dagobert," in Charles Cahier and Arthur Martin, eds., *Mélanges d'archéologie, d'histoire et de littérature* (Paris, 1847–49), 1:157–90, 239–44, pls. 26–30.

57. Hubert, "Le Fauteuil du roi Dagobert," *Demareteion* 1 (1935): 17–27; and Hubert, *L'Art pré-roman*, 135–36.

58. Peter Lasko, *Ars Sacra 800–1200* (Harmondsworth, 1972), 20–21. Martin Weinberger has suggested that the repairs were done after Suger's time in the late twelfth or early thirteenth century: "The Chair of Dagobert," in Lucy Sandler, ed., *Essays in Memory of Karl Lehmann* (New York, 1964), 382.

59. Both of the miniatures are illustrated in Hubert et al., *Carolingian Empire*, 119, fig. 106. The figure shows St. John in the Bible of Saint Emmeran of Regensburg, now in Munich, Bayerische Staatsbibliothek (Clm. 14000, fol. 97r). Possibly this manuscript was executed at Saint-Denis about 870. For the portrait of Lothaire I, see ibid., 285, fig. 296.

60. Peter Lasko believed that the heads were "a tradition that was probably no longer available in the twelfth century," *Ars Sacra*, 20, 262, nn. 33–39. I have in my possession an illustration cut out of an unidentified book which contains a drawing of the throne without the back or side arms, but with the two heads as upright terminals on each side at the back.

61. See W. Martin Conway, "The Abbey Church of Saint-Denis and its Ancient Treasures," pt. 3, *Archaeologia* 66, 2d. ser., 16(1915): 121.

62. The throne must have been kept in the treasury. At least it was there in the early eighteenth century, for it is mentioned by Félibien, *Histoire*, 545.

63. Léon Levillain wrote, "On peut, en effet, se demander jusqu'à quel point de tels renseignements sont historiques," and then in a note added, "Je compte établir ailleurs que l'auteur des *Gesta* n'ignorait pas, lui, la vérité, mais qu'il pouvait avoir intérêt à ne la point révéler." *Mém. de la Soc. de l'Hist. de Paris* 36 (1909): 157–58, n. 1. More recently Blaise Montesquiou-Fezensac has written that the author of the *Gesta Dagoberti* "ne mérite pas le dédain que Léon Levillain lui a témoigné." *Trésor* 1:4. Unfortunately, I have not been able to locate the intriguing exposé to which I alluded.

64. "Quamvis ecclesiam, quam ipse a fundamine construxerat," Krusch, ed., *Gesta Dagoberti* 17, *M.G.H., Script. rer. Mer.* 2, p. 406.

65. Ibid., "intrinsecus miro decore fabricaverit, foris quoque desuper absidam illam . . . ex argento purissimo mirifice cooperuit"; and ibid. 20, p. 407, "Nam et per totam ecclesiam auro textas vestes, margaritarum varietatibus multipliciter exornatas in parietibus et columnis atque arcubus suspendi devotissime

jussit." Reportedly the silver covering over the apse was removed by Dagobert's son, Clovis II, to give to the starving and the poor. Ibid. 50, p. 423. Félibien added that the silver originally was taken from the Visigoths, *Histoire*, 12. See also Erna Patzelt, *Die karolingische Renaissance* (Graz, 1965), 103, in which this description is accepted as a fact.

66. For numerous similar descriptions, see Joseph Gutmann, *The Temple of Solomon* (Missoula, Mon., 1976), passim.

67. Krusch, ed., *Gesta Dagoberti* 40, *M.G.H., Script. rer. Mer.* 2, p. 419: "Denique eodem tempore plumbum, quod ei ex metallo censitum in secundo semper anno solvebatur, libras octo millia ad cooperiendam eandem supradictorum beatorum martyrum ecclesiam . . . concessit." [**Ed. note:** Dagobert's gift probably provided the lead to cover the roof and was not for interior ornamentation as the author's text implies.]

68. See Levillain, *Mém. de la Soc. de l'Hist. de Paris* 36 (1909): 157–58.

69. Suger, *De Consecratione* 4, Lecoy de la Marche, ed., *Oeuvres*, 226; Panofsky, ed., *Suger*, 102–03.

70. Félibien, *Histoire*, 539, pl. II, R. [**Ed. note:** See also Montesquiou-Fezensac, *Trésor* 1:46, no. 84.]

71. Ibid., 46, no. 76 and n. 4; Félibien, *Histoire*, 539, pl. II, Q.

72. Montesquiou-Fezensac, *Trésor* 1:248, no. 234; Félibien, *Histoire*, 539, pl. II, E.

73. Montesquiou-Fezensac, *Trésor* 1:245, no. 221; Félibien, *Histoire*, 532. Another item supposedly taken from Saint-Hilaire in Poitiers by Dagobert was a pair of bronze doors. The incident was cited by Haymo in the ninth century as proof that Dagobert despoiled other churches in order to decorate Saint-Denis. In this instance no one took much notice, since one of the doors evidently fell into the Seine and was never seen again. Ibid., p. 20.

74. I have translated this legend from the text printed by Charles Liebman, "La Consécration légendaire de la basilique de Saint-Denis," *Le Moyen age* 6, 3d. ser. (1935): 253. [**Ed. note:** "Ung povre homme vint moult difforme et infect de leppre, priant le gardien de l'église qu'il luy souffrist passer la nuyt en icelle, ce que luy fut ottroyé: et luy estant esveillé perseverant en oraison, clairement veit Jhesuchrist accompagné de saint Pierre et saint Paul, avec les benoistz martyrs saint Denys, sainct Rustique et sainct Eleuthere venir en l'eglise par une fenestre: lequel vestu de blanc vestement fist le sacré office de dedication. De la vint Jesuchrist au lepreux: 'Toy homme (dist il) quant les evesques viendront demain au point du jour pour celle eglise dedier, annonce leur qu'elle est de moy consacree.' La garaison duquel homme fist foy de coste chose: car Jesuchrist touchant sa face: luy osta toute sa leppre, et la jecta contre la prochaine pierre, ou jusques aujourdhuy par tres grant admiration est veue conglutinee. Duquel myracle les prelatz estonnez se abstindrent de celle dedycace."]

75. Suger, *De Administratione* 29, Lecoy de la Marche, ed., *Oeuvres*, 191; Panofsky, ed., *Suger*, 50–51.

76. Levillain, *Bib. de l'Ec. des Ch.* 91 (1930): 8, n. 2.

77. Levillain, *Bib. de l'Ec. des Ch.* 86 (1925): 70; and Friedrich Prinz, *Frühes Mönchtum im Frankreich* (Munich, 1965), 106, 168–69.

78. "Preterire enim non debemus, quod [Bathilde] per seniores basilicas sanctorum domni Dionisii et domni Germani vel domni Medardi et sancti Petri vel domni Aniani seu et sancti Martini, vel ubicumque ejus perstrinxit notitia, ad pontifices seu abbates suadendo pro zelo Dei praecepit et epistolas pro hoc eis direxit, ut sub sancto regulari ordine fratres infra ipsa loca consistentes vivere deberent." Krusch, ed., *Vita sanctae Bathildis* 9, *M.G.H., Script. rer. Mer.* 2, p. 493.

79. This union of the two monastic rules was one of the most interesting events in the development of early western monasticism—"sub regula sancti Benedicti vel sancti Columbani conversari et vivere debeant," charter of Bertfrid of Amiens, 664. See Jean Martial Léon Besse, *Les Moines de l'ancienne France* (Paris, 1906), 290–93. Prinz, *Frühes Mönchtum*, 193.

80. Levillain, *Bib. de l'Ec. des Ch.* 86 (1925): 77–78.

81. The famous Foire du Lendit, which began the second Wednesday in June after the Feast of Saint John, was, according to the medieval tradition, founded by Charles the Bald. Levillain, however, has shown that it did not begin until the end of the ninth century. The confusion between the Lendit and St.-Denis fairs is owing to Robert Gaguin in the fifteenth century. See Levillain, *Revue historique* 155 (1927): 242; and Levillain, *Bib. de L'Ec. des Ch.* 91 (1930): 9–10.

82. The Foire de la Saint-Mathias was the least important of the fairs. It owed its origin to the celebration of the dedication of the church on 24 February. It may date from the end of the ninth century but is probably later. See Levillain, *Bib. de l'Ec. des Ch.* 91 (1930): 7–9.

83. Levillain has concluded that the analysis of the charter in the *Gesta Dagoberti* is authentic and that the original charter was consequently still at Saint-Denis when Hincmar and Hilduin were writing between 835 and 840. The existing charter of this concession by Dagobert is a forged document of the early tenth century. Ibid., 10–14, 37.

84. "Ad ipsa sancta fistivetate domni Dionisii ad illo marcado advenientes." Charter of Childebert III, 710 (Lauer and Samaran, eds., *Les Diplômes originaux des Mérovingiens,* 22). This charter does not mention Dagobert, but Levillain believed that his name was omitted by mistake. Levillain, *Bib. de l'Ec. des Ch.* 91 (1930): 11, 14.

85. "De illa festivitate sancti Dionisii in idipso pago Parisiaco de omnes necuciantes, tam Saxsones quam Frisones vel alias naciones promiscuas, de quascumque pagos vel provincias ad festivitate sancti Dionisii martyris, tam in ipso marcado quam et in ipsa civitate Parisius." Charter of Pepin the Short, 753, Mühlbacher, ed., *M.G.H., Diplomata Kar.* 1, p. 9, no. 6. "Et ostendebant praeceptum Dagoberti regis, qualiter ipsum marcatum stabilisset." Charter of Pepin the Short, 759, ibid., p. 17, no. 12.

86. "In ipso quoque tempore annuale mercatum, quod fit post festivitatem." Krusch, ed., *Gesta Dagoberti* 34, *M.G.H., Script. rer. Mer.* 2, p. 413.

87. The fair was undoubtedly at first merely a market of provisions for the faithful and the pilgrims during the celebrations of 9 October. All medieval fairs originated in some religious festival, but every fair had to be granted or allowed by the king. Levillain, *Bib. de l'Ec. des Ch.* 91 (1930): 50.

88. "Ad negociandum vel necocia plurima exercendum et vina conparandum." Charter of Pepin the Short, 753, Mühlbacher, ed., *M.G.H., Diplomata Kar.* 1, p. 9, no. 6.

89. Charter of Childebert III, 710 (Lauer and Samaran, eds., *Les Diplômes originaux des Mérovingiens,* 22). Levillain has defined "Saxones" as Anglo-Saxons of Great Britain; and by 753 the "Frisons," or Flemish, were mentioned. [**Ed. note:** Levillain, *Bib. de l'Ec. des Ch.* 91 (1930): 28–29.] In the tenth century merchants from Italy, Spain, and Provence were present at the fair. False charter of Dagobert I; Georg Heinrich Pertz, ed., *M.G.H., Diplomata Imperii* 1 (Hanover, 1872), Diplomata Spuria 23, pp. 140–41 (hereafter cited as Pertz, ed., *Diplomata Imp.* 1).

90. "Et quoniam ipsa eadem Ecclesia a tempore Dagoberti gloriosi Principis et Regis Francorum, primi ejusdem Ecclesiae fundatoris, et aliorum antecessorum nostrorum in Castro suo per septem septimanas." Charter of Louis VI, 1122. Doublet, *Histoire,* 851.

91. "Usque dum ipse mercatus finiatur." Charter of Charles the Bald, 862. Jules Tardif, *Monuments historiques* (Paris, 1866), 119.

92. "Et quatenus, antehactis temporebus, clade intercedente, de ipso vigo sancti Dionisii ipse marcadus fuit emutatus, et ad Parisius civetate, inter sancti Martini et sancti Laurente baselicis, ipse marcadus fuit factus." Charter of Childebert III, 710. Lauer and Samaran, eds., *Les Diplômes originaux des Mérovingiens,* 22. Levillain has shown that the location indicated in this passage must have been at the very "portes" of Paris, near the church of Saint-Martin-des-Champs. See Levillain, *Bib. de l'Ec. des Ch.* 91 (1930): 22–24.

93. The *Gesta Dagoberti* is accurate in stating that the revenues were given to Saint-Denis by Dagobert. This is substantiated by the number of disputes that arose with various royal officials concerning these revenues. The first dispute was between 673 and 675 with Guerin, count of Paris. The following ones were in 709 with Grimoald, mayor of the palace of Neustria, and in 753 and 759 with Gerard, count of Paris. See Levillain, *Bib. de l'Ec. des Ch.* 91 (1930): 38–49.

94. Charter of Theodoric III, 680–88. Lauer and Samaran, eds., *Les Diplômes originaux des Mérovingiens* no. 18, p. 13. This charter gave exemptions from all duties, such as: "pontaticus, portaticus, pulviraticus, roda[ti]cus, salutaticus, cispetaticus," and any other "redibicio," and covered not only boats on any French river and carts on any road, but also all beasts and even men carrying goods of the abbey or merchants acting for the monks. It applied to any place where taxes were levied, such as: "civitates, castella, vici, portus, pontes publici," and "reliqui

marcadi," or any market. See Levillain, *Bib. de l'Ec. des Ch.* 91 (1930): 264–76, esp. 267.

95. Archives Nationales, K3, no. 1; published by Doublet, *Histoire,* 443; and by Tardif, *Monuments historiques,* 8–10, no. 10. See Levillain, *Bib. de l'Ec. des Ch.* 87 (1926): 35–53, 330.

96. As the charter of Clovis II is the oldest and nearest to the original, I shall quote it: "Et nostra integra devocio et peticio fuit, ut apostolicus vir Landericus, Parisiaci aecclesiae episcopus, privilegio ad ipsum sanctum locum abbati vel fratrebus ibidem consistentebus, facere vel confirmare pro quiite futura deberit, quo facilius congregacioni ipsi licerit pro stabiletate regni nostri ad limena marterum ipsorum jugeter exorare: hoc ipse pontefex cum suis quoepiscopus iuxta peticionem devocionis nostrae plenissemam volontatem prestitisse vel confirmasse dinuscetur." Charter of Clovis II, 653. Pertz, ed., *M.G.H., Diplomata Imp.* 1, charter 19, p. 20. The charter of Theodoric IV, 724, is the same, adding a clause about the free election of the abbot; Havet, *Bib. de l'Ec. des Ch.* 51 (1890): 60–61. The charter of Pepin the Short, 768, follows Theodoric IV; Mühlbacher, ed., *M.G.H., Diplomata Kar.* 1, p. 34. The charter of Hilduin, 832, is of small value; Levillain, *Bib. de l'Ec. des Ch.* 87 (1926): 34, n. 3.

97. Marculfe, *Formulae* 1, 1, 2 (ed. Zeumer, pp. 39–41). Also, an analysis of the false charter of Landri proved that many clauses could not have been written in the seventh century. See Levillain, *Bib. de l'Ec. des Ch.* 87 (1926): 35–53.

98. "Ut dixemus, ipse sanctus locus videtur esse ditatus, nullus episcoporum, nec praesentes nec qui futuri fuerint successores, aut eorum ordenatores vel qualibet persona, possit quoquo ordene de loco ipso alequid auferre aut alequa potestate sibi in ipso monasthirio vindicare vel alequid quase per conmutacionis titulum, absque volontate ipsius congregacionis vel nostrum permissum, minoere." Charter of Clovis II, 653. Pertz, ed., *M.G.H., Diplomata Imp.* 1, charter 19, p. 20.

99. Levillain, *Bib. de l'Ec. des Ch.* 87 (1926): 341.

100. Charter of Dagobert I, 29, July 624; Pertz, ed., *M.G.H., Diplomata Imp.* 1, Documenta Spuria 43, p. 161. Pertz dated it to 637 and included it among a group of false charters. Charter of Dagobert I, c. 631–32; ibid., 143–44. Charter of Dagobert I, c. 633, ibid., 152–53.

101. Charter of Chilpéric II, 716; ibid., 72–73. [**Ed. note:** See below, nn. 106, 107.]

102. Krusch, ed., *Gesta Dagoberti* 39, 50, *M.G.H., Script. rer. Mer.* 2, pp. 418, 423.

103. Not only the medieval tradition, but the immunity has been upheld by such eminent scholars as Dom Mabillon, *De re diplomatica* 3, 2d ed. (Paris, 1709), 244–45; and more recently by Fustel de Coulanges, "Etude sur l'immunité mérovingienne," *Revue historique* 22 (1883): 252–53.

104. "Et ut hoc libenter adquiescerent, privilegium eis firmare iussit, vel etiam emunitates concessit, ut melius eis delectaret pro rege et pace summi regis Christi clementiam exorare." Krusch, ed., *Vita sanctae Bathildis* 9, *M.G.H., Script. rer. Mer.* 2, pp. 493–94.

105. See Levillain's detailed analysis of these charters in *Bib. de l'Ec. des Ch.* 87 (1926): 68–95.

106. "Iuxta quod anteriores parentis nostri vel precelsus avuncolus noster Theodoricus, seo et consobrini nostri Chlodovius, Childebercthus et Dagobercthus, quondam regis, per eorum aucturetatis ad ipsa baseleca hoc pristetirunt vel confirmaverunt." Charter of Chilpéric II, 716; Pertz, ed., *M.G.H., Diplomata Imp.* 1, charter 81, p. 72.

107. Levillain has interpreted the text of the charter of Chilpéric II, 716, in such a way that it supports the information of the *Vita Bathildis; Bib. de l'Ec. des Ch.* 87 (1926): 54–68. Although Levillain's arguments lack conviction, the statement of the *Vita Bathildis* remains the earliest authentic mention of immunity for Saint-Denis.

108. Bathilde married Clovis II about 650 or 651. He died in 657 and she remained in power, as regent, until her son Clotaire III attained his majority. See ibid., 53–54.

109. In addition to commercial privileges, Theodoric III (670–91) gave three *mansi* and a town to the abbey between 677 and 688 (charters of Theodoric III; Pertz, ed., *M.G.H., Diplomata Imp.* 1, charters 47, 48, 51, and 57, pp. 43–44, 46, 51). In 692 Clovis III (691–95) gave additional revenues (ibid., charter 64, pp. 56–57). Childebert III (695–711) gave four domains between 695 and 710 (ibid., charters 67, 68, 75, and 78, pp. 59–61, 66–67, 69–70). In 726 Theodoric IV (720–32) gave one domain (ibid., charter 94, p. 84).

110. The charter of Theodoric IV, 724, reestablishing the independence of Saint-Denis states that the charter of Landri had been confirmed by his predecessors: "ad anterioris rigis parentis nostrus de eu tempore usque nunc confirmatus," Havet, *Bib. de l'Ec. des Ch.* 51 (1890): 60. The charter of Chilpéric II, 716, proves that immunity had been confirmed by Theodoric IV, Clovis II, Childebert II, and Dagobert III (Pertz, ed., *M.G.H., Diplomata Imp.* 1, charter 84, p. 74). The charters of Childebert III, 710, and of Pepin the Short, 753, show that almost every Merovingian king had confirmed the right to hold the fair (ibid., charter 77, pp. 68–69; and Mühlbacher, ed., *M.G.H., Diplomata Kar.* 1, charter 6, pp. 9–11).

111. Evidence for this is naturally scarce; but the charter of Theodoric III, 680–88, granting complete commercial privileges (see above, n. 94), leaves no doubt that the abbey was actively engaged in commerce. An example of this is the sale of "4980 kilogrammes of oil and about 9 hectoliters of wine" to the bishop of Autun. See charter of Clovis III, 692 (Pertz, ed., *M.G.H., Diplomata Imp.* 1, charter 60, pp. 53–54). [**Ed. note:** Latin original published by Pertz reads, "olio milli quignentas liberas, et vino bono modios cento".]

112. An interesting example of this is the method employed to evade the law against loans at interest. By paying a debt of a certain noble, Ibbon, who later died insolvent, the abbey received lands in the "Beauvaisis." Charter of Childebert III, 695 (ibid., charter 68, pp. 60–61).

113. Tornoaldus was bishop of Paris from 693 or 694 until 718

or 719 (Duchesne, *Fastes episcopaux* 2:469). A charter of Chilpéric II, 717, shows that he was also abbot of Saint-Denis (Pertz, ed., *M.G.H., Diplomata Imp.* 1, charter 87, p. 77).

114. This office of a monastic bishop, whose duty it was to take charge of the "predication of pilgrims," did not survive. It seems to have been peculiar to the late Merovingian and Carolingian periods, before the introduction of the authentic Benedictine Rule. At Saint-Denis the office did not exist after 840. See Levillain, *Bib. de l'Ec. des Ch.* 87 (1926): 330–39.

CHAPTER 3. FULRAD'S CHURCH

1. The *Continuationes*, in Krusch, ed., *Chronica Fredegarii, M.G.H., Script rer. Mer.* 2, pp. 168–93; Friedrich Kurze, ed., *Annales Fuldenses* (Hanover, 1891); Georg Waitz, ed., *Annales Bertiniani* (Hanover, 1883); Nithardus, *De dissensionibus filiorum Ludovici Pii*, ed. Migne, *P.L.*, 116, cols. 45–76; Flodoardus (canonicus Remensis), *Annales, Historia Remensis*, and *Opuscula metrica*, ed. Migne, *P.L.*, 135, cols. 23–886; Ordericus Vitalis, *Historia ecclesiastica*, ed. Migne, *P.L.*, 188, cols. 17–984; Rudolfus Glaber (Cluniacensis monachus), *Historiarum sui temporis libri quinque*, Migne, ed., *P.L.*, 142, cols. 611–98; S. Abbo abbas Floracensis, *Opera*, Migne, ed., *P.L.*, 139, cols, 417–584; S. Fulbertus Carnotensis episcopus, *Opera*, Migne, ed., *P.L.*, 141, cols. 189–374.

2. Previté-Orton, *Shorter Cambridge*, 1:158.

3. See the introduction to Heinrich Fichtenau, *The Carolingian Empire*, trans. by Peter Munz (Oxford, 1963), 1–24; see also the charts in Previté-Orton, *Shorter Cambridge*, 1:154–55.

4. Ibid., 297.

5. Prinz, *Frühes Mönchtum*, 209; in regard to the decision to send Pepin and Carloman to be educated at Saint-Denis, see Pierre Riché, *Education and Culture in the Barbarian West—Sixth through Eighth Centuries*, trans. John J. Contreni (Columbia, S.C., 1975), 442; and Previté-Orton, *Shorter Cambridge*, 1:297.

6. [Ed. note: "Ils devaient 'consulter le pontife au sujet des rois,' et lui demander, 'lequel des deux il était juste d'appeler du titre de roi, ou le Mérovingien qui vivait sans rien faire dans son Palais, ou bien celui qui avait tous les soins du gouvernement et tout le fardeau des affaires.' "] Fustel de Coulanges, *Histoire des institutions* 6, *Les Transformations de la royauté* (Paris, 1892), 199. "Burchardus . . . et Folradus . . . missi sunt Romam ad Zachariam papam, ut consulerent pontificem de causa regum . . . qui nomen tentum regis sed nullam potestatem regiam habuerunt." Eginhardus, *Annales Laurissenses et Eginhardi*, Migne, ed., *P.L.*, 104, p. 373.

7. Most medieval historians treat this major event: see Lavisse, *Histoire de France*, 2:271–72; Levillain, "L'Avènement de la dynastie carolingienne et les origines de l'état pontifical (749–757). Essai sur la chronologie et l'interprétation des événements," *Bib. de l'Ec. des Ch.* 94 (1933): 226–29.

8. Levillain, *Bib. de l'Ec. des. Ch.* 94 (1933): 230, 250–54.

9. Buchner claimed that there is no proof that such an altar was dedicated, Maximillian Buchner, "Die Areopagitika des

Abtes Hilduin von St. Denis und ihr kirchenpolitischer Hintergrund. Studien zur Gleichsetzung Dionysius des Areopagiten mit dem hl. Dionysius von Paris sowie zur Fälschungstechnik am Vorabend der Entstehung der Pseudoisidorischen Dekretalen," *Historisches Jahrbuch* 56 (1936): 477–78; Levillain, however, believed that the consecration actually took place, Levillain, *Bib. de l'Ec. des Ch.* 94 (1933): 261, n. 1. Without explaining, Hubert considered that the consecration involved a church, Hubert et al., *Carolingian Renaissance*, 54, 310.

10. Levillain, *Bib. de l'Ec. des Ch.* 94 (1933): 294. [Ed. note: "Un citoyen de Rome, logé aux frais de la république, un abbé mitré 'prelatus nullius' et un prince de l'Eglise, attestent qu'il avait eu, dans l'avènement de la dynastie carolingienne et dans la fondation de l'Etat pontifical, une part telle qu'il mérite de voir son nom associé à ceux du pape et du roi."]

11. Fulrad is not identified in the *Catholic Encyclopedia* of 1909 or of 1967. See now Josef Fleckenstein, "Fulrad von Saint-Denis und der fränkische Ausgriff in den süddeutschen Raum," in Gerd Tellenbach, ed., *Studien und Vorarbeiten zur Geschichte des grossfränkischen und frühdeutschen Adels*, Forschungen zur oberrheinischen Landesgeschichte 4 (Freiburg im Breisgau, 1957), 9–39.

12. William Smith and Henry Wace, *A Dictionary of Christian Biography* (London, 1880), 2:585–86. This brief sketch identifies his parents as Riculfus and Ermengarda.

13. Levillain has suggested that Fulrad was only a priest when he was sent to Rome in 751, and that he was made abbot of Saint-Denis when he returned. Levillain, *Bib. de l'Ec. des Ch.* 94 (1933): 226–28.

14. Félibien, *Histoire*, 49.

15. These privileges included the right to have six deacons clothed in dalmatics for the celebration of the Mass; the personal right to wear a mitre though he was not a bishop; the right to wear the senatorial white stockings and slippers; and the special saddle covering when he was riding. All of these ornaments were to be placed in Fulrad's coffin when he was buried. Bull of Stephen III, ca. 755, Félibien, *Histoire*, pièces justicatives, p. xxvii, no. XXXVIII; Levillain, *Bib. de l'Ec. des Ch.* 94 (1933): 269.

16. Félibien, *Histoire*, 55.

17. Félibien, *Histoire*, pièces justicatives, pp. xxviii–xxxix, no. LVI. See Félicie Marie Emilie d'Ayzac, *Histoire de l'Abbaye de Saint-Denis en France* (Paris, 1861), 2:508–09; Tangl, *Neues Archiv* 32 (1907): 171–73; and Fleckenstein, "Fulrad von Saint-Denis," 10–17, map p. 16.

18. "Donamus pro anime nostrae remedio ad ecclesiam sancti Diunisii, ubi ipse praeciosus domnus cum sociis suis corpore quiescunt et venerabilis vir Fulradus abba praeese videtur et nos Christo propitio a novo aedificavimus opere et modo cum magno decore iussimus dedicare, donatumque in perpetuo ad ipsum sanctum locum esse volumnus." Diploma of Charlemagne, 25 Feb. 775 (Mühlbacher, ed., et al., *M.G.H., Diplomata Kar.* 1, 92, p. 133).

19. "Cum basilicam Sanctorum, diruta priore quae coepta a

Pippino Rege, augustius a Karolo Regni successore consummata est, opifices architectarentur, unus clavorum, quibus tecto tabulae adfigebantur, cecidit." *Miracula* or *Vita sancti Dionysii* 1, 14, ed. Mabillon, *Acta sanctorum Ord. Ben.*, saec. 3, pt. 2, p. 315; see also Julius von Schlosser, ed., *Schriftquellen zur Geschichte der karolingischen Kunst* (Vienna, 1896), 213.

20. Diploma of Pepin, 768 (Mühlbacher, ed., et al., *M.G.H., Diplomata Kar.* 1, no. 28, pp. 38–40).

21. "Quique cum quanta se humilitate ante limina basilicae sanctorum martyrum perfuncto huius vitae curriculo sepeliri preceperit, titulus etiam ipsius conditorii innotescit." Letter from Louis to Hilduin, ca. 835; Dümmler, ed., *Epistolae variorum inde a morte Caroli Magni usque ad divisionem imperii, M.G.H., Epistolarum* 5, *Karolini Aevi* 3 (Berlin, 1899), p. 326.

22. Levillain, *Mém. de la Soc. de l'Hist. de Paris* 36 (1909): 161.

23. "Et deponentes augmentum quoddam, quod a Karolo Magno factum perhibebatur honesta satis occasione (quia pater suus Pipinus imperator extra in introitu valvarum pro peccatis patris sui Karoli Martelli prostratum se sepeliri, non supinum, fecerat)." Suger, *De Administratione* 25, Lecoy de la Marche, ed., *Oeuvres*, 187; Panofsky, ed., *Suger*, 44–45. Although Suger's text probably reflected accumulated traditions, the letter from Louis the Pious to Hilduin proves that the idea of self-humiliation was current in the early ninth century.

24. [**Ed. note:** "L'abbatiale mérovingienne fut détruite; mais il nous est impossible de préciser les conditions et circonstances de sa démolition."] Levillain, *Mém. de la Soc. de l'Hist. de Paris* 36 (1909):159.

25. [**Ed. note:** "L'occasion était largement offerts aux Francs de s'initier aux fonctions cultuelles célébrées 'more romano'."] Cyrille Vogel, "La Réforme cultuelle sous Pepin le Bref et sous Charlemagne (deuxième moitie du VIIIe siècle et premier quart du IXe siècle," in Erna Patzelt, *Die Karolingische Renaissance,* 182.

26. The documents are: Alfred Boretius, ed., *Admonitio Generalis* (23 March 789) 80, *M.G.H., Legum Sectio II, Capitularia regum Francorum* 1 (Hanover, 1883), p. 61 (hereafter cited as *Cap. reg. Franc.*); Boretius, ed., *Karoli epistola generalis* (786–800), *M.G.H., Cap. reg. Franc.* 1, p. 80; Hubert Bastgen, ed., *Libri Carolini sive Caroli Magni Capitulare de Imaginibus* 1, 6, *M.G.H., Legum Sectio II, Concilia* 2, supplementum (Hanover, 1924), p. 21; *Capitulare de Imaginibus* 1, 6, Migne, ed., *P.L.,* 98, col. 1019–22; Walafrid Strabon, *Libellus de exordiis et incrementis quarundam in observationibus ecclesiasticus rerum ecclesiasticarum* 26, Boretius and Viktor Kraus, eds., *M.G.H., Legum Sectio II, Cap. reg. Franc.* 2 (Hanover, 1897), p. 508.

27. Vogel, "Réforme cultuelle," in Patzelt, *Karolingische Renaissance,* 179.

28. Sedlmayr, *Mitteilungen der Gesellschaft für Salzburger Landeskunde* 115 (1973): 145–48.

29. Centre de Recherches sur les Monuments Historiques (hereafter cited as C.R.M.H.), Prélèvements et analyses par C. Jaton, A. Blanc, Basilique de Saint-Denis: no. 93–14, M I and M II.

30. Levillain, *Mém. de la Soc. de l'Hist. de Paris* 36 (1909): 160.

31. On papal consecrations, see Francis Salet, "Cluny III," *Bull. mon.* 126 (1968): 239–47.

32. Archives Photographiques, 4 rue de Turenne, Paris, photo numbers 58.P.1054, 58.P.1055, 58.P.1058, 58.P.1059, 58.P.1060.

33. [**Ed. note:** See above, chap. 2, n. 8.]

34. "The excellence of the mortar points to the high grade of craftsmanship both in making the slaked lime and in mixing and placing the mortar," Professor Frederick K. Morris, Department of Geology, Massachusetts Institute of Technology, letter to author, 6 February 1951.

35. The dimensions—"28 centimètres de long sur 17 centimètres de haut"—given in my 1953 text are in error, Crosby, *L'Abbaye royale*, 16. Formigé's precise dimensions—"longs de 1 pied (0,324 m.), hauts d'un demi-pied (0,162 m.) environ"—compress the stones to fit his theory, Formigé, *Abbaye royale,* 59; Vieillard-Troïekouroff, *Karl der Grosse* 3:345.

36. Crosby, "A Carolingian Pavement at Saint-Denis—Preliminary Report," *Gesta* 9/1 (1970): 42–43.

37. Formigé, *Abbaye royale,* 63; Geneviève Aliette, marquise de Maillé, *Les Cryptes de Jouarre* (Paris, 1971), 125, n. 3.

38. On the theory and practice of using pulverized brick in mortar, see the long footnote with references in Forsyth, *The Church of St. Martin,* 26, n. 12; see also Paolo Verzone, *The Dark Ages,* 43–44, 60.

39. Formigé referred to the bevel as "un chapiteau à doucine," *Abbaye royale,* 163.

40. Crosby, 1942, 99–104.

41. Formigé, *Abbaye royale,* 159–63, fig. 143.

42. Crosby, 1942, 99 and n. 63. [**Ed. note:** For the plans by Jacques Cellérier and Viollet-le-Duc, see ibid., figs. 9 and 73.]

43. Formigé's measurements were "environ 3,50 m. sur 1,50 m." *Abbaye royale,* 159.

44. Ibid. [**Ed. note:** "Les accès à ces couloirs se retournaient d'équerre au nord et au sud où je les ai dégagés." See also App. H, fig. 11.]

45. One of the photographs in the Archives Photographiques—no. 58-V-1656—shows a series of three or four descending stones which might have been interpreted as steps, but these must have been in the apse above the crypt as shown by the fragment of painted drapery on the right of the photograph. This masonry is no longer visible. [**Ed. note:** See App. H, fig. 11.]

46. Formigé, *Abbaye royale,* 159.

47. Formigé assumed that these windows were enlarged at some later but undetermined time, *Abbaye royale,* 163. A workman at Saint-Denis warned me in 1961 that much of the southern side of the apse had been completely rebuilt, which was evidently common knowledge, for Vieillard-Troïekouroff noted that "Ce meneau subsistait dans une fenêtre. J. Formigé les a indiscrètement rétablis dans les autres." *Karl der Grosse* 3:353, n. 79. Formigé's workmen were so skillful that only an expert eye can detect their substitutes. The Archives photographs suggest that

the workmen began their restoration, or repairs, before the excavations were finished, possibly to impress visiting officials, but such complete reworking of the original masonry raises questions about all of the details.

48. [**Ed. note:** For an illustration of the blackened niche, see Formigé, *Abbaye royale,* fig. 137; for a plastered and painted window embrasure, see ibid., fig. 138; and concerning the wooden frame, ibid., 163.]

49. May Vieillard-Troïekouroff's attempt to interpret Formigé's plan, which she published in *Karl der Grosse* 3:340, fig. 1, has been copied by almost all subsequent authors, for example, Wolfgang Braunfels, *Die Welt der Karolinger und ihre Kunst* (Munich, 1968), 63, fig. 1, and Sedlmayr, "Politische Bedeutung," 155, abb. 1. Hubert chose to publish Formigé's completely imaginary plan, Hubert et al., *Carolingian Renaissance,* 305, fig. 375. [**Ed. note:** See also Formigé, *Abbaye royale,* 169: "Cette abside se termine sur deux épaulements en retour d'équerre dont la longueur n'est pas connue, parce qu'ils sont noyés dans les fondations postérieures."]

50. Formigé, *Abbaye royale,* 51, fig. 40.

51. Such chambers were often not recorded on plans of the crypt in the vain hope that they would escape violation. These particular rooms on the north side were, I was told, used by the French Resistance in 1944–45 to hide weapons.

52. [**Ed. note:** Crosby, 1942, 137; Crosby, *L'Abbaye royale,* 17]; and for one text, "Basilicae fabrica completa, impositaque turri, in qua signa, ut moris est, penderent; Fulradus venerandus abbas, qui operi magnanimiter institerat, dum diu desideratum opus consideraret adspexit necdum lignorum summota instrumenta, quibus nixi artifices praedictae turris cacumen erexerant," see *Miracula* or *Vita sancti Dionysii* I, 15 (Schlosser, ed., *Schriftquellen,* 213; Mabillon, ed., *Acta Sanct. Ord. Ben.,* saec. 3, pt. 2, p. 315). [**Ed. note:** See also, below, n. 83 for portions of a unique text, *Descriptio Basilicae Sancti Dyonisii* (Landesbibliothek Karlsruhe, ms. Augiensis CCXXXVIII, fols. 159v–160r), which also documents the existence of a tower ("casubula habet pedes de alto XXXIII"). Bound into a compilation of texts and dated in the thirty-first year of Charlemagne's reign, the *Descriptio* was first published in 1980 in an edited version with a French translation and brief commentary by Alain J. Stoclet, "La *Descriptio Basilicae Sancti Dyonisii.* Premiers commentaires," *Journal des savants* (1980): 103–17. See also the uncorrected or original text published by Bernhard Bischoff, "Eine Beschreibung der Basilika von Saint-Denis aus dem Jahre 799," *Kunstchronik* 34, no. 3 (1981): 97–103, with a German translation and explanatory notes.

This important text gives measurements for the plan, foundations, and elevation of Fulrad's church as well as the number of windows, columns and capitals, doors and arches, with distinctions made among the various media used for capitals and doors. Further study is needed to analyze and evaluate the information provided by the *Descriptio* in terms of the archaeological information presented in this chapter and of the author's reconstruction of the Carolingian basilica. See now Werner Jacobsen,

"Saint-Denis in neuem Licht: Konsequenzen der neuendeckten Baubeschreibung aus dem Jahr 799," *Kunstchronik* 36 (1983): 301–08; and Heitz, "Saint-Denis," in P. Périn and L.-C. Feffer, eds., *La Neustrie,* 165.]

53. I refer to a Carolingian foot [**Ed. note:** sometimes called the Gallic foot], as equaling 0.3329 m. See especially Forsyth, *The Church of St. Martin,* 23–24, n. 4.

54. On the narrow hall squeezed by towers, see Suger, *De Consecratione* 2, Lecoy de la Marche, ed., *Oeuvres,* 217–18; Panofsky, ed., *Suger,* 88–89. [**Ed. note:** "Quia igitur in anteriori parte, ab aquilone, principali ingressu principalium valvarum porticus artus hinc et inde gemellis, nec altis, nec aptis multum, sed minantibus ruinam." For Suger's reference to Charlemagne (Suger, *De Administratione* 25), see above, n. 23.]

55. Panofsky, ed., *Suger,* 225–29.

56. Crosby, *Proceedings of the American Philosophical Society* 93 (1949): 347–61.

57. Ibid., 358–59, nn. 15, 16. [**Ed. note:** See also the recent reference to this "embryonic" apse, Carol Heitz, "More romano. Problèmes d'architecture et liturgie Càrolingiennes," in *Roma e l'età carolingia. Atti della giornate di studio, 3–8 maggio 1976 a cura dello Istituto di storia dell'Arte dell'Università di Roma. Istituto Nazionale di Archeologia e Storia dell'Arte* (Rome, 1976): 27–37. Also E. Baldwin Smith, *Architectural Symbolism of Imperial Rome and the Middle Ages* (Princeton, 1956), 82–83.]

58. Crosby, *Gesta* 9/1 (1970): 42–45.

59. Earlier I believed that the eighth-century pavement was lower, Crosby, *Proceedings of the American Philosophical Society* 93 (1949): 357 (−0.75 m); Crosby, 1942, 132 (−1.10 m).

60. Hubert et al., *Carolingian Renaissance,* 4.

61. "L'autre, très considerable, en forme de dé, est décorée sur ses quatre faces d'ornements de style merovingien; ce cube a eu dans la suite une destination qui demeure inexpliquée; il a été creusé en forme de récipient peut-être dans le but d'en faire une cuve baptismale; toutes les faces sont bien conservées sauf la supérieure." Report of Jules Quicherat in "Séance du 11 mai 1881," Auguste Prost presiding, *Bull. de la Soc. Nat. des Antiq. de France* (1881): 177. As mentioned earlier, both the Carolingian base and the Gallo-Roman block have now been returned to Saint-Denis, where they may be seen in the Musée Lapidaire.

62. Ibid.

63. This base was still at the Cluny Museum when I saw it in 1936. It was moved back to Saint-Denis during the 1950s. For the original move in 1881, see François de Montrémy, "Base carolingienne conservée au musée de Cluny," *Bull. mon.* 81 (1922): 424–26.

64. Hubert, *Art pré-roman,* 161.

65. Crosby, "Fouilles executées récemment dans la basilique de Saint-Denis," *Bull. mon.* 105 (1947): 177.

66. Formigé, *Abbaye royale,* 53, 61.

67. Bibliothèque Municipale in Autun, dated 754. Hubert et al., *Carolingian Renaissance,* 70, fig. 61. Jean Porcher, ibid., 71, identified the Gundohinus Gospels as the beginning of Carolingian book illumination and noted the coincidence between

the date of the gospels, 754, and the crowning of Pepin the Short at Saint-Denis by Pope Stephen II. Even though the location of "Vosevium," where the gospels supposedly were completed, cannot be identified, I would suggest that the sculptor of the base at Saint-Denis shared the aesthetic preference of the illuminator of the gospels.

68. Formigé, *Abbaye royale*, 53, figs. 41, 42; see also Vieillard-Troïekouroff, *Karl der Grosse* 3:347, figs. 3, 4 (plaster cast).

69. [**Ed. note:** In June 1984 the editor had an opportunity to examine the four bases still visible and *in situ* (N1 and 2 and S2 and 3) and to take the measurements of plinth N1 and bases N1 and N2 given above. (None of the other dimensions recorded in this section were retaken.) For all four the examination indicated that, given the noncongruent measurements of the bases and plinths, the crucial statistic was the level at which the Carolingian pavement (established by the author as −0.71 m) had impinged on the base. With the excavated areas in question now underneath the pavement of the nave, that significant measurement had to be taken by sighting the level of −0.71 from the nearest opening in the nave floor where removable paving stones or grills permit entry into the excavations. Those openings also provided information about the varying thickness of today's pavement—a dimension crucial to establishing the −0.71 m level on each base.

All four bases examined bear a vestige or scar of the Carolingian pavement traceable at least in part on one or more of the visible faces. In each instance the base had been set so that all of the carved ornament was above that level; the amount of the base rising above and lying below the Carolingian pavement emerged as a variable dependent on the overall height of the block and of the area carved, as well as on the level of the footing of the base.

The degraded states of bases N1 and S2 noted by the author seem to reflect the poor quality of the stone. The quality differs noticeably from that used for N2 (the fleur-de-lys base), for S3 (the base still intact, but with its large fleur-de-lys ornament nearly effaced), and for the Cluny base in the Musée Lapidaire. Visual inspection suggested that laboratory tests would probably find the stone of the two degraded bases comparable and identify that of the three others as a stronger and better quality limestone.

The repairs in red mortar characteristic of Carolingian construction which the author observed on base N1 suggests that it was *spolia* from the Merovingian structure repaired and reused in the Carolingian period—a hypothesis which would explain the strikingly different composition and style of the decoration with the other known bases. Stone analysis is essential before that hypothesis can be extended to include bases S1 (no longer accessible but, as the author noted, also in fragments) and S2. The questions raised by the bases indicate an area for further research.]

70. [**Ed. note:** "magnorum capitellorum et basium columnas deportantium disruptionem exhilarati deaptare sollicitabamur.] Suger, *De Consecratione* 3, Lecoy de la Marche, ed., *Oeuvres*, 221, Panofsky, ed., *Suger*, 94–95.

71. [**Ed. note:** Leningrad, M. E. Saltykow-Schtschedrin State

Library, Lat. Fv. I. Nr. 6, fol. AB.], Braunfels, *Welt der Karolinger*, p. 63, abb. 27, where he also described the relief as "wie langobardischen Bandornamentik." Photographs of the base have been published by Montrémy, *Bull. mon.* 81 (1922): 425; Crosby, 1942, 135, fig. 35a; Vieillard-Troïekouroff, *Karl der Grosse* 3:347, fig. 1; Hubert et al., *Carolingian Renaissance*, 216, fig. 197.

72. Hubert et al., *Carolingian Renaissance*, 216, fig. 197.

73. [**Ed. note:** See the *Corpus della scultura altomedievale* 7, *La Diocesi di Roma*, 3 parts (Spoleto, 1974), which provides a visual survey of comparative material. See especially the eighth-century bases in the chapel of S. Zenone in S. Prassede, ibid., part 1, figs. 92 and 94. See also Rudolf Kautzsch, "Die langobardische Schmuckkunst in Oberitalien," *Römisches Jahrbuch für Kunstgeschichte* 5 (1941): 3–48.]

74. Formigé, *Abbaye royale*, 60, fig. 48. Vieillard-Troïekourouff, *Karl der Grosse* 3:348, fig. 6.

75. [**Ed. note:** "In novitate siquidem sessionis nostrae impedimentum quoddam, quo medium ecclesiae muro tenebroso secabatur." Suger, *De Administratione* 34, Lecoy de la Marche, ed., *Oeuvres*, 204; Panofsky, ed., *Suger*, 72–73. See also the "claire-voie transversale" of the priory church of Saint Généroux of the eastern end of the tenth-century nave, Carol Heitz, *L'Architecture religieuse carolingienne: Les Formes et leur fonctions* (Paris, 1980), 193, fig. 155.]

76. Thomas F. Mathews, "An Early Roman Chancel Arrangement and its Liturgical Functions," *Rivista di archeologia cristiana* 38 (1962): 79.

77. Suger, *De Administratione* 34, Lecoy de la Marche, ed., *Oeuvres*, 203; Panofsky, ed., *Suger*, 73.

78. Viollet-le-Duc, *Revue archéologique*, n.s. 3 (1861): 302. [**Ed. note:** "Traces des peintures représentant des tentures fort grossièrement tracées en gris sur un fond blanc." Formigé, *Abbaye royale*, 61, 161, figs. 138–40. Figure 138 shows the marbleized painting of a window embrasure.]

79. [**Ed. note:** Crosby, 1942, 160.]

80. Crosby, *Gesta* 9/1 (1970): 45.

81. [**Ed. note:** See René Louis, *Les Eglises d'Auxerre des origines au XIe siècle* (Paris, 1952), 111–24; and Jean Vallery-Radot, "Auxerre. La Cathédrale Saint-Etienne. Les Principaux textes de l'histoire de la construction," *Congrès Archéologique de France, Auxerre* 116 (1959): 43–45.]

82. Crosby, 1942, 131–34, 143–45.

83. [**Ed. note:** See above, note 52; also the recent publication of a text that recorded measurements and other statistics for the church of Fulrad, including the height of the church to the vault ("de alto usque ad camerato habet pedes LXXV. Excepto habet ille fundamentum pedes XIII"); the height of the roof ("diticus [read as *tictus*, a variant of *tectum*] habet de alto pedes XXX"); the tower ("casubula habet de alto pedes XXXIII"); and the total height ("totum de alto pedes CXL"). (N.B. The sum of the heights minus the thirteen pedes of the "fundamentum" equals pedes 138, not 140). See Stoclet, *Journal des savants* 10 (1980): 104; and Bischoff, *Kunstchronik* 34 (1981): 99–100.]

84. [**Ed. note:** See Bischoff, *Kuntschronik* 34 (1981)] 99–100; and Stoclet, *Journal des savants* 10 (1980): 104, which give the number of marble and stone columns and capitals within and without the church; also the number of arches ("arcus majores XLV"). During the summer of 1984 a square pier with Carolingian ornament was excavated on the site of the church of Les Trois Patrons. The local archaeologists, 8 rue Franciade, Saint Denis, have attributed the pier to the Carolingian building of Saint-Denis. See Olivier Meyer et al., *Saint-Denis recherches urbaines 1983–1985. Bilan et fouilles* (St.-Denis, 1985), 65, 67, fig. 48.]

85. [**Ed. note:** Crosby, 1942, 133.]

86. [**Ed. note:** Levillain, *Mém. de la Soc. de l'Hist. de Paris* 36 (1909):176.]

87. [**Ed. note:** Suger, *De Consecratione* 3, Lecoy de la Marche, ed., *Oeuvres*, 222; Panofsky, ed., *Suger*, 97. See also ibid., 235, n. for Suger's text, p. 96, line 9.]

88. Crosby, 1942, 153, n. 91.

89. "Fui sicut in oratione in aecclesia eiusdem beati martiris subtus campanas, et vidi ante altare bonum pastorem domnum Petrum et magistrum gentium domnum Paulum." George Waitz, ed., *Revelatio* (a fabricated story about Pope Stephen II by Abbot Hilduin), from *Ex Hilduini abbatis libro de S. Dionysio, M.G.H., Scriptores* 15, 1 (Hanover, 1887), p. 2; Maximillian Buchner, *Das Vizepapsttum des Abtes von Saint-Denis* (Paderborn, 1928), 250; Panofsky, ed., *Suger*, 159–60.

90. [**Ed. note:** On the tower of Fulrad's church, see also Richard Krautheimer's review, "The Abbey of Saint-Denis, 475–1122, Volume I, by Sumner McKnight Crosby," *American Journal of Archaeology* 48 (1944): 220, which, on the basis of Crosby's first excavation reports, proposed a round rather than a square tower over the transept. On the question of comparable crossing towers, see George Forsyth, "St. Martin's at Angers and the Evolution of Early Mediaeval Church Towers," *Art Bulletin* 32 (1950): 308–18; and Virginia Jansen, "Round or Square? The Axial Towers of the Abbey Church of Saint-Riquier," *Gesta* 21 (1982): 83–90.]

91. [**Ed. note:** See above, n. 54.]

92. Formigé, *Abbaye royale*, 52.

93. [**Ed. note:** On this, see inter alia Krautheimer, "The Carolingian Revival of Early Christian Architecture," *Studies*, 206–12.]

CHAPTER 4. FROM THE DEATH OF FULRAD TO THE BIRTH OF SUGER

1. Originating in France, not England, the existing documents concerning these early grants evidently bear some relationship to the terms of the actual grants; see Stevenson, *English Historical Review* 6 (1891): 342. See also Félibien, *Histoire*, 59–60, pièces justicatives LXII, pp. xlii–xliii; and Crosby, 1942, 83, n. 58.

2. Félibien, *Histoire*, 62–64; Fichtenau, *The Carolingian Empire*, 82, considered Saint-Denis "the most famous of all abbeys" and noted Fardulph's unusual authority as a *missi dominici*, ibid., 108.

3. Recorded by the *tituli* written by Hibernicus Exul, *Epitaphium Karoli Imperatoris, Carmina* 19, Ernst Dümmler, ed., *M.G.H., Poetae Latini medii aevi* 1, *Aevi Carolini* 1 (Berlin, 1881 and 1964), pp. 407–11; Adolf Katzenellenbogen, *The Sculptural Programs of Chartres Cathedral. Christ. Mary. Ecclesia.* (1959; repr. New York, 1964), 15, 110, n. 44.

4. Félibien, *Histoire*, 64–65.

5. Buchner, *Historisches Jahrbuch* 56 (1936): 441–80, and 57 (1937): 31–60. Most historians have regarded the reign of Louis the Pious, Charlemagne's son, as beginning the decay of the Carolingian Empire. See Previté-Orton, *Shorter Cambridge*, 1:335–42. François Louis Ganshof suggested, however, that improvements were made on Charlemagne's system and concept of government, "Louis the Pious Reconsidered," *History*, n.s. 42 (1957): 171–80.

6. Félibien, *Histoire*, 73–74.

7. Levillain, "Wandalbert de Prüm et la date de la mort d'Hilduin de Saint-Denis," *Bib. de l'Ec. des Ch.* 108 (1949–50): 5–35; Werner Ohnsorge, "Das Kaiserbündnis von 842–844 gegen di Sarazenen. Datum, Inhalt und politische Bedeutung des 'Kaiserbriefes aus St.-Denis,'" *Archiv für Diplomatik, Schriftgeschichte, Siegel- und Wappenkunde* 1 (1955): 117–27.

8. Gabriel Théry, *Etudes dionysiennes*, vol. 16 of *Etudes de Philosophie médiévale*, ed. Etienne Gilson (Paris, 1932) 1:12.

9. Ibid., 1:167.

10. Maïeul Cappuyns, *Jean Scot Erigène. Sa Vie, son oeuvre, sa pensée* (Louvain, 1933), 150–51.

11. [**Ed. note:** see Introduction to part I, n. 17.]

12. Buchner, "Zur Enstehung und zur Tendenz der 'Gesta Dagoberti'. Zugleich ein Beitrag zum Eigenkirchwesen im Frankreich," *Historisches Jahrbuch* 47 (1927): 252–74; Buchner, *Das Vizepapsttum des Abtes von St.-Denis*, 52–80; Buchner, *Historisches Jahrbuch* 56 (1936): 441–80, and 57 (1937). See the review by Levillain, "Compte rendu: Max Buchner, *Das Vizepapsttum des Abtes von St.-Denis*," *Le Moyen Age* 39, 2d ser. 30 (1929): 85–95. Théry, in announcing a third volume of his *Etudes Dionysiennes*, stated that it would be preceded by "une étude d'ensemble sur Hilduin, par M. Léon Levillain," Théry, ibid., 1, p. iii. In addition to the works of Buchner, see Félibien, *Histoire*, 66–81; Théry, *Etudes Dionysiennes*, 1:11–12; and Levillain, *Bib. de l'Ec. des Ch.* 86 (1925): 35–43. Those works served as sources for this summary of Hilduin's life.

13. Levillain, *Bib. de l'Ec. des Ch.* 86 (1925): 40–41.

14. Crosby, 1942, 165–87.

15. Formigé, *Abbaye royale*, 169–72, fig. 151; Vieillard-Troïekouroff, *Karl der Grosse* 3:336.

16. "Idcirco ego . . . criptam ante pedes sanctissimorum martyrum nostrorum ad laudem & gloriam nominis Domini, in honore sanctae & intemeratae semperque virginis genetricis Dei Mariae omniumque sanctorum aedificavi, in qua multa pretiosissima sanctorum pignora auxiliante Domino collocavi." Hilduin, letter fragment in Félibien, *Histoire*, pièces justicatives LXXV, p. lvi. [**Ed. note:** Félibien dated the letter c. 833.]

"Vir venerabilis Hilduinus . . . ecclesiam ante pedes eorundum beatissimorum martyrum . . . pro nostra, conjugis etiam prolis, ac salute sua perpetua, aedificavit; in qua auxiliante Domino suoque laudabili studio laborante per multa & preciosissima sanctorum pignora collocavit." Charter of Louis the Pious, 833, ibid., pièces justicatives LXXVI, p. lvii.

Since certain revenues were accorded to the upkeep of a chapel in 832, and since mention is made in Hilduin's undated letter of a dedication on 1 November 832 [**Ed. note:** Ibid., pièces justicatives 1, p. lvi], Levillain has concluded that this must have been the date of the dedication of Hilduin's chapel. See Levillain, *Mém. de la Soc. de l'Hist. de Paris* 36 (1909): 161, n. 4.

17. "Collocavitque (Dagobertus) post altare in cripta tantae profunditatis, ut usque ad genua omnino se intromittat, si quid inde voluerit abstrahere aliquis. Quinetiam antequam ad corpora sanctorum perveniatur, criptula quaedam aureis gemmis extrinsecus decorata habetur, in qua duabus seris diligenter munita Dominici clavi & coronae condita servantur pignora, nolloque alio aditu praeter hunc scrinia sanctorum videri, aut ab aliquo possunt ullatenus tangi. Ecce quomodo corpus sancti Dionysii munitum, nulla adimi possit arte latronum." Haymo, *Detectio corporum* 5, Félibien, *Histoire,* pièces justicatives, pt. 2, p. clxviii.

18. [**Ed. note:** Suger, *De Consecratione* 4, Lecoy de la Marche, ed., *Oeuvres,* 225; Panofsky, ed., *Suger,* 101; see also below, ch. 7.]

19. The *Miracula Sancti Dionysii,* written about this time, mentions an altar dedicated to the Holy Trinity which was placed in the church by Hilduin. But since the altar was in the church proper, the reference has no pertinence to his chapel. "Altare, quod Hilduinus Abba insigni admodum opere sanctae Trinitati, inter alia quae multa et praecipua Ecclesiae ornatui contulerat, statuit." *Miracula* or *Vita sancti Dionysii* 2, 32, *Acta Sanct. Ord. Ben.,* saec. 3, pt. 2, p. 323.

20. Lenoir, *Architecture monastique,* 2:163; Léon Maître, "Correspondance: La crypte de Saint-Denis," *Bull. mon.* 72 (1908): 137–45; and Levillain, "Correspondance: Réponse à M. Maître," *Bull. mon.* 72 (1908): 145–54. See also Crosby, 1942, 169–85, and figs. 40–41 for a discussion of earlier reconstructions of Hilduin's chapel.

21. Both Levillain and Hubert thought that Hilduin's chapel had two stories: Levillain, *Mém. de la Soc. de l'Hist. de Paris* 36 (1909): 170–171; Hubert, *L'Art pré-roman,* 20. [**Ed. note:** For the author's fourteen excavations in the crypt (CR1–CR14) made in 1938 and 1939, see Crosby, 1942, 171–75, and figs. 47–54, 79–85, 91.]

22. [**Ed. note:** On the proliferation and development in France in the ninth century of outer crypt systems for the veneration of relics, see Heitz, *L'Architecture religieuse carolingienne,* 161–82.]

23. The photogrammetric study of the crypt vaults included only the twelfth-century vaults; therefore only the north side of the *caveau royal* is shown. The vaults on the south side have been restored, but the deviation of the axis of the two parallel walls on the north side can be clearly seen. [**Ed. note:** See fig. 110c and Album no. 9.]

24. Crosby, 1942, 170.

25. Ibid., 128, 172.

26. Excavations CR 8 and 9 encountered water beneath the foundations, evidence that the present water table remains only about 0.60 m below the crypt pavement. [**Ed. note:** See Crosby, 1942, fig. 91.] The chamber dug under the center of the *caveau royal* by Formigé to shelter the royal remains proved so humid that recently everything had to be removed.

27. [**Ed. note:** Suger, *De Consecratione* 2, Lecoy de la Marche, ed., *Oeuvres,* 217; Panofsky, ed., *Suger,* 89.]

28. [**Ed. note:** Suger, *De Consecratione* 4, Lecoy de la Marche, ed., *Oeuvres,* 224–25; Panofsky, ed., *Suger,* 101.]

29. Formigé, *Abbaye royale,* 169–72. [**Ed. note:** See also Heitz, *L'Architecture religieuse carolingienne,* 165, who accepted the author's reconstruction rather than Formigé's as the one best supported by both the architectural and the liturgical evidence.]

30. Capital CS 7 [**Ed. note:** *caveau royal,* seventh capital from west on south side], for example, used to be SS 1 [**Ed. note:** south ambulatory, westernmost capital].

31. [**Ed. note:** "J'ai retrouvé en 1952 la base de son abside demi-circulaire, abside de 4,10 m de diamètre hors oeuvre. Elle se présente comme un plateau massif horizontal, dont la paroi extérieure est revêtue d'un enduit lisse." Formigé, *Abbaye royale,* 169.]

32. [**Ed. note:** "Cette abside se termine sur deux épaulements en retour d'équerre dont la longueur n'est pas connue." Ibid., 169 and fig. 151.]

33. Ibid., 170. As far as I can determine, the twelfth-century pavement was approximately at the level it is today; if the ninth-century pavement was 0.45 m lower, it would have been beneath some of the foundations presumably built to support it.

34. Ibid., 169.

35. Ibid., 169–72, figs. 154–55.

36. [**Ed. note:** Ibid., 169.]

37. It has been suggested that Haymo's reference to gilded stones and gems should be interpreted as a mosaic with a gold background. No remnants, of course, exist today. See Hubert, *L'Art pré-roman,* 115.

38. [**Ed. note:** For Latin quote, see above, n. 17.] Certain scholars are inclined to believe that Félibien's text of Haymo's *Detectio* was not copied from the original but rather from a much later manuscript of the life of Saint Denis, so that many of the details are inaccurate. This is the opinion of Charles Liebman. Yet since this particular passage refers to a part of the crypt that was rebuilt in the twelfth century, it is probable that the text was part of the original document. [**Ed. note:** See Charles Liebman, *Etude sur la vie en prose de Saint Denis* (Geneva, 1942), p. xiv, n. 2. For a full discussion of the date of the Haymo text, see Levillain, *Revue historique* 155 (1927): 267–70.]

39. [**Ed. note:** See Levillain, *Bull. mon.* 72 (1908): 152. For Levillain's interpretation of the archaeological evidence and the texts, most of which the author has accepted, see ibid., 145–54, and Levillain, "L'Eglise carolingienne de Saint-Denis," *Bull. mon.* 71 (1907): 238–45.]

40. [**Ed. note:** See above, n. 17.]

41. René Maere, "Cryptes au chevet du choeur dans les églises des anciens Pays-Bas," *Bull. mon.* 91 (1932): 81–119. [**Ed. note:** The basic work remains Albert Verbeek, "Die Aussenkrypta Werden einer Bauform des frühen Mittelalters," *Zeitschrift für Kunstgeschichte* 13 (1950): 7–38; see also Heitz, *L'Architecture religieuse carolingienne,* 161–85, and Warren Sanderson, "Monastic Reform and the Architecture of the Outer Crypt, 950–1100," *Transactions of the American Philosophical Society,* n.s. 61, part 6 (1971): 1–36.]

42. [**Ed. note:** Crosby, 1942, 179, 180, fig. 70a, and p. 183; also Krautheimer, "The Crypt of Santa Maria in Cosmedin and the Mausoleum of Probus Anicius," in *Essays in Memory of Karl Lehmann,* ed. Lucy Sandler, *Marsyas, Studies in the History of Art,* Supplement 1 (1964): 171–75 and fig. 2.]

43. Other similar structures existed at Saint-Maurice of Agaune and at the Cathedral of Lausanne, but the dates of these two are uncertain. Hubert, *L'Art pré-roman,* 61; and Louis Blondel, "Les Anciennes Basiliques d'Agaune: Etude archéologique," *Vallesia* 3 (1948): 40–48.

[**Ed. note:** On Saint-Maurice of Agaune, see also Heitz, *L'Architecture religieuse carolingienne,* 28, 235, n. 24; and Oswald et al., *Vorromanische Kirchenbauten,* 3:297–99. For Sainte-Croix of Chelles, see Hubert, *L'Art pré-roman,* 58; for Saint-Etienne of Saint-Amand, Paul Frankl, *Baukunst des Mittelalters: Die frühmittelalterliche und romanische Baukunst* (Wildpark-Potsdam, 1926), 31; and Hubert, *L'Art pré-roman,* 59–60; for the abbey of Jouarre, Maillé, *Les Cryptes de Jouarre;* Hubert, *L'Art pré-roman,* 15–18; and Frankl, *Baukunst des Mittelalters,* 9; for Saint-Martin of Autun, Hubert, *L'Art pré-roman,* 58, 61; for the cathedral of Châlons-sur-Marne, Hubert, *L'Art pré-roman,* 61; and more recently Jean-Pierre Ravaux, "Les Cathédrales de Châlons-sur-Marne avant 1230," *Mémoires de la Société d'Agriculture, Commerce, Sciences et Arts du département de la Marne* 89 (1974): 40; for the cathedral of Notre-Dame of Lausanne, Oswald et al., *Vorromanische Kirchenbauten,* 2:169–71.]

44. The crypt at Werden was enlarged after the death of Ludger in 809, but before 830, to accommodate Ludger's tomb. See Edgar Lehmann, *Die frühe deutsche Kirchenbau die Entwicklung seiner Raumordnung bis 1080* (Berlin, 1938), 143. Lasteyrie, "L'Eglise de Saint-Philbert-de-Grandlieu," *Mémoires de l'Académie des Inscriptions et Belles-Lettres* 38:2 (1909–11): 4–5. Levillain has indicated that the addition to the east of the early choir was begun in 836 but modified for greater protection of the relics after the ravages of the Normans in 847. Léon Levillain, "Compte rendu: R. de Lasteyrie, *L'Eglise Saint-Philbert-de-Grandlieu (Loire-Inférieure),*" *Le Moyen Age* 23, 2d ser., 14 (1910): 50. [**Ed. note:** For Werden, see also Oswald et al., *Die vorromanische Kirchenbauten,* 3:368–71; and Heitz, *L'Architecture religieuse carolingienne,* 142–45. For Saint-Philbert-de-Grandlieu, see Heitz, *L'Architecture religieuse carolingienne,* 161–65.]

45. [**Ed. note:** For a discussion of the development of eleventh-century outer crypts, especially in the Mosan region, see Luc-Francis Genicot, *Les Eglises mosane de XIe siècle* 1: *Architecture et société,* Université de Louvain: Recueil de travaux d'his-

toire et de philologie, 4th ser., fasc. 48 (Louvain, 1972), 128–63. See also Sanderson, *Transactions of the American Philosophical Society,* n.s., 61:6 (1971): 1–66. For Corvey, see Heitz, *L'Architecture religieuse carolingienne,* 116 and figs. 116, 118. Any investigation of outer crypts should also include Saint-Germain en Auxerre and Saint-Pierre at Flavigny, Heitz, *L'Architecture religieuse carolingienne,* 167–78.

46. [**Ed. note:** See Crosby, 1942, 182.]

47. [**Ed. note:** See ibid.; and Heitz, *L'Architecture religieuse carolingienne,* 43.]

48. [**Ed. note:** Jurgis Baltrušaitis, *L'Eglise cloisonnée en orient et en occident* (Paris, 1941), 22–48.]

49. [**Ed. note:** See Crosby, 1942, 182.]

50. Kenneth J. Conant, *Cluny, Les Eglises et la maison du chef d'ordre* (Mâcon, 1968), 54–56, pls. XXV–XVIII.

51. Félibien, *Histoire,* 81–92.

52. See the *Annales Bertiniani,* anno 867; Chrétien César Auguste Dehaisnes, ed., *Les Annales de Saint-Bertin et de Saint-Vaast* (Paris, 1871), 164, and the charter of Charles the Bald, 870, Félibien, *Histoire,* pièces justicatives C, p. lxxvii.

53. Arthur Giry, "La Donation de Rueil à l'abbaye de Saint-Denis. Examen critique de trois diplômes de Charles-le-Chauve," in *Mélanges Julien Havet. Recueil des travaux d'érudition dédiés à la mémoire de Julien Havet (1853–93)* (Paris, 1895), 702–03. Levillain, *Bull. mon.* 71 (1907): 225–26.

54. Félibien, *Histoire,* 69, 73–74, 80.

55. [**Ed. note:** Ferdinand Lot and Louis Halphen, *La Règne de Charles le Chauve: Première partie (840–51)* (Paris, 1909), 133–38.]

56. Waitz, ed., *Annales Bertiniani,* anno 857, p. 48.

57. Ibid., anno 858, p. 49.

58. Ibid., anno 859, p. 52; Charter of Charles the Bald, 859, Félibien, *Histoire,* pièces justicatives XC, p. lxvii.

59. Waitz, ed., *Annales Bertiniani,* anno 861, p. 54.

60. Ibid., anno 865, p. 80.

61. Levillain, *Bull. mon.* 71 (1907): 224.

62. Waitz, ed., *Annales Bertiniani,* anno 869, p. 98. This fortification was rebuilt under Charles the Simple. Diploma, 8 February 898, Tardif, ed., *Monuments historiques,* 139.

63. Waitz, ed., *Annales Bertiniani,* anno 876, pp. 132–34; Mabillon, ed., *Miracula s. Dionysii* 1, 1 and 2, *Acta Sanct. Ord. Ben.,* saec. 3, pt. 2, pp. 326–27.

64. Flodoardus, *Historia Remensis ecclesiae* 4, 8, Migne, ed., *P.L.,* 135, col. 288.

65. Félibien, *Histoire,* 100.

66. See, for instance, Wolfgang Friedrich Volbach, "Art Under Charles the Bald," in Hubert et al., *Carolingian Renaissance,* 239–60.

67. See Albert Mathias Friend, "Carolingian Art in the Abbey of St. Denis," *Art Studies. Medieval, Renaissance and Modern* 1 (1923): 67–75; Friend, "Two Manuscripts of the School of St. Denis," *Speculum* 1 (1926): 59–70; W. Martin Conway, "Some Treasures of the Time of Charles the Bald," *Burlington Magazine* 26 (March 1915): 236–41; Charles Rufus Morey, "The Illumi-

nated Manuscripts of the Pierpont Morgan Library," *The Arts* 7 (1925): 193. The theory was vigorously opposed by Georg Leidinger, *Der Codex aureus der Bayerischen Staatsbibliothek in München* (Munich, 1925), 6:121–22. [**Ed. note:** See also the recent study by Herbert L. Kessler, *The Illustrated Bibles from Tours* (Princeton, 1977), 7, n. 2.]

68. Levillain, *Bib. de l'Ec. des Ch.* 87 (1926): 245–99; C. van de Kieft, "Deux diplômes faux de Charlemagne pour Saint-Denis, du XIIème siècle," *Le Moyen age* 64, 4th ser. 13 (1958): 401–03.

69. Although I have found no direct reference concerning the extent of that reform, it is possible to infer that it was complete. See Ernst Sackur, *Die Cluniacenser in ihrer kirchlichen und allgemeingeschichtlichen Wirksamkeit* 2 (Halle, 1894), 32–33.

70. Félibien, *Histoire*, 120–22.

71. Guibert gives the only early reference to this tower, the foundations of which were discovered in 1946. Built against the northwest side of the eighth-century church of Abbot Fulrad, between the transept and the nave, King William's tower had a square base almost 10.50 m across. Ivo was the abbot of Saint-Denis from 1075–1094. Guibert of Nogent, *Self and Society in Medieval France. The Memoirs of Abbot Guibert de Nogent*, ed. with an intro. by John F. Benton, trans. C. C. Swinton Bland (New York, 1970), 228. Crosby, *L'Abbaye royale*, 21, 52, fig. 16.

72. Without any reference to the archaeological evidence, Hubert and Formigé arbitrarily located William the Conqueror's tower at the western entrance to Fulrad's church. Jean Hubert used the word "vraisemblablement," "Communication de la séance du 13 mars," *Bull. de la Soc. Nat. des Antiq. de France* (1945–47, published 1950), 137–40. Again without any explanation, Jules Formigé included this tower in his chapter on Dagobert's church of 630 and located it at the western entrance, Formigé, *Abbaye royale*, 52.

73. Just to the west in the same alignment is part of the well-preserved north side aisle exterior wall of Fulrad's church. The foundation *libages* rise to within 1.05 m of the present pavement. The top surface of the highest step lies 1.35 m below the present pavement, or 0.65 m below the eighth-century pavement.

74. For Saint-Hilaire-le-Grand, see Edouard Aubert, "Etude sur l'ancien clocher de l'église Saint-Hilaire-le-Grand à Poitiers," *Mém. de la Soc. Nat. des Antiq. de France* 42 (1881): 45–70; Paul Frankl, *Baukunst des Mittelalters*, 109, fig. 155; Louis Grodecki, Florentine Müterich, Jean Taralon, and Francis Wormald, *Le Siècle de l'an mil* (Paris, 1973), 43, 46, 48, figs. 50, 422 (plan). [**Ed. note:** See also Marcel Aubert, "Saint-Hilaire," *Congrès archéologique de France* 104 (1951): 44–57, for a brief discussion and earlier bibliography.] A north tower also existed at Fulbert's cathedral at Chartres. See reconstruction by Merlet, after an eleventh-century miniature by Andrew de Mici; Otto George von Simson, *The Gothic Cathedral. Origins of Gothic Architecture and the Medieval Concept of Order*, 2d ed. (Princeton, 1974), pl. 30.

75. Formigé claimed that my excavations in the north transept had been "recomblées" (filled in), so that he could not see

these steps. The pavement in this area has, indeed, been reinstalled, but the excavation remains open under a reinforced concrete slab and can still be inspected. The installation was made while Formigé was in charge of Saint-Denis, and the steps are still visible. Formigé identified them as the principal northern entrance to Fulrad's church from the cemetery and claimed that there were similar steps leading out to the cloister from the south side aisle wall. I have found no evidence of steps on the south side. Formigé, *Abbaye royale*, 54. All of these plans based on Formigé's work show these exits: Vieillard-Troïekouroff, *Karl der Grosse* 3:340, fig. 1; Hubert et al., *Carolingian Renaissance*, 305, fig. 375.

76. The location of the relics of Saint Hippolytus in the church at Saint-Denis before 1236 is uncertain. According to Félibien the relics were brought to Saint-Denis by Fulrad in about 763, Félibien, *Histoire*, 53. They are not mentioned again until the twelfth century, when Suger included them in his account of the dedication of the western bays in 1140 [**Ed. note:** Lecoy de la Marche, ed., *Oeuvres*, 223; Panofsky, ed., *Suger*, 99]. Panofsky analyzed the texts relative to these relics in some detail without solving the problem. Panofsky, ed., *Suger*, 151–54. Suger's choice of words is ambiguous about whether or not the relics were actually in the chapel dedicated to Saint Hippolytus on the north side on 9 June 1140. [**Ed. note:** See also Panofsky, "Postlogium Sugerianum," *Art Bulletin* 29 (1947): 121.]

77. [**Ed. note:** ". . . je serais tenté de la (the inscription) *situer vers la fin du deuxième tiers de ce siècle*."] Montesquiou-Fezensac, "Communication de la séance du 13 mars, 1946," *Bull. de la Soc. Nat. des Antiq. de France* (1945–47, published 1950): 136–37.

78. See Panofsky, ed., *Suger*, 159–62.

79. I am indebted to Professor Eric Carlson for this information.

80. Viollet-le-Duc, *Revue archéologique* n.s., 3 (1861): 302; Maître, *Revue de l'art chrétien* (1909): 179–81.

81. Camille Enlart, "Correspondance," *Bull. mon.* 71 (1907): 549.

82. Levillain, "Correspondance," *Bull. mon.* 71 (1907): 550–53; ibid., 72 (1908): 147–54; Eugène Lefèvre-Pontalis, "Le Caveau central de la crypte de Saint-Denis," *Bull. mon.* 71 (1907): 559.

83. Formigé, *Abbaye royale*, 172–77, fig. 159.

84. Ibid., 176.

85. Thomas E. Polk, *Saint-Denis: Suger's Choir and the Pre-Gothic Crypt*, a paper read at the Thirtieth Annual Meeting of the Society of Architectural Historians, 1977, quotation from the abstract.

86. Formigé, *Abbaye royale*, 175, 177, fig. 160.

87. Crosby, 1942, 174, fig. 54, p. 172 and figs. 85, 91.

88. References for the following details will be given in the next chapter.

INTRODUCTION TO PART II

1. Suger, *De Administratione* 24, Lecoy de la Marche, ed., *Oeuvres*, 186; and Panofsky, ed., *Suger*, 42–43.

2. [**Ed. note:** The author has explored these questions in the following articles: "Abbot Suger's St.-Denis. The New Gothic," in *Studies in Western Art* 1, *Romanesque and Gothic Art,* Acts of the Twentieth International Congress of the History of Art, New York, 1961 (Princeton, 1963), 85–91; "The Creative Environment," *Ventures* (*Magazine of the Yale Graduate School*) (Fall 1965): 10–15; and "An International Workshop in the Twelfth Century," *Cahiers d'histoire mondiale* (*Journal of World History*) 10 (1966): 19–30.]

3. Walter Gropius, "Idee und Aufbau des Staatlichen Bauhausen Weimar (1923)," the first proclamation of the Weimar Bauhaus, as translated and quoted in *Bauhaus 1919–1928,* ed. Herbert Bayer, Walter Gropius, and Ise Gropius (Boston, 1952), 23.

4. See inter alia, Achille Luchaire, *Les Premiers Capétiens (987–1137), Histoire de France depuis les origines jusqu'à la Révolution,* ed. Ernest Lavisse (Paris, 1901), 2, pt. 2:144–79.

5. For a detailed account of the life of Louis VI, see Achille Luchaire, *Louis VI le Gros, Annales de sa vie et de sa règne (1081–1137)* (Paris, 1890).

6. [**Ed. note:** See Marcel Aubert, *Suger* (Rouen, 1950), 4; and Panofsky, ed., *Suger,* 2–3.] The young prince Louis probably stayed at Saint-Denis no later than 1092 or 1093. Luchaire, *Louis VI,* xii.

7. [**Ed. note:** The author based his discussion of the increase of trade and the rise of towns on the work and conclusions of Henri Pirenne. See Henri Pirenne, *Medieval Cities. Their Origins and the Revival of Trade* (Princeton, 1925); Henri Pirenne, *Les Villes du Moyen Age. Essai d'histoire économique et sociale* (Brussels, 1927); and Henri Pirenne, *Economic and Social History of Medieval Europe* (New York, 1937), 39–50. The Pirenne thesis touched off great debate, and scholarship generated by that debate has undermined many of his conclusions. For a good survey of the debate and resulting scholarship up to 1958, see Alfred E. Havinghurst, ed., *The Pirenne Thesis: Analysis, Criticism and Revision* (Boston, 1958).

Robert S. Lopez, a pioneer in the modern study of medieval economics, is perhaps the most incisive critic of Pirenne's conclusions. Robert S. Lopez, "Mohammed and Charlemagne: A Revision," *Speculum* 18 (1945): 14–38; reprinted in Havinghurst, ed., *Pirenne Thesis,* 58–73. See also Lopez's *Festschrift,* Harry A. Miskimin, David Herlihy, Abraham L. Udovitch, eds., *The Medieval City* (New Haven, 1977), 329–34; Richard Hodges and David Whitehouse, *Mohammed, Charlemagne and the Origins of Europe: Archeology and the Pirenne Thesis* (Ithaca, N.Y., 1983); and André Chédeville, Jacques Le Goff, and Jacques Rossiaud, *La Ville médiévale des Carolingiens à la Renaissance, Histoire de la France urbaine,* 2, ed. Georges Duby (Paris, 1980).]

8. Achille Luchaire, *Les Communes françaises à l'époque des Capétiens direct* (Paris, 1890). [**Ed. note:** More recently, Chédeville et al., *La Ville médiévale,* 142–81.]

9. [**Ed. note:** For example, see a charter of 1145 signed by Suger in which he gave lands and privileges to those who were to live in the village of Vaucresson, a village which he had built. Lecoy de la Marche, ed., *Oeuvres,* 360–61.]

10. [**Ed. note:** On the classical curriculum in the twelfth century, see the study that itself remains a classic, Charles H. Haskins, *The Renaissance of the Twelfth Century* (Cambridge, Mass., 1927), esp. 93–126; also Raymond Klibansky, "The School of Chartres," in *Twelfth-Century Europe and the Foundations of Modern Society* (Proceedings of a Symposium Sponsored by the Division of Humanities of the University of Wisconsin and the Wisconsin Institute for Medieval and Renaissance Studies, November 12–14, 1957), ed. Marshall Clagett, Gaines Post, and Robert Reynolds (Madison, Wis., 1961), 3–14; Richard W. Southern, *Medieval Humanism and Other Studies* (New York, 1970), 61–85; and David Knowles, *The Evolution of Medieval Thought* (New York, 1962), esp. 131–40. The variety of intellectual life in the twelfth century is the subject of the seminal work by Marie-Dominique Chenu, *Nature, Man and Society in the Twelfth Century,* ed. and trans. Jerome Taylor and Lester K. Little (Chicago, 1968).]

11. Christopher Brooke, *The Twelfth Century Renaissance* (Norwich, 1969), 53–74. [**Ed. note:** On John of Salisbury, see also inter alia, Clement Charles Julian Webb, *John of Salisbury* (London, 1932).]

12. Christopher Brooke, *Europe in the Central Middle Ages 962–1152* (New York, 1964), 318–22. [**Ed. note:** See also Knowles, *Evolution of Medieval Thought,* 116–30.]

13. [**Ed. note:** Bernard of Clairvaux, *Epistola* 78, *P.L.* 182, cols. 191–99; also published in a French translation by Félibien, *Histoire,* 158–61.]

14. [**Ed. note:** "Solumque ac totum erat quod nos movebat, tuus ille scilicet habitus et apparatus cum procederes, quod paulo insolentior appareret." Bernard, *Epistola, P.L.* 182, col. 193.]

15. [**Ed. note:** "Sine cunctatione et fraude, sua Caesari reddebantur; sed non etiam Deo quae Dei sunt persolvebantur aeque fideliter. Quod audivimus, non quod vidimus, loquimur: claustrum ipsum monasterii frequenter, ut aiunt, stipari militibus, urgeri negotiis, jurgiis personare, patere interdum et feminis. Quid inter haec coeleste, quid divinum, quid spirituale poterat cogitari? . . . cujus studio et industria Vulcani officina studiis videtur mancipata coelestibus, imo sua Deo habitatio reddita; et, in id potius quod ante fuit, ex synogoga Satanae restituta." Ibid., 193–94.]

16. [**Ed. note:** For Bernard's other letters to Suger, see Migne, ed., *P.L.* 182:

Epistola 222 (1148), cols. 387–90.
Epistola 266 (1150), cols. 470–72.
Epistola 369 (1148), col. 574.
Epistola 370 (1148–9), col. 575.
Epistola 371 (1146), col. 575.
Epistola 376 (1149), col. 581.
Epistola 377 (1149), cols. 581–83.
Epistola 378 (1149), col. 583.
Epistola 379 (1149), col. 583.
Epistola 380 (1150), cols. 585–86.
Epistola 381 (1143), col. 584.

The dates for the letters indicated above follow the dating of

Lecoy de la Marche, which is more recent than that of Migne. See Lecoy de la Marche, ed., *Oeuvres*, 285, 286, 297, 300, 306, 311, 316.

For Suger's letter to Bernard of 1150 or 1151, see Lecoy de la Marche, ed., *Oeuvres*, 282–83. The other, mentioned by Suger in a letter dated 1150 to Peter the Venerable of Cluny, does not seem to have survived, ibid., 274.]

17. [**Ed.** note: Willelmus, *Sugerii Vita*, Lecoy de la Marche, ed., *Oeuvres*, 389.]

18. [**Ed.** note: Bernard of Clairvaux, *Apologia ad Guillelmum Sancti Theodorici Abbatem*, P.L. 182, cols. 914–16.]

19. [**Ed.** note: Arthur Kingsley Porter, *Romanesque Sculpture of the Pilgrimage Roads* 1 (Boston, 1923), 222–23.]

20. [**Ed.** note: von Simson, *Gothic Cathedral*, 111; see also 55–58 and 112–13.]

21. [**Ed.** note: On Hugh of Saint-Victor and the school, see Knowles, *Evolution of Medieval Thought*, 141–49; and the excellent survey by Joachim Ehlers, *Hugo von St. Victor. Studien zum Geschichtsdenken und zur Geschichtsschreibung des 12. Jahrhunderts*, Frankfurter Historische Abhandlungen, 7 (Weisbaden, 1973), 1–50 and bibliography, 216–35. For Rupert of Deutz, see John H. Van Engen, *Rupert of Deutz* (Berkeley, Los Angeles, London, 1983), passim, and bibliography, 377–85.]

22. Henri Focillon, *The Art of the West in the Middle Ages* 1, *Romanesque Art*, ed. Jean Bony, trans. Donald King, 2d ed. (London, 1969), 102–46; and Whitney S. Stoddard, *Art and Architecture in Medieval France* (New York, 1972), 69–90.

[**Ed.** note: See also Meyer Schapiro, "On Geometric Schematism in Romanesque Art," reprinted in Schapiro, *Romanesque Art* (New York, 1977), 265–84. In this study Schapiro examined some of Focillon's ideas about the Romanesque aesthetic as developed by Jurgis Baltrušaitis in *La Stylistique ornementale dans la sculpture romane* (Paris, 1931). Schapiro's collected essays in *Romanesque Art* expand our understanding of the variety in Romanesque art. Because of that variety, the aesthetic principles elude a single definition. See especially, "On the Aesthetic Attitude in Romanesque Art," ibid., 1–27.]

23. Focillon, *Art of the West*, 1:105.

24. [**Ed.** note: Bernard of Clairvaux, *Apologia*, P.L. 182, col. 916.]

25. Von Simson, *Gothic Cathedral*, 95. [**Ed.** note: But see now, Anne Prache, *Ile-de-France romane* (Zodiaque, 1983). In summing up the character of late Romanesque art in the Ile-de-France, the author noted, "sous l'impulsion d'une pensée spirituelle renouvellée, il a engendré des oeuvres à nulle autre part pareilles, dans lesquelles se conjuguent les procédés traditionels, inspirés des plus grands monuments romans, et une force créatrice, génératrice de formes neuves," ibid., 17. The inclusion by the editors of Suger's building campaigns at Saint-Denis and the western portals of Chartres among Romanesque monuments is at variance with the concepts signaled in this volume as hallmarks distinguishing the birth of the Gothic style.]

26. Panofsky, ed., *Suger*, 37.

27. His extant writings consist of: (1) *Vita Ludovici Grossi Regis*, a life of King Louis the Fat, Lecoy de la Marche, ed., *Oeuvres*, 5–149; Waquet, ed., *Vie de Louis* [**Ed.** note: See ibid., xvii–xxiv, for a discussion of the seven extant manuscript copies of the *Vita Ludovici*: Paris, Bibliothèque Mazarine, ms. 2013, fols. 232–66; Bib. nat. mss. lat. 17546; lat. 17656 (only a partial text); lat. 12710; lat. 5925; and also Vatican Library, Cod. Reg. ms. 461]; (2) the details of his own administration, *De Rebus in Administratione sua Gestis*, Lecoy de la Marche, ed., *Oeuvres*, 151–209; Panofsky, ed., *Suger*, 40–81 [**Ed.** note: The *De Administratione* survives in only one manuscript, Paris, Bib. nat. ms. lat. 13835. See Panofsky, ed., *Suger*, 143.]; (3) the small book about the consecration of the new portions of Saint-Denis, *Libellus alter de Consecratione Ecclesiae Sancti Dionysii*, Lecoy de la Marche, ed., *Oeuvres*, 211–38; Panofsky, ed., *Suger*, 82–121 [**Ed.** note: Lecoy de la Marche combined two major manuscripts of the text for his edition: Vatican Library, Cod. Reg. 571, fols. 119r–129v and Paris, Bibliothèque de l'Arsenal, ms. 1030, fols. 81r–82r, 137r–143r; see Panofsky, ed., *Suger*, 143–44.] Those works by Suger tell us as much about the author as they do about the history of his time. Twenty-six of his letters were published by Lecoy de la Marche, ed., *Oeuvres*, 238–84 [**Ed.** note: For the sources used by Lecoy de la Marche, see idem, ed., *Oeuvres*, xiii–xiv.] Thirteen official acts, or charters, including Suger's own *Testamentum* also survive, Lecoy de la Marche, ed., *Oeuvres*, 319–74. [**Ed.** note: For the date and manuscript source of each piece, see ibid., xiv–xv. Panofsky also published the charter, *Ordinatio A.D. MCXL vel XCXLI Confirmata*, idem, ed., *Suger*, 122–37, and see ibid., 144, for its manuscript sources.] For a number of other documents associated with Suger or written in his honor, see Lecoy de la Marche, ed., *Oeuvres*, 375–426. The most important in this last category is the *Sugerii Vita*, a eulogy written shortly after his death by brother Willelmus, who may have been his secretary, Lecoy de la Marche, ed., *Oeuvres*, 375–411. [**Ed.** note: See ibid., xv–xvii, for a discussion of the only manuscript source for this, Paris, Bib. nat. lat., 14192.]

28. For a complete list of all works about Suger from the seventeenth to the nineteenth centuries, see Ulysse Chevalier, *Répertoire des sources historiques du Moyen Age. Bio-bibliographie* (Paris, 1907) 2:4343–45.

29. Besides that of Lecoy de la Marche, ed., *Oeuvres* (see above, n. 27), the studies include the critical edition of Suger's *Vita Gloriossimi Ludovici* by Auguste Emile Louis Marie Molinier, ed., *Vie de Louis le Gros par Suger suivie l'Histoire du roi Louis VII publiées d'après les manuscrits* (Paris, 1887); and the very sound, objective doctoral thesis by Otto Cartellieri, *Abt Suger von Saint-Denis 1081–1151* (Berlin, 1898). Henri Waquet published the first in a series of translations of Suger's writings, in *Vie de Louis*, with a useful introduction, v–xxvi, followed by Dom Jean Leclercq's French translation of *De Consecratione* entitled *Comment fut construit Saint-Denis?* (Paris, 1945). Erwin Panofsky, ed., *Suger*, translated into English only those passages of interest to the historian of art. His introductory essay and his copious notes remain the most sensitive and evocative study of Suger's personality. Another substantial biography by Marcel Aubert, *Suger*,

presents the abbot as monk, historian, and artist; and most recently, Otto von Simson devoted a major chapter in his book *Gothic Cathedral*, 61–90, to a penetrating examination of Suger's motivations. Another French translation of his writings is in preparation by Philippe Verdier.

30. [**Ed. note:** Most recently, in celebration of the 900th anniversary of the birth of Suger, The International Center of Medieval Art and the Medieval Academy of America sponsored the conference "Abbot Suger and Saint-Denis: An International Symposium," held at Columbia University, New York, in 1981. Coinciding with this event, the Metropolitan Museum of Art, New York, mounted an exhibition at The Cloisters which focused on works of art from Saint-Denis dating to the time of Suger. For this, see the catalogue, Sumner McK. Crosby, Jane Hayward, Charles T. Little, and William Wixom, *The Royal Abbey of Saint-Denis in the Time of Suger (1122–1151)* (New York, 1981), hereafter cited as Crosby et al., *Saint-Denis*, 1981.]

31. Cartellieri, *Abt Suger*, 127, regs. 1–2; Aubert, *Suger*, 3. [**Ed. note:** See also Panofsky, ed., *Suger*, 30–31; and, on his oblation, see Suger, *De Administratione* 33, 34A, Lecoy de la Marche, ed., *Oeuvres*, 196–97, 208; Panofsky, ed., *Suger*, 61, 81.] For a recent article on the *oblatus* see: Ilene H. Forsyth, "The Ganymede Capital at Vézelay," *Gesta* 15:241–46.

32. Suger, *Testamentum Sugerii Abbatis*, Lecoy de la Marche, ed., *Oeuvres*, 339; see also Cartellieri, *Abt Suger*, 127, reg. 3.

33. Suger, *Vita Ludovici* 9, Lecoy de la Marche, ed., *Oeuvres*, 30; Waquet, ed., *Vie de Louis*, 48–49.

34. [**Ed. note:** Cartellieri, *Abt Suger*, 128, reg. 7.]

35. [**Ed. note:** Ibid., reg. 8.]

36. [**Ed. note:** Ibid., passim.]

37. Suger, *De Administratione* 23, Lecoy de la Marche, ed., *Oeuvres*, 184–85.

38. Ibid., 12, Lecoy de la Marche, ed., *Oeuvres*, 170–73; Suger, *Vita Ludovici* 20, Lecoy de la Marche, ed., *Oeuvres*, 82–84; Waquet, ed., *Vie de Louis*, 21, 152–57.

39. Suger, *Vita Ludovici* 26, Lecoy de la Marche, ed., *Oeuvres*, 110; Waquet, *Vie de Louis*, 208–09.

40. [**Ed. note:** "*de stercore erigens pauperem*, ut sedere cum principibus faceret, sublimavit"] Ibid., Lecoy de la Marche, ed., *Oeuvres*, 112; Waquet, ed., *Vie de Louis*, 212–13.

41. [**Ed. note:** "cujus abbas ipse quo ceteris prelatione major tanto vita deterior atque infamia notior erat." Peter Abelard, *Historia Calamitatum*, ed. Jacques Monfrin, 3d ed. (Paris, 1967), 81.]

42. For a summary of the incident, see Panofsky, ed., *Suger*, 17–18.

43. Ibid.

44. Cartellieri, *Abt Suger*, 131–33, regs. 34, 40, 46.

45. Lecoy de la Marche, ed., *Oeuvres*, 155–85.

46. Von Simson, *Gothic Cathedral*, 91, n. 2 and 171, n. 43; Louis Grodecki, *Les Vitraux de Saint-Denis. Etude sur le vitrail au XIIe siècle*, vol. 1 (Paris, 1979), p. 28, n. 44.

47. Levillain, *Revue historique* 155 (1927), 241–76; von Simson, *Gothic Cathedral*, 77–79.

48. [**Ed. note:** *Gesta Dagoberti I Regis Francorum* 34, *M.G.H., Scriptores*, 2:413, reported that Dagobert not only established the fair but also conceded to the abbey in perpetuity all revenues from the fair, including what would have normally gone to the king. On this document and on the history of the fair itself, see Levillain, *Bib. de l'Ec. des Ch.* 91 (1930): 7–65.]

49. [**Ed. note:** Levillain, *Bib. de l'Ec. des Ch.* 91 (1930): 23, n. 5; and Cartellieri, *Abt Suger*, 130, reg. 26.]

50. *De Hominibus Villae Beati Dionysii Liberatati Traditis*, 1125, Lecoy de la Marche, ed., *Oeuvres*, 319–22, esp. 320.

51. [**Ed. note:** "Videres reges et principes multosque viros praecelsos imitatione nostra digitos manuum suarum exanulare, et anulorum aurum et gemmas margaritasque preciosas, ob amorem sanctorum Martyrum eidem tabulae infigi praecipere. Nec minus etiam archiepiscopi et episcopi, ipsos suae desponsationis anulos ibidem sub tuto reponentes."] Suger, *De Administratione* 31, Lecoy de la Marche, ed., *Oeuvres*, 193; Panofsky, ed., *Suger*, 54–55.

52. [**Ed. note:** Suger, *De Consecratione* 4, Lecoy de la Marche, ed., *Oeuvres*, 226; Panofsky, ed., *Suger*, 102–03.]

53. Suger, *De Administratione* 34, Lecoy de la Marche, ed., *Oeuvres*, 206; Panofsky, ed., *Suger*, 76–77.

54. Grodecki, *Vitraux de Saint-Denis*, 1:31–32.

55. [**Ed. note:** Suger, *De Consecratione* 2, Lecoy de la Marche, ed., *Oeuvres*, 219–20; Panofsky, ed., *Suger*, 90–93.]

56. [**Ed. note:** Ibid., 3, Lecoy de la Marche, ed., *Oeuvres*, 221–22; Panofsky, ed., *Suger*, 94–97.]

57. [**Ed. note:** "monumentum aere perennius."] Suger, *Vita Ludovici*, prologus, Lecoy de la Marche, ed., *Oeuvres*, 6; Waquet, ed., *Vie de Louis*, 4–5.

58. [**Ed. note:** "ne post decessum nostrum . . . redditibus ecclesia minuatur."] Suger, *De Administratione* 1, Lecoy de la Marche, ed., *Oeuvres*, 156; Panofsky, ed., *Suger*, 40–41.

59. [**Ed. note:** See Lecoy de la Marche, ed., *Oeuvres*, xviii–xix.]

60. [**Ed. note:**

Bright is the noble work; but, being nobly bright, the work
Should brighten the minds, so that they may travel, through
    the true lights.]

Suger, *De Administratione* 27, Lecoy de la Marche, ed., *Oeuvres*, 189; Panofsky, ed., *Suger*, 46–47.

61. [**Ed. note:** "geometricis et aritmeticis instrumentis" Suger, *De Consecratione* 4, Lecoy de la Marche, ed., *Oeuvres*, 225; Panofsky, ed., *Suger*, 100–01].

62. Panofsky, ed., *Suger*, 26.

63. Crosby, *L'Abbaye royale*, 37.

64. Panofsky, ed., *Suger*, 17.

65. Emile Mâle, *Religious Art in France—The Twelfth Century: A Study of the Origins of Medieval Iconography*, ed. Harry Bober, trans. Marthiel Mathews (Princeton, 1978), 154 (hereafter cited as Mâle, *Twelfth Century*).

66. [**Ed. note:** Willelmus, *Sugerii Vita*, Lecoy de la Marche, ed., *Oeuvres*, 381–82.]

67. [**Ed. note:** "accitis fusoribus et electis sculptoribus."] Suger, *De Administratione* 27, Lecoy de la Marche, ed., *Oeuvres,* 188; Panofsky, ed., *Suger,* 46–47.

68. Cartellieri, *Abt Suger,* 128, reg. 14 (1112); 129, reg. 20 (1122); 131, regs. 34–36 (1123); 132, reg. 40 (1124); 135, reg. 63 (1129).

69. Ibid., 129, reg. 18 (1118); 139, regs. 92–96 (1137).

70. Ibid., 128, reg. 9 (1107). [**Ed. note:** Suger, *De Administratione* 23, Lecoy de la Marche, ed., *Oeuvres,* 184–85.]

71. Cartellieri, *Abt Suger,* 136, reg. 70 (1131).

72. Aubert, *Suger,* 81.

73. Cartellieri, *Abt Suger,* 128, reg. 7 (1107); 135, reg. 66 (1130); 138, reg. 87 (1135); 139, reg. 99 (1138); 140, reg. 102 (1138).

74. [**Ed. note:** "magistrorum multorum de diversis nationibus." Suger, *De Administratione* 34, Lecoy de la Marche, ed., *Oeuvres,* 204; Panofsky, ed., *Suger,* 72–74.]

75. [**Ed. note:** "optimorum palliorum repositione." Suger, *De Administratione* 1, Lecoy de la Marche, ed., *Oeuvres,* 155; Panofsky, ed., *Suger,* 40–41; also ibid., 34A, Lecoy de la Marche, ed., *Oeuvres,* 209; Panofsky, ed., *Suger,* 80–81.]

76. Crosby, *Cahiers d'histoire mondiale (Journal of World History)* 10 (1966): 28–30. [**Ed. note:** See also above, n. 2.]

77. Bernard, *Apologia* 11, *P.L.* 182, col. 914.

78. Suger, *De Administratione* 10, Lecoy de la Marche, ed., *Oeuvres,* 165–66.

79. Suger, *Vita Ludovici* 31, Lecoy de la Marche, ed., *Oeuvres,* 136–38; Waquet, ed., *Vie de Louis* 32, 262–67.

80. [**Ed. note:**

Mens hebes ad verum per materialia surgit,
Et demersa prius hac visa luce resurgit.]

Suger, *De Administratione* 27, Lecoy de la Marche, ed., *Oeuvres,* 189; Panofsky, ed., *Suger,* 48–49.

81. [**Ed. note:** "Unde, cum ex dilectione decoris domus Dei aliquando multicolor, gemmarum speciositas ab exíntrinsecis me curis devocaret, sanctarum etiam diversitatem virtutem, de materialibus ad immaterialia transferendo, honesta meditatio insistere persuaderet, videor videre me quasi sub aliqua extranea orbis terrarum plaga, quae nec tota sit in terrarum faece nec tota in coeli puritate, demorari, ab hac etiam inferiori ad illam superiorem anagogico more Deo donante posse transferri."] Ibid., 33, Lecoy de la Marche, ed., *Oeuvres,* 198; Panofsky, ed., *Suger,* 62–65.

82. [**Ed. note:** "Mihi fateor hoc potissimum placuisse, ut quaecumque cariora, quaecumque carissima, sacrosanctae Eucharistiae amministrationi super omnia deservire debeant. *Si libatoria aurea, si fialiae aureae, et si mortariola aurea ad collectam sanguis hircorum aut vitulorum aut vacae ruffae,* ore Dei aut prophetae jussu, deserviebant: *quanto magis ad susceptiornem sanguinis Jesu Christi* vasa aurea, lapides preciosi, quaeque inter omnes creaturas carissima, continuo famulatu, plena devotione exponi debent. Certe nec nos nec nostra his deservire sufficimus. . . . Opponunt etiam qui derogant, debere sufficere huic amministrationi mentem sanctam, animum purum, inten-

tionem fidelem. Et nos quidem haec interesse praecipue proprie, specialiter approbamus. In exterioribus etiam sacrorum vasorum ornamentis, nulli omnino aeque ut sancti sacrificii servito, in omni puritate interiori, in omni nobilitate exteriori, debere famulari profitemur."] Ibid., 33, Lecoy de la Marche, ed., *Oeuvres,* 199–200; Panofsky, ed., *Suger,* 64–67.

83. [**Ed. note:** "posteritati memoriae reservare."] Ibid., 1, Lecoy de la Marche, ed., *Oeuvres,* 155; Panofsky, ed., *Suger,* 40–41; also ibid., 29.

84. [**Ed. note:** Suger, *Testamentum,* Lecoy de la Marche, ed., *Oeuvres,* 333–36.] Panofsky, ed., *Suger,* 29.

85. [**Ed. note:** Suger, *De Consecratione* 4, 5, Lecoy de la Marche, ed., *Oeuvres,* 225, 230; Panofsky, ed., *Suger,* 100–01, 108–09.]

86. [**Ed. note:** See Stephen Bayley, *The Albert Memorial: The Monument in its Social and Architectural Context* (London, 1981), 71–72, 152, n. 27, and pls. 39–42.]

87. [**Ed. note:** "Cumque per terram nostram Capreolensis vallis transiremus, accitis servientibus nostris nostrarum custodibus et aliarum silvarum peritis, adjurando fide et sacramento eos consuluimus, si ejus mensurae ibidem trabes invenire quocumque labore valeremus. Qui subridentes, si auderent, potius deriderent; admirantes si nos plane nesciremus in tota terra nihil tale inveniri posse, maxime cum Milo Capreolensis castellanus homo noster, qui medietatem silvae a nobis cum alio foedo habet. . . . Nos autem quicquid dicebant respuentes quadam fidei nostrae audacia silvam perlustrare coepimus, et versus quidem primam horam trabem unam mensurae sufficientem invenimus. Quid ultra? usque ad nonam aut citius per fruteta, per opacitatem silvarum, per densitatem spinarum, duodecim trabes (tot enim necessariae erant) in admirationem omnium, praesertim circumstantium."] Suger, *De Consecratione* 3, Lecoy de la Marche, ed., *Oeuvres,* 221–22; Panofsky, ed., *Suger,* 94–97.

88. Ibid., 2, Lecoy de la Marche, ed., *Oeuvres,* 219–20; Panofsky, ed., *Suger,* 90–93.

89. [**Ed. note:** "quater centum libras, cum plus satis valerent, pro eis dedimus." Suger, *De Administratione* 32, Lecoy de la Marche, ed., *Oeuvres,* 195; Panofsky, ed., *Suger,* 58–59.]

90. Panofsky, ed., *Suger,* 17.

91. Suger, *De Administratione* 34, Lecoy de la Marche, ed., *Oeuvres,* 204–06; Panofsky, ed., *Suger,* 72–77.

CHAPTER 5. THE WESTERN BAYS

1. Suger, *De Administratione* 24, Lecoy de la Marche, ed., *Oeuvres,* 186; Panofsky, ed., *Suger,* 42–43.

2. [**Ed. note:** "mulieres super capita virorum, tanquam super pavimentum, ad altare dolore multo et clamoso tumultu currerent"] Ibid. 25, Lecoy de la Marche, ed., *Oeuvres,* 186; Panofsky, ed., *Suger,* 42–43.

3. [**Ed. note:** "Mulierum autem tanta et tam intolerabilis erat angustia, ut in commixtione virorum fortium sicut prelo depressae, quasi imaginata morte exsanguem faciem exprimere, more parturientium terribiliter conclamare, plures earum mis-

erabiliter decalcatas, pio virorum suffragio super capita hominum exaltatas, tanquam pavimento abhorreres incedere, multas
etaim extremo singultantes spiritu in prato fratrum, cunctis desperantibus, anhelare."] Suger, *De Consecratione* 2, Lecoy de la
Marche, ed., *Oeuvres*, 216–17; Panofsky, ed., *Suger*, 88–89. [**Ed.
note:** Also "promtas mulierculas, super capita virorum tanquam
super pavimentum incedendo, niti ad altare concurrere, pulsas
aliquando et repulsas et pene semimortuas virorum miseran-
tium auxilio in claustrum ad horam retrocedentes, pene extremo
spiritu anhelare."] Suger, *Ordinatio A.D. MCXL vel MCXLI
Confirmata*, Lecoy de la Marche, ed., *Oeuvres*, 357–58; and Panofsky, ed., *Suger*, 134–35.

4. [**Ed. note:** "Fratres etaim insignia Dominicae passionis
adventantibus exponente, eorum angariis et contentionibus succumbentes, nullo divertere habentes, per fenestras cum reliquiis
multoties effugerunt."] Suger, *De Consecratione* 2, Lecoy de la
Marche, ed., *Oeuvres*, 217; Panofsky, ed., *Suger*, 88–89.

5. Von Simson, *Gothic Cathedral*, 89.

6. [**Ed. note:** Ibid., 83–89.]

7. Dated by some before the First Crusade (1095–99), the
earliest of the three literary texts, the *Descriptio*, describes a
pelerinatio of Charlemagne in which he freed Jerusalem and
brought back to Aix-la-Chapelle one of the nails that held Christ
to the cross, eight thorns from the crown of thorns, and many
other relics, including a portion of the true cross. According to
the *Descriptio*, Charles the Bald then gave the thorns and one of
the nails to Saint-Denis, as well as a portion of the wood of the
cross. The *Descriptio* authenticated two of the abbey's most precious relics and also a third, the segment of the cross, which the
abbey did not even claim to own until after 1204, when Philip
Augustus gave a fragment to Saint-Denis. The nail and the
thorn provided a primary attraction, bringing pilgrims to the
abbey, especially during the great fairs.

[**Ed. note:** The only published text of the *Descriptio* is incomplete and based on a manuscript of uncertain provenance
dated before the end of the thirteenth century (Paris, Bib. nat.
ms. lat. 12710). See Gerhard Rauschen, ed., *Die Legende Karls des
Grossen in 11. und 12. Jahrhundert*, Gesellschaft für Rheinische
Geschichtskund, 7 (Leipzig, 1890), 103–25. The earliest
manuscript known is one of Saint-Ouen in Rouen dated 1100–
30. See Elizabeth Brown and Michael Cothren's forthcoming
article, "The Twelfth-Century Crusading Window of the Abbey of Saint-Denis: 'Praetertorum enim recordatio futurorum
est exhibitio," *Journal of the Warburg and Courtauld Institutes* 48
(1985) (hereafter cited as *J.W.C.I.*); and Marc du Pouget, "Recherches sur les chroniques latines de Saint-Denis: Edition critique et commentaire de la *Descriptio Clavi et Coroni Domini* et
deux séries de textes relatifs à la légende carolingienne," *Positions
des Thèses. Ecole des Chartes* (1978): 41–46.]

A parody of the *Descriptio*, the *Pèlerinage de Charlemagne*,
elaborates details of Charlemagne's fictitious trip to Jerusalem
and Constantinople. This early *chanson de geste* proposes that
Charlemagne himself brought the sacred relics of the Passion to
Saint-Denis. Most scholars of this century detect philological

details characteristic of mid-twelfth-century French and note
the close resemblance of many events to the ill-fated Second
Crusade (1147–49). The possibility that the *Pèlerinage* was writ-
ten by a monk of Saint-Denis is remote, and no serious attempts
have been made to involve Abbot Suger in its composition. See
Theodor Heinermann, "Zeit und Sinn der Karlsreise," *Zeitschrift für romanische Philologie* 56 (1936): 497–562; Robert
C. Bates, "Le Pèlerinage de Charlemagne: A Baroque Epic,"
Yale Romanic Studies 18 (1941): 1–47; and Alfred Adler, "The
Pèlerinage de Charlemagne in New Light on Saint-Denis," *Spec-
ulum* 22 (1947): 550–61.

[**Ed. note:** Were it not for the broadly comic element in the
work the *chanson* might be thought to enhance the prestige of the
abbey. Recent literature emphasizes the work as a comic parody
of the fictitious pretensions of the *Descriptio*—an aspect which
belies authorship by a monk of Saint-Denis. In addition, attribution to Saint-Denis overlooks the fact that in the twelfth century
there was no vernacular tradition at the abbey. See Ronald N.
Walpole, "The *Pèlerinage de Charlemagne*: Poem, Legend and
Problem," *Romance Philology* 8 (1954–55): 173–86; Hans-Jörg
Neuschäfer, "Le Voyage de Charlemagne en Orient als Parodie
der Chanson de Geste: Untersuchungen zur Epenparodie in
Mittelalter (1)," *Romanistisches Jahrbuch* 10 (1959): 78–102.
Jules Horrent, *Le Pèlerinage de Charlemagne. Essai d'explication
littéraire avec des notes de critique textuelle* (Paris, 1961), takes the
work seriously and opposes Walpole.]

The third text containing a deliberate exaggeration of Charlemagne's involvement in Spain, the *Pseudo-Turpin Chronicle*, is
the most complicated of these literary inventions. It enlarges
Charlemagne's disastrous campaign against the Moslems in
Spain in 778 into six campaigns. All details are exaggerated and
some are imaginary. Included among Charlemagne's most generous acts is the gift of France to Saint-Denis, made in terms
almost identical with those used in Charlemagne's false charter
of 813. On the charter, see van de Kieft, "Deux diplômes," 401–
36, esp. 416–36. Some authors have concluded that the author of
the *Pseudo-Turpin Chronicle* was a Cluniac monk originally from
southwestern France who was strongly under the influence of
Saint-Denis. See ibid., 402.

[**Ed. note:** The earliest surviving documentary evidence is in
Doublet, *Histoire*, 725–27. For the text of the false charter, see
M.G.H., Diplomata Karlinorum 1, ed. Englebert Mühlbacher
(Hanover, 1906), p. 428, no. 286, a reprint of Doublet's text; and
Barroux, *Le Moyen Age* 64, 4th ser. 13 (1958): 1–26. On all three
texts (*Descriptio, Turpin*, and the charter), see Jean-Pierre Poly
and Eric Bournazel, *La Mutation féodale Xe–XIIe siècles* (Paris,
1980), 288–92. The standard work with commentary on the
Latin versions of the *Pseudo-Turpin* remains that by Cyril Meredith-Jones, *Historia Karoli Magni et Rotholandi ou Chronique du
Pseudo-Turpin. Textes revus et publiés d'après 49 manuscrits* (Paris,
1936); see too Adalbert Hämel, "Los manuscritos latinos del
falso Turpino," in *Estudios dedicados Menéndez Pidal* (Madrid,
1953), 4:67–85; also Christopher Holher, "A Note on Jacobus,"
J.W.C.I. 35 (1972): 31–80, who viewed the eclectic manuscript

Codex Calixtinus as a schoolbook for teaching students Latin rather than as a serious composition. The *Pseudo-Turpin* is one of the five works bound together in the *Codex*.]

8. [**Ed. note:** "divinae supplicans pietati . . . bono initio bonum finem salvo media concopularet."] Suger, *De Administratione* 25, Lecoy de la Marche, ed., *Oeuvres,* 187; Panofsky, ed., *Suger,* 44–45.

9. [**Ed. note:**

Pars nova posterior dum jungitur anteriori,
Aula micat medio clarificata suo.]

Ibid., 28, Lecoy de la Marche, ed., *Oeuvres,* 190; Panofsky, ed., *Suger,* 50–51.

10. [**Ed. note:** "si interpolate in navi ecclesiae occasione turrium ageretur, aut temporibus nostris aut successorum nostrorum, tardius aut nunquam quocumque infortunio, sicut dispositum est, perficeretur."] Ibid., 29, Lecoy de la Marche, ed., *Oeuvres,* 191: Panofsky, ed., *Suger,* 52–53.

11. [**Ed. note:** "quibus summus pontifex Dominus Jesus Christus testimonio antiquorum scriptorum manum apposuerat."] Ibid., Lecoy de la Marche, ed., *Oeuvres,* 191: Panofsky, ed., *Suger,* 50–51.

12. Crosby, 1942, 43 and note 11; Liebman, *Le Moyen Age* 45, 3d. ser., 6 (1935): 252–64.

13. [**Ed. note:** "tam auro quam preciosis coloribus."] Suger, *De Administratione* 24, Lecoy de la Marche, ed., *Oeuvres,* 186; Panofsky, ed., *Suger,* 42–43.

14. One of the eighth-century bases, S2, was found bound by an iron band, which must have been installed when Suger's workmen made the repairs in the 1130s.

15. [**Ed. note:** "cum jam hoc ipsum multo sumptu compleretur inspirante divino nutu . . . ad augmentandum et amplificandum nobile manuque divina consecratum monasterium virorum sapientum consilio, religiosorum multorum precibus . . . adjutus."] Suger, *De Administratione* 25, Lecoy de la Marche, ed., *Oeuvres,* 186; Panofsky, ed., *Suger,* 42–45.

16. [**Ed. note:** "augmentum quoddam, quod a Karlo Magno factum perhibebatur."] Ibid., 44–45.

17. Suger, *Testamentum,* 1137, Lecoy de la Marche, ed., *Oeuvres,* 336.

18. Von Simson, *Gothic Cathedral,* 91.

19. When Louis VI took the *vexillum* from the high altar at Saint-Denis, he did so as the *signifer,* or standard bearer, of the abbey. The significance of Louis' act is best understood in the context of a tradition fully developed at a later date which held that the Vexin had been given to Saint-Denis by Dagobert or one of his successors, and that no later than the ninth century the abbey had infeudated the Vexin to counts who were recognized as the abbey's most important vassals. With the vexillum as their insignia, they were obligated to defend Saint-Denis. In this way the vexillum of the counts of the Vexin became the standard of the abbey. Many of these details have no corroboration in authenticated documents, nor is there a text to prove that the counts of the Vexin were vassals of the abbey. Yet in his writings

Suger twice called the Vexin a fief of the abbey [**Ed. note:** *De Administratione* 4, Lecoy de la Marche, ed., *Oeuvres,* 161–63; and *Vita Ludovici* 26, ibid., 116; Waquet, ed., *Vie de Louis* 28, 220–21], as does a charter signed by Louis VI in 1124 [**Ed. note:** *Diplôme de Louis VI,* 1124, Lecoy de la Marche, ed., *Oeuvres,* 417–18]. From the early Middle Ages the abbey had held important lands in the Vexin, but no document affirmed its control of the county. In fact, when William Cliton became count of the Vexin in 1127—three years after the ceremony at Saint-Denis—the king gave him the title, with no mention of any homage owed to the abbey.

Recognizing that Saint Denis "was the special patron, and after God, the unparalleled protector of the kingdom [**Ed. note:** "specialem patronum et singularem post Deum regni protectorem," Suger, *Vita Ludovici* 26, Lecoy de la Marche, ed., *Oeuvres,* 115; Waquet, ed., *Vie de Louis* 28, 220–21], Louis VI took the vexillum of the abbey in the manner of a vassal acknowledging the authority of his overlord. He summoned all of France—*tota Francia*—to rally behind him at Reims. In the face of such opposition Henry V withdrew, and the exultant French returned to their own lands. Suger proudly wrote, "Whether in our own times or in those of remote antiquity, France has never done anything more illustrious than this deed nor has she proclaimed more gloriously the glory of her power, when the strength of all her parts is united." [**Ed. note:** "Quo facto nostrorum modernitate, nec multorum temporum antiquitate, nihil clarius Francia fecit, aut potentiae suae gloriam viribus membrorum suorum adunatis, gloriosius propalavit." Suger, *Vita Ludovici* 27, Lecoy de la Marche, ed., *Oeuvres,* 121; and Waquet, ed., *Vie de Louis* 28, 230–31.] See Barroux, *Le Moyen Age* 64, 4th ser., 13 (1958): 1–26; also for the later development associating the vexillum with the oriflamme of France, see Laura Hibbard Loomis, "The Oriflamme of France and the War-cry 'Monjoie' in the Twelfth Century," in *Studies in Art and Literature for Belle de la Costa Greene,* ed. Dorothy Miner (Princeton, 1954), 67–82.

20. Suger, *De Hominibus Villae Beati Dionysii,* 1125, Lecoy de la Marche, ed., *Oeuvres,* 320.

21. Panofsky, ed., *Suger,* 150, note for p. 44, line 14.

22. Ernst Gall, *Die Gotische Baukunst in Frankreich und Deutschland,* 2d ed. (Braunschweig, 1955), 108.

23. Panofsky, ed., *Suger,* 148, note for 44, line 1 and 150, note for 44, line 14. [**Ed. note:** See also Domino DuCange's discussion of the usual meaning of *monasterium* adopted here by the author, *Glossarium mediae et infimiae Latinitas,* 2d ed. (Graz, 1954), 5:457–58; and Marcel Aubert, *L'Eglise de Saint-Benôit-sur-Loire* (Paris, 1931), 8, note 2.]

24. Martinet's engraving, as first published by Beguillet, is entitled *Fortifieé de tours bâties par Suger et abbatues en 1779* (Fortified by towers built by Suger and torn down in 1779). Edme Beguillet and J.-Ch. Poncelin de la Roche, *Description historique de Paris et de ses plus beaux monumens gravés en taille douce par F. N. Martinet . . .* (Paris, 1780), 2:122. See also Formigé, *Abbaye royale,* 34, fig. 26. [**Ed. note:** Ferdinand Albert Gautier (Gauthier), "Continuation de l'histoire de Félibien . . . Recueil d'anecdotes et autres objets curieux relatifs à l'histoire de l'ab-

baye de Saint-Denis en France," Paris, Bib. Nat. ms. fr. 11681, p. 43 (hereafter cited as Gautier, ms. fr. 11681), described the entrance and dated it to the time of Suger in the entry of that journal for August 1778, when the demolition of the old fortifications began.]

25. The view of the abbey published in the *Monasticon Gallicanum*, drawn about 1690 by Dom Germain, shows such buildings as part of the gate ensemble, but those structures could have been added or changed after the twelfth century. [**Ed. note:** M. Peigné-Delacourt and Leopold Delisle, *Monasticon Gallicanum* (Paris, 1871), xxi and pl. 66.] Panofsky insisted that 200 pounds was too large a sum for a "mere convent entrance." Panofsky, ed., *Suger,* 150, note 44, 14.

26. [**Ed. note:** "cum primum pauca expendendo multis, exinde multa expendendo nullis omnino indigeremus, verum etiam habundando fateremur."] Suger, *De Consecratione* 2, Lecoy de la Marche, ed., *Oeuvres,* 218; Panofsky, ed., *Suger,* 90–91.

27. "In aedificatione magnae et caritativae domus hospitum, in reparatione et renovatione dormitorii et refectorii, et in augmentatione obedientiae thesauri." Suger, *Testamentum,* 1137, Lecoy de la Marche, ed., *Oeuvres,* 336.

28. Von Simson concluded that "the west facade was not begun until 1137," *Gothic Cathedral,* 92.

29. A concise account of the restorations at Saint-Denis during the nineteenth century can be found in Paul Vitry and Gaston Brière, *L'Eglise abbatiale de Saint-Denis et ses tombeaux, notice historique et archéologique,* 2d ed. (Paris, 1925), 34–49; see also Crosby, 1942, 7–12; Louis Grodecki, *Vitraux de Saint-Denis,* 1:42–60.

[**Ed. note:** See also Crosby, *L'Abbaye royale,* 71. Documents indicate that Pierre Fontaine, Napoleon's imperial architect, directed the work but did not supplant Jacques Cellérier as architect-in-charge at Saint-Denis. Cellérier, successor in 1807 to Jacques-Guillaume Legrand, continued in that capacity through the spring of 1813. Then, after the minister of the interior had elevated Cellérier to the post of *inspecteur général* of the Conseil des Bâtiments Civils, François Debret became the architect-in-charge at Saint-Denis. See Paris, Archives nationales, Carton F13 1367, année 1813.]

30. [**Ed. note:** See Ferdinand François de Guilhermy, unpublished notes, Paris, Bibliothèque nationale, ms. nouv. acq. fr. 6121, fols. 14–15 (hereafter cited as Guilhermy, "Notes," Bib. Nat. ms. nouv. acq. fr. 6121).]

31. [**Ed. note:** See Viollet-le-Duc's drawing of this excavation, published by Formigé, *Abbaye royale,* 70, fig. 51.]

32. Pier no. 10 has not been fully excavated, but Formigé had part of the masonry on the south side above the pavement removed, which revealed that the twelfth-century pier was symmetrical, as was pier no. 11. [**Ed. note:** See Formigé's plan, *Abbaye royale,* 66, fig. 49.]

33. Sumner McK. Crosby, "The Plan of the Western Bays of Suger's New Church at Saint-Denis," *Journal of the Society of Architectural Historians* 27 (1968): 39–43 (hereafter cited as *J.S.A.H.*).

34. [**Ed. note:** In agendis siquidem hujusmodi, apprime de convenientia et cohaerentia antiqui et novi operis sollicitus."] Suger, *De Consecratione* 2, Lecoy de la Marche, ed., *Oeuvres,* 218; Panofsky, ed., *Suger,* 90–91.

35. I have restudied the plan of the western bays and completely rethought the interpretation I presented in 1968 in the article cited above in note 33. This chapter includes new evidence provided by the photogrammetric renderings of the twelfth-century vaults—information not available in 1968.

36. Suger, *De Administratione* 26, Lecoy de la Marche, ed., *Oeuvres,* 187; Panofsky, ed., *Suger,* 44–45.

37. The southeast socle has not been uncovered.

38. The southern bases were found in 1939, the northern ones in 1947–48.

39. The excavations at the base of the north tower, on the western and northern sides, were first opened by Viollet-le-Duc in 1847. [**Ed. note:** The architect, Mesnage, working with Viollet-le-Duc, kept a running record of the work: "Journal du travaux de l'église royale de Saint-Denis commencée au mois de Janvier 1847," Paris, Archives de la Commission des Monuments Historiques.] In 1939 I took the opportunity of extending an excavation begun at the base of the south tower by municipal workmen checking electrical outlets.

40. If the lines of the diagonal arches in the photogrammetric plan are extended, they do not all intersect precisely in the corners, as one might expect in modern geometric drawing, but the tolerances are not more than 0.30 m, which in massive piers is not excessive. [**Ed. note:** See, too, Sumner McK. Crosby, "Some Uses of Photogrammetry by the Historian of Art," in *Etudes d'art médiéval offertes à Louis Grodecki,* ed. André Chastel, Albert Chatelet, S. McK. Crosby, and Anne Prache (Paris, 1981), 119–28.]

41. Crosby, *L'Abbaye royale,* 32–42; Crosby, "Plan of the Western Bays," 42–43.

42. Originally formulated by Paul Frankl [**Ed. note:** See especially Paul Frankl, "Der Beginn der Gotik und das allgemeine Problem des Stilbeginnes," *Festschrift Heinrich Wölfflin, Beiträge zur Kunstund Geistesgeschichte zum 21 June 1924 überreicht* (Munich, 1924): 107–25]; more recently the concept of diagonality has been emphasized by Jean Bony, "Diagonality and Centrality in Early Rib-Vaulted Architectures," *Gesta* 15 (1976): 15–25; see also the article by Stephen Gardner, "Two Campaigns in Suger's Western Block," *Art Bulletin* 66 (Dec. 1984): 581.

43. It should be remembered that the columns of the eighth-century nave measured 4.00 m from center to center.

44. The outermost columns of the central portal, for instance, are in line with the diagonal arches of the north and south bays.

45. Piers nos. 10 and 11 were enlarged in the thirteenth century when the nave was rebuilt and again in 1841 when the new organ was installed. [**Ed. note:** See plan, Crosby, *L'Abbaye royale,* 68, fig. 25.]

46. Sumner McK. Crosby, "Excavations at Saint-Denis—July, 1967," *Gesta* 7 (1968): 48–50.

47. The soundings in the masonry of piers nos. 10 and 11 were done by Formigé's workmen. [**Ed. note:** See above, note 32.]

48. Since the first, or westernmost, column bases of the junction could not be completely excavated, their exact dimensions have not been verified, so that their precise distances from piers nos. 10 and 11 remain somewhat uncertain.

49. [**Ed. note:** See especially Gardner, *Art Bulletin* 66 (Dec., 1984): 574–87.]

50. "Malheureusement, Suger ne surveilla pas les fondations de son édifice avec toute l'attention qu'exige ce genre de travaux; ce qui est plus vraisemblable, pressé de jouir et ne voulant pas enfouir des sommes trop considérables dans ces oeuvres inférieures, il les fit faire précipitamment et avec parcimonie." Viollet-le-Duc, "Eglise de Saint-Denis," *Paris Guide* (Paris, 1867), 1:703.

51. Paris, Archives Photographiques, nos. 206158, 206165, 206163 (fig. 50). [**Ed. note:** Photographs of the original drawings, Inv. nos. 21.752, 21.753, and 21.751, respectively, in Paris, Archives des Monuments Historiques.]

52. Crosby, 1942, fig. 31b.

53. The lower part of the capital was exhibited in a case in the Métro station at Saint-Denis in 1978. [**Ed. note:** "On trouve à la fouille au pied de la tour nord un chapiteau en pierre dont il ne reste que la partie inférieure. . . . Ce chapiteau . . . présent (les pieds) l'extremité d'une figure couchée et le fragment d'un personnage qui se tient debout au pied d'un lite [*sic*] mortuaire." Mesnage, "Journal des Travaux," 24 avril 1847.]

54. The relieving arch may be seen in an excavation drawing published in Crosby, 1942, fig. 77.

55. Salin's summary description of the location of this burial reads: "Sous le narthex (face nord) un sarcophage de plâtre dont la tête seule apparaissait dans le remblai (qui forme les parois d'une sorte de puits creusé par Viollet-le-Duc)." Supposedly attached to a belt, a most unusual collection of seven iron tools was found, "qui ne sont pas sans analogie avec les instruments de chirurgie gallo-romaines," yet the burial was dated in the seventh century. Salin, *Monuments Piot* 49 (1957): 124–26, figs. 29, 30.

56. The most recent discussion stated: "I feel it reasonable to assume that Suger's *parvis* was 0.60 m below the present-day level." Paula Gerson, "The Lintels of the West Façade of Saint-Denis," *J.S.A.H.* 34 (1975): 194.

57. Doublet, *Histoire,* 285.

58. For a discussion of these measurements, see Gerson, *J.S.A.H.* 34 (1975): 190, n. 5.

59. I had hoped that the building of the Métro tunnels under the present *parvis* would provide definitive evidence, but I received no answers to my questions. Possibly the tunnels were too deep.

60. Viollet-le-Duc, "Eglise Impériale," 303.

61. Viollet-le-Duc, *Dictionnaire,* 7:52 and 52, n. 3.

62. The 1828 drawing by Debret of excavations made in front of the central portal also fails to give the levels. Paris, Archives Photographiques, no. MH 167–238.

63. Formigé, *Abbaye royale,* 37 and fig. 27. [**Ed. note:** See Gerson, *J.S.A.H.* 34 (1975): 191–94 (esp. fig. 7) for a critique of Formigé's calculations.]

64. The notation on Viollet-le-Duc's drawing reads: "sol tracé par une gîte en plâtre." [**Ed. note:** The drawing in Paris, Archives Photographiques, was published by Formigé, *Abbaye royale,* 70, fig. 51.]

65. The pavement was 0.71 m below the present pavement of the north side aisle of the nave. [**Ed. note:** On this, see Crosby, *Gesta* 9 (1970): 42–45.]

66. In order to excavate this area properly, the entire pavement must be removed. Unfortunately, an opportunity to do this has not as yet presented itself.

67. The pier bases visible today above the pavement are nineteenth-century (fig. 45a), and they bear no resemblance to the originals.

68. The normal, or most frequently used, bevel was 0.10 m high and receded 0.50 m. The upper bevel on pier no. 6 is 0.20 m high but recedes only 0.30 m.

69. [**Ed. note:** For those comparisons, see Pierre Héliot and Pierre Rousseau, "Communication sur l'âge des donjons d'Etampes et de Provins. Séance du 20 décembre," *Bull. de la Soc. nat. des Antiq. de France* (1967): 293–96.]

70. Formigé, *Abbaye royale,* 73, fig. 54; Sumner McK. Crosby, "Masons' Marks at Saint-Denis," in *Mélanges offerts à René Crozet,* ed. Pierre Gallais and Yves-Jean Riou (Poitiers, 1966), 2:711–17.

71. See, for instance, the plan of a pier from the nave of Exeter: Francis Bond, *Gothic Architecture in England. An Analysis of the Origin and Development of English Church Architecture from the Norman Conquest to the Dissolution of the Monasteries* (London, 1905), p. 661, no. 9.

72. Ibid., nos. 4 and 8.

73. [**Ed. note:** A thorough archaeological analysis needs to be done. Gardner's article suggested the importance of a detailed study from a scaffolding high enough to reach the uppermost capitals, *Art Bulletin* 66 (Dec. 1984): 584 n. 32. The editor's inspection of some capitals attainable from an eighteen-foot scaffolding indicated that the *badigeon* had been removed with a wire brush which has skinned all the carvings and left its marks over the entire surfaces of the capitals. Another problem which cannot be resolved involves the obvious differences in the color of the stone of the capitals. Even from the pavement the observer can see that some have a much yellower appearance than others which have the pale, creamy color associated with the stone used for the sculpture on the western portals. See Sumner McK. Crosby and Pamela Z. Blum, "Le Portail central de la façade occidentale de Saint-Denis," *Bull. mon.* 131 (1973): 211–17, esp. p. 214. The differences cannot be attributed to varying climatic conditions in the various bays, since capitals of contrasting hues are often side by side. The capital cited by the author as a paradigm for the foliate style is one of the yellower ones—a hue always associated with the nineteenth-century restorations in the study cited above.]

74. [**Ed. note:** Close comparisons exist in monuments either under construction at roughly the same time as Saint-Denis or dated slightly later. Similar handling of Corinthian type acanthus leaves occurs at Châteaudun, Chartres, Sens cathedral, Notre-Dame-de-Paris, and Saint-Germain-des-Prés—to name a few. Earlier comparisons have been cited in monuments further afield, in Italy and southwestern France. See the recent monograph on the twelfth-century foliate capitals at Saint-Denis: Walter Wulf, *Die Kapitellplastik des Sugersbau von Saint-Denis* (Frankfurt-am-Main, 1979). This study does not include an analysis of the condition of the capitals.]

75. These two capitals are located at the northern side of the window opening to the west over the north portal (fig. 55b). [**Ed. note:** Although comparable in their acanthus type, they differ slightly in the formation of the volutes. The repetition of identical forms frequently occurs above the triple colonnettes of the transverse arches, and the same motif may recur on the small capitals supporting the next order of the arch.]

76. [**Ed. note:** For other examples, see also inter alia, Appendix K 2a–c, 3a, 5b, and 6c.]

77. [**Ed. note:** In this group, see also Appendix K, 2a, right, and 12, third from right.]

78. [**Ed. note:** For the other "water-leaf" capital, see Appendix K 20a, third from left. A letter to the editor of 6 August 1984 from William Clark noted that this capital may not be a true "water-leaf" but instead has particular interest as an example of an unfinished carving.]

79. [**Ed. note:** See for other examples Appendix K 2, third from left; 3a, second and fourth from left; 9b, second from right; and 10b, far right.]

80. Formigé claimed that only two of the ground-level vaults were original, *Abbaye royale*, 68, 76.

81. Viollet-le-Duc wrote: "ces arcs (à Saint-Denis) sont tous en tiers-point, c'est-à-dire formés d'arcs de cercle brisés à la clef," *Dictionnaire*, 9:501.

82. Formigé believed that these window openings were enlarged in the thirteenth century or later, *Abbaye royale*, 73–76. He ignored the presence of several masons' marks on most of the top embrasures of the windows.

83. The northern opening has only four such steps because more recent masonry blocks the top portion.

84. Sumner McK. Crosby, "The Inside of St.-Denis' West Façade," in *Gedenkschrift Ernst Gall*, ed. Margarete Kühn and Louis Grodecki (Munich, 1965), 63.

85. The excavation has recently been filled in.

86. For photographs of these nave piers, see Crosby, *L'Abbaye royale*, pls. 56, 57.

87. For a restoration of the interior of the choir of Saint-Germain-des-Prés, see William W. Clark, "Spatial Innovations in the Chevet of Saint-Germain-des-Prés," *J.S.A.H.* 38 (1979): 359, fig. 20. For a photograph of the nave of Sens cathedral, see von Simson, *Gothic Cathedral*, fig. 21.

88. An addition to the eleventh-century church of Saint-Martin at Angers encountered similar difficulties. See Forsyth, *The Church of St. Martin*, 161–67.

89. Similar finished masonry with a bevel must have been underground or out of sight under the pavement in front of the western portals and inside the western bays.

90. [**Ed. note:** According to Gardner only the triple capital survives from the twelfth century; the three shafts, bases, and lower figure are later work, Gardner, *Art Bulletin* 66 (1984), n. 32.]

91. Suger, *Ordinatio,* enacted in 1140 or 1141, Lecoy de la Marche, ed., *Oeuvres,* 356–60; Panofsky, ed., *Suger,* 132–35. Panofsky translated *superius* as "upstairs" and *inferius* as "downstairs," which led to some confusion about the "exact location" of the two lateral chapels, particularly that of Saint Hippolytus. See ibid., 151–54. Since, however, the two lateral chapels are in fact lower than the central one, I have assumed that all three chapels were in the upper stories above the entrance bays. Crosby, in *Gedenkschrift Ernst Gall,* 66.

92. [**Ed. note:** "ad id peragendum multimodam laudem . . . decantabamus . . . pulcherrimum et angelica mansione dignum superius oratorium, in honore sanctae Dei Genitricis semperque virginis Mariae et sancti Michaelis archangeli omniumque Angelorum, sancti Romani ibidem quiescentis aliorumque multorum sanctorum quorum ibi nomina subtitulata habentur, dedicantes; inferius vero in dextro latere oratorium in honore sancti Bartholomaei multorumque aliorum sanctorum; in sinistro autem, ubi sanctus requiescere perhibetur Hippolitus, oratorium in honore ejusdem et sanctorum Laurentii, Sixti, Felicissimi, Agapiti aliorumque multorum."] Suger, *De Consecratione* 4, Lecoy de la Marche, ed., *Oeuvres,* 223; Panofsky, ed., *Suger,* 96–99.

93. [**Ed. note:** "Qui locus quam secretalis, quam devotus, quam habilis divina celebrantibus, qui ibidem Deo deserviunt, ac si jam in parte dum sacrificant eorum in coelis sit habitatio, cognorunt." Suger, *De Administratione* 26, Lecoy de la Marche, ed., *Oeuvres,* 187; Panofsky, *Suger,* 44–45.

94. Ibid. [**Ed. note:** See Panofsky's discussion of this passage, *Suger,* 151–54; also idem, "Postlogium Sugerianum," *Art Bulletin* 29 (1947): 121, for an analysis of texts relevant to the location of relics of Saint Hippolytus which suggests reasons for Suger's uncertainty about where the body of the saint rested.]

95. Crosby, *L'Abbaye royale,* 59–60; Robert Branner, *St Louis and the Court Style in Gothic Architecture* (London, 1965), 45–51. [**Ed. note:** For a text of the *Chronicon,* see Elie Berger, "Annales de Saint-Denis, généralement connues sous le titre de Chronicon Sancti Dionysii ad cyclos paschales," *Bib. de l'Ec. des Ch.* 40 (1879): 261–95. The passages in question are on pp. 281 and 290–91.]

96. Paul Frankl, *Gothic Architecture* (Middlesex, 1962), 28.

97. Vitry and Brière, *Eglise Abbatiale,* 2d ed., 56.

98. The sounding made in the floor of the southwest corner of the south upper chapel uncovered a bevel, but it is not clear how this was intended to function.

99. See, for instance, Charles Seymour, Jr., *Notre-Dame of*

Noyon in the Twelfth Century: A Study in the Early Development of Gothic Architecture (New Haven, 1939), 156–57.

100. Bond, *Gothic Architecture in England*, 246–49.

101. Bond suggested that "It is probably because these sharp edges were often broken in transit or in working, that the practice of chamfering arose," ibid., 278. At Saint-Denis the chamfers are so extensive that they must have been for deliberate visual effect.

102. Crosby, *Studies in Western Art*, 1:86–87.

103. [**Ed. note**: See too Gardner, *Art Bulletin* 66 (1984): 584–87.]

104. Suger, *De Consecratione* 2, Lecoy de la Marche, ed., *Oeuvres*, 217–18; Panofsky, ed., *Suger*, 88–89.

105. [**Ed. note**: "ad turrim anterioris partis prosecutionem studium nostrum contulissemus, jam in altera parte peracta"] Suger, *De Administratione* 29, Lecoy de la Marche, ed., *Oeuvres*, 191; Panofsky, ed., *Suger*, 50–51.

106. See the *Attachements* nos. 14, 18 prepared by Geffrier, Entrepreneur in 1838, Paris, Archives de la Commission des Monuments historiques. Formigé stated that the north tower must have been finished before 1151 because Suger used the plural *turria* as being "already completed," *Abbaye royale*, 77. [**Ed. note**: Formigé paraphrased Suger, *De Administratione* 25, Lecoy de la Marche, ed., *Oeuvres*, 187, but used Suger, *De Consecratione* 2, ibid., 218.] Panofsky noted, however, that the term can mean a single tower as well as the twin-towered superstructure as a whole, *Suger*, 163. [**Ed. note**: Panofsky's note refers to a passage in *De Administratione* 29 in which Suger said Divine will diverted him from work on the second tower to begin the renewal of the central body of the church, ibid., Lecoy de la Marche, ed., *Oeuvres*, 191; Panofsky, ed., *Suger*, 50–51.] Viollet-le-Duc, in his discussion of *chainage*, assumed that the north tower was built in the mid-twelfth century, but this was a general, not a specific, reference, *Dictionnaire*, 2:398.

The fire, which burned for two whole days "with a terrible odor" (une tres-mauvaise odeur) in 1219, must have damaged details as well as masonry. [**Ed. note**: See Félibien, *Histoire*, 221.]

107. Debret wrote: "En attaquant la restauration des créneaux construits sous Charles VI, et qui surmontent la partie lisse dans laquelle je devais placer mes figures, je reconnus qu'elle menaçait ruine, par le peu d'incrustement de ses terrassons dans la masse principale de la construction primitive. Obligé d'y faire des reprises importantes, je decouvris à 0.30 m. de profondeur une autre façade plus ancienne, sans doute celle des fortifications de Charles VI. Pour en conserver le témoignage, je fis tracer une forte feuillure à la hauteur où elle me parait s'arrêter." *Notice sur les diverses constructions et restaurations de l'église de St.-Denis, Séance publique annuelle des cinq académies*, 1842, Institut Royale de France du lundi 2 Mai 1842 (1842):23. Although I have examined this upper masonry, I can find no trace of what Debret mentioned and do not know how to interpret his statement. Viollet-le-Duc stated simply: "on les [crénellations] a refaits en totalité en 1839 et 1841." Guilhermy, "Notes," Bib. Nat. ms. nouv. acq. fr. 6121, fol. 78.

CHAPTER 6. THE WEST FAÇADE AND THE WESTERN PORTALS

1. See Grodecki, *Vitraux de Saint-Denis*, 1:47–51.

2. "Façade défigurée, dépourvue à tout jamais d'intérêt historique, et fort laide d'ailleurs." Didron, *Annales archéologiques* 5 (1846): 109.

3. Richard Hamann McLean in his article "Les Origines des portails et façades sculptés gothiques," *Cahiers de civilisation médiévale Xe–XIIe siècles* 2 (1959): 157–75, made no mention at all of the sculpture of Saint-Denis.

4. At the end of the Hundred Years' War the abbey was under attack by both sides, and in 1567 it was pillaged by the Huguenots. Vitry and Brière, *Eglise abbatiale*, 2d ed., 18–49, gave a concise history of the abbey from the fourteenth through the nineteenth centuries; see also Crosby, 1942, 4–12; and Grodecki, *Vitraux de Saint-Denis*, 1:29–60.

5. Repairs and modifications of 1771 also affected much of the extant sculpture on the portals.

6. Debret's *attachements*, or graphic studies, are on file in the archives of the Monuments Historiques, 3, rue de Valois, Paris.

7. The *attachements* include many details not to be found on the façade today. Among them are medallions in the spandrels of the north and south portals; a large band of relief sculpture over the central portal; elaborate figures and frames on the faces of all four buttresses; medallions over the two center blind lancets; and very elaborate ornaments filling the four corners around the rose window.

8. [**Ed. note**: For a survey of Debret's work and the problems created thereby, see Vitry and Brière, *Eglise abbatiale*, 2d ed., 38–42.]

9. [**Ed. note**: "sub musivo, quod et novum contra usum hic fieri et in arcu portae imprimi elaboravimus." Suger, *De Administratione* 27, Lecoy de la Marche, ed., *Oeuvres*, 188; Panofsky, ed., *Suger*, 46–47.]

10. [**Ed. note**: See below note 100.]

11. [**Ed. note**: Evidence, both architectural and sculptural, indicates a date of ca. 1150 for the rose window at Saint-Etienne, Beauvais, and the sculptural program around it. See M. Fillmore Hearn, "The Rectangular Ambulatory in English Medieval Architecture," *J.S.A.H.* 30 (1971): 195, and n. 22; and Annie Henwood-Reverdot, *L'Eglise Saint-Etienne de Beauvais. Histoire et Architecture* (Beauvais, 1982), 131–32. Chantal Hardy, in a recently completed dissertation for the University of Montréal (Canada), also dated the rose at Saint-Etienne ca. 1150. (The editor thanks William Clark for this information.) Elaine Beretz of Yale University is preparing a dissertation on the iconography of this early rose window which will also include a study of the restorations to the rose and sculpture.

Eudes (Odo), bishop of Beauvais, was one of the three celebrants in the consecration of the narthex of Saint-Denis in 1140. See Suger, *De Consecratione* 4, Lecoy de la Marche, ed., *Oeuvres*, 223; Panofsky, ed., *Suger*, 96–97. With the church of Saint-Etienne under construction at that time, perhaps Eudes or one of his retinue suggested the inclusion of the rose window in the north façade.

In addition to the rose window, scholars have seen other influences from Saint-Denis in the architecture and sculpture of Saint-Etienne. For example, the capitals of the columns that form the spokes of the rose at Saint-Etienne closely resemble those in the western bays at Saint-Denis, Wulf, *Kapitellplastik,* 93–94; also, a sequence of masks in foliage in the outer voussoir of Saint-Etienne's north door (of the same campaign as the rose) compare well with those in the outer order (now recut) framing the Saint-Denis rose, Henwood-Reverdot, *L'Eglise Saint-Etienne,* 147. Information supplied by E. Beretz.]

12. [**Ed. note:** Inter alia, the seventeenth-century drawing by Martellange of the west façade (fig. 83), the late eighteenth-century drawing by Martinet (both in Paris, Bib. nat., Cabinet des Estampes), as well as that by Cellérier (ca. 1818, Archives des Monuments Historiques) and one by Viollet-le-Duc (1831, collection of Madame la Marquise de Maillé) all show a stringcourse making the transition to the greater salience of the crenellations. For these and other prerestoration drawings, see Formigé, *Abbaye royale,* figs. 65, 66, 68–70.]

13. Two *attachements* (one of them, fig. 70) prepared by Geffrier, Entrepreneur, and countersigned by F. Debret in 1838 show the design of the north tower in detail. [**Ed. note:** See above, n. 6.]

14. The use of mirror images as a basic design principle has been noted in the plan of the western bay.

15. Crosby, in *Gedenkschrift Ernst Gall,* 59–60.

16. [**Ed. note:** See Crosby and Blum, *Bull. mon.* 131 (1973): 211–12.]

17. That peculiarity at Saint-Denis was also noted by Formigé, *Abbaye royale,* 87. On the irregularity of the coursing of the mural masonry, see Whitney S. Stoddard, *The West Portals of Saint-Denis and Chartres. Sculpture in the Ile-de-France from 1140 to 1190. Theory of Origins* (Cambridge, Mass., 1952), 9–10.

18. Gerald Allen, "A Report on the West Facade of Saint-Denis," seminar paper, Yale University, 10 January 1971.

19. Crosby, *Etudes d'art médiéval offerts à Louis Grodecki,* 119–28.

20. Although Suger did not mention them, he must have seen the arch at Orange on his way to Italy, as well as the arches in Rome and such Roman city gates as those at Autun, Reims, and Trier. [**Ed. note:** See also Paula Gerson, "The West Facade of Saint-Denis: An Iconographic Study," (Ph.D. diss., Columbia University, 1970, University Microfilms, Ann Arbor, Mich., no. 73-76, 428), 71–73.

21. E. Baldwin Smith, *Architectural Symbolism of Imperial Rome and the Middle Ages* (Princeton, 1956), 30, 37.

22. [**Ed. note:** "Quorum trium una et gloriosa processio, cum per ostium sancti Eustachii egrederetur, ante principales portas transiliens cum ingenti cleri decantantis et populi tripudiantis turba, episcopis praeeuntibus et sanctae insistentibus consecrationi, per singularem atrii portam." Suger, *De Administratione*

26, Lecoy de la Marche, ed., *Oeuvres,* 188; Panofsky, ed., *Suger,* 44–47.]

23. Panofsky, ed., *Suger,* 154, note for p. 44, lines 28–46, 2; also Crosby, *L'Abbaye royale,* 36.

24. For diagrams showing the restorations affecting details of the central archivolts, see Crosby and Blum, *Bull. mon.* 131 (1973), pl. VIII.

25. Adelheid Heimann, "Trinitas Creator Mundi," *J.W.C.I.* 2 (1938): 42.

26. I have relied heavily on two unpublished studies and wish to express my sincere appreciation to the authors for their permission to do so: Gerson, "The West Façade," and Ellen D'Oench, "The Trinity at Saint-Denis," graduate seminar paper, Yale University, Spring 1975.

27. The fresco at Saint-Paul's-Outside-the-Walls has been dated to the fifth or sixth century, but there is some doubt about its validity, since it is known only through seventeenth-century drawings, some of which do not include the Lamb. See Heimann, "Trinitas Creator Mundi," 44, n. 4; and Alfred Backel, *Die Trinität in der Kunst. Eine ikonographische Untersuchung* (Berlin, 1931), 22. Such a depiction of the Trinity was known in the twelfth century, for Hildegard of Bingen so described it in her *Liber Scivias,* written 1141–51 and illustrated between 1160 and 1180. See Louis Baillet, "Les Manuscrits du 'Scivias' de Sainte Hildegarde conservé à la Bibliothèque de Wiesbaden," *Monuments Piot* 19 (1911): 116 and fig. 26; Gerson, "West Façade," 132; D'Oench, "The Trinity," 7.

28. Montague Rhodes James, *The Apocalypse in Art* (London, 1931), 32–33.

29. Mâle, *Twelfth Century,* 6–8.

30. Ibid.

31. [**Ed. note:** On the significance of the bust of Christ in the inner archivolt below the Trinity, who is flanked by souls presented by angels for judgment, see Crosby and Blum, *Bull. mon.* 131 (1973): 232–33.]

Other connotations for the representation of God holding the medallion, or disk, with the Lamb include possible cosmological significance; see Anna C. Esmeijer, "La macchina dell'universo," in *Album Discipulorum aangeboden aan Professor Dr. J. G. van Gelder* (Utrecht, 1963), 5–15; Gerson, "West Façade," 132, n. 2. In the later twelfth century, following a long oral tradition, the Holy Grail is described as a disk large enough to hold the Paschal Lamb eaten by Jesus and his Apostles at the Last Supper; see Jean Marx, *La Légende arthurienne et le Graal* (Paris, 1952), 241–50; Roger S. Loomis, *The Grail from Celtic Myth to Christian Symbol* (New York, 1963), 28–29; and D'Oench, "The Trinity," 19.

32. [**Ed. note:** "La figure monumentale du Christ, l'une des sculptures les plus controverées et dénigrées à Saint-Denis, domine le portail entier."] Crosby and Blum, *Bull. mon.* 131 (1973): 217.

33. [**Ed. note:** "garde sa pose originelle et, en général, la forme et la disposition stylisée de draperies du XIIe siècle."] Ibid.

34. [**Ed. note:** With veiled hands, the fourth angel at the right

of Christ now holds three nails in his right hand and a block-shaped object in his left. See n. 37.]

35. [**Ed.** note: For that Augustinian interpretation of the imagery of this representation of Christ, see Gerson, "West Façade," 119–23.]

36. On the symbolism of the Apostles, see Sumner McK. Crosby, *The Apostle Bas-Relief at Saint-Denis* (New Haven, 1972), 53, 63–64.

37. The restoration, a partially striated, boxlike object carried by the upper angel on Christ's right (see above, n. 34), defies interpretation. Also it is impossible to know whether the original number of nails in his right hand was four or one. The latter might have been the case because among its most venerated possessions the abbey treasured a nail as the relic of the Passion. See Crosby and Blum, *Bull. mon.* 131 (1973): 229–30.

38. The Virgin was only slightly restored. [**Ed.** note: On the various restorations, see ibid., 225–29 and pl. Vb.]

39. Although there can be no proof that this figure seated to the left of Christ was intended to be Saint John the Divine [**Ed. note:** first proposed by Crosby, *L'Abbaye royale,* 37] scholars have accepted the likelihood that it was. Gerson, "West Façade," 125–26.

40. Katzenellenbogen, *Sculptural Programs of Chartres,* 84.

41. [**Ed.** note: Mâle, *Twelfth Century,* 179–81.]

42. [**Ed.** note: Yves Christe, "Le portail de Beaulieu: Etude iconographique et stylistique," *Bulletin archéologique du Comité des travaux historiques et scientifiques* 56 (1970): esp. 76.]

43. Mâle, *Twelfth Century,* 407, and 510, note 88.

44. [**Ed.** note: "Elles ont la prétention d'offrir une restitution des oeuvres que Suger avait installées à cette place. . . . Il va sans dire que cette restitution, faite en 1842–43 [sic], sans aucun document, est de nulle valeur: c'est un assemblage composé de motifs empruntés à quelques sculptures en pierre ou à des vitraux et le style, comme la technique, en sont déplorables."] Vitry and Brière, *Eglise abbatiale,* 2d ed., 63.

45. Félibien, *Histoire,* 534.

46. Pierre Ferdinand Albert Gautier (Gauthier), "Recueil d'anecdotes et autres objets curieux relatifs à l'histoire de l'abbaye royale de Saint-Denis . . . ," Paris Bib. Nat. ms. suppl. fr. 2803, p. 121, cited by Montesquiou-Fezensac, *Bull. de la Soc. Nat. des Antiq. de France* (1945–47, published 1950), 128–37. [**Ed.** note: Montesquiou-Fezensac cited the Gautier ms. by its old designation. That handwritten copy of Gautier's journal is now classified as ms. fr. 11681. The original holograph survives in the Bibliothèque Municipale de St.-Denis. On this see Gerson, "West Façade," 13, n. 1.]

47. [**Ed.** note: Suger, *De Administratione* 27, Lecoy de la Marche, ed., *Oeuvres,* 188; Panofsky, ed., *Suger,* 46–47.] Panofsky commented on this distinction between the casters, who were "summoned (*accitis*)," and the artists, sculptors, who were "chosen (*electis*)," but he noted that if *electis* is understood as an adjective rather than a participle, the translation would read: "Bronze casters and outstanding sculptors having been summoned," which would eliminate the distinction. Panofsky,

ed., *Suger,* 158, note for p. 48, lines 7f. I do not know of other medieval distinctions between technicians and artists.

48. [**Ed.** note: "Valvas siquidem principales, accitis fusoribus et electis sculptoribus, in quibus passio Salvatoris et resurrectio vel ascensio continetur, multis expensis, multo sumptu in earum deauratione, ut nobili porticui conveniebat, ereximus; necnon et alias in dextera parte novas, in sinistra vero antiquas.] Ibid., 46–47.

49. [**Ed.** note: "L'on entre en ce devant, appellé le Parvis, & de là en l'Eglise par trois grandes portes, qui contiennent tout le bas du frontispice, qui ont chacune deux battans: icelles revestuës de fonte à personnages, le tout jadis doré de fin or. La porte du milieu contient en hauteur quinze pieds, & en largeur douze & demy: l'autre à main droite, en entrant, contient 13. pieds de haulteur, & 8. pieds & demy de largeur: la troisieme à senestre, porte 14. pieds de haulteur, & 8. pieds de largeur."] Doublet, *Histoire,* 285.

50. [**Ed.** note: "Il dit . . . qu'il fit venir plusieurs fondeurs & sculpteurs bien experimentez, pour ornez & enrichir les battans de la porte principale de l'entree de l'Eglise, sur laquelle se void la Passion, Resurrection, Ascension, & autres histoires (avec la representation dudit Abbé prosterné en terre) le tout de fonte: & qu'il luy a convenu faire de grandes frais, tant pour le metail, que pour l'or qui y a esté employé: pareillement aussi pour les battás de la porte de main droite, en entrant, qu'il a fait enricher de metail, or & esmail, laissant les anciens battans de la troisieme porte de main gauche, qui estoient au premier bastiment de l'Eglise."] Ibid., 240.

51. [**Ed.** note: "Sur les anciens battans de la porte ancienne de l'Eglise que fit bastir le Roy Dagobert, cecy est escrit en lettres tres-antiques & entrelacees l'unes dans les autres, aussez difficiles a lire: . . . Et plus bas, au dessous de deux figures, l'une d'un Evesque, & l'autre d'un Religieux, sont escrits ces mots en mesme lettres tres-antiques: . . . Lequel Airard présente à S. Denis deux portes. Icelles deux grandes portes, sont pardessus le bois couvertes de fonte."] Ibid., 241.

Early in the eighteenth century, Félibien repeated Suger's description but added, "Suger y est représenté de la même maniere que dans la vitre du chevet dont nous avons parlé," *Histoire,* 173. Later, to be certain that he omitted nothing, he added, "Une petite figure en bas-relief d'un goust fort gothique est sur la grande porte de bronze du même costé. Elle représente un religieux de Saint-Denys nommé Airard. On lit ces mots au dessous: *Airardus monachus,* & ces deux vers en lettres entrelassées les unes dans les autres:

Hoc opus Airardus caelesti munere fretus,
Offert, ecce tibi Dionysi pectore miti.

Cet Airard vivoit du temps de l'abbé Fulrad sous le regne de Pepin, comme nous l'apprenons du premier livre des miracles de S. Denys. Ainsi l'image qui le représente, est une des plus anciennes d'ou l'on puisse connoître qu'elle estoit pour lors la forme de l'habit des religieux de Saint-Denys. On voit encore sur le ceintre de la porte de l'autre collatéral un religieux en habit de chanoine, tel que le porterent les religieux de Saint-Denys sous la fin du regne de Charlemagne, lorsqu'ils quitterent l'habit monastique. La porte du milieu qui est du temps de l'abbé Suger & où l'on voit sa figure, est aussi de bronze, & paroist avoir esté dorée autrefois. On y voit en divers cartouches l'histoire des principaux mysteres de Notre-Seigneur. Les armes du Cardinal Mazarin & celles de l'Abbaye y ont esté mise sur les deux battans depuis qu'elle fut reparée, le Duc de Mazarin son héritier ayant donné à cet effet la somme de deux mille livres en 1663," Ibid., 534.

52. Simon Germain Millet, *Le Trésor sacré ou inventaire des sainctes reliques et autres précieux joyaux qui se voyent en l'église et au trésor de l'abbaye royale de S. Denis en France,* 4th ed. (Paris, 1645[1646]), 27, 482 [**Ed note:** See also Montesquiou-Fezensac, *Trésor,* 1:129 n. 6.].

53. Vincenzo Scamozzi, ms. c. 42, Museo Civico Vicenza. See Scamozzi, *Tacchino di viaggi da Parigi a Venezia (14 marzo–11 maggio 1600),* ed. Franco Barbieri (Venice, 1959), 38–39 and pl. I; also Franco Barbieri, "Vincenzo Scamozzi, studioso ed artista," *Critica d'Arte* 8 (1950): 218, fig. 171, 226 and 229, note 20.

54. Ad decus ecclesiae, quae fovit et extulit illum,
  Suggerius studuit ad decus ecclesiae.
  Deque tuo tibi participans martyr Dionysi,
  Orat ut exores fore participem Paradisi.
  Annus millenus et centenus quadragenus
  Annus erat Verbi, quando sacrata fuit.

Suger, *De Administratione* 27, Lecoy de la Marche, ed., *Oeuvres,* 188–89; Panofsky, ed., *Suger,* 46–47.

The repetition of *ad decus ecclesiae* with two different allusions, the first to the ecclesiastical institution and the second to the architectural structure, is characteristically Sugerian, as noted by Panofsky, ed., *Suger,* 163–64, note for p. 46, lines 18f.

55. Portarum quisquis attollere quaeris honorem,
  Aurum nec sumptus, operis mirare laborem.
  Nobile claret opus, sed opus quod nobile claret
  Clarificet mentes, ut eant per lumina vera
  Ad verum lumen, ubi Christus janua vera.
  Quale sit intus in his determinat aurea porta:
  Mens hebes ad verum per materialia surgit,
  Et demersa prius hac visa luce resurgit.

Suger, *De Administratione* 27, Lecoy de la Marche, ed., *Oeuvres,* 189; Panofsky, ed., *Suger,* 46–49.

56. [**Ed. note:** On the mastic that coats the surfaces of the jambs, see Crosby and Blum, *Bull. mon.* 131 (1973): 213–14.]

57. Gerson, "West Façade," 106–08.

58. For the bas-relief, see Crosby, *Apostle Bas-Relief,* 53–55. [**Ed. note:** For the medallions of the windows, see fig. 43a, and inter alia, Grodecki, *Vitraux de Saint-Denis,* 1: figs. 106–18, where some of the inscriptions also occur on an inner band that follows the contours of the roundel.]

59. Panofsky, ed., *Suger,* 164, note for p. 46, line 26. For his perceptive commentaries on the verses, see ibid., 163–65, and von Simson, *Gothic Cathedral,* 114–15.

60. "I am the door. By me if any man enter in, he shall be saved: and he shall go in, and out, and shall find pastures (John 10:9)." [**Ed. note:**

  Et in superliminari:
  Suscipe vota tui, judex districte, Sugeri;
  Inter oves propias fac me clementer habieri.

Suger, *De Administratione* 27, Lecoy de la Marche, ed., *Oeuvres,* 189; Panofsky, ed., *Suger,* 48–49. See also Gerson, "West Façade," 110–11.]

61. Panofsky, ed., *Suger,* 23.

62. "Sur les costez de chaque portique sont de grandes statuëes de rois, de reines & d'autres principaux bienfacteurs de cette église," Félibien, *Histoire,* 529.

63. [**Ed. note:** Bernard de Montfaucon, "Dessins et gravures pour *Les monumens de la monarchie françoise,*" Paris. Bib. Nat. ms. fr. 15634, fols. 33–77. See also below, notes 68 and 74.]

64. Gautier, Paris, Bib. Nat. ms. fr. 11681, p. 20. See also H. Herluisson and P. Leroy, "Le manuscrit de Ferdinand Albert Gautier, organiste de l'abbaye de Saint-Denis," *Réunion des Sociétés savantes des Départements, section Beaux-Arts* 19 (1905): 236–49. [**Ed. note:** The ornamented columns now in place that replaced the eighteenth-century statue columns date from the nineteenth-century restorations directed by Debret. See "Réponse de M. Debret, architecte, aux critiques de la Commission des Monuments Historiques," 14 janvier 1842, in "Seine—Saint-Denis. Dossier de l'Administration 1841–76," Archives de la Commission des Monuments Historiques, fol. 19 (hereafter cited as Dossier de l'Administration 1841–1876).]

65. Quinette, "Note des objects qui restent à recueillir dans la ci-devant abbaye de Saint-Denis, d'après l'authorisation du ministre de l'intérieur. . . . 3° Dans l'église, vingt-quatre têtes environ, débris de monuments du moyen-âge, provenant de la demolition du portail," cited by Marvin C. Ross, "Monumental Sculpture from Saint-Denis: An Identification of Fragments from the Portal," *The Journal of the Walters Art Gallery* 3 (1940): 103, n. 18. See also Louis Courajod, *Alexandre Lenoir: Son Journal et le Musée des Monuments Français* (Paris, 1887), 3:401.

66. "Mais ce que l'on ignorait encore, c'est que cette statue, qui passait au temps de Dom Plancher pour représenter Dagobert, fut transportée en Bourgogne, tout près de Dijon en 1774. En effet à la démolition du cloître de Saint-Denis, entreprise en 1771, elle avait été acquise par le marquis de Migieu pour son château de Savigny-les-Beaune, où l'on montre encore la place qu'elle occupait dans un angle du grand escalier," Pierre Quarée, "L'Abbé Lebeuf et l'intérpretation du portail de Saint-Bénigne de Dijon," in *L'Abbé Lebeuf et le Jansénisme. XXXIe Congrès de l'Association Bourguignonne des Sociétés Savantes, Auxerre, 1960* (Auxerre, 1962), 283. [**Ed. note:** For the thirty-six years following the purchase of the statue from the Paris dealer, Lucien Demotte, by The Metropolitan Museum of Art, the provenance of the statue column had not been confirmed. Finally in 1955 Vera Ostoia associated the sculpture with the engraving published by Montfaucon. See below, n. 73.]

67. A. Lenoir, *Aquarelles et dessins,* 4: St.-Denis, sheet #17,

Paris, Musée du Louvre, Cabinet des Dessins. This watercolor was brought to my attention by Professor Frank Ludden, who also sent me the photograph of the original. [**Ed. note:** "La montagne" at Saint-Denis, located by Lenoir as "sur la place qui précède celle de l'église de l'abbaye," probably was on the "Place aux Gueldes (or Geuldres)," the name formerly given the square located "à gauche en arrivant de Paris." It was also known as "place des Récolets." When "la montagne" was destroyed, the square resumed its former name "place aux Gueldres," popularly known as "Guêtres." See "Documents" [excerpted from the Gautier ms.], "La Ville de Saint-Denis pendant la Révolution. Récit contemporain," *Le Cabinet historique* 21 (1874): 118. See also above, n. 63. Gautier also mentioned "une Espèce de Belvedaire [summer house] en forme de montagne" when "le jardin du fonds" was enlarged in 1780, Gautier, ms. fr. 11681, p. 47.]

68. "Notes tirés de (R)aquefort [Roquefort] édition de Legrand d'Aussy: Legrand l'Aussy déclare, d'après son expérience, que les dessins de l'ouvrage de Montfaucon n'ont pas le moindre ressemblance avec les originaux, poses changés, accessoires et emblêmes supprimés, draperies modifiées, têtes différentes." Guilhermy, "Notes," Bib. Nat. ms. nouv. acq. fr. 6121, fol. 233. I have not been able to consult this edition of Legrand d'Aussy. [**Ed. note:** Legrand d'Aussy, *Des Sépultures nationales et particulièrement celles des rois de France . . . suivi des funérailles des rois, reines, princes et princesses de la monarchie française, depuis son origine jusques et y compris elles de Louis XVIII, par M. de Roquefort* (Paris, 1824), 266, 268-69. In that text cited by Guilhermy, the author's comments referred not to the statue columns as reproduced by Montfaucon but to drawings of the tomb effigies which Legrand d'Aussy had the opportunity to compare with the sculptures still extant and then on display in Paris at the Musée des Monumens Français.]

69. "Si pourtant ou veut bien triompher d'une répugnance trop légitime [because of the restorations], on s'apercevra qu'un des portails, celui du milieu, conserve ses dispositions primitives." Emile Mâle, "La Part de Suger dans la création de l'iconographie du moyen âge," *Revue de l'art ancien et modern* 35 (1914): 339. [**Ed. note:** See also Mâle, *Twelfth Century*, 178, 221-22.]

70. Ross, *Journal of the Walters Art Gallery* 3 (1940): 90-109.

71. Stephen K. Scher, *The Renaissance of the Twelfth Century* (Providence, 1969), 153-55 and pl. 53; and Stephen K. Scher, "The 'Renaissance of the Twelfth Century' Revisited," *Gesta* 9 (1970): 60. [**Ed. note:** At the time of its acquisition in 1920 the head reputedly came from Saint-Denis.]

72. Léon Pressouyre, "Une Tête de reine du portail central de Saint-Denis," *Gesta* 15 (1976): 151-60.

73. Vera K. Ostoia, "A Statue from Saint-Denis," *The Metropolitan Museum of Art Bulletin* 13/10 (June 1955): 298-304. [**Ed. note:** For the bibliography of the statue column, see Crosby et al., *Saint-Denis*, 1981, 46; also above, n. 66.]

74. [**Ed. note:** Some of the originals as well as an incomplete set of close copies and equally close reversed copies of the drawings made *in situ* by Antoine Benoist are preserved among the papers of Bernard de Montfaucon (see above, n. 63). See also

André Rostand, "La Documentation iconographique des Monumens de la Monarchie françoise de Bernard de Montfaucon," *Bulletin de la Société d'Histoire de l'Art français* (1932): 119-23; and Pressouyre, *Gesta* 15 (1976): 151-52.]

75. [**Ed. note:** See, for example, Katzenellenbogen, *Sculptural Programs of Chartres*, 28, 34, who subsumes the validity of the order in the Montfaucon plates in his identification of the statue columns. This is justified because on a good number of the drawings preserved in the Montfaucon papers there are indications of the portal, the embrasure, and also the place within the embrasure of the statue columns. See Montfaucon, Bib. Nat. ms. fr. 15634, fols. 63, 64, 66-68, 70, 71, 76, 77. The figures are also numbered consecutively from one to twenty-three, numeration beginning, according to a note, with the outermost statue in the left embrasure and proceeding in order from left to right across the portals. Some of these identifying numbers also appear on the copies.]

76. Wilhelm Vöge, *Die Anfänge des monumentalen Stiles im Mittelalter. Ein Untersuchung über die erste Blütezeit französische Plastik* (Strasbourg, 1894), esp. 80-90 and 197-200; Wilhelm Vöge, "Uber die Bamberger Domsculpturen," *Repertorium für Kunstwissenschaft* 22 (1899): esp. 102.

77. Marcel Aubert, "Le Portail royal et la façade occidentale de la cathédrale de Chartres. Essai sur la date de leur exécution," *Bull. mon.* 100 (1941): 177-218.

78. Cecile Goldscheider, "Les Origines du portail à statues colonnes," *Bulletin des Musées de France* 11, nos. 6-7 (1946): 22-25 (résumé du thèse de l'Ecole du Louvre); Marcel Aubert, "Têtes de statues-colonnes du portail occidental de Saint-Denis," *Bull. mon.* 103 (1945): 243-48. [**Ed. note:** See also Marcel Aubert, "Séance du 17 janvier," *Bull. de la Soc. Nat. des Antiq. de France* (1945-47, published 1950): 26.]

79. Louis Grodecki, "La Première sculpture gothique, Wilhelm Vöge et l'état actuel des problèmes," *Bull. mon.* 117 (1959): 271-75, 281.

80. See inter alia, William Wixom, *Treasures from Medieval France* (Cleveland, 1967), 72-74, 354, and nos. III-14 and III-15.

81. [**Ed. note:** Bernard de Montfaucon, *Les Monumens de la Monarchie françoise* (Paris, 1729), I: pl. X.]

82. [**Ed. note:** Katzenellenbogen identified the headless female figure among the statue columns of the left portal as a queen; see Katzenellenbogen, *Sculptural Programs of Chartres*, 28 and 115, n. 4. The fourth figure identified as a woman is also headless. Montfaucon, *Monumens*, I: pls. XVI, XVII.]

83. The heads of the Apostles under arches on the bas-relief were large with, in general, a proportion of 1 : 4.5 in relation to the total height of the figure. (The exaggerated size of the head may have compensated for the eye-level of the viewer, who was probably looking up from below.) Similar large heads may be seen on the capitals of the crypt, but there they seem to vary according to the style of the artist responsible for the carving. In the stained glass windows the heads of the figures varied in size according to the relative importance of the personage involved. As for comparisons with the carvings of the central portal, all

heads but one now *in situ* are nineteenth-century replacements. [**Ed. note:** See diagrams of restorations, Crosby and Blum, *Bull. mon.* 131 (1973): pls. IIIb, Vb, VIb, VIII, XIV, XVI, X, XII, XVIIb, XVIIIb.]

84. [**Ed. note:** Gerson, "West Façade," 141, 150–53.]

85. Pressouyre, *Gesta* 15 (1976): 151–60.

86. Gerson, "West Façade," 153–58, cited the long braided hair bound with ribbon as the particular attribute of Sheba.

87. [**Ed. note:** Félibien, *Histoire,* 529.]

88. [**Ed. note:** Montfaucon, *Monumens,* 1:193–94; then see also Jacques Vanuxem, "The Theories of Mabillon and Montfaucon on French Sculpture of the Twelfth Century," *J.W.C.I.* 20 (1957): 45–58; reprinted by Robert Branner, *Chartres Cathedral* (New York, 1969), 168–85, esp. 176–78.]

89. See the précis of the 1751 *Mémoire,* Abbé Lebeuf, "Conjectures sur la reine Pédauque," *Histoire de l'Académie royale des Inscriptions et Belles-Lettres* 23 (1756): 231–34.

90. Vöge, *Anfänge,* esp. 177, n. 1, and 182; more recently Marie-Louise Thérel has linked the statue columns to the *Glossa Ordinaria* and the sacred columns in front of Solomon's temple, "Comment la patrologie peut eclairer archéologie. A propos de l'Arbre de Jesse et des statue-colonnes de Saint-Denis," *Cahiers de civilisation médiévale Xe–XIIe siècles* 6 (1963): 145–58.

91. Mâle, *Twelfth Century,* 392.

92. Louis Hourticq, *La Vie des images* (Paris, 1927), 36–39; Marcel Aubert, *La Sculpture française au moyen âge* (Paris, 1946), 178; Louis Grodecki, *Chartres* (New York, 1963), 26. [**Ed. note:** These interpretations focused on Chartres rather than on Saint-Denis.]

93. The abbé Bulteau came close to asserting this same idea when he attempted to combine the ideas of Montfaucon and Lebeuf. Marcel J. Bulteau, *Monographie de la cathédrale de Chartres* (Chartres, 1888), 2:62–68; see also Ernst Kitzinger, "The Mosaics of the Cappella Palatina in Palermo: An Essay on the Choice and Arrangement of Subjects," *Art Bulletin* 31 (1949): 291–92; also Katzenellenbogen, *Sculptural Programs of Chartres,* 27–36.

94. [**Ed. note:** Instead of following the conventional horizontal reading of the statue columns, Gerson was the first to attempt to interpret the statue columns within each portal with respect to the iconographical meaning of the tympanum and archivolts above. Her brilliant exegesis showed how the right portal program stemmed from the concepts in the *Ecclesiastical Hierarchy* by Dionysius the Pseudo-Areopagite. Gerson, "West Façade," 150–53. Looking for and finding the same correlation between the statue columns, the jamb sculptures, and the figures surviving in the outer archivolt of the north, or left, portal, the editor has proposed a unified program for that pendant portal also based on the *Ecclesiastical Hierarchy.* The integrated iconographical statement made by the lost royal statue columns, plus the extant sculptures on the jambs and the figures in the outer archivolt also led to a new proposal for the subject matter of the lost mosaic. Pamela Z. Blum, "The Lateral Portals of the West Façade of the Abbey Church of Saint-Denis. Archeological

and Iconographical Considerations," paper presented at the conference *Abbot Suger and Saint-Denis: An International Symposium,* held at Columbia University, New York, 10–12 April 1981. In an expanded version, the paper, now at press, will appear in the proceedings of the conference, ed. Paula Gerson, to be published by The Metropolitan Museum of Art, New York. A summary of the findings will be included in the editor's volume in preparation, *The Twelfth-Century Figurate Sculpture of the Building Campaigns of Abbot Suger.*

95. [**Ed. note:** The church at Lincoln built by the Norman bishop Remigius was "so like a fortress . . . [walls of the apse ca. 8 ft. thick] that [King] Stephen used it as such . . . when the castle opposite was held by his enemies." Albert F. Kendrick, *The Cathedral Church of Lincoln: A History and Description of its Fabric and a List of the Bishops* (London, 1898), 8.]

96. [**Ed. note:** The theme of *regnum/sacerdotium* as the meaning of the statue columns had its most recent exponent in M. Fillmore Hearn, *Romanesque Sculpture: The Revival of Monumental Stone Sculpture in the Eleventh and Twelfth Centuries* (Ithaca, N.Y., 1981), 192–97. For a contrary opinion, see Willibald Sauerländer, *Gothic Sculpture in France 1140–1270* (New York, 1972), 379.]

97. [**Ed. note:** The archaeological examination of the lateral portals indicated that the extent of the restorations to the twelfth-century jamb carvings and to the one original archivolt surviving in each of those portals was roughly comparable, but cutting back of the carved surfaces in the upper zones of those portals was greater than that in the central portal. The weathering in the left, or north, portal far exceeded that in both the central and right portals—a phenomenon which made the analysis of the restorations to the Signs of the Zodiac much more difficult to identify and the identification of repairs a bit less certain. See Blum, "The Lateral Portals."]

98. Guillaume Le Gentil de la Galaisière, "Observations sur plusieurs monumens gothiques que j'ai remarqués dans cette capitale, sur lesquels sont gravés les signes du zodiaque & quelques hyérogliphes égyptiens relatifs à la religion d'Isis," *Histoire de l'Académie Royale des Sciences 1788* 91: *Avec les mémoires de mathématique & de physique* (1790): 406; and May Vieillard-Troïekouroff, "Les Zodiaques parisiens sculptés d'après Le Gentil de la Galaisière astronome du XVIIIe siècle," *Mém. de la Soc. Nat. des Antiq. de France* 84, 9th ser., 4 (1968): 183, n. 1. [**Ed. note:** See also Gerson, "West Façade," 47.]

99. Guilhermy in his notes and Johann E. von Borries in his thesis both suggested that the missing signs were placed on a lintel which they assumed was part of the original portal; Guilhermy, "Notes," Bib. Nat. ms. nouv. acq. fr. 6121, fols. 26–27; and von Borries, "Die Westportale der Abteikirche von Saint-Denis. Versuch einer Rekonstruction" (Ph.D. diss., Hamburg, 1957), 73–74. Gerson proved that there was no room for such a lintel, "West Façade," 45–50. She proposed that the signs were placed on corbels under each end of the tympanum. Vieillard-Troïekouroff suggested that the old bronze doors were high enough to have allowed the inclusion of the missing

signs, *Mém. de la Soc. Nat. des Antiq. de France,* 9th ser., 4 (1968): 183, note. 1.

100. Le Gentil de la Galaisière, *Histoire de l'Académie Royal des sciences 1788* 91 (1790): 406. Similar irregularities may be seen on the western portal of the cathedral of Senlis and on the western portals of Chartres. Viollet-le-Duc noted simply that the workmen "did not always follow the order in which they should have been placed [**Ed. note:** "Les oeuvriers ne suivaient pas toujours l'ordre dans lequel ils devait être placés"], *Dictionnaire,* 9:552.

101. Cellérier's drawing of the west façade about 1818 shows the inner archivolt of the north portal bare. Debret clearly stated that the carving now to be seen on the inner archivolt was done by the sculptor Joseph-Sylvestre Brun.

[**Ed. note:** For Cellérier's drawing, see Formigé, *L'Abbaye royale,* fig. 68. The drawing postdates the 1770–71 restorations to the portals, which according to Debret replaced the voussoir stones of the archivolts in question. Responding to his critics, who in attacking his work condemned him for two blank archivolts of the lateral portals, Debret wrote, "Ces deux bandeaux d'archivoltes non ornés de figures et irregulièrement placés au dessus des deux portes latérales étaient de l'époque de cette restauration [1771]; non en forme de tores, et non réservés à dessein comme on le suppose, ce qui est sans exemple à mon connaissance, mais construites par assises beaucoup plus régulières que celle qui les accompagnaient; de plus, d'une qualité de pierre différente de nature, et avec ciselures levées sur leur jointes ce qui attest une reconstruction beaucoup plus moderne que l'édifice," Dossier de l'Administration 1841–1876, fol. 18v.

Corroborating Debret's assertion, an eighteenth-century drawing by Charles Percier preserves evidence of a decorative band of pierced, abstract ornament on one of the archivolts enframing the north portal. The decoration would have embellished either the inner archivolt or the outermost order, or possibly both, as at Rouen cathedral. There the late twelfth-century decoration provides the only comparable example of abstract pierced work. Cf. Blum, "Lateral Portals"; and for the Rouen ornament, Sauerländer, *Gothic Sculpture in France,* pl. 182; see also for the Percier drawing, Archives Photographiques, MH 167208.]

102. [**Ed. note:** C. Jaton and A. Blanc, "Etude pétrographique des prélèvements effectués en décembre 1971," Façade occidentale, nos. 93–25 to 93–30. Crosby archives, and also the Centre de Recherches sur les Monuments Historiques, Paris, Palais de Chaillot.]

103. [**Ed. note:** Guilhermy first proposed that the figures should be identified as Peter and Paul; very tentatively Gerson examined the possibility of their identification as Ecclesia and Synogoga. The archaeological examination made by the editor in 1973 has left no doubt about the authenticity of the attributes of the two figures: the tablet of the law received by Moses (on the Deity's left), and to his right a flowering rod (usually associated with Aaron). See Ferdinand le Baron de Guilhermy and Adolphe N. Didron, "Saint-Denys, restauration de l'église roy-

ale," *Annales archéologiques* 1 (1844): 233; Gerson, "West Façade," 80–82; and Blum, "Lateral Portals."]

104. Von Borries, "Westportale," 175–76. [**Ed. note:** von Borries interpreted the group in the center of the archivolt as the *traditio legis.* Although he thought that he recognized another Apostle in the lower groups, he concluded that the figures did not enrich the meaning of the central theme and like the lower figures in the inner archivolt of the right portal filled primarily a compositional function. For a different identification with a reading that integrates those figures with the rest of the portal's program, see Blum, "Lateral Portals."]

105. Sumner McK. Crosby, "A Relief from Saint-Denis in a Paris Apartment," *Gesta* 8 (1969): 45–46.

106. Von Borries, "Westportale," 180–89.

107. [**Ed. note:** Suger, *De Administratione* 27, Lecoy de la Marche, ed., *Oeuvres,* 188; Panofsky, ed., *Suger,* 47.]

108. Panofsky, ed., *Suger,* 162.

109. [**Ed. note:** See above, n. 94, 104.]

110. Grodecki, *Vitraux de Saint-Denis,* 1:98–102.

111. [**Ed. note:** See above, n. 103.]

112. Possibly Suger's most delicate role was as mediator between the king and the pope. The bitter investiture struggle between *imperium*—the secular, or imperial, authority to appoint bishops—and *sacerdotium*—the religious, or papal, authority—had dominated German and Roman relations in the eleventh and twelfth centuries, but the conflict was less momentous in France. The compromise devised by the great bishop Ivo of Chartres and implemented by Suger rested first on a firm alliance with the pope against the emperor; and second, on an alliance of the bishops against the predatory nobility of the kingdom. Fully backed by Suger, the compromise also gave the king's endorsement to the basic ideas on ecclesiastical reform. In his turn the pope recognized the king's continued domination of the "royal bishoprics." [**Ed. note:** For a lucid summary and a basic bibliography, see von Simson, *Gothic Cathedral,* 67–70.] Friendly with the popes of his era, Suger was particularly intimate with Calixtus II and may even have been instrumental in formulating the Concordat of Worms in 1122, which resolved the investiture problem at least momentarily.

113. [**Ed. note:** See above, n. 106.]

114. Walter Cahn, "The Tympanum of the Portal of Saint-Anne at Notre Dame de Paris and the Iconography of the Division of Powers in the Early Middle Ages," *J.W.C.I.* 32 (1969): 72.

115. [**Ed. note:** "in aeternae sapientiae rationis fonte . . . salubriter exhauriunt"] Suger, *De Consecratione* 1, Lecoy de la Marche, ed., *Oeuvres,* 213: Panofsky, ed., *Suger,* 82–83.

116. Seeking an overall theme for the north, or left, portal, Gerson proposed that the "old" doors and the statue columns recalled the history of the abbey and that two of the kings might be identified as early benefactors such as Clovis II and Dagobert. Gerson, "West Façade," 159–60, 160, n. 1. [**Ed. note:** On the identification of the headless female figure as a queen, see above n. 82.]

117. Panofsky reproduced a drawing, after the engraving in

Mabillon's *Annales,* supposedly showing the monk Airardus holding the doors; Panofsky, ed., *Suger,* 161. [**Ed. note:** Johann Mabillon, *Annales ordines S. Benedicti occidentalium monarchorum patriarchae* (Lucca, 1739), 2:237.]

118. [**Ed. note:** le Gentil de la Galaisière, *Histoire de l'Académie Royale des Sciences, 1788,* 91 (1790): pls. XVII and XVIII; and for the Cellérier drawing, see Formigé, *L'Abbaye royale,* fig. 68.]

119. Among the most comprehensive studies of the Works of the Months are Olga Koseleff, *Die Monatsdarstellung der französischen Plastik des 12. Jahrunderts* (Marburg, 1934); James C. Webster, *The Labors of the Months in Antique and Medieval Art to the End of the Twelfth Century* (Evanston, 1938); and Curt Gravenkamp, *Monatsbilder und Tierkreiszeichen an Kathedralen Frankreichs* (Heidelberg, 1949).

120. Koseleff commented that the iconography of this medallion is "die einzig bekannte in der Plastik des 12. Jhts.," *Monatsdarstellungen,* 11. Von Borries does not comment on the iconography but merely points out that it is badly preserved, "Westportale," 44. The recent washing of this medallion and of the two above it has clearly identified the insets and other repairs to the predominantly twelfth-century forms.

121. The Works of the Months were frequently carved in southwestern France, but the dating of the early ones there is uncertain, and the divergent iconography indicates a different source from that informing the cycle at Saint-Denis. [**Ed. note:** For the scenes at Autun, see Denis Grivot and George Zarnecki, *Giselbertus, Sculptor of Autun* (London, 1961), 28–29, pls. B and O 1–29; and for Vézelay, Francis Salet, *La Madeleine de Vézelay* (Melun, 1948), 129–39, 177–79, pl. 16.]

122. I am indebted to Paula Gerson for recognizing this interesting detail, "West Façade," 89–90.

123. For the original portions of these colonnettes, for the portals where each belonged, and for the often extensive restorations to them, see the forthcoming study by Pamela Z. Blum. [**Ed. note:** See also Stoddard, *West Portals of Saint-Denis and Chartres,* 2–3; Marcel Aubert and Michèle Beaulieu, *Paris. Musée du Louvre. Description raisonnée des sculptures du Moyen Age, de la Renaissance et des temps moderns, I: Moyen Age* (Paris, 1950), figs. 57a, b; and Crosby and Blum, *Bull. mon.* 131 (1973): 249 n. 1.]

124. [**Ed. note:** In a French dissertation in progress under the direction of Anne Prache, Bella Meier will investigate the literary sources and the iconographical significance of the Atlas figures in monumental sculptural programs.]

125. Crosby, *L'Abbaye royale,* 36.

126. Von Borries and Gerson stated that both of these reliefs were inserted into the south portal either during the restorations in 1771 or in 1839–40. Von Borries, "Westportale," 65; Gerson, "West Façade," 44–45.

127. See, for instance, Vitry and Brière, *Eglise abbatiale,* 2d ed., 61.

128. Vöge, *Anfänge,* 225, n. 2; Mâle, *Twelfth Century,* 178, 221–22; von Borries, "Westportale," 155, 262, n. 300. Guilhermy, in his "Notes," Bib. Nat. ms. nouv. acq. fr. 6121, fols. 57–58,

described the figures of the archivolt and of the tympanum briefly but did not mention the restorations.

129. Victor Leroquais, *Les Sacramentaires et les missels manuscrits des bibliothèques publiques de France* (Paris, 1924), 4: pl. 2; and V. Leroquais, *Paris. Bibliothèque nationale. Les Manuscrits à peintures en France du VIIe–XIIe siècles* (Paris, 1954), no. 239, fig. 24; Mâle, *Twelfth Century,* 222, fig. 176.

130. Ibid.

131. Grivot and Zarnecki, *Gislebertus,* 146–49.

132. Gerson, "West Façade," esp. 95–97 and 150–53. [**Ed. note:** See above, n. 94.]

133. Katzenellenbogen, *Sculptural Programs of Chartres,* 28–30; Ernst H. Kantorowicz, *Laudes Regiae: A Study of Liturgical Acclamations and Medieval Ruler Worship* (Los Angeles, 1946), 56–64. See also Gerson, "West Façade," 145–46.

134. Félibien, *Histoire,* 534. [**Ed. note:** For the text, see above, n. 51.]

135. [**Ed. note:** Panofsky, ed., *Suger,* 160–61, holds with Mabillon's and (following him) Félibien's identification. For the dating of the doors to the eleventh century—the date accepted by the author—see also Montesquiou-Fezensac, *Bull. de la Soc. des Antiq. de France* (1945–47, pub. 1950), 128–37.]

136. [**Ed. note:** Smith, *Architectural Symbolism,* 81–96. On the liturgical uses of the west work after the Carolingian period, see Carol Heitz, *Recherches sur les rapports entre architecture et liturgie à l'époque carolingienne* (Paris, 1963), 169–239.]

137. [**Ed. note:** "multimodam laudem," Suger, *De Consecratione* 4, Lecoy de la Marche, ed., *Oeuvres,* 223; Panofsky, ed., *Suger,* 96–97.]

138. [**Ed. note:** "angelica mansione dignum."] Ibid., Lecoy de la Marche, ed., *Oeuvres,* 223; Panofsky, ed., *Suger,* 96–97. [**Ed. note:** "in parte dum sacrificant eorum in coelis sit habitatio." Suger, *De Administratione* 26, Lecoy de la Marche, ed., *Oeuvres,* 187; Panofsky, ed., *Suger,* 44–45.

139. Smith, *Architectural Symbolism,* 186–88.

140. Heitz, *Architecture et liturgie,* 145–61.

141. Ibid., esp. 145–50.

CHAPTER 7. THE CRYPT AND CHOIR

1. [**Ed. note:** "Qu'il s'agisse donc de l'architecture, de la sculpture ou de la peinture sur verre, le problème stylistique majeur que pose le chantier de Saint-Denis est la même; c'est celui de l'origine de l'art gothique. Pour l'architecture, ce problème a déjà été souvent abordé; on peut même le considerer comme résolu."] Grodecki, *Vitraux de Saint-Denis,* 1:20.

2. [**Ed. note:** "tam sancto et tam fausto opere exhilarati."] Suger, *De Administratione* 28, Lecoy de la Marche, ed., *Oeuvres,* 189; Panofsky, ed., *Suger,* 48–49.

3. [**Ed. note:** "ut, cum primum pauca expendendo multis, exinde multa expendendo nullis omnino indigeremus."] Suger, *De Consecratione* 2, Lecoy de la Marche, ed., *Oeuvres,* 218; Panofsky, ed., *Suger,* 90–91.

4. Suger, *De Consecratione* 4, Lecoy de la Marche, ed., *Oeuvres,* 226; Panofsky, ed., *Suger,* 102–03.

5. [**Ed. note:** "ad defossa faciendis fundamentis praeparata."] Ibid., Lecoy de la Marche, ed., *Oeuvres,* 226; Panofsky, ed., *Suger,* 100–01.

6. [**Ed. note:** "ipsis sacratis lapidibus tanquam reliquiis deferremus."] Ibid., Lecoy de la Marche, ed., *Oeuvres,* 225; Panofsky, ed., *Suger,* 100–01.

7. Ibid., Lecoy de la Marche, ed., *Oeuvres,* 224; Panofsky, ed., *Suger,* 98–99. [**Ed. note:** Panofsky defines "Sancti Sanctorum locus" as "the monks' choir which enclosed both the Main Altar and the Altar of the Trinity," ibid., 258, note for p. 134, line 12.]

8. Erwin Panofsky, "A Note on a Controversial Passage in Suger's *De Consecratione Ecclesiae Sancti Dionysii,*" *Gazette des Beaux-Arts* 26, 6th ser. (1944): 105.

9. [**Ed. note:** "decretum est illam altiori inaequalem, quae super absidem sanctorum dominorum nostrorum corpora retinentem operiebat, removeri voltam usque ad superficiem criptae cui adhaerebat; ut eadem cripta superioritatem sui accedentibus per utrosque gradus pro pavimento offerret, et in eminentiori loco Sanctorum lecticas auro et preciosis gemmis adornatas adventantium obtutibus designaret (it was decided to remove that vault, unequal to the higher one, which, overhead, closed the apse containing the bodies of our Patron Saints, all the way [down] to the upper surface of the crypt to which it adhered; so that this crypt might offer its top as a pavement to those approaching by either of the two stairs, and might present the chasses of the Saints, adorned with gold and precious gems, to the visitors' glances in a more elevated place)"] Suger, *De Consecratione* 4, Lecoy de la Marche, ed., *Oeuvres,* 225; Panofsky, ed., *Suger,* 100–01. [**Ed. note:** See also the slightly different version and translation by Panofsky, *Gazette des Beaux-Arts* 26, 6th ser.(1944): 100–01.]

Suger's phrase "illam altiori inaequalem," which Panofsky identified as the "problem vault," must certainly have referred to the vault over the eighth-century apse. Panofsky, ed., *Suger,* 220, note for p. 100, lines 7–14; and idem, *Gazette des Beaux-Arts* 26, 6th ser. (1944): 101–05.

10. [**Ed. note:** "Ut autem sapienti consilio, dictante Spiritu sancto cujus unctio de omnibus docet, luculento ordine designatum est quid prosequi proponeremus, collecto virorum illustrium tam episcoporum quam abbatum conventu, accita etiam domini ac serenissimi regis Francorum Ludovici praesentia, pridie idus julii, die dominica, ordinavimus ornamentis decoram, personis celebrem processionem. Quin etiam manibus episcoporum et abbatum insignia Dominicae Passionis, videlicet clavum et coronam Domini, et brachium sancti senis Simeonis, et alia sanctarum reliquiarum patrocinia praeferentes, ad defossa faciendis fundamentis praeparata loca humiliter ac devote descendimus. Dein paraclyti Spiritus sancti consolatione invocata, ut bonum domus Dei principium bono fide concluderet, cum primum ipsi episcopi ex aqua benedicta dedicationis factae proximo quinto idus junii propriis confecissent manibus cementum, primos lapides imposuerent, hymnum Deo dicentes, et *Funda-*

menta ejus usque ad finem psalmi solemniter decantantes. Ipse enim serenissimus rex intus descendens propriis manibus suum imposuit; nos quoque, et multi alii tam abbates quam religiosi viri lapides suos imposuerunt; quidam etiam gemmas, ob amorem et reverentiam Jesu Christi, decantantes: *Lapides preciosi omnes muri tui.*" (Thus, when, with wise counsel and under the dictation of the Holy Ghost Whose unction instructs us in all things, that which we proposed to carry out had been designed with perspicuous order, we brought together an assembly of illustrious men, both bishops and abbots, and also requested the presence of our Lord, the Most Serene King of the Franks, Louis. On Sunday, the day before the Ides of July, we arranged a procession beautiful by its ornaments and notable by its personages. Carrying before ourselves, in the hands of the bishops and abbots, the insignia of Our Lord's Passion, viz., the Nail and the Crown of the Lord, also the arm of the aged St. Simeon and the tutelage of other holy relics, we descended with humble devotion to the excavations made ready for the foundations. Then, when the consolation of the Comforter, the Holy Spirit, had been invoked so that He might crown the good beginning of the house of God with a good end, the bishops—having prepared, with their own hands, the mortar with the blessed water from the dedication of the previous fifth day before the Ides of June—laid the first stones, singing a hymn to God and solemnly chanting the *Fundamenta ejus* to the end of the Psalm. The Most Serene King himself stepped down [into the excavation] and with his own hands laid his [stone]. Also we and many others, both abbots and monks, laid their stones. Certain other persons also [deposited] gems out of love and reverence for Jesus Christ, chanting: *Lapides preciosi omnes muri tui.*"] Suger, *De Consecratione* 4, Lecoy de la Marche, ed., *Oeuvres,* 225–26; Panofsky, ed., *Suger,* 100–03.

11. Panofsky's translation "with perspicuous order" emphasizes the lucidity of the plan but does not stress the luminous quality which "luculento" also implies. [**Ed. note:** Panofsky, ed., *Suger,* 101 and n. 10 above]

12. Panofsky cited as a comparison Roman Breviary, *Commune Dedicationes Ecclesiae,* 5th Antophon, continuing: "et turris Jerusalem gemmis aedificabuntur" (and the towers of Jerusalem shall be built of gems), Panofsky, ed., *Suger,* 102, n. 43.

13. [**Ed. note:** "Insistentes igitur per triennium multo sumptu, populoso operariorum conventu, aestate et hieme, operis perfectioni, ne nobis conqueri Deo."] Suger, *De Consecratione* 5, Lecoy de la Marche, ed., *Oeuvres,* 227; Panofsky, ed., *Suger,* 104–05.

14. [**Ed. note:** "Quod quidem gloriosum opus quantum divina manus in talibus operosa protexerit, certum est etiam argumentum, quod in tribus annis et tribus mensibus totum illud magnificum opus, et in inferiore cripta et in superiore voltarum sublimitate, tot arcuum et columnarum distinctione variatum, etiam operturae integrum supplementum admiserit."] Suger, *De Administratione* 28, Lecoy de la Marche, ed., *Oeuvres,* 190; Panofsky, ed., *Suger,* 48–51.

15. [**Ed. note:** Quorum quidem operturarumque impul-

sionem cum episcopus expavesceret, saepe manum benedictionis in ea parte extendebat, et brachium sancti senis Simeonis signando instanter opponebat, ut manifeste nulla sui constantia, sed sola Dei pietate et Sanctorum merito ruinam evadere appareret. Sicque cum multis in locis firmissimis, ut putabatur, aedificiis multa ruinarum incommoda intulisset . . . titubantis in alto solis et recentibus arcubus nihil proferre praevaluit incommodi.] Suger, *De Consecratione* 5, Lecoy de la Marche, ed., *Oeuvres,* 230; Panofsky, ed., *Suger,* 108–09.

16. Levillain, *Mém. de la Soc. de l'Hist. de Paris* 56 (1909): 191–92.

17. See inter alia Aubert, *Suger,* 157, n. 97.

18. [**Ed. note:** "regiae majestatis serenissimi regis Francorum Ludovici placido favore (desiderabat enim sanctos Martyres suos protectores ardentissime videre), diem agendi secunda junii dominica, videlicet III idus, quod est Barnabae Apostoli, consulte assignavimus."] Suger, *De Consecratione* 6, Lecoy de la Marche, ed., *Oeuvres,* 232; Panofsky, ed., *Suger,* 110–13.

19. Panofsky, *Gazette des Beaux-Arts* 26, 6th ser. (1944): 104, n. 19.

20. See above, n. 15.

21. [**Ed. note:** "Invitatorias itaque nuntiis multis, etiam cursoribus et praeambulis pene per universas Galliarum regiones litteras delegavimus; archiepiscopos, episcopos, ex parte Sanctorum et debito apostolatus eorum tantae interesse solemnitati votive sollicitavimus."] Suger, *De Consecratione* 6, Lecoy de la Marche, ed., *Oeuvres,* 232; Panofsky, ed., *Suger,* 112–13.

22. [**Ed. note:** "archidiaconis et abbatibus et aliis honestis personis."] Ibid., Lecoy de la Marche, ed., *Oeuvres,* 234; Panofsky, ed., *Suger,* 114–15.

23. Suger, *De Administratione* 26, 32, Lecoy de la Marche, ed., *Oeuvres,* 177–78, 201; Panofsky, ed., *Suger,* 44–45, 68–69; Suger, *De Consecratione* 4, 7, Lecoy de la Marche, ed., *Oeuvres,* 223, 236–37; Panofsky, ed., *Suger,* 96–97, 118–19; Suger, *Ordinatio,* Lecoy de la Marche, ed., *Oeuvres,* 357; Panofsky, ed., *Suger,* 132–33.

24. Panofsky translated "perendie" as "on the third day," which is difficult to understand. The third day after what? Since the literal translation is "the day after tomorrow," I have assumed that Suger meant two days before the consecration on Friday, 9 June.

25. [**Ed. note:** "Ipse dominus rex Ludovicus, et regina conjux ejus Aanor, et mater ejus, et regni optimates perendie adventarunt. De diversis nationum et regnorum proceribus, nobilibus, et gregariis militum et peditum turmis, nulla suppetit computatio."] Suger, *De Consecratione* 6, Lecoy de la Marche, ed., *Oeuvres,* 232–33; Panofsky, ed., *Suger,* 112–13.

26. [**Ed. note:** "Nos autem non tantum exterioribus (ea enim affluenter sine querela exhiberi praeceperamus)."] Ibid., Lecoy de la Marche, ed., *Oeures,* 233; Panofsky, ed., *Suger,* 112–13.

27. [**Ed. note:** "(mense enim junio pene omnia victualia cara erant) . . . propter ovium quae eodem anno extiterant morticinia. . . . 'Paternitati vestrae adduco, ut quod vobis placuerit

retineatis, et quod non placeruit nobis dimittatis.' "] Ibid., Lecoy de la Marche, ed., *Oeuvres,* 231; Panofsky, ed., *Suger,* 110–11.

28. [**Ed. note:** "sequente mane, cum de camerula nostra ad sancti sacrificii ex consuetudine accelerarem celebrationem, subito quidam de fratribus albis monachus renitentem ad cameram me retrahit. In quem aliquantisper, quia nos a tanto impediebat opere, commotus, cum minus bene respondissem."] Ibid.

29. [**Ed. note:** "quo intenta tantarum personarum, tam sancta expedite ecclesiam intus et extra perlustrare posset processio, componebamus."] Suger, *De Consecratione* 6, Lecoy de la Marche, ed., *Oeuvres,* 233; Panofsky, ed., *Suger,* 112–13.

30. [**Ed. note:** "sanctorum corpora de suis assumentes oratoriis, ex consuetudine in palliatis tentoriis in exitu chori decentissime reponendo locavimus."] Ibid.

31. Panofsky, ed., *Suger,* 246, note for p. 114, lines 3f. [**Ed. note:** The text in question reads: "Pernoctantes itaque tota nocte vespertina matutinorum synaxi in laudem Divinitatis." Suger, *De Consecratione* 6, Lecoy de la Marche, ed., *Oeuvres,* 234; Panofsky, ed. *Suger,* 114–15.]

32. [**Ed. note:** "Jesum Christum Dominum nostrum . . . sanctum locum misericorditer visitare et sacris actionibus non tantum potentialiter, sed etiam personaliter adesse dignaretur, devotissime flagitabamus."] Ibid., Lecoy de la Marche, ed., *Oeuvres,* 234; Panofsky, *Suger,* 114–15, and 246, note for p. 114, line 8.

33. [**Ed. note:** "episcopaliter se componebant . . . superius, inter sanctorum Martyrum sepulturas et sancti Salvatoris altare."] Ibid., 114–15.

34. [**Ed. note:** "tot tantorum choream pontificum vestibus albis decoram, mitris pontificalibus et circinatis aurifrisiis pretiosis admodum comatam, pastorales virgas manibus tenere, circumcirca dolium ambire . . . potius chorus coelestis quam terrenus, opus divinum quam humanum, tam regi quam assistenti nobilitati videretur apparere. Populus enim pro intolerabili magnitudinis suae impetu foris agebatur, et dum chorus praefatus aquam benedictam extra, hysopo ecclesiae parietes virtuose aspergendo, projiciebat, rex ipse ejusque decuriones tumultuosum impetum arcebant, et virgis et baculis regredientes ad portas protegebant."] Ibid.

35. [**Ed. note:** "ventum est ad sanctarum reliquiarum repositionem, ad sanctorum dominorum nostrorum antiquos et venerandos tumulos accessimus (neque enim adhuc de loco suo mota erant). Prosternentes autem se tam ipsi pontifices quam dominus rex, et nos omnes, quantum pro loci angustia permittebamur, inspectis . . . venerandis scriniis. . . . Protinus lacerti moventur, brachia extenduntur, tot et tantae manus iniiciuntur, quod nec etiam septima manus ipsa sancta scrinia attingere valeret. Eapropter ipse dominus rex se medium eis ingerens, lecticam argenteam specialis patroni de manu episcoporum, sicut videtur, de manu Remensis archiepiscopi, Senonensis, Carnotensis et aliorum assumens, tam devote quam honeste praevius egrediebatur. Mirabile visu! Nunquam talem, praeter illam quae in antiqua consecratione coelestis exercitus visa est."] Ibid., Lecoy de la Marche, ed., *Oeuvres,* 235–36; Panofsky, ed., *Suger,* 114–17.

36. [**Ed. note:** On the problem of locating this door, see Panofsky, ed., *Suger,* 248, note for p. 116, lines 33ff. The recently published *Descriptio Basilicae Sancti Dionysii* of 799 lists a total of three doors decorated with ivory and silver, but does not give their locations. See Stoclet, *Journal des savants* (janvier–juin 1980): 104; and Bischoff, *Kunstchronik* 34/3 (1981): 100.]

37. [**Ed. note:** For the identification of the altars and their locations, see Panofsky, ed., *Suger,* 249–50, note for p. 118, lines 8–34, and plan preceding the plates.]

38. [**Ed. note:** "per claustrum cum candelabris et crucibus et aliis festivis ornamentis, cum odis et laudibus multis processerunt. . . .

Revertentes igitur ad ecclesiam, et per gradus ad altare superius quieti Sanctorum destinatum ascendentes . . . de nova ante novam eorum sepulturam consecranda agebatur principali ara, quam domino Remensi archiepiscopo Samsoni imposuimus consecrandam. Agebatur etiam de aliis tam gloriose quam solemniter aris viginti consecrandis. . . .

Qui omnes tam festive, tam solemniter, tam diversi, tam concorditer, tam propinqui, tam hilariter ipsam altarium consecratione missarum solemnem celebrationem superius inferiusque peragebant, ut ex ipsa sui consonantia et cohaerente harmoniae grata melodia potius angelicus quam humanus concentus aestimaretur."] Suger, *De Consecratione* 7, Lecoy de la Marche, ed., *Oeuvres,* 236–38; Panofsky, ed., *Suger,* 116–21.

39. Formigé, *Abbaye royale,* 120–23, and plan, fig. 86; Panofsky, ed., *Suger,* 249–50, note for p. 118, lines 8–34, and plan preceding the plates.

40. Simon de Vermandois, bishop of Noyon from 1123 to 1148.

41. Alvisius, bishop of Arras from 1131 to 1148.

42. Algerius, bishop of Coutances from 1132 to 1150.

43. Rotrodus (Rotrou) de Beaumont-le-Roger, bishop of Evreux from 1139 to 1148.

44. [**Ed. note:** *"mons Syon . . . civitas Regis magni,* cujus in *medio Deus non commovebitur,* sed peccatorum incitamentis *commotus,* odorifero poenitentium holocausto placari et propitiari non dedignabitur. *Medium* quippe duodecim columnae duodenorum Apostolorum exponentes numerum, secundario vero totidem alarum columnae Prophetarum numerum significantes, [in] altum repente subrigebant aedificium."] Suger, *De Consecratione* 5, Lecoy de la Marche, ed., *Oeuvres,* 227; Panofsky, ed., *Suger,* 104–05.

45. *Ephesians* 2 : 19–22.

46. [**Ed. note:** *"In quo et nos* quanto altius, quanto aptius materialiter aedificare instamus, tanto per nos ipsos spiritualiter *coaedificari in habitaculum Dei in Spiritu* sancto edocemur" (*In Whom we, too* are taught *to be builded together for an habitation of God through the* Holy *Spirit* by ourselves in a spiritual way, the more loftily and fitly we strive to build in a material way).] I have freely interpreted Suger's text in *De Consecratione* 5, as edited and annotated by Panofsky, *Suger,* 104–05 and p. 223.

47. Suger, *De Consecratione* 4, Lecoy de la Marche, ed., *Oeuvres,* 225; Panofsky, ed., *Suger,* 100–01.

48. A critical study of the thirteenth-century rebuilding of the upper portions of the choir and the transept and nave is being prepared by Caroline Bruzelius for publication by the Yale University Press. [**Ed. note:** Bruzelius, *The Thirteenth-Century Church at St-Denis* (New Haven, 1986).]

49. Guilhermy, *Monographie,* 195. [**Ed. note:** See also below, note 67.]

50. No decorative details or distinctive masonry help to suggest a possible date for the construction of these rooms. The "secret" caverns provided storage room for arms and supplies of the French Resistance at the end of World War II.

51. Vitry and Brière, *Eglise abbatiale,* 2d ed., 101; also Félibien, *Histoire,* 509–10.

52. In Crosby, 1942, 100, I wrote that this passage was "pierced through the massive foundations to the east and north." Now that this entire area has been excavated to reveal the foundations of Sainte Geneviève's chapel, it is clear that there were no such massive foundations.

53. See Félibien, *Histoire,* 517. Although Félibien must have been alive when Marie-Thérèse died, his account of the location of the royal burials is difficult to understand.

54. Guilhermy, *Monographie,* 188.

55. Ibid., 52.

56. [**Ed. note:** For reproductions of Robert's painting, see Hubert Burda, *Die Ruine in den Bildern Hubert Roberts* (Munich, 1967), fig. 106, and p. 85; and one in color reproduced by Jean Starobinski, *1789, les emblèmes de la raison* (Paris, 1973), pl. 39. Today the original is in the collection of the Musée de Carnavalet, inv. no. P. 1477.]

57. François Auguste René, vicomte de Chateaubriand, *Génie du Christianisme ou Beautés de la Religion Chrétienne,* 7th ed. (Paris, 1823), 4:98.

58. For the most recent and accurate account of Lenoir's activities at Saint-Denis, see Grodecki, *Vitraux de Saint-Denis,* 1:42–46. [**Ed. note:** See also Courajod, *Alexandre Lenoir,* 3 vols.]

59. See Crosby, 1942, 8; also the good account of these restorations in Vitry and Brière, *Eglise abbatiale,* 2d ed., 34–36.

60. [**Ed. note:** see below, n. 63]

61. Photographs of two different plans of the crypt dated 1811 and signed by Cellérier existed in the Archives Photographiques before World War II. I have no record of where the originals are. [**Ed. note:** See fig. 98b.]

62. Vitry and Brière, *Eglise abbatiale,* 2d ed., 36–37.

63. Eugène Viollet-le-Duc, Dossier de l'Administration, 1841–1876, Paris, Archives des Monuments Historiques, pp. 95–96.

64. Projecting bosses on the exterior of the crypt are also supposed to record the depth of the nineteenth-century recutting.

65. I have not been able to corroborate the statement I made in Crosby, 1942, 147–48.

66. The numbers 1.90 m and 1.60 m, for example, written in the two curving passages presumably of the eighth-century annular crypt are unintelligible, especially since Formigé has excavated there.

67. On 18 January 1817, a workman found the ditch into which the royal remains had been thrown. The ditch was between the mausoleum of the Valois and the wall of the cemetery. The remains, according to Louis Flamand-Grétry, were put into coffins—four for the Valois and one for the Bourbons—which were sealed into the small chamber to the north of the present northern entrance to the crypt. Louis V. Flamand-Grétry, *Description complète de la ville de Saint-Denis* (Paris, 1840), 172. Large, black marble slabs inscribed with the names of the kings and queens buried at Saint-Denis are attached to the wall of the crypt outside the iron grill to the chamber. Guilhermy, "Notes," Bib. Nat. ms. nouv. acq. fr. 6121, fol. 21.

68. The relics were kept in Hilduin's crypt in the eleventh century and were still there when Suger began to rebuild the crypt. See Suger, *De Consecratione* 2, Lecoy de la Marche, ed., *Oeuvres*, 216–17; Panofsky, ed., *Suger*, 86–89. They were lost in 1233, see Félibien, *Histoire*, 228–32. The reliquary for the nail was still in the treasury in 1706, see ibid., 537, pl. I, D.

69. Lefèvre-Pontalis, *Bull. mon.* 71 (1907): 556–58, and plan opposite 556. Formigé's excavations at the eastern end of the "caveau central" evidently did not uncover any foundations for such a flat wall. At least he did not leave in place any evidence for such a wall. The only early nineteenth-century published plan of the caveau royal with a flat eastern end that I have discovered prefaces the text in Guilhermy, *Monographie*, plan no. 3. [**Ed. note:** See also fig. 98a showing the crypt as of 1793.] There is also a section, drawn and signed by Viollet-le-Duc on 5 March 1859, with a flat eastern end. In the late 1930s I photographed the drawing when it was still with his manuscript pages in the care of his grandson, rue Condorcet, Paris. I do not know the current location of the drawing.

70. [**Ed. note:** "Dans la restauration de cette crypte, je me suis efforcé de supprimer toutes les additions qui la défiguraient et je n'ai refait que des parties de dallages qui manquaient. Elle se présente donc dans son état ancien qui permet d'admirer cet ensemble magnifique auquel rien peut être comparé, ni en France ni ailleurs."] Formigé, *Abbaye royale*, 186.

71. Ibid., 171, figs. 154, 155.

72. The apse shown in ibid., fig. 154, was built by Viollet-le-Duc.

73. Lefèvre-Pontalis, *Bull. mon.* 71 (1907): 556–57, and plan opposite 556.

74. The photograph of the caveau royal published by Formigé was taken after the transverse arch and the two capitals had been removed, *Abbaye royale*, fig. 154.

75. I recall this as a surprising disclosure. The abacus in question is located above the second capital from the west on the north side of the caveau royal.

76. The north arch had been filled with a masonry wall. The southern one was closed by bronze doors that had been reinstalled by Inspector Général Louis Sallez after World War I. Crosby, 1942, 12.

77. Lefèvre-Pontalis admitted that the plans of the crypt at Saint-Denis were filled with errors and that he could not establish the different axes exactly because the "mesure est très difficile à prendre." "Le Caveau central," *Bull. mon.* 71 (1907): 555–56.

78. Crosby, 1942, fig. 12, opp. p. 101.

79. [**Ed. note:** "Fratres etiam insignia Dominicae passionis adventantibus exponentes, eorum angariis et contentionibus succumbentes, nullo divertere habentes, per fenestras cum reliquiis multoties effugerunt." Suger, *De Consecratione* 2, Lecoy de la Marche, ed., *Oeuvres*, 217; Panofsky, ed., *Suger*, 88–89.]

80. [**Ed. note:** "nullus aliud ex ipsa sui constrictione quam sicut statua marmorea stare, stupere, quod unum supererat, vociferare. Mulierum autem tanta et tam intolerabilis erat angustia, ut in commixtione virorum fortium sicut prelo depressae, quasi imaginata morta exsanguem faciem exprimere, more parturientium terribiliter conclamare, plures earum miserabiliter decalcatas, pio virorum suffragio super capita hominum exaltatas, tanquam pavimento abhorreres incedere, multas etiam extremo singultantes spiritu in prato fratrum, cunctis desperantibus, anhelare."] Ibid., Lecoy de la Marche, ed., *Oeuvres*, 216–17; Panofsky, ed., *Suger*, 88–89.

81. [**Ed. note:** "in eminentiori loco Sanctorum lecticas auro et preciosis gemmis adornatas adventantium obtutibus designaret."] Ibid. 4, Lecoy de la Marche, ed., *Oeuvres*, 225; Panofsky, ed., *Suger*, 100–01.

82. See below, n. 84.

83. [**Ed. note:** "potius angelicus quam humanus concentus aestimaretur."] Ibid. 7, Lecoy de la Marche, ed., *Oeuvres*, 238; Panofsky, ed., *Suger*, 120–21.

84. [**Ed. note:** "Provisum est etiam sagaciter ut superioribus columnis et arcubus mediis, qui in inferioribus in cripta fundatis superponerentur, geometricis et aritmeticis instrumentis medium antiquae testudinis ecclesiae augmenti novi medio aequaretur, nec minus antiquarum quantitas alarum novarum quantitati adaptaretur; excepto illo urbano et approbato in circuitu oratoriorum incremento, quo tota clarissimarum vitrearum luce mirabili et continua interiorem perlustrante pulchritudinem eniteret."] Ibid. 4, Lecoy de la Marche, ed., *Oeuvres*, 225; Panofsky, ed., *Suger*, 100–01.]

85. The 10.00 m dimension is constant from east to west on the new, enlarged plan of the eighth-century church.

86. The exterior walls of the north and the south eighth-century side aisles were not parallel, so that the width varies from east to west.

87. Von Simson, *Gothic Cathedral*, 100, fig. 4, which reproduces the plan from Gall, *Gotische Baukunst*, 52, fig. 15.

88. [**Ed. note:** For a diagram of this, see Sumner McK. Crosby, "Crypt and Choir Plans at Saint-Denis," *Gesta* 5 (1966): 7, fig. 1.

89. The fifth, or median, rib of the central eastern chapel is 2.60 m long. The median ribs of the western chapels measure 2.20 m.

90. The existing keystone dates to the thirteenth century, but since dimensions of the hemicycle are the same as they were in the twelfth century, the keystone must be approximately in its original position.

91. [**Ed. note:** Et demersa prius . . . resurgit."] Suger, *De Ad-*

ministratione 27, Lecoy de la Marche, ed., *Oeuvres,* 189; Panofsky, ed., *Suger,* 48–49.

92. Panofsky, *Suger,* 238–39, note 100 for lines 14–20.

93. Since the bases are placed on the curved arcs of the hemicycle and ambulatory, their inner faces are oblique to each other. Measurements vary from spot to spot, but the axial dimension, that is, between the centers of the columns, averages 2.50 m.

94. Formigé, *Abbaye royale,* 182. Formigé was so impressed by these overhangs that he had them incised in the pavement of the crypt.

95. Jean Hubert observed that Hilduin's crypt was correctly oriented exactly to the east and that probably Sainte Geneviève's early chapel was also so oriented. See "Communication de la Séance du 10 juillet 1946," *Bull. de la Soc. Nat. des Antiq. de France* (1945–47, published 1950), 177; and Formigé, *Abbaye royale,* 170. The discovery of the foundations of the fifth-century chapel has disproved such a theory.

96. The slight deviation of the axis to the north would have been noticeable as soon as the eighth-century apse had been lowered to the level of the ninth-century vaults.

97. These deviations are particularly evident in the photogrammetric plans of the vaults, which demonstrate how studies of the superstructure often prove valuable in determining a ground plan.

98. The buttresses on either side of the eastern axial chapel are the same but reversed, as are those between the successive chapels farther to the west.

99. Crosby, *Studies in Western Art,* 1:89; also Crosby, *Gesta* 5 (1966): 5.

100. Richard Gould, a young architect who worked for some time on the plan of Saint-Denis, persuasively reproduced the dimensions and angles between the radiating chapels of the crypt. Based on a specific module and the geometric use of a golden section triangle, the results appear to be extraordinarily precise, but they involved the use of a digital computer and complicated geometrical ratios. I doubt whether even the latter were available to a twelfth-century mason.

101. Crosby, *Studies in Western Art,* 1:88–89.

102. Crosby, *Gesta* 5 (1966): 6.

103. Sergio Luis Sanabria, while a student at the University of Colorado, proposed such an *ad quadratum* system for the plan of Saint-Denis, but the photogrammetric plans were not available to him. I do not know whether he has continued his research on Saint-Denis. [**Ed. note:** For a detailed discussion of the principle of *ad quadratum,* see Fredrik M. Lund, *Ad Quadratum: A Study of the Geometrical Bases of Classic and Medieval Religious Architecture* (London, 1921).]

CHAPTER 8. CRYPT STRUCTURE

1. In spite of the time and energy expended on his restoration of the crypt at Saint-Denis, Viollet-le-Duc made only the briefest mention of it in his article "Crypt," *Dictionnaire,* 4:452. Robert de Lasteyrie, *L'Architecture religieuse en France à l'époque romane,* 2d ed. (Paris, 1929), 304–11, did not mention Saint-Denis at all.

2. Crosby, 1942, fig. 85.

3. This small sondage, done in 1977, was the last one I made at Saint-Denis.

4. Ibid., for that excavation made in 1939.

5. This was uncovered by Formigé when he excavated the eastern end of the caveau royal.

6. [**Ed. note:** *"Lapides preciosi omnes muri tui."*] Suger, *De Consecratione* 6, Lecoy de la Marche, ed., *Oeuvres,* 226; Panofsky, ed., *Suger,* 102–03.

7. The bases average 1.10 m square by 0.30 m high. There is a plinth 0.05 m high, a flat band 0.04 m high, a slight scotia 0.03 m high, and a small torus molding 0.02 m high. The shafts, or vertical portions, are 1.10 m high, 0.84 m in diameter. The large, curved blocks of which they are constructed average 0.60 m long and vary in height from 0.18 m to 0.32 m. The carved capitals with their astragals are 0.38 m high, and the molded abaci above them are 0.20 m high.

8. These piers average 1.50 m wide with a pilaster 0.60 m wide that projects 0.30 m. They are less than 0.10 m lower than the ambulatory piers. The walls between the chapels are 0.80 m thick, increasing to a thickness of 2.40 m on the exterior.

9. The buttresses are 0.30 m wide and project 0.80 m to the exterior.

10. [**Ed. note:** With reference to the foundations of the nave and towers, Suger wrote, "robusto valde fundamento materiali." Suger, *De Consecratione* 2, Lecoy de la Marche, ed., *Oeuvres,* 218; Panofsky, ed., *Suger,* 88–89.]

11. The transverse arches over the ambulatory are 0.60 m wide. The broken, or pointed, arches between the hemicycle piers measure 0.80 m in width, and the arches over the openings into the radiating chapels are 0.90 m wide. The wall arches in the radiating chapels are 0.30 m wide.

12. For a general description of early medieval groin vaults, see Bond, *Gothic Architecture in England,* 290–95.

13. Jean Bony, "Gloucester et l'origine des voûtes d'hémicycles gothiques," *Bull. mon.* 98 (1939): 329–31. Bony called attention to the six-part vaults in the crypt at Gloucester as well as to the three-, four- and five-part vaults built in 1079 at Winchester cathedral.

14. For the *anse de panier* arch, see Viollet-le-Duc, *Dictionnaire,* 1:45, fig. 2. For oval profiles, see René Chappuis, "Utilisation du tracé ovale dans l'architecture des églises romanes," *Bull. mon.* 134 (1976): 6–36.

15. Similar carved overlapping arches can be seen on the towers of Mainz cathedral, where Suger was in 1124.

16. The knobs that project from the masonry, as seen in photographs of the exterior of the crypt, are evidence of the degree of recutting, or shaving back, of the stone surfaces when Debret's workmen "cleaned" the masonry in the nineteenth century. The spouts that project from each chapel below window level were for the disposition of surplus holy water after the celebration of the mass.

CHAPTER 9. CHOIR STRUCTURE

*[**Ed. note:** An earlier, more comprehensive but unannotated version of this chapter is in the Crosby files Box VIII[1]. William W. Clark, in his paper, "Suger's Church at Saint-Denis: State of the Question," which he presented at the 1981 conference, "Abbot Suger and Saint-Denis: An International Symposium" took that version as the basis for his discussion of the twelfth-century choir. Soon to appear in an expanded form in the proceedings of the symposium (at press, The Metropolitan Museum of Art, New York), his summaries and comments provide a valuable addendum to this chapter, particularly because of the consideration given to significant material deleted by Sumner Crosby in this final version. See also in the same publication, Jean Bony, "What Sources for the Choir of Saint-Denis?" The editor has added Appendix J to this volume in order to include the author's table of statistical information on the choir structure and his comments on the comparative figures which he compiled for the crypt and choir.]

1. [**Ed. note:** On the earlier experiments in the 1130s and early 1140s which resulted in the "genesis" of the Gothic chevet in the Parisian abbey of Saint-Martin-des-Champs, see Jean Bony, *French Gothic Architecture of the 12th and 13th Centuries* (Berkeley, 1983), 49–60.]

2. [**Ed. note:** "superioribus columnis et arcubus mediis, qui in inferioribus in cripta fundatis superponerentur." Suger, *De Consecratione* 4, Lecoy de la Marche, ed., *Oeuvres*, 225; Panofsky, ed., *Suger*, 100–01.

3. Formigé, *Abbaye royale*, 182.

4. The bases of the slightly larger colonnettes between the chapels, diameter 0.20 m, are obviously nineteenth-century replacements. [**Ed. note:** On the details of the radiating chapels, particularly variations from chapel to chapel in the treatment of the plinth, see Clark, "Suger's Church."]

5. Excerpts from manuscript notes recording information about nineteenth-century restorations indicate how complicated the problem of reconstructing and authenticating details remains: "les six colonnes, en marbre noir, placées entre les chapelles, proviennent des grands Augustins de Paris. Napoléon en fit présent à l'église de Saint-Denis. Leurs chapiteaux en pierre, imité de la forme corinthienne, ont été sculptés sous la direction de l'architect, Legrand.

"M. Viollet-le-Duc les faits enlever et remplacer par des colonnes de pierre, pareilles aux autres du chevet." Guilhermy, "Notes," Bib. Nat. ms. nouv. acq. fr. 6121, fol. 137. One of Viollet-le-Duc's notes reads: "Le 15 février l'architect de l'Eglise de Saint-Denis avant reconnu que les murs d'appuis des fenêtres des chapelles du tour du choeur se lézardaient et perdaient leur aplomb en s'inclinant vers le dehors, a fait enlever une portion de la balustrade aveugle posée en 1806 en dedans de ces appuis pour les décorer probablement, il a reconnu que derrière ces fausses balustrades il existe des vides garnis, à peine, de gravois et que le parement extérieur des appuis pose à faux sur les arcs des fenêtres de la crypte, en conséquence il a immédiatement donné les ordres nécessaires pour rétablir ces appuis avec de bonnes

assises faisant l'épaisseur du mur, afin d'éviter ces mouvemens, et en leur rendant leur forme primitive." Saint-Denis, Dossier de l'Administration 1841–1876, Paris, Archives de la Commission des Monuments Historiques, p. 219. Possibly those repairs also affected interior details.

6. These monolithic shafts of the ambulatory columns are among the largest such shafts known to me.

7. In the photogrammetric elevation of chapel number three the ambulatory shaft is shown incorrectly with drums.

8. Until a scaffolding is available to allow examination of each capital at close range, no statement about the authenticity of these capitals can be considered trustworthy.

9. Frankl, *Gothic Architecture*, 35.

10. For identification of original fragments of glass still in place, see Grodecki, *Les Vitraux de Saint-Denis*, 1:63–103.

11. [**Ed. note:** Louis Grodecki, "Suger et l'architecture monastique," *Bulletin des relations artistiques France-Allemagne* (Mayence, 1951) unpaginated. See also, below, note 12.]

12. Grodecki, *Les Vitraux de Saint-Denis*, 1:125–26.

13. [**Ed. note:** Ibid., passim.]

14. Suger, *De Consecratione* 5, Lecoy de la Marche, ed., *Oeuvres*, 227; Panofsky, ed., *Suger*, 104–05.

15. Suger, *De Administratione* 28, Lecoy de la Marche, ed., *Oeuvres*, 190; Panofsky, ed., *Suger*, 48–51.

16. [**Ed. note:** Félibien, *Histoire*, 227; Marcel Aubert, *L'Architecture normande. Son Influence dans le nord de la France aux XIe et XIIe siècles* (Paris, 1939), 101; Frankl, *Gothic Architecture*, 35; Viollet-le-Duc, *Paris Guide*, 703; and idem, "Eglise imperiale," 303.

The ultimate source would be the comment of Abbot Eudes Clément (1230–45), who undertook the rebuilding of the choir in 1231. He wrote, "in reparatione ecclesie nostre tam utili quam necessaria cum ruinam minaretur." Paris, Archives nationales LL 1157, p. 85. See also Félibien's paraphrase of that statement, *Histoire*, 227; and Branner, *St Louis and the Court Style*, 45–46, esp. 46, note 28. The question remains whether that statement encompassed the choir as well as the Carolingian nave.]

17. Viollet-le-Duc, *Dictionnaire*, 2:304.

18. Georg G. Dehio and Gustav von Bezold, *Kirchliche Baukunst des Abendlandes. Historisch und systematisch dargestellt* (Stuttgart, 1961), 2:56–68, esp. 65–68; and Seymour, *Notre-Dame de Noyon*, 112–13.

19. [**Ed. note:** "Il est toutefois une question sur laquelle tous les archéologues sont d'accord c'est l'existence de vast tribunes sur les collatéraux de la nef."] Anfray, *L'Architecture normande*, 99. For example, see Marcel Aubert, *Notre-Dame de Paris* (Paris, 1929), 19; and idem, "Les Plus anciennes croisées d'ogives. Leur rôle dans la construction," *Bull. mon.* 93 (1934): 172.]

20. Panofsky, ed., *Suger*, 1st ed. (1946), 221.

21. Crosby, *L'Abbaye royale*, 46.

22. Panofsky, ed., *Suger*, 239.

23. [**Ed. note:** A. K. Porter, *Medieval Architecture*, 1:264–66, and 2:86–88; Clarence Ward, *Medieval Church Vaulting* (Princeton, 1915), 67; Dehio and von Bezold, *Kirchliche Baukunst des Abendlandes*, 2:65; and Frankl, *Gothic Architecture*, 35.]

24. [**Ed. note:** Bony, *French Gothic Architecture*, 93–95, fig. 87, and 479, n. 16.]

25. [**Ed. note:** Ibid., 479, n. 16.]

26. [**Ed. note:** "dum praefatum novi augmenti opus capitellis et arcubus superioribus et ad altitudinis cacumen produceretur, cum necdum principales arcus singulariter voluti voltarum cumulo cohaererent, terribilis et pene intolerabilis obnubilatione nubium, inundatione imbrium, impetu valdissimo ventorum subito tempestatis exorta est procella; quae usque adeo invaluit, ut non solum validas domos, sed etiam lapides turres et ligneas tristegas concusserit. Ea tempestate, quadam die, anniversario gloriosi Dagoberti regis, cum venerabilis Carnotensis episcopus Gaufredus missas gratiarum pro anima ejusdem in conventu ad altare principale festive celebraret, tantus oppositorum ventorum impetus praefatos arcus nullo suffultos podio, nullis renitentes suffragiis impingebat, ut miserabiliter tremuli, et quasi hinc et inde fluctantes, subito pestiferam minarentur ruinam."] Suger, *De Consecratione* 5, Lecoy de la Marche, ed., *Oeuvres*, 230; Panofsky, ed., *Suger*, 108–09.

27. John Fitchen, *The Construction of Gothic Cathedrals* (Oxford, 1961), Appendix L, pp. 289–95; Kenneth J. Conant, "Edifices marquants dans l'ambiance de Pierre le Vénérable et Pierre Abélard," *Pierre Abélard, Pierre le Vénérable. Les Courants philosophiques, littéraires et artistiques en occident au milieu du XIIe siècle*, ed. Réné Louis, Jean Jolivet, and Jean Châtillon (Paris, 1975), 727–32; and Panofsky, ed., *Suger*, 242–43.

28. [**Ed. note:** It is now generally assumed that the first flying buttresses were those built at Notre-Dame de Paris in the late 1170s. William W. Clark and Robert Mark, "The First Flying Buttresses: A New Reconstruction of the Nave of Notre-Dame de Paris," *Art Bulletin* 64 (1984): 47–65; also Bony, *French Gothic Architecture*, 179–86.]

29. Anne Prache, "Les Arcs-boutants au XIIe siècle," *Gesta* 15 (1976): 38.

30. [**Ed. note:** For Saint-Martin-des-Champs, see now Bony, *French Gothic Architecture*, 49–60; and for comparisons with Saint-Denis, ibid., 62–63.]

31. [**Ed. note:** See Prache, *Gesta* 15 (1976): 38, fig. 7.]

32. Clark, *J.S.A.H.* 38 (1979): 349. [**Ed. note:** On the basis of comparisons of capitals with those of Saint-Denis the author suggested a date "soon after 1144," ibid.]

33. [**Ed. note:** Ibid., 348–65.]

34. [**Ed. note:** Ibid., 363.]

35. [**Ed. note:** Ibid., 365, fig. 26.]

36. [**Ed. note:** Louis Barbier, "Etude sur la stabilité des absides de Noyon et des Saint-Germain des Prés," *Bull. mon.* 89 (1930): 515–29.]

37. [**Ed. note:** Clark, *J.S.A.H.* 38 (1979): 365.

38. [**Ed. note:** See ibid., 360, and figs. 2 and 20. The reconstruction published here as figure 118 was drawn by Donald Sanders under the supervision of William W. Clark and incorporates the author's final opinions which correct the earlier sketch published in Panofsky's second edition cited above, n. 22.]

39. [**Ed. note:** See also Bony's reconstruction, which accords with the author's hypothesis, *French Gothic Architecture*, 95, fig. 87.]

CHAPTER 10. SUGER'S UNFINISHED TRANSEPT AND NAVE

1. Formigé, *Abbaye royale*, 96–100; Viollet-le-Duc, *Dictionnaire*, 9:228–29. [**Ed. note:** The author had discussed his excavations in the nave and transept in detail in some of his earlier studies. See, for example, Sumner McK. Crosby, "Communication sur ses fouilles de la basilique de Saint-Denis," Séance du 9 juillet 1947, *Bull. de la Soc. Nat. des Antiq. des Fr.* (1945–49, published 1950): 253; "New Excavations in the Abbey Church of Saint-Denis," *Gazette des Beaux-Arts* 6th ser., 26 (1944, published 1947): 115–26; *Bull. mon.* 105 (1947): 167–81; "Early Gothic Architecture—New Problems as a Result of the St. Denis Excavations," *J.S.A.H.* 7 (1948): 113–16; "Sous le dallage de l'Abbaye royale de Saint-Denis," *Archéologia* 14 (1967): 34–38, and 15 (1967): 71–75; and *Gesta* 7 (1968): 48–50.]

2. Suger, *De Administratione* 28–29, Lecoy de la Marche, ed., *Oeuvres*, 189–92; Panofsky, ed., *Suger*, 48–53.

3. [**Ed. note:** "Promptus igitur urgere successus meos . . . ad executionem operis nos ipsos contulimus, et cruces collaterales ecclesiae ad formam prioris et posterioris operis conjungendi attolli et accumulari decertavimus." Panofsky translated the infinitives as "to raise and to enlarge" as opposed to the author's rendering.] Ibid. 28, Lecoy de la Marche, ed., *Oeuvres*, 190–91; Panofsky, ed., *Suger*, 50–51.

4. [**Ed. note:** Ibid.] See, for instance, Formigé's conclusion, "Le transept était achevé en 1148," *Abbaye royale*, 97.

5. This lacuna in the transcription of the Latin text came to my attention thanks to a photostatic copy of Bib. nat. ms. lat. 13835 which E. Panofsky kindly sent to me after he had finished editing it. For the pertinent phrase, see fol. 44. [**Ed. note:** The manuscript, the basis for all published versions, dates from the twelfth century and apparently came from Saint-Denis itself. On this see Panofsky, ed., *Suger*, 143.]

6. Formigé, *Abbaye royale*, 97, fig. 81.

7. Suger, *De Consecratione* 5, Lecoy de la Marche, ed., *Oeuvres*, 227; Panofsky, ed., *Suger*, 105.

8. [**Ed. note:** "plaqué un contrefort d'angle à trois redents, et, plus loin, une bande à faible ressaut."] Formigé, *Abbaye royale*, 98.

9. Suger, *De Administratione* 29, Lecoy de la Marche, ed., *Oeuvres*, 191; Panofsky, ed., *Suger*, 50–53; Formigé, *Abbaye royale*, 98.

10. [**Ed. note:** See ibid.]

11. The royal funerary monuments that fill the northwest corner of the transept today, as well as the fourteenth-century chapels between the nave buttresses on the north side, allowed only limited soundings along this side.

12. The upper surfaces of two additional buttresses were uncovered when the pavement of the last, or easternmost, fourteenth-century chapel between the northern buttresses was

lowered. I have been told that the pavement level in this area has been changed again.

13. The two socles that were uncovered are uniformly built. These finished blocks, with slanting bevel, enclose a rubble core.

14. The only significant object discovered in the fill of this area was a small, mutilated limestone fragment of the head of a man in chain mail. Found alone loose in the fill with no relation to anything around it, it appears to date to the thirteenth or fourteenth century.

15. Formigé's comments on the north transept portal as well as on the two towers flanking the choir are incomprehensible. His confusion between twelfth- and thirteenth-century masonry cannot be explained, and he totally misunderstood the foundations under the north transept, which he referred to as proof that there was a porch opening into the northern cemetery. Formigé, *Abbaye royale,* 98–100, 102–05.

16. Crosby, *Bull. mon.* 105 (1947): 170–71; see also Crosby, *Gazette des Beaux-Arts* 6th ser., 26 (1944): 120.

17. Similar large, polygonal socles, which may date from 1150–60, may be seen under the compound piers of Sens cathedral; and continuous, superimposed "benches" support the blind arcades around the Sens ambulatory. The benches may date from the previous decade. See Gall, *Gotische Baukunst,* figs. 68–71.

18. [**Ed. note:** "l'oeuvre de Suger se bornait à noyer les colonnes carolingiennes dans ses piliers et à fortifier les arcs pour leur permettre de supporter les murailles surélevées." | Levillain, *Mém. de la Soc. de l'Hist. de Paris* 36 (1909): 208.

19. [**Ed. note:** Formigé, *Abbaye royale,* 97–98.]

20. I last saw this capital in the entrance vestibule to the offices of Madame la Commandante of the Maison de la Légion d'Honneur at St. Denis.

21. The same design was proposed by Robert C., comte de Lasteyrie, *L'Architecture religieuse en France à l'époque gothique* (Paris, 1926), 1:22; and by von Simson, *Gothic Cathedral,* 102, 119.

CONCLUSION

1. [**Ed. note:** Because at his death the author's manuscript lacked a conclusion, this recent essay, first published in *Monasticism and the Arts,* ed. Timothy G. Verdon (Syracuse, N.Y., 1984), 189–206, is reprinted here with the permission of the editor. The essay provides a summary in his own words of aspects of the monument which the author considered of paramount importance.]

2. Jurgis Baltrušaitis, *Réveils et Prodiges: Le gothique fantastique* (Paris, 1960), 236–64.

3. Suger, *De Administratione* 33, Lecoy de la Marche, ed., *Oeuvres,* 198; Panofsky, ed., *Suger,* 62–65. [**Ed. note:** "Unde, cum . . . aliquando multicolor, gemmarum speciositas ab extrinsecis me curis devocaret, sanctarum etiam diversitatem virtutum, de materialibus ad immaterialia transferendo, honesta meditatio insistere persuaderet, videor videre me quasi sub aliqua extranea orbis terrarum plaga, quae nec tota sit in terrarum

faece nec tota in coeli puritate, demorari, ab hac etiam inferiori ad illam superiorem anagogico more Deo donante posse transferri."]

4. Ibid. 28, Lecoy de la Marche, ed., *Oeuvres,* 190–91; Panofsky, ed., *Suger,* 50–51. [**Ed. note:** "Promptus igitur urgere successus meos, cum nihil mallem sub coelo quam prosequi matris ecclesiae honorem, quae puerum materno affectu lactaverat, juvenum offendentem sustinuerat, aetate integrum potenter roboraverat, *inter* Ecclesiae et regni *principes* solemniter *locaverat,* ad executionem operis nos ipsos contulimus, et cruces collaterales ecclesiae ad formam prioris et posterioris operis conjungendi attolli et accumulari decertavimus."]

5. Ibid. [**Ed. note:**

Pars nova posterior dum jungitur anteriori,
Aula micat medio clarificata suo.
Claret enim claris quod clare concopulatur,
Et quod perfundit lux nova, claret opus
Nobile, quod constat auctum sub tempore nostro,
Qui Suggerus eram, me duce dum fieret.]

APPENDIX A

1. Formigé published Viollet-le-Duc's drawing of his excavation of the interior of pier no. 2 and one photograph of the bases of the northwest side of pier no. 6, *Abbaye royale,* 50–51, figs. 51, 53. The accompanying text indicates how little he understood about these excavations.

2. I published a report of these excavations in *Gesta* 7 (1968): 48–50.

APPENDIX B

1. Formigé, *Abbaye royale,* 53; Vieillard-Troïekouroff, *Karl der Grosse* 3:346.

2. Panofsky, ed., *Suger,* 95.

APPENDIX D

1. A summary account of these excavations appeared in 1967: Sumner McK. Crosby, "Sous le dallage de l'abbaye royale de Saint-Denis," *Archéologia* 14 (1967): 34–38.

2. For one unusual circumstance, see Crosby, *The Apostle Bas-Relief,* 7–9.

3. Crosby, 1942, 87–164.

APPENDIX F

1. Crosby, *Gesta* 9 (1970): 42–45.

APPENDIX G

1. Suger, *De Administratione* 29: Lecoy de la Marche, ed., *Oeuvres,* 191; Panofsky, ed., *Suger,* 50–51.

2. See Crosby, *The Apostle Bas-Relief,* for a complete description and analysis.

3. Ibid., 9–10.

4. *The Royal Abbey of Saint-Denis in the Time of Abbot Suger (1122–1151)*, 50–53. [**Ed. note:** The recurrence of precisely the Apostles' facial type on a capital in the westernmost chapel on the south side of the choir supports the author's dating. The editor is grateful to Stephen Gardner for this observation.]

APPENDIX J

1. Frankl, *Gothic Architecture*, 35.

APPENDIX K

1. [**Ed. note:** See now Wulf, *Die Kapitellplastik*, passim.]

2. In 1938, when I was beginning to examine the fabric of the twelfth-century portions of the abbey church, we tried to get accurate measurements of the interiors of the western bays, including the heights of the vaults. We had neither adequate equipment nor experience and reached the keystones of the vaults by means of a long bamboo fishing pole stretched out from the top of a double extension ladder. A tape measure attached to the end of the pole provided what I assumed would be a satisfactory overall vertical height. The process involved moving the heavy extension ladder along the walls of each bay. When we reached the northeast bay, where the holy water font was installed at the entrance to the south side aisle, I was suddenly urgently called down from the top of the ladder by my assistant, who pointed excitedly to the font, which was frothing vigorously. Fragments of the *badigeon* covering the walls had fallen from the wall above the font directly into it. We were horrified by the possible reaction of the clergy and quickly dismounted all equipment to return to Paris for the next few days. On our return to the church no one commented on the unusual condition of the holy water, so we resumed our examination.

3. See our detailed article: Crosby and Blum, *Bull. Mon.* 131 (1973): 209–66.

4. Formigé, *Abbaye royale*, 73.

5. [**Ed. note:** Blum, *The Twelfth-Century Figurate Sculpture of the Building Campaigns of Abbot Suger*, forthcoming. See also Blum, *Gesta* 21 (1981): 73–87.]

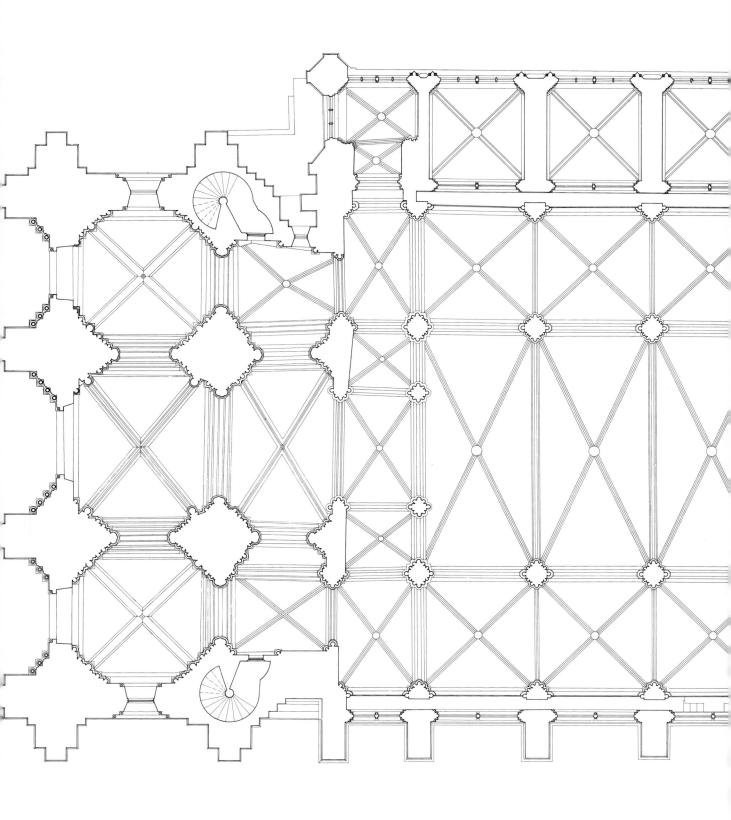

0

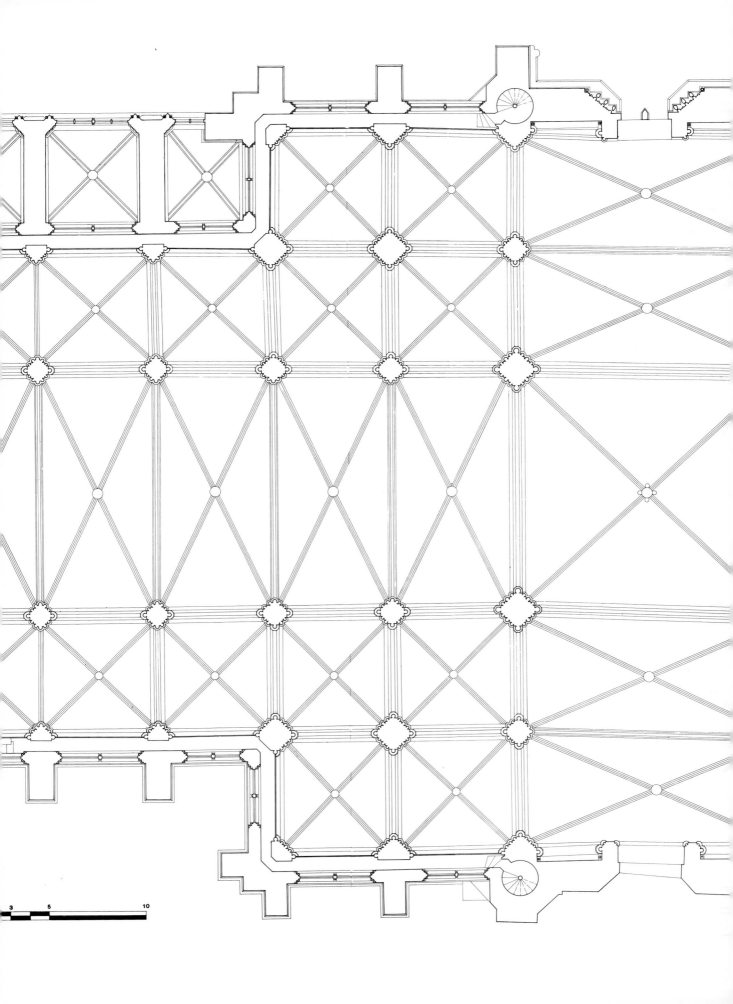

3 5 10

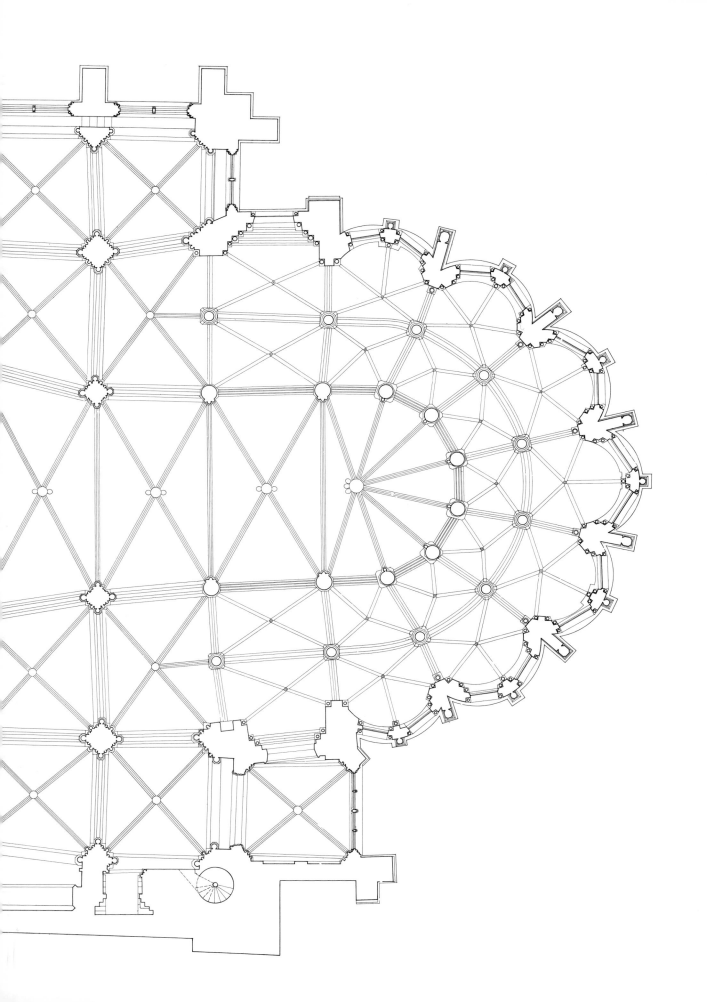

Bibliography

The bibliography was compiled by Elaine Beretz and Faye Hirsch from the author's citations in the footnotes. It includes additional references provided by the editor's notes.

ARCHIVAL SOURCES

Paris. Archives de la Commission des Monuments Historiques. Seine-Saint-Denis. "Dossier de l'Administration, 1841–76."

Paris. Archives de la Commission des Monuments Historiques. Mesnage (architect). "Journal des travaux de l'église royale de St. Denis commencé au mois de Janvier 1847."

Paris. Archives nationales. Carton F [13], 1367. "Travaux de Paris et du département de la Seine: Etats de distribution d'acomptes (classement par établissements), 1808–33."

Paris. Bibliothèque nationale ms. fr. 11681. Gautier (Gauthier), Pierre Ferdinand Albert. "Recueil d'anecdotes et autres objets curieux relatifs à l'histoire de l'abbaye royale de Saint-Denis en France, pour faire suite à l'histoire de D. Félibien."

Paris. Bibliothèque nationale ms. fr. 15634. Montfaucon, Bernard de. "Dessins et gravures pour *Les Monumens de la monarchie françoise.*"

Paris. Bibliothèque nationale ms. lat. 13835. Suger. *Liber de rebus in administratione sua gestis.*

Paris. Bibliothèque nationale ms. nouv. acq. fr. 6121. Guilhermy, Ferdinand François le Baron de. "28 Notes historiques et descriptives sur l'abbaye & basilique de St. Denis."

Paris. Musée du Louvre. Cabinet des dessins. Lenoir, Albert. *Aquarelles et dessins.* RF 1870 5279-5282.

Paris. Palais de Chaillot. Centre de Recherches sur les Monuments Historiques. Jaton, C., and A. Blanc. "Dossier monument n° 9. Etude pétrographique des prélèvements effectués en décembre 1971."

PRINTED PRIMARY SOURCES

Abbo monachus S. Germani a Pratis Parisiensis (Abbo of St. Germain). *Le Siège de Paris par les Normands.* Edited and translated by Henri Waquet. Paris, 1942.

Abbo abbas Floriacensis (Abbo abbot of Fleury). *Epistolae et Apologeticus.* Edited by Jacques-Paul Migne. In *P.L.,* 139, cols. 417–584.

Abelardus, Petrus (Peter Abelard). *Historia calamitatum.* Edited by Jacques Monfrin. 3d ed. Paris, 1967.

Admonitio generalis. Edited by Alfred Boretius. In *M.G.H., Legum Sectio II: Capitularia regum Francorum* 1:52–62. Hanover, 1883.

Aimoinus monachus Floriacensis (Aimon of Fleury). *De gestis*

503

regum Francorum. Edited by Martin Bouquet. In *Rec. des hist. de France,* 3:21–143. Paris, 1741.

Annales Bertiniani. Edited by Georg Waitz. In *Scriptores rerum Germanicarum in usum scholarum ex Monumentis Germaniae Historicis recusi,* 31. Hanover, 1883.

Les Annales de Saint-Bertin et de Saint-Vaast. Edited by Chrétien César Auguste Dehaisnes. Paris, 1871.

Annales Fuldenses. Edited by Friedrich Kurze. In *Scriptores rerum Germanicarum in usum scholarum ex Monumentis Germaniae Historicis,* 39. Hanover, 1891.

Berger, Elie, ed. "Annales de Saint-Denis, généralement connues sous le titre de Chronicon sancti Dionysii ad cyclos paschales." *Bib. de l'Ec. des Ch.* 40 (1879): 261–95.

Bernardus Clareavallensis (Bernard of Clairvaux). *Apologia ad Guillelmum Sancti-Theoderici abbatem.* Edited by Jacques-Paul Migne. In *P.L.,* 182, cols. 895–918.

———. *Epistola.* Edited by Jacques-Paul Migne. In *P.L.,* 182, cols. 67–716.

Bischoff, Bernhard, ed. "Eine Beschreibung der Basilika von Saint-Denis aus dem Jahre 799." *Kunstchronik* 34 (1981): 97–103.

Bollandus, Johannes, and the Bollandists, eds. *Acta Sanctorum quotquot toto orbe coluntur, vel a catholicis scriptoribus celebrantur quae ex latinis et graecis.* . . . Paris, 1643ff, Venice, 1734ff, and Paris, 1863ff.

Bouquet, Martin, et al., eds. *Recueil des historiens des Gaules et de la France.* 24 vols. Paris, 1738–1904.

Codex carolinus. Edited by Wilhelm Gundlach and Ernst Dümmler. In *M.G.H., Epistolarum* 3: *Merowingici et Karolini aevi* 1:469–657. Berlin, 1892.

Die nona octobris: De SS. Dionysio ep., Rustico presbyt. et Eleutherio diacono martyribus Parisiis in Francia. Edited by Cornelius Byeus. In *Acta Sanctorum* 52: Oct. 4:865–987. Paris, Rome, 1868.

Dionysius Areopagitus (Dionysius the Pseudo-Areopagite). *Oeuvres complètes du Pseudo-Denys l'Aréopagite.* Edited and translated by Maurice Patronnier de Gandillac. Paris, 1943.

Diplomata Karolinorum 1. Edited by Engelbert Mühlbacher. In *M.G.H.* Hanover, 1906.

Diplomata regum Francorum e stirpe Merowingica et maiorum domus e stirpe Arnulforum. Edited by Georg Heinrich Pertz. In *M.G.H., Diplomata Imperii* 1. Hanover, 1872.

Eginhardus abbas. *Annales Laurissenses et Eginhardi.* Edited by Jacques-Paul Migne. In *P.L.,* 104, cols. 367–508.

Epistolae variorum inde a morte Caroli Magni usque ad divisionem imperii. Edited by Ernst Dümmler. In *M.G.H., Epistolarum* 5: *Karolini aevi* 3:299–360. Berlin, 1899.

Eusebius. *The Ecclesiastical History.* Translated by Kirsopp Lake. 2 vols. London, 1926–32.

Ex Hilduini abbatis libro de S. Dionyso. Edited by Georg Waitz. In *M.G.H., Scriptores* 15, pt. 1:2–3. Hanover, 1887.

Flodoardus canonicus Remensis (Flodoardus of Reims). *Annales.* Edited by Jacques-Paul Migne. In *P. L.,* 135, cols. 417–90.

———. *Historia Remensis ecclesiae.* Edited by Jacques-Paul Migne. In *P. L.,* 135, cols. 23–418.

———. *Opuscula metrica.* Edited by Jacques-Paul Migne. In *P. L.,* 135, cols. 491–886.

Fortunatus, Venantius Honorius Clementianus, presbyter, postea episcopus Pictavensis (Fortunatus). *Carminum epistularum expositionum libri undecim.* Edited by Fridericus Leo. In *M.G.H., Auct. Antiq.* 4, pt. 1:1–270. Berlin, 1881.

[Fortunatus]. *Carminum spuriorum appendix.* Edited by Fridericus Leo. In *M.G.H., Auct. Antiq.* 4, pt. 1:371–86. Berlin, 1881.

[Fortunatus]. *Passio sanctorum martyrum Dionysii, Rustici et Eleutherii [Gloriosae].* Edited by Bruno Krusch. In *M.G.H., Auct. Antiq.* 4, pt. 2:101–105. Berlin, 1885.

Fredegarius. *Chronicarum quae dicuntur Fredegarii scholastici libri IV cum continuationibus (ann. 627).* Edited by Bruno Krusch. In *M.G.H., Script. rer. Mer.* 2:1–193. Hanover, 1888.

Fulbertus Carnotensis episcopus (Fulbert, bishop of Chartres). *Opera.* Edited by Jacques-Paul Migne. In *P.L.,* 141, cols. 189–374.

Gandillac, Maurice de, ed.
See Dionysius Areopagitus.

Gesta Dagoberti I. Regis Francorum. Edited by Bruno Krusch. In *M.G.H., Script. rer. Mer.* 2:396–425. Hanover, 1888.

Glaber, Rudolfus.
see Rodulfus Glaber.

Gloriosae. Edited by Bruno Krusch.
See [Fortunatus]. *Passio sanctorum martyrum Dionysii, Rustici et Eleutherii [Gloriosae].*

Gregorius episcopus Turonensis (Gregory of Tours). *Histoire des Francs, livres I–IV: Texte du manuscrit de Corbie, Bibliothèque nationale ms. lat. 17655.* Edited by Henri Omont. Collection de textes pour servir à l'étude et à l'enseignement de l'histoire, 2. Paris, 1886.

———. *Liber in Gloria martyrum: Gregorii episcopi Turonensis libri octo miraculorum.* Edited by Bruno Krusch and Wilhelm Arndt. In *M.G.H., Script. rer. Mer.* 1, pt. 2:484–561. Hanover, 1885.

———. *Libri historiarum X.* Edited by Bruno Krusch. In *M.G.H., Script. rer. Mer.* 1, pt. 1. Hanover, 1885; reprinted 1951.

———. *The History of the Franks by Gregory of Tours.* Edited and translated by Ormonde M. Dalton. 2 vols. Oxford, 1927.

———. *The History of the Franks.* Translated by Lewis Thorpe. Harmondsworth and Baltimore, 1974.

Guibert de Nogent. *Self and Society in Medieval France. The Memoirs of Abbot Guibert of Nogent (1064?–c.1125).* Edited with an introduction by John F. Benton. Translation by C. C. Swinton Bland, rev. by editor. New York and Evanston, 1970.

Hibernicus Exul. *Carmina.* Edited by Ernst Dümmler. In *M.G.H., Poetarum latinorum medii aevi* 1: *Aevi carolini* 1:393–413. Berlin, 1881 and 1964.

Hilduinus abbas S. Dionysii (Hilduin abbot of Saint-Denis). *Areopagitica sive Sancti Dionysii vita.* Edited by Jacques-Paul Migne. In *P.L.,* 106, cols. 13–24. Paris, 1851.

———. *Passio sanctissimi Dionysii.* Edited by Jacques-Paul Migne. In *P.L.,* 106, cols. 23–50. Paris, 1851.

Historia Karoli Magni et Rotholandi ou Chronique du Pseudo-Turpin: Textes revues et publiés d'après 49 manuscrits. Edited by Cyril Meredith-Jones. Paris, 1936.

Jacobus de Voragine (Varagine). *La Légende dorée.* Translated by Jean-Baptiste Marie Roze. Introduction by Hervé Savon. 2 vols. 2d ed. Paris, 1967.

————. *La Légende dorée.* Translated by Téodor Wyzewa. 3 vols. Paris, 1929.

————. *The Golden Legend of Jacobus de Voragine.* Translated and edited by Granger Ryan and Helmut Ripperger. New York, 1969.

Karoli epistola generalis (786–800). Edited by Alfred Boretius. In *M.G.H., Legum Sectio II: Capitularia regum Francorum* 1: 80–81. Hanover, 1883.

Kohler, Charles Alfred, ed.

See *Vita beatae Genovefe virginis.* . . .

Lauer, Philippe, and Charles Samaran, eds. *Les Diplômes originaux des Mérovingiens: Fac-similés phototypiques avec notices et transcriptions.* Paris, 1908.

Leclercq, Jean, ed. and trans.

See Suger, *Comment fut construit Saint-Denis?*

Lecoy de la Marche, Auguste, ed. *Oeuvres complètes de Suger recueillies, annotées et publiées d'après les manuscrits pour la Société de l'Histoire de France.* Paris, 1867.

Libri carolini sive Caroli Magni capitulare de imaginibus. Edited by Hubert Bastgen. In *M.G.H., Legum Sectio II: Concilia* 2, Supplementum. Hanover, 1924.

Ludowicus imperator (Louis the Pious). *Epistola ad Hilduinum.* Edited by Ernst Dümmler. In *Epistolae variorum inde a morte Caroli Magni usque ad divisionem imperii* 19. *M.G.H., Epistolarum* 5: *Karolini aevi* 3:325–27. Berlin, 1899.

See also *Epistolae Variorum.* . . . Edited by E. Dümmler.

Mabillon, Jean, and Luc d'Achéry, eds. *Acta Sanctorum Ordinis S. Benedicti in saeculorum classes distributa.* 3 vols. Venice, 1668–1772; reprinted, 1935.

Mandach, André de. *Naissance et développement de la chanson de geste en Europe.* 4 vols. Geneva, 1961–80.

Meredith-Jones, Cyril, ed.

See *Historia Karoli Magni et Rotholandi.*

Miracula Sancti Dionysii. Edited by Jean Mabillon. In *Acta Sanctorum Ordinis S. Benedicti, saec.* III, pt. 2: 343–64. Paris, 1772.

————(or *Vita S. Dionysii episcopi Parisiensis.* Edited by Luc d'Achéry and Jean Mabillon. In *Acta Sanctorum Ord. Ben. saec.* III, pt. 2: 311–29. Paris, 1734.

Molinier, Auguste Emile Louis Marie, ed.

See Suger, *Vie de Louis le Gros.*

Mouskés (Mousket), Philippe de. *Chronique rimée de Philippe Mouskes.* Edited by Frédéric Auguste Ferdinand Thomas, baron de Reiffenberg. 2 vols. Collection des chroniques belges inédites. Brussels, 1836–38.

Nithardus S. Richarii abbas (Nithard of Saint-Riquier). *De dissensionibus filiorum Ludovici Pii.* Edited by Jacques-Paul Migne. In *P.L.,* 116, cols. 45–76.

Ordericus Vitalis Uticensis monachus (Orderic Vitalis of Saint-Evroult). *Historia ecclesiastica.* Edited by Jacques-Paul Migne. In *P.L.,* 188, cols. 17–984.

Panofsky, Erwin, ed. and trans. *Abbot Suger on the Abbey Church of Saint-Denis and its Art Treasures.* Princeton, 1946. 2d ed. Edited by Gerda Panofsky-Soergel. Princeton, 1979.

Pseudo-Dionysius Areopagitus.

See Dionysius Areopagitus.

Rodulfus Glaber Cluniacensis monachus (Rodolf Glaber). *Historiarum sui temporis libri quinque.* Edited by Jacques-Paul Migne. In *P.L.,* 142, cols. 611–98.

Scamozzi, Vincenzo. *Tacchuino di viaggio da Parigi e Venezia (14 marzo–11 maggio 1600).* Edited by Franco Barbieri. Venice, 1959.

Schlosser, Julius von, ed. *Schriftquellen zur der Karolingischen Kunst.* Vienna, 1896.

Stoclet, Alain J., ed. "La *Descriptio Basilicae Sancti Dyonisii:* Premiers commentaires." *Journal des savants* (1980): 103–17.

Sugerius abbas S. Dionysii (Suger abbot of Saint-Denis). *Comment fut construit Saint-Denis?* Translated by Jean Leclercq. Paris, 1945.

————. *Libellus alter de consecratione ecclesiae Sancti Dionysii.* In Lecoy de la Marche, ed., *Oeuvres,* 213–38.

————. *Libellus alter de consecratione ecclesiae Sancti Dionysii (The Other Little Book on the Consecration of the Church of St.-Denis).* In Panofsky, ed., *Suger,* 82–121.

————. *Liber de rebus in administratione sua gestis.* In Lecoy de la Marche, ed., *Oeuvres,* 155–209.

————. *Liber de rebus in administratione sua gestis (On What was Done under His Administration).* In Panofsky, ed., *Suger,* 40–81.

————. *De Hominibus villae beati Dionysii libertati traditis,* 1125. Lecoy de la Marche, ed., *Oeuvres,* 319–22.

————. *Epistolae.* In Lecoy de la Marche, ed., *Oeuvres,* 238–84.

————. *On the Abbey Church of St.-Denis and its Art Treasures.* See Panofsky, Erwin.

————. *Ordinatio A.D. MCXL vel MCXLI confirmata.* In Lecoy de la Marche, ed., *Oeuvres,* 349–60.

————. *Ordinatio A.D. MCXL vel MCXLI confirmata (Ordinance Enacted in the Year 1140 or in the Year 1141).* In Panofsky, ed., *Suger,* 122–37.

————. *Testamentum Sugerii abbatis,* 17 June 1137. In Lecoy de la Marche, ed., *Oeuvres,* 333–41.

————. *Vie de Louis VI le Gros.* Edited and translated by Henri Waquet. Les Classiques de l'histoire de France au moyen age, 11. Paris, 1929.

————. *Vie de Louis le Gros par Suger, suivie de l'histoire du roi Louis VII publié d'après les manuscrits.* Edited by Auguste Emile Louis Marie Molinier. Paris, 1887.

————. *Vita Ludovici Grossi regis 12.* In Lecoy de la Marche, ed., *Oeuvres,* 1–149.

Tardif, Jules. *Monuments historiques.* Paris, 1866.

Vita beatae Genovefe virginis: Etude critique sur le texte de la vie latine de Sainte Geneviève de Paris avec deux textes de cette vie. Edited with commentary by Charles Kohler. Bibliothèque de l'Ecole des Hautes Etudes, 48. Paris, 1881.

Vita Eligii episcopi Noviomagensis. Edited by Bruno Krusch. In *M.G.H., Script. rer. Mer.* 4:634–761. Hanover, 1902.

Vita Genovefae virginis Parisiensis. Edited by Bruno Krusch and Ernst Dümmler. *M.G.H., Script. rer. Mer.* 3:204–38. Hanover, 1896.

Vita sanctae Bathildis. Edited by Bruno Krusch. In *M.G.H., Script. rer. Mer.* 2:475–508. Hanover, 1888.

Vita S. Dionysii episcopi Parisiensis. Edited by Luc d'Achéry and Jean Mabillon. See *Miracula Sancti Dionysii.*

Walafridus Strabonus abbas Augiensis (Walahfrid Strabo of Augia Dives or Reichenau). *Libellus de exordiis et incrementis quarundam in observationibus ecclesiasticis rerum.* Edited by Alfred Boretius and Victor Krause. In *M.G.H., Legum Sectio II: Capitularia regum Francorum* 2:474–516. Hanover, 1897.

Waquet, H., ed. *Vie de Louis.*
See Suger, *Vie de Louis VI le Gros.*

Willelmus. *Sugerii vita.* In Lecoy de la Marche, ed., *Oeuvres,* 375–411. Paris, 1868.

SECONDARY WORKS

Adler, Alfred. "The *Pèlerinage de Charlemagne* in New Light on Saint-Denis." *Speculum* 22 (1947): 550–61.

Alföldi, Maria R. "Zum Ring der Königin Arnegunde." *Germania* 41 (1963): 55–58.

Allen, Gerald. "A Report on the West Facade of Saint-Denis." Unpublished seminar paper, Yale University, January 1971 (Crosby archives).

André, Florence, and Gilbert Mangin. "Les Bijoux d'Arégonde." *Dossiers de l'archéologie* 32 (1979): 50–65.

Anfray, Marcel. *L'Architecture normande: Son Influence dans le nord de la France aux XIe et XIIe siècles.* Paris, 1939.

Arbellot, François, ed. *Etude sur les origines chrétiennes de la Gaule: Première partie, Saint Denys de Paris.* Paris, 1880.

Aubert, Edouard. "Etude sur l'ancien clocher de l'église Saint-Hilaire-le-Grand à Poitiers." *Mém. de la Soc. Nat. des Antiq. de France* 42 (1881): 45–70.

Aubert, Marcel. "Communication de la séance du 17 janvier 1945." *Bull. de la Soc. Nat. des Antiq. de France* (1945–47, published 1950): 26.

―――. *L'Eglise de Saint-Benôit-sur-Loire.* Paris, 1931.

―――. *Notre-Dame de Paris: Sa Place dans l'histoire de l'architecture du XIIe au XIVe siècle.* 2d ed. Paris, 1929.

―――. "Les Plus Anciennes Croisées d'ogives: Leur rôle dans la construction." *Bull. mon.* 93 (1934): 5–67 and 137–237.

―――. "Le Portail royal et la façade occidentale de la cathédrale de Chartres: Essai sur la date de leur exécution." *Bull. mon.* 100 (1941): 177–218.

―――. *La Sculpture française au moyen-âge.* Paris, 1947.

―――. *Suger.* Rouen, 1950.

―――. "Têtes de statues-colonnes du portail occidental de Saint-Denis," *Bull. mon.* 103 (1945): 243–48.

―――, and Michèle Beaulieu. Paris. Musée national du Louvre. *Description raisonnée des sculptures du moyen age, de la Renaissance et des temps moderns, I: Moyen age.* Paris, 1950.

Aubert, Roger. "Denys (Saint), premier évêque de Paris." *D.H.G.E.* 14:263–65. Paris, 1960.

d'Ayzac, Félicie Marie Emilie. *Histoire de l'abbaye de Saint-Denis en France.* 2 vols. Paris, 1860–61.

Baillet, Louis. "Les Miniatures du 'Scivias' de Sainte Hildegarde conservé à la Bibliothèque de Wiesbaden." *Monuments Piot* 19 (1911): 49–149.

Baltrušaitis, Jurgis. *L'Eglise cloisonnée en orient et en occident.* Paris, 1941.

―――. *La Stylistique ornementale dans la sculpture romane.* Paris, 1931.

Barbier, Louis. "Etude sur la stabilité des absides de Noyon et de Saint-Germain des Prés." *Bull. mon.* 89 (1930): 515–29.

Barbieri, Franco. "Vincenzo Scamozzi, studioso ed artista." *Critica d'arte* An. 8, ser. 3, fasc. 29 (Sept. 1949): 222–30. Fasc. 30 (Nov. 1949): 300–13.

Barroux, Robert. "L'Abbé Suger et la vassalité du Vexin en 1124: La Levée de l'oriflamme, la Chronique du Pseudo-Turpin et la fausse donation de Charlemagne à Saint-Denis de 813." *Le Moyen Age* 64, 4th ser., 13 (1958): 1–26.

―――. *Dagobert, roi des Francs.* Paris, 1938.

Barthélémy, Anatole de. "Compte rendu: Charles Kohler, *Vita beatae Genovefe virginis: Etude critique sur le texte de la vie latine de Sainte Geneviève de Paris.*" *Bulletin du Comité d'Histoire et d'Archéologie du Diocèse de Paris* 1 (Jan. 1883–June 1885): 97–99.

Bates, Robert C. "Le Pèlerinage de Charlemagne: A Baroque Epic." *Yale Romanic Studies* 18 (1941): 1–47.

Baudot, Jules L., Léon Chaussin, eds., and the Benedictines of Paris. *Vies des saints et des bienheureux selon l'ordre du calendrier, avec l'historique des fêtes.* 13 vols. Paris, 1935–59.

Bayer, Herbert, Walter Gropius, and Ise Gropius, eds. *Bauhaus 1919–1928.* 2d ed. Boston, 1952; reprinted, 1959.

Bayley, Stephen. *The Albert Memorial: The Monument in its Social and Architectural Context.* London, 1981.

Beckwith, John. *Early Medieval Art: Carolingian, Ottonian, Romanesque.* London, 1964.

Bédier, Joseph. *Les Légendes épiques: Recherches sur la formation des chansons de geste.* 4 vols. 3d ed. Paris, 1926–29.

Beguillet, Edme, and J.-Ch. Poncelin de la Roche. *Description historique de Paris et de ses plus beaux monumens gravés en taille douce par F. N. Martinet. . . .* 3 vols. Paris, 1779–81.

Benedictines of Paris, eds. *Vies des saints.*
See Baudot and Chaussin, ed.

Benoit, Fernand. "La Basilique Saint-Pierre et Saint-Paul à Arles: Etude sur les cancels paléochrétiens." *Provence historique* 7 (1957): 8–21.

Bernard, Eugène. *Les Origines de l'église de Paris: Etablissement du christianisme dans les Gaules. Saint Denys de Paris.* Paris, 1870.

Besse, Jean-Martial Léon. *Les Moines de l'ancienne France (période gallo-romaine et mérovingienne).* Paris, 1906.

Birchler, Linus. *Die Kunstdenkmäler des Kantons Schwyz: Gersau, Küssnach und Schwyz.* Vol. 2 of *Die Kunstdenkmäler der Schweiz.* Basel, 1930.

Blanchet, Adrien. *Etude sur la décoration des édifices de la Gaule romaine.* Paris, 1913.

PLATE 2. Overall ground plan with crypt and all excavations.

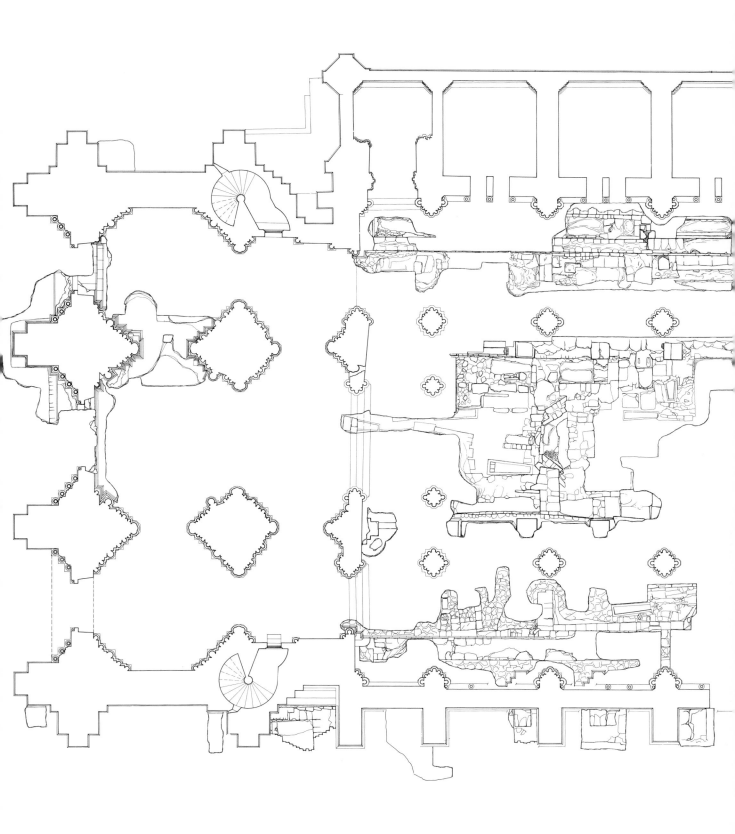

0

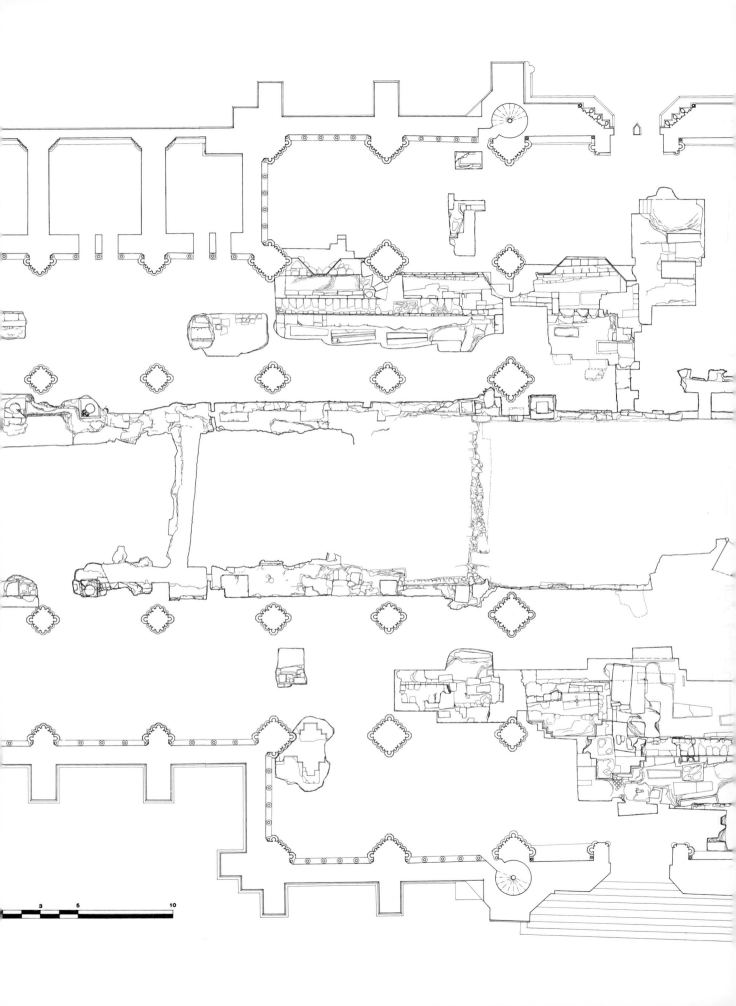

3   5   10

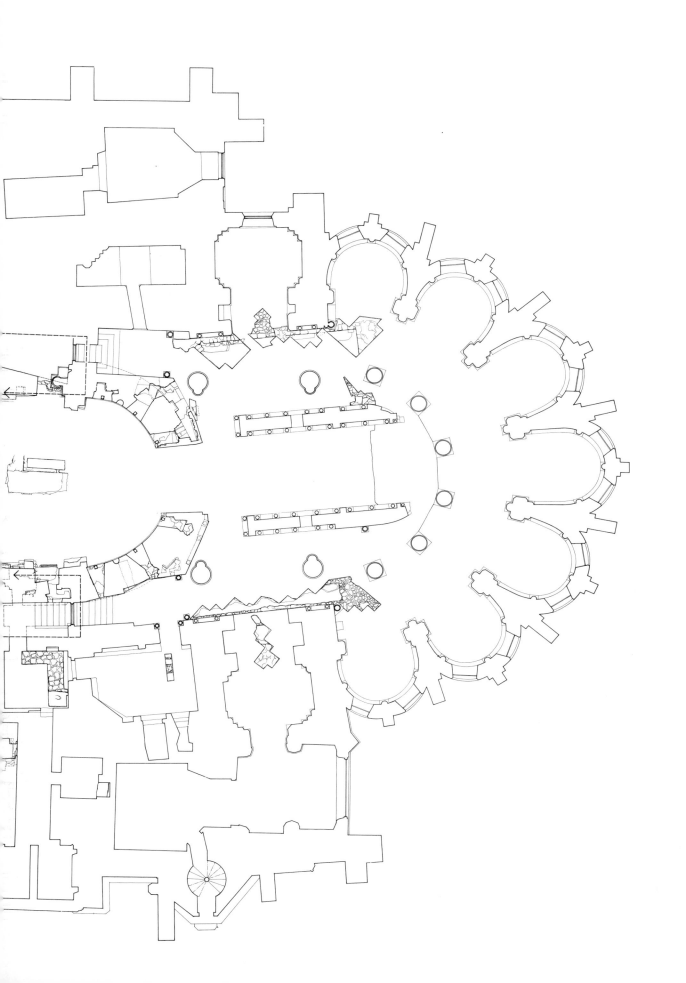

————, and Adolf Edmond Dieudonné. *Manuel de numismatique française.* 4 vols. Paris, 1912–36.

Blondel, Louis. "Les Anciennes Basiliques d'Agaune: Etude archéologique." *Vallesia* 3 (1948): 9–57.

Blum, Pamela Z. "The Lateral Portals of the West Façade of the Abbey Church of Saint-Denis: Archeological and Iconographical Considerations." In *Abbot Suger and Saint-Denis: An International Symposium.* Edited by Paula Gerson. The Metropolitan Museum of Art, New York, 1986.

————. *The Twelfth-Century Figurate Sculpture of the Building Campaigns of Abbot Suger.* Forthcoming.

————. "The Saint-Benedict Cycle on the Capitals of the Crypt at Saint-Denis." *Gesta* 21 (1981): 73–87.

Bober, Harry. "On the Illumination of the Glazier Codex: A Contribution to Early Coptic Art and Its Relation to Hiberno-Saxon Interlace." In *Homage to a Bookman: Essays on Manuscripts, Books and Printing Written for Hans P. Kraus on his 60th Birthday Oct. 2, 1967,* edited by Hellmutt Lehmann-Haupt, 31–49. Berlin, 1967.

Bond, Francis. *Gothic Architecture in England: An Analysis of the Origin and Development of English Church Architecture from the Norman Conquest to the Dissolution of the Monasteries.* London, 1905.

Bony, Jean. "Diagonality and Centrality in Early Rib-Vaulted Architectures." *Gesta* 15 (1976): 15–25.

————. *French Gothic Architecture of the 12th and 13th Centuries.* Berkeley, Los Angeles, London, 1983.

————. "Gloucester et l'origine des voûtes d'hémicycle gothiques." *Bull. mon.* 98 (1939): 329–31.

————. "What Sources for the Choir of Saint-Denis?" In *Abbot Suger and Saint-Denis: An International Symposium.* Edited by Paula Gerson. The Metropolitan Museum of Art, New York, 1986.

Boussuat, Robert. "Traditions populaires relatives au martyre et à la sépulture de saint Denis." *Le Moyen Age* 62, 4th ser., 11 (1956): 479–509.

Branner, Robert. *Chartres Cathedral.* New York, 1969.

————. *St Louis and the Court Style in Gothic Architecture.* London, 1965.

Braunfels, Wolfgang. *Die Welt der Karolinger und ihre Kunst.* Munich, 1968.

————, Helmut Beumann, Bernhard Bischoff, Herman Schnitzler, and Percy Ernst Schramm, eds. *Karl der Grosse: Lebenswerk und Nachleben.* 5 vols. Düsseldorf, 1965–68.

Brooke, Christopher N. L. *Europe in the Central Middle Ages 962–1152.* New York, 1964.

————. *The Twelfth Century Renaissance.* Norwich, 1969. New York, 1970.

Brown, Elizabeth, and Michael Cothren. "The Twelfth-Century Crusading Window of the Abbey of Saint-Denis: 'Praetertorum enim recordatio futurorum est exhibitio.'" *J.W.C.I.* 48 (1985): forthcoming.

Bruzelius, Caroline. *The Thirteenth-Century Church at St-Denis.* New Haven, London, 1986.

Buchner, Maximilian. "Die Areopagitika des Abtes Hilduins von St. Denis und ihr kirchenpolitischer Hintergrund: Studien zur Gleichsetzung Dionysius' des Areopagiten mit dem hl. Dionysius von Paris sowie zur Fälschungstechnik am Vorabend der Entstehung der pseudoisidorischen Dekretalen." *Historisches Jahrbuch* 56 (1936): 441–80, and 57 (1937): 31–60.

————. "Zur Entstehung und zur Tendenz der 'Gesta Dagoberti:' Zugleich ein Beitrag zum Eigenkirchwesen im Frankreich." *Historisches Jahrbuch* 47 (1927): 252–74.

————. *Das Vizepapsttum des Abtes von Saint-Denis.* Paderborn, 1928.

Bulteau, Marcel J. *Monographie de la cathédrale de Chartres.* 3 vols. Chartres, 1887–92.

Burda, Hubert. *Die Ruine in den Bildern Hubert Roberts.* Munich, 1967.

Cabanot, Jean. "Chapiteaux de marbre antérieurs à l'époque romane dans le département des Landes." *Cahiers archéologiques* 22 (1972): 1–18.

Cabrol, Fernand, and Henri Leclercq. *Dictionnaire d'archéologie chrétienne et de liturgie.* 15 vols. Paris, 1907–53.

Cahier, Charles, and Arthur Martin. *Mélanges d'archéologie, d'histoire et de littérature.* 4 vols. Paris, 1847–56.

Cahn, Walter. "The Tympanum of the Portal of Sainte-Anne at Notre Dame de Paris and the Iconography of the Division of Powers in the Early Middle Ages." *J.W.C.I.* 32 (1969): 55–72.

Cappuyns, Maïeul. *Jean Scot Erigène: Sa Vie, son oeuvre, sa pensée.* Louvain, Paris, 1933.

Cartellieri, Otto. *Abt Suger von Saint-Denis 1081–1151.* Berlin, 1898.

Chappuis, René. "Utilisation du tracé ovale dans l'architecture des églises romanes." *Bull. mon.* 134 (1976): 6–36.

Chateaubriand, François Auguste René, vicomte de. *Génie du christianisme, ou Beautés de la religion chrétienne.* 5 vols. 7th ed. Paris, 1822–23.

Chédeville, André, Jacques Le Goff, and Jacques Rossiaud. *La Ville médiévale des Carolingiens à la Renaissance.* Vol. 2 of *Histoire de la France urbaine,* edited by Georges Duby. Paris, 1980.

Chenu, Marie-Dominique. *Nature, Man and Society in the Twelfth Century: Essays on New Theological Perspectives in the Latin West.* Edited and translated by Jerome Taylor and Lester K. Little. Chicago, London, 1968.

Chevalier, Cyr Ulysse Joseph. *Répertoire des sources historiques du moyen âge:* 2 vols. 2d. ed. Paris, 1905–07.

Christe, Yves. "Le Portail de Beaulieu: Etude iconographique et stylistique." *Bulletin archéologique du Comité des Travaux Historiques et Scientifiques* 56, n.s., 6 (1970): 57–76.

Clark, William W. "Spatial Innovations in the Chevet of Saint-Germain-des-Prés." *J.S.A.H.* 38 (1979): 348–65.

————. "Suger's Church at Saint-Denis: State of the Question." In *Abbot Suger and Saint-Denis: An International Symposium,* edited by Paula Gerson. The Metropolitan Museum of Art, New York, 1986.

————, and Robert Mark. "The First Flying Buttresses: A New

Reconstruction of the Nave of Notre-Dame de Paris," *Art Bulletin* 66 (1984): 47–65.

Conant, Kenneth. *Cluny: Les Eglises et la maison du chef d'ordre.* Mâcon, 1968.

———. "Edifices marquants dans l'ambiance de Pierre le Vénérable et Pierre Abélard." In *Pierre Abélard, Pierre le Vénérable: Les Courants philosophiques, littéraires et artistiques en occident au milieu du XIIe siècle,* edited by Réné Louis, Jean Jolivet, and Jean Châtillon, 727–32. Paris, 1975.

Conway, W. Martin. "The Abbey of Saint-Denis and its Ancient Treasures." *Archaeologia* 66, 2d ser., 16 (1915): 103–58.

———. "Some Treasures of the Time of Charles the Bald." *Burlington Magazine* 26 (March 1915): 236–41.

Corpus della scultura altomedievale 7, *La Diocesi di Roma.* 3 parts. Spoleto, 1974.

Courajod, Louis Charles Jean. *Alexandre Lenoir: Son Journal et le Musée des Monuments Français.* 3 vols. Paris, 1878–87.

Crosby, Sumner McKnight. *L'Abbaye royale de Saint-Denis.* Paris, 1953.

———. *The Abbey of St.-Denis, 475–1122.* Vol. 1. New Haven, 1942.

———. "Abbot Suger's Program for his New Abbey Church." In *Monasticism and the Arts.* Edited by Timothy Gregory Verdon, 189–206. Syracuse, N.Y., 1984.

———. "Abbot Suger's St.-Denis: The New Gothic." In *Studies in Western Art,* Vol. I: *Romanesque and Gothic Art.* Acts of the Twentieth International Congress of the History of Art, New York, 1961, edited by Millard Meiss, et al., 85–91. Princeton, 1963.

———. *The Apostle Bas-Relief at Saint-Denis.* New Haven, London, 1972.

———. "A Carolingian Pavement at Saint-Denis: Preliminary Report." *Gesta* 9/1 (1970): 42–45.

———. "Communication sur ses fouilles de la basilique de St.-Denis. Séance du 9 juillet 1947." *Bull. de la Soc. Nat. des Antiq. de France* (1945–47, published 1950): 253.

———. "The Creative Environment." *Ventures (Magazine of the Yale Graduate School)* (Fall 1965): 10–15.

———. "Crypt and Choir Plans at Saint-Denis." *Gesta* 5 (1966): 4–8.

———. "Early Gothic Architecture—New Problems as a Result of the St. Denis Excavations." *J.S.A.H.* 7/3–4 (1948): 13–16.

———. "Excavations at Saint-Denis—July, 1967." *Gesta* 7 (1968): 48–50.

———. "Excavations in the Abbey Church of St.-Denis 1948: The Façade of Fulrad's Church." *Proceedings of the American Philosophical Society* 93 (1949): 347–61.

———. "Fouilles exécutées récemment dans la basilique de Saint-Denis." *Bull. mon.* 105 (1947): 167–81.

———. "The Inside of St.-Denis' West Façade." In *Gedenkschrift Ernst Gall,* edited by Margarete Kühn and Louis Grodecki, 59–68. Munich, Berlin, 1965.

———. "An International Workshop in the Twelfth Century."

Cahiers d'histoire mondiale (Journal of World History) 10 (1966): 19–30.

———. "Masons' Marks at Saint-Denis." In *Mélanges offerts à René Crozet,* edited by Pierre Gallais and Yves-Jean Riou, 2:711–17. Poitiers, 1966.

———. "New Excavations in the Abbey Church of Saint-Denis." *Gazette des Beaux-Arts,* 6th ser., 26 (1944, published 1947): 115–26.

———. "The Plan of the Western Bays of Suger's New Church at St. Denis." *J.S.A.H.* 27 (1968): 39–43.

———. "A Relief from Saint-Denis in a Paris Apartment." *Gesta* 8/2 (1969): 45–46.

———. "Some Uses of Photogrammetry by the Historian of Art." In *Etudes d'art médiéval offertes à Louis Grodecki,* edited by Sumner McK. Crosby, André Chastel, Anne Prache, and Albert Chatelet, 119–28. Paris, 1981.

———. "Sous la dallage de l'abbaye royale de Saint-Denis." *Archéologia* 14 (1967): 34–38, and 15 (1967): 71–75.

———, and Pamela Z. Blum. "Le Portail central de la façade occidentale de Saint-Denis." *Bull. mon.* 131 (1973): 209–66.

———, Jane Hayward, Charles T. Little, and William D. Wixom. *The Royal Abbey of Saint-Denis in the Time of Abbot Suger (1122–51).* New York, 1981.

Davin, Vincent. *Les Actes de Saint Denys de Paris. Etude historique et critique.* Paris, 1897.

Debret, François. "Notice sur les diverses constructions et restaurations de l'église de Saint-Denis." Institut Royal de France. *Séance publique annuelle des cinq académies du lundi 2 Mai 1842.* (1842): 11–28.

Dehio, Georg G., and Gustav von Bezold. *Die kirchliche Baukunst des Abendlandes: Historisch und systematisch dargestellt.* 7 vols. Stuttgart, 1887–1901; reprinted 1961.

Delaborde, Henri-François. "Le Procès du chef de Saint Denis en 1410." *Mémoires de la Société de l'Histoire de Paris et de l'Ile-de-France* 11 (1884): 297–409.

Deshoulières, François. "L'Eglise Saint-Pierre de Montmartre." *Bull. mon.* 77 (1913): 5–30.

Dictionnaire d'histoire et de géographie ecclésiastique. 19 vols. Paris, 1912–.

Didron, Adolphe Napoléon. "Achèvement des restaurations de Saint-Denis." *Annales archéologiques* 5 (1846): 107–13.

D'Oench, Ellen. "The Trinity at Saint-Denis." Unpublished seminar paper, Yale University, Spring 1975 (Crosby archives).

Doublet, Jacques. *Histoire de l'abbaye de S. Denys en France.* Paris, 1625.

Dubois, Jacques. "L'Emplacement des premiers sanctuaires de Paris." *Journal des savants* (1968): 5–44.

Duby, Georges, ed. *Histoire de la France urbaine.*
See Chédeville, André, et al., *La Ville médiévale.* . . .

DuCange, Charles DuFresne. *Glossarium mediae et infimae Latinitatis.* 10 vols. 2d ed. Graz, 1954.

Duchesne, Louis Marie Olivier. "A propos du *Martyrologe Hiéronymien.*" *Analecta bollandiana* 17 (1898): 421–47.

————. *Les Fastes épiscopaux de l'ancienne Gaule.* 3 vols. Paris, 1900–15.

Dufour, Valentin. "Les VII stations de Saint Denis." *Bulletin du bouquiniste* 29 (1872): 211–19, 243–46.

Dumoulin, André. "Recherches archéologiques dans la région d'Apt (Vaucluse)." *Gallia* 16 (1958): 197–241.

Duval, Paul-Marie. *Paris antique des origines au troisième siècle.* Paris, 1961.

Ehlers, Joachim. *Hugo von St. Victor: Studien zum Geschichtsdenken und zur Geschichtsschreibung des 12. Jahrhunderts.* Frankfurter Historische Abhandlungen, 7. Weisbaden, 1973.

Enlart, Camille. "Correspondance." *Bull. mon.* 71 (1907): 546–49.

Erlande-Brandenburg, Alain. *Le Roi est mort: Etude sur les funérailles, les sépultures et les tombeaux des rois de France jusqu'à la fin du XIIIe siècle.* Geneva and Paris, 1975.

Esmeijer, Anna C. "La macchina dell'universo." In *Album discipulorum aangeboden aan Professor Dr. J. G. van Gelder,* 5–15. Utrecht, 1963.

Ewig, Eugen. "Résidence et capitale pendant le haut Moyen Age." *Revue historique* 230 (1963): 25–72.

Eygun, François. "Le Baptistère Saint-Jean de Poitiers." *Gallia* 22 (1964): 137–72.

Félibien, Michel. *Histoire de l'abbaye royale de Saint-Denys en France.* Paris, 1706.

Fichtenau, Heinrich. *The Carolingian Empire.* Translated by Peter Munz. Oxford, 1963.

Fitchen, John. *The Construction of Gothic Cathedrals: A Study of Medieval Vault Erection.* Oxford, 1961.

Flamand-Grétry, Louis V. *Description complète de la ville de Saint-Denis.* Paris, 1840.

Fleckenstein, Josef. "Fulrad von Saint-Denis und der fränkische Ausgriff in den süddeutschen Raum." In *Studien und Vorarbeiten zur Geschichte des grossfränkischen und frühdeutschen Adels,* edited by Gerd Tellenbach, 9–39. Forschungen zur oberrheinischen Landesgeschichte, 4. Freiburg im Breisgau, 1957.

Fleury, Michel. "Les Fouilles de la basilique depuis Viollet-le-Duc." *Dossiers de l'archéologie* 32 (1979): 19–26.

————. "Le Monogramme de l'anneau d'Arégonde." *Dossiers de l'archéologie* 32 (1979): 43–45.

————, and Albert France-Lanord. "Les Bijoux mérovingiens d'Arnégonde." *Art de France* 1 (1961): 5–18.

————, and Albert France-Lanord. "La Tombe d'Arégonde." *Dossiers de l'archéologie* 32 (1979): 27–42.

Focillon, Henri. *Romanesque Art.* Vol. 1 of *The Art of the West in the Middle Ages,* edited by Jean Bony and translated by Donald King. 2 vols. 2d ed. London and New York, 1969.

Formigé, Jules. *L'Abbaye royale de Saint-Denis: Recherches nouvelles.* Paris, 1960.

————. "Comptes rendus des dernières découvertes dans la basilique de Saint-Denis. Séance du 3 Avril 1957." *Bull. de la Soc. Nat. des Antiq. de France* (1957): 75–76.

————. "Séance du 3 avril 1957: Communication sur les travaux récents de la basilique de Saint-Denis." Institut de France. *Académie des Beaux-Arts, années 1956–57* (Paris, 1957): 77–92.

Forsyth, George H. *The Church of St. Martin at Angers: The Architectural History of the Site from the Roman Empire to the French Revolution.* Princeton, 1953.

————. "St. Martin's at Angers and the Evolution of Early Mediaeval Church Towers." *Art Bulletin* 32 (1950): 308–18.

Fossard, Denise. "Les Chapiteaux de marbre du VIIe siècle en Gaule—Style et évolution." *Cahiers archéologique* 2 (1947): 69–85.

France-Lanord, Albert. "La Fouille en laboratoire: Méthodes et résultats." *Dossiers de l'archéologie* 32 (1979): 66–91.

Frankl, Paul. "Der Beginn der Gothik und das allgemeine Problem des Stilbeginnes." In *Festschrift Heinrich Wölfflin: Beiträge zur Kunst- und Geistesgeschichte zum 21. Juni 1924 überreicht von Freunden und Schülern,* 107–25. Munich, 1924.

————. *Baukunst des Mittelalters: Die frühmittelalterliche und romanische Baukunst.* Wildpark-Potsdam, 1926.

————. *Gothic Architecture.* Middlesex, Baltimore, 1962.

Friend, Albert Mathias. "Carolingian Art in the Abbey of St. Denis." *Art Studies: Medieval, Renaissance and Modern* 1 (1923): 67–75.

————. "Two Manuscripts of the School of St. Denis." *Speculum* 1 (1926): 59–70.

Fustel de Coulanges, Numa Denis. "Etude sur l'immunité mérovingienne." *Revue historique* 22 (1883): 249–90.

————. *Histoire des institutions politiques de l'ancienne France.* 6 vols. Paris, 1888–92.

Gall, Ernst. *Die gotische Baukunst in Frankreich und Deutschland.* 2d. ed. Braunschwieg, 1955.

Ganshof, François Louis. "Louis the Pious Reconsidered." *History,* n.s., 42 (1957): 171–80.

Gardner, Stephen. "Two Campaigns in Suger's Western Block," *Art Bulletin* 66 (Dec. 1984): 574–87.

Gaucher, E.-M. (pseud.). *Saint Denis, martyr, sa sainte vie, ses reliques, avec invocations; historique et courte description de la basilique; tombe célèbre; les funérailles royales (Louis XVI et Marie-Antoinette),* 1: *Saints patrons du diocèse de Paris.* Saint-Juste-en-Chausée, Oise, 1900.

Gautier (Gauthier), Pierre Ferdinand Albert. "La Ville de Saint-Denis pendant la Révolution: Récit contemporain." *Le Cabinet historique* 20/1 (1874): 280–303, and 21/1 (1875): 118–34.

Genicot, Luc-Francis. *Les Eglises mosanes du XIe siècle,* 1: *Architecture et société.* Université de Louvain: Recueil de travaux, d'histoire et de philologie, 4th ser., fascicule 48, Louvain, 1972.

Le Gentil de la Galaisière, Guillaume Joseph Hyacinthe Jean Baptiste. "Observations sur plusieurs anciens Monumens gothiques que j'ai remarqués dans cette Capitale, sur lesquels sont gravés les signes du Zodiaques, & quelques hyéroglyphes Egyptiens relatifs à la religion d'Isis." *Histoire de l'Académie Royale des Sciences 1788,* 91: *Avec les mémoires de mathématique & de physique.* Paris, 1790: 390–438.

Germain, Michel. *Monasticon Gallicanum: Collection de 168 planches de vues topographiques répresentant les monastères de l'Ordre de saint Benoît.* Edited by Achille Peigné-Delacourt and Leopold Delisle. Paris, 1871; reprinted, 1984.

Gerson, Paula. "The Lintels of the West Façade of Saint-Denis." *J.S.A.H.* 34 (1975): 189–97.

———. "The West Façade of St. Denis: An Iconographic Study." Ph.D. dissertation, Columbia University, 1970; University Microfilms, Ann Arbor, Mich., no. 73-76, 428.

Giry, Arthur. "La Donation de Rueil à l'abbaye de Saint-Denis: Examen critique de trois diplômes de Charles-le-Chauve." In *Mélanges Julien Havet. Recueil des travaux d'érudition dédiés à la mémoire de Julien Havet (1853–93),* 683–717. Paris, 1895.

———. *Manuel de diplomatique.* Paris, 1894.

Goldscheider, Cécile. "Les Origines du portail à statues-colonnes." *Bulletin des Musées de France* 11/6 and 7 (1946): 22–25.

Gravenkamp, Curt. *Monatsbilder und Tierkreiszeichen an Kathedralen Frankreichs.* Heidelberg, 1949.

Griffe, Elie. *La Gaule chrétienne à l'époque romaine.* 3 vols. Paris, 1947–65.

———. "Les Origines chrétiennes de la Gaule et les légendes clémentines." *Bulletin de littérature ecclésiastique* 56 (1955): 3–22.

Grivot, Denis, and George Zarnecki. *Gislebertus, Sculptor of Autun.* London, 1961.

Grodecki, Louis. *L'Architecture ottonienne: Au Seuil de l'art roman.* Paris, 1958.

———. *Chartres.* Translated by Katherine Delavenay. New York, 1963.

———. "La Première Sculpture gothique: Wilhelm Vöge et l'état actuel des problèmes." *Bull. mon.* 117 (1959): 265–89.

———. *Les Vitraux de Saint-Denis: Etude sur le vitrail au XIIe siècle* 1. Paris, 1976.

———, Florentine Mütherich, Jean Taralon, and Francis Wormald. *Le Siècle de l'an mil.* Paris, 1973.

Guilhermy, Ferdinand François le Baron de. *Monographie de l'église royale de Saint-Denis: Tombeaux et figures historiques.* Paris, 1848.

———, and Adolphe N. Didron. "Saint-Denys, restauration de l'église royale." *Annales archéologiques* 1 (1844): 230–36.

Gutmann, Joseph, ed. *The Temple of Solomon: Archeological Fact and Medieval Tradition in Christian, Islamic, and Jewish Art.* Missoula, Montana, 1976.

Hackel, Alfred. *Die Trinität in der Kunst: Eine ikonographische Untersuchung.* Berlin, 1931.

Hämel, Adalbert. "Los manuscritos latinos del falso Turpino." In *Estudios dedicados a Menéndez Pidal.* Edited by Marcelino Menéndez y Pelayo. Vol. 4:67–85. Madrid, 1953.

Hardy, Chantal. "La Fenêtre circulaire en l'Ile-de-France au XIIe et XIIIe siècles." Dissertation, Université de Montréal, 1983.

Haskins, Charles H. *The Renaissance of the Twelfth Century.* Cambridge, Mass., 1927.

Hatt, Jean-Jacques. "Circonscription d'Alsace." *Gallia* 28 (1970): 317–43.

Havet, Julien Pierre Eugène. *Oeuvres.* 2 vols. Paris, 1896.

———. "Questions mérovingiennes, V: Les Origines de Saint-Denis." *Bib. de l'Ec. des Ch.* 51 (1890): 5–62.

Havinghurst, Alfred F., ed. *The Pirenne Thesis: Analysis, Criticism and Revision.* Boston, 1958.

Hearn, Millard Fillmore. "The Rectangular Ambulatory in English Medieval Architecture." *J.S.A.H.* 30 (1971): 187–208.

———. *Romanesque Sculpture: The Revival of Monumental Stone Sculpture in the Eleventh and Twelfth Centuries.* Ithaca, N.Y., 1981.

Heimann, Adelheid. "Trinitas Creator Mundi." *J.W.C.I.* 2 (1938): 42–52.

Heinermann, Theodor. "Zeit und Sinn der Karlsreise." *Zeitschrift für romanische Philologie* 56 (1936): 497–562.

Heitz, Carol. *L'Architecture religieuse carolingienne: Les Formes et leur fonctions.* Paris, 1980.

———. "Communication sur le chancel de Saint-Pierre-aux-Nonnains à Metz." *Bull. de la Soc. Nat. des Antiq. de France* (1975): 95–114.

———. "More romano. Problèmes d'architecture et liturgie carolingiennes." In *Roma e l'età carolingia. Atti delle giornate di studio, 3–8 maggio 1976 a cura dello Istituto di storia dell'Arte dell'Università di Roma. Istituto Nazionale di Archeologia e Storia dell'Arte* (Rome, 1976): 27–37.

———. *Recherches sur les rapports entre architecture et liturgie à l'époque carolingienne.* Paris, 1963.

———. "Saint-Denis." In *La Neustrie. Les Pays au nord de la Loire de Dagobert à Charles le Chauve (VIIe-IXe siècles,* edited by Patrick Périn and Laure-Charlotte Feffer, 164–65. Paris, 1985.

Héliot, Pierre, and Pierre Rousseau. "Communication sur l'âge des donjons, d'Etampes et de Provins. Séance du 20 décembre." *Bull. de la Soc. Nat. des Antiq. de France* (1967): 289–308.

Henwood-Reverdot, Annie. *L'Eglise Saint-Etienne de Beauvais: Histoire et architecture.* Beauvais, 1982.

Herluisson, Henri, and Paul Leroy. "Le Manuscrit de Ferdinand Albert Gautier, organiste de l'abbaye de Saint-Denis." *Réunion des Sociétés Savantes des Départements à la Sorbonne. . . . Section des Beaux-arts* 29. France. Ministère de l'instruction publique et des Beaux-arts. Direction des Beaux-arts (1905): 236–49.

Héron de Villefosse, René. *Histoire de Paris.* Paris, 1948.

Hinkle, William M. *The Portal of the Saints of Reims Cathedral: A Study in Medieval Iconography.* New York, 1965.

Hodges, Richard, and David Whitehouse. *Mohammed, Charlemagne & the Origins of Europe: Archaeology and the Pirenne Thesis.* Ithaca, N.Y., 1983.

Hohler, Christopher. "A Note on Jacobus." *J.W.C.I.* 35 (1972): 31–80.

Horrent, Jules. *Le Pèlerinage de Charlemagne: Essai d'explication littéraire avec des notes de critique textuelle.* Paris, 1961.

Hourticq, Louis. *La Vie des images.* Paris, 1927.

Hubert, Jean. *L'Art pré-roman.* Paris, 1938.

PLATE 3. Composite reconstructed plan of Sainte Geneviève's chapel, including excavated remains (Merovingian Saint-Denis, ca. 475); of the church in the time of Dagobert, including excavated remains (Merovingian Saint-Denis, ca. 620); and of the church showing William the Conqueror's tower (Romanesque Saint-Denis, ca. 1080).

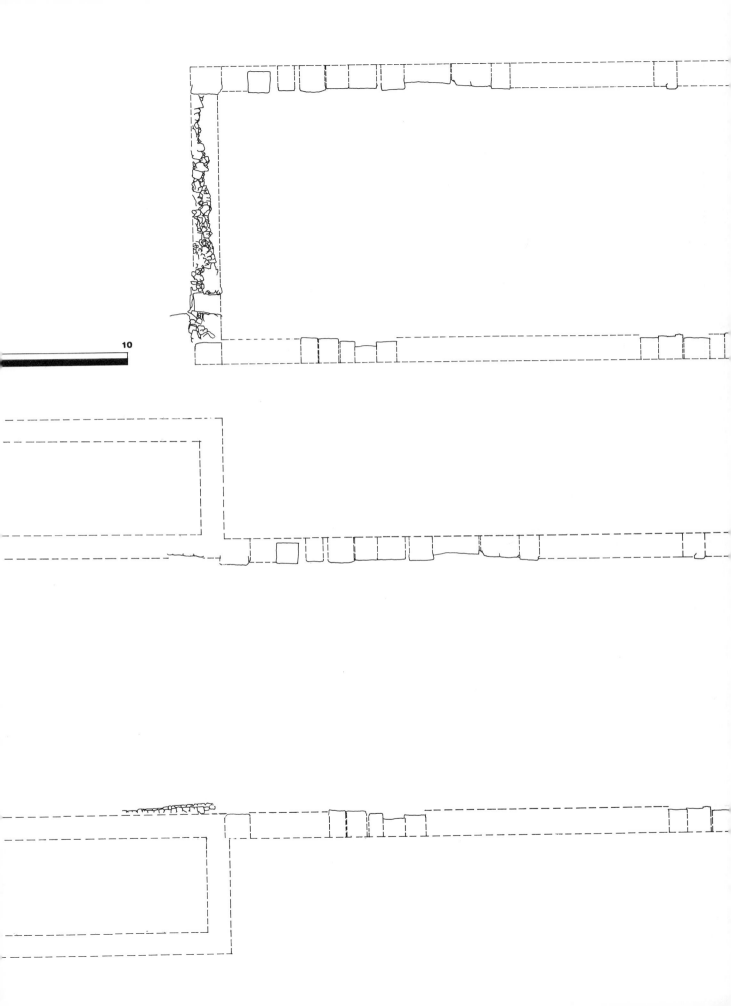

10

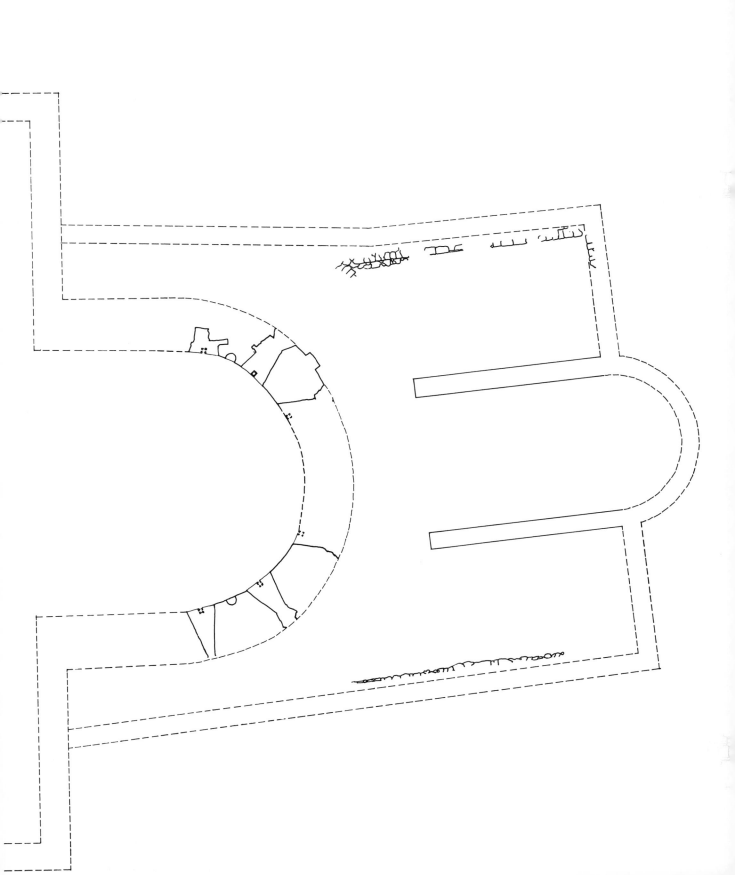

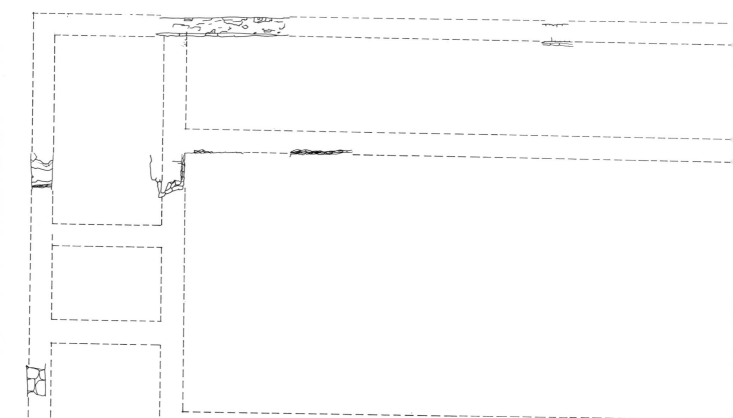

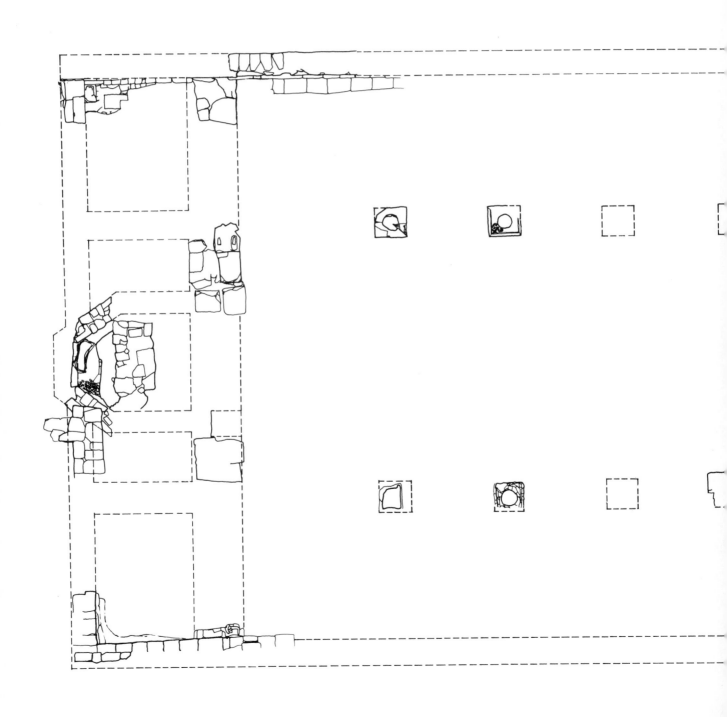

————. "Communication de la séance du 13 mars 1946." *Bull. de la Soc. Nat. des Antiq. de France* (1945–47, published 1950): 137–40.

————. "Communication de la séance du 10 juillet 1946." *Bull. de la Soc. Nat. des Antiq. de France* (1945–47, published 1950): 176–77.

————. "Le Fauteuil du roi Dagobert." *Demareteion* 1 (1935): 17–27.

————, Jean Porcher, and Wilhelm F. Volbach. *The Carolingian Renaissance*. Translated by James Emmons, Stuart Gilbert, and Robert Allen. New York, 1970.

————. *Europe of the Invasions*. Translated by Stuart Gilbert and James Emmons. New York, 1969.

Huvelin, Paul. *Essai historique sur le droit des marchés & des foires*. Paris, 1897.

Jacobsen, Werner. "Saint-Denis in neuem Licht: Konsequenzen der neuentdeckten Baubeschreibung aus dem Jahre 799." *Kunstchronik* 36 (1983): 301–08.

Jalabert, Denise. *La Flore sculptée des monuments du Moyen âge en France: Recherches sur les origines de l'art français*. Paris, 1965.

James, Montague Rhodes. *The Apocalypse in Art*. London, 1931.

Jansen, Virginia. "Round or Square? The Axial Towers of the Abbey Church of Saint-Riquier." *Gesta* 21 (1982): 83–90.

Kantorowicz, Ernst H. *Laudes Regiae: A Study in Liturgical Acclamations and Mediaeval Ruler Worship*. Berkeley, Los Angeles, 1946.

Kaplan, Barry A. "Bursae Eleganter Gemmatae: The History of an Abandoned Liturgical Instrument." Master's thesis, Yale University, 1972.

Katzenellenbogen, Adolf. *The Sculptural Programs of Chartres Cathedral: Christ. Mary. Ecclesia*. Baltimore, 1959; reprinted, New York, 1964.

Kautzsch, Rudolf. "Die langobardische Schmuckkunst in Oberitalien." *Römisches Jahrbuch für Kunstgeschichte* 5 (1941): 3–48.

Kendrick, Albert F. *The Cathedral Church of Lincoln: A History and Description of its Fabric and a List of the Bishops*. Lincoln, 1898.

Kieft, C. van de. "Deux diplômes faux de Charlemagne pour Saint-Denis, du XIIème siècle." *Le Moyen Age* 64, 4th ser., 13 (1958): 401–36.

Kessler, Herbert. *The Illustrated Bibles from Tours*. Studies in Manuscript Illumination 7. Princeton, 1977.

Kitzinger, Ernst. "The Mosaics of the Cappella Palatina in Palermo: An Essay on the Choice and Arrangement of Subjects." *Art Bulletin* 31 (1949): 269–92.

Klibansky, Raymond. "The School of Chartres." In *Twelfth-Century Europe and the Foundations of Modern Society*. Proceedings of a Symposium Sponsored by the Division of Humanities of the University of Wisconsin and the Wisconsin Institute for Medieval and Renaissance Studies, November 12–14, 1957, edited by Marshall Clagett, Gaines Post, and Robert Reynolds, 3–14. Madison, Wis., Milwaukee, and London, 1961; reprinted, 1966.

Knowles, David. *The Evolution of Medieval Thought*. New York, 1962.

Koseleff, Olga. *Die Monatsdarstellungen der französischen Plastik des 12. Jahrhunderts*. Marburg, 1934.

Kötting, Bernhard. *Der frühchristliche Reliquienkult und die Bestattung im Kirchengebäude*. Cologne and Opladen, 1965.

Krautheimer, Richard. "The Crypt of Santa Maria in Cosmedin and the Mausoleum of Probus Anicius." In *Essays in Memory of Karl Lehmann*. Edited by Lucy Sandler. *Marsyas, Studies in the History of Art, Supplement 1* (1964): 171–75.

————. Review, *"The Abbey of St.-Denis 475–1122, volume I*, by Sumner McKnight Crosby. . . ." In *Supplement to the American Journal of Archaeology* 48 (1944): 218–21.

————. *Studies in Early Christian, Medieval and Renaissance Art*. Translated by Alfred Frazer, et al. New York, 1969.

Kreusch, Felix. "Im Louvre wiedergefundene Kapitelle und Bronzebasen aus der Pfalzkirche Karls des Grossen zu Aachen." *Cahiers archéologiques* 18 (1968): 71–98.

Krüger, Karl Heinrich. *Königsgrabkirchen der Franken, Angelsachsen und Langobarden bis zum Mitte des 8. Jahrhunderts*. Munich, 1971.

Krusch, Bruno. "Nochmals das Martyrologium Hieronymianum." *Neues Archiv* 26 (1901): 349–89.

————. "Zum Martyrologium Hieronymianum." *Neues Archiv* 20 (1895): 437–40.

————. "Zur Afralegende und zum Martyrologium Hieronymianum." *Neues Archiv* 24 (1899): 289–337.

Kubach, Hans Erich. "Die vorromanische und romanische Baukunst in Mitteleuropa." *Zeitschrift für Kunstgeschichte* 18 (1955): 157–98.

Kurth, Godefroid Joseph François. *Etudes franques*. 2 vols. Paris, 1919.

Larrieu, Mary. "Chapiteaux en marbre antérieurs à l'époque romane dans le Gers." *Cahiers archéologiques* 14 (1964): 109–57.

Lasko, Peter. *Ars Sacra, 800–1200*. Harmondsworth, Baltimore, 1972.

Lasteyrie, Robert Charles, comte de. *L'Architecture religieuse en France à l'époque gothique*. 2 vols. Paris, 1926–27.

————. *L'Architecture religieuse en France à l'époque romane*. 2d ed. Paris, 1929.

————. *L'Eglise de Saint-Philbert-de-Grandlieu (Loire-Inférieure)*. Paris, 1909. Extrait des *Mémoires de l'Académie des Inscriptions et Belles-Lettres* 38.

László, Gyula. *Steppenvölker und Germanen: Kunst der Völkerwanderungszeit*. Vienna and Munich, 1970.

Lavisse, Ernest. *Histoire de France depuis les origines jusqu'à la Révolution*. 9 vols. Paris, 1900–11.

Lebeuf, Jean. "Conjectures sur la reine Pédauque." (*Mémoire* of 1751, excerpted and described in) *Histoire de l'Académie Royale des Inscriptions et Belles-Lettres* 23 (1756): 227–35.

Lefèvre-Pontalis, Eugène Amédée. "Le Caveau central de la crypte de Saint-Denis." *Bull. mon.* 71 (1907): 554–62.

Legrand d'Aussy, Pierre-Jean-Baptiste. *Des Sépultures nationales et particulièrement celles des rois de France . . . Suivi des funé-*

railles des rois, reines, princes et princesses de la monarchie française, depuis son origine jusques et y compris elles de Louis XVIII,
par M. de Roquefort. Paris, 1824.

Lehmann, Edgar. Die frühe deutsche Kirchenbau die Entwicklung
seiner Raumanordung bis 1080. Forshungen zur deutschen
Kunstgeschichte, vol. 27. Berlin, 1938.

Leidinger, Georg. Der Codex aureus der bayerischen Staatsbibliothek in München. 6 vols. Munich, 1921–25.

Lenoir, Albert. Architecture monastique. 2 vols. Paris, 1852–
56.

Lenormant, Charles. "Notice sur le fauteuil de Dagobert."
Mélanges d'archéologie, d'histoire et de littérature. Edited by
Charles Cahier and Arthur Martin, 1:157–90 and 239–44.
Paris, 1847–49.

Leroquais, Victor. Paris. Bibliothèque nationale. Département
des manuscrits. Les Manuscrits à peintures en France au VIIe–
XIIe siècles. 2d ed. Paris, 1954.

——. Les Sacramentaires et les missels manuscrits des bibliothèques publiques de France. 4 vols. Paris, 1924.

Levillain, Léon. "L'Avènement de la dynastie carolingienne et
les origines de l'état pontifical (749–757): Essai sur la chronologie et l'interprétation des événements." Bib. de l'Ec. des
Ch. 94 (1933): 225–95.

——. "Compte rendu: Maxmilian Buchner, Das Vizepapsttum des Abtes von Saint-Denis." Le Moyen Age 39, 2d ser., 30
(1929): 85–95.

——. "Compte rendu: R. de Lasteyrie, L'Eglise de Saint-
Philbert de Grandlieu (Loire-Inférieure)." Le Moyen Age 23, 2d
ser., 14 (1910): 49–50.

——. "Correspondance à M. Maître." Bull. mon. 71 (1907):
550–53.

——. "Correspondance: Réponse à M. Maître," Bull. mon. 72
(1908): 145–54.

——. "L'Eglise carolingienne de Saint-Denis." Bull. mon. 71
(1907): 211–62.

——. "Essai sur les origines du Lendit." Revue historique 155
(1927): 241–76.

——. "Etudes sur l'abbaye de Saint-Denis à l'époque
mérovingienne,"
I: "Les Sources narratives." Bib. de l'Ec. des Ch. 82 (1921): 5–
116;
II: "Les Origines de Saint-Denis." Bib. de l'Ec. des Ch. 86
(1925): 5–99.
III: "Privilegium et Immunitates ou Saint-Denis dans l'église et
dans l'état." Bib. de l'Ec. des Ch. 87 (1926): 20–97 and 245–
346.
IV: "Les Documents d'histoire économique (suite)." Bib. de
l'Ec. des Ch. 91 (1930): 5–65 and 264–300.

——. "Les Plus Anciennes églises abbatiales de Saint-Denis."
Mémoires de la Société de l'Histoire de Paris et de l'Ile de France
36 (1909): 143–222.

——. "Wandalbert de Prüm et la date de la mort d'Hilduin
de Saint-Denis." Bib. de l'Ec. des Ch. 108 (1949–50): 5–35.

Liebman, Charles J. "La Consécration légendaire de la basilique

de Saint-Denis." Le Moyen Age 45, 3d ser., 6 (1935): 252–
64.

——. Etude sur la vie en prose de Saint Denis. Geneva and New
York, 1942.

Loenertz, Raymond J. "La Légende parisienne de S. Denys
l'Aréopagite: Sa Genèse et son premier témoin." Analecta
bollandiana 69 (1951): 217–37.

Loomis, Laura Hibbard. "The Oriflamme of France and the
War-Cry 'Monjoie' in the Twelfth Century." In Studies in Art
and Literature for Belle de Costa Greene, edited by Dorothy
Miner, 67–82. Princeton, 1954.

Loomis, Roger S. The Grail, from Celtic Myth to Christian Symbol.
New York, 1963.

Lopez, Robert S. "Mohammed and Charlemagne: A Revision."
Speculum 18 (1945): 14–38. Reprinted in The Pirenne Thesis:
Analysis, Criticism and Revision, edited by Alfred F. Having-
hurst, 58–73. Boston, 1958.

Lot, Ferdinand, and Louis Halphen. Le Règne de Charles le
Chauve: Prèmiere partie (840–51). Paris, 1909.

Louis, René. "XIXe circonscription—Sens." Gallia 8 (1950):
178–80.

Luchaire, Achille. Les Communes françaises à l'époque des Capétiens directs. Paris, 1890.

——. Louis VI le Gros: Annales de sa vie et de sa règne (1081–
1137) avec une introduction historique. Paris, 1890.

——. Les premiers Capétiens (987–1137). Vol. 2, pt. 2 of Histoire
de France depuis les origines jusqu'à la Révolution, edited by
Luchaire and Ernest Lavisse. Paris, 1901.

Lund, Fredrik M. Ad Quadratum: A Study of the Geometrical
Bases of Classic and Medieval Religious Architecture. . . . London, 1921.

Mabillon, Jean, ed. Annales ordinis S. Benedicti occidentalium
monarchorum patriarchae. In quibis non modo res monasticae,
sed etiam ecclesiasticae historiae . . . continetur. . . . 6 vols. Lucca, 1739–45.

Maillé, Geneviève Aliette, marquise de. Les Cryptes de Jouarre.
Paris, 1971.

Maere, René. "Cryptes au chevet du choeur dans les églises des
anciens Pays-Bas." Bull. mon. 91 (1932): 81–119.

Maître, Léon, "Le Culte de saint Denis et de ses compagnons."
Revue de l'art chrétien 51 (1908): 361–70, and 52 (1909):
80–94 and 175–83.

——. "Correspondance: La Crypte de Saint-Denis." Bull.
mon. 72 (1908): 137–45.

Mâle, Emile. "La Part de Suger dans la création de l'iconographie du moyen âge." Revue de l'art ancien et moderne 35
(1914): 91–102, 161–68, 253–62, and 339–49.

——. Religious Art in France—The Twelfth Century: A Study
of the Origins of Medieval Iconography. Edited by Harry Bober.
Translated by Marthiel Mathews. Princeton, 1978.

Marx, Jean. La Légende arthurienne et le Graal. Paris, 1952.

Mathews, Thomas F. "An Early Roman Chancel Arrangement
and its Liturgical Functions." Rivista di archeologia cristiana 38
(1962): 73–95.

McLean, Richard Hamann. "Les Origines des portails et façades sculptés gothiques." *Cahiers de civilisation médiévale Xe–XIIe siècles* 2 (1959): 157–75.

McClendon, Charles B. "Review of Carol Heitz. *L'Architecture religieuse carolingienne: Les Formes et leur fonctions.* Paris, 1980." In *J.S.A.H.* 41 (1982): 58–59.

Meyer, Olivier, Laurent Bourgeau, David Coxall, Nicole Meyer, and Caroline Relier. *1981 Bilam d'une année de recherches à Saint-Denis.* Saint-Denis, 1982.

————, Michaël Wyss, David Coxall, and Nicole Meyer. *Saint-Denis recherches urbaines 1983–1985. Bilan des fouilles.* Saint-Denis, 1985.

Millet, Simon Germain. *Le Trésor sacré ou inventaire des sainctes reliques et autres précieux joyaux, qui se voysent en l'église et au trésor de l'abbaye royale de S. Denis en France. . . .* 4th ed. Paris, 1646.

Miskimin, Harry A., David Herlihy, and Abraham Udovitch, eds. *The Medieval City.* New Haven, London, 1977.

Montesquiou-Fezensac, Blaise de. "Communication de la séance du 13 mars 1946. Les Portes de bronze de Saint-Denis." *Bull. de la Soc. Nat. des Antiq. de France* (1945–47, published 1950): 128–37.

————. "Une Epave du trésor de Saint-Denis: Fragment retrouvé de la croix de saint Eloi." In *Mélanges en hommage à la mémoire de Fr. Martroye,* 289–301. Société Nationale des Antiquaires de France. Paris, 1940.

————. "'In sexto lapide:' L'Ancien Autel de Saint-Denis et son inscription." *Cahiers archéologiques* 7 (1954): 51–60.

————. *Le Trésor de Saint-Denis.* 3 vols. Paris, 1973–77.

Montfaucon, Bernard de. *Les Monumens de la Monarchie françoise.* 5 vols. Paris, 1729–33.

Montrémy, François de. "Base carolingienne conservée au musée de Cluny." *Bull. mon.* 81 (1922): 424–26.

Moretus-Plantin, Henri. "Les Passions de saint Denys." In *Mélanges offerts au R. P. Ferdinand Cavallera . . . à l'occasion de la quarantième année de son professorat à l'Institut catholique,* 215–30. Toulouse, 1948.

Morey, Charles Rufus. "The Illuminated Manuscripts of the Pierpont Morgan Library." *The Arts* 7 (1925): 189–214.

Neuschäfer, Hans-Jörg. "Le Voyage de Charlemagne en Orient als Parodie der Chanson de Geste: Untersuchungen zur Epenparodie im Mittelalter (I)." *Romanistisches Jahrbuch* 10 (1959): 78–102.

Nourry, Emile [Pierre Saintyves]. *En Marge de la Légende dorée, songes, miracles et survivances: Essai sur la formation de quelques thèmes hagiographiques.* Paris, 1931.

Ohnsorge, Werner. "Das Kaiserbündnis von 842–44 gegen die Sarazenen: Datum, Inhalt und politische Bedeutung des 'Kaiserbriefes aus St.-Denis.'" *Archiv für Diplomatik, Schriftgeschichte, Siegel- und Wappenkunde* 1 (1955): 88–131.

Ostoia, Vera K. "A Statue from Saint-Denis." *The Metropolitan Museum of Art Bulletin,* n.s., 13 (June 1955): 298–304.

Oswald, Friedrich, Leo Schaefer, and Hans Rudolf Sennhauser. Zentralinstitut für Kunstgeschichte (Munich). *Vorromanische Kirchenbauten: Katalog der Denkmäler bis zum Ausgang der Ottonen.* 3 vols. Munich, 1966–71.

P. V. (Philippe Verdier). "Suger, 1081–1151." *Encyclopaedia Universalis* 15 (1968): 506–07.

Pachtère, Felix-Georges de. *Paris à l'époque gallo-romaine.* Paris, 1912.

Panofsky, Erwin. "Note on a Controversial Passage in Suger's *De Consecratione Ecclesiae Sancti Dionysii.*" *Gazette des Beaux-Arts* 6th series, 26 (1944, published 1947): 95–114.

————. "Postlogium Sugerianum." *Art Bulletin* 29 (1947): 119–21.

Patzelt, Erna. *Die karolingische Renaissance.* Graz, 1965.

Pirenne, Henri. *Economic and Social History of Medieval Europe.* London, 1936.

————. *Medieval Cities: Their Origins and the Revival of Trade.* Princeton, 1925; revised edition, 1939.

————. *Les Villes du moyen âge: Essai d'histoire économique et sociale.* Brussels, 1927.

Poly, Jean-Pierre, and Eric Bournazel. *La Mutation féodale: Xe et XIIe siècles.* Paris, 1980.

Porter, Arthur Kingsley. *Medieval Architecture: Its Origins and Development.* 2 vols. New Haven, 1912.

————. *Romanesque Sculpture of the Pilgrimage Roads.* 10 vols. Boston, 1923.

Pouget, Marc du. "Recherches sur les chroniques latines de Saint-Denis: Edition critique et commentaire de la *Descriptio Clavi et Corone Domini* et de deux séries de textes relatifs à la légende carolingienne." *Positions des Thèses: Ecole des Chartres* (1978): 41–46.

Prache, Anne. "Les Arc-boutants au XIIe siècle." *Gesta* 15 (1976): 31–42.

————. *Ile-de-France romane.* Zodiaque: La Nuit des temps, 60. Paris, 1983.

Pressouyre, Léon. "Une Tête de reine du portail central de Saint-Denis." *Gesta* 15 (1976): 151–60.

Previté-Orton, Charles William. *The Shorter Cambridge Medieval History.* 2 vols. Cambridge, 1952.

Prinz, Friedrich. *Frühes Mönchtum im Frankreich: Kultur und Gesellschaft in Gallien, den Rheinlanden und Bayern am Beispiel der monastischen Entwicklung (4. bis 8. Jahrhundert).* Munich, Vienna, 1965.

Prost, Auguste. "Communication de la séance du 11 mai 1881." *Bull. de la Soc. Nat. des Antiq. de France* (1881): 173–85.

Quarré, Pierre. "L'Abbé Lebeuf et l'interprétation du portail de Saint-Bénigne de Dijon." In *L'Abbé Lebeuf et le Jansénisme: XXXIe Congrès de l'Association Bourguignonne des Sociétés Savantes, Auxerre, 1960,* 281–87. Auxerre, 1961.

Quicherat, Jules. "Communication de la séance du 11 mai 1881." M. Prost presiding. *Bull. de la Soc. Nat. des Antiq. de France* (1881): 176–78.

Rauschen, Gerhard, ed. *Die Legende Karls des Grossen in 11. und 12. Jahrhundert.* Gesellschaft für Rheinische Geschichtskund, 7. Leipzig, 1890.

Ravau, Jean-Pierre. "Les Cathédrales de Châlons-sur-Marne -

avant 1230," *Mémoires de la Société d'Agriculture, Commerce, Sciences et Arts du Département de la Marne* 89 (1974): 31–70.

Rice, David Talbot, ed. *The Dawn of European Civilization: The Dark Ages.* London, 1965.

Riché, Pierre. *Education and Culture in the Barbarian West, Sixth through Eighth Centuries.* Translated by John J. Contreni. Columbia, South Carolina, 1975.

Roblin, Michel. *Le Terroir de Paris aux époques gallo-romaine et franque: Peuplement et défrichement dans la Civitas des Parisii (Seine, Seine-et-Oise).* Paris, 1951.

Rolland, Henri. "Les Fouilles de Glanum (Saint-Rémy-de-Provence) de 1945 à 1947." *Gallia* 6 (1948): 140–69.

Roques, René, et al. "Denys le Pseudo-Aréopagite." *D.H.G.E.* 14: 265–310.

Ross, Marvin C. "Monumental Sculptures from St.-Denis: An Identification of Fragments from the Portal." *The Journal of the Walters Art Gallery* 3 (1940): 90–109.

Rostand, André. "La Documentation iconographique des *Monumens de la Monarchie françoise* de Bernard de Montfaucon." *Bulletin de la Société de l'Histoire de l'Art Français* (1932): 104–49.

Sackur, Ernst. *Die Cluniacenser in ihrer kirchlichen und allgemeingeschichtlichen Wirksamkeit bis zur Mitte des elften Jahrhunderts.* 2 vols. Halle, 1892–94.

Sainte-Beuve, Charles Augustin. *Portraits contemporains.* 2 vols. Paris, 1846.

Salet, Francis. "Cluny III." *Bull. mon.* 126 (1968): 235–92.

———. *La Madeleine de Vézelay.* Melun, 1948.

Salin, Bernhard. *Die altgermanische Thierornamentik: Typologische Studie über germanische Metallgegenstände aus dem IV. bis IX. Jahrhundert, nebst einer Studie über irische Ornametik.* Stockholm, 1935.

Salin, Edouard. "Sépultures gallo-romaines et mérovingiennes dans la basilique de Saint-Denis." *Monuments Piot* 49 (1957): 93–128.

———. "Les Tombes gallo-romaines et mérovingiennes de la basilique de Saint Denis (fouilles de janvier–février 1957)." Académie des Inscriptions et Belles-Lettres. *Mémoires de l'Institut National de France* 44/1 (1960): 169–263.

Sanderson, Warren. "Monastic Reform in Lorraine and the Architecture of the Outer Crypt, 950–1100." *Transactions of the American Philosophical Society,* n.s., 61:6 (1971): 3–36.

Sauerländer, Willibald. *Gothic Sculpture in France 1140–1270.* Translated by Janet Sondheimer. New York, 1972.

Schapiro, Meyer. *Romanesque Art.* New York, 1977.

Scher, Stephen K. *The Renaissance of the Twelfth Century.* Providence, 1969.

———. "'The Renaissance of the Twelfth Century' Revisited." *Gesta* 9/2 (1970): 59–61.

Schlosser, Julius von. *Schriftquellen zur Geschichte der karolingischen Kunst.* Vienna, 1896.

Schramm, Percy Ernst, and Florentine Mütherich. *Denkmale der deutschen Könige und Kaiser: Ein Beitrag zur Herrschergeschichte von Karl dem Grossen bis Friedrich II, 768–1250.* Munich, 1962.

Sedlmayr, Hans. "Die politische Bedeutung des Virgildomes." *Mitteilungen der Gesellschaft für Salzburger Landeskunde* 115 (1975): 145–60.

Seymour, Charles. *Notre-Dame of Noyon in the Twelfth Century: A Study in the Early Development of Gothic Architecture.* New Haven, 1939.

Smith, Earl Baldwin. *Architectural Symbolism of Imperial Rome and the Middle Ages.* Princeton, 1956.

Smith, William, and Henry Wace. *A Dictionary of Christian Bibliography.* 4 vols. London, 1877–87.

Southern, Richard W. *Medieval Humanism and Other Studies.* Oxford, New York, Evanston, 1970.

Spiegel, Gabrielle M. *The Chronicle Tradition of Saint-Denis: A Survey.* Brookline, Mass. and Leyden, 1978.

———. "The Cult of Saint Denis and Capetian Kingship." *Journal of Medieval History* 1 (1975): 43–69.

Stevenson, William Henry. "The Old English Charters to St. Denis." *English Historical Review* 6 (1891): 736–42.

Stoddard, Whitney S. *Art and Architecture in Medieval France. Medieval Architecture, Sculpture, Stained Glass, Manuscripts, the Art of the Church Treasuries.* 2d ed. of *Monastery and Cathedral in France.* . . . Middletown, Connecticut, 1966. Evanston, San Francisco, London, 1972.

———. *The West Portals of Saint-Denis and Chartres: Sculpture in the Ile-de-France from 1140 to 1190, Theory of Origins.* Cambridge, Mass., 1952.

Tangl, Michael. "Das Testament Fulrads von Saint-Denis." *Neues Archiv* 32 (1907): 167–217.

Taracena Aguirre, Blas, Pedro Batlle Huguet, and Helmut Schlunk. *Ars hispaniae: Historia universal del arte hispánico,* 2. Madrid, 1947.

Thérel, Marie-Louise. "Comment la patrologie peut éclairer l'archéologie: A propos de l'Arbre de Jessé et des statues-colonnes de Saint-Denis." *Cahiers de civilisation médiévale Xe-XIIe siècles* 6 (1963): 145–58.

Théry, Gabriel. *Études dionysiennes.* 2 vols. Vols. 16 and 19 of *Etudes de Philosophie médiévale,* edited by Etienne Gilson. Paris, 1932 and 1937.

Van Engen, John H. *Rupert of Deutz.* Berkeley, Los Angeles, London, 1983.

Vanuxem, Jacques. "The Theories of Mabillon and Montfaucon on French Sculpture of the Twelfth Century." *J. W.C.I.* 20 (1957): 45–58.

Verbeek, Albert. "Die Aussenkrypta. Werden einer Bauform des frühen Mittelalters." *Zeitschrift für Kunstgeschichte* 13 (1950): 7–38.

Verzone, Paolo. *The Art of Europe: The Dark Ages from Theodoric to Charlemagne.* Translated by Pamela Waley. New York, 1968.

Vieillard-Troïekouroff, May. "L'Architecture en France du temps de Charlemagne. Fouilles récents." In *Karl der Grosse* 3:336–68. Düsseldorf, 1966.

———. "Les Chapiteaux de marbre du Haut Moyen-Age à Saint-Denis." *Gesta* 15 (1976): 105–11.

———. "Les Zodiaques parisiens sculptés d'après Le Gentil de

la Galaisière astronome du XVIIIe siècle." *Mém. de la Soc. Nat. des Antiq. de France,* 84, 9th series, 4 (1968): 161–94.

————, Denise Fossard, et al. "Les Anciennes Eglises suburbaines de Paris (IVe–Xe siècles)." *Paris et Ile-de-France: Mémoires publiès par la Fédération des Sociétés Historiques et Archéologiques de Paris et de l'Ile-de-France* 11 (1960): 17–282. *Vies des saints.*

See Baudot and Chaussin, eds.

Viollet-le-Duc, Eugène. *Dictionnaire raisonné de l'architecture française du XIème au XVIème siècle.* 10 vols. Paris, 1854–68.

————. "Eglise de Saint-Denis." *Paris Guide par les principaux écrivans et artistes de la France,* 1:702–11. Paris, 1867.

————. "L'Eglise impériale de Saint-Denis." *Revue archéologique,* n.s., 3 (1861): 301–10 and 345–53.

Vitry, Paul, and Gaston Brière. *L'Eglise abbatiale de Saint-Denis et ses tombeaux: Notice historique et archéologique.* 2d ed. Paris, 1925.

Vöge, Wilhelm. *Die Anfänge des monumentalen Stiles im Mittelalter: Eine Untersuchung über die erste Blütezeit französischer Plastik.* Strasbourg, 1894.

————. "Über die Bamberger Domsculpturen, I." *Repertorium für Kunstwissenschaft* 22 (1899): 94–104.

Vogel, Cyrille. "La Réforme cultuelle sous Pepin le Bref et sous Charlemagne (deuxième moitié du VIIIe siècle et premier quart du IXe siècle)." In *Die Karolingische Renaissance,* Erna Patzelt, ed., 173–242. Graz, 1965.

von Borries, Johann E. "Die Westportale der Abteikirche von Saint-Denis: Versuch einer Rekonstruction." Ph.D. dissertation, Hamburg, 1957.

von Simson, Otto George. *The Gothic Cathedral: Origins of Gothic Architecture and the Medieval Concept of Order.* New York, 1956; 2d ed., New York, 1962 and Princeton, 1974.

Walpole, Ronald N. "The *Pèlerinage de Charlemagne:* Poem, Legend and Problem." *Romance Philology* 8 (1954–55): 173–86.

————. *Philip Mouskés and the Pseudo-Turpin Chronicle.* Berkeley and Los Angeles, 1947.

Ward, Clarence. *Mediaeval Church Vaulting.* Princeton, 1915.

Webb, Clement Charles Julian. *John of Salisbury.* London, 1932.

Webster, James Carson. *The Labors of the Months in Antique and Mediaeval Art to the End of the Twelfth Century.* Evanston, Chicago, 1938.

Weinberger, Martin. "The Chair of Dagobert." In *Essays in Memory of Karl Lehmann,* edited by Lucy Sandler, 375–82. New York, 1964.

Wilson, David McKenzie. "A Ring of Queen Arnegunde." *Germania* 42 (1964): 265–68.

Wixom, William. *Treasures from Medieval France.* Cleveland Museum of Art. Cleveland, 1967.

Wulf, Walter. *Die Kapitellplastik des Sugerbaus von Saint-Denis.* Frankfurt-am-Main, Bern, Las Vegas, 1979.

Index

Italic numbers refer to illustrations. Churches are listed under city where located, followed by church name.